THE PRINCES IN THE TOWER

THE
PRINCES
IN THE
TOWER

Solving History's Greatest Cold Case

PHILIPPA LANGLEY

PEGASUS BOOKS
NEW YORK LONDON

'We find but few historians, of all ages, who have been diligent enough in their search for truth; it is their common method to take on trust what they deliver to the public, by which means, a falsehood once received from a famed writer, becomes traditional to posterity.'[1]

John Dryden (1631–1700), poet, translator, critic, playwright.
Created first Poet Laureate in 1668.

THE PRINCES IN THE TOWER

Pegasus Books, Ltd.
148 West 37th Street, 13th Floor
New York, NY 10018

Copyright © 2023 by Philippa Langley

First Pegasus Books cloth edition November 2023

ISBN: 978-1-63936-627-9

10 9 8 7 6 5 4 3

Printed in the United States of America
Distributed by Simon & Schuster
www.pegasusbooks.com

Contents

Foreword

In September 2017, on a small bench in the Cramond Inn in Edinburgh, we sat gazing at the late fifteenth-century handwriting that had just appeared on my laptop screen. This was a remarkable archival find from the National Archives in The Hague, only recently discovered by a Dutch team of researchers. I translated the Middle Dutch on the screen into English for Philippa. Line after line, the words, penned in Holland by a clerk more than 500 years ago, revealed in detail the journey of 'The White Rose', in the northern part of Holland, to the Island of Texel …

Uncovering this, and proving that the events surrounding the Yorkist invasion in 1495 were not handed down through history as they actually happened, was exciting and full of promise. We had only just begun to investigate the archives on the continent, and now it dawned on me just how much potential there was in neglected archival material and pieces of evidence that could lie outside the UK. It seemed that answers to Britain's age-old mystery were waiting to be found in the archives of the Low Countries, which made perfect sense because there had been precedents: in 1470 King Edward IV and his brother Richard had fled to Bruges via Texel, while nine years earlier Richard and his other brother George were sent to Utrecht as children. The reason? To find shelter in the Burgundian Netherlands in times of uncertainty and danger in the kingdom.

Returning to the Netherlands from Edinburgh, and infected by Philippa's enthusiasm, I couldn't wait to continue searching in the archives on the continent. As a lawyer myself, I leaned on the historical expertise of my fellow Dutch team members and the kindness of archivists who were so willing to offer me the help I needed.

How I loved those ancient sources and their medieval handwriting. Slowly, I learnt to decipher and transcribe texts that, at first sight, appeared unreadable – and what a joy the moment was when their contents revealed themselves to me. Just to hold those magnificent leatherbound books and scrutinise city accounts, letters and receipts – all the while eager to find that one snippet of evidence that could possibly shed new light on this enduring mystery – was enough to become passionately involved in Philippa's project.

Over the years, it did turn out that the archives on the continent were indeed real treasure troves, containing a wealth of previously neglected material from the key years. Philippa, while undertaking her own original research and analysing in minute detail the reign of Richard III and subsequent Yorkist uprisings in Henry VII's reign, once joked that thanks to the Dutch project members all she had to do was 'sit back and open her inbox to get another avalanche of new finds coming in from Europe'.

Recently, Philippa asked me if I would write the foreword for her new book. This is a great honour and, indeed, I would like to pay tribute to all the other contributors, specialists, experts, Latinists and researchers, from the UK and overseas, who selflessly and generously dedicated their time and energy to help make The Missing Princes Project a success.

This unprecedented work that is now before you is an absolute must-read for anyone interested in history and historical mysteries. Its completeness and the astonishing breadth of sources it makes use of define this as a landmark study in British history. It is the result of what can be achieved when forces are brought together for the same cause by an inspirational woman, tireless in her quest to uncover the truth about what happened to the sons of King Edward IV, last seen in the summer of 1483, playing in the Tower grounds.

Nathalie Nijman-Bliekendaal
Member of the Dutch Research Group
Formerly a criminal lawyer, now a passionate historical researcher

Preface

This work represents the first five-year report of The Missing Princes Project (2016–21). The project is a cold-case investigation into the disappearance of Edward V and Richard, Duke of York, in 1483, employing the same principles and practices as a modern police enquiry. The project's remit, assisted by members of the police and investigative agencies, is to follow the basic tenet of any modern investigation, ABC:

Accept Nothing – **B**elieve Nobody – **C**hallenge Everything

This work, therefore, makes no apologies for upsetting any long-established apple carts, including those of famed and famous writers.

Our only objective is the truth.

Philippa Langley MBE

Family Trees

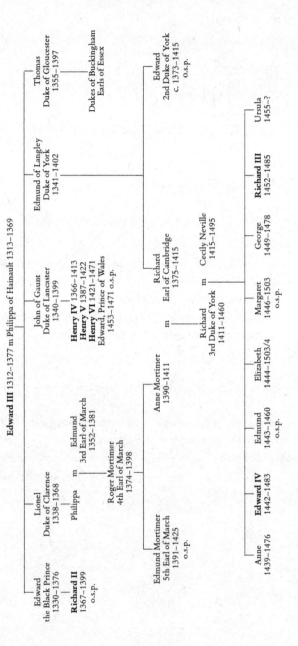

Royal Houses of York and Lancaster (simplified)

Edward III 1312–1377 m Philippa of Hainault 1313–1369

Edward
the Black Prince
1330–1376

Richard II
1367–1399
o.s.p.

Lionel
Duke of Clarence
1338–1368

Philippa m Edmund
3rd Earl of March
1352–1381

Roger Mortimer
4th Earl of March
1374–1398

Edmund Mortimer
5th Earl of March
1391–1425
o.s.p.

Anne Mortimer
1390–1411

John of Gaunt
Duke of Lancaster
1340–1399

Henry IV 1366–1413
Henry V 1387–1422
Henry VI 1421–1471
Edward, Prince of Wales
1453–1471 o.s.p.

Edmund of Langley
Duke of York
1341–1402

Edward
2nd Duke of York
c. 1373–1415
o.s.p.

Thomas
Duke of Gloucester
1355–1397

Dukes of Buckingham
Earls of Essex

Richard
Earl of Cambridge
1375–1415

m

Richard
3rd Duke of York
1411–1460

m Cecily Neville
1415–1495

Anne
1439–1476

Edward IV
1442–1483

Edmund
1443–1460
o.s.p.

Elizabeth
1444–1503/4

Margaret
1446–1503
o.s.p.

George
1449–1478

Richard III
1452–1485

Ursula
1455–?

o.s.p. = *died childless*
Appreciation to Annette Carson

Houses of Tudor and Beaufort

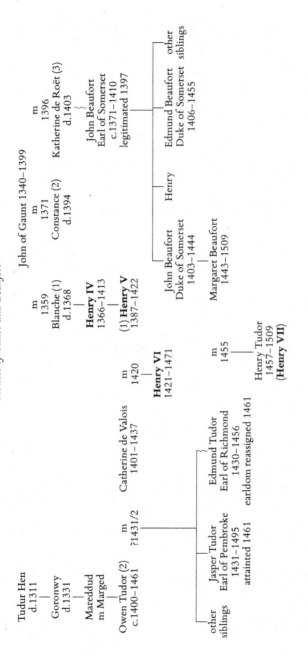

Appreciation to Annette Carson

Royal House of York

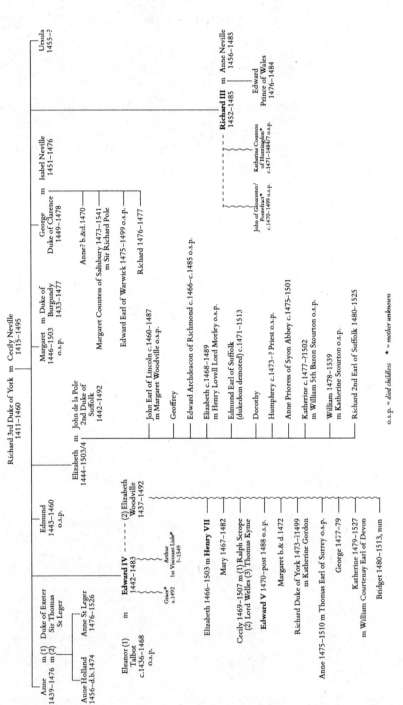

Richard 3rd Duke of York m Cecily Neville
1411–1460 | 1415–1495

Anne m (1) Duke of Exeter m (2) Anne St Leger 1476–1526 — **Edmund** 1443–1460 o.s.p. — **Elizabeth** m John de la Pole 2nd Duke of Suffolk 1442–1492 — **Margaret** m Duke of Burgundy 1446–1503 o.s.p. 1433–1477 — **George** m Isabel Neville Duke of Clarence 1451–1476 1449–1478 — **Ursula** 1455–?

Anne 1439–1476 m (1) Sir Thomas St Leger

Anne Holland 1456–d.b.1474

Edward IV 1442–1483 - - - - (2) Elizabeth Woodville 1437–1492

Eleanor (1) Talbot c.1436–1468 o.s.p.

Arthur 1st Viscount Lisle ?–1549

Grace★ a.1492

John Earl of Lincoln c.1460–1487 m Margaret Woodville o.s.p.

Geoffrey

Edward Archdeacon of Richmond c.1466–c.1485 o.s.p.

Elizabeth c.1468–1489 m Henry Lovell Lord Morley o.s.p.

Edmund Earl of Suffolk (dukedom demoted) c.1471–1513

Dorothy

Humphrey c.1473–? Priest o.s.p.

Anne Prioress of Syon Abbey c.1475–1501

Katherine c.1477–?1502 m William 5th Baron Stourton o.s.p.

William 1478–1539 m Katherine Stourton o.s.p.

Richard 2nd Earl of Suffolk 1480–1525

Anne? b.&d.1470

Margaret Countess of Salisbury 1473–1541 m Sir Richard Pole

Edward Earl of Warwick 1475–1499 o.s.p.

Richard 1476–1477

Richard III m Anne Neville 1452–1485 | 1456–1485

John of Gloucester/ Pontefract★ c.1470–1499 o.s.p.

Katherine Countess of Huntingdon★ c.1471–1487? o.s.p.

Edward Prince of Wales 1476–1484

Elizabeth 1466–1503 m **Henry VII**

Mary 1467–1482

Cecily 1469–1507 m (1) Ralph Scrope (2) Lord Welles (3) Thomas Kyme

Edward V 1470–post 1488 o.s.p.

Margaret b.& d 1472

Richard Duke of York 1473–?1499 m Katherine Gordon

Anne 1475–1510 m Thomas Earl of Surrey o.s.p.

George 1477–79

Katherine 1479–1527 m William Courtenay Earl of Devon

Bridget 1480–1513, nun

o.s.p. = *died childless*   ★ = *mother unknown*

Family of Peirse of Bedale

Peter Peirse of Bedale
Standard Bearer to King Richard the third at Bosworth field
where he lost a leg but lived many years after

Henry Peirse of Bedale d.1487 (Portugal) o.s.p.	Thomas Peirse of Bedale	

Thomas Peirse of Bedale:

| Richard Peirse of Bedale d.1573 | Christopher of Burrell bur. 16 August 1597 | Anne? |

Marmaduke Peirse of Bedale d.1609 — m — Dorothy, daughter of Gale of Scruton, d.1599

| George a.1581 | Anne a.1581 | Anne |

Henry Peirse of Bedale d.a.1602 — m — Isabella, sister of Matthew Pickering of Richmond

| Richard b.1602 o.s.p. | Elizabeth 1591–1610 | Dorothy b.1596 |

John Peirse of Bedale, Gent. Sewer to Charles I 1593–1658 — m — Sarah, daughter of Peter Chamberlayne

| Dorothy, married Ralph Dowson of Lofthouse | Elizabeth, Sarah, Hannah | Isabella, married 1660, Abraham Clough of Kingston upon Hull |

Richard Peirse of Lazenby, Hutton Bonville, etc., d.1708 — m — Mary, daughter of Matthew Hutton of Markse.

John of Bedale d. unm.

Appreciation to Lady Judranka Beresford-Peirse

Maps

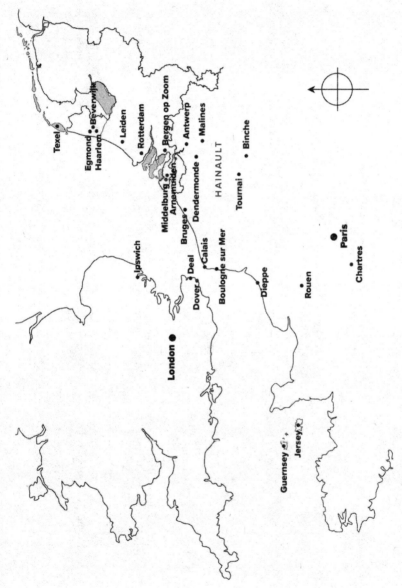

England, France and the Low Countries (Belgium and Holland). (Philippa Langley)

UK, Ireland and the Channel Islands. (Philippa Langley)

Introduction

The Inspiration

On 25 August 2012, the mortal remains of Richard III of England (1452–85) were discovered beneath a car park in Leicester. News of the discovery and the king's eventual reburial went viral, reaching an estimated global audience of over 366 million.[1] The return of the king captured the world's imagination, but how had this come about? The search for Richard III had been instigated and led not by an academic or archaeologist, but by a writer.

The Looking For Richard Project was a research initiative which questioned received wisdom and dogma. It proved the 'bones in the river' story to be false. For centuries, it had been believed that at the time of the Dissolution of the Monasteries (in the late 1530s), Richard III's remains were exhumed from their resting place, carried through the streets of Leicester by a jeering mob and reburied near the River Soar. Later, it was claimed they were exhumed again and thrown into the river.[2] Without any supporting evidence, the story had been repeated as truth and fact by leading historians.

We also disproved the local projection that the lost Greyfriars Church was probably inaccessible, being under the buildings and road of Grey Friars (street). This was suggested in 1986, with a plaque erected four years later to mark the location. It would be further supported in 2002.[3]

The Looking For Richard Project also examined Richard III's character by commissioning the first-ever psychological analysis by two of the UK's leading experts, Dr Julian Boon and Professor Mark Lansdale. Their eighteen-month study, based on the known details of Richard's life, revealed that he was not psychopathic, narcissistic or Machiavellian – three of the traits long employed by traditional writers to describe the king.

In physical terms, analysis of Richard's remains by scientists at the University of Leicester revealed that the king was not, as Shakespeare depicted, a 'hunchback' afflicted by kyphosis (a forward bend of the spine). Richard suffered from a scoliosis (a sideways bend), which resulted in uneven shoulders. As there is no record in the king's lifetime of any disparity in shoulder height, the condition was not readily apparent.[4]

Analysis also discovered that Richard, contrary to Shakespeare, did not walk with a limp. His hips were straight and his legs normal. He was not lame and was not described in such terms during his lifetime. Similarly, he did not suffer from a withered arm as alleged by the Tudor writer Thomas More. Both arms were of equal length and size.

In addition, the story that the king's head had struck Bow Bridge when his body was brought to Leicester over the back of a horse following the Battle of Bosworth was also proved false. There were no marks on the king's skull to suggest that it had come into contact with anything resembling a stone or bridge.

The Looking For Richard Project heralded a new era of evidence-based Richard III research and analysis. It was a major opportunity for the academic community and leading historians to employ this new knowledge as the basis for further discoveries.

We didn't have to wait long. As we headed towards the king's reburial, two key members of the team were undertaking their own evidence-based investigations.

Dr John Ashdown-Hill was investigating the king's dental record, revealing that Richard's teeth showed no consanguinity (blood relationship) with the 'bones in the urn' in Westminster Abbey, said to be those of the Princes in the Tower. The story promulgated by historians for centuries was now open to question.[5]

Richard III had no congenitally missing teeth, a condition known as hypodontia. This was in direct contrast to the bones in Westminster Abbey, where both skulls presented this genetic anomaly. Previously, it had been argued that this inherited dental characteristic had proved the royal identity of the remains.[6]

So, was this story yet another myth; as great a historical red herring as the 'bones in the river' story?

Another key member of the Looking For Richard Project was undertaking her own enquiries. Annette Carson, a leading biographer of Richard III, published an important constitutional examination of Richard's legal authority in 1483. *Richard, Duke of Gloucester as Lord Protector and High Constable of England* (2015) revealed that Richard's actions during the protectorate were fully compliant with his official position as Protector and Constable of England. This included the execution of William, Lord Hastings, where Richard is traditionally accused of overstepping his rightful authority. So, it seemed that the Looking For Richard Project had been the catalyst for a new era of evidence-based research that would lead to significant discoveries concerning the debate around Richard III.

It would be important for traditional historians to raise their own questions. In May 2014, a year after the announcement of the identification of the king, Professor Michael Hicks, Emeritus Professor of Medieval History at the University of Winchester, was the first.[7]

Despite the overwhelming evidence supporting a positive identification, Hicks contested that the remains could belong to 'a victim of any of the battles fought during the Wars of the Roses'. He questioned the DNA evidence and singled out the carbon-14 dating analysis, which covered a period of eighty years, as 'imprecise'. University of Leicester scientists responded firmly, explaining how the identification had been made by 'combining different lines of evidence'. They would 'challenge and counter' Professor Hicks' views in follow-up papers, 'demonstrating that many of his assumptions are incorrect'.

In December 2014, the university published a paper on the DNA investigation, explaining that 'analysis of all the available evidence confirms identity of King Richard III to the point of 99.999% (at its most conservative)'.[8] Genealogist Ashdown-Hill examined Hicks' suggestion and established that no other individual satisfied the criteria as an alternative candidate.[9] Hicks felt that the remains were those of an illegitimate family member whose name is now lost to us.

On Tuesday, 24 March 2015, during reburial week, a headline in the *Daily Mail* proclaimed, 'It's mad to make this child killer a national hero: Richard III was one of the most evil, detestable tyrants ever to walk this earth.' The writer, Michael Thornton, presented no verification or proof. His piece drew online comments from around the world, best summed up by Catherine from Chicago, United States, 'This article shows a complete disregard for what counts as historical evidence'.

Thornton's article had been prompted by a TV programme screened a few days earlier. On Saturday, 21 March 2015, the day before the king's coffin made its historic journey to Leicester Cathedral, Channel 4 broadcast *The Princes in the Tower* by Oxford Film & Television,[10] promoted as 'a new drama-documentary … in which key figures … debate one of English history's darkest murder mysteries'. An extended release from Oxford Film & Television stated:

> More than 500 years after the Princes disappeared the arguments about their fate rage as fiercely as ever. No bodies were produced, no funeral was performed. This is the ultimate medieval whodunit: there are villainous tyrants, scheming rivals, and two young boys in the Tower who meet a grisly end. Was the dastardly Richard to blame as Shakespeare says? Or was Richard framed by a powerful enemy? By unpicking the events that led to the boys' disappearance, and exploring the murderous power struggle at court, this film cuts through centuries of propaganda to examine the real evidence …[11]

The programme was a strange mish-mash. Despite an apparent intention to engage in meaningful debate, the broadcast failed to live up to its billing. Most historians and writers gave pertinent and important material insights, particularly Janina Ramirez, who was at pains to offer fact over reported fiction. But sadly, instead of following the known facts, the programme took the road most travelled: evil schemers in dark corners leading the viewer to the requisite conclusion – the boys were murdered, and by their uncle Richard. Indeed, the finale claimed that the mystery of the disappearance of the Princes in the Tower had been solved, a conclusion erroneously reached by a Tudor historian misrepresenting a later Tudor source. The *Daily Telegraph* reviewed it as a 'flimsy documentary drama which served as hype … with little reference to any evidence'.[12]

I nevertheless held out hope that the traditional community might embrace a new era of evidence-based history. However, what happened next would act as a catalyst for an entirely new research initiative.

On Monday, 22 March 2015, as Richard's coffin was received by Leicester Cathedral in preparation for reburial, Channel 4 TV presenter Jon Snow asked a Tudor historian for the evidence of Richard's murder of the Princes in the Tower. 'The evidence', the historian replied, 'is that he would have been a fool not to do it.'

In another of Snow's television interviews on 26 March, the evening of King Richard's reburial, I was asked, 'What next?'

'There's a big question to answer now', I replied. 'What happened to the sons of Edward IV?'

I had seen how asking questions changes what we know and is a key to greater understanding and important new discoveries. This was how the king had been found.

Historical enquiry is littered with the unpicking of received wisdom. Antonia Fraser helped to debunk the myth that Marie Antoinette said 'Let them eat cake'; Virginia Rounding refuted the claim that Catherine the Great had been killed by having sexual relations with a horse; William Driver Howarth disproved that the right of 'prima nocta' (*Droit de seigneur*) existed in medieval Scotland (as depicted in the film *Braveheart*); and Guilhem Pépin established that the brutal massacre of 3,000 men, women and children at Limoges in 1370, believed for centuries to have been carried out by England's Black Prince, was in fact perpetrated by French forces on their own people.[13] All had asked searching questions, thrown out old mythology and started with a clean sheet. It was exactly as my Looking For Richard Project had proceeded, irrevocably changing what we know. Could this approach apply to the mystery surrounding the Princes in the Tower?

While I considered my next steps, I watched with interest *The Imitation Game* (2014), starring Benedict Cumberbatch, the actor who had read the evocative poem 'Richard' at the reburial in 2015. Loosely based on Andrew Hodges' biography of Alan Turing, this highly acclaimed award-winning feature film retells the breaking of the Enigma code during the Second World War.

When you ask the right questions, the smallest detail can form the key to a major discovery. For Turing and his team, it was the realisation that his new 'computer' machine (named Christopher) and two words of German ('*Heil Hitler*') were all that was required to break the unbreakable code. It gave hope to my new search to uncover the truth about the disappearance of the sons of Edward IV. Could a small and perhaps seemingly insignificant discovery be the key to solving this most enduring of mysteries?

Philippa Langley

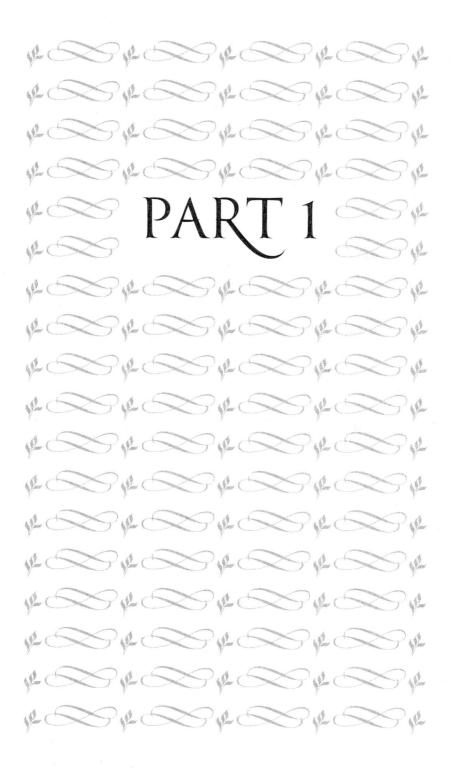

PART 1

1

The Missing Princes Project

A Cold-Case Investigation

Before we investigate the traditional story of the murder of the sons of King Edward IV, it is important to introduce The Missing Princes Project and to explain its methodology. Some of those involved in the project have written papers for this work, presenting archival discoveries and evidence. As a result, this publication represents the project's first five-year report (2016–21).

It is also important, as the project's lead, to clarify my position and role. I have studied the life and times of Richard III for nearly thirty years. It is a fascinating period of history, inspiring George R.R. Martin's *Game of Thrones* fantasy series, and, of course, William Shakespeare's famous play. And therein, it seems, lies the dichotomy of the two representations of Richard III: the loyal lord of the north (one interpretation),[1] and the murdering psychopath. Two extremes certainly, but as we may all attest, life is many shades of grey. As a result, it was important to begin this investigation with a clean sheet. Yes, I am a Ricardian and revisionist. I hold this position on the basis of years of analysis of the contemporary source materials created during Richard's lifetime. While much of that evidence has survived, a great deal more has been lost or destroyed since his death at the Battle of Bosworth.

However, I was clear from the outset that I had to be prepared for whatever might be uncovered. The Looking For Richard Project had sought to lay the king to rest. It was now time to investigate the final question surrounding Richard III – in the hope of making peace with the past, on both sides of the debate.

My role was that of the investigation's operations room – its hub – part of which involved launching a new website designed to attract volunteer members, the project's boots on the ground. Intelligence gathering would be paramount if the project was to succeed in its primary aim of unravelling the mystery surrounding the boys' disappearance. There is considerable archival material in America and Europe, particularly France, Germany and the Low Countries. I would need help if the project was to have any hope of uncovering new and neglected evidence.

I also had to prepare for the possibility that many searches would probably prove fruitless. The ravages of time and the effects of two world wars were clearly a concern. It was also possible that after years of searching nothing new might be found. However, it was important that we were looking for the very first time.

In the summer of 1483, two children disappeared: a boy of 12 and his brother, aged 9. The enquiry into their disappearance would, therefore, fall into the category of a cold-case missing person investigation, employing the same principles and practices as a modern police enquiry. Although it was not an academic study or exercise, it would naturally involve examination of all contemporary and near contemporary material. Intelligence gathering would be key.

Cold-case procedure would introduce modern police investigative techniques to facilitate forensic analysis of existing material. This would inform the production of detailed timelines and new lines of investigation. It would also involve the application of 'means, motive, opportunity and proclivity' analysis to create a 'person of interest' enquiry and employ criminal search methodology and profiling systems. Significantly, the investigation would search for new and neglected archival material outside the main search locations and engage leading experts including police and Crime Scene Investigation (CSI) specialists.

The term 'missing' would be central because this was all we knew for certain based on the available evidence. The project could be nothing other than a missing person investigation, albeit one that was over 500 years old. It was not, by any stretch of the imagination, an easy task. Initial analysis revealed a Gordian knot of information that would have to be unravelled and scrutinised so that nothing was missed. Apparent red herrings seemed to litter the stories surrounding the disappearance and each would have to be analysed and investigated. The project could not afford to miss anything, no matter how seemingly insignificant. Everything was on the radar.

So, how could a cold-case investigation help move our knowledge forward? Hadn't the events that led to the disappearance taken place too long ago for any meaningful modern analysis?

I had come to Richard's story as a screenwriter. Screenwriters are not in the business of writing about saints but about the human condition – the complex, conflicted, flawed – the real, or the 'as real' as the source material might allow. As I learnt more, I discovered that the working practices of modern screenwriters are not dissimilar to those of the police and investigative agencies.

Specialists confirmed that the human element is critical to understanding and progressing an enquiry. This is achieved by first employing facts which are corroborated by the available contemporary material extracted at the location. There are three key elements: facts, as opposed to rumour, hearsay and gossip; location, proximity to the place under investigation; and contemporary, proximity to the time under investigation. Second, we extrapolate that key information in terms of what is known about the actions of those involved. People do not act one-dimensionally. For screenwriters and investigative specialists alike, actions speak louder than words. We must study what people do in order to understand what they know or believe.

After specialist consultation, I discovered that successful cold-case enquiries are based on what I termed the HRH system of investigative analysis. That is, the removal of **H**indsight; **R**ecreating the past as accurately and realistically as possible by drilling down into that moment; and the introduction of the **H**uman element in order to more properly understand the intelligence gathered. In short, this is the analysis of who was doing what, where, when, why, with whom and with what consequences. Such a strategy provides modern police specialists and investigative agencies with the means of unlocking a historical enquiry, particularly a cold-case missing person investigation.

The advice of police investigators suggested the use of well-regarded methods such as TIE and ABC. TIE is the police acronym for 'Trace, Investigate, Eliminate'. As witnesses to the disappearance are clearly unavailable for interview, timelines and an extensive database would reference and cross-check movements and begin to trace and eliminate individuals from the investigation. The second police acronym, ABC (Accept nothing. Believe nobody. Challenge everything), would ensure that evidence was properly corroborated.

The project would also employ Occam's Razor: a problem-solving device in which the simplest explanation is generally correct. For many years, a key member of my local branch of the Richard III Society was prize-winning novelist David Fiddimore. Before Dave sadly passed away in June 2015, he had been the head of Customs and Excise Intelligence in Scotland, investigating crimes of piracy, smuggling (usually drug related), fraud and money laundering. At many of our meetings Dave would arrive with black eyes and on one occasion fractured ribs. He would not, he said, send his team into a situation that he himself would not face. It had been one of the reasons he was interested in Richard III; a leader who also led from the front. His years of experience also taught him one important investigative lesson – not to over-complicate a situation – Occam's Razor worked.

I had employed the problem-solving device in my search for the king. Eighteenth- and nineteenth-century accounts of the location of the lost Greyfriars Priory in Leicester had described it as being 'opposite St Martin's Church' (Leicester Cathedral). 'Priory' had been taken to mean the extensive precinct quarter encompassing an area equivalent today to five international football fields. I had challenged this view, believing it to mean the Priory church itself, its most important building. As a result, my mantra for the search for the king and at the 2012 dig was 'church-road-church'. It proved accurate.

At the Battle of Bosworth commemorations in Leicestershire on Saturday, 22 August 2015, the new research initiative was announced. I was asked for my initial thoughts. Having consulted a wide range of specialist police investigators, particularly those involved in cold-case missing person enquiries, my view was simple: could the application of Occam's Razor shed new light on the mystery? This raised an important question: a former King Edward and a former Prince Richard disappeared during the reign of Richard III, and a 'King Edward' and a 'Prince Richard' reappeared during the reign of Richard's successor, Henry VII. This simple narrative now formed a key line of enquiry.

The Missing Princes Project set out in the summer of 2015 with three lines of investigation. This quickly developed into 111 lines of enquiry – some of which you will read about in this work.

In July 2016, at the Middleham Festival, The Missing Princes Project was formally launched. Previously, on 15 December 2015, the website went live. Within a few short hours the project secured its first eight members. In the weeks and months that followed over 300 volunteers from around the world would join. Ordinary people were prepared to investigate archives, many with specialist knowledge of palaeography (ancient writing) and Latin, others with European language skills. Members of police forces and Ministry of Defence specialists also joined, as did medieval historians and specialists across a number of fields, including input from a number of the world's leading forensic anthropologists. It was exciting and daunting in equal measure.

The search for the truth had begun.

2

The Missing Princes

Edward V and Richard, Duke of York

We begin our investigation by scrutinising what is known about the two missing persons at the heart of our enquiry. By examining all available materials, we can construct profiles, analyse movements and consider those closest to them. This will allow us to delve back in time and open significant lines of investigation. We must recognise, however, that as they were children, contemporary references and evidence prior to their disappearance may be brief and lacking in detail.

The two missing persons at the centre of our endeavours are the sons of Edward IV of England (1442–83) – Edward (b. 1470) and Richard (b. 1473). Let us now examine what we know about both boys: their lives and movements, physical appearance and character, and those closest to them, particularly at the time of the disappearance. At this remove, the boys are believed to have disappeared in the summer of 1483 when Edward was 12 and Richard 9. It is also understood that they were last seen in the same location – the palace of the Tower of London.

Edward, Prince of Wales

Edward was born on Friday, 2 November 1470,[1] at Cheneygates Mansion, home of the Abbot of Westminster, which formed part of the Abbot's House complex adjoining Westminster Abbey. Edward's mother, Queen Elizabeth

Woodville, had taken sanctuary in the mansion with her three royal daughters (4-year-old Elizabeth, 3-year-old Mary and 18-month-old Cecily). Edward IV had been deposed and driven into exile in Burgundy by forces loyal to the Lancastrian king, Henry VI.

The baby was baptised in the abbey with the abbot and prior and Elizabeth, Lady Scrope, acting as godparents.[2] On St George's Day (Tuesday, 23 April) 1471, twelve days after Edward IV's restoration to the throne, the king reserved a Garter stall for his son and heir, Prince Edward, at St George's Chapel, Windsor.[3]

On 26 June 1471, Edward of Westminster was proclaimed Prince of Wales, Duke of Cornwall and Earl of Chester, and on 3 July in the Parliament chamber, the Lords Spiritual and Temporal swore an oath of allegiance to him as heir to the throne.[4] Prominent among them were Thomas Bourchier, Archbishop of Canterbury; Robert Stillington, Bishop of Bath and Wells; Anthony Woodville, Earl Rivers; William, Lord Hastings; John, Lord Howard; Henry Stafford, Duke of Buckingham (aged 15); and the king's younger brothers, George, Duke of Clarence (22) and Richard, Duke of Gloucester (19). On 8 July, by King's Patent, the rule of the prince's household and estates, was entrusted to his Council until he reached his majority at 14.[5]

On Tuesday, 29 September 1472 (Michaelmas Day), Edward was created Prince of Wales, Duke of Cornwall and Earl of Chester. On Tuesday, 13 October, the 11-month-old prince was carried by his chamberlain, Sir Thomas Vaughan, to meet Lord Gruthuyse, a Burgundian noble who had aided Edward IV during his recent exile. Later, at the investiture of Gruthuyse as Earl of Winchester, the baby was carried by the queen and wore 'robes of estate'. A surviving contemporary account of the prince's clothing includes yards of velvets and silks for doublets, gowns and bonnets.[6]

On 27 September 1473, detailed ordinances were drawn up governing Edward's household and daily life, and the toddler prince was taken to live at Ludlow Castle on the Welsh Marches.[7] Ludlow, which had been the former childhood home of Edward IV, was a Duchy of York possession, so it seems that the decision was his father's, who had been brought up in the Marches. The prince's 'Master' and 'governor and ruler' was the queen's brother, Anthony Woodville, Earl Rivers.[8]

President of the Prince's Council was John Alcock, Bishop of Rochester (later Bishop of Worcester). Alcock was also entrusted with the prince's education. The Prince's Council consisted of the queen; the Archbishop of Canterbury; the prince's paternal uncles, the Dukes of Clarence and

Gloucester; Robert Stillington, Bishop of Bath and Wells; Lawrence Booth, Bishop of Durham; and (later) Edward Storey, Bishop of Carlisle, the queen's Chancellor. Other members of the Council included the Earl of Shrewsbury, Lords Devereux and Dacre, and the prince's maternal cousins, Sir John Fogge and Richard Haute. Due to other responsibilities and distances, many may have attended on an irregular basis, if at all, 'whilst six of those who certainly did attend were the prince's maternal relatives and family appointees'.[9]

Sir Richard Grey, second son of the queen by her first marriage to Sir John Grey of Groby and Prince Edward's maternal half-brother, joined the Council in 1476.[10] On 25 February 1483, Sir William Stanley was made the Prince's Steward; Sir Richard Croft, his Treasurer; and Richard Haute, Controller of his Household.[11]

The prince's estate in Wales, together with Chester (and Flint) and the Duchy of Cornwall comprised the largest block of land owned by the Crown. This gave the Prince's Councillors control of an income conservatively estimated at £6,000 a year, about 10 per cent of the ordinary revenue of the king.[12] The profits of the prince's estates were paid into a coffer to which only the queen, Bishop Alcock and Earl Rivers had a key.[13] Rivers, the prince's maternal uncle, became the leading lord in the region; his personal signet seal replaced the prince's Great Seal in authenticating the majority of princely warrants.

Prince Edward occasionally visited one or both of his parents. In May 1474, he was with the king at Windsor, and in August 1477 he was at Windsor with the queen. The prince also journeyed to Warwick to his paternal uncle, George of Clarence in 1474 and to Haverfordwest, Coventry, Chester, Shrewsbury, Worcester, Wigmore Castle and Bewdley.[14] Early in 1483, the prince was due to visit Canterbury with the queen but the event was cancelled due to an outbreak of measles in the city.[15] Edward also spent Christmas with his family, variously at Windsor, Woking, Eltham and Greenwich, and in 1478 attended Parliament following the Great Council (see pp. 30 and 35). It seems the young prince was well used to travelling.

In June 1475, an event of international importance took place, which the 4-year-old prince may have remembered. Edward IV embarked on an invasion of France with his brothers and appointed, as was customary, the king's heir as 'keeper of the realm and lieutenant in the King's absence'. Although queen regents were not the norm in England (as they were in France), the queen would nevertheless exercise significant influence. For the thirteen weeks of the invasion, 7 July to 22 September, all government acts were witnessed in Prince Edward's name.[16] England's nobility accompanied the king to France, including John, Lord Howard, Earl Rivers and Thomas Grey, Marquess of Dorset (the prince's elder maternal half-brother). Prior to the invasion, on Tuesday, 18 April, at Westminster, Prince Edward was knighted and on Monday, 15 May made a Knight of the Garter.[17]

In preparation for the invasion, at Sandwich on Tuesday, 20 June 1475, Edward IV made his will. As heir to the throne, the prince would come of age at 14. Edward, however, inserted in his will a number of phrases which appeared to suggest some uncertainty over the succession of his eldest son. Whether the young prince was sickly or had a sickly constitution[18] or his young age prompted a natural concern in a time of high infant mortality is not clear.

On Sunday, 9 November 1477, during King Edward's imprisonment of his brother, George, Duke of Clarence, the 7-year-old prince was in London. In the presence of the Great Council, his paternal uncle, Richard, Duke of Gloucester, led the lords and nobles in pledges of fealty to the Yorkist heir. Gloucester was followed by the Duke of Buckingham and John de la Pole, Duke of Suffolk, husband of King Edward's elder sister, Elizabeth, and thereafter, Dorset, Rivers and Lord Lisle, among others.

It is here that we have what may be the only officially recorded conversation between Prince Edward and Gloucester, taken from a contemporary account in the British Library,[19] 'on both his knees, putting his hands between the prince's hands, [Gloucester] did him homage for such lands as he had of him and so kissed him'. The prince thanked 'his said uncle that it liked him to do it so humbly'.[20]

In 1479, Edward, Prince of Wales, was created Earl of March and Earl of Pembroke.[21] Two years later, in May 1481, the 10-year-old prince joined the king at Sandwich to review the English fleet. John, Lord Howard, was leading a naval campaign against Scotland.[22] Sandwich was an important Cinque Port, and the prince would have greeted the fleet's leading officers.

On Friday, 22 June 1481, Prince Edward's marriage to Anne of Brittany was ratified. This was an important political alliance intended to ensure Brittany's continued independence from its powerful neighbour of France. Previously, in 1476–78, King Edward had approached Isabella and Ferdinand of Spain for a marriage alliance, but negotiations came to nothing. Two of the Spanish monarchs' daughters had been proposed: Isabella, the Infanta, and later, Katherine of Aragon.[23] The apparent reluctance of the Spanish monarchs remains a mystery.

Prince Edward's Character

In December 1483, the Italian chronicler Domenico Mancini declared that Prince Edward was 'so much like his great father in spirit and in innate gifts as well as remarkable in his learning'.[24] In about 1490, the Burgundian chronicler Jean Molinet reported that Edward was 'undemanding and greatly melancholic'.[25] It is possible, therefore, that Edward may have followed his father's predisposition to melancholia.[26] It also seems that he was devout. As a child, the young prince's routine was structured around his daily devotions, from morning prayer in his chamber, followed by Mass, and then, in the evening, Vespers before bed at 8 p.m.

On 25 February 1483, Edward IV revised the instructions for the Prince's Household and Council. These provide a window into the character of young Edward as the 12-year-old pre-teen began to assert himself, push boundaries and 'chafe against his tutelage'.[27] The new instructions of February 1483 (about five months prior to his disappearance) reveal a prince who was developing fast.

At all times during the day, Prince Edward was to be accompanied by at least two 'discrete' persons:

> ... he was not to order anything to be done without the advice of Alcock, Grey or Rivers, and none of his servants was to encourage him to do anything against the household instructions. If he did so, or acted in an unprincely way, the three men were to warn him personally and to tell the king and queen if he refused to amend.[28]

The new instructions also ensured that nothing 'should move or stir him to vices'.

The original 1473 instructions similarly required that no one in the household should be a 'Swearer, Brawler, Back-biter, commune hazarder [gambler], Avowter [adulterer] nor fornicator or use Abawdry [bawdy] words' in his presence.[29] At night, several servants were to attend the prince in his chamber and make him 'joyous and merry' for his bedtime. A nightly watch would also ensure the prince's safeguarding, and a doctor and surgeon were to be always on hand.[30]

If these stipulations appear somewhat cloying to our modern sensibilities, it was the recognised regime of instruction for noble children at the time. We also know that Edward was not alone and enjoyed the company of other sons of the nobility who were receiving their education with him. Edward was not in seclusion.

Sadly, in about 1478, one of his companions died. Edmund Audley's family inscribed their son's honoured position in the Prince's Household on his tomb monument.[31]

Although Mancini never met Prince Edward, he described in some detail the boy's education and accomplishments, including an apparent love of literature and poetry.

> … how profuse were the signs of his liberal education and how agreeably, indeed judiciously he brought together words and deeds beyond his years … he was especially accomplished in literature, so that he possessed the ability to discuss elegantly, to understand fully and to articulate most clearly from whatever might come to hand, whether poetry or prose, unless from the most challenging authors.[32]

Mancini's informant was Dr John Argentine, the prince's physician, who was probably with him at Ludlow. Argentine seems to have fled to France at the time of the October 1483 uprising against Richard III when Mancini was preparing his report on English affairs for the French government. Mancini tells us the physician was 'the last of the attendants employed by the young king' (prior to his disappearance).

In November 1485, the Crowland chronicler described Edward and Elizabeth's children as 'handsome and most delightful'.[33]

Edward's Appearance
The recognised contemporary image of Edward V (Lambeth Palace Library) shows the young prince with his parents in 1477 as Earl Rivers presents a book to the king (see Plate 3).[34] The *Dictes and Sayings of the Philosophers* had been translated from the French by the earl. This image reveals a young boy with blond hair, with perhaps a slightly reddish tinge, similar to the depiction of his mother, Queen Elizabeth. Edward would have been 6 or 7 at the time.

The figure in the blue robe with light brown hair is thought to be his uncle, Richard of Gloucester. Post-discovery analysis of Richard III's genome revealed that he had a 77 per cent probability of having blond hair. This is thought to have been the type of blond hair that darkened with age. The earliest known (copy) portrait of Richard at the Society of Antiquaries shows the king with light brown hair (see Plate 1).[35]

An image of Edward V can be seen at Canterbury Cathedral with his family. Originally dating from about 1482, the Royal Window was considerably damaged during the Civil War by a Puritan minister wielding a pike. However, following the restoration of the monarchy, it was restored and replaced from the 1660s, when it was kept within the magnificent Rose Window but placed higher up,[36] perhaps for increased protection. Both boys are portrayed with blond hair. It is not known whether this hair colour reflected the original stained-glass images. Later nineteenth-century artists (Millais and Delaroche) followed the same colouring. What is unusual, however, in terms of our investigations, is that the restored upper portions of Edward V (and his brother) in Canterbury are shown wearing the closed crown of a king (see Plates 6 and 7).

We do have one surviving contemporary image from the Royal Window at Canterbury, which resides in the Burrell Collection in Glasgow and depicts Prince Edward's elder sister, Cecily. This reveals a young woman with reddish-blonde hair wearing an open circlet crown.

The earliest known portrait of Edward IV, also at the Society of Antiquaries, depicts the king with very light brown, almost dark blond hair. However, the Lambeth Palace image of 1477 portrays Edward IV with dark brown hair.

Several sixteenth- and seventeenth-century images of Edward V exhibit blond, reddish blond or light brown hair. However, a contemporary depiction at Little Malvern Priory in Worcester from around 1482 (see Plate 4) shows the prince in an open circlet crown with medium blond hair. As a result, it seems that Edward had blond hair as a child which slightly darkened with age.

In terms of Edward's physicality, Mancini tells us that the prince 'indulged in horses and dogs and other useful exertions to build bodily strength'.[37] Although Richard III's remains were described as 'gracile' (slender), it is not known if young Edward possessed a similar build. 'He had such dignity in his whole person and in his countenance such charm,' continued Mancini, 'that, however much they might feast their eyes, he never surfeited the gaze of observers.'[38] In 1482, Italian poet Pietro Carmeliano met Prince Edward (aged 11) and stated that he was the 'most comely of princes ... and all the stars rejoice in your face. Justly do you have the king's visage, best of dukes, for the kingly sceptre awaits you after your father.'[39] This is perhaps the most important physical description we have of the young prince – that, prior to puberty, he resembled his father.

Richard, Duke of York

Richard was probably born on Tuesday, 17 August 1473, at the Dominican Priory, Shrewsbury, on the Welsh borders.[40] He was the sixth child of King Edward and Queen Elizabeth, and their second son. The date of Richard's birth is uncertain since it was not recorded in the chronicles of the time. However, seven years later, on 17 August he received the regalia for the noble Order of the Garter, which seems to confirm the assumed birth date.[41]

On Saturday, 28 May 1474, 9-month-old Prince Richard was created Duke of York in a magnificent ceremony in London with celebratory jousts. Almost a year later, on Tuesday, 18 April 1475, the infant prince was knighted with his elder brother,[42] and a month later, made a Knight of the Garter with his brother. The little Duke of York had already received a Garter stall at St George's Chapel in April, vacated by the death of Lord Beauchamp. He is listed as one of the Scrutiners, an honorary title for the toddler.[43]

Edward IV's will, made in June 1475 when Richard was almost 2, indicates that the prince was a healthy and active child. The document, cautious in terms of young Edward's survival, is much more positive about his younger brother.[44] At the age of 16 in August 1489, he would reach maturity and take possession of his lordships and inheritances.[45]

Richard's wedding to Anne Mowbray on Monday, 15 January 1478, was perhaps the most extraordinary event of the prince's infant life. Anne had inherited the considerable estates of the dukedom of Norfolk following her father's death on 17 January 1476. The bride was 5 and the groom 4 years old when their nuptials were celebrated at St Stephen's Chapel in Westminster Abbey. The marriage itself would not, naturally, be consummated until the bride and groom had reached 'nubile years'.

The wedding was timed to coincide with a Parliament, allowing the nobility to gather en masse to honour the couple. An eyewitness testimony records, 'The press was so great … the abundance of the noble people so innumerable.'[46] Anne was escorted to the chapel by Earl Rivers and the young John de la Pole, Earl of Lincoln (aged about 15). Lincoln was Edward IV's nephew by the king's elder sister, Elizabeth, Duchess of Suffolk.

The young bridegroom and his family, including his elder brother and grandmother, Cecily, Dowager Duchess of York, waited to receive his bride under a canopy of cloth of gold. The king gave away the bride. Following Mass at the high altar, Prince Richard's uncle, the Duke of Gloucester, threw gold and silver coins to the onlookers. Gloucester and Buckingham led the bride to the king's great chamber for the wedding feast. Three great jousting tournaments were held, with Rivers one of the victors.[47]

As Anne Mowbray's mother, the Dowager Duchess of Norfolk, had failed to produce a male heir, Anne's young husband was created Duke of Norfolk and Earl of Warenne on Friday, 7 February 1477.[48] By 1478, Richard had also become Earl Marshal of England – a title generally associated with the Norfolk dukedom. Eleanor Talbot (d. 1468) (see Chapter 7) was the elder sister of Anne's mother.

On Wednesday, 12 June 1476, a further Mowbray title was granted to Richard when he became Earl of Nottingham, and the following year he received his own council chamber in preparation for his ducal Council. In November 1477, 4-year-old Richard attended the Great Council with his 7-year-old brother, the Prince of Wales. Edward received the fealty of the lords and nobles, led by Gloucester. The Prince of Wales was seated on a bed beneath the cloth of estate, while his brother, Richard, 'sat on the bed's foot beside the cloth of estate'.[49]

By 1478, as the holder of many great offices, estates and lordships, 5-year-old Richard, Duke of York and Norfolk, had his own Council, including a Chancellor, lawyer, treasurer and Chamberlain, Sir Thomas Grey.[50] He also had his own seal and several gentlemen servants including John Roden, Thomas Galmole[51] and (by 1483) Poynes, who 'dwelled' with him.[52]

On 5 May 1479, Richard of York was appointed Lord Lieutenant of Ireland for two years, an appointment renewed in August the following year for a further twelve years.[53] This would take Richard's role in Ireland to his twentieth birthday in 1493. Previously, in December 1479, the young prince had travelled to Ireland, undertaking what seems to have been his first official visit, with the 6-year-old witnessing the appointment of the Constable of Dublin Castle. Placed in this key role in Dublin was Sir James Keating, a staunch Yorkist.[54]

Sadly, Richard and Anne's marriage was not to last. In November 1481, Anne died, aged 8, at Greenwich Palace and was buried in the Chapel of St Erasmus at Westminster Abbey.[55] The chapel had been founded by Queen Elizabeth Woodville, following the birth of Edward, Prince of Wales, in Westminster sanctuary.

The vast Mowbray estates should now pass to Anne's heirs, cousins William, Viscount Berkeley, and John, Lord Howard. However, in January 1483, by Act of Parliament, Edward IV gave his youngest son the rights to the estates, with a reversion to his male heirs. Failing that, the estates would revert to the king himself. As historian Charles Ross commented, this provided 'a colour of legality to a situation which violated the rules of landed inheritance'.[56]

Edward IV died on 3 April 1483,[57] leaving Edward V as king and Richard, Duke of York and Norfolk, heir presumptive. Two months later, on Monday, 16 June, young Richard left his mother's side to join Edward in the Tower of London, 'for the comfort of his brother the king' prior to his coronation.[58] On this occasion, we learn of the only recorded conversation with his uncle, Gloucester. It was reported on 21 June, five days later, when the priest, Canon Simon Stallworth, wrote to Sir William Stonor.

As Stallworth was in the service of the Lord Chancellor, John Russell, Bishop of Lincoln, he was probably an eyewitness, or received a first-hand account, possibly from Russell himself. He reported that Gloucester received his young nephew at the Star Chamber door at Westminster 'with many loving words'. The letter goes on to add that the young prince is 'blessed be Jesus, merry'.[59] Despite having his own Council, the little Duke of York had always lived with his mother and his acts were subject to her assent and advice.[60] Gloucester's work for the government brought him regularly to court and the boy would have known his youngest royal uncle as a familiar figure.

Richard's Character

We have three contemporary and near-contemporary accounts of Richard of York's character and demeanour. First, Stallworth's letter of June 1483, mentioned above, in which Richard is 'blessed be Jesus, merry'. The second, dating to 1496, in which Rui de Sousa, the Portuguese Ambassador to England from 1481 to 1489,[61] described the young prince as 'a very noble little boy and that he had seen him singing with his mother and one of his sisters and that he sang very well'. De Sousa added that Richard was 'playing very well at sticks and with a two-handed sword'.[62]

The third account was provided by the Burgundian chronicler Jean Molinet in about 1490. Molinet is confused, calling Edward 'Peter' and Richard 'George'. While at the Tower with his brother, 'the second son was greatly joyous and spirited, keen and prompt to dance and play'. Molinet adds that the younger son then asked his brother to dance to cheer his spirits, saying, 'My brother, learn to dance'. The request was rebuffed, and Edward responded, 'It would be better if you and I learn to die, because I believe that we will not be of this world for long.'[63] Although Molinet's version is probably apocryphal, the eyewitness accounts of Stallworth and de Sousa appear authentic.

We may, therefore, deduce that Richard seems to have been a lively and happy child. He enjoyed music, singing and dancing and was also considered athletic, being good at sports, sticks and a two-handed sword. He also seems to have possessed a certain natural charm. De Sousa was so taken with him that the old ambassador could remember him with clarity some fifteen years later.

Growing up as the only boy, following the death of his younger brother George in 1479, historian Ann Wroe suggests he may well have been petted and adored by his sisters, all of whom except Catherine were older. Aristocratic boys aged 7 were normally educated in other noble households, usually some distance from their homes and families. However, from what little information we have, it seems that Richard may have had his own household in London. Whether he was separated at the age of 7 from his mother and sisters is not known. Like his elder brother, however, he would have been educated and trained with noble companions of a similar age. In January 1483, John Howard presented Richard with a bow, so it's likely the 9-year-old prince also enjoyed shooting arrows.[64]

Richard's Appearance

We have two accounts of Richard's appearance. In 1496, de Sousa described the young prince as 'very pretty and the most beautiful creature he had ever seen'.[65] In 1493, Richard's aunt, Margaret of Burgundy, recalled the prince in the summer of 1480 during a visit to England. She writes, having met a young man purporting to be the adult Richard:

> I recognised him as easily as if I had last seen him yesterday or the day before … and that was not by one or two general signs, but by so many visible and specific signs that hardly one person in ten hundred thousand [a million] might be found who would have marks of the same kind.[66]

For Richard of York's distinguishing physical marks, see Chapter 14, note 84, Chapter 17, note 241, and Appendices 4 and 7.

Profiles

From this, we can construct profiles of both missing individuals. Edward was clearly intelligent and seems to have had a particular love and understanding of literature and poetry. He had blond hair and resembled his father. He may also have been physically slight. At the time of his disappearance, he was a pre-teen and seems to have begun pushing boundaries and asserting himself. He may have had a predisposition to melancholia or a susceptibility to pre-teen sulks.

His brother, Richard, seems to have been healthy and physically active, with a more robust constitution. He enjoyed singing and dance and may have had a natural aptitude for music and some sport. He also seems to have been a particularly happy and exuberant child. He probably had fair colouring. Both boys were considered handsome, particularly Richard, who seems to have been 'the most beautiful creature'. They also possessed charm and were clearly memorable, particularly in terms of their appearance and personalities. Both boys also lived in large, busy households.

The next stage of the enquiry will reconstruct events immediately prior to the boys' disappearance, allowing us to delve back in time and open new lines of investigation.

3

1483

Two Weeks, One Summer

On Monday, 16 June 1483, Thomas Bourchier, Archbishop of Canterbury, and John, Lord Howard, escorted Edward IV's youngest son, Richard, Duke of York, from sanctuary at Cheneygates Mansion[1] at Westminster Abbey to the Royal Palace of the Tower of London.[2] Travelling in a flotilla of boats along the Thames with these two stalwarts of his father's court, the young prince may have taken the opportunity to wave to the people on the quaysides as they passed.[3] London was always busy but now it was teeming with visitors.

In the Royal Apartments at the Tower, Richard of York would join his elder brother, Edward, for his brother's coronation in six days' time, on Sunday, 22 June. The following day, however, everything would change.

On Tuesday, 17 June, the King's Council postponed Edward V's coronation until 9 November.[4] What had caused this unprecedented event?

Five days later, on the day the coronation was due to take place, news of Edward IV's bigamous marriage and the illegitimacy of his children was announced.[5] As a bastard, Edward was barred from the succession. He could not be anointed with the Holy Chrism and crowned. An unparalleled constitutional crisis had erupted. On Wednesday, 25 June, the Lords, Church and Commons, the Three Estates of the Realm, petitioned the next Yorkist heir to accept the throne.[6] The following day, on Thursday, 26 June, Richard, Duke of Gloucester, the children's paternal uncle, accepted the throne. England now had a new king.[7]

On Sunday, 6 July 1483, Richard III was crowned at Westminster Abbey, his wife, Anne Neville, beside him. It was the first double coronation since Edward II and Isabella of France in 1307. It was also the first-ever coronation of northerners. Sometime afterwards, it seemed that the whereabouts of the sons of the late king Edward IV were no longer known.

The events of the summer of 1483 are among the most contested in British history. Foreign and Tudor chroniclers (and Shakespeare) describe a ruthless grab for power, planned in the north following Edward IV's death in early April. From this moment on, Richard, Duke of Gloucester, Edward's erstwhile loyal brother, would stop at nothing until he had taken the throne.

This is the traditional story, devoid of context and detail, but is it supported by contemporary sources from Gloucester's own lifetime? If we follow our police methodology, drill down into the moment, eliminating all hindsight reporting, what might this reveal?

Today, the Tudor account of 1483 is still the generally accepted version of events, promulgated for centuries by prominent traditional historians – and they may be correct. However, if we are to attempt to uncover the truth, we must reconstruct events from the start and investigate where contemporary evidence suggests a far more nuanced version.

As an example, in April 2015 new research was published by historical biographer Annette Carson which changed perceptions by expanding what we know. It revealed one small detail that has been hitherto forgotten or omitted by our leading historians. In 1483, Richard, Duke of Gloucester, was Lord High Constable of England.[8] He had been granted the office for life on 17 October 1469 at the age of 17. Within an overall span of fourteen years,[9] he had carried out this role for his brother with apparent responsibility, prudence and judiciousness, as indeed (the sources attest) he had performed all offices awarded to him by the king. These included Warden of the West Marches, Lord Great Chamberlain of England, Lord High Admiral of England and, since 1480 and the Scottish wars, Lieutenant General of England's land forces.[10]

So, what powers did the Constable of England exercise? Carson reveals:

> The High Constable of England, as one of the Great Officers of State, wielded national powers which included some that were second only to the king himself, principally when dealing with rebellion, insurrection or any of the many other activities deemed to be treasonable.[11]

The role was military and judicial, with powers to arrest, try, condemn and sentence without appeal. The Constable operated through the Constable's Court, also known as the Court of Chivalry or Court of Knighthood. A knight was a member of an international Christian fellowship of honour, a knight of Christ. Thus, if he breached a solemn promise made on his honour, he could be charged with 'treason to his knighthood'.[12] In dealing with treason, the Constable's Court could supersede the right of the nobility to trial by their assembled peers. It also extended to encompass not only the ranks of *miles* (knights) but all levels of society.[13] The Constable also had the power to appoint a deputy or deputies.

Richard's authority as High Constable will be new to many readers, which is why, in terms of our enquiry, it is important that the role of the High Constable is taken into serious consideration.

In order to investigate the disappearance of the Princes in the Tower in 1483, we must first contextualise the events that led to the boys' presence in the Tower, and the wider events surrounding what we now know as the Wars of the Roses, or the Cousins' War, as it is perhaps better understood. This is important in order to form and inform potential lines of enquiry.

We'll begin by discussing briefly the background to the conflict and then consider the events of 1483, based on our police methodology and most recent research.

Background: The Cousins' War

In the mid-fifteenth century, there arose contention during the disastrous reign of the Lancastrian King Henry VI (1421–71). Henry suffered from a condition which resulted in prolonged bouts of mental instability and catatonia (a combination of symptoms causing lack of movement and communication, confusion, mutism and agitation). In 1455, on the king's latest return to relative stability, his cousin Richard, 3rd Duke of York (1411–60) found himself and his circle discarded by Henry and under political attack from the bewildered king's favoured advisors. Violence on both sides erupted into sporadic battles, until in 1460 York saw his only recourse was to assert his claim to the throne through his family line, a line senior to Henry's House of Lancaster.

The Duke of York (father of Edward IV and Richard III) was, like Henry, a direct descendant of Edward III (1312–77), who had several surviving sons (see family tree on p. 10). Henry was descended from the third son, John of Gaunt, Duke of Lancaster. Gaunt's son took the throne in 1399 as Henry IV. Richard of York inherited his ducal title from Edward III's fourth son, but his senior royal lineage descended from Edward's second son, Lionel, Duke of Clarence, whose entitlement to the succession had been disenfranchised when Henry IV took the throne.

In order to understand why a descendant of a third son of Edward III was king, instead of the descendant of a second son (following the established right of male primogeniture), we have to go back to the end of 1376 and the beginning of 1377. At this time, following the death of Edward III's eldest son and heir, Edward, the Black Prince, and subsequent accession of the prince's heir, Richard II, a boy of 10 years, Edward III amended the right of succession by removing the heirs of Lionel, Duke of Clarence. The reason for this removal was because Lionel's heir was a female (Philippa). Philippa had married Edward Mortimer, 3rd Earl of March.

As historian Ian Mortimer clarifies, 'King Edward [III] and others at his court believed that he had the right to establish the line of succession without reference to Parliament as this is implicit in his entail of the throne on his heirs male.'[14] As a result, John of Gaunt and his son, Henry Bolingbroke, now established their right to the throne. It is important to note here, however, that Edward III was pursuing a claim to the crown of France, where there existed a Salic Law of succession. Had he been successful, his descendants would have been affected by this Salic Law, which excluded women and their descendants from the throne. England had no such law, and indeed, attempts at entailing the throne were viewed dubiously by the English Parliament.

Richard II, despite two marriages, remained childless, and in the Parliament of 1386, Roger Mortimer, 4th Earl of March (son of Philippa), was declared his heir. The Westminster chronicler also recorded that Roger's young sons, Edmund and Roger, were the heirs presumptive.

Richard was adept at using the succession as a political weapon, and by January 1398 had changed his mind. Mortimer, unlike his cousins, received no dukedom, but at the prorogued Parliament of January 1398 he received a 'hero's reception when he arrived at Westminster'. Ian Mortimer adds:

Twenty thousand turned out to see him, according to Usk, which even though it is probably a gross exaggeration, is probably sufficient indication to conclude that many of the populace still believed that the rightful line of succession lay in the Mortimer family, and wished to demonstrate in his favour as a protest against Richard.[15]

By 1394, Richard, suspicious of Gaunt and harbouring a deep hatred of Gaunt's son Henry Bolingbroke, decided that his new heir was to be 'his very dear uncle', Edmund of Langley, 1st Duke of York (Edward III's fourth son). Richard believed that he had finally eradicated the Lancastrian claim to the throne.[16]

Henry Bolingbroke thought otherwise. After his father's death, he took up arms and seized the throne from Richard II, having secured Edmund of Langley's capitulation. Bolingbroke, now Henry IV, the first Lancastrian king, would witness rebellions against his reign, most famously by his erstwhile supporter Henry Percy (Hotspur). Percy was a revered and respected noble in the north who had married Elizabeth Mortimer, granddaughter of Lionel, Duke of Clarence.

Henry IV's son, Henry V, would also experience rebellion and conspiracy, significantly by Richard, Earl of Cambridge, Edmund of Langley's second son (see the family tree on p. 10), whom he executed. As to the young Mortimer heirs, Edmund and Roger, you can read more about them and their neglected significance in Chapter 11.

It seems apparent that Edward III sowed the seeds of the Cousins' War with his unilateral attempt in 1376–77 to erect a barrier to the descendants of Clarence, who would otherwise be heirs presumptive after his death – thus providing cover for Henry IV's seizure of the crown. The disruption of the line of succession by the Lancastrian dynasty in 1399 was still remembered in the 1450s by those who, like Richard, Duke of York, sought remedy for being dispossessed and ostracised under his grandson, Henry VI. York's claim to the throne was adjudicated and found valid by Parliament, resulting in the dynasty of Yorkist kings.

With this in mind, let us now place under the microscope the events of summer 1483, which led to the presence of the sons of Edward IV in the Tower of London.

1483

On Thursday, 3 April 1483,[17] King Edward IV died at his Palace of Westminster in London. The day previously, Edward had sent a letter to John Howard at his home at Stoke-by-Nayland, Suffolk. The letter was received by Howard on Friday, 4 April.[18] We do not know the contents of the letter.

It seems that Howard now prepared a large contingent of men to travel with him to the king at Westminster.[19] Howard left for London on Monday, 7 April.[20]

In London, no announcement was made regarding the king's death. We do not know why. Edward was only 40 years of age, his illness was short and his death unexpected.[21] He also left a very young heir, aged 12. It seems that Edward prepared for the eventuality of his death because he added a number of codicils to his will at this time.[22]

In York, on Sunday, 6 April, news of his demise was received by the Dean of York Minster, who immediately notified the city's mayor. The following morning, Monday, 7 April, the mayor informed the City Council and a dirge for the deceased king was organised at the Minster for noon that day.[23] As no service was offered for the king on the Sunday, it seems that York Minster received the news very late that day, possibly at night.

Chronology suggests that Edward may have died in the early hours of the morning. General travel times to York from London were approximately four or five days. The messenger arrived within three days. We do not know who this messenger was, or why someone at court sent the news north, or indeed, if this had been the dying king's command. It seems, at this remove, to have been the only message sent at this time (see p. 46), other than the earlier letter to Howard. It seems probable that the message was also destined for the king's brother in the north, Richard, Duke of Gloucester. As the chronicler Mancini informs us, later communications were despatched to Gloucester by William, Lord Hastings, the King's Chamberlain and close confidant in London. It is therefore possible that the message which reached York on 6 April may have been delivered at his command.[24]

On Wednesday, 9 April, John Howard arrived in London and headed to Westminster.[25] The king's death was now announced in the capital.[26] On Thursday, 17 April, the second week's anniversary of King Edward's death, the solemn rituals for the king's burial at Windsor began and Edward's coffin was moved from St Stephen's, the king's private chapel at Westminster Palace, to Westminster Abbey.

Howard carried the king's personal banner of arms. Thomas Bourchier, Archbishop of Canterbury, did not take part in the ceremonies. We do not know why, but he was old and possibly quite frail.[27] After a night vigil in the abbey, the cortège set out for Windsor the following day. Edward IV was buried at St George's Chapel, Windsor, on Friday, 18 April.[28]

Having recently received a palatinate kingdom in the north (including parts of Scotland),[29] it seems Gloucester may have been somewhere in the north-west or Scottish borders when news was received in York of the king's death. By 14 April, he had received news of the king's death.[30] His first act was to write to the queen (and King's Council) in London, conveying his condolences, assurances of loyalty and acknowledgement of his rightful position in the future government of the young king.[31] He also wrote to the new king, Edward V, at Ludlow on the Welsh border to ascertain where to rendezvous for the journey to London.[32]

On or around Thursday, 17 April, the second week's anniversary, Gloucester attended a funeral ceremony and Requiem Mass for the king at York Minster, the mother church of the northern province. Here, 'full of tears', he led the north in mourning but also in swearing fealty to the new king, Edward's son and heir, Edward V.[33]

Before 24 April,[34] Gloucester and a delegation of 200 or 300 gentlemen[35] left York to journey south to meet the young king at Northampton. Northampton was a major conurbation and key staging post on the Great North Road, with its own abbey, castle and town walls. In earlier reigns it had also hosted Parliaments.[36] Here, it seems reasonable to suggest that Gloucester and the northern retinue would join the town's mayor, civic and church leaders, burghers and other dignitaries for the new king's Royal Entry and official welcome. The welcome would have been doubly important for Northampton as it lay in close proximity to the seat of the young king's maternal relatives at Grafton Woodville (later renamed Grafton Regis).[37]

Following the rendezvous at Northampton, Gloucester and the men of the north would accompany the young King Edward to London. The journey from York to Northampton appears to have been slow and respectful; the duke's contingent dressed in the deepest black of mourning for the recently departed king. By Saturday, 26 April, Gloucester and the men of the north had reached Nottingham.[38]

Meanwhile, Edward V was travelling to Northampton from the Welsh borders. As the new monarch, his mourning colour was blue. As Prince of Wales, Edward had lived with his own household at Ludlow from about the age of 3. Here, Edward was under the guidance and tutelage of his 'governor and ruler' and 'Prince's master', his maternal uncle, Anthony Woodville, Earl Rivers.[39] Also travelling with the young king was his Chamberlain (as Prince of Wales), Sir Thomas Vaughan, and the rest of his household. It has previously been assumed that Edward's maternal half-brother, Sir Richard Grey (aged about 26) also travelled from Ludlow but Mancini reveals this was not the case (see p. 49).

It is not known where or when Earl Rivers received the news of Edward IV's death, but it is presumed to have been at Ludlow. However, it is known that Rivers was on his estates in Norfolk at Middleton near Lynn on Thursday, 20 March, and then further east towards the coast at Walsingham on Tuesday, 25 March, the medieval New Year. On both occasions, Rivers met with a neighbouring landowner in an attempt to settle a long-running dispute. They 'agreed to put some of their conflicting claims before the Duke of Gloucester's council for arbitration'.[40] Walsingham was the famous Shrine of Our Lady and place of pilgrimage.

Previous to this, Rivers had been on his estates at Norfolk during the Christmas period and then attended the Parliament in London, which was dissolved on or by Tuesday, 18 February. This gives a period from 26 March when Rivers' location was unknown. It is possible, therefore, that the earl travelled directly to Ludlow at around this time. It is also possible that Rivers was on his Norfolk estates when he received news of the king's illness or death. King Edward fell ill on 28–30 March.[41] Stopping in London, the earl would then have been able to consult with his sister, the queen, receive any instructions and personally deliver her message of the king's death to her son at Ludlow.

Edward V received news of his father's death at Ludlow on Monday, 14 April.[42] This suggests the passage of more than a week before he was informed (allowing for general travel times from London to Ludlow). Does this length of time suggest that Rivers was elsewhere and had to be informed first, or that arrangements needed to be agreed in London? It also seems appropriate that news of his father's death should come directly from his mother, the Queen Mother, Elizabeth Woodville. The Crowland chronicler tells us that Elizabeth wrote to her son prior to the burial of King Edward, informing him that he should not have more than an agreed force of 2,000 men when he came to London.[43]

In London, the size of the retinue which was to accompany the new king had caused heated debate in the King's Council, prompting Lord Hastings to threaten to retire to his fortress at Calais if the king's escort consisted of an 'immoderate number of horse'. The Crowland chronicler records:

The more foresighted members of the Council, however, thought that the uncles and brothers on the mother's side should be absolutely forbidden to have control of the person of the young man until he came of age. They believed that this could not easily be achieved if those of the queen's relatives who were most influential with the prince were allowed to bring his person to the ceremonies of the coronation with an immoderate number of horse.[44]

An armed force of 2,000 was finally agreed by Queen Elizabeth.[45] Edward would now wait in Ludlow for the troops to be summoned and provisioned for the journey, and his household prepared for this significant relocation. Civic arrangements for the new king's arrival in the capital will have also taken time to organise, including preparations for a meeting with his paternal uncle, Gloucester, and the men of the north. The new monarch and his escort left Ludlow for Northampton on Thursday, 24 April, after celebrating St George's Day on the previous day.

In London, the king's coronation had been hastily arranged for Sunday, 4 May.[46] This left little time for the nobility, Church and civic dignitaries from around the country to reach the capital in time. Edward's arrival in London was planned for Thursday, 1 May, just three days beforehand.[47]

Immediately upon arrival, he would be lodged in the Tower – the royal palace where England's kings resided prior to coronation. The hurried date also meant there would be little time for such customary duties as meetings with the King's Council. A further cause for concern was the clear snub that an early coronation date presented to his uncle. As England's Great Chamberlain, it was Gloucester's role to organise the coronation.

An even more troubling development was that Gloucester's military offices were also being usurped in his absence. According to all chroniclers who mention the matter, Edward IV had named his brother Gloucester, Protector of the Realm. The role of Protector is best described by its full title: 'Protector and Defender of the Realm and Church in England and Principal Councillor of the King'.

Edward V was a child of 12, who was not scheduled to come of age until his fourteenth birthday, and even then, would probably be too immature to be allowed untrammelled kingly powers. In the fifteenth century, a protectorate had been put in place on three occasions for Henry VI: first when underage and twice when, as an adult, he became mentally indisposed. All such creations took place when the king was deemed unable to exert personal rule.[48]

Knowing Edward V was underage, Edward IV had sought to ensure that his brother would be the new king's Councillor-in-Chief, while continuing in his military capacity as head of homeland security. According to precedent, it was not obligatory to honour the late king's wishes, but statutes passed by Parliament three times in recent years had established the mode of governance during a king's incapacity to rule, which was a protectorate with clearly defined roles for the various participants. An alternative regime could be proposed and sanctioned by Parliament, but in May 1483 Parliament could not pass new statutes because no Parliament had been called. The ritual of a coronation did not in itself render the king able to rule if he was otherwise incapacitated, as demonstrated by the two protectorates of the adult Henry VI. Such weighty decisions were expected to be made for the public good by men experienced in administration of the realm.

On Wednesday, 16 April, at Ludlow, the new king, Edward V, wrote to the Mayor of Lynn in Norfolk, mentioning the news of his father's death received two days previously and requesting that the peace be kept.[49] The letter stated his intention to 'be at our city of London in all convenient haste by God's grace to be crowned at Westminster'.[50] It made no mention of Edward IV's codicil establishing a protectorate. There is little doubt the letter will have been composed for the new king, but it is written in his own name and bears the new king's signet. This seems to suggest that the young king was not informed about his late father's codicil, or he chose (or was advised) to ignore it. It also seems the new king was aware of the hasty coronation plans.[51]

In London, around Sunday, 20 April, some members of the King's Council met to discuss the late king's will. 'Two resolutions were put forward, the losing one being that the Duke of Gloucester should govern because Edward IV had so directed in his will and because by law he ought to do so. The successful resolution, voted for by the Queen Mother's party, was in favour of government by a council of which Gloucester would be the chief member.' Although the foregoing comment uses the words 'government by a council', the accurate Latin translation is 'government by many persons' (*administratio per plures*), without designating their status. Mancini would certainly have written 'by a council' had this been his understanding.[52]

This local group of interim councillors, dominated by the Woodville family, had thus set aside the former king's wishes for a protectorate and opted instead for an unspecified group controlling the government, within which Gloucester (when he eventually arrived) would evidently be marginalised and outnumbered. Without any submission to Parliament, those who expected to surround Edward V were making unsanctioned decisions designed to be set in place as a fait accompli. There would be nothing to prevent these 'many persons' from assuming the power to declare an end to Edward V's minority, giving the 12-year-old boy nominal authority to rule and govern as king.[53]

Northampton, Stony Stratford and Grafton Woodville

On Tuesday, 29 April, Gloucester and the men of the north arrived at Northampton. It is not known what information Gloucester was apprised of by this time, nor indeed what he may have believed. We can thank Mancini (and his likely informant, Dr Argentine) for the most circumstantial account of what followed, with Crowland supplying some useful details.

The king's party had arrived nearby but instead of heading to Northampton as planned, Edward positioned his force at Stony Stratford, 15 miles further south on the road to London. It seems probable that Edward himself detoured to overnight comfortably at Grafton Woodville, the nearby estate of his mother's family, a few miles from Stony Stratford. Probably by prior arrangement, it was here that his maternal half-brother, Sir Richard Grey, now arrived from London to join his escort with a further contingent of men.[54] The strength of this new contingent is unknown, but it was significant enough to be mentioned by both Mancini and Crowland. Meanwhile, Rivers, aware that explanations were in order, proceeded to Northampton with his companions to greet Gloucester, Buckingham and their companions.[55]

What now took place in Northampton changed everything. Rivers welcomed Gloucester and they 'spent most of the night feasting'.[56] It seems reasonable to assume that the conviviality included the town's dignitaries, who were probably saddened (and possibly bristling) by the royal snub.

Very late that evening, Henry Stafford, 2nd Duke of Buckingham, arrived. He had also arranged to join the king's entourage to London.[57] Buckingham, a royal duke directly descended from Edward III, was the young king's uncle through his marriage to Katherine Woodville, younger sister of the Queen Mother. Mancini records their 'large force of soldiers', although it is not known how many of these men had travelled with Gloucester and the gentlemen of the north, nor how large was Buckingham's retinue and escort. The *Great Chronicle* states that Gloucester and Buckingham's contingent was 'well & strongly accompanied with Sundry men of worship, as knights and other'.[58]

The next morning, Wednesday, 30 April, Mancini reports that Rivers was taken and placed under guard in Northampton before the combined ducal parties hastened to catch up with the king and his escort, who were about to leave for London. There may have been two reasons for this. First, Gloucester, while on the road, must have been receiving intermittent items of news relating to the Council's actions in London, and indeed Mancini confirms he was writing letters requesting his due position by precedent and by what he had now learnt were his late brother's codicils. Evidently, the intelligence lately brought by his cousin Buckingham confirmed that his letters had been ignored and his offices usurped. He would now be deeply suspicious of what Rivers and his family may have planned.

Second, Gloucester's scouts on the road would have alerted him to the presence of Sir Richard Grey and his men ahead. Rivers had permitted this augmentation of numbers beyond the agreed limit of 2,000 men, while leaving his command to visit Northampton. There were now several thousand men at arms congregated on the open road. Taking the initiative in his military capacity, Gloucester assumed overall command, arrested Grey and others, including (according to Crowland) Sir Thomas Vaughan, and dispersed most of the men to where they had come from.[59] Taking the young Edward V in his charge, he led the royal party back to Northampton. It was now his responsibility to bring the king safely to London. Crowland described the event in the following terms:

> The duke of Gloucester ... did not put off or refuse to offer to his nephew, the king, any of the reverence required from a subject such as a bared head, bent knee, or any other posture. He said that he was only taking precautions to safeguard his own person because he knew for certain that there were men close to the king who had sworn to destroy his honour and his life. Having said that, he had it publicly proclaimed that anyone of the king's household should withdraw from the place at once and that they should not come near any places where the king might go, on pain of death.[60]

Gloucester, Buckingham and the king then remained in Northampton overnight. At some point, Rivers and Grey were sent north and imprisoned at Sheriff Hutton and Middleham respectively, Grey with his servants.[61]

It is reported that Vaughan was also taken prisoner (and executed at Pontefract), but no evidence of his incarceration exists, whether at Pontefract or elsewhere. Mancini makes no mention of him, and no record exists in *Harleian Manuscript 433* alongside the expenses during imprisonment for Rivers and Grey. Analysis of the 'Honour of Pontefract' also fails to record any expenses for Vaughan, despite his supposed eight-week incarceration.[62]

At present, the only clue rests in the will of Lord Rivers (23 June 1483), which directs that a debt be paid to Thomas Vaughan, of which Rivers had already paid 'xx marcs here in the north'. This might imply that Vaughan was, at least for a while, at Sheriff Hutton, unless messengers and servants were permitted between the different northern locations. Furthermore, although Rivers and Grey were tried[63] and buried at Pontefract, Vaughan was apparently buried or reburied at Westminster Abbey where he has a tomb monument; unfortunately, the abbey's muniments have revealed no further information.[64]

It is important, at this point, to say something about the sources for the events of 29–30 April. Both are chronicles written after the event and thus include a great deal of hindsight. They are also generally hostile to Gloucester and Buckingham. No chronicles from the perspective of the two royal dukes or their retinues exist, although a search is currently under way. As a result, events have been reconstructed by cross-referencing the facts that can be gleaned from both accounts, together with other sources and a corroborative timeline of events and movements.

Medieval scribe at work.

The two chronicles in question are Mancini and Crowland (they are examined in greater detail in Chapter 5). Mancini wrote his account in hostile France on 1 December 1483 for a member of the French government. This followed the October uprising against King Richard in some southern counties of England, after which several rebels had fled to the continent. Our other chronicle was written at Crowland Abbey in Lincolnshire around November 1485. This was after the death of Richard III at the Battle of Bosworth, when power was now in the hands of Henry VII, the Lancastrian pretender, who had been previously exiled with those rebels on the continent in Brittany and France. Mancini was reporting what he saw as Gloucester's grab for the throne, and the author of the Crowland Chronicle harboured a deep prejudice against those from the north of England.

It must be noted, however, that certain information has a ring of authenticity. For example, Mancini tells us that when Edward V was informed about the arrest of his maternal relatives (Rivers and Grey), he spoke forcefully on their behalf. This seems very likely considering his probable closeness to these relatives. However, other information intended to conjure an atmosphere of brooding menace is known to be inaccurate, such as Mancini's claim that Gloucester and Buckingham conspired as they supposedly travelled the same route together to Northampton.

Let us now return to the events following 30 April and King Edward's arrival in Northampton with Gloucester and Buckingham. On or by the following day, Thursday, 1 May, it seems likely that the young king received the town's official welcome and condolences on the death of his father. Gloucester now wrote to the Council and Mayor of London. Mancini reports:

Meanwhile the Duke of Gloucester wrote to the Council and to the chief officer of the city whom they call mayor, since an ill rumour was being circulated that he had brought his nephew not under his care but into his power, with the aim that the realm should be subjected to himself. Both letters conveyed the following or similar message: there was no question of his having detained his nephew the King of England, rather had he released him and the realm from ruination; because the young lad would have gone straight into the hands of those who, since they had not spared either the honour or the life of the father, could not be expected to have more consideration for the youthfulness of the son.[65] The action had been taken by reason of his own preservation and to provide for that of the king and kingdom. No man but he alone had such concern for the welfare of King

Edward and the security of the realm. At an early date it would be arranged that he and the boy would be present in the city so that the crowning and all that pertained to the ceremonials might be more honourably performed.[66]

Mancini adds his own view that this was a stratagem by which Gloucester planned to 'win the goodwill of the people' and, through this, 'supreme power against their wishes'. The Italian's take on events needs to be reported for the sake of balance, and as a useful example of hindsight colouring his report. Mancini adds, 'After these letters had been read aloud to the Council and the populace, they all praised the Duke of Gloucester by reason that he was dutiful to his nephews and that he purposed not to fail in punishing their enemies.'[67]

Three times Mancini asserts that claims were made of *insidiae* ('ambushes') against Gloucester 'both in the city and on the roads'. These assertions are hard to pin down and unfortunately, as Carson notes, the Latin word '*insidiae*' is not just translatable as ambushes 'but as any kind of trap, snare, treachery or plot'.[68]

Sometime on Friday, 2 May, the royal party left Northampton for London. Immediately prior to this, Edward had written to the Archbishop of Canterbury asking him to safeguard the Great Seal of England.[69] The Great Seal symbolised the sovereign's approval of state documents on behalf of the governance of the realm. Considering Edward's young age, this step must have been advised by Gloucester. It seems likely that the young king had by now been informed of the codicil in his father's will creating a protectorate.

It is not known where they rested overnight but by Saturday, 3 May, the royal party had arrived at St Albans. Here, King Edward appointed John Geffrey, his favourite chaplain at Ludlow, to the nearby parish church at Pembrigge.[70] St Albans was another staging post on the road to the capital, so it seems reasonable to suggest that the new king would have received a royal welcome from the town's dignitaries.

It may have been on this day that Edward, Gloucester and Buckingham autographed their names together (see p. 54). This is a remarkable contemporary record. Edward signed the paper as king at the top and, with a respectful distance, Gloucester recorded his name and motto, 'loyalty binds me', beneath, followed by Buckingham, 'remember me often'. This surviving scrap of paper reveals, at face value, Gloucester's loyalty to the new king and Buckingham's wish for Edward to remember him. We cannot guess whether the latter was

May 1483, during progress with Edward V to London. *Top*: signature of Edward V with royal monogram, 'R Edwardus quintus' (R=Rex). *Middle*: autograph motto Loyaulté me Lie (loyalty binds me) and signature of Richard, Duke of Gloucester (Richard Gloucestre). *Bottom*: autograph motto Souvente me Souvene (remember me often) and signature of Henry Stafford, Duke of Buckingham (Harry Bokingham). (BL, MS Cotton Vesp. F xiii, f. 123. Redrawn: Philippa Langley)

intended to garner future rewards and grants or a personal touch as the boy's uncle by marriage.

On Sunday, 4 May, the day that had previously been arranged for Edward's coronation, the royal party set off on the short journey to London.

London

What had transpired in London during this short period, however, was extraordinary. By the late evening of Tuesday, 30 April, and following morning, news had reached the capital alerting the Queen Mother to the events at

Northampton and Stony Stratford, probably brought by a returning member of Sir Richard Grey's contingent. It's also possible that Gloucester sent a messenger. So, what had taken place in London that was so extraordinary?

On 1 May, the Queen Mother fled with her children and other family members into sanctuary at Cheneygates Mansion at Westminster Abbey. Mancini records that she was accompanied by the king's other half-brother, the Marquess of Dorset (aged 28) and her brother, Lionel Woodville, Bishop of Salisbury.[71] So what had caused a queen of England (and a bishop) to flee to sanctuary in a time of peace?

The previous day, she and Dorset had attempted to raise an army against Gloucester but had failed signally. Mancini reports:

> But when they had incited certain nobles who had come to the city, along with others, to take up arms, they perceived that all men's hearts were not only irresolute but deeply inimical to themselves. Several even said publicly that it was more just and beneficial for the boy-king to be with his paternal uncle than with his maternal uncles and uterine brothers.[72]

At face value, this action seems to support the theory that Elizabeth Woodville feared for her life, but if we drill down into the moment, we see that there was unrest in London with the Queen Mother's party and the followers of Lord Hastings openly squaring up against each other.

Elizabeth Woodville had taken sanctuary before, in the dangerous times when Edward IV had been forced out of his kingdom, and it seems to have been her first instinct to take herself and her immediate family into sanctuary again. Her actions at this time, and those of her menfolk, including her brother Rivers, are examined in Chapter 16.

On Tuesday, 29 April, the Queen Mother's youngest brother, Sir Edward Woodville had officially been given command of the English fleet by the Interim Council in the absence of England's Lord High Admiral, Richard of Gloucester. Woodville led twenty vessels to face an apparent threat posed by marauding French ships, but 'piracy in the channel was nothing new' and was regularly settled via diplomacy.[73] An amount of £3,670 was taken from the Treasury by Woodville and Dorset to provision the fleet with men and equipment, and Woodville himself would go on to abscond with two royal ships that included 200–300 soldiers and archers. He also requisitioned £10,250 in gold coin from an unnamed vessel in harbour, confiscated in the name of the Crown. This figure amounted to 15 per cent of royal revenues with a similar figure having financed 22,500 soldiers and the invasion of Scotland the previous year.[74] As Elizabeth, the Queen Mother, headed to sanctuary, Mancini reports that the Treasury 'is believed to have been divided between the queen, the marquess [Dorset] and Edward [her brother]'.[75]

On Sunday, 4 May 1483, Edward V entered London and received a royal welcome from the city's Mayor, Council, civic dignitaries, prelates and nobility. The king was accompanied by two royal uncles, his household and an escort of 'no more than' 500 men. Mancini describes the escort as 'soldiers', but it would be highly unlikely that the gentlemen of the north had returned home. It is therefore probable that Mancini's soldiers were mainly part of Buckingham's contingent.[76]

The entourage entered the outskirts of the city accompanied by four cartloads of weapons 'bearing the devices of the queen's brothers and sons', while proclamations were made describing how they were to have been used against the king's uncle.[77] Edward V was conveyed in triumph through the city and safely ensconced at the Bishop of London's Palace in (medieval) St Paul's churchyard.[78] In all likelihood, the young king received an equally warm welcome from the citizens of London and was cheered enthusiastically through the streets.

From Monday, 5 May, to Saturday, 10 May, a lengthy Council was held over several days. This confirmed Gloucester in his role of Protector. Gloucester and Buckingham now 'compelled all the lords spiritual and temporal and mayor and aldermen of the city of London to take the oath of fealty to the king … it was performed with pride and joy by all'. The Council also decided upon the new date of the coronation. This would now take place on Sunday, 22 June, with Edward V's first Parliament the following Wednesday, 25 June.

It was also decided that the king be moved to a more spacious residence. Several places were suggested. Buckingham proposed the Tower, and this was agreed upon.[79] Mancini asserts that Gloucester now attempted to obtain the Council's consent to punish Rivers and Grey for treason, but this was denied. However, Gloucester, as we have seen, could have arraigned and punished them himself as Constable of England and had no need to apply to the Council, who had no authority to determine such a matter. Mancini was clearly unaware of the Council's position in this regard or Gloucester's judicial powers as Constable and Admiral, claiming that he held 'no public office'. As Carson records, 'Their incarceration was doubtless an item of business that he [Gloucester] brought to the Council's attention, but not as a supplicant.'[80]

On Saturday, 10 May, the Council gave orders for Sir Thomas Fulford to take control of the English fleet from Sir Edward Woodville.[81] With all Council business completed, on 9–10 May, John Howard now sent thirty-eight of his men home.[82] It seems likely that these were the men who had set off for London with Howard a month earlier, following Howard's receipt of King Edward's letter immediately prior to his death.

All was now well. On 14 May, Howard was made Chief Steward of the Duchy of Lancaster (south of the Trent) and further orders were issued against Edward Woodville, directing several naval commanders and ship's captains to put to sea to arrest him and return the fleet.

The rest of the month followed customary procedure and protocol. On Monday, 19 May, Edward V and his household were moved to the Royal Apartments at the Tower of London.[83] On the same day, Gloucester signed a letter from 'Richard Duke of Gloucester, brother and uncle of kings, protector and defensor, great Chamberlain, Constable and Admiral of England'.[84] On Friday, 23 May, the King's Council offered the wording of an oath of safety to Elizabeth Woodville if she would agree to leave sanctuary. The declaration was led by the Archbishops of Canterbury and York, with the Royal Dukes of Gloucester and Buckingham and various other lords.[85] The Queen Mother preferred to remain.[86]

By early June 1483, plans for the coronation and Parliament were well advanced. Calls to attend had been sent to the country's nobility, prelates and civic leaders. Howard's wife had arrived, as had Gloucester's. On Monday, 9 June, an extended Council meeting took place from ten in the morning until two in the afternoon with the coronation discussed and preparations proceeding at pace.[87]

On the following day, however, Gloucester wrote to the city of York to prepare and send armed men to London. The cause of the alarm was the queen, her kin and affinity, who 'daily intend to murder and utterly destroy us and our cousin, the duke of Buckingham, and the old royal blood of this realm'. Gloucester issued the request in the same terms as the letter instanced above, from the 'brother and uncle of kings, protector and defensor, great Chamberlain, Constable and Admiral of England'.[88]

So, what had prompted this unexpected request? Taken as read, it tells us that some form of plot had apparently been uncovered at around this time, coinciding with Dorset having secretly quit the Westminster sanctuary.[89] Sir Edward Woodville was also still at large with two vessels of the English fleet and well over £10,000 in gold coin.

By the following day, Gloucester had sent another letter north requesting aid. As we have seen, an armed force takes time to assemble and provision. To travel to London from the north would take about four days for a company of horse and longer with infantry. The city of York would assemble 200 men at Pontefract Castle to 'attend on my lord of Northumberland to go to my said lord of Gloucester good grace'.[90] It would, therefore, be up to ten days or more before the northern arrays could arrive in the capital. This would certainly be in time for peace-keeping at the coronation and Parliament, but not for any immediate peril.

It's likely that the men of the north who were already with Gloucester in London would have been on hand for any localised and immediate threat, but whatever future fears he had are difficult, at this remove, to comprehend. Perhaps he did not yet know much more than to raise the level of alarm to severe: as a seasoned general and battle commander, this response would be in keeping with any level of perceived threat. The duke, as Protector of the Realm, could not afford to be caught unprepared. Presumably, some information had come to light that propelled him to take action. Though some commentators, looking at events from hindsight, have viewed Gloucester's appeals for assistance as predatory, other, more objective, assessments see them as precautionary.

Meanwhile, plans for the coronation and Parliament continued unabated. The only significant political move at this time was a change to the governance of the realm made by the King's Council, which may have formed part of the Council's business on 9 June.

By this date, the Council had reached a decision which is recorded in the draft sermon (which has survived) to be given by the Lord Chancellor at the opening of Edward V's Parliament: a speech which set out government policy for parliamentary approval. Should we need any confirmation that Richard's Chancellor and Council were wholly in accord, it will be found in the text by Chancellor John Russell, Bishop of Lincoln, who goes out of his way to make pointed remarks regarding the queen's family, specifically, the ambitions of Earl Rivers, and possibly referring to his former influence on the young king – 'great waters and tempestuous Rivers' that 'by breaches and inundations the firm land and isles may be oftentimes lost and annihilated, or at the least greatly diminished'.[91]

The Council's decision was to formalise the protectorate in an enactment that would set its term to continue until Edward V came of age on his fourteenth birthday, in eighteen months' time.[92] With the 12-year-old king an unknown quantity, it made sense, as the speech emphasised, to ensure he received tutelage for the demanding responsibilities of sovereignty.

On Friday, 13 June, an event occurred that logic suggests was not unconnected with Gloucester's alarmed letters two or three days earlier. At a Council meeting at the Tower of London (where the young king resided in the Royal Apartments), Lord Hastings was accused of plotting against the Protector's life and summarily executed.[93]

Domenico Mancini, writing about five months later and having been in London to hear (and/or read) the explanatory proclamation, wrote as follows:

> The Protector by prearrangement called out that a trap had been set for him, and that these men had come with concealed weapons so that they could be the first to unleash a violent attack. At that, soldiers who had been stationed there by their lord came running in with the Duke of Buckingham and beheaded Hastings by the sword under the false name of treason; the others they detained, out of respect for their lives, it is supposed, for reasons of religion and holy orders.[94]

Among those present, Mancini names two prominent figures, the Archbishop of York, Thomas Rotherham (arrested, later released), and the Bishop of Ely, John Morton (arrested, later turned rebel), being co-conspirators known to have been meeting with Hastings privately, 'and several others'. To set his account against the historical record, we do know the names of some others present, including Buckingham and John Howard – John Howard's son, Sir Thomas Howard, Sir Charles Pilkington and Sir Robert Harrington, 'men of knightly rank with a number of their followers', who were nearby.[95] Others known to have been rounded up in connection with the same plot included the king's secretary, Oliver King, and, on the following day, John Forster, a leading official of Elizabeth Woodville and close associate of Hastings and Morton, who was arrested at his country house in Hertfordshire and committed to the Tower (both were later released).[96] Forster had been Elizabeth Woodville's Receiver-General since 1466.

Concealed weapons had no place in the council chamber, and Mancini was clearly aware of reports that hidden arms had been brought to the meeting, the accusation being that this was an attempt on the life of the Protector (as announced in the subsequent public proclamation).[97] Mancini's report, in hindsight – the alleged trap and false charge – is attributable to his task of constructing a coherent narrative for readers in France explaining what he knew of how Richard III came to be king. The drama would have likely given rise to stories in the streets of London, and it is questionable whether Mancini was intimate enough with events in the Tower to have had positive knowledge that a trap had been laid.

Unfortunately, like so much of the documentation that survives, his account is both flawed and biased. 'Beheaded by the sword' is discounted by historians and may simply have been conjecture, perhaps arising from the French method of execution at this time for the nobility in France. It is generally agreed that Hastings alone suffered execution, while the number of those arrested would seem to confirm that Hastings was not singled out as the only target, as later narratives (Thomas More and Shakespeare) have taught us to believe.

In a thronged palace like the Tower of London there were certainly enough people present or in the vicinity to have known the truth of the matter. Inferences may be drawn from the fact that although there must have been considerable alarm, contemporary correspondence reports no unrest in the capital. Readers who recall Gloucester's powers as High Constable of England will appreciate that he would have been able to form a tribunal from among those present and conduct a summary trial.[98]

In chronicles and stories written after the death of Richard III, the execution of Hastings is portrayed as illegal. In particular, there is considerable distortion by Henry VII's historian, Polydore Vergil, who in his original manuscript records the actual names of the knights of the realm who were close by these events, but would later remove these details from the texts of his history that went into print, describing them anonymously as 'a sort right ready to do a mischief'.[99] As a result, modern historians have described these knights as 'guards', and the execution as murder. Hastings' younger brother, Richard, Lord Welles, attended King Richard's coronation and fought for him at Bosworth.[100] Though not attainted (received judgement of death or outlawry), he was pardoned by Henry VII on 18 September 1485. He lost the Welles title but was compensated by a land grant. He was never summoned to Parliament under Henry VII and died without issue in 1503.

In contemporary accounts, there is no mention of the presence or arrest of Thomas, Lord Stanley, which is an addition attributable to Vergil.[101] Vergil also changes the chronological sequence of events to follow an error originally made by Mancini, in which both sons of Edward IV had been taken to reside in the Tower prior to Hastings' execution.

Amid the swirl of misreporting, both ancient and modern, around the developments of mid-June, it is the Crowland account that stands out in recording the correct sequence of events – i.e., that the execution of Lord Hastings occurred on 13 June, while the Woodville contingent, including the Duke of York and his mother, were still occupying the Westminster sanctuary. The widespread error in chronology has a significance to which we will return shortly.[102]

Meanwhile, we now arrive at the events of Monday, 16 June, described at the beginning of this chapter, when Richard, Duke of York, left sanctuary to join his elder brother in the Royal Apartments at the Tower of London. Mancini reports that 'it became of concern to the Council that it would be seen as unseemly for the king to be crowned in the absence of his brother'. He adds an apparent report attributed to Gloucester that it was 'the wish of the boy himself to be with his brother'. His account then continues, 'with the consent of the Council', Gloucester 'blockaded the sanctuary with soldiers'.[103]

There had been guards around those parts of the Abbey being occupied by the Woodvilles for some time, since the Council had been concerned that those menfolk who refused to reconcile, like Lionel Woodville and the Marquess of Dorset, should not be allowed to abscond with the wherewithal to foment trouble (which, as events would prove, they eventually did). Crowland adds:

> The following Monday they came by boat to Westminster with a great crowd, with swords and clubs and compelled the Lord Cardinal of Canterbury to enter the sanctuary, with many others, to call upon the queen, in her kindness, to allow her son Richard, duke of York, to leave and come to the Tower for the comfort of his brother, the king. She willingly agreed to the proposal and sent out the boy who was taken by the Lord Cardinal to the king in the Tower of London.[104]

That the king's younger brother was apparently happy to join his elder brother comes from a contemporary letter written by Canon Stallworth, a priest in the service of the Lord Chancellor, Bishop Russell. Stallworth may have been an eyewitness to the events, or in receipt of a first-hand account, possibly from the Lord Chancellor himself, who was present:

> On Monday last was at Westminster great plenty of harnest men: there was the deliverance of the Duke of York to my lord Cardinal, my lord Chancellor, and other many lords Temporal and with him met my lord of Buckingham in the middle of the hall of Westminster: my lord protector receiving him at the Star Chamber Door with many loving words and so

departed with my lord Cardinal to the tower, where he is, blessed be Jesus, merry. [21 June 1483][105]

This witness testimony contradicts the later accounts of Mancini and Crowland, who imply that Elizabeth Woodville was compelled by the threat of force to release the boy and the Archbishop of Canterbury was similarly compelled to remove him. To remove a child from sanctuary by force, in the full view of innumerable onlookers, would have been wholly unprecedented and a major misjudgement, particularly given the presence of two of the country's most respected elders of the Church and leading Councillors.[106]

As we know, John, Lord Howard, was also present and would accompany the boy by boat along the Thames. So, the picture generally painted of York being removed from his mother's arms is very far from the truth. Equally far from the truth is Mancini's false memory, repeated by numerous other chroniclers, as we have observed, that the Hastings episode only happened after the boy had left sanctuary. This is a classic example of hindsight dictating perceptions, in this case, the perception that the mother would never have relinquished her child knowing that the Protector had just committed a cynical public murder.

This section, 'Two Weeks, One Summer', is so called in order to highlight, for the first time, a significant development in events. This, as we have seen, occurred on Tuesday, 17 June, when the Council felt it had no choice but to move Edward V's coronation to Sunday, 9 November, a postponement of nearly five months. The traditional account of this key period is heavily reliant on hindsight. However, as a police investigation we do not have the luxury of the rear-view mirror. At all times, we must examine events as they happened, placing ourselves in the very moment while accessing what facts can be gleaned by cross-referencing all reliable sources and timelines. As a result, a period of three months boils down to two crucial weeks.

Let us investigate these critical weeks to attempt to understand why everything now changed.

Two Weeks, One Summer

The five-month postponement of a coronation, the supreme ceremony of the Church and State, was wholly unprecedented. It suggests nothing less than a constitutional crisis had occurred which required time and careful consideration. So, what could have caused the postponement of the coronation and Parliament?

It seems that the very act of transferring Edward IV's youngest son to the Tower in preparation for the coronation prompted someone to come forward, or some information to come to light, requiring investigation by the King's Council for fully five more days. Only on 22 June was any information allowed to be made public, and we shall soon see why it was sufficient to set everything on its head.

All this time Elizabeth Woodville remained in sanctuary, while her refusal to reach an accommodation with the present government imperilled the fate of her relatives presently held hostage in the north. Solemn oaths for her safety had been rebuffed, and she had refused to accompany her youngest son as he joined her other young son for his coronation. Why was this?

Two suppositions immediately come to mind. Was her protected location at Westminster, with so many resources at hand, too useful a centre in terms of the armed resistance her family was presently fomenting? Or was there something she feared – and feared so greatly that she left her two young sons to face it alone?

On Wednesday, 18 June, Edward V signed what would be, according to extant records, his last warrant as king.[107] Two days later, on Friday, 20 June, the last surviving London documents name him as king (the final documents referring to Edward as king are at Cambridge on 27 June, some 55 miles from the capital).[108]

Our first understanding of what was going on behind the scenes at Westminster comes from another letter by Canon Stallworth, written on Saturday, 21 June, and describing recent events to his patron, Sir William Stonor. Stallworth confirms the execution of Hastings on 'Friday last' and the deliverance of the Duke of York from sanctuary, adding that Hastings' men have now become Buckingham's men. He then comments, significantly, that Lord Lisle, brother-in-law to the queen, has 'come to my lord Protector and waits upon him'.[109]

On Sunday, 22 June, in London, came the thunderclap. Sermons were preached at St Paul's Cross and elsewhere in the city announcing the bastardy of the offspring of Edward IV and Elizabeth Woodville. Amid general confusion, the preachers recorded the legal outcome, which was that Richard of Gloucester was now the legitimate Yorkist heir.[110] Many who heard the news, including Mancini, could make no sense of the legal quagmire. We shall examine the importance of these two paragraphs in depth in Chapter 7.

By this time, with the Queen Mother and members of her now scattered adult family still holding out against the government, instructions would have been sent for the trial (and inevitable execution) of Rivers, Grey and (possibly) Vaughan.

On Wednesday, 25 June, Richard of Gloucester was petitioned to become king by the Three Estates of the Realm (Lords, Church and Commons). The Bill of Petition was presented at Baynard's Castle, the home of his mother, Cecily, Duchess of York.

The following day, Thursday, 26 June 1483, at Baynard's Castle, Gloucester accepted election as king. As Richard III, he now performed the ritual assumption of the seat of justice in King's Bench, Westminster, then proceeded to St Paul's. His reign is dated from this day.

News was soon being officially disseminated, and on Saturday, 28 June, a letter was sent to Lord Mountjoy at the English garrison at Calais 'referring to recent events and enclosing a copy of the petition requesting the Duke of Gloucester to accept the crown and the reasons for this request. It was sent under the King's signet from the City of London.'[111]

The sons of Edward IV remained in the Tower of London. Richard and Anne took up temporary residence in the Tower on Friday, 4 July, in preparation for their coronation on Sunday, 6 July. It seems likely that the boys would have been moved to a new suite of rooms at or around this time. It is certain that this would have been a difficult and extremely unsettling time for both boys (and their sisters in sanctuary). Whether 9-year-old Richard of York understood the implications of recent events is doubtful. In contrast, it is probable that his elder brother, Edward, fully appreciated the personal ramifications of this wholly unparalleled constitutional crisis.

4

The Disappearance

A Timeline

In the previous chapter, we traced the events which placed Edward V and his brother, Richard, Duke of York, in the Tower of London: potentially their last known location. In this chapter, we will construct a timeline of the events surrounding their disappearance and consider the effectiveness of a chronological approach.

What do we know? In the summer of 1483, two male children apparently vanished. They were brothers. The elder boy was 12, the younger 9. Both had last been seen playing in the Palace Gardens of the Tower of London. They may be described as celebrities. Both boys lived in large households with servants and retainers. At the time of their disappearance, their paternal uncle was the new Head of State. These are the bare facts as we know them.

It is clear from this basic analysis that the prime suspect in the disappearance is the new king, Richard III. As Head of State, it is probable that he was involved in some capacity or, at the very least, made aware of it.

Establishing the exact time of the disappearance is key. We will therefore examine the period immediately after Richard III's coronation on 6 July. Although both boys were no longer considered princes, they will, however, continue to be described as 'Edward V' and 'Richard, Duke of York' throughout this work for ease of understanding.

Summer 1483

Following the coronation on 6 July, it seems likely that the king and queen moved to Greenwich Palace to enjoy the customary post-coronation tournaments. On Sunday, 13 July, following the removal of the anointing coif and the celebration of a Mass,[1] Richard III began the business of government.[2] On Tuesday, 15 July, the Duke of Buckingham was appointed Constable of England, and on Thursday, 17 July, Robert Brackenbury, King Richard's former Treasurer when he was Duke of Gloucester, was appointed Constable of the Tower of London.[3] Brackenbury's role would encompass responsibility for the two boys in the Tower.

Previously, King Richard had corrected a dubious act of Edward IV's administration. On 28 June, John Howard was created Duke of Norfolk and Earl Marshal of England and Howard's cousin was created Earl of Nottingham.[4] Edward IV's youngest son, while no longer Duke of Norfolk, retained the title Duke of York.

On Friday, 18 July, seventeen former servants of Edward IV and Edward V were paid for their service. Although the men are named, it is not known why they were dismissed. It is probable that due to Edward IV's recent death their tenure had come to a natural conclusion. The payment records:

> Richard etc. For as much as we certainly understand that the sum of Fifty and two pounds & xx d [pence] remains due to the persons following for their services done to our dearest Brother late king whom god absoille [absolve] and to Edward Bastard late called king Edward the Vth.[5]

The payment is important for two reasons. Firstly, it records the way Edward V was now described in official documents – 'Edward Bastard late called king Edward the Vth' – and, secondly, it strongly suggests that Edward V was alive on Friday, 18 July 1483. J.A.F. Thomson drew attention to the phrase 'whom god absoille' to underline the distinction 'between the pious prayer for Edward IV's soul and the absence of any such for his son's'.[6]

It seems probable, as a royal bastard, that Edward's fifty servants[7] as Prince of Wales were no longer deemed appropriate. However, there is no documentary evidence to suggest that the King's Council removed all of Edward's servants at this time, or that his education and religious devotions were discontinued.[8] This would have been particularly harsh considering recent events. It also seems that the royal tutor, John Giles, Archdeacon of London, continued in his role.[9]

On Saturday, 19 July, King Richard left London on a royal progress to the north. Travelling 22 miles, the first stop was Windsor Castle. On Monday, 21 July, the king left for Reading Abbey, 17 miles further west.[10] Queen Anne remained at Windsor with her household to celebrate her feast day on Saturday, 26 July.[11]

However, the king's progress was disturbed by worrying developments. On Tuesday, 22 July, at Caversham near Reading, John Howard, Duke of Norfolk and Earl Marshal of England, left Richard's entourage and returned urgently to London, travelling partly at night.[12] On the way, he arrested several men at Bray (near Maidenhead).[13] Evidently, news of trouble had reached the royal party and a dangerous plot had been nipped in the bud. We have this from a letter written in King Richard's own hand, a week later, instituting due process against the perpetrators (see quote below, note 17).

Meanwhile, Howard (newly appointed Admiral of England)[14] had reached London by Thursday, 24 July.[15] The following day, his Household Books reveal he was present at Richard's London mansion, Crosby's Place, making preparations for an event of some note.[16]

The week's developments culminated in the king's official letter, written on Tuesday, 29 July at Minster Lovell, home of King Richard's close friend, Francis, Viscount Lovell. It was addressed to the Lord Chancellor of England, John Russell, Bishop of Lincoln, desiring him to consult with the Royal Council in London and institute judicial proceedings against certain prisoners:

> certaine personnes (of such as of late had taken it upon thaym the fact of an enterprise, as we doubte nat ye have herd) bee attached and in ward we desir' and wol you that ye doo make our letters of commission to such personnes as by you and our counsaille shalbe advised forto sitte upon thaym, and to procede to the due execucion of our laws in that behalve. Faille ye nat hereof as our perfect trust is in you.[17]

Russell clearly knew of the obliquely named 'enterprise', and the absence of any official legal records suggests he ensured the case was dealt with quickly and quietly. Those present at the hearing can no longer be ascertained because King Richard's *Baga de Secretis*[18] was either lost or destroyed following the king's death at Bosworth.[19]

The circumstances described in the king's letter are strictly contemporary with a plot described over a century later in John Stow's *Annales of England* (1592): a foiled attempt to abduct the sons of Edward IV from the Tower of

London. John Howard, in his office as Earl Marshal, had jurisdiction to preside over treason cases such as this in the Summary Court of the High Constable of England (which was not a court of common law).[20] Howard's construction of a 'sege' (a ceremonial chair or throne) at Crosby's Place tends to confirm that this was where the court was convened.[21]

John Stow names the executed men: Robert Russe, Sergeant of London; William Davy, Pardoner of Hounslow; John Smith, Groom of Edward IV's Stirrup; and Stephen Ireland, Wardrober of the Tower of London.[22] The conspiracy reported by Stow was clearly an inside job and, as such, confirms that the sons of Edward IV were alive and lodged at the Tower.

On Thursday, 7 August, following events at Crosby's Place, Howard sent a letter to his son, Thomas Howard, Earl of Surrey. Surrey, the King's Steward, was with King Richard at Warwick on progress. Queen Anne now also left Windsor to join the king at Warwick, her name day having been celebrated some twelve days previously.[23] On Monday, 11 August, Howard left the capital for his home in Suffolk, to begin his own (ducal) progress to the Shrine of Our Lady at Walsingham in Norfolk.[24]

From 29 August to 20 September, the royal progress was at York. On Monday, 8 September, Richard's heir, Edward of Middleham (age 7), was knighted with the king's nephew, Edward of Warwick (8), the king's illegitimate son, John of Gloucester (around age 13), and the Spanish Ambassador, Galfridus (Geoffrey) de Sasiola.[25] In addition, Edward of Middleham was ceremonially invested as Prince of Wales.[26] Edward IV's eldest son retained his former titles, Earl of March and Pembroke.

On or around 14 September 1483, at Bristol, the Recorder (a legal appointee responsible for keeping the record of the city's courts and transactions) completed the city's Kalendar for the mayoral year (15 September 1482 to 14 September 1483). The Kalendar recorded the death of Edward IV and accession of Richard III but failed to include any reference to the sons of Edward IV.[27]

On Saturday, 11 October, at Lincoln, King Richard received news of an uprising in several southern counties.[28] He also discovered that his cousin, Buckingham, was involved. By the end of October, the uprising was suppressed, and on Sunday, 2 November, at Salisbury, Buckingham was executed. On 25 November, Richard returned to London.[29] Two days later, on Thursday, 27 November 1483, the royal tutor, John Giles, was awarded a yearly grant of £40, a significant sum.[30]

These are the bare facts relating to events at or around the time of the disappearance. As we shall see from an analysis of sources in Chapter 5, two chroniclers, Crowland and Vergil, believed the princes to have been alive when King Richard was at York in September 1483. The *Great Chronicle* records the boys were seen shooting arrows in the gardens of the Tower of London sometime during the capital's mayoral year of 29 October 1482 to 28 October 1483.[31]

As contemporary evidence shows that Richard of York joined his brother in the Tower Palace on 16 June 1483, the window for the boys' disappearance is therefore 17 June to 20 September 1483, when King Richard and the court left York. This timeline could be extended to 28 October 1483. As government records fail to include customary prayers for the souls of Edward V (or his brother), it seems reasonable at this stage in the enquiry to conclude that both boys were alive on 18 July. This date may be supported by the possible attempts to remove them on or around 21 July. On or around 14 September, Bristol's Kalendar made no mention of the sons of Edward IV.

The likely timeframe for the disappearance is therefore sometime after 18 July, possibly after 21 July,[32] and up to a potential end date of 20 September 1483. This end date could be extended to 28 October 1483 to take account of the London mayoral year. This offers a window of two (possibly three) months for the investigation.[33] The investigation timeframe ends here as there are no reported sightings of the boys at the Tower after that mentioned in the *Great Chronicle*.

The chronological approach has demonstrated that a window for the disappearance can be established. The timeline reveals that the boys were alive in September (and possibly October) with the window for the disappearance sometime after 18 July or possibly 21 July 1483.

In the next chapter, attention will turn to the surviving evidence and a full examination of all the available sources.

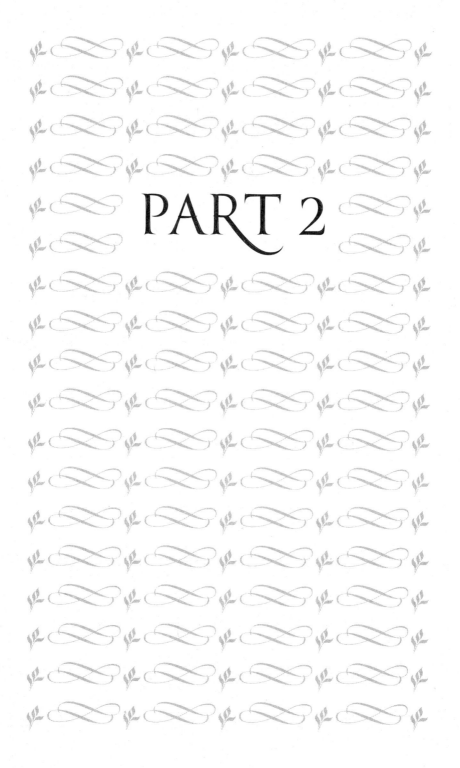

PART 2

5

The Sources

Missing, Murdered, Maintained

At the heart of the project's investigations stands the process of intelligence gathering. Information is extracted from the primary sources, the ordinary, day-to-day administrative records which allow us to drill down into our key period of investigation and recreate the past as accurately as possible. These records are featured throughout this work as endnotes. They include the Privy Seal, Signet Office, Exchequer and Chancery Rolls, Household Accounts, receipts, grants, commissions, writs, wills, Inquisitions Post Mortem (IPMs) and legal cases. Their importance derives from the fact that they are administrative records (compiled by clerks and lawyers) and, as a result, have no reason to lie. They were not written for public consumption.

The most contemporary chronicles are also important but, as with any account compiled by those not directly involved, exhibit a potential for author bias, dramatic inventions and reports of rumour, hearsay and gossip. A chronicle is akin to our investigative agencies today accessing newspaper articles as part of their enquiries. Here, they need to retrieve information that can be corroborated.

This too is our task. Rumour, hearsay and gossip is not evidence. It is not accepted by a court or the Crown Prosecution Service. However, in a cold-case investigation of a disappearance that is more than 500 years old, we do not have the luxury to ignore any potential information. As a result, rumour, hearsay and gossip are also scrutinised for leads and new lines of investigation. No stone can be left unturned.

It is also important to give greater weight to accounts written close to the key period under investigation. This helps to minimise the contaminating potential hindsight. Later sources can be helpful but only when they can provide information that can be corroborated and derived, where possible, from the ordinary, day-to-day recording systems.

It is also important to know where a source originated and how this might inform its content, particularly foreign sources. Foreign governments had agendas. If we know what these agendas are we can analyse new information in context. Our police and investigative agencies also take into account foreign sources, but only when they have a direct connection to the key period of investigation. Again, we do not have this luxury so all foreign sources will be analysed.

Our analysis of the sources is therefore chronological. This will allow us to observe the development of trends, which can act as important signifiers. The analysis will also consist of four distinct periods of enquiry.

First, King Richard's reign and second, Henry VII's reign. The death of Richard III, the person most likely to have known what happened, is an important factor in the investigation. Can we see anything of note following his death? Did the story change? Did witnesses come forward? Was new information brought to light?

The third stage of the analysis examines materials from the Tudor period post-Henry VII, and the final area of examination commences in 1603 when the Tudor dynasty ended. Did the story change? Was any significant information brought to light following the accession of the Stuarts?

Our examination focuses specifically on materials relating to the disappearance of Edward V and Richard of York, the Princes in the Tower. Materials relating to the identity of the two Yorkist pretenders to the English throne who emerged during Henry VII's reign are examined in Chapters 12 and 14.

Missing, Murdered, Maintained

Based on our four timeline categories, we will now consider who said what, when and where, and what this might reveal.

The Reign of Richard III (d. 22 August 1485)

As we have seen in previous chapters, important primary sources are those recorded by eyewitnesses at the time of the events they describe. In this category, we have several letters. Canon Stallworth's letters of 9 and 21 June 1483 record unfolding events but do not mention a disappearance or death of King Edward's sons.[1] This is important as Stallworth, through his connection with Chancellor Bishop Russell, was at the heart of events. We can therefore assume that both boys were known to be alive at this time.

We can also assume that they were alive at the time of King Richard's coronation (see Chapter 4). The coronation was well attended, with 3,000 guests at the banquet, and included the King's Council, nobility, Church and commons.[2] That the princes were alive at the time of the coronation is an important factor in our investigation (see note 125 and Chapter 6).

Similarly, a private letter written by Thomas Langton, Bishop of St David's, to his friend, William Selling, the Prior of Christ Church, Canterbury, in mid-September is also significant.[3] Langton was in York on progress with the king and court. He was much-respected and close to King Richard as one of his chaplains. He was also Rector of All Hallows, Bread Street, and Gracechurch (Lombard Street) in London, parishes which included Baynard's Castle and the Tower.[4] He would later go on to serve Henry VII (see Chapter 10).

Langton's (private) communication does not mention the princes. After discussing the issue of shipments of Communion wine from France and a potential confrontation with Scotland over Dunbar, Langton records:

> I trust to God soon, by Michaelmas [29 September], the King shall be in London. He contents the people where he goes best that ever did a prince; for many a poor man that has suffered wrong many days has been relieved and helped by him and his commands in his progress. And in many great cities and towns were great sums of money given him which he has refused. On my troth I never liked the conditions of any prince so well as his; God has sent him to us for the welfare of us all.[5]

But Langton's communication should not be understood as a purely panegyrical description of Richard, for the bishop adds a cautionary note about King Richard's court, 'And I am not overlooking the fact that pleasure reigns to some degree'.[6]

In France, on 1 December 1483, the first detailed chronicle concerning the events in England during the spring–summer of 1483 was completed by an agent acting for the French government, Domenico Mancini. Following Louis XI's annulment of the long-standing marriage agreement between the dauphin and Elizabeth of York, which would incite Edward IV's subsequent intention to invade France in order to punish Louis, Mancini was sent to England to report on English affairs. Mancini's patron was Angelo Cato, Archbishop of Vienne, Louis XI's physician and counsellor and a powerful figure at the heart of the French government.[7]

Mancini arrived in London at the end of 1482 and returned to France at the time of Richard III's coronation on 6 July.[8] He was therefore present in the capital as key events unfolded, but he probably spoke no English and had no known connections with English government circles. However, Mancini mentions reports from one of Edward V's doctors, John Argentine, who obviously had inside knowledge about Edward's household.[9] Argentine, having lost his post as physician, seems to have fled to the continent at the time of the October 1483 uprising against King Richard, when Mancini may have received information or been brought up to date.[10] In France, Mancini was happy to recite what he knew of English affairs to French officials but reticent to put pen to paper, only doing so at the insistence of his patron.[11]

Before we consider Mancini's account, it is important to note that Argentine's information relating to Edward IV's sons concerned Edward V only. While Mancini was compiling his report, the long-expected death of Louis XI of France occurred, and his 13-year-old heir, Charles VIII, succeeded. Mancini will have been aware of the similarities between the situations of minority rule in England and France (see Chapter 7).

Mancini's account, completed by 1 December 1483, reports the following in respect of the fate of Edward V:

> But after the removal of Hastings all the attendants who had served the young king were barred from access to him. He and his brother were conducted back into the more inward apartments of the Tower itself, and day by day came to be observed more rarely through the lattices and windows, up to the point that they completely ceased to be visible. The physician Argentine, who was the last of the attendants employed by the young king, reported that, like a victim prepared for sacrifice, he sought remission of sins by daily confession and penitence, because he reckoned that his death was imminent ... I have seen several men break out in tears and lamentation when mention was made of him after he was removed from men's sight and now there was suspicion that he had been taken by death. Whether, however, he has been taken by death, and by what manner of death, so far I have not at all ascertained.[12]

Mancini offers the first suspicion, on the part of men he has observed, that Edward V may have died. The date of such observation is difficult to extrapolate, but on this reading would be sometime after the execution of Hastings on 13 June. There is, from current searches, no extant record of the removal of Edward V's attendants. All we have are the seventeen names who were paid off on 18 July, by which time Mancini had left the country. The relocation of the boys to the 'inward apartments of the Tower itself' (possibly the White Tower) until they were seen 'more rarely' and then not at all, strongly suggests a disappearance around this time.

Since Mancini could not personally have viewed the boys' movements and given the available documentary evidence (see Chapter 4), the most likely deduction seems that he was given this information after his return to France.[13] He is also unclear as to where he saw the 'several men break out in tears and lamentation when mention was made of [Edward V]', whether in England or later, on the continent. His circumspect comment, that 'so far' he has ascertained nothing, sits alongside his protestation that his written report will be a poor effort and 'not complete in all particulars'. This may further support his reluctance to put pen to paper, with key pieces of intelligence in want of verification.

As for the death of Edward V, a foreboding is clearly implied, but the cleric fails to elucidate further: he clearly didn't know if Edward V was alive or not. Death is therefore hinted at, but no unnatural means are mentioned in his report. So was Edward V unwell or sickly, prompting an intensification of religious devotion, as historian John Ashdown-Hill has posited?[14]

It seems not untoward to suggest that the stress of recent events and Edward's fall from grace had a significant impact. We must also consider whether it was Argentine who strongly implied or believed Edward had been 'taken by death' (yet made no reference to his brother). The doctor had been removed from office, so his comments may have been politically motivated. In summary, therefore, the factual content of Mancini's account indicates that the boys were taken into close confinement and subsequently disappeared. Moreover, events had taken their toll on Edward V, possibly affecting his health. It is not known if a new doctor was assigned to the children (with the surgeon apparently keeping his role) or if any potential illness or melancholia subsequently abated.

At Tours on Thursday, 15 January 1484, the French Chancellor, Guillaume de Rochefort, delivered the opening address at the assembly of the *Estates-General* of France.[15] It is not known whether Rochefort was in receipt of new intelligence, nor did he quote Mancini, but he seems to suggest that Mancini's account (and those who informed it) was considered to be 'testimony [evidence]' originating in England.

However, Rochefort's statements went much further than Mancini was prepared to concede in writing. Rochefort announced:

> … that it suffice to quote the testimony [evidence] from our neighbours the English. Look at, I beg you, the events which, after the death of King Edward, happened to that country. Behold his children, already great and brave, murdered unpunished and the crown transferred to the murderer by the favour [approval, *faventibus*][16] of the people.[17]

This is an important heightening of rhetoric, taking place six weeks after Mancini's report was submitted. We are informed that all of Edward IV's children have been murdered, and by the king who now rules.

As Edward IV's daughters were in sanctuary at Westminster, Rochefort's account is clearly inaccurate in this respect. We are informed that the murder took place prior to the new king's coronation (6 July), and this allowed the crown to be transferred with the approval of the people. Rochefort's statement seems to have been accepted on the continent as truth, or at least part-truth.

In January 1484, Thomas Basin, Bishop of Lisieux (1412–91), in his history of Louis XI, reported the following for the year 1483:

> Whether the royal children were still alive or whether they had been killed by order of their uncle, one cannot know with certainty but the second theory is by far the most likely because so long as they survived nothing could guarantee an imposter inciting rebellion or conspiracies, given how much the English are inclined towards revolts and factions, which in the alternative case would certainly not happen.[18]

In his notes for the year 1483, Caspar Weinreich, a merchant from Danzig (Gdańsk) in Poland recorded that '[King Richard] had his brother's children killed'.[19] We cannot be sure when he actually wrote this down, as all we have is an edited copy of his notes, and if he had put his seafaring life behind him at this point in time, as is suggested, the gossip he received could have been quite cold news.

Early the following year, on 1 March 1484, the mother of the princes, Elizabeth Woodville, left sanctuary. Reaching an agreement with King

Richard and his Council, Elizabeth's eldest daughters would join the royal court. It is likely that, at certain times, Elizabeth may have also attended. As the original Oath of Safety made in May 1483 (see Chapter 3) has been lost or destroyed, we've been unable to make a comparison. The agreement of 1 March 1484 does not mention Elizabeth's sons but does state King Richard's intentions concerning her daughters:

> I shall see that they shall be in surety of their lives and also not suffer any manner of hurt by any manner of person or persons to them or any of them in their bodies and persons to be done by way of Ravishment or defouling contrary to their will / nor them or any of them imprison within the Tower of London or other prison / but that I shall put them in honest places of good name & fame.[20]

The agreement adds that when Elizabeth's daughters come of age they will be married to 'gentlemen born', and Elizabeth Woodville herself will receive 700 marks a year from government revenues for her own endowment (*'exibicione'*). The agreement was sworn on the Bible by King Richard in full view of the Lords Spiritual and Temporal and the Mayor and Aldermen of the City of London (for the full text of the agreement, see Appendix 1).

This is a significant document as it opens a window into this key moment. There are several important factors. The reference to the Tower of London as a prison seems to confirm Mancini's report that the princes were placed in confinement – possibly in the White Tower – for a period of time (see the *Great Chronicle*, p. 94). Also, this was known to Elizabeth Woodville while in sanctuary – though she would have known that Edward V was in the Tower's Royal Apartments while awaiting his coronation, for which purpose she had agreed with the Archbishop of Canterbury that his younger brother could join him on 16 June. It is not known when she subsequently received information about her sons, or from whom, nor whether she demanded a full account of their whereabouts or fate as a preliminary to leaving sanctuary, or what she and her daughters were told. Additionally, it is not known if Elizabeth played any role in the abduction attempt from the Tower Palace the previous summer, or if any such involvement had subsequently been uncovered by the new government.

The lack of any mention of Elizabeth's sons is a significant omission. The agreement offers no prayers or observances for them. The oath was conducted openly and in full view of key witnesses, including leading members of the Church.

Six weeks later, on or around 17–24 April 1484,[21] Edward, Prince of Wales, died at the age of 7 at Middleham Castle in North Yorkshire. At the time, King Richard and Queen Anne were at Nottingham Castle. The Crowland chronicler reports:

> ... this only son ... died at Middleham castle after a short illness ... You might have seen the father and mother, after hearing the news at Nottingham where they were then staying, almost out of their minds for a long time when faced with the sudden grief.[22]

There is no evidence that Edward's death was the result of foul play, nor any suspicion of it.

For the year ending 8 September 1484 (Nativity of the Virgin), the Annals of Cambridge record a payment to the Duke of York. The payment probably refers to King Richard's visit to the university earlier that year from 9–11 March.[23] John Howard, Duke of Norfolk, was in attendence. The town Treasurer's accounts record:

> For the servants[24] of the Lord the King, Richard the Third, this year, 7s.; and in rewards to the servants of the Lord the Prince, 7s.; and in rewards to the servants of the Queen, 6s. 8d.; and in rewards to the servants of the Duke of York, 6s. 8d.[25]

It is unclear whether this payment relates to the servants of Edward IV's youngest son (age 10), or is a scribal error for those of Edward, Earl of Warwick (age 9), who was in Queen Anne's household.[26] Whether or not a scribal error, this suggests that in Cambridge, on or by 8 September 1484, Richard, Duke of York, was believed to be alive.

For the remainder of King Richard's reign, the Signet, Privy Seal, Colchester Oath Book, Chancery, Close Roll and Royal Exchequer records describe Edward V as the 'bastard king' (Colchester Oath Book, September 1483)[27] or 'bastard' (grant of 16 December 1483).[28] On 5 January 1484, under a Privy Seal from the Royal Exchequer, an item refers to a fee to be paid to a John Belle in Cambridge that had been due to him from the time of 'the Coronation of the bastard son of King Edward'.[29] Similarly, a second document from the Royal Exchequer around 7–25 June 1484, relating to a tax collection, reads, 'Edward bastard late said king of England the fifth'.[30] A third document comes from the Close Rolls of the Royal Chancery from 1 December 1484 and records an indenture made between Thomas Ormond, knight, and William Catesby on 13 June 1483 in 'the first year of the reign of Edward bastard, late called king of England the fifth'.[31] These three records from 1484 are the last specific administrative references to the elder boy in official government documents and do not record Edward V as deceased, nor offer any appropriate prayers or observations for his soul.

In the summer and autumn 1484, there are ten IPMs for the death of William, Lord Hastings. As historian Gordon McKelvie informs us, 'IPMs differ from the documents found in the patent rolls and the privy seal because they were produced in the localities by the local escheator, not by clerks at Westminster.'[32] An escheator was a local legal officer formally appointed to look into any reversion of property or lands in their area following a death.

The IPMs for Hastings cover counties across the Midlands and in the north and south where the Royal Councillor owned estates. The documents record the death of Hastings on '13 June in the year of Edward V, the bastard', the local legal officers describing Edward V as a bastard, 'either by their own volition or after being instructed to by the Hastings family themselves'.[33] None of the IPMs record Edward V's death or offer any prayers or observances.

There are two further references to the 'Lord Bastard' in 1484–85, in the Canterbury City Archives and King's Signet Office at Westminster. In November 1484, in Canterbury, there is a reference to payments for an allowance of wine and leavened bread 'for the Lord Bastard riding to Calais', and a pike and wine for 'Master Brakynbury Constable of the Tower of London', returned from Calais at that time 'from the Lord Bastard'.[34] The document is dated Michaelmas 1484 to Michaelmas 1485. Michaelmas is 29 September. The entry is specific about Brackenbury's role as Constable of the Tower of London. From late 1484, to his death at the Battle of Bosworth in August 1485, Brackenbury held several roles (see Chapter 17). It is not known why his Tower role was singled out in this record.

On Wednesday, 9 March 1485 the King's Signet Office records, 'A warrant to Henry Davy to deliver to John Goddeslande fotemane [footman] unto the lord Bastard two dublettes of silk oon jaket of silk oone gowne of gloth two shirtes and two bonetes [hats].'[35] Many writers have attributed this entry as a grant of clothing for King Richard's bastard son, John of Gloucester. John was about 15 at the time and would be awarded the Captaincy of Calais two days later, on 11 March. King Richard's award of the captaincy very clearly describes John as his bastard son.[36] John was not a lord, a fact the king and his Signet Office knew well.[37] It seems probable that the king's tailor (Henry Davy) will have known this too.[38]

In contrast, Edward V had been a lord, the Earl of March and Pembroke, as well as erstwhile King of England, a fact generally remembered when he was referred to. This is recorded in the Wardrobe Account where Edward is described as 'the said Lord Edward'.[39] Administrative work relied on accurate record keeping. If 'lord' was a clerical error, as some believe, then the recorders for the Wardrobe Account, Signet Office and at Canterbury made the identical mistake. It may also be important for our enquiry to note that the surname Goddesland is unusual, originating within 15 miles of Coldridge and, until only recently, 'restricted to North Devon'[40] (see Appendix 3).

In 1485, further information comes from the continent. Henry Tudor, a pretender to the English throne exiled in France, sent an open letter to his allies in England calling King Richard a 'homicide and unnatural tyrant',[41] a possible reference to the continental allegations of the murder of Edward IV's children. In December 1483, Henry had promised to marry Elizabeth of York so was aware of her survival. He fled to the French court in September 1484 (from Brittany) which transformed Henry into a significant threat. The French government lent him 50,000 crowns, 2,000 mercenaries and a fleet of ships for an attempt on the English throne.[42]

The final source recorded during King Richard's reign concerning the sons of Edward IV dates from May to early June 1485. This comes from a Silesian envoy, Niclas von Popplau. Popplau visited King Richard and his court at York for three or four days, 1–5 May 1484, meeting the king on a number of occasions. His diary was written a year later in Nuremberg, Germany, prior to the envoy falling ill.[43] Popplau's report is an eyewitness account. He records in his diary:

> Ten miles from Doncaster, en route to York, there is also a castle stronghold. **Inside are held in safekeeping the king's treasure and all great lords, such as the king's children and sons of princes, that are kept just as close as if in captivity.** And the said castle is named in Latin *pons fractus* [Pontefract], as I was later given to understand from the mouth of the king himself, by name Richard, King of England ... [Emphasis added.][44]

It is likely that Richard's illegitimate children, Katherine and John (of Gloucester/Pontefract) resided at Pontefract Castle in early May 1484. Katherine would marry only at the end of that month.[45] Did Edward IV's illegitimate children, and potentially one or more of his sons, also reside at the castle for a period of time? And is this what Popplau inadvertently records?

As we have seen, King Richard's heir had died in mid-April at Middleham and, as Prince of Wales, would have kept his own household. Piotr Radzikowski, editor of Popplau's diary, interprets 'kept just as close as if in captivity' as referring to royal prisoners historically kept at Pontefract.[46] However, this exhibits the editor's own knowledge of Pontefract Castle and its long history, rather than the limited information available to the foreigner, Popplau, who states that he derived knowledge of Pontefract Castle from personal discussions with King Richard and wrote about it in terms of that particular king only.[47]

Immediately prior to his visit with King Richard, at the end of February 1484, Popplau had met Gui de Rochefort (Guillaume's brother) in Burgundy and,[48] more recently, Charles VIII of France and Henry Tudor at Rouen on 23 April 1485.[49] Popplau is the first to identify 'the sons of King Edward' specifically (rather than 'the children'). He further records in his diary:

> And King Richard, who reigns now, had put to death the sons of King Edward, they say, so that not they but he was crowned. But many say (and I count myself amongst them) they still live and are kept in a very dark cellar.[50]

The envoy records no noble women or children at King Richard's court at York in 1484.[51] It is not known where, or from whom Popplau received his information. Popplau also follows the French/Rochefort assertion in placing the rumoured deaths prior to King Richard's coronation.

The Reign of Richard III: Summary

Analysis of material from King Richard's reign is important for what it reveals about the position in England, and abroad. English government and county records suggest that Edward V was alive or thought to be alive. He had, at some point, been confined in the Tower of London with his younger brother. This had angered the Queen Mother, Elizabeth Woodville, who received a new, or updated, oath of safety for her daughters from the king and government in order for them to leave sanctuary. This was witnessed by the Lords, Church and Commons. It is not known who drew up the agreement, or what relation it had to the original from May 1483. In the 1484 agreement, Elizabeth would not allow nor countenance what she saw as imprisonment in the Tower or 'other prison' for her daughters.

At face value, the actions of the Queen Mother in coming to terms with Richard, Church and government suggest one or both boys may have been alive, or thought to be alive – or at least, this is what she and her daughters were told by English officials. No evidence can be found of any prayers or masses being said for the boys, or any formal burials taking place.[52] The fate of Richard of York is (currently, bar the record at Cambridge) absent from English government records of Richard's reign. Searches in this regard are ongoing.

Abroad in France, an agent acting for the French government, Domenico Mancini, reports that both boys were taken into some form of close confinement (possibly the White Tower), where they were 'observed more rarely through the lattices and windows, up to the point that they completely ceased to be visible'. This seems to confirm a disappearance – and for both boys. Mancini records Argentine's report that Edward 'reckoned that his death was imminent', observing suspicions that he might have died, though has nothing concrete to add. In mid-January 1484, the French government declares the children (of Edward IV) to have been murdered by the new (Yorkist) king prior to his coronation, with the English king then acceding to the throne with the favour (approval) of the people. Thereafter, foreign accounts follow the French/Rochefort narrative for the alleged killing of Edward IV's children, with only one (Basin) questioning it.

The account of Niclas von Popplau is of interest as it straddles home and abroad and suggests a disparity between English and continental reports regarding the fate of the boys. The English royal nurseries at this time were based in the north at Sandal and Sheriff Hutton in Yorkshire. It is not known how Popplau's six weeks in England persuaded him that the boys were alive, albeit held in 'a very dark cellar' (an idiom for 'a secret place'). Popplau did not visit Sandal or Sheriff Hutton but may have passed by Pontefract Castle.[53]

The envoy's account suggests that no obvious exhibition of the boys had taken place in England during Richard's reign.[54] It is not known whether this was because the government felt there was no need, it was considered a security risk, they didn't know where they were or what had become of them, or they didn't have one or more of the boys to exhibit (either by way of death or removal to out-of-reach locations).

Government and county records did not record the death of Edward V or prayers or observances for his soul. With leading churchmen occupying key roles in English government and witnessing the agreement with the boys' mother, such an omission may be significant.

The Reign of Henry VII (d. 21 April 1509)

On Monday, 22 August 1485, Richard III died at the Battle of Bosworth. This is an important marker for the enquiry. Had any witnesses previously been reluctant to come forward with significant information, the change of regime presented them with their opportunity. We will therefore now examine materials from the twenty-four-year reign of Henry VII to see what this might reveal.

Late August 1485

Our first source is Dafydd Llwyd's poem, written just after King Richard's death at Bosworth. The pretender, Henry Tudor, with his Welsh descent, made landfall in Wales and consulted Llywd on his way to the confrontation. Llwyd, a Welsh bard, lived at Mathafarn, 5 miles east of Machynlleth, Powys,[55] where Henry was stationed on 14 August 1485.[56] In translation, his (untitled) poem refers to King Richard as a Jew, Saracen, mole, dog, fettered boar, little 'R', little boar, caterpillar, ape and evil shepherd. Likening someone to a Jew or Saracen was an established form of medieval disparagement. Llwyd's verse speaks of the princes:

> A fettered boar who in his ward, Punished sons of Edward, If he slew, without judges leave, His two youthful nephews ... Shame upon the wretched Saracen For killing angels, Christ's own. An atrocity he did, by St Non's miracles, An exploit of cruel Herod.[57]

Henry was crowned King Henry VII at Westminster on 30 October 1485. His first Parliament opened on 7 November. This is a significant moment in the project's investigations. If Henry's Parliament believed Edward IV's sons had been killed, this represented an opportunity to present a detailed account, to investigate and interrogate all those with information (including Bosworth prisoners), launch an enquiry and authorise a full search of the Tower and royal nurseries. Among the many crimes attributed to King Richard in an Act of Attainder, Parliament reported the 'shedding of infants blood', but nothing more specific.[58]

Parliament, as we have seen, consisted of the Lords, Church and Commons who had, until very recently, known and served King Richard. Declining the opportunity to expose Richard's possible regicide afforded by the national stage of political life is significant. Moreover, Henry had promised to marry the princes' sister, Elizabeth of York, for which he needed to repeal the 1484 Act of Parliament which established the bastardy of King Edward's children. In repealing that Act, he would automatically reinstate Elizabeth's brothers as the legitimated heirs to the English throne. To prove their decease was, therefore, of the utmost importance to the new king and government.

In November 1485, the Crowland Abbey chronicler set down an account of King Richard's reign. Crowland Abbey is in Lincolnshire, in eastern England. Its author (the most likely candidate is cleric Richard Langport)[59] reported the situation in London while King Richard was investing his son as Prince of Wales at York in September 1483:

> In the meantime and while these things were happening the two sons of King Edward remained in the Tower of London with a specially appointed guard. In order to release them from such captivity the people of the South and of the West of the kingdom began to murmur greatly, to form assemblies and to organise associations to this end.

For the events concerning the uprising itself, the Crowland chronicler added:

> … a rumour arose that King Edward's sons, by some unknown manner of violent destruction, had met their fate. For this reason, all those who had begun this agitation, realising that if they could not find someone new at their head for their conquest it would soon be all over with them, remembered Henry earl of Richmond …[60]

This is an important account as it states that the boys were alive in September 1483 when King Richard was at York but were rumoured to have 'met their fate' sometime after the 'agitation' began. Significantly, this uprising against King Richard was in October 1483, when Henry Tudor first attempted to invade. The chronicler's wording echoes King Henry's Parliament where Henry was declared to have acceded to the throne by right of conquest. It seems that the Crowland chronicler, or someone close to him, was present at the first Tudor monarch's Parliament and began writing his account shortly thereafter.[61] This may suggest a dissemination by the new government of information not found in any official document.

September 1485 or Later[62]

The next piece in the jigsaw comes from Robert Ricart, the Recorder of Bristol. Ricart compiled a Kalendar of city proceedings that included national events. Events were recorded for each mayoral year, which ran from 15 September to 14 September. A marginal note next to the civic year September 1483 to September 1484 was evidently added at a later date, perhaps in September 1485 when writing the entry for the mayoral year 1484–85 which encompassed Bosworth (although it was perhaps added even later). It states, 'And this yere the two sonnes of King E. were put to scylence [silence] in the Towre of London'.[63]

It is not known if 'put to silence' meant death or if the boys had been removed from contact with other people. If death or murder was meant, no pious hopes for their souls were included. As Ricart was located in a part of the country which experienced the October uprising, he may have been recording the same rumour mentioned by Crowland, though the rebellion is not mentioned. This seems to suggest that Ricart, or a member of the City Council, attended Henry VII's first Parliament.

In the mayoral year 1483–84, Ricart correctly records Buckingham's execution (2 November 1483). Since we know the marginal note for the princes was placed there at least a year *after* Buckingham's execution, this raises the possibility that at the time of the October uprising this key western port may have had no knowledge that the 'agitation' against King Richard had anything to do with King Edward's sons.

On 1 March 1486, Diego de Valera wrote to the Spanish monarchs, Ferdinand and Isabella. A former Spanish Ambassador, Valera wrote from his home at Puerto de Santa Maria, having come into receipt of information from 'trustworthy merchants' returning to the Spanish port from England. Valera reported that his information covered 'all that happened (in England) … up to the end of January':

> … that, as your Royal Majesty knows well enough, this Richard killed two innocent nephews to whom the kingdom belonged after the life of his brother; moreover, although King Edward, the father of these, was making war in Scotland and Richard remained in England, it is claimed that he ordered them to be killed with herbs.[64]

This is the first instance in which we are offered a description of the killing: an allegation of poisoning. Valera is misinformed about events concerning the Scottish invasion of 1482 – it was Richard who waged the war in Scotland and Edward who remained in England. He or his informants seem to have no knowledge of the illegitimacy of Edward IV's children – or failed to record it.

Richard is said to have killed his nephews while Edward IV was still alive, and during the Scottish war (in the summer of 1482).

It is not known where this story originated or from which English port the 'trusted merchants' embarked. As London was England's major port city, it may be hypothesised that this story was current in the capital by the end of January 1486. This was five months after King Richard's death, but within a couple of months of the commencement of Henry VII's Parliament.

The first session of Parliament was prorogued on Saturday, 10 December 1485.[65] The proximity of Henry VII's Parliament seems to be further supported by the content of Valera's letter, which follows contemporary Tudor propaganda in describing Henry as Earl of Richmond in exile 'to whom the realm [England] lawfully belonged'. By March 1486, Valera surmises that the Spanish monarchs had been informed of the deaths.

19–27 September 1486

Our next source is provided by the Italian poet, Pietro Carmeliano.[66] Carmeliano resided in London from 1481.[67] During Richard's reign he had written in praise of the Yorkist monarch but received only modest patronage.[68] Directly after the submission of his new poem, Carmeliano would benefit from Tudor patronage for the rest of his life. His poem to King Henry was the poet's first political writing.[69] Carmeliano likened the new monarch to Apollo, 'the people say that this is not a man's likeness, but a God's'. Richard is described as 'a criminal tyrant, habituated to evil-doing', 'savage' and 'ready for every wickedness'. As for the princes, the poet (through the ghost of Henry VI) has Richard 'put them to the sword'.[70]

Carmeliano's poem escalates what seems to be a fast-developing narrative. In just over a year since the Yorkist monarch's death, he offers a sense of certainty surrounding the demise (murder) of the princes. Although allegorical, the source of Carmeliano's information (as a foreign national) is not known.

1488

Álvaro Lopes de Chaves was a secretary to Afonso V and John II of Portugal. In some notes, he stated:

… in the year of 83 … the Duke of Gloucester had in his power the Prince of Wales and the Duke of York, the young sons of the said king his brother, and turned them to the Duke of Buckingham, under whose custody the said Princes were starved to death. And the said Gloucester, author of this murder out of his desire to be king, wishing to clear himself of so ugly an event, beheaded the Duke of Buckingham and rose to kingship …[71]

This is the first time the Duke of Buckingham is implicated as an accomplice to murder (starvation), an act said to have occurred prior to Gloucester's coronation (6 July). Buckingham was, of course, executed on 2 November 1483, after Richard's coronation. His execution took place on Edward V's thirteenth birthday (see Chapter 6).

Before his death in 1489, Jan Allertzs, the Recorder of Rotterdam, wrote, 'after king Edward's death he [Duke of Gloucester] killed two of his brother's children, boys, or so he was accused: but anyway they were killed, and he himself became king'.[72]

Around 1490[73]

Our next informant is John Rous, the Warwickshire priest and Neville family retainer. Like Carmeliano, Rous had written in praise of King Richard during the Yorkist monarch's lifetime. Around five years after the king's death, Rous describes Richard as the 'Antichrist', 'retained within his mother's womb for two years and emerging with teeth and hair to his shoulders'.[74] As for the fate of the princes, Rous writes (following the execution of Rivers, Grey and Vaughan on 25 June 1483):

And shortly he imprisoned his lord King Edward V, king in deed but not crowned, together with his brother Richard who had been taken from Westminster on the promise of safety. In this way it was afterwards known to very few by what manner of death they had suffered. The usurper King Richard III then ascended the throne of the slaughtered children whose protector he was himself.[75]

Rous' account ignores the illegitimacy of the princes and the 1484 Act of Parliament (see Chapter 6) and follows the foreign theme that both boys died prior to Richard's coronation. Though Richard is accused of imprisoning them, he is not named as the perpetrator of their presumed deaths. The Tower as a location is perhaps implied, since Rous also mentions the imprisonment of both boys and the promise of safety as a condition of Richard of York's emergence from sanctuary to join his brother. This was made by Thomas Bourchier, Archbishop of Canterbury (although Rous does not name him). Bourchier had died in 1486.

Rous adds what may be new information – that the manner of death was known to 'very few'. It is not clear whether this means at the time of writing or at the time of the 'slaughter'. This suggests the new Tudor regime had not yet disseminated an agreed story about the events which led to the boys' apparent deaths. It might also mean that Rous assumed those at the top of government knew 'what manner of death they suffered' but were keeping it from public consumption, or it had somehow been implied that they knew. Either way, nothing has been found in official records of this period.

25 April 1496

Spanish investigations were conducted in Setúbal, Portugal, pursuant to Spain negotiating for Catherine of Aragon to marry Henry VII's heir, while demanding that there must be no living pretender to the English throne. Testimonies about a young man claiming to be the Duke of York were taken from witnesses, with the Portuguese Ambassador Rui de Sousa first to be interrogated. The notary recorded:

> And then he [de Sousa] heard it said that they had put him [York] and his brother too, the Prince of Wales, in a fortress where a body of water passed by, and that they bled them, and they died from the forced bleeding.[76]

As de Sousa had been Ambassador to England from 1481 to 1489 it is unclear why he didn't name the Tower of London, unless he believed it to be another location. He did not indicate why the boys would have been bled – generally an indication of illness. It is further uncertain if de Sousa was suggesting a deliberate or accidental death.

1500

Our next source comes from the Burgundian chronicler, Jean Molinet. Edward and Richard are called 'Pierre' and 'George'. Molinet writes:

> They were prisoners for about five weeks; and through the Captain of the Tower, the Duke Richard had them secretly killed and made to disappear. Some say that he took them to a large place and enclosed them with nothing to drink or eat. Others say that they were pressed between two quilts, sleeping in the same chamber. And when came the execution, Pierre, the eldest son, was sleeping, and the young one woke up, and when he realised the malicious deed, he started to say: 'Ha, my brother, wake up, as one

90

is coming to kill you!' then he started to say to those who appeared, 'why are you killing my brother? Kill me and let him live!' Then one after the other were executed and killed, and their corpses were moved to some secret place; then they were recovered, and after the death of the King Richard were given royal funerals. The same day arrived in the Tower of London, the Duke of Buckingham, then misbelieved at having killed the said children, because he was pretending to the crown.[77]

[...]

Because of the said murder of his two nephews, and the other enormous and foul acts, the princes and noble of England, sovereignly those of the Church, rose against him and deployed the banner of Saint Gilbert, bishop; and many barons and knights that gathered to descend on France, worked at finding the corpses of the said children, born of royal blood. And when they were found, were interred in the Church of the Preachers in London; and then, entered the Royal Palace and imprisoned the Duke Richard; but he talked softly and promised so many beautiful gifts, that he escaped the hand of his enemies. Then after, more by force than love, he was crowned King of England, the day of Saint Michael, in one thousand four hundred and eighty two.[78]

[...]

The Count of Richmond seeing the King trampled on[79] [vanquished], and that God gave him victory over a tyrant, took the oath in towns near London where he entered as a victor; and was received in a great triumph; and had a proclamation before his coronation published everywhere, that if there were a claimant to the crown by descent from the King Edward. He was to show himself; and he would help him to get crowned; but no soul appeared.[80]

There is a lot of information to unpick in Molinet's chronicle. The boys were prisoners for 'about five weeks'.[81] Both were executed in the Tower by Richard, as duke, and this was done through the 'Captain of the Tower'.[82] We have a murder committed by starvation or smothering between quilts (mattresses or cushions). Starvation takes place in a 'large place'. The bodies were buried in a secret place, but following King Richard's death they were recovered and given royal funerals. The murder incites the rebellion against

Richard. Those who rebelled and went to France returned, searched for the bodies, found them and buried them in the 'Church of the Preachers in London' (i.e., medieval St Pauls).[83] 'Duke Richard' was alive at the time of the burial and was then crowned king. His coronation took place in 1482. Buckingham arrived at the Tower at the time of the murders but was incorrectly implicated in the crime due to his pretensions to the crown.

This is an important account to disentangle because it contains new information about an apparent proclamation published everywhere before Henry's coronation, allegedly seeking to find any male descendants of Edward IV. Although it seems to undermine the chronicler's earlier information regarding murder, significantly, it offers the first account of any public statement made by Henry in respect of the princes, circulated in and around London. The proclamation was issued prior to Henry's coronation and suggests that at this time (September–October 1485), it was assumed Edward V (or some other offspring) was alive, or thought to be alive (see Chapter 12).

1502

Our next source is Bernard André, Henry VII's court poet and tutor to Arthur, Prince of Wales.[84] Originally from Toulouse in France, André arrived in England after Henry VII's accession and was invited to write the new king's biography, in which he says:

> Richard, then, who had been called and declared Protector by the king, concealing the tyrannical plan he had in mind, at first ordered his nephews to be summoned from Wales. But Queen Elizabeth, King Edward's prudent wife, took care for herself and her children and sought sanctuary in a sacred place. What more can I say? After the tyrant, safe in his London stronghold, slew the lords he knew were faithful to his brother, he ordered that his unprotected nephews secretly be dispatched with the sword.[85]

Like Carmeliano, Rous, Allertzs and Molinet, André follows the French/Rochefort line, asserting that the boys were 'dispatched' prior to Richard's accession. Following Carmeliano, we are again given the method of the sword (shorthand for a violent death). This was carried out at Richard's command and undertaken in secret. No speculation regarding who committed the act (either rumoured or surmised) is offered. André's account may suggest information (or rumour) circulating at King Henry's court, although we must note, once again, this appears in no official record.

1502–03

London merchant Richard Arnold published a book, which included some brief city annals. For 1483, he recorded, 'This year deceased the king, in April, entering into the twenty-third year of his reign, and the two sons of King Edward were put to silence. And the Duke of Gloucester took upon him the crown in July [*sic*].'[86]

1508

Richard Pynson's *Magna Carta cum aliis Antiquis Statutis* was published in London. This presumes the date of Edward V's death as 22 June 1483 and place of burial, the Tower of London.[87]

Henry VII died on 21 April 1509.

The Reign of Henry VII: Summary

What is perhaps of most interest following the death of King Richard is the lack of any official record or statement concerning the disappearance or fate of the princes. Henry VII failed to order any recorded enquiry or make use of the national platform his first Parliament (or subsequent Parliaments) afforded. This would have secured his reign (by right of conquest) and quelled any potential future uprisings (two Yorkist pretenders emerged in 1486 and 1491). In contrast, the Burgundian chronicler Molinet relates that a proclamation was made by Henry in September–October 1485, prior to coronation. No known copy of this exists but searches are ongoing.

At this point, our intelligence gathering suggests that rumours were allowed to take hold, or deliberately spread, at or around the time of Henry's first Parliament in November 1485. These rumours supported existing foreign accounts of the princes meeting an untimely end. No account of the princes' demise existed at this time from an English writer.

Henry's proclamation, uniquely mentioned by Molinet, may also explain the lack of any indictment in his Parliament. Having proclaimed the possibility that Edward V was alive (if a genuine invitation for his rival claimants to come forward), Henry might look somewhat foolish or, at best, badly informed (see Chapter 10). Crowland now reported his recollection that 'a rumour arose' at the time of the October uprising but this was not recorded at Bristol, a port involved in the rebellion.

During Henry's reign, the boys are said to have been killed by poison, starvation, smothering or the sword (violent death) or by being bled. Molinet relates that the bodies were found by those returning from France (i.e., Henry and his rebels) and given a royal burial in (probably) St Paul's Church in London. No known English record of this discovery, or burial, exists.

One account (1508) mentions burial in the Tower of London. The date of both murders is variously recorded in unofficial texts as taking place before King Richard's coronation on 6 July 1483, including Molinet. Confusingly, Molinet adds, 'They were prisoners for about five weeks.' Five weeks from 16 June (when Richard of York joined Edward V at the Tower) takes us to 21 July and the abduction attempt.

We will now place under the microscope our next important timeline. This will take us to 1603 and the end of the Tudor dynasty.

The Tudor Dynasty Continued: 1509–1603

In the spring of 1509, Henry VII was succeeded by his only surviving son, Henry VIII (d. 1547). Henry was followed by Edward VI (d. 1553), Mary I (d. 1558) and Elizabeth I (d. 1603).

Around 1512

The next source is *The Great Chronicle of London*. The *Great Chronicle* was an account of events in the capital recorded for each mayoral year. Mayoral years ran from 29 October to 28 October. In around 1496, the *Great Chronicle* came into the hands of Robert Fabyan, who inserted entries post-1438 where it had left off. He then continued work on it from 1502–12 – it is this final 1512 manuscript which survives.[88]

In the mayoral year of October 1482 to October 1483, York's transfer to the Tower is recorded as follows, 'Whom the said protector conveyed straight unto the king, where both were well treated within the king's lodging being within the Tower, a certain of time after.'

Following Gloucester's request for the northern force, and prior to the sermons announcing the illegitimacy of Edward's children (22 June), the Chronicle adds, 'And after this were the prince & the duke of York held more straight [closely]'.[89]

It then records, 'And during this mayor's year, The children of king Edward were seen shooting & playing In the garden of the Tower by sundry times [meaning on separate, different occasions]'.[90]

For the next mayoral year of October 1483–October 1484, the *Great Chronicle* records, 'But after Easter much whispering was among the people that The king had put the Children of king Edward to death.'[91]

For the first mayoral year of Henry VII, from 29 October 1485 to 28 October 1486, the *Great Chronicle* has this to say:

> Considering the death of king Edward's children, Of whom as men feared openly to say that they were Rid out of this world, But of their manner of death was many opinions, for some said they were murdered between ii feather beds, Some said they were drowned In malmsey and some said they were stikked with a Venomous potion. But how so ever they were put to death, Certain It was that before that day [Henry Tudor's invasion] they were departed from this world, Of which Cruel deed sir James Tyrell was Reported to be the doer. But others put that weight upon an old servant of king Richard's named ____ [name left blank].[92]

According to the chronicle, the children were well treated and then held more straitly. After October 1483 they had disappeared. It was rumoured the following Easter (Sunday, 18 April 1484) that King Richard had put them to death. As the chronicle describes the children shooting and playing in the Tower garden, it seems explicit that the rumours of murder referred to the two princes. The 'children' were said to have been smothered between two feather beds, drowned in Malmsey wine or 'stikked' (put out/stifled) with a poison.

Significantly, we are also given a new alleged perpetrator, Sir James Tyrell (executed in 1502). This is what the compiler in London, Robert Fabyan, was able to recall by 1512. The *Great Chronicle* reported the rumours of the princes' deaths arose at Easter 1484 and not, as Crowland indicated, during the October uprising of 1483. Easter is an important and notable time of year. This suggests that the October uprising against King Richard may not have had a direct connection with the disappearance (or deaths) of King Edward's sons or was a new Tudor/rebel narrative following Bosworth. Searches of Town Accounts are ongoing in an attempt to corroborate Crowland's account.

1513–19

A London citizen recorded in his notes for 1483,[93] 'Item: this year King Edward the vth, late called Prince Wales, and Richard duke of York his brother, King Edward iiij sons, were put to death in the Tower of London be the vise [advice or design] of the duke of Buckingham.'[94] This is the first English allegation that the princes were put to death by the Duke of Buckingham, or on his advice.

1516

After reporting the accession of Richard III, Fabyan's New Chronicles recorded, 'In which pass time the prince, or of right king Edward the v., with his brother the duke of York, were put under sure keeping within the Tower, in such wise that they never came abroad after.'[95]

1517

The next account comes from the *Dutch Divisie Chronicle*. Written in 1500, it was published in 1517:

> ... they were trusted to the care of the Earl [*sic*] of Buckingham. Now some would say that the Duke of Gloucester their foresaid uncle made them starve to become king himself. Some others will say that the Duke of Buckingham killed these children hoping to become king himself ... And some say that this Henry Earl of Buckingham killed only one child and spared the other which he had lifted from the font and had him secretly out of the country. This child was called Richard ... The Duke of Gloucester, these two children being thus secretly hidden and put out of the way, made himself King of England, and ordered the foresaid Henry Earl of Buckingham to be killed as a traitor.[96]

Buckingham is again implicated, with Gloucester secretly hiding both children so they are 'put out of the way'. This is the second time the survival of either of the princes is suggested (following Molinet's alleged proclamation).

1524

Our next chronicle source originates in France from the work of Philippe de Commynes. Commynes was a former Councillor to the courts of Burgundy and France. He completed his *Mémoires* in about 1491, reporting events in England. They were published in 1524:[97]

> The duke had his two nephews murdered and made himself king, with the title King Richard ... as soon as King Richard had had his two nephews cruelly murdered, as I said before, he lost his wife.[98]

He signed his letters 'Richard' and he had the two sons of his brother, Edward, put to death ... the duke of Gloucester had done homage to his nephew as his king and sovereign lord: then immediately he had committed this murder ... King Richard did not last long, nor did the duke of Buckingham who had put the two children to death.[99]

This alleges that Gloucester had his nephews murdered so he could become king, with Buckingham named as the perpetrator of the killing (not merely by his advice, see the London citizen report mentioned previously).

1529

Our next account comes from John Rastell in London. Rastell was an author, printer and publisher, and brother-in-law of Thomas More. Rastell writes:

... the said protector, by the council of the duke of Buckingham, as it was said, caused this young king and his brother to be conveyed to ward [guarded or kept safe]; which were never after seen but there put to death.

But of the manner of the death of this young king, and of his brother, there were divers opinions; but the most common opinion was, that they were smothered between two featherbeds, and that, in the doing, the younger brother escaped from under the featherbeds, and crept under the bedstead, and there lay naked a while, till that they had smothered the young king, so that he was surely dead; and, after this, one of them took his brother from under the bedstead, and held his face down to the ground with his one hand, and with the other hand cut his throat bolle [throat-ball – Adam's apple] a souder [asunder] with a dagger. It is a miracle that any man could have so hard a heart to do so cruel a deed, save only that necessity compelled them, for they were so charged by the duke, the protector, that if they showed not to him the bodies of both those children dead, on the morrow after they were so commanded, that then they themselves should be put to death. Wherefore they that were so commanded to do it, were compelled to fulfil the protector's will.

And after, that the bodies of these two children, as the opinion ran, were both closed in a great heavy chest, and by the means of one that was secret with the protector, they were put in a ship going to Flanders; and, when the ship was in the black deeps, this man threw both those dead bodies, so closed in the chest, over the hatches into the sea; and yet none of the mariners, no none in the ship, save only the said man, knew what things it was that was there so enclosed. Which saying divers men conjectured to be true, because that the bones of the said children could never be found buried, neither in the Tower nor in no other place.

Another opinion there is, that they which had the charge to put them to death, caused one to cry suddenly, 'Treason, treason'. Wherewith the children being afeared, desired to know what was best for them to do. And then they bad them hide themselves in a great chest, that no man should find them, and if anybody came into the chamber they would say they were not there. And according as they counselled them, they crept both into the chest, which, anon after, they locked. And then anon they buried that chest in a great pit under a stair, which they before had made therefore, and anon cast earth thereon, and so buried them quick. Which chest was after cast into the black deeps, as is before said.

Then, the 20th day of June [*recte* 26th], the said protector took upon him as king of the realm, proclaiming himself King Richard III.

Immediately after his coronation, the grudge, as well of the lords as of the commons, greatly increased against him [King Richard], because the common fame went that he had secretly murdered the two sons of his brother, King Edward IV in the Tower of London.[100]

This is an important account as it represents the first time that several narratives are ascribed to the disappearance and widely published in England. Both boys were put to death by Richard as Protector, 'as it was said' by the 'council' of the Duke of Buckingham (not by Buckingham himself, compare Commynes' and the London citizen's notes). Following this, Richard proclaimed himself king. Edward V had been smothered and Richard of York's throat cut by unnamed men. The following day, the bodies were to be shown to Richard or the men undertaking the task would also be killed. The bodies were then put in a great chest, placed on a boat to Flanders and thrown into the River Thames in an area on the estuary known as the 'black deeps'. One man undertook this task and none aboard the ship were aware of what was taking place.

Another scenario describes both boys placed alive in the great chest, which is locked and buried in a great pit under a stair (in the Tower). The pit had been specifically made for this task. The chest was then exhumed, taken on the ship to Flanders and thrown into the river at black deeps. Significantly, Rastell adds, 'Which saying divers men conjectured to be true, because that the bones of the said children could never be found buried, neither in the Tower nor in no other place.' The timeline for this account of the boys' murder is on or around 26 June when Gloucester accepted the throne.

Undated

The next mention, in the Middleton Collection at Nottingham University, appears in a list of kings similar to the Anlaby Cartulary (see below). Handwritten notes on the folio can be dated to sometime after 1521. It states, 'Edward the fifth reigned as a child from the aforesaid 9th day of April until the 25th day of June, whereupon the following day he was slain and his body submersed underwater.'[101] This seems to follow Rastell for Edward V's death on 26 June and the body being cast into the 'black deeps'.

1530

The next mention appears in the Anlaby Cartulary. This includes a list of monarchs, their length of reign and dates of death. Edward V is recorded as reigning for two months and eight days;[102] his death is given as 22 June.[103] Edward's entry was included sometime during the Tudor period, following the death of Henry VII in 1509.[104] It states, 'The death of Edward v[th] on 22nd June, reigned 2 months and 8 days but was not crowned, slain and no one knows where he was buried.'[105]

1532

Our next account occurs in the records of the Armourers and Braziers Company in London. It relates, 'After Edward IV reigned Prince Edward V from the 9th day of April to the 22nd day of June privately destroyed and lie buried in the tower of London.'[106] This again offers a date of death of 22 June 1483 and a second mention of burial location in the Tower of London (see 1508, Pynson, p. 93).

1534

Our next commentator is Polydore Vergil. Vergil was an Italian cleric, writer and author and came to reside in London around 1502. Vergil became friends with Thomas More and Erasmus, among others. Encouraged by Henry VII, the Italian began a complete history of England (his *Anglica Historia*) in around 1506–07. The first unpublished manuscript covered events to 1513 and was completed in that year. Later, it was published in revised form in 1534 at Basel.[107] Vergil states:

Henry VII's historian, Polydore Vergil (*c*.1470–1555).

For when Richard heard that the constable [of the Tower] was delaying the execution of his command, he immediately gave to another, namely Sir James Tyrell, the task of swiftly despatching his nephews. Obliged to execute these orders, Tyrell left York for London and at once had the boys put to death. Thus perished Prince Edward alongside his brother Richard. But what manner of death the poor innocents met is not known for certain.[108]

Later, in his 1534 edition, Vergil observed that long after Richard's reign there remained 'those among the common people' who suspected that Edward IV's sons were still living in secret (see also the 1546/55 editions).

This is the first account to state that the boys were put to death while King Richard was at York (Richard left York on 20 September 1483). The perpetrator was Sir James Tyrell.

1543

In this year a new literary style of writing about history emerged, complete with imagined scenes and dialogue. *The Chronicle of John Hardyng* (1378–1465) was published by Richard Grafton with an unattributed continuation which comprised a narrative on Richard III in English taken from Thomas More's unpublished proto-drama on the subject.[109] More had been executed seven years earlier by Henry VIII, on the fifty-second anniversary of King Richard's coronation (6 July 1535).

More's nephew, William Rastell (also a publisher), later discovered another version of the same untitled, unfinished narrative among his uncle's papers which he published in 1557, entitling it *The History of King Richard the Third* and claiming it as the authentic version. The contents are essentially the same, but Rastell's version is more commonly known and is quoted here. Rastell believed More wrote it in 1513 when he was one of the under-sheriffs of London, but in fact it has survived in various versions, with internal indications revealing that he continued working on them to a much later date. More was a humanist writer, lawyer and politician, holding the post of Lord Chancellor three years prior to his execution. He had been a page in the household of Dr John Morton (d. 1500), Henry VII's advisor and chief administrator.[110]

More writes that at Gloucester on royal progress (2 August 1483), King Richard sends a John Green, whom he specially trusts, to kill the princes, but Sir Robert Brackenbury, Constable of the Tower, refuses to allow it to take place. Green returns to King Richard, who is now at Warwick (8–13 August 1483). A page tells Richard that a certain James Tyrell will undertake the deed. Richard doesn't know the man[111] but rises from the draught (privy/toilet) to engage him in the task.

Tyrell arrives at the Tower and delivers a letter to Brackenbury commanding him to give the keys of the Tower to Tyrell for one night. Brackenbury does so and leaves. Edward and Richard are 'shut up' in the Tower with all servants removed other than a Black Will, or William Slaughter. The murder now takes place:

> Sir James Tyrell devised that they should be murdered in their beds, to the execution whereof he appointed Miles Forest ... a fellow fleshed in murder before time. To him he joined one John Dighton, his own horse-keeper, a big, broad, square, strong knave. Then, all the other being removed from them, this Miles Forest and John Dighton about midnight ... came into the chamber and suddenly lapped them up among the clothes – so bewrapped them and entangled them, keeping down by force the featherbed and pillows hard into their mouths, that within a while, smored [smothered] and stifled their breath falling, they gave up to God their innocent souls ... and long after lying still ... they laid their bodies naked out upon the bed and fetched Sir James to see them. Which, upon the sight of them, caused those murderers to bury them at the stair foot, meetly deep in the ground, under a great heap of stones.

> Then rode Sir James in great haste to King Richard and showed him all the manner of the murder, who gave him great thanks and, as some

say, there made him a knight.[112] But he allowed not, as I have heard, the burying in so vile a corner, saying that he would have them buried in a better place because they were a king's sons. Lo the honourable courage of a king! Whereupon they say that a priest of Sir Robert Brackenbury took up the bodies again and secretly interred them in such place as, by the occasion of his death which only knew it, could never since come to light. Very truth it is and well known that at such time as Sir James Tyrell was in the Tower for treason ... both Dighton and he were examined and confessed to the murder in manner above written, but wither the bodies were removed they could nothing tell. And thus shut up in prison, and privily slain and murdered; their bodies shut up and cast God wot where ...

Prior to this, More had added, '... that some remain yet in doubt whether they were in his [Richard's] days destroyed or no'.[113]

More's narrative offers the first literary account from an English author, including a number of new names: Green, Slaughter, Forest and Dighton (see Chapter 17). Significantly, he includes the only account of a confession by the alleged perpetrator, Sir James Tyrell, which More says he made in 1502 at his execution (see Chapter 8).

1546

Polydore Vergil reprinted his *Anglica Historia* with a slightly stronger variation to the 1534 text about the survival of the princes, a variation which was also included in his best-known 1555 reprint at the time of his death, 'A report prevailed among the common people that the sons of Edward the king had migrated to some part of the earth in secret, and there were still surviving'.[114]

1548 and 1550

Following Grafton's publication of the new literary-style narrative (More's account), his *Union of the Two Noble and Illustre Families of Lancaster and York* (by Edward Hall) followed More's account.

1551

In Holland, the Dutch chronicler, Jan Reygersbergh, wrote:

In the same year King Edward the fourth, with this name king of England died. And he left two sons and one daughter behind. And these rightful heirs were expelled from England.[115]

1577 and 1587

In England, Hall's work (as above) was followed by Raphael Holinshed's *Chronicles of England, Scotland and Ireland* ('*Holinshed's Chronicles*') which again borrowed heavily from More. Uniquely, Holinshed's narrative included a public declaration of innocence made by King Richard at the time of his Parliament (23 January–20 February 1484), 'For what with purging and declaring his innocence concerning the murder of his nephews toward the world, and what with cost to obtain the love and favour of the communality (which outwardly glossed, and openly dissembled with him) ...'[116]

As the Queen Mother left sanctuary on 1 March 1484, the timing of the declaration may be significant. It is not known why Holinshed is the only Tudor chronicler to record the declaration.

In 1592, historian John Stow in his *Annales of England*, accepted More's account of murder by Tyrell (see 1611, p. 104, John Speed). In 1592–93, Holinshed was the principal source material for a new play by William Shakespeare: *The Tragedie of King Richard the Third*.[117]

The Tudor Dynasty Continued: Summary

During this period, Edward V's death is recorded in some unofficial accounts as being 22 June 1483. Towards the middle of the Tudor era, John Rastell (More's brother-in-law) published the English account of the disappearance of the princes – as murder on 26 June 1483. Following More's execution, this was built on by William Rastell (More's nephew), who published the best-known narrative of King Richard's reign, discovered among More's papers and given the title *The History of King Richard the Third*. This was extensively 'borrowed' by Hall and Holinshed and was eventually taken up by William Shakespeare as the basis of a play about King Richard.

More's account became embellished in the retelling, but in his original he recorded that doubts about the princes' deaths existed in King Richard's time. He locates the deaths of both princes at on or around 8–13 August 1483, when Richard was at Warwick. During the Tudor period (after 1485), the government failed to publish or proclaim any statement accounting for the disappearance of the princes.

In 1534, 1546 and 1555 (during the reigns of Henry VIII and Mary I), Vergil has the deaths take place when King Richard was in York (September 1483). He also recorded a common report of survival, where Edward V and Richard of York had travelled in secret to a foreign land, although this did not appear in his original text of 1513. In 1551, this narrative seemed to be supported by a Dutch chronicler who recorded the children of Edward IV (two sons and a daughter) were 'expelled from England'. In 1557, Holinshed recorded a public declaration of innocence made by King Richard in 1484. In 1592–93, Shakespeare based his play on More's narrative.

1603 Onwards – The Post-Tudor Period
The demise of the Tudor dynasty is an important point in the enquiry. Did the story change, or new information come to light?

1611
In this year, historian John Speed published *The Historie of Great Britaine* and Bertram Fields writes:

> According to the seventeenth-century historian John Speed, his fellow historian John Stow, who adopted More's account in his *Annals*, published in 1592, maintained orally on a number of occasions that the princes had not been murdered at all, but were living incognito beyond the sea.[118]

1616
Essayist, courtier and MP Sir William Cornwallis published *The Encomium of Richard III* in 1616. This considered what was known about Richard and the princes and 'sought to demonstrate that a proposition generally accepted as true, was in fact, false'.[119] A pamphlet by John Morton was still in circulation in the 1590s and early 1600s, which Cornwallis believed to have been the basis for More's account.[120] Cornwallis' intellectual exercise added no new information regarding the disappearance, other than the existence of Morton's pamphlet (with More and Morton critiqued).[121]

1619
Sir George Buc held the office of Master of the Revels to James I of England. His ancestors were retainers of the Howard family. His great-grandfather, Sir John Buck, fought for King Richard at Bosworth and was executed at Leicester. An antiquarian and historian, Buc examined all records and documents (and consulted the families of those involved in Richard's reign). He completed his defence of Richard, *The History of King Richard the Third*, in 1619. Buc also believed that More's account stemmed from an original work by Morton.[122] In considering the contradictory nature of More's work, Buc

found no evidence for Tyrell's confession. After recording the various allegations of murder, Buc summarised:

> Thus the murder is reported by some of the accusers, but some others vary from them and say that these young princes were embarked in a ship at Tower wharf, and that they were conveyed from hence into the seas, and so cast into the deeps and drowned. But some others say that they were not drowned, but were set safe on shore beyond the seas.

Buc added, 'For some say that they were shipped alive and conveyed over the seas. Here you see that it was held and believed that they were living after the death of King Richard.'[123]

1622

Sir Francis Bacon, former Lord Chancellor of England, published his *History of the Reign of Henry the Seventh*. In late 1485, as King Henry prevaricated over his promise to marry Elizabeth of York who, if legitimated, would have a greater claim to the throne, Bacon agreed with Vergil that there were doubts as to the demise of the princes:

> ... even at that time secret rumours and whisperings – which afterwards gathered strength and turned to great troubles – that the two young sons of King Edward the Fourth, or one of them, which were said to be destroyed in the Tower, were not indeed murdered but conveyed secretly away, and were yet living: which if it had been true, had prevented the title [coronation] of the Lady Elizabeth.[124]

1674

In 1674, bones were discovered at the Tower of London and said by the government of Charles II to be the princes. They were placed in an urn in Westminster Abbey and identified as such. In 1933, the contents of the urn were examined (see Chapter 9).

1768

In this year, Sir Horace Walpole, 4th Earl of Orford, antiquarian, art historian and Whig politician, published *Historic Doubts on the Life and Reign of Richard the Third*. Walpole was the youngest son of the British Prime Minister, Sir Robert Walpole. *Historic Doubts* included a critical factual analysis of the fate of the princes, with specific reference to More's account. After presenting the Wardrobe Account for the clothing for 'the Lord Edward' as evidence that Edward V was alive at the time of King Richard's coronation (and possibly present at the ceremony),[125] Walpole stated:

> ... for it appears by the roll of parliament, which bastardised Edward the Fifth, that he was then alive, which was seven months after the time assigned by More for his murder. If Richard spared him seven months, what could suggest a reason for the murder afterwards? To take him off then was strengthening the plan of the earl of Richmond [Henry Tudor].[126]

King Richard's Parliament ran from 23 January to 20 February 1484. The text from the Parliament roll was copied by Buc. The roll of 1484 recorded, 'Also it appeareth that *all* the issue of the said king Edward *be* bastards and unable to inherit or claim anything by inheritance, by the law and custom of England.'[127]

Conclusion

A broad-brushstroke analysis of materials in *England* concerning the disappearance of Edward V and Richard, Duke of York, suggests that during Richard III's reign both boys were alive. A later chronicler asserts that a public declaration (of innocence) was made by King Richard around 23 January to 20 February 1484. During the reign of Henry VII, the princes were said to be put to death by Richard (as duke), although no official record, statement or proclamation condemning the Yorkist king was made. Henry's first Parliament offered an oblique reference to 'the shedding of infants blood' but did not touch upon regicide.

In and around London, prior to his coronation on 30 October 1483, Henry Tudor is said to have issued a proclamation challenging any offspring of Edward IV to come forward if alive. During Henry's reign and after his death, murder becomes the popular report,[128] either by Richard (as king) or the Duke of Buckingham (whether by design or advice).

The date of death for Edward V was given as either 22 or 26 June 1483. Evidence (as previously shown) suggests that Edward was alive at this time. Thomas More records rumours of survival but relates the death of both boys around 8–13 August 1483, while uniquely claiming that Sir James Tyrell confessed to organising it; Vergil locates their deaths in September 1483 (when King Richard was at York); Crowland and a (private) letter from Thomas Langton, Bishop of St David's, suggest both boys were alive on or around 20 September 1483 when Richard left York; *The Great Chronicle of London* believed the princes disappeared on or by 28 October 1483.

A chronicler in the Low Countries described the survival of the younger prince, another that both sons (and a daughter) had been 'expelled from England' following the death of Edward IV. Editions of Vergil recorded a common belief in the survival of both boys, who had secretly travelled abroad. Following the demise of the Tudor dynasty, one or both princes were said to have survived and been sent overseas during King Richard's reign.[129]

Our intelligence gathering exposes a significant trend in England. This can be summarised as:

Maintained – Murdered (duke) – Murdered (king) – Maintained

The Missing Princes Project's key period of investigation is now extended to 1509 (King Henry's death). This will allow scrutiny of the period covering the two pretenders to Henry's throne: 'Lambert Simnel' (1486–87) and 'Perkin Warbeck' (1491–99) – see Chapters 12 and 14.

A further trend reveals how allegations among foreign sources were transferred to England following the invasion of French and rebel forces with the pretender, Henry Tudor, in 1485.[130] During Henry's reign, this was further supported by key foreign nationals at his court (Carmeliano, André and Vergil). In relation to foreign and Tudor allegations that the princes were put to death and a crime committed, it is of equal importance that we now also consider all potential suspects.

6

The Suspects

Means, Motive, Opportunity, Proclivity to Kill

An important trend uncovered in our investigation of sources reveals how foreign assertions of the deaths of the princes as a 'known fact' were transferred to England in 1485 following the invasion of French forces supporting Henry Tudor. The new certainties were supported by key foreign nationals who were given patronage at King Henry's court. In respect of these foreign and Tudor allegations, it is important to examine all persons accused of being responsible. This will follow accustomed modern procedures: means, motive, opportunity and proclivity to kill analysis.

We will begin by examining hypotheses suggested in later times and conclude with the two main suspects put forward by the sources we examined earlier: Richard, Duke of Gloucester (as duke and king), and Henry Stafford, Duke of Buckingham.

Named Suspects from Later (Modern) Period

Although not documented in contemporary or near-contemporary accounts (see Chapter 5), we must consider all potential suspects. This may inform ongoing lines of investigation.

Dr John Argentine (c. 1443–1508)

John Argentine was a physician who began his medical practice at the royal court in 1478.[1] Mancini reports that he was the last-known individual to attend Edward V, who believed that 'death was facing him'. As a physician with access to poisons, Argentine had the means and the opportunity.[2] We have no information regarding any proclivity to kill.

In 2021, crime writer and military historian Mei Trow proposed Argentine as the murderer of the princes, and of Prince Arthur (age 15), King Henry's heir. Trow revealed that depression (as exhibited by Edward V) is a symptom of mercury poisoning, with Prince Arthur's death being consistent with arsenic poisoning. Arthur is thought to have died of tuberculosis, but Trow uncovered no evidence to support this view. For motive, Trow posited that Argentine had a 'God complex' (similar to Dr Harold Shipman, a notorious British serial killer in the 1990s) and killed because he could.[3]

Margaret Beaufort, Countess of Richmond and Derby (1443–1509)

Margaret Beaufort was descended from an illegitimate line of the House of Lancaster through an adulterous union between John of Gaunt and his mistress, Katherine Swynford (née de Roet). Gaunt was the third son of Edward III (see family tree on p. 11). Gaunt's Beaufort offspring were legitimated in Richard II's Parliament of 1397 and given rights to receive and pass on certain honours and dignities, but their barrier as bastards to any rights of inheritance was not lifted. Later, their exclusion from royal succession was cemented by edict of Henry IV, their half-brother.[4]

Henry Tudor was a Beaufort great-grandson and only child of Margaret Beaufort.[5] Beaufort was wealthy and well connected, so had the means. She took part in the coronation of 6 July but did not join the royal progress north. Later Tudor accounts place her in London during the summer of 1483, so she may have had the opportunity.

A murder at this time rests on two propositions: Margaret Beaufort's belief that Edward IV's sons were the rightful heirs to the throne (thereby ignoring King Richard's election and coronation) and a belief in the overthrow (and/or demise) of Richard and all legitimate Plantagenet heirs. Both events would open a path to the throne for her son.

Edward of Warwick, the king's nephew, accompanied the royal progress to the north in 1483, so Beaufort had no access to this potential Plantagenet male line claimant.[6] Warwick's royal claim would come into force should a future

Parliament reverse the 1478 attainder of his father, George, Duke of Clarence, Edward IV's brother.

Warwick was legitimate. As were the de la Poles (heirs of Edward IV's sister), with no attainder and seven sons.[7] At this remove, it seems Beaufort's position as a suspect to a murder in 1483 is based on later reporting after King Richard's death and a promotion of her role at this key time in Tudor histories.

It might be important to note Beaufort's likely participation in the attempt to capture or remove the princes from the Tower in July 1483. On 13 August, her half-brother, John Welles, was arrested in Cambridge as 'the king's rebel'.[8]

In January 1486, Henry VII married Elizabeth of York and subsequently repealed the 1484 Act of Parliament ratifying the bastardy of Edward IV's children. Thus, Edward's sons (age 12 and 15), if alive, and now no longer bastardised, became an immediate threat to her son's reign. From 23 January 1486, Beaufort had a clear motive.

Following Tudor's successful invasion in the summer of 1485 and seizure of the Plantagenet children from the northern nurseries, Beaufort took the children into her London household for a short while (see Chapter 10). This was probably intended to assess them, put them at ease and gain intelligence. No children disappeared or were known to have been hurt at this time.

Shortly afterwards, one of the children, Edward of Warwick (10), an orphan, was imprisoned in the Tower of London. Warwick remained in the Tower for nearly fourteen years until his execution in 1499.

Margaret Beaufort was a skilled politician with an unwavering ambition to advance her son,[9] but displayed no known proclivity to kill. At Warwick's execution (a legal form of killing), he was a young adult (24). It was suggested he may have had learning issues.[10] As she was a key advisor to Henry, we have no information regarding Beaufort's stance on Warwick's (orchestrated) trial and execution or whether she may have exerted any influence behind the scenes concerning the trials and executions in London during King Henry's reign; similarly, for Tyrell's trial and execution in 1502.

However, Beaufort wielded considerable power in the Midlands and north through her judicial court at Collyweston Palace in Northamptonshire, where she built a new prison. Signing herself 'Margaret R', Beaufort protected the new dynasty in the region, sending felons and those who had spoken against King Henry to London prisons.[11]

There is no evidence to suggest Beaufort was involved in any murders or considered a danger to children. It may, however, be important to note that following the demise of the Tudor dynasty, Cardinal John Morton was seen by Sir George Buc and members of his circle as a treacherous conspirator against the ruling house of York. Buc had read in an old manuscript book that 'it was held for certain that Dr Morton and a certain countess' conspired to use poison to do away with the princes. Buc's editor (Kincaid) added, 'the countess' is 'undoubtedly the Countess of Richmond [Beaufort]'.[12]

John Howard, Duke of Norfolk (1421–85)

John Howard was a Yorkist lord, soldier, ship owner and merchant. He was wealthy, so he had the means. Howard was in London for the coronation of King Richard, leaving on 19 July with the king and court on royal progress. As we have seen in Chapter 4, he returned to London for two weeks from 24 July to 11 August. He therefore had the opportunity.

Howard fought in many battles, so was able to kill. Battle and war, then as now, was an accepted form of killing, including the rout. If an enemy surrendered or was captured and killed without any form of summary trial (whether on the battlefield or elsewhere), it was considered murder.[13] As a leading magnate and Earl Marshal of England, Howard took part in trials that resulted in execution. Howard was a respected figure who was loyal to both Yorkist monarchs.

In 1844, John Payne Collier noticed that Howard's Household Books contained an entry for works at the 'Tower' on 21 May 1483. These included the purchase of two sacks of lime. Lime can be used to dissolve bodies. Collier suggested this may have had a sinister connotation.

A century later, in 1964, historian Melvyn J. Tucker used the household entry to propose Howard as the murderer of the princes. Tucker's theory was also based on Howard's motive to obtain the Norfolk dukedom and Mowbray estates from the younger prince, Richard of York (9), which, in Tucker's view, required the boy's death.

In 1980, historian Anne Crawford investigated Tucker's hypothesis. Crawford revealed that Howard had little to do with the Tower of London at the time in question. In all likelihood, the 'Tower' was a house in Stepney, London, rented by Richard, Duke of Gloucester in 1483 and given to Howard later that year.

The timeline for the supposed murder was also problematic as the young Duke of York and Norfolk was in sanctuary. In addition, Howard's inheritance of the dukedom and Mowbray estates did not require York's death but the reversal of an Act of Parliament. Crawford concluded that, based on this and other contemporary evidence, Howard was not the perpetrator he was alleged to be.[14] There is no evidence to suggest Howard was involved in any murders, or considered a danger to children.

Henry Tudor/Henry VII (1457–1509)

As mentioned in the context of his mother, Margaret Beaufort, the sons of Edward IV (if alive and no longer officially bastards) became a threat to King Henry after 23 January 1486 following the repeal of the 1484 Act of Parliament. As the victor at Bosworth, from 22 August 1485 Henry Tudor had the means and opportunity to dispose of the princes.

Henry was insecure and known for cruelty,[15] but could also be merciful.[16] Although he was present at the Battle of Bosworth, he is not known to have taken part in combat.[17] Following his victory at Bosworth, Henry ordered a number of executions.[18] There is no record of conviction by trial but no associated outrage either. A later local account from Leicester stated that the executions took place 'without any ceremony or decency'.[19]

As king, Henry was responsible for many trials and executions but there is no evidence that he was involved in any murders (illegal killings or assassinations). The illegal capture of Sir James Tyrell by breach of the king's safe conduct and his subsequent trial, which may have been orchestrated, indicates a degree of ruthlessness that might attract such an accusation, as does Warwick's execution, generally held to have been on a manufactured charge.[20] On the available data, Henry was not considered to be a danger to children,[21] although his incarceration of Warwick for fourteen years can certainly be viewed as severe.[22]

Conclusion

The brief evaluation of suspects suggested by the later commentators discussed offers a potential motive to Henry VII and his mother after 23 January 1486. At this time, the princes were 12 and 15 and no longer classed as bastards. As Edward V had reached his majority at the age of 14, he was, by November 1484, legally an adult.

No further information regarding the death (or trial) of King Richard's bastard son in the Tower of London in 1499 currently exists. This is thought to have been John of Gloucester. John would have been in his late twenties.[23] Without further evidence, Argentine remains a person of interest but not a suspect.

Named Contemporary Suspects

We will now consider Henry Stafford, Duke of Buckingham, and Richard, Duke of Gloucester (Richard III), both named as suspects in the alleged murder of Edward V and Richard, Duke of York, in foreign and Tudor reports.

Henry Stafford, 2nd Duke of Buckingham (1455–83)

Henry Stafford was a royal duke descended from Edward III through the male Plantagenet line (junior branch). He was married to Katherine Woodville, Edward V's aunt. They had four children. His home and affinity were in Wales and the west. As a royal duke, he was wealthy so he had the means. He was present in London during the spring–summer of 1483 so had the opportunity. Buckingham was not present on the king's progress.[24] More's narrative reports he joined it at Gloucester (2 August), where he and Richard parted on good terms.[25]

At this time, Buckingham was Constable of England (appointed 15 July), so he had the power to pass a sentence of execution.

By early October, he had joined the uprising against King Richard. He had no military experience and did not fight in battle, possibly due to his youth (at the time of the battles of Barnet and Tewkesbury in 1471 he was 15). In 1475, Buckingham joined Edward IV's invasion of France, which suggests he was prepared to fight, although no military engagement took place. He did not join Edward IV's wars against Scotland.

Although he was distanced from Edward IV and excluded from court, in 1478 Buckingham read the death sentence at the trial of George, Duke of Clarence, a duty for which Edward IV had made him High Steward.

The motive attributed to Buckingham for murdering the princes is ambition: to further his own claim to the crown.[26] This motive ignores the illegitimacy of Edward IV's children and the prior claims of the other senior line Plantagenet children. There is no evidence to suggest Buckingham had any sinister intent towards Clarence's heir, Edward of Warwick (8).

It might be significant that following his rebellion against Richard, Buckingham was tried and executed on Edward V's thirteenth birthday (2 November 1483). It was a Sunday. It was unusual for an execution to take place on the holy day of the week. Edward V's birthday was also All Soul's Day, when the dead were remembered.

It is not known if execution on this day meant anything – whether to send a message of swift punishment for his recent betrayal, any pretensions to the throne[27] or for anything that may have involved Edward V and Richard of York in London (perhaps abduction or something more disturbing). This latter view seems unlikely as Buckingham could have been arrested and tried at any point but remained trusted by the king and government. News of his rebellion in October 1483 came as a significant and unexpected shock.[28]

There is no evidence to suggest Buckingham was involved in any murders or considered a danger to children.

Richard, Duke of Gloucester (Richard III) (1452–85)

Richard, Duke of Gloucester was a royal duke descended from Edward III through two Plantagenet lines (Clarence and York, see family tree on p. 10). His home and affinity were in the north. He was wealthy, so he had the means. In 1483, he was present in London until 19 July, so he also had the opportunity.

Gloucester fought in battle, so was able to kill. As Constable of England and in several other judicial roles, he presided over trials and executions. Prior to the death of Edward IV, Gloucester was considered a loyal brother and commander. Following his death, he was reputed to be a murderer responsible for a number of deaths that were said to have been illegal, including Hastings, Rivers, Grey and Vaughan. As we have seen, these latter accusations failed to take into account Gloucester's national role as Constable (see Chapter 3).

By some, he was also reputed to have assassinated Henry VI in May 1471.

Gloucester had returned from the battles of Barnet and Tewkesbury with his personal bravery recorded; Henry was nearly 50 years old, frail and confused.[29] The murder of an ageing individual in physical decline with a recognised mental condition suggests potential psychopathy in the perpetrator and is an important pointer for the investigation. It is necessary, therefore, to place the circumstances of Henry VI's death under the microscope to see what this might reveal.

Following his capture in 1464, Henry had been kept in the Royal Apartments at the Tower of London by Edward IV. On King Edward's return to London from Tewkesbury on 21 May 1471, the *Arrival of Edward IV* reports:

… the said Henry, late called King, being in the Tower of London; not having, before that, knowledge of the said matters [death of his supporters and son] he took it to so great despite, ire and indignation that, of pure displeasure and melancholy, he died the xxiiij. [24] day of the month of May.[30]

Edward and his government asserted that the former monarch died of 'pure displeasure and melancholy'.

To our modern sensibilities, this seems suspiciously woolly. When subjected to scrutiny, however, 'melancholy' is used today in autopsy reports but is more commonly known as 'broken heart syndrome' or 'takotsubo cardiomyopathy'. This is an abrupt form of heart failure brought about by emotional or physical stress, caused, for example, by bereavement.

In 1471, the former monarch was informed of his queen's imprisonment, the deaths of his supporters and, most importantly, the death of his son in battle. Modern medical knowledge understands 'melancholy' as a plausible (and possibly accurate) report of the former monarch's demise. The date given for Henry's death is Thursday, 24 May, the Feast of the Ascension. The short form of Edward IV's *Arrival* was in circulation two days later, on 26 May 1471, and sent abroad to Burgundy and Bruges on 28 and 29 May.[31] This is the most contemporaneous account of the former monarch's death.

Following King Richard's death at Bosworth, foreign and Tudor accounts reported Henry VI's decease as a murder committed by Richard as Duke of Gloucester. A chronicle[32] claims that Henry was put to death on the night of Tuesday, 21 May 1471, between eleven and twelve o'clock, adding that the Duke of Gloucester was at the Tower that day with 'many other'. The others are not named. The date of this chronicle is sometime after March 1482 to 1500.[33]

The convenient timing of Henry VI's death is today viewed with suspicion, with most traditional commentators supporting the view of murder, or judicial killing, by Edward IV. The motive is that Henry's death brought the direct Lancastrian line to an end. This report places Gloucester at the scene of the crime. Gloucester was in London on 21 May but left the following day. For Gloucester to be considered a suspect, the king's death would need to take place on the 21st.

Henry's death is variously reported in later accounts as 20, 21, 22, 23 and 24 May.[34] Polydore Vergil, Henry VII's historian, attributes the murder to Gloucester but places the crime at the end of May (when Gloucester was no longer in the capital). Most significantly for the enquiry, in 1483 the French agent Domenico Mancini records no murder of Henry VI. This is important because the killing of a former monarch (particularly one who was considered saintly by this time) was an opportunity to denigrate both the English and the new Yorkist king.

Henry was later said to have been stabbed to death by Gloucester with a dagger or sword.[35] When Henry's tomb was opened in 1910, no attempt was made by the specialist (Dr MacAlister) to determine a cause of death by analysis of the bones, a notoriously difficult undertaking. A lay person who was present (Mary Clive) pointed out that Henry's remains had proved 'neither death by violence or a fractured skull'.

The king's skull was in pieces, but this was thought to have arisen from later exhumation, transference and reburial.[36] If Henry VI suffered from porphyria (through his French antecedents), the result of this genetically transmitted mental condition would have been an abnormally thin skull. This was noticed in the king's remains. Henry could have died instantly if he fell on a hard surface, or perhaps his heart stopped beating on receipt of the news from Tewkesbury. A later suggestion by another lay person that Henry's hair was 'matted with blood' was not corroborated by an anatomist. Based on an unattributed report of blood or material from decomposition processes, it is conjecture whether this might suggest Henry fell, potentially after his heart stopped.

Do we know who may have delivered the bad news to Henry, and when? If delivered on 21 May, it is possible this was Gloucester. This would be unusual as Henry was attended by ten people, two of whom were named as William Say and Robert Radclyf.[37] The confused monarch may have been more familiar with these individuals and recognised them, although it is recorded that some weeks earlier Henry, 'far gone in simplicity', had recognised the newly returned Edward IV from exile as 'My cousin of York'.[38]

Among the 'many other' at the Tower on 21 May were King Edward, Queen Elizabeth and their children, the king's family and Council having resided at the Tower at this time for safety. Very likely, the queen's brother, Anthony Woodville, Earl Rivers was also present. Rivers had been placed in charge of London and the Tower by Edward IV. The Constable of the Tower, John Sutton, 1st Baron Dudley, and Lieutenant, Richard Haute were also likely to have been there. As key Tower officials, it would have been appropriate (and customary) for one of them to have delivered the news to Henry. Their names, along with Rivers, Say and Radclyf,[39] have never been associated with Henry's death. This may further suggest that no murder took place.

It may also be significant that the first recorded attribution of murder was made by the Welsh bard Dafydd Llwyd, shortly after the Battle of Bosworth.

As we have seen in Chapter 5, Llwyd met Henry Tudor a few days before the confrontation. Llwyd labelled Gloucester as the murderer but added that the Lancastrian monarch died on the Thursday (24 May).[40] Previously in France, Henry Tudor had been (incorrectly) proclaimed as the son of Henry VI and, as a result, feted as the heir of the House of Lancaster.[41] In this light, Richard's alleged murder of Tudor's 'father' can perhaps be viewed as not unexpected in terms of foreign and Tudor propaganda (also see Carmeliano's poem of 1486, Chapter 5).

Other crimes attributed to King Richard by later accounts have been found to be unfounded. These include a role in Clarence's death in 1478 and the murder of his wife and queen in 1485. A more recent crime attributed to Gloucester has also been investigated and found to be unsubstantiated. This was the alleged mistreatment of Elizabeth Howard, the ageing Countess of Oxford, in 1472–73.[42] The countess was John Howard's cousin.

In hindsight, it is evident that once Gloucester was labelled as a murderer (and illegal king), a growing catalogue of crimes was added to the charge sheet. However, the charge we are examining is that of ordering the deaths of his nephews, the sons of Edward IV.

As a comparison, we have examined what happened to Edward of Warwick during the reign of Henry VII. As King Richard's nephew and potential claimant to the throne (should the attainder against Warwick's father have been reversed by Parliament), it's important to consider the young man's fate.

In 1478, following the death of his parents, 3-year-old Warwick became an orphan. In 1481, King Edward awarded the 6-year-old's wardship to Thomas, Marquess of Dorset (Queen Elizabeth's eldest son).[43] In June 1483, with Dorset in sanctuary, Gloucester brought the 8-year-old to the capital and placed him in his wife's household.[44]

Anne Neville was Warwick's aunt (his mother was Anne's sister). He was present at Richard and Anne's coronation and joined the royal progress at the town of Warwick with Queen Anne and her household. Warwick was knighted in York and remained in the royal household, possibly travelling with his servants and the king and queen.[45]

After King Richard's death, Warwick was discovered by Henry Tudor's supporters, unharmed in the royal nursery at Sheriff Hutton in Yorkshire. Richard's other nephews and nieces, eighteen Plantagenet claimants to the throne, also survived his reign. There is no evidence of them being harmed.

Modern specialists have established through experience and case study that we are all capable of killing, given the right circumstances.[46] The killing of children, then as now, is a particularly heinous crime, most generally focused on concerns relating to character (psychiatry and psychopathy) and criminality. Narratives that described the killing of the princes depicted it as premeditated with malice aforethought, recognised today as murder in the first degree.

If we consider Richard as the main suspect in this depiction of the murder of Edward IV's sons, it is of primary importance to establish his motive (as duke and king). In the absence of motive, there is no evidence to suggest he was involved in any murders (illegal killings or assassinations) or considered a danger to children.

Foreign and Tudor accounts state that Richard had the princes killed because his own claim to the throne was based on a lie. As a consequence, he was an illegal king (usurper). This rendered Edward V the rightful king and a direct threat to Richard's accession and reign. It also made Edward's younger brother, Richard of York, heir presumptive to his brother.

In the next chapter, we will examine this important question to establish whether Richard, Duke of Gloucester (Richard III) had a motive to murder the sons of Edward IV.

7

Richard III

King by Right – The Evidence

Many of the specialist investigators involved in The Missing Princes Project have raised the importance of Edward IV's first marriage to Eleanor Talbot as potential evidence in the disappearance of the sons of Edward IV. Put simply, if the Talbot marriage was a fabrication (as stated in the later Tudor narrative), then Richard III had a clear motive to eliminate the sons of Edward IV as the true heirs to the throne. However, if the Talbot marriage – and its implications – were true, then Richard III had no clear motive.[1] Consequently, we have now brought together all available marriage evidence.

On 25 June 1483,[2] a petition was drawn up asking Richard, Duke of Gloucester to become king on the following four grounds:

1 The existence of a secret pre-contract [because Edward IV subsequently married Elizabeth Woodville, his first marriage to Eleanor Talbot is known as a 'pre-contract'] without subsequent annulment
2 A second secret marriage (which constituted bigamy in modern terms), of which the fact of secrecy compounded the first sins and rendered them incapable of expiation
3 This resulted in the bastardisation of Edward IV's offspring of the second (Woodville) marriage
4 The ineligibility of Edward, Earl of Warwick (aged 8), due to his father's attainder.[3]

The next day, he accepted his election as King Richard III.

What is a Pre-Contract?

A pre-contract is a legal contract that precedes another contract. In medieval canon law, a pre-contract refers to an existing contract of marriage that pre-dates a subsequent contract of marriage. A pre-contract with a living partner would, unless dissolved, legally nullify any later marriages into which either party entered.[4] Therefore, Edward IV's contract of marriage with Eleanor Talbot became a pre-contract when he subsequently entered into a second (and consequently bigamous) contract of marriage with Elizabeth Woodville while Eleanor was still alive.[5] As a result, the children of Edward IV and Elizabeth Woodville were declared illegitimate. Bastard children were unable to inherit anything and therefore they were barred from succession to the throne.

It must be emphasised that a pre-contract is therefore a *previous and legally binding* contract of marriage and not a form of betrothal or engagement prior to a later contract of marriage. The term 'pre-contract' in medieval matrimonial law meant 'marriage'.[6]

The Pre-Contract (the Talbot Marriage): Supporting Evidence[7]

The validity of the pre-contract and, therefore, the legitimacy of Richard III's royal title is, in fact, supported by a range of contemporary and near-contemporary sources. In June 1483, the Three Estates of the Realm accepted the legality of Edward IV's secret marriage with Lady Eleanor Talbot and, consequently, ruled that the bigamous and clandestine nature of Edward IV's subsequent union with Elizabeth Woodville rendered Edward V and his siblings illegitimate. There being no senior legitimate heir, the Three Estates petitioned Richard to take the throne. Evidence authenticating this account of Richard III's accession is set out below.

There are six principal sources for the pre-contract (the Talbot marriage):

1 The *Titulus Regius*
2 Richard III's letter of 28 June 1483 to the Captain of Calais
3 The Crowland Chronicle
4 Philippe de Commynes

5 Eustace Chapuys
6 The Year Book, 1486.

The Titulus Regius

The *Titulus Regius* of January 1484 is an Act of Parliament ratifying Richard III's royal title. The Act stated that before the coronation of Richard III (6 July 1483), the Three Estates of the Realm presented to Richard, Duke of Gloucester a petition detailing his rightful title to the crown of England. In this 'roll of parchment', the Three Estates stated that Edward IV had made a contract of matrimony with Eleanor Talbot, daughter of the Earl of Shrewsbury, long before he contracted a second, 'feigned' marriage with Elizabeth Woodville. The children of this second 'marriage' were therefore bastards, 'unable to inherit and claim anything by inheritance by the law and custom of England'.[8] Thus, Richard, Duke of Gloucester ascended the throne as King Richard III.

Richard III's Letter of 28 June 1483 to the Captain of Calais

Richard III's letter of 28 June 1483 to the Captain of Calais stated that two days earlier, on 26 June, the king's 'sure and true title' was 'declared in a bill of petition which the lords spiritual and temporal and the commons of this land solemnly porrected [delivered] unto the king's highness at London'. Richard duly enclosed a copy of the bill of petition with the letter to Calais, 'there to be read and understanded' by the garrison. Richard III thus dated his reign from 26 June 1483. This is the petition presented to Gloucester by the Three Estates of the Realm and subsequently ratified in the *Titulus Regius* by the Parliament of January 1484 as the Act of Succession.[9]

The Crowland Chronicle

In November 1485,[10] the Crowland Chronicle confirmed the testimony of *Titulus Regius* and Richard's letter to Calais. The chronicler reported that Richard became king 'by means of a supplication contained in a certain parchment roll, that King Edward's sons were bastards, by submitting that he had been precontracted to a certain Lady Eleanor Boteler [née Talbot] before he married Queen Elizabeth'.[11]

Taken together, the *Titulus Regius*, Richard's letter to Calais and the Crowland Chronicle collectively establish that on 26 June 1483 the Three Estates of the Realm had presented to Richard a petition in the form of a parchment roll, requesting him to take the throne on the basis of Edward IV's invalid marriage with Elizabeth Woodville and the consequent illegitimacy of their offspring. However, these sources are silent on the origin of the information which convinced the Three Estates of Edward IV's pre-contract (see notes 2 and 3).

Philippe de Commynes

It was Philippe de Commynes, a Flemish knight and the leading diplomat in the service of the French king, Louis XI, who reported that Robert Stillington, the Bishop of Bath and Wells,[12] had revealed to Richard, Duke of Gloucester, that he (Stillington) had married King Edward 'to a certain English lady' when 'only he and they were present'. 'Later,' Commynes added, 'King Edward fell in love again and married the daughter of an English knight, Lord Rivers' (Elizabeth Woodville). It should be noted that Commynes states Edward IV's marriage 'to a certain English lady' to be a real event and does not attempt to discredit the pre-contract (the Talbot marriage) as a political fiction. According to Commynes, Stillington's revelation provided the grounds for Edward IV's Woodville offspring to be declared illegitimate.[13]

Eustace Chapuys

Two letters written in 1533 and 1534 by Eustace Chapuys, Imperial Ambassador in England to the Holy Roman Emperor Charles V, support Commynes' identification of Bishop Stillington as the source of the pre-contract. Chapuys stated that 'many respectable people' in England told him that Henry VIII 'only claims [the crown] by his mother, who was declared by sentence of the Bishop of Bath a bastard, because Edward [IV] had espoused another wife before the mother of Elizabeth of York'.[14] As Chapuys refers specifically to the Bishop of Bath – which the *Titulus Regius* does not – he cannot have obtained his information from the *Titulus Regius*. Chapuys' evidence therefore represents a corroborative English source, independent of both the *Titulus Regius* and Philippe de Commynes.

The Year Book of 1486

A Year Book is a legal record compiled by lawyers. It is broken down into four terms: Hilary, Easter, Trinity and Michaelmas. The Year Book of 1486 (Hilary term) provides further supporting evidence. The relevant passage describes the process by which Henry VII's first Parliament planned to annul the *Titulus Regius* of 1484.

Several lords wished to question Stillington, as 'they said that the Bishop of B made the bill'.[15] As Stillington's eyewitness knowledge of the pre-contract underpinned the petition presented to Richard in June 1483, it therefore follows that he should play a principal role in drafting the *Titulus Regius*. Stillington was a former Chancellor of England and a Doctor of Civil and Canon Law. With a wealth of legal, diplomatic and administrative expertise, Stillington possessed the necessary skills to compose the 'parchment roll' of 1483, later passed into law as the *Titulus Regius*. Stillington's role as pre-contract witness and principal author of the *Titulus Regius* is therefore logical and substantiated.

Even though Stillington's offences against Henry VII are described as 'horrible and heinous', 'imagined and done',[16] Henry refused to allow the lords to interrogate Stillington. Henry stated instead that 'he had pardoned him, and therefore he didn't want any more to put it to him'.[17]

Henry's reticence is entirely consistent with his nervous approach to the pre-contract (the Talbot marriage). He ordered the destruction of the enrolled parliamentary copy of the *Titulus Regius*, as well as additional documentary evidence described as appendices, ensuring their dangerous content 'may be forever out of remembrance and also forgot', 'cancelled, burned and put into oblivion'.[18] In addition, all remaining copies of the Act were to be returned to the Chancellor on pain of imprisonment. Furthermore, on the advice of Henry's justices, the *Titulus Regius* was repealed unread; a highly unusual (possibly unprecedented) event. James Gairdner argued that a point 'which is perhaps rather an evidence of the truth of the story [of the pre-contract], is the care afterwards taken [by Henry VII] to suppress and pervert it'.[19]

There are six supplementary sources:

1 Legal and Clerical Documents from King Richard's Reign
2 The Family Connection (Grey-Talbot)
3 The Recognition Ceremony
4 Royal European Relations
5 Domenico Mancini
6 Estates-General of France.

Legal and Clerical Documents from King Richard's Reign

As we have seen in Chapter 5, clerical and legal documentary evidence from King Richard's reign reveals that the bastardy of King Edward's children was accepted. The Inquisitions Post Mortem of the Hastings family declared 'Edward V, the Bastard' across ten counties.

The Family Connection

On 21 June 1483, Canon Stallworth, a priest in the service of John Russell, Bishop of Lincoln, Chancellor of England, reported, significantly, that Lord Lisle, brother-in-law to Queen Elizabeth Woodville, has 'come to my lord Protector and waits upon him'.[20] In doing so, Lisle effectively joined the Duke of Gloucester's affinity.[21] Lord Lisle was Sir Edward Grey and his wife, Elizabeth Talbot, Baroness Lisle, was the niece of Eleanor Talbot. Elizabeth was the elder daughter of Eleanor's deceased brother, John Talbot.[22]

The importance of this connection between Lisle and Eleanor Talbot and Lisle's allegiance to Gloucester becomes clear considering the following day's events. As we have seen in Chapter 4, on 22 June the bastardy of King Edward's children was announced. It is also important to note that the Duchess of Norfolk, Eleanor Talbot's sister, took a prominent role in Richard's coronation.

The Recognition Ceremony[23]

Further documentary evidence is provided by an element of the coronation ceremony known as the Recognition. The Recognition is the enquiry made by the Archbishop of Canterbury, requesting the people to consent to the king's coronation before he can vest himself for the Mass and begin the service.[24]

The text of the Recognition, found in a contemporary manuscript drawn up in 1483[25] for King Richard's coronation, includes the date 6 July and the name 'Richard' in the Acclamation.[26] It also includes marginal notes that may have been written by Richard, his Earl Marshal and/or his Chamberlain.[27] It survives in a collection of documents relating to the coronation of Richard III, in particular, a manuscript known as the Little Device.[28] The Little Device was the plan or Order of Service for Richard's coronation,[29] later used by Henry VII at his own coronation on 30 October 1485.[30] It is therefore quite remarkable that this source has survived.

The Little Device contains the text of the Recognition to be delivered at the coronation of Richard and his queen on 6 July 1483 by England's senior officiating cleric, Cardinal Thomas Bourchier, Archbishop of Canterbury.[31] After outlining various specifics about the double coronation, the text of the manuscript records:

This done the Cardinal as Archbishop of Canterbury showing the King the people at the 4 parties of the said pulpit shall say in this wise, Sirs here (cometh Richard the third) is present Richard rightful and undoubted inheritor by the laws of God and man to the crown and royal dignity of England with all things thereunto annexed and appertaining, elected chosen and required by all the 3 estates of this same land to take upon him the said crown and royal dignity, where upon you shall understand that this day is prefixed and appointed by all the peers of this land for the consecration enuncion and coronation of the said most excellent prince Richard. Will you sirs at this time give your wills and assents to the same consecration enuncion and coronation, whereunto the people shall say with a great voice King Richard, King Richard, King Richard yea yea yea so be it etc., King Richard King Richard King Richard.[32]

There are here several significant phrases. The first confirms that Richard is present and is the 'rightful and undoubted inheritor by the laws of God and man to the crown and royal dignity'. This clearly expresses Richard's rightful claim to the throne (as heir of Richard, Duke of York) and as the 'undoubted successor', he is awarded his position by the two powers in the land – Church and State.

A further explanation of the king's accession is then offered in similarly unambiguous language, 'elected chosen and required by all the 3 estates of this same land to take upon him the said crown and royal dignity'. This not only verifies Richard's election as king (chosen by and required by), but also by all Three Estates of the Realm. It also publicly proclaims the sequence of events in Richard's election as king, enacted by right of the nobility, Church and Commons (the collective body known as the Three Estates, which the king would periodically assemble as a Parliament). Additionally, in declaring 'this day is prefixed and appointed by all the peers of this land', it is made clear to all present that the peers have not only instigated this reign but have chosen and actively engaged with it. Finally, those present are asked to give their 'wills and assents' in 'great voice' in acclamation of the aforesaid statements.

It is important to note those present at the Recognition and Acclamation. We know from surviving documents that Richard's coronation was well attended and included prominent representatives of the noble families and clergy,[33] as well as key members of the Commons.[34] We also know that the coronation banquet catered for 3,000 guests.[35] Clearly, not everyone could be named.[36] Today, Westminster Abbey seats 2,000 but we've been unable to ascertain if all those who attended the banquet also attended the coronation ceremony.[37]

Royal European Relations

Richard followed royal protocol by writing to foreign rulers informing them of his accession.[38] On 7 July 1483, English merchants in Bruges provided 'lavish entertainment in honour of the coronation'.[39] By 21 July, Louis XI of France had responded, noting that he had seen Richard's letters, thanked him for his news and confirmed a desire for friendship.[40] This initial communication with Louis seems sadly to no longer exist, but Richard's communication of 20 August – 'my servant Blanc Sanglier, who is presently over with you'[41] – reveals that the king's herald had stayed a month or more at Louis' court. Richard's earlier letter of 18 August also reveals the presence of Buckingham Herald at King Louis' court.

Communications between Richard and Ferdinand and Isabella of Spain were lengthy and warm. The Spanish queen quickly expressed a desire for a new and meaningful friendship.[42] This is significant. A monarch's reputation was not to be risked on the international stage.[43] And as Galfridus (Geoffrey) de Sasiola, the Spanish Ambassador, accompanied Richard on his royal progress,[44] the Spanish monarchs would have been well informed of events in England.

Domenico Mancini

Such positivity is further supported by the account of Domenico Mancini, who was in London during the pre-contract crisis. Although relatively hostile to Richard, Mancini reports:

> No one survived of the royal line save Richard, Duke of Gloucester, who by law was entitled to the crown and, by virtue of his ability, could bear its burden of responsibilities. His past career and blameless morals were the surest pledge of his good governance: and though he would refuse such a burden, yet he might change his mind if asked by the lords.[45]

He adds, 'By these three orders of men, whom they call the three estates, are all matters of difficulty decided and their decrees carry authority. This being accomplished, a date was fixed for the coronation.'[46]

Mancini's account echoes the Recognition. He makes it clear that Richard was legally entitled to the crown but would refuse the 'burden' unless asked 'by **the** lords' (i.e., the peers; emphasis added). Moreover, he confirms the legality of Richard's accession by deliberation of the three estates as their 'decrees carry authority'.

Mancini also confirms the basis of Richard's royal title, stating, 'His [Edward V's] illegitimacy arose by reason that his father King Edward [IV], when he took Elizabeth in marriage, was contracted in all legality to another wife.'[47]

Estates-General of France[48]

A French source further supports the transparency of Richard III's accession by election. It is, somewhat surprisingly, the speech made by Guillaume de Rochefort to the Estates-General of France in Tours on 15 January 1484.[49]

The Estates-General was a legislative and consultative assembly acting as an advisory body to the French king, to which petitions from various separate estates, including nobles, clergy and commons, could be presented. In its composition it was not dissimilar to the English Parliament, but, as an advisory body, lacked power in its own right.

From 1483 to 1492, Guillaume de Rochefort was the Lord Chancellor of France, the officer of state responsible for the judiciary and a leading member of the French government. His speech on 15 January 1484 opened the Estates-General at a time of national crisis.

Louis XI had died on 30 August 1483, leaving his 13-year-old son and heir, Charles VIII, as the country's new monarch. As the king was underage, a regency government was established under the guidance of Charles' older sister, Anne of Beaujeu. However, Louis XI's second cousin, Louis of Orleans, and several feudal lords had attempted to seize the regency in open revolt. This grab for power was 'rejected by the Estates-General of Tours'.[50]

The parallels with the political situation in England at this time are remarkable. As the Valois monarchy came under increasing pressure from their Orleanist cousins, the political future of a child king, as two of its leading families vied for position and power, must have been a concern.[51]

Consequently, Rochefort's opening address is significant. His speech, understandably, is a long-winded justification of France as a great nation, loyal to its kings, and the young Valois king as its undisputed leader. It is also, understandably, deeply hostile to the English propensity to overthrow their kings and equally hostile to England's new (warrior) king, Richard III. Both countries had recently experienced failed rebellion attempts, and many English rebels had fled to the continent. Rochefort reports on events in England:

… that it suffice to quote the testimony [evidence] from our neighbours the English. Look at, I beg you, the events which, after the death of King Edward, happened to that country. Behold his children, already great and brave, murdered unpunished and the crown transferred to the murderer by the favour [approval, *faventibus*][52] of the people.[53]

It is Rochefort's comments about the accession of Richard III which are most revealing. He confirms that the crown was 'transferred' to Richard by the favour (approval) of the people. No negative constitutional connotation is applied to Richard's accession. Additionally, Rochefort confirms that Richard was not only given the crown by the favour (approval) of the people – a direct reference to lawful election by the Three Estates of the Realm – but also that the testimony [evidence] of the English was sufficient confirmation.

Testimony is defined by the *Oxford English Dictionary* as 'a formal written or spoken statement, especially one given in a court of law' and 'evidence or proof of something'. Did this evidence come from Richard's early communication with Louis or from his herald, Blanc Sanglier, and was this supported and given further credence by the presence of Buckingham Herald? In whatever manner this information was received, the French government and its Chancellor were clear on two things: Richard's lawful and transparent accession.

Further evidence acknowledging King Richard's legal title to the throne is contained in the grant in Ireland of 13 August 1486. For more on this, see Chapter 12, note 25.

Conclusion

There thus survives a considerable body of evidence testifying both to the veracity of the pre-contract (the Talbot marriage) and to its central role in the accession of Richard III. The *Titulus Regius* is, in effect, the retrospective proof of Edward IV's legitimate marriage to Eleanor Talbot, accepted by the Three Estates of the Realm and presented to Richard in the form of a petition on 26 June 1483. Two days later, Richard sent a copy of the petition to the Calais garrison and, in January 1484, Parliament ratified the document by incorporating it into the *Titulus Regius* (Act of Succession). As far as the political community were concerned, the *Titulus Regius* itself enshrined the proof of the pre-contract and the consequent legitimacy of Richard's title.

The evidence strongly supports Stillington's role as both witness to Edward IV's secret marriage to Eleanor Talbot and his subsequent participation in composing the *Titulus Regius*.

Until relatively recently, historians questioned the very existence of Eleanor Talbot, a situation remedied by the research of historian Dr John Ashdown-Hill. Significantly, Richard III did not reward Stillington during his reign, quashing any suggestion that Richard bribed the bishop to connive in a plot to take the throne.

It is also important to note that Elizabeth Woodville's brother-in-law, Edward Grey, Lord Lisle, who was married to Eleanor Talbot's niece, placed himself at the service of the Protector and government immediately prior to the public announcement of King Edward's children's bastardy. This strongly suggests Lisle family witness testimony in support of the Talbot marriage. As does the prominent role of Eleanor's sister, the Duchess of Norfolk, at King Richard's coronation.

Did these and Stillington's testimony form part of the Appendices to the *Titulus Regius*, which were destroyed by Henry VII in January 1486? No copies of these important documents have ever been found.

Further documentary evidence is provided by the coronation ceremony itself, in particular, the Recognition. Later printed versions of King Richard's coronation ceremony were, as historians Anne Sutton and Peter Hammond note, not 'wholly accurate, omitting some lines, and some of the marginal notes'.[54] This later editing process seems to have gone further, with printed versions removing King Richard's Recognition (and Acclamation), and in one instance only mentioning it in passing while placing it in the account of the coronation of his successor, Henry VII.[55] It is also important to note (as above) that Henry VII copied Richard's Recognition in his own coronation, and this was delivered not by the Archbishop of Canterbury but by Henry's supporter, Peter Courtenay, Bishop of Exeter.[56]

Another intriguing element is the publication of a further manuscript relating to King Richard's coronation, which was published by the Tudor chronicler (and publisher) Richard Grafton, in his John Hardyng's *Chronicle* of 1543.[57] It is not clear if this manuscript (now lost) contained Richard's Recognition or if Grafton decided not to include it.[58] Grafton did, however, include Sir Robert Dymoke's challenge as the King's Champion in Westminster Hall and the Heralds' largesse.[59] As a result, later versions of Grafton's work and other Tudor chroniclers followed this previously edited format.[60]

In coronation documents from the time of Richard II, the Recognition is outlined in general terms only.[61] Whether this is suggestive of either a recognised or open format I've been unable to discover because there are no earlier Recognition texts with which to make a comparison.

As we stand, it would seem that Richard's Recognition was not only allowed to survive but was subsequently used by Henry VII – not, ostensibly, the act of someone who believed his predecessor had obtained the throne through illegal or fraudulent means. Additionally, and significantly, there is a marked difference between the parliamentary ratification of Richard III's royal title in 1484 and Henry VII's royal title in 1485. Whereas Parliament declared Richard king on the basis of a full exposition of the line of succession, Henry eschewed such formalities and simply declared himself king.[62] The bill presented by Henry to Parliament, unlike that presented by Parliament to Richard, bears no resemblance to the Recognition.[63] Henry simply tells Parliament he is king, because he is king.[64]

It must be noted that the Recognition element of a coronation was (and still is) considered a formality. In earlier records, this is made clear in its perfunctory description.[65] However, it is in King Richard's detailed Recognition that its importance is gleaned.

It is apparent that King Richard's Recognition was of great personal importance to him and to the realm. In it, the process that led to his acceptance of the throne is clearly expressed. It is significant that no contemporary English source appears outraged by what they had heard or witnessed,[66] and transparency seems to have been a key objective. This is further supported by the statement at the French Estates-General of January 1484.

Richard followed royal protocol and wrote to continental rulers informing them of his accession, which was well received. This positivity is further supported by Mancini, who reports the bastardy of King Edward's children and legality of Richard's accession. This position is reinforced by documentary evidence from King Richard's reign.

It is also important to consider the actions of European governments and monarchies during Richard's reign. France, which was well versed in anti-English propaganda[67] and no friend to the Yorkist dynasty and its warrior kings, failed to denounce Richard's kingship. Although the French stated in January 1484 that Richard had 'murdered his brother's children' (see Chapter 5), they failed to censure his kingship. All the European powers – Burgundy, the Holy Roman Empire, Brittany, Spain and Portugal – maintained strong and cordial relations with King Richard. We could perhaps attribute these diplomatic links to realpolitik. However, governments and particularly monarchies were highly jealous of their reputations and to openly cultivate dealings with a known usurper king, particularly without censure, would have been extraordinary.

In addition, following the death of Richard's queen in March 1485, both Spain and Portugal entered marriage negotiations with King Richard. Ferdinand and Isabella of Spain offered their eldest daughter and King John II of Portugal offered his sister, the Holy Princess Joanna.[68] The Portuguese monarchy, by virtue of the marriage of John of Gaunt's daughter to King John I, was the senior legitimate royal Lancastrian line. The planned marriage between Richard and Joanna would, therefore, unite the Houses of York and Lancaster. As we considered earlier, it's also important to note that the Spanish monarchs, for whatever reason, failed to accept Edward IV's heir as a potential royal spouse for one of their daughters (see Chapter 2).

Finally, it is perhaps significant, in terms of our enquiries, to consider one further point. Early in Henry VII's reign, when he would have welcomed any proof that the pre-contract was a slanderous lie, he chose to destroy and suppress it rather than openly challenge and disprove it. Henry's actions demonstrate that he lacked the evidence to refute Edward IV's Talbot marriage. His heavy-handed approach shows that it was too dangerous to investigate the matter further and his own claim to the throne rested on a policy of ruthless censorship.

From the documentary evidence presented, it is clear that Richard III was the legal King of England. He was petitioned and elected by the Lords, Church and Commons, otherwise known as the 'Three Estates of the Realm', which formed a Parliament when convened in session by a monarch.

Consequently, in terms of our enquiries, Richard, as duke and king, had no clear motive to murder his nephews, Edward V (12) and Richard, Duke of York (9). The secondary motive – to prevent the boys becoming figureheads of any potential insurgency – is examined in Chapter 11.

8

Sir James Tyrell's Confession

Fact or Fiction?

Sir James Tyrell (1456–1502)[1] is a significant person of interest for The Missing Princes Project, not least for an unspecified journey undertaken by him to Flanders on behalf of Richard III in late 1484 'for diverse matters concernyng gretely our wele',[2] and shortly afterwards, in January 1485, for his receipt of the quite astonishing sum of £3,000 on the continent.[3]

More generally, Tyrell enjoyed a long-standing closeness to Richard, as both duke and king. However, he is also prominent because of the number of enquiries that have been received by the project questioning the need for a research initiative into the mystery of the princes when it is known that Tyrell confessed to their murder. Many cite as proof a Channel 4 TV documentary first broadcast on 21 March 2015, just before the reinterment of Richard III in Leicester, and repeated since.

After briefly introducing Sir James Tyrell, we will consider his alleged confession in light of the historical record and establish precisely what is known. We will also look at the conclusion reached by the television programme.

The following analysis also brings to light what seems to be new information regarding Sir James Tyrell: that he was appointed Gloucester's Chamberlain in 1479 (at the same time that Robert Brackenbury was the duke's Treasurer), and that his likeness may adorn the walls of St Nicholas' Chapel in Gipping, Suffolk.

Sir James Tyrell

Very truth is it and well known that at such time as Sir James Tyrell was in the Tower for treason committed against the most famous prince, King Henry the Seventh, both Dighton and he were examined and confessed the murder in manner above written ...[4]

Sir James Tyrell was the son of Sir William Tyrell of Gipping, Suffolk, and Margaret Darcy of Maldon, Essex. In 1462, his father was executed for his involvement in a conspiracy against Edward IV. Tyrell's wardship was given to Cecily, Duchess of York, who shortly returned it to Tyrell's mother, Margaret, and her feoffees (trustees of her estate) for a token £50.[5]

In May 1471,[6] James Tyrell fought for the House of York at the Battle of Tewkesbury and was knighted on the field by King Edward. By 1473, he had joined Richard of Gloucester's retinue and was entrusted to escort the duke's mother-in-law, the widowed Dowager Countess of Warwick (1426–92), from sanctuary in Beaulieu Abbey to Yorkshire. By 1474, he was one of the challengers at the tournament to celebrate the creation of King Edward's youngest son as Duke of York, and he was also part of the army that invaded France the following year. By 1477, Tyrell was Gloucester's Sheriff of Glamorgan and Morgannwg in Wales, and in April 1479 he was appointed the duke's Chamberlain.[7]

By January 1480, his cousin, Elizabeth Tyrell (*c.* 1436–1507) had been appointed Lady Mistress of the Royal Nursery by Elizabeth Woodville.[8] In 1482, Gloucester made Tyrell knight-banneret during the Scottish campaign and by mid-November, he was appointed Vice Constable of England (Richard held the office of Constable of England).[9] As Vice Constable, Tyrell was responsible for the short custody of Thomas Rotherham, Archbishop of York, following the discovery of William Hastings' conspiracy on 13 June 1483.

Tyrell had five children with his wife, Anne, who was the daughter of Sir John Arundel and Elizabeth Morley.[10]

Sir James Tyrell and Richard III

Following King Richard's accession in June 1483, Tyrell was made a Knight of the Body, Master of the Horse and Master of the Henchmen. During the

October uprising, he was largely responsible for the Duke of Buckingham's capture in Wales and escorted him to Salisbury for execution. With the aid of his gentleman servant, Christopher Wellesbourne, Tyrell was also responsible for the discovery of Buckingham's 5-year-old son and heir.[11]

Tyrell was given authority to seize and administer Buckingham's forfeited Welsh estates and to reassert the king's authority over crown lands in Wales.[12] He was also rewarded with the stewardship of the Duchy of Cornwall for life and given the Cornish lands of the rebel Thomas Arundel.[13]

By early January 1485, Tyrell was made Lieutenant of Guînes Castle in the Marches of Calais, a key strategic stronghold. As a result, he was not present at the Battle of Bosworth.

Sir James Tyrell and Henry VII

Tyrell's absence from Bosworth may account for the fact that he was not attainted for his support of King Richard. He seems to have made his peace with Henry VII, keeping his office at Guînes but losing his positions in Wales[14] and Cornwall and the Arundel lands. By 16 June and 12 July 1486, Tyrell had secured two royal pardons for a possible association with the first Yorkist rebellion, headed by the Stafford brothers and Francis, Viscount Lovell,[15] and which included Tyrell's gentlemen servants, Giles and Christopher Wellesbourne. The first pardon was for himself and the second for himself and those in the Guînes garrison, including its former chaplain.[16]

By 1488 Tyrell was a Knight of the Body, and by 1495, a Royal Councillor and feoffee to the use of Henry VII's will.

In November 1499, the executions of the Earl of Warwick and the pretender known as Perkin Warbeck took place (Tyrell was not named in the pretender's confession thereby suggesting no apparent connection between them). In 1501, Tyrell attended the Lord Steward (Sir Robert Willoughby) at the reception of Catherine of Aragon in London.

Following the death of Henry VII's heir, Prince Arthur, in April 1502, Tyrell was lured out of Guînes Castle by a safe custody and indicted for his support of the Plantagenet Yorkist heir, Edmund de la Pole. Imprisoned in the Tower of London, Tyrell was tried for treason at the Guildhall in London on 2 May 1502 and executed on Tower Hill four days later. He was 46. His son Thomas, who was arrested with him, had his sentence commuted to imprisonment.

Sir James Tyrell was posthumously attainted for high treason on 25 January 1504.[17] The attainder was reversed three years later, on 19 April 1507.[18] He was buried in the Austin Friars, in London.

Sir Thomas More: Tyrell's Confession

The account of Tyrell's confession that has been quoted was written by Sir Thomas More (1478–1535), see Chapter 5. Written as a dramatic narrative,[19] it was first published (without acknowledgement) eight years after More's death by the printer Richard Grafton, who copied it as a continuation to his publication of John Hardyng's *Chronicle* (1543).[20] The unfinished manuscript was found posthumously among More's papers by his brother-in-law, John Rastell (d. 1536) and published in 1557 as the 'authentic' version by his nephew, William Rastell (d. 1565).[21]

Concerns have been raised over the fact that More failed to publish this account during his lifetime.[22] For a prolific writer to keep a manuscript unfinished, untitled and unpublished is perhaps a first warning sign; that he never referred to it in his many letters is perhaps another.

A further significant alert is provided by its innumerable errors,[23] William Hastings is named 'Richard' Hastings and Henry, Duke of Buckingham, 'Edward'. Additionally, More's opening line detailing Edward IV's age at his death is incorrect and seems to follow the age of Henry VII at his demise. As a result of many decades of scholarship, More's manuscript is today viewed as a literary narrative and early humanist treatise on royal tyranny.[24]

More's sources are important. Although he states of Tyrell and Dighton's confession, 'Very truth is it and well known', he offers no evidence to corroborate his claim. Prior to this, he makes a number of statements describing his sources as local rumour and gossip. He also claims to have heard a number of differing accounts of the princes' deaths, 'I shall rehearse you the dolorous end of those babes, not after every way that I have heard, but after that way I have heard by such men and by such means as me thinketh it were hard but it should be true'.[25]

More's work is peppered with statements such as 'as some say', 'as I have heard', 'they say',[26] 'I have learned of them that much knew and little cause to lie', and 'I have heard by credible report of such as were secret with his chamberers that, after this abominable deed done, he [Richard] never had quiet of mind'.[27] He also asserts 'that some remain in doubt whether they were in his [Richard's] days destroyed or no'.[28]

In terms of Dighton (the second named confession), More goes on to reveal that he 'yet walketh on alive in good possibility to be hanged ere he die'. At this remove, this seems a rather astonishing and scarcely credible claim – a man who confessed to a double murder and regicide is nevertheless at liberty and permitted to walk free. Moreover, there is no evidence that a 'Dighton' was in the Tower during Tyrell's confinement[29] or that Tyrell and Dighton were ever examined.[30]

The Sources

Given these concerns, what can we establish regarding the veracity of More's account of Tyrell and Dighton's confessions? Is it supported by other sources of the period? It is important that we now consider these sources in some detail.

Robert Fabyan, The Great Chronicle of London *(c. 1512)*
The first connection between Tyrell and the presumed death of Edward IV's sons occurs in *The Great Chronicle of London*. After reciting various rumours concerning the manner of the children's demise, the text says:

> But howsoever they were put to death, certain it was that before that day [Henry Tudor's invasion] they were departed from this world, of which cruel deed Sir James Tyrell was reported to be the doer, but others put that weight upon an old servant of King Richard's named ____ [name left blank, modernised].[31]

Polydore Vergil, Anglica Historia *(First Published in 1534)*
Fabyan's continuation of the *Great Chronicle*, along with other sources, would have provided material for Polydore Vergil's history of England, *Anglica Historia* (1512, published in 1534, 1546 and 1555).[32] Henry VII's historian would certainly have noted the reference to Tyrell, as, indeed, would Thomas More, who had access to both works.

Vergil refers thus to King Richard's royal progress visit to York in September 1483:

> But when Richard heard that the constable [of the Tower] was delaying the execution of his command, he immediately gave to another, namely

Sir James Tyrrell, the task of swiftly despatching his nephews. Obliged to execute these orders, Tyrrell left York for London and at once had the boys put to death. Thus perished Prince Edward alongside his brother Richard. But what manner of death the poor innocents met is not known for certain.[33]

Later, while introducing the uprising launched on behalf of the Yorkist pretender known as 'Lambert Simnel' (April 1486), Vergil says, 'Henry VII had (as soon as he had gained power) flung Edward, the only son of the duke of Clarence, into the Tower of London, and ... it was popularly rumoured that Edward [V] had been murdered in that place'.[34]

Vergil then states that Lambert Simnel was an impostor for claiming to be the Duke of Clarence's son, Edward of Warwick, adding that Simnel's followers in Ireland would '**restore** the boy to the throne [of England; emphasis added]'.[35]

Vergil goes on to discuss at some length the next Yorkist uprising, which was in the name of another pretender, Peter (or Perkin) Warbeck, who was a 'deception' or believed to be the 'resuscitated duke of York',[36] the younger Prince in the Tower. Vergil relates that the 'youth' had:

> falsely assumed the person and name of Richard duke of York, who had many years before been murdered with his brother Edward in the Tower of London on the orders of his uncle Richard, as was known beyond doubt. And to assert or to believe otherwise would be the height of folly.[37]

In discussing the pretender's time with James IV in Scotland in 1495–97, Vergil adds, 'if he [Peter] were **restored** to the kingdom with the king's help [emphasis added]'.[38]

With 'Peter' executed for treason by King Henry in November 1499, Vergil moved on to discuss a new Yorkist pretender to Henry's throne, Edmund de la Pole, the son of Edward IV and Richard III's sister, Elizabeth Plantagenet, Duchess of Suffolk. Here, in 1502, Tyrell is again named as the murderer of King Edward's sons: 'At length even James Tyrell came to the scaffold. He was that same James to whom King Richard deputed the business of arranging the deaths of the two wretched sons of King Edward; which business he thoroughly performed.'

Vergil adds:

> On that occasion James could – without danger to his own life – have spared the boys, rescued them from death and carried them to safety ...

But he would not do this in order that he might afterwards try, against all human and divine injunctions, to help Earl Edmund, son of Edward's sister; for this at length he paid by his own death the appropriate penalty for his previous crimes.[39]

There is no record in Vergil of a confession by Tyrell, nor of an individual named Dighton.

Despite recording these alleged murders, as we have seen, Vergil commented that doubts persisted as to the demise of Edward IV's sons, 'A report prevailed among the common people that the sons of Edward the king had migrated to some part of the earth in secret, and there were still surviving'.[40]

More's account of Tyrell's (and Dighton's) confession now informed the many histories published during the reigns of the Tudor monarchs. Through Holinshed (2nd edition, 1587), it became the principal source material for Shakespeare's play in 1593.

Consequently, following the demise of the Tudor dynasty, it is important to now consider what the early Jacobean historians had to say about Sir James Tyrell and the confession.

Sir George Buc, The History of King Richard the Third *(1619)*

Sir George Buc believed More's account to stem from an original work by Cardinal John Morton (*c.* 1420–1500),[41] Henry VII's advisor and chief administrator.[42] In considering the contradictory nature of More's work, Buc observed:

> For they [Morton and More] say in one place, as I have cited it before, that it was held in doubt whether they were murdered. But they say afterward that Tyrell and Dighton, being examined, confessed plainly and certainly the murder of the two princely brothers, the sons of King Edward IV, and all the manner of it. These be contraries. And by these contraries their speech falleth.
> [...]
> And then in regard that the confession of those was such as that it might not be disclosed nor the crime called in question and to justice but left unpunished (as the said authors confess), then it was but a counterfeit confession.[43]

After considering how all those named by More (and Morton) in connection with the murder died of natural causes (see Chapter 17), Buc concludes:

But Tyrell may be excepted in one respect, because he died not his natural death but a violent death. But yet that was not inflicted upon him for the murder of the two princes, but for other treason long afterward committed by him, and against King Henry himself. Moreover, John Green,[44] who was said to be a party in the practice of this foul treason against the young princes, was never called in question.[45]

Sir Francis Bacon, History of the Reign of King Henry VII *(1622)*

Shortly after Buc's commentary was completed, Sir Francis Bacon, former Lord Chancellor of England, published *The Historie of the Reign of King Henry the Seventh*. After twice mentioning the rumoured survival of one or more of the sons of King Edward IV,[46] Bacon records the deaths of two of the four named individuals involved in the murder. These are given as Miles Forest[47] and the Tower of London's priest – who is said to have buried the boys.[48] Bacon adds:

> ... and there remained alive only Sir James Tyrell and John Dighton. These two the king caused to be committed to the Tower, and examined touching the manner of death of the two innocent princes. They both agreed in a tale, as the king gave out to the effect ... [the narrative then follows More's account of the murder] ... This much was then delivered abroad, to be the effect of those investigations, but the king, nevertheless, made no use of them in any of his declarations; whereby, as it seems, those examinations left the business somewhat perplexed. And as for Sir James Tyrell, he was soon after beheaded in the Tower-yard for other matters of treason. But John Dighton, who, it seemed, spoke best for the king, was forthwith set at liberty, and was the principal means of divulging this tradition.[49]

Summary

1. Thomas More goes so far as to concede that 'some remain in doubt' that the princes were murdered and that it 'should be true', but he then goes on to say of the Tyrell confession, 'Very truth is it'. More identifies his anonymous sources as 'such men' and those who 'much knew and had little cause to lie'. The only real clue to his informants comes from 'such as were secret with his chamberers', meaning those who were close to those who served King

Richard in his chamber. However, More also tells us that he had heard many versions of the story, 'after every way that I have heard'.

2. The *Great Chronicle* does not record Tyrell's confession (nor mention a Dighton). It states that Tyrell was 'reported to be the doer' but fails to record the source of the rumour condemning Tyrell as the murderer. It then adds to the confusion, saying that 'others' put 'that weight' on someone else committing the crime, 'an old servant of King Richard's named ____' (presumably planning to name this unidentified individual). It is unclear whether 'old' referred to the advancing age of this servant as it was now some twenty-nine years later, or if it meant an aged servant, or a servant of many years standing.

3. Vergil's account, like the *Great Chronicle*, also fails to include any confession or a figure named Dighton. Vergil attributes the murder to Tyrell but then claims that Tyrell killed the sons of Edward IV because he wanted the son of King Edward's sister to reign. He tells us it was 'popularly rumoured' that Edward V was killed and then, paradoxically, uses the words 'restore' and 'restored' when discussing both Lambert Simnel's claim to the throne as the 'King Edward' crowned in Ireland, and Peter Warbeck's claim as the Duke of York, the youngest son of Edward IV. Vergil also states the murders of both boys were 'known without doubt' and to 'assert or to believe otherwise would be the height of folly'. He offers nothing in aid of identifying the sources of his information, or the rumours.

Vergil's timeline for the murders also requires scrutiny. His account says that Tyrell returned to London from York (29 August–20 September), when the alleged crime was committed. Today, this is said to be supported because Tyrell visited London at this time to collect items of clothing. In 1983, historians Anne Sutton and Peter Hammond published the original documents of the Great Wardrobe Accounts. Two deliveries of clothing to York relate to Tyrell. One is designated to Tyrell as Master of the Horse to his office and was received by its Clerk of the Stable, a John Frisley.[50] The second order was delivered to the seven henchmen of the king and Tyrell, 'their master', for their 'apparel and array' for the investiture of the Prince of Wales (8 September) and '**delivered** unto them for theire were [wear] [emphasis added]'.[51] As Sutton and Hammond confirm, the original Wardrobe Accounts do not say that Tyrell collected the goods. They added, 'It is inconceivable that the important Master of the Horse and Henchmen would have ridden several hundred miles to pick up clothes which could have been delivered by a menial.'[52]

4. The Jacobean writer Sir George Buc questions the veracity of More's confession story on account of its many contradictions, particularly the lack of written evidence and the failure of King Henry to publish the alleged confession. Buc, an antiquarian, diligently identifies his sources in his *History*, among them the Howard family, including Lord William Howard and Thomas Howard, Earl of Arundel and Surrey (great-great-grandson of John Howard and great-grandson of Thomas Howard). Both John and Thomas served Richard III and fought for him at Bosworth.

Buc acquired information from heralds, who were his acquaintances, many contemporary records of the time and members of families involved in the events of Richard's reign. Manuscript sources included a letter written by Elizabeth of York in his patron's collection (Thomas Howard, Earl of Arundel and Surrey) and a certain 'old manuscript book', which he had seen but was later unable to locate.[53]

Buc, while roundly dismissing More's account of a group of murderers led by Tyrell, protests that the truth ought to have been discovered 'by due examination' of those who remained alive.

5. Francis Bacon concurs with Buc in questioning the confessions but believes that Tyrell and Dighton were examined in the Tower, where they 'both agreed in a tale'. Bacon offers a most intriguing royal source, revealing that the confession story was 'as the king gave out', and that Dighton, set at liberty, was the 'principal means of divulging this tradition'.[54]

The Princes in the Tower by Oxford Films

Let us now turn to the TV documentary *The Princes in the Tower* (Channel 4, 2015), considered by some to be twenty-first-century proof of Tyrell's alleged confession:

> More is 99 per cent right. There is some sort of confession. What we have here is as near as we can get to the truth.

With this verdict, the documentary concluded that 'we may finally have solved the mystery of the Princes in the Tower'.[55]

The documentary followed the suggestion that the truth of More's confession story was confirmed by the fact that Henry VII and his queen were staying in the Tower of London, where Tyrell was on trial, and were therefore present in person to witness Tyrell's admission of guilt. If this were true, it represented a considerable step forward.

However, that argument failed to report three significant points. First, Tyrell's trial had nothing to do with the sons of Edward IV; he was, in fact, arraigned for committing high treason in support of the Yorkist heir, Edmund de la Pole.[56] Second, the trial had not taken place at the Tower of London but was heard at the Guildhall in central London, so there is no evidence for the claim that Henry and his queen were present to witness proceedings. And third, the Tower was a palace and royal residence.[57] Sadly, none of these pertinent facts were presented or scrutinised.

Conclusion

The veracity of More's account of the confession of Sir James Tyrell (and Dighton) to the murder of the sons of Edward IV is dependent upon the following factors.

First, is there any confirmatory evidence? As England's former Chancellor Sir Francis Bacon informs us, this does not exist. No declarations or proclamations were made by King Henry, nothing reported in Parliament or recorded and published by the government of the day. What accounts we do have are contradictory and incoherent. Polydore Vergil claimed that Tyrell murdered the sons of King Edward IV so that a younger son of King Edward's sister could rule at some future date. Such remarkable foresight and political cunning is not borne out by the historical evidence nor supported by Tyrell's long and faithful service to three reigning monarchs.[58]

In confirmation that More's 'evidence' was not generally accepted, we have Vergil's recorded admission that at the time the pretender Lambert Simnel appeared – barely eight months after Bosworth Field – it was commonly believed that the sons of Edward IV were not dead but safely hidden.[59] The words printed in Vergil's publications of 1546 and 1555 are worth repeating here:

> ... in vulgus fama valeret filios Edouardi regis aliquo terrarum secreto migrasse, atque ita superstites esse.

[... a report prevailed among the common people that the sons of Edward the king had migrated to some part of the earth in secret, and there were still surviving.][60]

It is seldom remarked that Vergil's text was contemporary with the first pla-giarised appearances in print of More's experimental drama. Another point often overlooked is Vergil's use of the words 'restore' and 'restored' when reporting the identities of the two pretenders to the English throne. Did these terms – which actually suggest the authenticity of the pretenders – slip through the net?

We also have the considerable evidence provided by Tyrell's wider fam-ily's support for the pretender Perkin Warbeck, who claimed to be the youngest son of Edward IV. In 1498, Sir John Speke was fined the enormous sum of £200 by Henry VII for 'aiding and comforting' the pretender.[61] W.E. Hampton records:

> Speke's adherence to Warbeck suggests that even that branch of the Arundell family which was hostile to Richard III had no knowledge of the certain deaths of the sons of Edward IV nor suspicion of Sir James's responsibility in the matter ...[62]

Significantly, we also have evidence of Tyrell's close family's support of Warbeck, and their confirmation that he was the son of Edward IV. Tyrell's first cousin,[63] Sir Thomas Tyrell of Essex and Hertfordshire (c. 1453–1510), was one of several conspirators in the Warbeck rebellion, which aimed to assassinate Henry VII.

One of Henry's spies recorded a remarkable conversation in which Sir Thomas Tyrell stated unequivocally that the boy was King Edward's son.[64] Sir Thomas had been an Esquire of the Body to Edward IV and Richard III[65] and was also the nephew of Elizabeth Tyrell, Mistress of the Royal Nursery. It seems, therefore, that Sir Thomas, like many others in the Warbeck conspiracy, had connections with the Yorkist royal family, its household and nursery.[66]

Despite written evidence of his treason, together with two witnesses, it is quite remarkable that Sir Thomas was never brought to trial, whereas Sir William Stanley, King Henry's Chamberlain, had been summarily exe-cuted for uttering some words in support of the boy. Interestingly, the *Oxford Dictionary of National Biography* (*ODNB*) records no mention of Sir Thomas

Tyrell's part in the conspiracy nor the family's identification of Warbeck as King Edward's son.[67] We must also add to this the Tyrell family tradition that both princes stayed at Gipping with their mother (Elizabeth Woodville) 'by permission of the uncle [Richard III]'.[68]

Additionally, as Annette Carson established, no records survive of contemporary Requiem Masses for the souls of the boys.[69] This, in terms of the period's religiosity, is highly significant.

Second, we must consider chronology. Henry VII had been king and master of the Tower of London from the summer of 1485, but it had apparently taken seventeen years to produce a story of any kind which accounted, 'as the king gave out', for the disappearance of the princes. Importantly, the story appeared at a time of genuine crisis for the early Tudor dynasty. Henry VII's son and heir had died unexpectedly (as had his third son, Prince Edmund), while the king himself was ill and deeply unpopular. The marriage of Catherine of Aragon to Henry's remaining son (Prince Henry) therefore assumed some importance in securing the dynasty's future.

Did Henry VII therefore feel compelled to reassure the Spanish monarchs of his continued hold on the throne by finally bringing the mystery of the princes to a definite conclusion, thereby securing the ground for this strategic marriage?

Third, we must take into account what we know about Sir James Tyrell. He served three kings faithfully and was placed in positions of trust. King Richard described him as 'oure trusty and welbeloved knighte for oure body and Counsaillor'.[70] His biographer, the Reverend Sewell, said of him, 'We have abundant evidence of the greatness, reputation and personal bravery of

Signature of Sir James Tyrell (1456–1502), 8 January 1501, from deed of agreement, originally amongst muniments at Redgrave Hall, Suffolk. (Rev. W.H. Sewell, 'Memoirs of Sir James Tyrell', *Proceedings of the Suffolk Natural History and Archaeological Society*, Vol. 5, Part 2, 1878, p. 167. Redrawn: Philippa Langley)

Sir James Tyrell. He was one of the foremost, and certainly one of the ablest men of his day.'[71]

So, was it one of Tyrell's royal duties that made him the ideal candidate for an alleged confession? As Master of the Henchmen, Tyrell was in charge of the young boys and teenagers at King Richard's court – they were the squires and pages required for ceremonial duties and knightly training. Did this role provide a connection that afforded the story a degree of credence? Or was it because Tyrell's cousin, Elizabeth, was Mistress of the Royal Nursery? Both positions would have placed Tyrell within the orbit of the children of Edward IV.

Or was it because he was responsible for the discovery and delivery of Buckingham's young heir during Richard's reign? However, no source during Tyrell's lifetime raised any concern regarding his proximity to children or their safety in his care. Today, the *ODNB* fails to record any mention of Tyrell's own children, four of whom married.[72]

Finally, we must also consider what we know about More's unfinished manuscript; specifically, that it was written as a dramatic narrative and remained unfinished, untitled and unpublished. That it was not taken seriously as a 'history' can perhaps be further deduced from the written work of More's brother-in-law, John Rastell in 1529. As C.S.L. Davies and Matthew Lewis establish,[73] Rastell published his history of England in *The Pastime of People*,[74] yet failed to record Tyrell, his confession or involvement in any murder. This despite the fact that Rastell, like his brother-in-law, was a prolific writer and publisher. Would More not have known about Rastell's forthcoming great publication, nor mentioned the stories which formed part of his own writing? This would have been a considerable scoop for his publisher brother-in-law. At the time, More had also been made Lord Chancellor with access to all official records.

As a result, it seems that Sir James Tyrell has been cemented in the collective conscience as the undoubted murderer of the Princes in the Tower on the strength of two dramatic narratives that became immensely popular and remained so for centuries: those of More and Shakespeare. The publication of More's account in the middle of the sixteenth century provided the key source for Shakespeare in 1593.

Until reliable evidence is forthcoming, or new materials uncovered, we must conclude that there are no grounds to support the validity (or veracity) of Sir James Tyrell's alleged confession to the murder of King Edward IV's sons.

However, we can perhaps conclude from this analysis that some connection was made between Tyrell and the sons of Edward IV, at or before the time of Tyrell's death. Is this connection explained by the two pardons granted to Tyrell by King Henry in the summer of 1486, which in turn added an indirect degree of credence to what the king later 'gave out' in respect of Tyrell's guilt?

PART 3

9

Windsor Coffins and a Westminster Urn

In respect of foreign and Tudor allegations that the princes were killed, it is important to consider physical evidence. This relates primarily to any discovery of human remains, thereby establishing that a missing person has died, whether by natural causes, accident or homicide. Homicide may be defined as death resulting from the action (or inaction) of another person (or persons).

Place and time of discovery may also be important. Are the remains found at a location and a time consistent with the enquiry?

As we have seen previously, foreign and Tudor accounts either fail to provide details of searchable burial locations (giving, for example, the river as a possible place) or state that the location is not known (1530, 1543). Two accounts suggest burial locations for Edward V (12) and Richard, Duke of York, (9) at medieval St Paul's Church (1500) and the Tower of London (1508, 1532).

Accounts in 1529 and 1619 state that a full search at the Tower and other places was made but nothing was found. With accounts of the alleged disposal of the bodies confused and disparate, today two discoveries are said to be evidence of their death in childhood, one by homicide (suffocation). The locations are St George's Chapel, Windsor, and the Tower of London. It is important to examine both accounts for potential evidence.

The Windsor Coffins

In 1789–90 at St George's Chapel, Windsor, restoration work on Edward IV's burial vault revealed a nearby additional vault. As two of Edward IV's other children were known to have been buried at the chapel, a ledger stone was therefore placed in the floor marking their burial.[1] The children were Mary (14) and George (2). George died in March 1479, Mary in May 1482.

In 1811, during works in the Tomb House of the Wolsey Chapel (the Albert Memorial Chapel today), two coffins were discovered. These were found to contain King Edward's children, with George's coffin exhibiting a name plate.[2] On Friday, 30 July 1813, the coffins were 'deposited in a vault (in the presence of the Dean) constructed for the purpose immediately under the stone which bears their names, and adjoining the tomb of King Edward the 4th, in the North Aisle of St George's Chapel'.[3]

In 2012, a blog on the chapel's website suggested that two coffins found in 1790 in the vault close to that of Edward IV might be those of the Princes in the Tower.[4] This suggestion took hold, prompting independent researchers Dr A.J. Hibbard (2015) and Eileen Bates (2016) to investigate.

In November 2016, the chapel archivist revealed that the original information on their website was inaccurate and 'if there were any coffins in the vault it is not known how many there were or when they dated from'.[5] The archivist explained that the 1790 report mentioned that a small vault was noticed at the time when Edward's vault was opened but the former was not explored,[6] and it was thought it could contain the coffins of King Edward's children (George and Mary). This position was confirmed for the project in 2021 by Kate McQuillian, archivist at the chapel. Additionally, when the coffins of George and Mary had been interred in the vault adjoining King Edward's in 1813 nothing of note was remarked upon. At this point, we can only conclude that no other coffins of children were observed there.

For St George's Chapel to be considered a potential burial place for the sons of Edward IV during King Richard's reign, it is also important to consider the most recent research in this regard.[7] This examined the allocation of the Order of the Garter stalls in the chapel. Examination revealed that the stalls for Edward V and Richard, Duke of York, were not reassigned during King Richard's reign. Reassignment was (and still is) a necessary requirement for the royal order following death, degradation (attainder) or voluntary surrender. Indeed, on Henry Tudor's arrival into London and his first visit to the royal chapel, he would have been greeted by both Yorkist stalls. The Garter stalls of Edward V and Richard,

Duke of York, would be reassigned during his reign (8 May 1491 and before 16 November 1489 respectively).[8] Additionally, the Order of the Garter records from King Richard's reign form a significant part of those innumerable documents either lost or destroyed following his death at Bosworth.

The Westminster Urn

In 1674, bones were discovered at the Tower of London while workmen were demolishing several structures abutting the south face of the White Tower, in the Inmost Ward, including a forebuilding and jewel house, which had been erected during the previous five centuries. This was to make way for a new open area and outer staircase.[9] The bones had been found at a depth of 10ft when digging down to the foundations at the south-east corner. Initially, they were thrown onto a nearby rubbish heap with other building detritus. Sometime later, when news of the discovery became known to the authorities at the Tower, they were retrieved on the orders of Charles II and said to be the remains of Edward V and Richard, Duke of York. The now partial remains were placed in General Monck's tomb in Westminster Abbey.

Four years later, in 1678, they were exhumed and reinterred in an urn in the abbey, complete with a Latin inscription stating they were the princes.[10] It is not known what caused the four-year delay.[11]

On 6 July 1933, the urn was opened, and the contents were investigated by historian Lawrence Tanner and anatomist Professor William White (White was assisted by dental surgeon Dr George Northcroft). Their report states that they identified the skeletal remains of two male children – the elder was 12–13 years old and the younger was 9–11 years old. Assessing evidence of consanguinity (blood relationship), they found features 'of no small significance' in the bones and jaws. Based on Thomas More's story (their chosen reference), it was concluded from these assumptions that they were the right ages for the princes in 1483 and so they were given the names Edward and Richard. A red stain on the older skull was thought to be blood and evidence of suffocation.

This is an important scientific paper for the enquiry. Since its publication, leading traditional historians have relied on its findings as evidence of murder, although many specialists have questioned its findings. To help clarify this, experts have been engaged by the present project to investigate the bones in the urn. They are Professor George Maat (August 2017) and Professor Dame Sue Black (August 2019).

Report 1 (Maat)

Professor George Maat is a leading Dutch bio-anthropologist specialising in archaeological and forensic anthropology and based at Leiden University Medical Centre. Maat is involved in the identification of victims, including the mass graves in Kosovo, the Tsunami in Thailand and several air disasters including MH-17 in Ukraine.

To undertake his analysis, Maat was furnished with all available materials from the only first-hand examination on record. These included fifteen black and white photographs of the remains (1933); five X-ray images (1933); and the Tanner and Wright report (1935). For the analysis to be blind, the 1935 report was redacted to include factual information only. This eliminated any historical references and any early twentieth-century bias.[12]

For the Maat report, see Appendix 10. What follows is a precis:

> The Minimum Number of Individuals present is 2 (with a possibility of 3), with the elder set of remains more likely to be female. Consanguinity between the two main sets of remains is possible via the age range. Age range of the remains is indicated at 9.5–12.5 years (older set) and 7–11 years (younger set). No cause of death indicators were present, and no antiquity for any of the remains was identifiable.

Report 2 (Black and Hackman)

Professor Dame Sue Black is one of the world's leading anatomists and forensic anthropologists. In 1999, she was the lead anthropologist for the British Forensic Team in Kosovo. Her expertise has been crucial in adjudicating many high-profile criminal cases. Based at Lancaster University, in April 2021 she was created Baroness Black of Strome.

Assisting Black was Professor Lucina Hackman, who is also a leading forensic anthropologist specialising in living age and human identification. She has given expert evidence in court in relation to trauma analysis, identification and age estimation, and is based at Dundee University.

To undertake the analysis, Black and Hackman were furnished with all available materials from the only first-hand examination on record (with no redactions), and with papers by Theya Molleson (1984),[13] P.W. Hammond and

W.J. White (1986),[14] John Ashdown-Hill (2018),[15] and Glen Moran (2018)[16] – all later commentators who had not handled the remains. Following the events of the pandemic, the final report was submitted on 11 November 2021, with some follow-up questions on 16 November.

Black and Hackman's report was 'based only on the papers above and in light of forensic standards'.[17] For the report (and subsequent questions), see Appendix 10. What follows is a precis:

> In terms of Tanner and Wright's identification of the remains, the 2021 report noted confirmation bias. The remains are human, incomplete and fragmentary with at least two individuals represented. These are juvenile. The oldest individual whose age can be estimated from some of the remains is between 9–15 years, the youngest is estimated at between 8–12 years. There is no evidence to support the suggestion that all remains are male. There is no scientific evidence to support a date of death. There is no strong evidence to support consanguinity. We would question the stain being blood. We would not comment on whether such staining could be evidence of suffocation using a pillow.[18]

Other Physical Evidence

With no scientific evidence to support Tanner and Wright's conclusion that the remains were those of King Edward's sons, can we look to other disciplines to provide relevant information?

Archaeological investigation at the Tower over many decades has revealed sub-strata levels with remains dating from the Iron Age, Roman, Saxon and Norman periods. The Tower's location at a strategic point on the River Thames has ensured habitation over many centuries, prior to construction of the Norman fortress in the 1070s.

In 1965, the complete skeleton of a 13–16-year-old boy was discovered close to that of the 1674 discovery.[19] Modern techniques dated the skeleton to the Iron Age. At the depth the bones in the urn were discovered, archaeological experts agree that the remains in the urn will most probably date to a pre-medieval period.[20]

And what of the anonymous note cited in Tanner and Wright's historical narrative which stated that 'there were pieces of rag and velvet about them'? Might this help to date the remains?[21] The undated note, mentioned in a book on the Tower by Richard Davey (1910), is said to be from an unidentified manuscript on heraldry.[22]

Velvet was in production in Europe in the twelfth and thirteenth centuries, with church vestments known to have been made of velvet by 1250.[23] While searches continue, could the discovery of the unidentified manuscript on heraldry (with its seventeenth-century marginalia) indicate an early medieval foundation burial?

Foundation burials were common across Europe in the early Middle Ages as a means of offering protection to new buildings against possible collapse.[24] By 1170, new royal lodgings had been added to the White Tower on its southern side.[25] These were part of the palace buildings (including the Jewel House, see the 1597 plan at Plate 15), which were demolished from 1668[26] to make way for the new open area and outer staircase. Could this suggest an early medieval foundation burial for the Royal Apartment buildings themselves?

This is, of course, pure speculation. Both accounts of the original discovery of the bones, penned by John Knight, surgeon to Charles II, do not mention velvet, and the first of these, Knight's 'official' account, was signed by him.[27] No velvet (or other material) was found in the urn when it was opened in 1933. Moreover, foundation sacrifices were common during the Roman and Saxon periods.

The southern aspect of the White Tower is built on the foundation of earlier Roman structures at its south-east corner.[28] The Normans were known to utilise Roman foundations in several of their buildings. Colchester Castle, for example, was constructed on the foundation of a Roman temple.[29] In the sixteenth century, John Stow stated that the Tower of London had originated as a Roman stronghold. This tradition was later supported by archaeological investigation.[30] The 1674 remains were 'ten foot' down (foundation level) beneath a newly demolished set of exterior stairs which had risen to the second bay along from the left, accessing entrances in the southern elevation of the White Tower.[31]

Discoveries of remains of children (and animals) at the Tower have been many and varied over the centuries, perhaps not wholly surprising in an ancient site. Some from the early seventeenth century were tentatively identified as the princes before being disregarded.[32]

Today, the remains in the abbey urn are said to be those of the princes on account of Thomas More's sixteenth-century narrative. As we have seen, More claimed the princes were buried in the Tower at the 'stair foot' (which stair is not stated), but shortly afterwards, again according to More, the bodies were exhumed and reinterred secretly in a 'better place', 'God wot where' (see Chapter 5).

For more on Henry Tudor's unsuccessful search of the Tower in the immediate aftermath of Bosworth and analysis of potential witnesses, see Chapter 10.

Our investigation has uncovered a lack of both physical and documentary evidence in support of foreign and Tudor allegations of death or homicide. As a result, it is important to widen the enquiry to examine any relevant information from King Richard's reign regarding the potential survival of the princes and any later traditions that may support this position. This may inform new lines of investigation.

The Wider-Ranging Investigation – The Whereabouts of King Edward's Sons During King Richard's Reign

The question of where various royal children were domiciled during King Richard's reign is itself uncertain, with few clues available. Still fewer are any clues as to the specific location of Edward IV's sons.

Surviving records from the King's Signet Office describe household ordinances for a royal nursery at Sandal Castle with the 'Children togeder at oon brekefast' on 24 July 1484. Which children is not made clear, although Francis Lovell's teenage nephew, Henry Lovell, Lord Morley (a minor),[33] is said to be at his breakfast with John de la Pole, Earl of Lincoln.

Viewed objectively, the domiciled presence of the Yorkist children in Richard's heartlands of Yorkshire would make strategic and political sense.[34] Additionally, several events may suggest that one or more of the boys were taken north. These include the payment and dismissal of a number of Edward V's attendants on 18 July 1484,[35] just before the royal progress left the capital on 19 July,[36] and the presence on the progress of the former tutor and President of Edward V's Prince of Wales Council, John Alcock, Bishop of Worcester.[37]

Did the Accounts Clerk at Cambridge misremember King Richard and Queen Anne's visit of 9–11 March 1484 and mistake the Earl of Warwick for Edward IV's youngest son? And what did Popplau mean in his report after visiting the royal court in York in early May 1484 (compiled a year later), when he referred to the safekeeping at Pontefract Castle of the king's treasure, children and sons of princes, kept as close as they would be if in actual captivity? And why did Popplau consider the boys to be alive but hidden in a secret place?

We must also consider several traditions surrounding the possible whereabouts of Edward IV's sons during King Richard's reign. Perhaps one of the most well known is the Tyrell family tradition that the boys stayed at Gipping

Manor in Suffolk with their mother 'by permission of the uncle'.[38] At this remove, the tradition sounds plausible as a story that may have been recounted by subsequent generations of the Tyrell family following Sir James' execution and Thomas More's story about his later confession to their murder.

Other locations with modern local traditions concerning the residence of one or more of the princes during King Richard's reign include Llandovery in Wales, and its connection to Tyrell (and Buckingham);[39] and Barnard Castle in County Durham, with its connection to Sir Richard Ratcliffe, its Constable,[40] Miles Forest, its Keeper of the Wardrobe (see Chapter 17) and its Brackenbury Tower. An oral tradition states that Robert Brackenbury was in charge of one or more of the princes being moved to Barnard Castle.[41] There is also a tradition at Scarborough Castle,[42] Bedale in North Yorkshire (see Chapter 14)[43] and Mottram in Longdendale, Lancashire.[44]

Longdendale is particularly interesting. Once a possession of Francis Lovell, the king's close friend and Chamberlain, an information panel on display at the Portland Basin Museum in Ashton-under-Lyne records, 'A persistent local story claims that the two "Princes in the Tower" were not murdered but were secretly moved to Longdendale by Francis Lovell, Lord of Longdendale, who was Chamberlain to Richard III.'

Longdendale was later granted to Sir William Stanley.[45] Sir William, who played a crucial part at Bosworth, became King Henry's Chamberlain, was not present at Stoke Field and rebelled ten years after Bosworth in the name of Edward IV's youngest son, Richard, Duke of York.[46] William was summarily executed after many of the rebels had been brought by deception to the Tower of London.[47] As Vergil and Buc confirm, the rebellion in 1495 in the boy's name was extensive and included a number of leading nobles from Henry's court under Sir William's titular leadership.[48]

A tradition which has recently come to prominence is the one at Coldridge in Devon and its connection to Edward V. For more on this, see Appendix 3.

With a lack of both physical and documentary evidence in support of the deaths or homicides of the princes – and several potential signifiers for their survival – it is important to again widen the enquiry and return to the immediate period following the death of King Richard, the person most likely to have known what happened. What might this reveal?

We will now place under the microscope the immediate aftermath of Bosworth and undertake a detailed examination of potential witnesses.

10

To Kill a King
The Aftermath of Bosworth

As a cold-case police enquiry, an important facet of The Missing Princes Project is to attempt the recreation and forensic examination of events as they happened – that is, without the contamination of so many unverifiable accounts that were written in retrospect by persons who had no personal insight into what took place. One such example is the period immediately post-Bosworth when the worlds of Richard III and Henry Tudor collided. What Henry and his forces investigated at this key moment may help to illuminate the mystery of the missing princes.

Henry's Delayed Arrival into London

One of the project's significant questions concerns Henry's delayed arrival into London and apparent change in strategy following King Richard's death. Securing the capital was a vital military objective, so why did Henry spend twelve days undertaking a journey that should have been completed in three?[1] Moreover, why did Henry's focus turn north at this crucial juncture? We are told that Henry (and his army) wished to enjoy the progress and acclamation. This may be partly true.[2]

However, in postponing his arrival the new uncrowned and self-proclaimed king risked finding the gates of London closed to his invading foreign army and rebel force. London had rallied to King Richard, providing 3,178 men[3] and imposing martial law to protect the city from the invaders.[4] The fact that London stood down and eventually welcomed Henry, following confirmed reports of King Richard's death[5] and a show of strength by Henry,[6] suggests no Yorkist force or heir was present in the capital at the time of Richard's defeat.

Post-Bosworth Events – Under the Microscope

It is important to note that Henry VII's historian, Polydore Vergil, devoted only two lines of text to this crucial time, describing it as a triumphant progress. The later Tudor chroniclers followed his lead. To replace this lack of record, we will examine surviving contemporary sources to shine a new light on Henry's preoccupations during this key period, when he focused his attentions on the north.

In Leicester by the early morning of 23 August, Henry Tudor's immediate focus was York, signing arrest warrants for Robert Stillington, Bishop of Bath and Wells, and the late king's close friend and confidant, Sir Richard Ratcliffe. Henry also sent a proclamation to the city, detailing the death and defeat of King Richard and his supporters.[7] This was delivered by Windsor Herald.[8] The proclamation included (incorrectly) the deaths of Francis Lovell, Thomas Howard and John de la Pole. Interestingly, it also included (correctly) the death of Richard Ratcliffe.

Forces were now despatched from Leicester, carrying these communications and arriving near York the following day, 24 August, a distance of some 100 miles. Afraid to enter, Sir Roger Cotton[9] sent word to the city fathers requesting a meeting on the outskirts of the city at 'the sign of the boar'.[10] They complied and the following day, King Henry's proclamation was read throughout York. On the same day, the city fathers sent a delegation to the new king with letters for 'several' people.

On 27 August the arrest warrant for Stillington and Ratcliffe (signed four days earlier on the 23rd) was delivered to the city. By 30 August, Sir Robert Halewell arrived carrying an intriguing letter requesting the city's 'assistence and aide', for which it would receive Henry's 'especial thankes'. The letter had been signed by Henry at Leicester on 24 August, six days earlier.[11]

What was this 'assistence and aide', and why did Henry's letter arrive some considerable time after signature, along with the arrest warrants for

Stillington and Ratcliffe? Moreover, where was Robert Willoughby? A Wiltshire landowner, Willoughby had fled to the continent in October 1483 following the failed uprising against King Richard and fought for Henry Tudor at Bosworth.[12]

Henry VII's historian, Vergil, writing thirty years later, states that at Leicester, Willoughby had been charged to remove Richard's 10-year-old nephew Edward, Earl of Warwick, from the northern castle of Sheriff Hutton where Elizabeth of York was also discovered[13] (Vergil makes no mention of the official royal nursery at Sandal Castle).[14] The City of York records mention no visit by Willoughby or indeed any information regarding his mission.[15] It seems that this information was on a need-to-know basis only.

Analysis of Henry's communications with York suggests either some form of travel disruption on the northern roads or, more likely (considering Cotton and Windsor Herald's prompt arrival and the erroneous content of Henry's proclamation), that Henry planned their delivery to ensure the city was carefully managed and compliant, which may have been part of a wider strategy. Henry VII was a deeply suspicious and cautious man who, throughout his reign, employed an extensive network of spies to keep him fully informed at all times. It therefore seems logical for Henry to sign two important documents on 23 August and give them to two separate forces to deliver; each would then be able to keep tabs on the other and report back.

The actions of the city fathers suggest suspicions surrounding a drip-feed of information from the new king, prompting an immediate deputation carrying letters for a number of people (including the Earl of Northumberland[16] and Lord Stanley).[17] The deputation would hope to secure Henry's good offices, but considering the city fathers' later actions,[18] might also serve as an urgent fact-finding mission. As Henry's northern prisoners included Northumberland, the Warden of the Eastern and Middle Marches, his intelligence in the region should have been wide-ranging and straightforward,[19] yet his delay in northern parts implies otherwise.

Events at this time also suggest the simultaneous despatch of forces from Leicester, carrying similar communications for other northern locations, intended to ensure their submission and compliance while also gathering intelligence.[20] This intelligence gathering may explain Henry's delayed arrival into London, pointing to a search for information concerning the location of royal children, particularly those with a claim to the throne. Certainly, Molinet's description of Henry's post-Bosworth proclamation in London would suggest as much (see Chapter 5). Is this what Halewell's 'assistence and aide' letter alluded to? Possession of the royal children secured at northern nurseries[21] may have been a priority in helping ensure London's welcome and compliance.

What Did Henry Do?

As we have seen, Henry signed a letter in Leicester on 24 August intended for York. Later that day, he was in Coventry, 24 miles away. Coventry, which had been visited by King Richard on his royal progress in 1483,[22] sent troops to King Richard[23] and fought in what seems the heaviest action at Bosworth.[24] As the city's *Annals* report that Richard was 'shamefully Carryed to Leicester',[25] Henry's visit may have been intended to quell any lingering loyalty to the Yorkist king.[26]

Henry's tenuous claim to the throne, which was inferior to thirty or more Plantagenet claimants, may have been a factor. He may also have used the Dun Cow[27] as a device for the visit.

Coventry was a known militia city,[28] with Henry's generals keen to secure it before their move south. Moreover, Coventry was also associated with Edward V as the Prince of Wales.[29] Ultimately, Henry's demonstration of force was successful. After Coventry, rather than press on to London (where he would have arrived on or about 28 August after a three-day journey),[30] it is likely Henry returned to Leicester to witness King Richard's burial and the execution of Catesby and others.

He actually arrived in London some six days later. Bernard André, who was present, tells us that Henry reached London after leaving St Albans on 3 September.[31] Therefore, attention now turns to the important eight-day period from 25 August to 2 September to ascertain whether Robert Willoughby's activities in the north explain Henry's delay.

Robert Willoughby's Mission

Henry's historian tells us that Willoughby's mission to secure the Earl of Warwick at Sheriff Hutton Castle was undertaken 'without delay'.[32] As Sir Roger Cotton and Windsor Herald arrived on the outskirts of York on 24 August, it is likely that Willoughby took the same amount of time, skirting York and arriving at Sheriff Hutton the same day. With Willoughby's escort departing the following day, the journey from Sheriff Hutton to Shoreditch in London (some 205 miles) would have taken about five days.[33] However, a chariot for the 10-year-old Earl of Warwick (and any other children with him) would extend the journey time to six or seven days.

Willoughby would have reached London between 31 August and 1 September, well before Henry. It therefore seems likely that Henry deliberately paused so that he could rendezvous with Willoughby, perhaps at Northampton or St Albans, thus ensuring he had royal children in his possession when he entered the capital.

Sir Edward Woodville

A further significant question is why Robert Willoughby was chosen for the mission to the royal nursery[34] when it would seem that Henry had the perfect person with him at Leicester. Sir Edward Woodville (c. 1454–28 July 1488)[35] knew the north, having taken part in the 1482 invasion of Scotland,[36] and was also well known to Edward IV's children as their uncle. Woodville had arguably provided Henry Tudor with the ability to launch his bid for the English throne and fought bravely for him at Bosworth.[37]

So why was Woodville passed over? No contemporary account suggests that he sustained any injury.[38] Was he sent to Sandal (and nearby Pontefract) instead? Later events suggest this to be unlikely.

Woodville was a skilled soldier but his lack of advancement under Henry is significant. As C.P. Wilkins remarks, he possessed 'little or nothing by way of landed estates'. Indeed, King Henry's solitary gift to Woodville suggests he wanted him out of the way.[39] He would only be recognised by Henry after the Battle of Stoke in June 1487 despite the fact that he took no part in the conflict.[40] Ten months later, Woodville was admitted to the Order of the Garter.[41]

However, almost immediately, he defied the king's orders by taking nearly 800 men to fight in Brittany, where he died on 28 July at the Battle of St Aubin du Cormier.[42] Does this suggest a lack of respect for Henry, or perhaps Henry's mistrust of Woodville?[43]

By 1487, Henry had a spy in Woodville's household when Woodville failed to attend his niece's coronation and planned to travel to Portugal.[44] Or did Henry retain Woodville in his entourage in 1485 as a means of allaying any fears as the army moved south, particularly through Northampton and Stony Stratford and the nearby Woodville manor of Grafton? Might

Grafton have been the rendezvous point with Willoughby (and others), with Woodville acting as a lure for a compliant Princess Elizabeth and any other siblings?

Post-Bosworth Interrogations

The death of Richard III allowed surviving witnesses or informants to come forward once Henry Tudor had made himself king. We may assume that high on Henry VII's agenda was to carry out interrogations to discover the fate of Edward IV's sons. Who might have been potential witnesses, and what information might they provide?

Using police methodology to recreate the past as accurately as possible enables an investigation, particularly a cold-case enquiry, to identify persons of interest. We will consider four well-placed individuals and examine not only their apparent knowledge of events, but also what became of them. This will help establish who was where, when and doing what – an important signifier for potential witnesses.

William Catesby (c. 1446–85)

Catesby was a lawyer and one of King Richard's Councillors and closest advisors. He fought for the king at Bosworth and was captured after the battle.[45] Two days later, on 25 August, he was executed by beheading in Leicester. Prior to execution, he was permitted to write a new will,[46] which provides an important window into the immediate post-battle period. Its contents prove beyond doubt that while atoning for previous transgressions, he was doing whatever he could to survive.[47]

Given Henry VII's personal involvement in prisoner interrogation,[48] it seems inconceivable that Catesby was not questioned. Whatever he knew or confessed, if he had revealed anything about the death or killing of the sons of Edward IV the new government would undoubtedly have made it public. In his will, Catesby records a deep regret that Thomas, Lord Stanley's family had failed to help him in his hour of need (which led directly to his execution). This suggests that on arrival in Leicester on 24 August, when the elder Stanley first met Henry Tudor,[49] he actively distanced himself from Catesby.

Writing of Catesby's execution, Henry VII's sixteenth-century historian (Vergil) records that a number of others were executed with him, 'Two days after at Leycester, William Catesby, lawyer, with a few that wer his felowys, were executyd'.[50]

In the eighteenth century, local historian John Throsby added what may have been a local story – that the executions were conducted 'without any ceremony or decency'.[51] This might suggest that Catesby and his 'fellows' were not allowed a customary few words on the scaffold. His failure to name the other executed prisoners implies they were of little political or local significance. This helps inform events surrounding our investigation's second potential witness.

Thomas Howard, Earl of Surrey (1443–1525)

Howard was a leading supporter of King Richard and Steward of his household. According to Crowland and the later Tudor narrative, he was captured at Bosworth,[52] which might indicate that he was interrogated at Leicester. As a seasoned soldier, Howard may have been less forthcoming than Catesby.[53] Perhaps the execution in Leicester of his retainer John Buck[54] on 24 August might suggest a rather sinister attempt to encourage Howard to talk,[55] or a warning about what might await him, his family and affinity.[56]

This inference seems probable considering what we know about Howard from Sir George Buc, whose family enjoyed long-standing connections with the Howards.[57] Buc makes it clear that although 'sorely hurt and wounded', Howard managed to escape the battle and 'came by night to the house of a gentleman not far from Nottingham', where he was given (secret) succour while his wounds were 'cured'. Only after hearing of an amnesty[58] (and possibly the execution of his retainer) did Howard give himself up[59] sometime after the November 1485 Parliament.[60]

As a fugitive, Howard could not protect his family and affinity. In addition, the new king had issued a proclamation listing those who had perished in battle, and it must have seemed that the Yorkist cause was all but over.[61] Paradoxically, Henry's proclamation, which lists Howard among the fallen, supports Buc's assertion that he escaped the battle. If Howard had been captured and held prisoner in Leicester (as Crowland and the later Tudor histories would have us believe), it would have stretched credulity to list him among the dead.[62]

Howard was kept imprisoned in the Tower (and Queenborough Castle, Kent) for over three years. It is not known why Howard was singled out.

Northumberland was released in December 1485 after three months of captivity in the Tower.

Following the deaths of his father and king, it seems likely that Howard had no reason to keep any information from the new administration. His apparent co-operation and oath of allegiance would become a key part of his eventual release and subsequent rise to leading roles in King Henry's army and government. As to the sons of Edward IV, if Howard had provided any intelligence, it would have been known to the new regime by 9 December 1485, when his imprisonment in the Tower began. But nothing was placed on record or made public regarding Howard's knowledge of or culpability in their disappearance or deaths.

Thomas Bourchier, Cardinal Archbishop of Canterbury (1404–30 March 1486)

Thomas Bourchier was enthroned as Archbishop of Canterbury during the reign of Henry VI (24 January 1455) and made cardinal by request of Edward IV on 18 September 1467. On 16 June 1483, during the reign of Edward V, Bourchier gave Elizabeth Woodville, the Queen Mother, a commitment to return her youngest son to her following his emergence from sanctuary.[63] Bourchier sat on King Richard's Council during the key period surrounding the disappearance of the princes, stepping down on 8 December 1483.[64] At no point in the much-respected cardinal's career, whether after King Richard's death, Tudor's arrival into London, Henry's coronation (by the Bishop of Exeter) or the sitting of Parliament, was it mentioned that Bourchier had reported or repented any former transgression or made reparation to the Queen Mother or before God.[65] As Bourchier continued in the role of England's leading primate until his death, it seems he was not censured for any potential involvement in, or knowledge of, the demise of the princes.

Thomas Langton, Bishop of St David's, Salisbury, Winchester and Archbishop of Canterbury (c. 1430–1501)

Previously a royal chaplain, Langton was provided to the Bishopric of St David's on Richard of Gloucester's recommendation from 21 May 1483.[66] He then accompanied the royal progress north. In 1484–85, following Bishop Lionel Woodville's attainder and flight to sanctuary, Langton was translated to the Bishopric of Salisbury. Prior to his assumption of

St David's on 4 July 1483, Langton had held two rectorates in London,[67] where his responsibilities encompassed Baynard's Castle (where Gloucester accepted the crown) and the Tower of London (the residence of King Edward's sons).

As a royal chaplain, he probably had access to Edward V and Richard, Duke of York. If the boys had been killed or made to disappear under suspicious circumstances before Richard's coronation, it is highly likely that Langton would have known about it.

As King Richard's 'very dear and faithful counsellor and spokesman who knows the secrets of our heart' (see Chapter 14), Langton would have been considered an invaluable source of intelligence for Henry VII's government. Langton was at Bosworth[68] and very likely taken to Leicester, but it seems that whatever intelligence he held, it was neither placed on record nor pleasing to the new regime.

Placed in custody,[69] on 6 October 1485 Langton forfeited the temporalities [properties and revenues] of the Bishopric of Salisbury and was excluded from King Henry's first Parliament, though on 6 November he was granted a full pardon. In 1493, he was translated to Winchester, and on 22 January 1501, Henry VII secured his election as Archbishop of Canterbury. Five days later, Langton fell ill and died of the sweating sickness.

Throughout King Henry's reign, Langton distanced himself from the king and government, visiting the royal court only when summoned to Parliament or convocation.[70] Langton's role relating to his support of the Yorkist pretenders is discussed in Chapters 12 and 14. In his will, Langton released Sir James Tyrell from a considerable loan of £100.[71]

Henry's Arrival in London

Henry's delayed post-Bosworth arrival in the capital, and his subsequent delayed marriage to Elizabeth of York,[72] creates an impression of uncertainty and insecurity surrounding the fate of King Edward's sons which seems to have persisted throughout his reign. This is supported by the inability (or failure) of prominent figures who survived King Richard to provide useful evidence concerning the sons of Edward IV.

Upon his arrival in London, Henry's searches at the Tower were described by Sir George Buc, who had painstakingly accessed the documentary collections of his fellow antiquaries and heralds of the College of Arms, 'There was much and diligent search made for their bodies in the Tower. And all these places were opened and digged where it was said or supposed their bodies were laid. But they could never be found by any search.'[73]

We may therefore propose that in the aftermath of King Richard's death, and despite the fullest of investigations, Henry Tudor was unable to find any clear evidence of the princes' fate, nor persons able to provide necessary information. As well as those mentioned, we may assume Henry questioned John Alcock, Bishop of Worcester (the former tutor and President of Edward V's Council, who joined King Richard on his 1483 progress); Chancellor John Russell, Bishop of Lincoln (who remained in London that summer and acted discreetly for the king in the sensitive matter of the trial of conspirators); Thomas Lynom, King Richard's Solicitor General (pardoned by Henry on 26 September 1485 and subsequently appointed Surveyor and Receiver of Middleham);[74] and the Stanley brothers, who had been members of Richard's circle and supported him during the 1483 uprising. If any had come forward with useful intelligence, Henry VII would have made capital of it. It is striking that there is not any general belief in their death, but rather an apparent general ignorance of their fate.

Conclusion

Failing any new evidence to the contrary, our investigation of surviving informants, and what they might have told Henry VII, has revealed nothing that appears to have been used by his government or propaganda. By the same token, it strongly suggests that Henry himself either remained in ignorance or had reason to conceal any clues he did discover. With confirmation of death strikingly absent, we must now consider a new line of enquiry: that Edward IV's sons survived King Richard's reign or were believed to have survived it.

11

In Living Memory

The Mortimer Heirs – A Blueprint

As we have seen, one of the most important aspects of any cold-case missing person enquiry is the need to drill down into the key period when the individuals went missing. By recreating the past in this way, an investigation can develop critical lines of investigation. In terms of The Missing Princes Project, this represents an attempt to uncover what specific individuals knew at the time of the disappearance. If we can enter their world at this key moment, we can begin to understand the actions of those involved, which then allows a better understanding of motive.

Motive may be defined as self-interest. It is also important to examine a possible secondary motive concerning King Richard and his government: the need to prevent the boys becoming figureheads in any potential uprising.

Furthermore, in view of the project's new line of enquiry regarding the survival of Edward IV's sons beyond King Richard's reign, do we have a historical blueprint for times when royal heirs were set aside?

Remarkably, we do, and it relates to Richard III and Edward IV's grandmother, Anne Mortimer (aged 7), her brothers, Edmund, 5th Earl of March (6) and Roger (5), and their sister Eleanor (3). As we have seen (Chapter 3), Edmund Mortimer was the named heir of the childless King Richard II. After him, his younger brother Roger would have been the next heir. However, in 1399, their claim was set aside by the usurpation of the first Lancastrian king, Henry IV. Henry was the boys' uncle.

So, what happened to the Mortimer children, and how might this inform the investigation?

Edmund and Roger Mortimer

On Henry IV's accession, Edmund and Roger's estates were transferred to the Percy family and the boys placed at Windsor Castle (Berkshire) and Berkhamsted Castle (Hertfordshire), in the custody of Henry's most loyal supporters. Fifteen months later, the eldest, Edmund, was granted a small inheritance.[1]

Six years later, there was a plot to free the boys, now aged 13 and 12, and deliver them to their uncle, Sir Edmund Mortimer, in Wales. On 13 February 1405, the boys were removed from Windsor Castle by their aunt, Constance of York, Countess of Gloucester. Close to Cheltenham, the party was apprehended by forces loyal to Henry IV. During interrogation at Westminster, Constance implicated her elder brother, Edward, Duke of York, as the 'principal instigator' in the royal kidnapping.[2]

The boys were placed under strict supervision at Pevensey Castle on the south coast, almost directly opposite Calais, where they stayed for the next four years.[3] Their uncle, Edward of York, was imprisoned in the Tower of London and at Pevensey for about seven months.[4] Constance was imprisoned in the Midlands at Kenilworth Castle for eighteen months.

In February 1409, the boys, now 18 and 17, were transferred to the custody of the king's heir, Henry of Monmouth (23). The boys remained in royal custody for fourteen years until the death of Henry IV. At the time of their release in 1413, Edmund Mortimer was 21 and Roger was 20. Both were made Knights of the Bath by the new Lancastrian king, Henry V (Monmouth), with Edmund kept in close attendance.

In 1415, despite his status as senior claimant to the throne, Edmund informed Henry V of a Yorkist plot. The conspiracy named Edmund as rightful king. The Southampton Plot involved Edmund's brother-in-law, Richard, Earl of Cambridge. Cambridge was caught and executed.

Edmund now married Anne, daughter of the Earl of Stafford, who was descended from Edward III (see the family tree on p. 10). This infuriated Henry V, who fined Edmund 10,000 marks, leaving him 'bound to the king and deeply in debt'.[5]

Edmund Mortimer, 5th Earl of March, died aged 33 in Ireland without issue. Roger had died shortly after release, apparently of natural causes.

During their long incarceration, the boys had been kept variously at secure locations away from London, and at a time of crisis, on the coast. They seem to have been well treated, and for part of the time at Windsor and Berkhamsted, brought up with Henry IV's children in the Royal Nursery.[6]

Documentation of the period describes Edmund as the king's 'ward' (May 1400, 1411, 1412), 'kinsman' (September 1400, 1401, 1413), in the 'king's custody' (February 1402) and 'keeping' (February 1408, 1411).[7] It also seems that both boys were allowed a servant[8] and the presence of a nursemaid.[9]

Anne and Eleanor Mortimer

Anne and Eleanor Mortimer were allowed to stay with their mother but within five years were orphans. The girls were not well treated by Henry IV, and Anne (12) and Eleanor (8) became destitute.[10] In spite of this, both eventually made good marriages.

In 1408 Anne (20) married Richard, Earl of Cambridge (executed 1415). Anne died on 22 September 1411 after giving birth the previous day to Richard, Duke of York (father of Richard III and Edward IV).

Eleanor married Sir Edward Courtenay, who died in 1418 and was the heir of the Earl of Devon. They had no issue. She next married Sir John Harpenden and moved to Normandy, France. Harpenden was granted a general pardon by Henry V for marrying Eleanor without royal consent. Eleanor is believed to have died in 1422.[11]

Conclusion

The fate of Edmund Mortimer and his brother Roger is important for the enquiry. It reveals that, within living memory, King Richard and all those at his court were aware of an obvious example of how to set aside a child heir. It was also clear that in times of crisis, it was of the utmost importance to conceal their whereabouts. There was a precedent for an abduction attempt, but also an apparent rapprochement and, over time, loyalty to the new regime.

It is of further significance that all this was undertaken on behalf of two *legitimate* heirs, who were a far greater threat to Henry IV, a supremely ruthless king. We must also note that within five years of Henry IV's accession, the

Mortimer children were orphans; something Elizabeth Woodville will have been aware of with regard to her own situation as a single parent.

Does this new intelligence provide a window onto why in May 1483 the King's Council, led by Richard, Duke of Gloucester as Protector, prepared an oath of security for Elizabeth and her daughters so they could leave sanctuary? An oath that Richard swore to as king in March 1484 in full view of the Three Estates of the Realm: the King's Council, prelates, and Mayor and Aldermen of London.

Richard's promise to marry the girls to gentlemen and provide for their wellbeing seems to have persuaded Elizabeth of the government's sincerity (see Chapter 16). Is this why only the girls were mentioned in the oath (see Chapter 5 and Appendix 1)? Were the Royal Council aware that Elizabeth Woodville would not countenance the release of her daughters if they faced the possibility of destitution following her death, a fate that had befallen the Mortimer girls?

Given the apparent attempt, on or around 21 July 1483, to abduct Edward V and Richard, Duke of York, from the Tower of London while King Richard was on royal progress, the project now needed to widen its investigation to consider the removal of the princes to secure locations outside London. These would encompass Richard's heartlands in the north, including the royal nurseries (see Chapter 10), the Yorkist Channel Islands of Jersey and Guernsey and Yorkist Ireland. It would also consider key locations on the continent.

What the project now uncovered was astonishing.

PART 4

12

Edward V: Proof of Life

by Nathalie Nijman-Bliekendaal and Philippa Langley

The Missing Princes Project cold-case investigation now brings to light two remarkable discoveries supporting the survival of the sons of King Edward IV, the Princes in the Tower, thereby offering proof of life. The importance of these discoveries cannot be overstated.

In this chapter, Nathalie Nijman-Bliekendaal and Philippa Langley consider a discovery made by Albert Jan de Rooij in the Archives Départementales du Nord in Lille on 5 May 2020. In Chapter 14, Nathalie and Philippa consider a further discovery made by Nathalie in the Gelderland archive in the Netherlands on 21 November of the same year.

With special thanks to the project's Dutch Research Group in bringing to public attention these important new discoveries.

'The Dublin King'

'... to serve her nephew, son of king Edward, late her brother ...'

What a Receipt from 1487 Tells Us About the Identity of the 'Dublin King'
In the first years of his reign, Henry VII was confronted with a serious Yorkist uprising. Its military preparation took place in Flanders and Zeeland in the

173

spring of 1487. The Dowager Duchess of Burgundy, Margaret of York, sister of Edward IV and Richard III, played an active role in the organisation of the invasion force, together with Yorkist nobles John de la Pole, Earl of Lincoln; Francis, Viscount Lovell; and other supporters of the House of York.[1] Their aim was to overthrow the new regime in England and replace Henry VII with an heir of the House of York who held a superior claim to the English throne.

On 15 May 1487, a Yorkist fleet left the small harbour town of Arnemuiden in the municipality of Middelburg in Zeeland and set sail for Ireland.[2] The ships carried a professional army of German mercenaries (*Landsknechte*) and Zeeland soldiers – raised with financial support from Margaret of York and led by Commander Martin de Zwarte and Lords Lincoln and Lovell.

Twelve days later, on Sunday, 27 May 1487,[3] a young man, the Yorkist heir was crowned King of England, France and Ireland in Christ Church Cathedral, Dublin. He would also be known as the 'Dublin King'.

Shortly after the coronation and Parliament, on 4 June 1487, the Yorkist army invaded England. On 16 June 1487, the 'Dublin King' lost his fight for the English throne at the Battle of Stoke.[4] He may have also lost his life,[5] or escaped and been injured.[6]

There are remarkably few surviving contemporary sources with which to reconstruct this important historic event. Although several sources confirm the Yorkist invasion took place in the name of 'King Edward', the true identity of the young man crowned in Dublin is still shrouded in mystery and remains a subject of debate.

The Lambert Simnel Affair

For Henry VII, in contrast, the identity of this Yorkist pretender was not in doubt, at least as presented to the outside world.[7] At an early stage of the conspiracy, the 'Dublin King' was characterised as an impostor, the son of an organ maker from Oxford who claimed to be Edward, Earl of Warwick.[8] According to an Act of the November 1487 Parliament, which followed the Battle of Stoke, the boy impostor was identified as one Lambert Simnel.[9] Somewhat confusingly, the boy was also described variously by the Tudor government as the son of a joiner, tailor, baker and shoemaker.[10]

Although the official English account of the uprising stated that he was an impostor claiming to be the Earl of Warwick, in records of the Habsburg Netherlands, the individual in whose name the revolt took place was seldom viewed as an impostor: his identity was usually simply recorded as 'the son of Clarence'. This is documented in the Danzig Chronicle (see note 5) and in two contemporary Flemish sources and a Dutch source from 1487.

One of the Flemish sources concerns an entry in the City Accounts of Malines, in which 'the son of Clarence' is mentioned as the recipient of a gift of wine.[11] The '*Chronicon ab anno 1465 usque ad 1487*', written by the Flemish monk Adrian De But, refers to 'the count of Warwick' and 'son of Clarence' as the Yorkist pretender.[12] In the County Accounts of Holland, we find the name of 'the duke of Clarence' as the challenger to Henry VII.[13] Unlike these documents from continental Europe, there are no surviving close contemporaneous sources in England (and Ireland), other than the official government accounts, connecting the name of Edward, Earl of Warwick to the Yorkist uprising (which is intriguing in itself).

To support his claim of this Edward being an impostor, Henry was quick to provide evidence of fraud. Early in the conspiracy, he 'exhibited' Warwick, who he kept imprisoned in the Tower of London, to the inhabitants of London and the nobles in the capital.[14] Henry thus made it clear that the real Earl of Warwick was in his custody and the Yorkist pretender was therefore an impostor.[15]

This is the traditional and generally accepted story of the identity of the first Yorkist pretender. It is hard to understand just how easily this Tudor narrative, the 'Lambert Simnel Affair', is so universally accepted, given the lack of objective evidence. The possibility that this pretender really was a descendant of the House of York with a legitimate claim to the throne has rarely been subjected to serious study.[16]

The Missing Princes Project

The Missing Princes Project seeks to challenge this type of historiography, based as it is on non-objective sources and hearsay. Consequently, there is an active search for new and neglected archival material to reconstruct events surrounding the disappearance of the sons of King Edward IV and to clarify the identity of the two Yorkist claimants to the English throne – in 1486, 'King Edward', alias Lambert Simnel, and in 1491, 'Prince Richard, Duke of York', alias Perkin Warbeck. At face value, this seems to present a scenario, as previously proposed in Chapter 1, in which a former King Edward and a former Prince Richard disappeared, and a King Edward and a Prince Richard reappeared.

Therefore, is this simple correlation what actually happened?

Both attempts on the English throne were largely prepared on the continent in the Habsburg Netherlands, with the support of the Burgundian-Habsburg monarchs and leading nobles. The archives in the Low Countries are therefore an important source of new information. Much of the archive material in England and Ireland was destroyed during the reign of Henry VII.[17] The archives on the continent, by contrast, seem to have survived relatively intact.

A Receipt from the Year 1487

The Archives Départementales du Nord in Lille, France, is just such an archive. It contains a considerable quantity of late-medieval documentation from the Burgundian (1384–1482) and Habsburg (1492–1581 and 1795) periods.

A remarkable document was recently discovered in this archival treasure trove which confirms that at least one of the sons of King Edward IV was alive in 1487.[18]

It is a proof of payment located among the accounting documents of the '*Recette de l'Artillerie*'.[19] The receipt, written in French and dated 16 December 1487, records the payment of 120 livres made by Laurens le Mutre, Counsellor and Receiver of 'The Artillery of the king of the Romans and his son the Archduke', to a certain Jehan de Smet, who, according to the document, was a merchant and maker of wooden objects living in Malines. De Smet was paid for supplying 400 long pikes to King Maximilian in June 1487. The receipt then states that the long pikes were taken away by King Maximilian himself and delivered to one of his highest and most trusted courtiers, Jan van Bergen, Lord of Walhain.[20]

The content of the receipt leaves no doubt as to which expedition these weapons were intended for: the first great Yorkist rebellion of 1487 against Henry Tudor. What makes this document so valuable and of great historical importance, however, is the fact that it not only describes the purpose of the expedition in great detail, but it also reveals the identity of the person in whose name the military support was intended: 'the son of King Edward'.

Translated into modern English the receipt runs as follows:

[These pikes were] to be distributed among the German-Swiss pikemen, who were then under the command of my lord Martin de Zwarte, a knight from Germany, to take and lead across the sea, whom Madam the Dowager[21] sent at the time, together with several captains of war from England, **to serve her nephew – son of King Edward, late her brother (may God save his soul), [who was] expelled from his dominion** – and obstruct the King of the forementioned England in his activities. [Emphasis added.] [22]

This is a most remarkable find, not only because it is the first close contemporary source to identify a son of the late King Edward IV as the beneficiary of the uprising of 1487, but also because of the relevance and weight of the evidence offered.

The receipt in which Jehan de Smet declares that he received the sum of 120 livres from the 'Kings councillor and receiver of the Artillery' ('with which sum I am satisfied') was witnessed, signed and dated by another leading official from the Burgundian-Habsburg court, namely one of King Maximilian's own secretaries, Florens Hauweel. We may assume that the secretary drew up this document personally and was responsible for its textual content, clearly detailing the purpose of the weapons.

It is hard to imagine that someone in such a position, so close to the political centre of power (and on top of the events of the day), would have made a mistake regarding the identity of the person for whom the weapons were ultimately intended, namely 'the son of King Edward'. Indeed, in a brief, written and signed statement at the bottom of the document, two other high-ranking officials reconfirm the accuracy of the receipt and conclude that the payment and distribution of the weapons had actually taken place 'in the manner, contained and extensively described in the receipt above'.

This short, added statement is an accounting control to ensure the reliability and accuracy of the Artillery's financial statements. It is signed by Lienart de la Court, Chamberlain and Master of the Artillery of the Kings of the Romans, and Andrieu Schaffer, Controller of the same Artillery.

The fact that the document was drawn up, inspected and signed by three leading officials at the Burgundian court, including a secretary to King Maximilian, renders the possibility of an error in the identification of the royal claimant for whom the weapons were intended extremely unlikely. Furthermore, there is no reason to assume that erroneous information was intentionally incorporated, as the receipt served no purpose other than that of an internal accounting mechanism validating a payment for the purchase of weapons. The probative value of this piece of evidence is therefore considerable, providing a probability bordering on certainty that the first Yorkist rebellion took place in the name of one of the sons of King Edward IV.

King Edward V

There is documentary evidence from two English sources and one Irish source, all contemporary with these events, that the uprising which culminated in the Battle of Stoke took place in the name of a King Edward. First, an account of the Battle of Stoke, laid down in the *Heralds' Memoir*, reveals that the rebels called their leader 'King Edward'.[23] Second, a memorandum of the City of York, written in June 1487, reports that the rebels shouted the name 'King Edward'.[24] Finally, an Irish patent was issued in the name of 'Edwardus, King of England, France and Ireland' and witnessed by the Earl of Kildare, dated to the first regnal year of this King Edward. This is an important example of where our forensic searches need to avoid assumptions made in the past.[25]

These documents offer good evidence to believe that the name of the Yorkist 'rebel king' was Edward. When we connect this name to the Lille Receipt, which refers to 'the son of King Edward IV' and to 'her nephew', it is patently clear that the eldest son of the late King Edward IV is intended – namely Edward V. That Edward V is the individual in question is further supported by the statement that he was 'expelled from his dominion'.

One of the first acts of Henry VII's Parliament on 23 January 1486[26] was to repeal Richard III's Act of Succession in which the children of Edward IV were declared illegitimate. The repeal had the direct consequence that Edward IV's children could resume their royal titles. If, as stated in the evidence from Lille, the former (bastard) King Edward V was indeed *expelled* from his dominion, then from 23 January 1486 he could be deemed king *in exile*.

That he was most probably exiled in Ireland we can now deduce from the letter patent, which was issued in Dublin on 13 August 1486. Other possible clues to his exile in Ireland are recorded in the Annals of Ulster for the 1480s. In the year 1485, the aftermath of Bosworth is described, 'And there lived not of the race of the blood royal that time but one young man, who came, on being exiled the year after to Ireland'.[27]

This supports the hypothesis previously advanced by Gordon Smith and, more recently, Matthew Lewis, that the 'Lambert Simnel Affair' was not an uprising in favour of Edward, Earl of Warwick, but an uprising in support of Edward V, the elder of the Princes in the Tower.[28]

Furthermore, Smith draws attention to other accounts which also give the age of the pretender as around 15, which fits the deposed monarch Edward V, who was 16 at the time (while Warwick had only just reached the age of 12).[29] These accounts correspond with the words from the Annals of Ulster, which describe the pretender as a young man.

In addition, because rumours circulated at an early stage that the Yorkist claimant who had surfaced in Ireland was a son of Edward IV, Henry VII had obvious reasons to create confusion regarding the claimant's identity. As Lewis aptly describes, Henry would face a crisis of support if the pretender's true identity became known:

> If he claimed to be Edward V, it would be a far more problematical incident for Henry ... whose rise to the throne had relied heavily on Yorkists who would abandon him for Edward V in a heartbeat.[30]

Smith also emphasises that Henry had a clear motive in alleging fraud because the justification of his kingship depended heavily on the belief that both sons of Edward IV were no longer alive.[31]

'One of King Edward's Sons'

Despite its removal from official records, it seems to have been known that the Yorkist claimant was 'one of King Edward's sons'. As Lewis reveals, Henry VII's poet, Bernard André, in his *Life of Henry VII*, 'appears to utterly ignore the official story'. André records that the pretender 'was the son of Edward the Fourth', adding that he was:

> accepted as Edward's son by many prudent men, and so strong was this belief that many did not even hesitate to die for him.[32]

André stated that the information had come from a herald sent to question the pretender in order to determine his identity. This conforms with contemporary records. On or around Michaelmas (29 September) 1486, Henry VII sent John Yonge, Falcon Pursuivant, to Ireland on 'his secret business'.[33]

Following the death of Henry VII, Lewis spotlights a remarkable briefing involving Henry's son, Henry VIII, which also 'deviates from the official version of events'. The passage admits that Lambert Simnel was named as 'one of King Edward's sons'.[34] In 1488, Pope Innocent VIII, while following the official account of Simnel as an impostor claiming to be the son of the Duke of Clarence, remarkably wrote that the pretender was of illegitimate birth.[35]

We may also be able to shed light on why Henry VII's November 1487 Parliament stated, quite incorrectly, that the coronation of the Yorkist king in Ireland took place on a Thursday (24 May). In the fifteenth and sixteenth centuries, kings and queens were crowned on Sundays. The Yorkist king had actually been crowned on 27 May 1487, the Sunday after Ascension. Twenty-two years earlier, Edward V's mother, Elizabeth Woodville, had been crowned on this same (holy) Sunday. It seems that the Yorkist claimant was sending a very clear message regarding his true identity,[36] which had to be expunged in the English Parliament.

Henry VII subsequently destroyed all records in Ireland pertaining to the Yorkist king's coronation and Parliament. Anyone 'concealing or receiving them [would be] deemed traitors attainted'.[37]

Truth is the Daughter of Time

As established above, given the nature of the document and the context in which it was drawn up at the time, the recently discovered Lille Receipt can be qualified as truthful and credible. The document provides good evidence to seriously challenge the traditional story that the 1487 Yorkist claimant to the English throne was an impostor who claimed to be Edward, Earl of Warwick. With this in hand, there is every reason to reinterpret those Irish records along with other surviving documentation which the Henrician government was unable to expunge.

Perhaps the most important consequence of the Lille document is that it shows that at least one of the Princes in the Tower was alive four years after his disappearance. This, in turn, lends plausibility to the observation that the second Yorkist uprising, seven years later, took place under the leadership of the second prince who disappeared from the Tower in 1483, namely the younger son of Edward IV: Prince Richard, Duke of York.[38] In this case too, Henry quickly declared that the young man was an impostor; this time, 'the son of a boatman from Tournay'.[39]

The evidence from Lille stands on its own, but one thing is certain: this important discovery has revealed that the traditional account of the murder of the Princes in the Tower no longer stands up to scrutiny.

In Summary

- In May 1487, a Yorkist armada sailed from Middelburg in the Low Countries to Ireland where a young 'King Edward' was crowned King of England. (See notes 2 and 4.)
- These forces (including large numbers from Burgundy and the Low Countries) formed an army to be led by this newly crowned king. They proceeded to England to challenge Henry VII for the throne he had seized from Richard III in 1485 at Bosworth.
- This 'King Edward' has now been positively identified as Edward V, the elder of the Princes in the Tower, sons of Edward IV (died 1483).
- The evidence for this identification is a receipt for weaponry delivered in June 1487 to King Maximilian (ruler of Burgundy) to equip the men of the Yorkist army. The weapons were required by Margaret of York, sister of Edward IV, Dowager Duchess of Burgundy 'to serve her nephew, son of King Edward, late her brother'. (See notes 18–22 and Appendix 2.)
- Notes on the identity of 'King Edward' – previously conflicting stories:
  i.   In sources not expunged by Henry VII's government, reports state that he was named 'King Edward' by his supporters. (See notes 23–25, 27–29 and 32–34.)
  ii. The official story spread by Henry VII, and believed by tradition, was that he was posing as Edward, Earl of Warwick (aged 12 in 1487), son of the late Duke of Clarence. Since little Warwick had long been Henry's prisoner in the Tower, it was easy to allege this imposture and 'prove' it by publicly exhibiting the boy. (See notes 8–10 and 15.)
  iii. In continental sources, where the armada was assembled, he was generally referred to as the 'son of Clarence' and was not given the name 'Edward'. (See notes 6, 11–13 and 35.)
  iv. In the aftermath of his defeat at the Battle of Stoke, there are conflicting reports as to whether he was killed or survived. (See notes 6, 23 and Appendix 3.)

For more on Edward V and what kind of a king he may have been, see Chapter 19.

13

The Yorkist Invasion of 1487

Edward V and the Second Fleet
by Zoë Maula, Dutch Research Group[1]

During the fifteenth century, the city of Bergen op Zoom was known as one of the leading trade cities of the Low Countries, rivalled only by Antwerp, Bruges and Middelburg. As a result of the wealth it accumulated, its rulers, the Van Glymes family, acquired both economic and political status at the Burgundian court during the late fifteenth century. For their unwavering support during the Flemish uprising of 1483–85, the Van Glymes earned a position in the inner circle of King Maximilian and the Dowager Duchess, Margaret of York. Both depended on each other to maintain and advance their influence nationally and internationally.[2]

The Van Glymes' proximity to Maximilian during the Flemish uprising, the favourable geographical location of Bergen op Zoom, and their military movements strongly suggest that the Van Glymes took part in the formulation of battle plans, and that Bergen op Zoom actively operated as a naval base for Maximilian's campaigns.[3] For this reason, it shouldn't be wholly unexpected that the Van Glymes were involved in Margaret's plans in 1486–87 to restore a Yorkist to the throne of England. The rulers of Bergen op Zoom were John II of Glymes (1417–94) and his heir, John III of Walhain (1452–1531). In early May 1484, John II had attended the court of King Richard III at York.[4]

On 1 January 1486, Henry VII, with suspicions aroused about the involvement of Burgundy in a Yorkist plot, renewed the commercial treaty with the

182

country for only a year. Then, when Henry became aware of the plan to oust him, which was spearheaded by Margaret, who gave sanctuary to many of the English rebels in 1486, his suspicions against Burgundy and the Low Countries were confirmed. From this point, the situation quickly escalated.

Less than two months after the commercial treaty was renewed on 20 February 1487, Henry VII cancelled the agreement and reduced the term of the treaty to six months.[5] This action was probably instigated by the arrival in Burgundy of Margaret's nephew, John de la Pole, Earl of Lincoln, at this time.

Maximilian, who by then understood that an alliance with England against France wasn't possible with Henry VII as king, gave his assent to Margaret, leaving no obstacle for the Van Glymes to give the Yorkist invasion their full support. In this context, it is therefore likely that the Van Glymes were involved in the 1487 invasion from the beginning.

Equipment, Loans and Distributions

From the moment Henry VII became aware that Lincoln had fled to Flanders, his suspicion against Burgundy and the Low Countries crystallised. On 4 March 1487 Henry gave a commission to Thomas Brandon, ordering him to take command of an armed force, mustered to proceed to sea against the king's enemies.[6] It's likely that Henry VII wanted to prevent others from following Lincoln and joining forces against him. Either that or the increased activity across the Channel aroused suspicion of an impending invasion from Flanders or Zeeland. This suspicion was well founded. From March 1487, the city of Bergen op Zoom and the Van Glymes appear to have been busy on behalf of Margaret of York.

An entry from the accounts of Margaret's dower lands records interesting movements, which supports the view that Bergen op Zoom operated as a naval base for the Yorkist invasion. On 27 March 1487, the Domain Accounts of Voorne (one of Margaret's dower lands) record a payment to messengers travelling from the city of Den Briel to Malines with 3,375 livres. Here they were to pay the full 6,375 livres, which the steward owed on behalf of Margaret, to the city of Bergen op Zoom. The same entry also records an order from Margaret to the Steward of Goedereede to deliver money from Malines to Bergen op Zoom.[7] In addition, another entry records a payment from March 1487 to a messenger sent from Den Briel bearing a letter from

Margaret to the Bailiff of Goedereede containing her instructions to have an abandoned pirate ship without mast and crew sent to Bergen op Zoom.[8] Considering the circumstances, it is likely that Margaret wanted the ship to be brought to Bergen op Zoom for compensation: this, and the money she sent there, may have been to supply funds for the Yorkist expeditionary force, though, of course, we cannot be sure.

The fact that these movements correspond to Christine Weightman's timeline of the Yorkist invasion, however, does strengthen this view. According to Weightman, the expeditionary force was ready to set sail from the Low Countries by April 1487, of which Henry VII was informed, thanks to his extensive intelligence network.[9]

Nathen Amin further strengthens this view by stating that the increased activity in Zeeland at the end of March might be what spurred Henry VII to order an extensive commission of array to the Duke of Suffolk to raise men to defend the eastern coastal counties of England on 7 April.[10] It might also have been Henry VII's quick response to these hostile movements in the Low Countries that hastened the invasion's preparations.

On 10 April, for example, Margaret writes a letter to the Receiver of Artillery, ordering him to immediately deliver 60 *pavois*, shields used for ships.[11] The urgent tone of the letter reflects a need for action, and could also be the reason why Margaret made a last-minute request for a loan from the city of Bergen op Zoom. An entry from the Register of Letters and Recognitions of 1487–88 records on 12 April 1487:

> On the desire of my dear lord of Bergen and my lord of Walhain, when selling the rents for 5000 crowns of 6 schellings, the city will loan the obtained sum to our lady of Burgundy dowager, which she hastily needed for certain difficult business.[12]

According to Korneel Slootmans, city archivist of Bergen op Zoom, the sum of 5,000 crowns amounted to 2,500 livres, which is a significant sum, equating to approximately £2.1 million in today's money.[13] The City Accounts of 1487–88 similarly record an entry, in which the City Council is gathered to meet on the request of Lord John II of Glymes and his son, John III of Walhain, to issue a loan of '1,500 livres to my lady the dowager'.[14]

Similar to the order for *pavois*, there appears to be an urgent undertone to Margaret's requests. This urgency can be illustrated by the fact that the money was handed over to Margaret personally, when she visited Bergen op Zoom on 14 April,[15] only two days after the City Council gave their agreement for the loan.

Knowing that the expeditionary force was ready to set sail by April, one can only conclude that the money Margaret requested from John II and John III was required for last-minute purchases for the invasion. A move most likely made in reaction to Henry VII's latest countermeasure. As such, the information detailed above can therefore be taken as evidence of the Van Glymes and their city's financial support of the Yorkist invasion, making them Margaret's close collaborators. This is proved by a receipt of weapons discovered in the Archives Départementales du Nord in Lille that clearly points to such involvement, as discussed in Chapter 12.[16]

The receipt from the archive states the following:

> For the quantity of 400 long pikes ... bought from me in the said place in the month of June, the year one thousand four hundred and eighty-seven and delivered to the Lord of Walhain, to be distributed among the German-Swiss pikemen, who were then, to take and lead across the sea

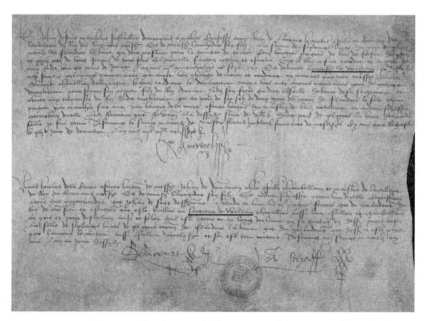

Fig. 1. Receipt of weapons dated 16 December 1487, with 'Monsieur de Walhain' and 'Seigneur de Walhain' underlined. (In Archives Départementales du Nord, Lille)

by ship, under the command of my lord Martin de Zwarte, a knight from Germany, whom Madam the Dowager sent at the time, together with several captains of war from England, to serve her nephew – son of King Edward, late her brother.[17]

In this receipt, John III of Walhain is clearly assigned to personally distribute the weapons that were purchased for the Yorkist invasion. As such, the receipt therefore provides conclusive evidence of the Van Glymes' involvement in the invasion and active support of Margaret's endorsement of the Yorkist King Edward. Yet, one aspect of the receipt remains vague. That is, the purchase is dated from 'the month of June', well after the expeditionary force departed the Low Countries. According to the *Chronicle of Zeeland*, the expeditionary force departed from Arnemuiden on 15 May 1487.[18] Furthermore, it is also known that the Yorkist king was crowned in Dublin on 27 May. This raises the question whether there was another force for which these weapons were purchased?

The City Accounts from 1487–88 of Bergen op Zoom might provide an answer to this question. Specifically, an entry from May 1487, which records the arrival of certain captains and riders before the city gates, as well as the expenses for their ships and provisions.[19]

At first glance, these men were clearly set to travel to Brittany, which was being invaded by France at the time. Though Burgundy was still trying to push back the French armies from its own southern borders, Maximilian was allied with Brittany and would have sent troops to aid Brittany. However, a closer look at the entry (see Fig. 2) suggests a link to the Yorkist invasion. That is, the word 'Brittany' is written above the word '*Ingelant* (England)', which has been crossed out. The entry reads:

> In May, when certain captains and riders came to the gates to travel to ~~England~~ Brittany … Paid for bread, cheese and for the captain on behalf of the burgomasters and aldermen because they were not allowed to enter the city.

One might suppose this was the clerk's correction of a mistake. Yet, considering the context already described, a much more likely explanation would be that the French invasion of Brittany was unexpected and the troops before the city gates were hastily reassigned to travel to Brittany.

As shown by the deletion, these men were initially intended to be sent to England to join the main expeditionary force from Ireland to meet

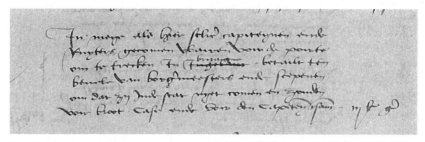

Fig. 2. City accounts of Bergen op Zoom 1487–1488, Archive of West-Brabant, Bergen op Zoom. (West-Brabants Archief, City accounts, Bergen op Zoom 1487–1488: boz – 0005, inv. nr. 759)

Henry VII's army at Stoke on 16 June 1487. This would certainly explain why the long pikes were bought and distributed in June. Sending the main expeditionary force to their Irish allies, followed by another force to attack Henry VII's army from two fronts, seems like something Margaret would do. It would also explain why John III of Walhain was assigned as distributor of weapons and why these men arrived before the gates of the city of Bergen op Zoom in May 1487.

With Bergen op Zoom acting as a naval base for the Yorkist invasion, then following the same procedure as with the first expeditionary force, this second force was also to be armed and equipped in Bergen op Zoom and gather in Arnemuiden to depart for England. This pincer movement against Henry VII could have produced a very different outcome.[20]

Still, the Van Glymes, who appear to have been one of the main forces among the Dutch nobles to support the Yorkist invasion, did see their efforts rewarded, despite the invasion being unsuccessful. From the Domain Accounts 1487–88 of the island of Voorne, an entry records Margaret awarding John II of Glymes and his son the governorship of the city of Den Briel and the lands of Voorne, from which they would receive a yearly sum of 3,000 livres from 26 February 1489.[21] Not only does this illustrate how valuable the Van Glymes were to Margaret, it can also be viewed as the final piece of evidence of their unfailing support for the Yorkist invasion.

Conclusion

From these findings, we can conclude that the Van Glymes actively supported the Yorkist invasion of 1487. But more importantly, once again, we see the Van Glymes appearing at an important moment in one of the key years within The Missing Princes Project, acting on behalf of the prince's main supporter, Margaret of York. Moreover, it reveals the level of support (financial and otherwise) for Edward V and the plan to send out another force to attack Henry VII's army from two fronts. Had this force been sent as intended, the Battle of Stoke might very well have turned out differently.

Richard, Duke of York: Proof of Life

by Nathalie Nijman-Bliekendaal and Philippa Langley

This is the first examination of a unique contemporary document rediscovered in the Gelderland Archive in the Netherlands in November 2020 by Nathalie Nijman-Bliekendaal of the Dutch Research Group.[1] It concerns the fate of the younger Prince in the Tower, Richard, Duke of York, second son of King Edward IV (also known as Richard of England or Richard Plantagenet) who – according to the text of the manuscript – was brought to safety (delivered) from the Tower of London to the continent with the help of John Howard, 1st Duke of Norfolk (*c.* 1425–85).

Preface

In the early 1950s, the Dutch historian Professor Diederik Enklaar, at the University of Utrecht, received a letter from the Gelderland Archive concerning the discovery of a rather curious document. The Master of the Charters, Mr P.J. Mey, wrote that a colleague had recently found a document in the archive, of which the origin is not clear.[2] According to Mey, it concerned a manuscript from about the year 1500, in which the fortunes of 'Richard', the younger brother of Edward V, are told; but the brothers, as Mey continued, 'according to literature – I have at hand here, were both murdered in the Tower'. Clearly intrigued by the manuscript, Mey wrote to Enklaar:

> However, the story I have here before me states that Richard was taken from the Tower under the direction of Hinrijck and Thomas Parcij and that he is staying in Paris and later goes to Middelburg via Brabant. To Lisbon, to Ireland, France and finally to the Duchess of Burgundy. The question now is: Is this reading 'of the Richard case' known in English literature? The Great Encyclopedia only says that there have been doubts about the truth of the mainstream story.

A short exchange of letters between Mey and the professor followed.[3] Mey suggested having the document examined by an expert on the matter as he had noticed that several (unknown) names are mentioned in the manuscript. However, Enklaar's response was rather discouraging: 'Is the case of the false York "Perkin Warbeck" not already sufficiently known? If you want to make a publication, it will only be due to the fact/importance of a new Dutch source.'

Although Professor Enklaar eventually provided the names of two experts in the field, namely the English Professors Grierson (Cambridge) and Bindoff (London), it seems that Mey lost his initial enthusiasm and the sense that he held an extraordinary manuscript.

As far as is known, no further research has been undertaken into this remarkable document. Shortly after this brief exchange of letters in February 1951, the manuscript was returned to the archive repository.

Introduction

The mainstream story to which Mey alluded concerns Thomas More's well-known dramatic narrative, based on the alleged confession of Sir James Tyrell, that the two sons of King Edward IV, known today as the Princes in the Tower, were murdered in the Tower of London by a certain Miles Forest and various henchmen, including John Dighton, on the orders of Richard III.

This popular story, first published under More's name in 1557, twenty-two years after his death, culminated in Shakespeare's 1593 play *The Tragedie of Richard the Third*. As a result, More's narrative continues to be widely accepted as the truth.[4]

The same uncritical acceptance is true of the story of the young man who arrived in Ireland in 1491 and was recognised there as one of the missing princes – Richard, Duke of York.[5] This Richard, who was supported in his claim to the English throne by European rulers in the years that followed, has gone down in history as the impostor named by Henry VII 'Perkin Warbeck', the son of a Tournai boatman.[6]

This traditional story, based on a single confession, is still widely taken to be proven history.[7] A good example is the response of Professor Enklaar, who, unreservedly and without inspecting the manuscript, concluded that it was the story of the 'false York'.

Diana M. Kleyn remarked on this 'false York' bias in her 1990 work *Richard of England*, noting that 'no one who has ever written anything about Perkin Warbeck has equally regarded him as other than an impostor'.[8]

According to the first line of the Gelderland manuscript, the narrator of the recorded events is none other than the '*Hertoghe van Jorcks, soene ins erffgename van Conynck Edward de vierde Rychart* [The Duke of York, son and heir of King Edward the Fourth, Richard]'.

In this manuscript, Richard recalls his secret departure from the Tower of London, including those who were present and responsible. He also records chronologically the events of his life from the time he was delivered from sanctuary in Westminster Abbey by his mother, the Dowager Queen, Elizabeth Woodville, to the Archbishop of Canterbury (and other nobles), up to and including his arrival at the court of his aunt, Margaret of York, in Burgundy at the end of 1492/early 1493.

Since the disappearance of Edward V and his brother, Richard, different stories have circulated about their potential survival. Some historians have recorded these, among them Polydore Vergil, who writes that 'a report prevailed among the common people that the sons of Edward the king had migrated to some part of the earth in secret, and there were still surviving'[9] and Sir George Buc, who, in his *History of King Richard the Third*, points out that 'some write that they were both secretly taken out of the Tower and both set afloat in a ship and conveyed together over the seas'.[10]

The Zeeland chronicler Jan van Reijgersbergh (*c.* 1510–91) simply states in his *Dije Cronijcke van Zeelandt* (Antwerp, 1551) that both sons were expelled from England after the death of their father, King Edward IV, in 1483.[11]

In a proclamation issued in Scotland in September 1496, Richard of England described the circumstances of his survival: 'and whereas we in our tender age escaped by god's might out of the tower of London and were secretly conveyed over the sea into other divers countries there remaining certain years as unknown'.[12]

However, no decisive evidence supporting their survival has ever been found, just as none has been found of the traditional murder story.

The Gelderland manuscript describes for the first time, in a personal account, the events surrounding the disappearance of Richard, Duke of York, and his brother Edward V in 1483. It also tells how and by whom one of the princes is secretly moved from the Tower of London and sheltered in safety on the continent.

Consequently, major question marks can now be placed against the traditional narrative. It may also confirm that one of the alternative stories – that the princes were taken from the Tower and sent abroad – is the true version of events, and that the man known as Perkin Warbeck was indeed the son of King Edward – Prince Richard, Duke of York – as many have argued.[13]

The period surrounding Richard's departure from the Tower of London is described in considerable detail. This not only is quite remarkable but also provides a relatively easy means of checking the various names and places mentioned in the narrative. In this way, the veracity of the account can be tested, and its credibility and reliability assessed.

The English translation of the original Middle Dutch text of the manuscript[14] is included in its entirety in this chapter and subjected to an analysis of its most significant details. As a result, this examination represents the first exploration of the manuscript.

Its origin, language, date and handwriting will be briefly examined in order to assess its authenticity. The text will then be presented in full, and its contents analysed.

The Authenticity of the Document

It is likely that the Gelderland Archive acquired the manuscript in the nineteenth or early twentieth century through a gift or deposit. It is also possible that it was purchased as a separate item by the archive itself at auction or from a vendor. For this reason, it is difficult to trace its provenance.[15]

The manuscript consists of four bound pages. It is neither dated nor signed. The dating of the piece to around the year 1500 by the Gelderland Archives appears to be correct, partly in view of the typical late-fifteenth-century handwriting. It is probable that the Gelderland document is a copy of an original.

The text provides some internal evidence regarding the date of composition. The narration ends when Richard leaves Charles VIII's court in France and arrives with his aunt, Margaret of York, in Malines. This would have been at the end of 1492 or the beginning of 1493 (see Appendix 5 and Timeline).

It seems likely that Richard's personal story was recorded shortly after his arrival in Malines, possibly at the insistence or request of Margaret of York. On 25 August 1493, Richard Plantagenet, as he called himself at that time, also wrote a letter from Dendermonde to the Spanish Queen Isabella.[16]

This letter, which will be discussed in more detail, appears to be a shortened, but more or less identical, rendition of events in the Gelderland document, which is an indication that both documents were written around the same time.

Another dating clue is the fact that the narration in the Gelderland manuscript was written in the past tense, except for the very last sentence, which reads, 'And by the Grace of God, I received help, honour and comfort ... that in a short time I will obtain my rights to which I was born.' Richard thus speaks at the moment he arrives at the court of Margaret of York, about the (near) future and what has still to take place.

The language in which the narrative is written is Middle Dutch or Middle Low German. It also resembles *Dietsch*, the language spoken by the ordinary people in the Burgundian Netherlands, which at the time had many local variants.[17] The style is narrative and it is told in an almost neutral and emotionless way by Richard himself. The death of his father, the flight into sanctuary and the sudden farewell from his mother, sisters and brother must have been traumatic for the 9-year-old; however, nowhere in this narrative do we get an impression of despair, fear or grief.

The Manuscript Text

Please note that names, capitals and punctuation have been modernised.

1–3:   Here we follow the Duke of York, son and heir to king Edward the fourth, Richard ('Rychart'), his son, delivered from the Tower of London where he has been for a while.

4–8:   First of all, I remember that my dearest lady and mother, queen Elizabeth ('elysabett'), delivered me from sanctuary of Westminster into the hands of the Archbishop of Canterbury ('cantelberch'), and other men, also from the states of the country, under commitment of certain promises made by him under oath to bring me back to the same sanctuary.

9–11:　Which Archbishop brought me to my uncle of Gloucester ('gloessester'). And so I was brought to my brother who was already there, in the Tower of London.

11–18:　[... several knights?] and squires were waiting for us there, of whom I think I remember that John Norris ('johan norijssche') was one, and William Tyrwyth ('tyrwijte') another. On the first night, shortly after these guards were relieved, they took leave of us with great melancholy and sadness. To these guards my brother often said melancholic words. Among other things he said and prayed my uncle of Gloucester ('glossestre') to have mercy on him, for he was just an innocent person.

19–21:　And then we were delivered to Brackenbury ('Braekeberij'), and then to sir James Tyrrell ('jacob tyrrijll'), and then to the Duke of Buckingham ('Hertoghe van Buckgegen'), by whose orders we were separated.

22–33:　And so they ordered my lord Foriest, Hamelett Maleven and Wylliam Puche by whom I was secretly taken into a room in a place where the lions are kept. There I was for such a long time, that Lord Howard ('heer halbard'), later made Duke of Norfolk ('hertoghe van nortfolck'), came to me and encouraged me. [At last?], he ordered the guards – described above – to leave and then brought two other men to me. They were called, they said so themselves: 'hinrijck (Henry) Parcij' and 'thomas (Thomas) Parcij'. They swore by honour and oath to Duke Howard ('hertoge halbard'), as mentioned before, to hide me secretly until certain years were past and that I would be placed under supervision by them for certain years. Then they shaved my hair and put a poor and drab skirt ('rockesgen') on me.[18]

34–36:　And shortly after that they left the Tower with me and went to Saint Katherine's ('sinte katrijns'). There they took a boat and rowed aboard a small and narrow ship already waiting there.

37–38:　And sailed to the sea and came ashore in the dunes of Boulogne-sur-Mer ('boene').[19]

39–44:　And from there we went to Paris ('Parijs'). We stayed there for a long time. Till the moment I was noticed by English folks there. And so we travelled from there to a city called Chartres ('charters') and from there to Rouen ('ruwan'), to Dieppe ('deijpen') and various other cities and places in France ('vranckrijk'). And finally, we got to Hainaut ('hennegaw').

45–49: From there in Brabant [...?] Malines (mechelen), Antwerp ('andwerpen'), Bergen ('berghen')[20] for a period of certain years. And from there I went to Zeeland ('Selant') [...?] Middelburg ('mydelborch') until Edward Brampton's[21] ('eduwart bramtons') wife was ready to sail us to Portugal.

49–53: [I sailed together with the prescribed Parcijs in a ship of their own.. ?]. To be able to tell [later?] [that they were on the same ship (with me), they knew a distinguishing feature ('lyckteyken') of me, namely that I played the clavichord.]

53–63: And then we arrived in Lisbon ('lysseboene'). From there I sent the aforementioned Thomas Parcij to England, to my lady my mother with certain distinguishing features ('lycktekenen') and also with certain messages. Shortly afterwards Henry Parcij became ill with the plague. During his illness, he told me that when he died, I would have to travel to Ireland to the lords of Kyldare[22] and Desmond[23] and also told me how I should rule the country. Then he died, may God save his soul.

64–65: Shortly afterwards I found a ship from Brittany ('bartayne') that wanted to sail to Ireland ('ierlant'). The master of the ship sailed me to Ireland ('ierlant') as he himself has testified and will testify more fully – at all times – when questioned.

70–72: There I found several of my acquaintances, among them the lord of Kyldare ('de here van kyldare'), Garret the Great ('gylbart de braven') and many others.[24] There I was recognised for who I was and treated as such.

73–85: And there I stayed for a while until my cousin the King of France ('konyng van vranckrijk')[25] contacted me and made a firm promise to assist and help me to claim my rights. However, when I arrived in France, I found the opposite. So I left, and went to my dearest aunt, the duchess of Burgundy ('myne leyffste moye de herthoginne van Burghoenen'). She recognised my rights and honesty. And by the grace of God, I received help, honour and comfort from my dear friends and servants that in a short time I will obtain my right to which I was born.

Content and analysis

The document begins, 'Here we follow the Duke of York, son and heir to King Edward the fourth Rychart his son delivered from the Tower of London where he has been for a while.'

The title of the text is written in the third person. It has the same handwriting as the young duke's personal narrative, which follows, suggesting that the document in question is a written copy of an original. It seems most likely that around the time the Duke of York was received at the Burgundian court, his story was recorded in an official document, possibly in Latin or French, the official language of the court.

Although Margaret of York could vouch for the 'authenticity' and identity of her royal nephew,[26] such a statement was required to support his credibility. Copies of the original may have been distributed throughout Burgundy. The Gelderland document could be such a copy.

It is beyond dispute that in the years following his arrival in the Burgundian Netherlands, Richard, Duke of York, was unreservedly recognised as the son of Edward IV and rightful heir to the English throne.[27] It cannot be ruled out, therefore, that Richard's recorded narrative contributed to this firm belief.

It is known that the Duke of York received military and financial support from King Maximilian to regain his kingdom. This support seems to have taken greater form than previously assumed. Recent archival research has revealed that several nobles in prominent positions at the Burgundian court supported Richard's ambitions with large sums of money. Both Albert of Saxony[28] and Engelbert II of Nassau,[29] who held leading military and administrative roles in the service of King Maximilian, lent to 'Richard of England' quite astonishing sums of 30,000 gold florins and 10,000 golden ecus respectively.[30] In these two rediscovered charters, Richard of England promises to repay them once he becomes sovereign ruler of England. This strongly suggests that both Burgundian nobles believed him to be the true son of Edward IV and rightful heir to the English throne. One of the charters mentioned was found to bear the royal seal and monogram of Richard of England, which appeared to be in extremely good condition.

The well-known Dutch chronicler Cornelius Aurelius (1460–1531), a contemporary of Richard, writes extensively about the presence of the Duke of York in Holland in 1495 in his *Dutch Divisie Chronicle* (published in 1517).[31] Aurelius, who consistently refers to the duke as 'The White Rose', seems to have had absolutely no doubt regarding his identity as the real prince and heir

Signature of Richard of England, 4 October 1493, with monogram. Sächsisches Staatsarchiv, Hauptstaatsarchiv Dresden, 10001, Nr 9005. Redrawn: Philippa Langley)

to the English throne. Illustrative of this firm belief is the fact that he (albeit mistakenly) writes that Richard was publicly executed with the sword in London in 1499. This is a punishment generally reserved for the nobility on the continent.[32]

Lines 4–18: What is particularly striking is the detail of Richard's report, especially during the period he resided in the Tower of London. Although, as a then 9-year-old, he does not provide dates, he does mention the names of guards and squires, who on closer examination can be identified as Edward IV's former household servants.

For example, he mentions the names of two guards: John Norris (Johan Norijssche) and William Tyrwhyt (William Tyrwijte). John Norris was Esquire of the Body for Edward IV and Edward V[33] and Tyrwhyt [Tyrwhite] was also a servant and Esquire of the Body for Edward IV,[34] so a young Richard, Duke of York, may have known both men.

It may be important to note the comments of Henry VII's French poet-biographer, Bernard André, concerning the detailed knowledge of the 'impostor prince'. In his life story of King Henry, composed a few years after Perkin Warbeck officially confessed his deception and eventually paid for it with his life, André writes:

> He could recall all the circumstances of Edward IV and recited by heart all the names of his household and servants, as though he had been taught these and had known them from the time he was a little boy. In addition he gave details of locations, dates and persons ... He even (as fine player he was) fortified these facts with a veil of such deceit that ... men of wisdom and great nobility were induced to believe him.[35]

Of course, André, in the service of Henry VII, had little choice but to assume that the person who pretended to be the Duke of York was indeed a fraud, but reading between the lines, it is clear that he was impressed by Richard's accurate knowledge of his time at the English court.

Both Norris and Tyrwhyt appear to have been the regular attendants and guards of Edward V and Richard (after the latter joined his older brother in the Tower on 16 June 1483). It can be inferred from the text that the brothers had been together for at least a while, and Mancini records that Edward V often conversed in melancholic terms with his attendants.[36] It was also reported elsewhere that the boys were seen shooting arrows in the Tower garden at 'sundry times', meaning on a number of occasions.[37]

Lines 19–21: Unfortunately, it is not clear from the text how much time Edward and Richard spent together in the Tower. A clue may be the date of Brackenbury's appointment as Constable of the Tower of London on 17 July 1483, just before King Richard left on his royal progress. It is possible that the two boys may have been together until that date, or perhaps longer, since Brackenbury was only the first person to whom they were delivered. Apparently, shortly after the handover to Brackenbury, Sir James Tyrell takes care of the two boys.

Finally, Buckingham orders the boys to be separated. This is a key moment: why are they separated at this point? Were there rumours of an impending attempt to kidnap the two boys from the Tower?[38] And were they separated for that reason?

Lines 22–33: Following separation from his brother, three new guards are appointed to watch over Richard: 'Mylorde Foriest', 'Hamelett Maleven' and 'William Puche'. Until now, no 'Mylorde Foriest', living in 1483, has been found. What immediately catches the eye is the striking resemblance to the name 'Miles Forest'. In medieval texts, names and words are often written phonetically (see for example 'Buckingham', given in the document as 'Buckgegen'). When 'Mylorde Foriest' is spoken aloud, it sounds like 'Miles Forest'. Furthermore, it is rather peculiar that the English word 'Mylorde' is used in the original text, since in the rest of the manuscript the middle Dutch word *'Heer'* or *'Here'* (which means 'Lord') is consistently used. For example, the original text says, 'Here Halbard', for 'Lord Howard'. It does not say, 'Mylorde Halbard'.

Therefore, it cannot be ruled out that 'Mylorde' concerns a first name but spelled or written down incorrectly and that 'Miles' (Foriest) was intended. This thought is supported by the fact that all the other guards mentioned in the manuscript are consistently referred to by their first and surnames.

As to the identity of the other two guards, a comprehensive search for 'Hamelett Maleven' produced no results but he was probably Halneth Mauleverer. Mauleverer was an Usher to the Chamber for Edward IV, and with his brother Robert and elder brother, Sir Thomas, fought for King Richard at Bosworth.[39]

The Chronicles of London also record 'one Malyverey' among the captains who were arrested at Deal in Kent, during the first invasion attempt by Richard, Duke of York, on 3 July 1495. It is not known which Mauleverer this was.[40] Most of those captured at Deal were killed or executed. André recorded that the prisoners entered London 'bound with ropes in a row like thieves' and 'after several days, about four hundred lost their lives; some lost their head, others died by the noose'.[41] Four Dutchmen were hanged in the river at St Katherine's.[42]

Halneth and Thomas' uncle, William Mauleverer of Kent (d. 1498), may have also been involved, having received a 'little ring with a diamond' from King Richard'.[43]

William Poche was a Yeoman of the Crown and, in the Report of the Deputy Keeper of the Public Records, served in the office of 'the keeper of the beds and other furniture, aka the small wardrobe in the Tower of London'.[44] He was granted the position for life on 8 March 1484 (replacing John Wharff). Nothing further is recorded for Poche and it is possible that he may have died at Bosworth.

If Richard of York did indeed indicate 'Miles Forest', rather than 'Mylorde Foriest', then his role as guardian of one of the princes was already on record in 1493. This also implies that Miles Forest and the other two guards were the last persons to see the young prince alive shortly before his disappearance from the Tower.[45]

Remarkably, thirty years later, a Miles Forest was named by Thomas More as one of the murderers in his story of the Princes in the Tower. Later discoveries at Henry VIII's court reveal that Forest was innocent of any involvement in the supposed murders (or regicides) of the king's uncles.[46]

Thomas More and Erasmus

Although More may, of course, have obtained his information in many other ways, it is at least noteworthy that his friend Desiderius Erasmus may have witnessed the arrival of Richard Plantagenet at the Burgundian court in 1492–93.

Erasmus worked from 1492 to 1495 as secretary to the Bishop of Cambrai, Henry of Glymes.[47] The bishop had been Margaret of York's court chaplain and confessor since 1479, and was a close confidant.[48]

Erasmus' stay at the court of the bishop thus overlaps exactly with the Duke of York's residence in the Burgundian Netherlands (under the auspices of his aunt). It is therefore quite possible that Erasmus was aware of Richard's presence through the bishop. Erasmus may have even witnessed Richard's arrival at Malines. Although a great deal of Erasmus' correspondence has been preserved, nothing seems to have survived from his time in the bishop's service. Significantly, in his later letters, Erasmus remains remarkably silent about this specific period.[49]

In 1499, the year in which Perkin Warbeck was executed on the orders of Henry VII at Tyburn, Erasmus was in England as a guest of More. They will certainly have discussed the whole affair, and Erasmus may have provided his good friend with information about the alleged impostor.[50]

The Lions Tower

After he is separated from his brother, Richard is secretly brought into a room, 'in a place where the lions are kept'. This new location must be somewhere near the Lions Tower.[51]

It is difficult to ascertain exactly when the separation of the boys took place. However, the very reason for their separation may have been the July abduction attempt. Around 21–22 July 1483, an attempt was made to remove Edward and his brother from their royal lodgings. This, as described previously, involved servants working within the Tower. Among them was a Stephen Ireland, Wardrober and member of the royal household, and one John Smith, Groom of King Edward IV's Stirrup.[52] It seems the Tower staff had been infiltrated and there was a potential risk to the boys.

At first glance, this new location near the Lions Tower seems like an odd and illogical place. However, if the intention was to safely conceal Richard, then the decision makes sense. It was at the entrance, within the secure fortifications and moat, away from the general business of the Tower Palace, but easily vacated in a quick getaway. It was also right next to Wharf Gate (now destroyed).[53]

John Howard, 1st Duke of Norfolk

According to the Gelderland manuscript, it was John Howard, close confidant of King Richard and staunch supporter of the House of York, who ensured that Richard of York, together with his supervisors, could leave the Tower unseen for the continent.

In the scarce literature on John Howard, he is described as a loyal and trusted confidant who carried out his duties at the English court, including a French ambassadorship under both Edward IV and Richard III, with ability and competence. He seems to have avoided court life as much as possible and was therefore, as far as is known, not involved in political intrigues during his long and distinguished career. He was created Duke of Norfolk on 28 June 1483, shortly before Richard III's coronation, and died with Richard at the Battle of Bosworth in August 1485, where he led the king's vanguard.[54]

By the time of the July abduction attempt, Howard was with King Richard, having left London on 19 July 1483 on the king's royal progress to the north. It is therefore not inconceivable that King Richard, upon learning of the (failed) attempt to kidnap the boys, may have felt it wise to protect his nephews and relocate them immediately for their own safety. It would also be crucial that their presence in the Tower could no longer give rise to further political plots.[55]

We do know that John Howard returned urgently to London from the royal progress on 22–23 July and remained in the capital until 11 August (see Chapter 4). Given his hasty departure, it appears that Howard may have been entrusted with King Richard's plan to relocate his nephews.

Howard had become one of the most powerful men in the kingdom and was given a wide range of supervisory powers from 16 July onwards, including, significantly, the office of Admiral of England on 25 July.[56] Howard was back in London on 24 July. His Household Books reveal that he left London for his Suffolk home at Stoke-by-Nayland on 11 August 1483.[57] It is likely that sometime during this period Howard visited young Richard in his new accommodation 'near the lions' together with Henry and Thomas Parcij, who swore by honour and oath to Howard to supervise the young duke and hide him secretly for a certain number of years. Their departure from the Tower should therefore have occurred sometime during this period. This was probably in the first week of August as several preparations were required: arranging two reliable supervisors, acquiring a ship and crew for the crossing and arranging a place to stay in Boulogne and Paris.[58] An entry in Howard's Household Books indicates that he may also have arranged the poor (drab) clothing for both boys.[59]

Hinrijck and Thomas Parcij/Henry and Thomas Percy (Peirse)

It would be an enormous step forward if we could discover the identity of Henry and Thomas Parcij (Percy, Parcy, Percie, Persey, Pearsy or Peirse). As their absence would have raised questions, it seems likely they were unmarried men in everyday positions, and probably members of either Howard's[60] or King Richard's trusted circle.

An inspection of Howard's Household Accounts reveals a number of individuals with the surname Percy or Perse. These include a Nycollas Percy (17 December 1464 and 25 May 1465); a Lady Percy (25 July 1482), probably Maud Herbert, wife of Henry Percy, Earl of Northumberland; a Master Percy (28 August 1482); and Anthony Percy (27 November 1482), in addition to a number of local East Anglian tradesmen named Perse. If the name Percy or Perse was a pseudonym for their real name, perhaps we must look for brothers with the names 'Henry and Thomas'. There is a Henry (Harry) and Thomas Daniel in Howard's service (his nephews) but it seems that Thomas was still in Howard's service in Suffolk in October 1483.[61]

Significant consideration must also be given to Sir Robert Percy of Scotton in Yorkshire (*c.* 1445–85), Comptroller of King Richard's Household and Marshal of the Marshalsea,[62] and Henry Percy, 4th Earl of Northumberland (*c.* 1449–89).[63] Extensive searches of both Percy households in the north failed to yield any likely candidates.[64]

However, when we turned to those associated with King Richard, in particular, the king's close friend and confidant, Francis, Viscount Lovell, was also Lord of Bedale,[65] a manor neighbouring the king's lordship of Middleham in Yorkshire, a Thomas Peirse was identified (see p. 13, the Family of Peirse of Bedale).[66] Further investigation also uncovered a Thomas and Henry Peirs (Peirse or Percy) in Bedale on 15 April 1483 at Francis Lovell's manorial court. This includes a record of a 'Pearsy'.[67] This reference strongly suggests Lovell's knowledge of the Peirses, their loyalty (and fealty) to him and his involvement in recommending them as York's guardians.

The Peirses of Bedale would have been well known to King Richard and Francis Lovell. That they were trusted servants is apparently demonstrated by

Thomas' father, Peter Peirse (*c.* 1440s–1510), who acted as the King's Standard Bearer at Bosworth. It may be significant that Thomas' grandson was called Henry, potentially denoting a family name and possible connection to Henry Percy, 4th Earl of Northumberland, of whom Peter is said to be a brother,[68] or more likely a distant relative.[69]

Interestingly, Thomas' son and heir was named Marmaduke. The name's connection to the story of Madoc, the twelfth-century illegitimate prince who took to the sea to flee internecine violence would have been well known in the fifteenth century.[70] Was this Thomas Peirse's way of honouring his own service to another illegitimate prince who had taken to the sea? It seems that Thomas may have gone further and named another son Richard. Richard Peirse died without issue and was buried in Bedale on 14 April 1573,[71] but the name would go on to become a Peirse family Christian name (see the family tree on p. 13).

Lines 33–36: Together with the two Peirses, young Richard leaves for St Katherine's. Immediately to the east of the Tower, St Katherine's was a poor community outside the city wall of London, with a hospital and church established by Queen Mathilda of Boulogne around 1148.[72] It was a spiritual place but also a place for sailors, seafarers and trading. It had a great deal of land surrounding it and several wharfs on the river.

The ship in which Richard and his two supervisors leave for France is already waiting on the River Thames. In this context, it may be important to note that Howard was one of the greatest ship owners in England, so the ship might have been one of his own.[73]

Lines 37–38: The main question is, of course, why France was chosen as the destination. The north of England (loyal to Richard III), Burgundy (the presence of his aunt, Margaret of York), and Ireland (which was pro-Yorkist) seem to be more logical destinations.

Certainly, Paris was the largest, most populated and overcrowded European city where a young boy and his two guardians could live incognito. Moreover, if there was someone at the English court who had strong ties to France, it was John Howard. He was a respected Ambassador to France from 1467 and seems to have had a good relationship with the French King Louis XI. In early 1483, Howard travelled to France in a diplomatic capacity.[74] But France was also important in terms of his mercantile interests, where he developed a network of trade connections. In short, Howard was familiar with France like no other, and from that perspective, it may have been a carefully considered choice.

In this context, it is important to consider that Boulogne-sur-Mer was a famous and important pilgrimage site in Europe and one of the oldest in

France. Medieval pilgrims, especially from England, France and Flanders, journeyed to worship our Lady of Boulogne-sur-Mer. Fourteen kings of France, including Louis XI, and many kings of England travelled to this northern French city on pilgrimage.[75] This route, also popular with English pilgrims, may therefore have been chosen very deliberately, offering the means to travel safely and unnoticed into France.

Lines 39–44: Paris was the place where the young duke, with Henry and Thomas Peirse, lived a secret life for an extended period of time. It is likely that Howard arranged the hiding place, making use of his connections in a city he had visited many times during a long ambassadorial (and mercantile) career. Richard states in the Gelderland manuscript that they 'stayed there for a long time'. How long is not clear – and from a young child's perspective, it is difficult to judge what he may have meant by 'a long time'.

The reason for leaving Paris was a significant one – the presence of the Duke of York had been noticed by 'English folks there'. From this moment, Paris was no longer considered a secure hiding place by the two Peirse guardians. This was certainly the case from September 1484 to August 1485 when Henry Tudor and his adherents fled Brittany and received asylum in Paris at the court of the new young French king, Charles VIII.[76] As there were several former Yorkists among Henry's followers, including young Richard's half-brother and former Chamberlain to Edward IV, Thomas Grey, Marquess of Dorset, and his uncle, Sir Edward Woodville, there was an obvious risk of recognition.

Leaving Paris, they kept to northern France, staying from time to time in diverse cities until they finally arrived in Hainaut. The county of Hainaut was in the hands of the Burgundian dukes, except the town of Tournai, which was still under French rule. It seems that France was clearly preferred, which may indicate that the new destination was the city of Tournai.[77] The exact moment of their arrival in Hainaut province remains unclear but it was probably towards the end of 1484.

If the ultimate goal was to provide Richard with a temporary refuge in a more secure and secluded place until peace and stability were restored in England, then a whole new situation arose for Richard of York and his supervisors with the deaths of King Richard and John Howard at the Battle of Bosworth on 22 August 1485[78] and the subsequent imprisonment of Howard's son and heir, Thomas, Earl of Surrey.[79]

In January 1486, Henry VII's marriage to Elizabeth of York[80] and the subsequent reversal of the *Titulus Regius* – King Richard's royal title – gave an important new twist to the situation. From this moment, Richard's and

Edward's rights to the English throne would take precedence over the claim of the new English king.

Lines 45–49: The wanderings, with the sole purpose of secrecy and the preservation of the Yorkist royal bloodline, continued and Richard finally reached Middelburg in the County of Zeeland (via Malines, Antwerp and Bergen op Zoom). For the first time, we see an overlap with the confession of Perkin Warbeck.[81] The story and timeline of both the Gelderland manuscript and that of the confession seem to coincide at this juncture. It was in the spring of 1487 that Perkin sailed with Edward Brampton's wife to Portugal.[82]

It is interesting to note that, at this point, Richard, Duke of York, is resident in Bergen op Zoom and Middelburg, the location of the military preparations for the first Yorkist invasion in 1487 under the command of Martin Zwarte and other Yorkist leaders.[83]

Lines 50–52: The transcribed Middle Dutch text is very difficult to understand here. It seems that the Peirses and Richard leave Middelburg in a ship other than the ship belonging to Edward Brampton's wife. The reason is hard to understand from the currently indecipherable text.

Also, the Middle Dutch word '*leyckteken*' is difficult to translate, but it presumably means a scar (wound), physical sign (sign) or personal characteristic. Most likely, Richard was referring to several natural distinguishing marks on his body and face 'by which those who knew him in his youth would recognize him', proving him to be the true Duke of York.[84]

Apparently another 'distinguishing feature' of York was an ability to play the clavichord. This was a popular western European keyboard instrument in the late Middle Ages. Seemingly, Richard possessed a love of dance (and 'play'), which may have included music.[85] As we have seen, Rui de Sousa, the Portuguese Ambassador to England (1481–89), met the young prince and saw him 'singing with his mother and one of his sisters and [said] that he sang very well' (see Chapter 2).

In this context, it is relevant to note that the version of the Perkin Warbeck confession recorded in French contains a separate appendix, documenting a completely different childhood, which is absent in the English confession.[86] According to the French confession, Perkin was not sent away but kept in Tournai, where he studied at the cathedral choir school. Historian Ann Wroe was the first to pay extensive attention to this alternative version of Perkin's life:

Piers [Perkin] was deliberately placed on the ladder to a better higher life: tuition in music, service in the church, perhaps university. / Latin grammar

/ ... if this version of his life was true ... / Piers' days at school would have been largely taken up with music of one kind or another. The [French] appendix said he was taught the manicordium: in French, this meant the clavichords [clavichord] or some sort of keyboard instrument, possibly the organ that Brampton had mentioned. / The confession took great care to give a plausible chronology for Piers's life until he sailed for Portugal. **But the fact remained that there were two distinct versions of his life**. [Emphasis added.][87]

This raises the significant question whether it was the Duke of York who received his education at the cathedral choir school in Tournai.

Lines 53–63: This paragraph spans a period of at least four years, in which Richard remains remarkably silent about his life in Portugal. Wroe's rediscovery of the 'Setúbal Testimonies' revealed that the pretender had been at the Portuguese court not for one year, as the official confession of Perkin Warbeck alleged, but for more than three years.[88] At the same time, Wroe also discovered a fifteenth-century poem remembering the 'White Rose' at the Portuguese court (and lamenting his fate at Henry's hands).[89]

It is striking that between 1488 and 1491, Henry VII suddenly paid special attention to Portugal, 'attention he had not shown before and was not to show again'.[90] In 1489, he sent an English Embassy to Portugal which included Richmond Herald, Roger Machado. Machado would become one of Henry VII's most important and trusted spies in the Warbeck affair.[91]

From Portugal, Richard sends Thomas Peirse back to his mother, Elizabeth Woodville, in England. He no longer sounds like a child: he now appears to be issuing commands. This would make Richard, Duke of York, 14 years of age when Peirse returned to England in the late summer of 1487.

The timing of Richard's personal message to his mother is also significant, despatched shortly after the unsuccessful first Yorkist invasion in 1487 (the so-called 'Lambert Simnel Affair'). This suggests that news of Edward V's defeat at Stoke Field in the summer of 1487 had filtered through to Portugal and reached Richard of York and the Peirses. Is this why he now sent formal word to his mother, reassuring her, despite his brother's death or injury, that he was still alive?

Henry Peirse died of the plague in Portugal. In 1488 and 1489, there was a great outbreak of plague in Lisbon and in 1491 it raged around the country.[92] On his deathbed, he instructed Richard to travel to Ireland, to the Lords of Kildare and Desmond. There was still much support for the Yorkist cause in

Ireland. What better way to cement lingering loyalty than by showing himself to the Irish lords so that they could see with their own eyes that he was King Edward's son. These same lords had only recently supported his elder brother.

Lines 64–69: Although Richard does not mention the name of the master of the Breton ship which took him to Ireland, it was probably Pregent (Pierre Jean) Meno, mentioned in Warbeck's confession.[93] Richard emphasises in the Gelderland manuscript that 'the master of the ship' testified that he had carried Richard to Ireland. This testimony seems to be very important to him, probably as proof of his identity.[94] Apparently, he was informed that the Breton was captured by Henry VII in December 1491 and seems to rely almost naively on Meno's honest testimony.

Nothing could be further from the truth. Wroe discovered that Pregent Meno, after his capture, does not appear to have been punished and eventually reaped considerable rewards. Presumably, this was for information, or silence. She notes that Henry VII – again – performed the trick of transforming a close acquaintance of the 'feigned lad' into a 'bastion of his own defences, well-mortared with rewards' (as he did a few years later with Sir Robert Clifford).[95]

Lines 70–72: Richard must therefore have arrived in Ireland around November 1491. He tells us nothing of his apparently tumultuous arrival in Cork, despite being recognised as the Duke of York in the 'official' confession. However, it is clear from the description in the Gelderland manuscript that his royal lineage was recognised and honoured by the Irish lords. Significantly, the Duke of York, as Lieutenant of Ireland, seems to have been in Ireland in 1479, witnessing at Dublin the appointment of the Prior of the Hospital of Jerusalem, Sir James Keating, as Constable of Dublin Castle.[96] If so, then we may assume that the young duke was honourably received by his deputy in Ireland, the Earl of Kildare (and other powerful lords).

At that time, Richard may have already had some notable distinctive facial marks, the same by which Margaret of York claimed to recognise him as her nephew in 1493.[97] She had last seen the Duke of York in 1480 during her trip to England, less than six months after his visit to Ireland in December 1479. Not much would have changed about the young duke's appearance in that short time. The above might explain why York went to Ireland first in 1491 and chose to reveal himself there as the Irish lords could possibly still recognise him by these marks and consequently acknowledge and support him as the heir of the House of York.

Lines 73–85: From Ireland, he left for France in the summer of 1492 at the invitation of the young French King Charles VIII, who promised support.

Richard did not stay at the French court for long. On 3 November 1492, Charles VIII and Henry VII signed the peace treaty of Étaples, a condition of which was that both sides promised not to support any claimants, rebels or traitors of the other.[98]

Richard then left for his aunt, Margaret of York, who received her nephew with open arms:

> At last the Duke of York himself came to me out of France, seeking help and assistance ... I indeed for my part, when I gazed on this male Remnant of our family – who had come through so many perils and misfortunes – was deeply moved, and out of this natural affection ... I embraced him as my only nephew and my only son.[99]

Here, Margaret seems to confirm York's superior claim to the throne (over her other nephew, the Earl of Warwick) and thus her support for him on these terms. She may also have been speaking figuratively as clearly York was not her 'son' (nor her only nephew).

The Dendermonde Letter: Richard Plantagenet to Isabella, Queen of Spain, 25 August 1493

Shortly after his arrival at the court of Margaret of York, Richard writes a letter to the Spanish Queen Isabella. In it, he asks Isabella to use her influence to help him regain the kingdom that is rightfully his. The remarkable feature of this letter is that although much less detailed, it corresponds in many aspects with the story recorded in the Gelderland manuscript. (See Appendix 5.)

There is, however, one striking difference with the Gelderland manuscript. In the letter, Richard writes that his brother, '... the Prince of Wales that is, had been killed in a pitiable death and I too being about nine years of age had been handed over to a certain lord to be killed'. The Gelderland narrative, which – as noted – must have been written about the same time, makes no mention of his older brother's (violent) death. Richard only talks about their separation after being handed over to Buckingham.

Emphasising the death of 'The Prince of Wales' in the Dendermonde letter seems understandable and easy to explain: it was of the greatest importance to present the Duke of York as the only surviving rightful heir to the English throne. Margaret's last hope of a glorious resurrection of the House of York in England now rested on Richard, second son of Edward IV.[100] It is also very likely, as Christine Weightman writes, that Maximilian was the power behind the Dendermonde letter.[101]

It may have also been important to claim that Edward died seemingly as a child rather than remind York's potential backers that his brother had lost at Stoke and that Maximilian's second fleet for him had ultimately been redeployed. Perhaps Margaret consented to the inclusion of Edward V's 'pitiable death' on the understanding that Richard III wasn't mentioned as a perpetrator. Thus, Margaret would not sacrifice her brother's posthumous reputation in order to support the new heir.

The safeguarding of King Richard's reputation seems to be further supported by York's proclamation from Scotland in September 1496. Here, he styled himself Richard of England and presented his claim, 'Richard by the grace of gode kinge of England and of France lorde of Ireland Prince of Wales', while associating his rule with the 'virtues and competence' of the old Yorkist order.[102]

On 8 May 1495, Margaret would cause her lawyer and proctor, Lord Valasius of Portugal, to write to Pope Alexander VI. The legal supplication, witnessed by leading members of Burgundian Church and state, including Margaret's Head of Household, Pierre de Lannoy, and two Papal Notary Publics, was clear in its confirmation of her nephew's credentials and identity.

Margaret's purpose was to seek revocation of the papal sentence of excommunication which Henry VII had procured from Alexander, and Innocent VIII before him, in March 1486, to be threatened on all who might dispute his right to reign. Even the pope himself, it was observed, could be 'deceived and duped' by one who had:

> ... usurped the realm itself and occupied it *de facto*, when he could not do so *de jure* ... claiming untrue things, namely that the right of the same realm of England indubitably and by right belonged to him ... notwithstanding that the most illustrious lord Richard survives in this life, the legitimate son of the said late king Edward, and successor and heir to his father's realm.

Nor could Henry VII hide behind his marriage to Edward IV's daughter, since **'a daughter cannot and should not succeed in any way ... when a son ... is in existence'** and in plain terms, **'no one should reign in another's realm'** (emphasis added). The result being that the 'alleged subjects of the same Henry' would be liable for this ultimate threat to their immortal souls if 'they, or any of them, should … presume to incite or cause to be incited [opposition to his reign], personally or through any other or others'.

This drew in the potential wrath of the Church on any who were likely to assist or support the young Richard of York, so that 'she with her adherents seems to be forbidden, contrary to the needs of nature, to give her nephew aid, counsel or support'. Indeed, as the argument on her behalf proceeded, if the truth had been known to these two popes, or the falsehoods not put forward, 'without doubt they would not have granted' the Tudor king's wishes, 'but would rather have ordered the said most illustrious lord Richard, the son of King Edward, to be restored to his realm and enthroned in possession of it'.

Margaret's arguments were set out as an urgent request for a reply to previous calls upon the pope which had gone unanswered, and the notarised document stated that there were 'subjoined letters of attestation from … my said lady and those aforesaid persons who adhere or will adhere to her'. Such letters must also have accompanied Margaret's previous appeal(s) to Pope Alexander and will have included depositions attesting to her nephew's identity and bona fides.

The document followed King Richard's proclamations of 7 December 1484 and 23 June 1485 in describing Henry as 'claiming to be the blood of Lancaster, although he knows that he was born … from adulterous embraces on the part of both parents'. It ends with Margaret's descriptor as 'the most illustrious lady Margaret of England'.[103]

The first Borgia pope seems to have responded with new condemnations.[104] By 22 September, Maximilian had interceded and despatched his own legal supplication on York's behalf (see Appendix 8).[105]

Searches are ongoing for previous or subsequent correspondence with the Vatican.

Further Thoughts: 1. Men of the Sea

In order to form a balanced opinion of the accuracy of the Gelderland text, the manuscript was subjected to close examination. The initial findings and results, as described in the 'content and analysis' section, reveal that much of the information provided is correct and verifiable.

The surprising statement that Richard III's confidant John Howard, 1st Duke of Norfolk, was trusted with the secret removal of the young Duke of York from the Tower of London seems to be explained and substantiated by existing evidence. For example, we first note Howard's urgent return to London from the royal progress on 22 July, a journey that may have been undertaken partly at night and included the arrest of a number of men at Bray. It also seems likely that the Percy retainer, Sir John Everingham of Birkin, North Yorkshire, may have accompanied him.[106]

Howard's Household Books record how England's Earl Marshal now took control of London, conducting a trial at Crosby's Place, King Richard's London residence. By 7 August, York (and his brother) could have been safely away.

Howard now writes to his son and heir, Thomas Howard, Earl of Surrey, King Richard's Steward, who is able to inform the king at Warwick.[107] This letter, together with most of King Richard's correspondence, would be lost or destroyed during the reign of Henry VII.

By 8 August, Howard's Books confirm that he is 'all content un to this day'[108] and by 11 August, Howard has left the capital to return to his home in East Anglia and lead his own ducal progress to My Lady's Shrine at Walsingham to give thanks. It might also be significant that at this precise moment, Queen Anne left Windsor to rejoin the king at Warwick. As with King Richard, however, no correspondence with his queen at Windsor survives from this time.

Why Howard was chosen for such a sensitive and secret mission is perhaps explained by his loyalty to the House of York and years of faithful service both on and off the field of battle. It is also very likely that Howard had developed a personal connection with King Edward's youngest son, who had been created Duke of Norfolk before him. We can see that Howard was present at Westminster, with the Archbishop of Canterbury, to help convey the young boy to the Royal Apartments in the Tower to await his brother's coronation. Also, and perhaps more significantly, Howard purchased a bow for the young boy. Howard had seven children of his own and it seems he knew young Richard well enough to know that he enjoyed shooting arrows (for the foregoing, see Chapters 3 and 4).

However, it is perhaps most remarkable that Howard was made Admiral of England with the 'certain specified powers' related to that office on 25 July,[109] at the very stage he and King Richard required control of the seas. Tight control of maritime activities at this time seems to be further supported by the surviving records of the Hanseatic League.[110]

It may also be important to note that Robert Langton was made Petty Customs Officer for the Port of London on 24 July 1483.[111] Robert was the brother of Thomas Langton, Bishop of St David's (Bishop of Salisbury in February 1485 and supporter of Richard III and Richard of England). It was Thomas who knew the 'secrets' of King Richard's heart.[112] Robert was also a long-standing associate of George Neville, who had close connections to John Howard,[113] and also seems to have been associated with Howard himself.[114]

Moreover, on 25 July 1483 Sir Edward Brampton, another leading Yorkist seafarer knighted by King Richard, was awarded the quite staggering sum of £350 on the same day that Howard was made admiral (equivalent to over £320,000 today). This award was without explanation.[115]

In 1481, during the Scottish campaign, Howard and Brampton had served together in the English fleet.[116] Here we see two men, both loyal Yorkists, who knew and trusted each other (and were trusted by the Yorkist kings), who were ship owners and knew the seas and ports. Was Howard relied upon to carry the younger boy to safety on one of his vessels, and Brampton, the elder boy on one of his? Current evidence suggests this may have been the case.

Further investigation has also revealed the potential involvement of a third individual. Christopher Colyns, a merchant and citizen of London, was a Gentleman Usher to Edward IV and a mourner at the king's funeral along with John Howard. Colyns was also a ship owner and master, a business associate of Howard's and a local agent in the Thames Estuary for both Edward IV and Richard III (Edward had been particularly involved in mercantile trade). He would also be tasked by King Richard to patrol the seas, outfit ships and men for war, ensure payments reached key English fortresses across the Channel in France, control a strategic fortress in Kent at Queenborough Castle (with the help of his brother), and command significant numbers of men.

Of particular interest is an annuity of £100 granted to Colyns by Richard on 20 August 1484, which was to last for twenty years (from Easter 1485). This was payment for services yet to be provided by Colyns according to indenture. It was a substantial sum, and for a prolonged period of time. However, the services in question were not specified. Remarkably, an identical indenture was granted to Brampton on the same day (20 August 1484).[117]

Cecil Roth makes a similar mention of this peculiar grant. He writes:

But the next grant was the most surprising of all. In consideration of 'services to be rendered according to certain indentures' he (i.e. Brampton) and another person named Christopher Colyns were each awarded an annuity of the then very considerable sum of £100 a year for twenty years. What those mysterious services were which Richard did not wish to make public, but for which he was willing to pay so dearly, must remain a matter of conjecture.[118]

It is highly probable that Colyns, like Brampton and Howard, had significant contacts in France and the Low Countries. Do these simultaneous indentures indicate the potential involvement of Colyns and Brampton in the transport of the princes, or at least some knowledge, given that their ships and captains were used? Like Howard and Brampton, the ports of London and the continent would have been well known to Colyns.

It also appears that Colyns, with Howard and Brampton, conducted an operation against pirates and rebels in mid-May 1483. This was ordered by the King's Council (under the advice of Richard, Duke of Gloucester, as Protector and Admiral) to apprehend the English fleet after it had been taken to sea by Sir Edward Woodville. It seems that these three men – Howard, Colyns and Brampton – must have known (and trusted) each other, and were similarly relied upon by Richard, as duke and king.[119]

Further Thoughts: 2. Implications for Other Key Individuals

The Gelderland manuscript also seems to explain several hitherto inexplicable events, not least the actions of the princes' mother, Elizabeth Woodville: first, in allowing her daughters to come out of sanctuary under King Richard's protection in March 1484, and second, requesting her son, Dorset (in France with Henry Tudor), to return to England and make his peace with Richard. And finally, following King Richard's death, Elizabeth apparently supported the uprising on behalf of Lambert Simnel, an impostor purporting to be the son of her former enemy, the Duke of Clarence (though Henry VII invented a different cover story). For this, her lands, possessions and jointures were removed, and she lived in poverty in Bermondsey Abbey (see Chapter 16).

It may also explain the imprisonment of two noblemen during the early reign of King Henry. First, the princes' half-brother, Dorset, who was incarcerated for what may have been over two years in the Tower of London at the time of King Edward's emergence. Second, the uniquely long captivity of John Howard's son and heir, Thomas Howard, confined in the Tower (and Queenborough Castle in Kent) following King Richard's death. Howard would remain a prisoner for over three years, released only upon an oath of loyalty to the new regime. Howard would be denied his inheritances, with the dukedom of Norfolk only restored to him twenty-eight years later by King Henry's son (Henry VIII) following the Battle of Flodden in 1513. The bafflement of the Howard family over Tudor stories about King Richard would be relayed in the years that followed,[120] leading to Sir George Buc's seminal *History of King Richard the Third* (1619), written after the demise of the Tudor dynasty when it was safe to openly question their version of events.[121]

Furthermore, these extraordinary discoveries shed light on King Richard's public declaration of innocence in the alleged murder of his nephews. The declaration was recorded at the time of Richard's Parliament (23 January to 20 February 1484), the sincerity of which almost certainly explains Elizabeth Woodville's decision on 1 March 1484 to place her daughters in his care. The declaration is recorded by Raphael Holinshed, who, despite his Tudor take on the event, informs us that the people accepted King Richard's declaration. Holinshed records, 'For what with purging and declaring his innocence concerning the murder of his nephews toward the world, and what with cost to obtain the love and favour of the communality (which outwardly glossed, and openly dissembled with him) ...'[122]

This may also explain a unique surviving record from the King's Signet Office at this time in a letter of recommendation for the king's close confidant and counsellor, Thomas Langton, Bishop of St David's. On 10 March 1484, King Richard wrote to Pope Sixtus IV (d. 12 August 1484):

> We send in person to your holiness the venerable father in Christ the lord Thomas bishop of St Davids our very dear and faithful counsellor and spokesman who knows the secrets of our heart. We have committed to him certain matters to be explained to your holiness and we humbly ask and beg that with your customary goodwill to us and our kingdom you will listen with ready and willing ears.[123]

The following day, Richard wrote to Charles VIII of France in a similar letter of recommendation for Langton, 'He will explain to your majesty in our name certain matters concerning us'.[124]

In view of this, Thomas Langton's remarkable presence in Malines in 1486 (most likely accompanied by Margaret of York) is worth mentioning,[125] particularly given his strong Yorkist sympathies and subsequent involvement in the second Yorkist conspiracy (1492–97) in favour of the second son of King Edward IV, Richard, Duke of York. During this period, Langton took an active part in the Yorkist 'Kendal Cell' in England.[126]

The project's discoveries explain Henry Tudor's post-Bosworth delay in the north of England, searching for news of King Edward's children and taking those he could locate into his immediate care and custody (see Chapter 10). On arrival in London, Henry issued a notable proclamation, which was delivered 'everywhere' in the capital and surrounding areas, 'that if there were a claimant to the crown by descent from the King Edward. He was to show himself; and he [Henry] would help him to get crowned; but no soul appeared.'[127]

It seems that Henry may have suspected that Francis Lovell was involved in the removal of the princes. Remarkably, within a year of Bosworth, King Henry ensured that one of his key enforcers, Simon Digby, was awarded the office of Steward of the Lordship of Bedale for life.[128] It's also possible that by 1494, Henry was in receipt of a copy of Richard of York's detailed narrative.

Significantly, in the spring of that year, Henry paid for an 'inquisition and investigation' at Middleham and Sheriff Hutton.[129] Certainly, by the time of Richard of England's proclamation from Scotland and subsequent invasion of England in the autumn of 1496, Digby and the heirs of his body were, 'for diverse considerations', granted for life the 20 marks annual rent of the Lordship of Bedale.[130] Digby, now Lieutenant of the Tower of London, was King Henry's key man in the capture, imprisonment and execution of the followers of Richard, Duke of York.[131] Richard himself, thanks to Digby's efforts, would be entrapped, beaten and kept in shackles and chains within the Tower, eventually to suffer execution along with his young Yorkist cousin, Edward, Earl of Warwick.[132]

In December 1497, Bedale was awarded to Digby's younger brother, Sir John Digby.[133] The payment required by Henry VII amounted to a knight's fee and a red rose. In 1542, following the death of both Digby brothers, Simon's grandson was awarded Bedale in a family covenant.[134] The covenant stated that Bedale had come into Henry VII's hands 'by forfeiture, treason of Sir Francis Lovell, Viscount Lovell'. The payment required by Henry was restated as a knight's fee and a single red rose. It also stated that the red rose rent was to be paid annually at the feast of the Nativity of John the Baptist. Was this date a cryptic reference to the recent capture (and eventual torture and execution) of Richard of England? Or was it simply an appreciation of the Digby family's allegiance to the Lancastrian cause; a cause in which the Battle of Towton had claimed the life of Simon Digby's father and three of his uncles.[135] Was Digby's entrapment and execution of Richard of England a thirty-eight-year payback for Towton? Perhaps it was both. Unlike his younger brother, Simon Digby never received the honour of knighthood.[136]

That Simon Digby was awarded Bedale, the manor of Francis Lovell and home of the Peirse family, reveals Henry VII's suspicions, and likely intelligence, of Lovell's involvement in the removal of the princes. By the time of Thomas Peirse's return to Bedale and the publication of Richard of England's account as the son of Edward IV and rightful king, Henry VII needed the services of a man who not only had powerful scores to settle, but little or no compunction in carrying them out. The Tudor and Elizabethan eras would see the Digby family rise to great wealth and prominence, despite the execution in 1570 of Sir John Digby's grandson, Simon Digby, Lord of Bedale, for his role in the Rising of the North against the last Tudor monarch, Elizabeth I.[137]

Conclusion

Tudor destruction of documents relating to the reign of Richard III, including the emptying of King Richard's *Baga de Secretis*, means we have to search in those places now left to us in order to uncover the truth. Document destruction and Henry VII's anti-Ricardian propaganda are perhaps the clearest indications of what Henry and his close adherents wished to conceal. By the time of the Lambert Simnel uprising, a great many at Henry's court believed the king's version of events. However, by the time Perkin Warbeck arrived, Henry's Yorkist servants and nobles no longer believed the official account en masse, and many died for it.[138]

Fortunately, the Gelderland Archive in the Netherlands proved to be one of those repositories still containing new evidence with which to support an alternative narrative. The manuscript rediscovered there in 2020 is unique and without precedent.

This authentic document, dated *c.* 1493, gives new, previously unknown and detailed information about the disappearance from the Tower of London in 1483 of the Duke of York (and his brother Edward V), together with further information concerning the young duke's wanderings on the continent in the years that followed.

A correlation of John Howard's actions with the chronology of events and information given in the Gelderland manuscript reveals an extraordinary sequence of events. However, perhaps most striking is the fact that Richard, Duke of York, in allowing this report to be recorded, with (verifiable) names and whereabouts, took the most enormous risk. In 1493, he officially stepped forward as the second son of King Edward IV and heir to the English throne, supported and recognised by the powerful Habsburg-Burgundy dynasty. If, at that moment, the information provided by him turned out to be incorrect, he would have placed his entire credibility at immediate risk before the whole expedition concerning the attainment of his English kingship had begun. It is therefore the case that he dared disseminate this detailed information at the time because he knew it was true and verifiable. (For Margaret of York, see Chapter 17.)

Another important factor is the recent discovery of the Lille Receipt, revealing that Edward V, the eldest son of King Edward IV, was alive in 1487,[139] significantly increasing the probability that his younger brother Richard had also survived and from 1493 onwards attempted to regain his right to the English throne.

It also strongly suggests the role of Francis Lovell in recommending Henry and Thomas Peirse as guardians to the young prince. Lovell's involvement post-Bosworth in the rebellion inspired by the crowning of King Edward in Ireland further strengthens the case for the survival of the elder prince, for whom both Lovell and Lincoln fought; the latter, though heir presumptive to Richard III, preferring to die on the field of battle for the Yorkist king.

It follows, therefore, that the rediscovery of the Gelderland manuscript is of unique historical importance. It supports the alternative story that both sons of King Edward IV were taken from the Tower and sent abroad into safety and hiding. It also provides many exciting new leads in the continuing search for further supporting evidence, particularly on the continent.

15

The Journey of the White Rose

To the Island of Texel, April–July 1495[1]
by Nathalie Nijman-Bliekendaal and Jean Roefstra

Introduction

On 3 July 1495, soldiers and captains of the Yorkist claimant to the throne, Richard, Duke of York, who had proclaimed himself 'King Richard (IV) of England' earlier that year,[2] set foot in England. The men were part of a fleet which York, with the support and assistance of the Habsburg-Burgundian princes, had amassed in the Low Countries in the preceding months. The 'new young king' had only one goal in mind: to reclaim the English throne which rightfully belonged to him as the son and heir of Edward IV.

Various sources describe this failed Yorkist invasion, which took place near the coastal town of Deal in Kent.[3] However, the exact place from which Richard's fleet left the continent was unknown, or at least uncertain.

In the extant chronicles and literature, the place of departure has always been unspecified, but some modern authors suggest the fleet departed from the county of Zeeland.[4] A logical conjecture, since some contemporary sources pointed towards Zeeland, which was close to the Habsburg-Burgundian centre of power at Malines.[5] Moreover, the crossing to the east coast of England from the ports in Zeeland was a relatively short one. There was also a precedent: on two previous occasions Yorkist military expeditions had set sail from Zeeland with the aim of conquering England – Edward IV in 1471 and Edward V in 1487.[6]

Despite this, our analysis reveals that the Duke of York, or 'The White Rose', as he was known (referring to his descent from the royal House of York), did not depart from Zeeland or Flanders but from the remote Dutch island of Texel. This followed a stay of two months or more in the far north of the County of Holland.

The *Divisie Chronicle* of Cornelius Aurelius (1460–1531)

Both English and Dutch historiographers[7] seem to have overlooked an important near-contemporary source illuminating the Yorkist expedition of 1495: the *Divisie Chronicle* of the Dutch chronicler Cornelius Aurelius.[8] Published in 1517, but probably written around 1500, it is considered the most important and reliable late medieval chronicle of the Low Countries. Aurelius describes in detail York's journey through the County of Holland during the months of April, May and June 1495, on his way to its northernmost point, the island of Texel.[9]

The relevant text reads:

In the year 1495 on Monday after the octave of Easter late in the evening, has arrived in the Town of Haarlem Richard [*sic Ritzaert*], the son of King Edward, who is called 'The White Rose' [*die Witte Rose*]. There he stayed for a while with the Knights of the Order of St John to wait for his people and other military equipment, because he wanted to go to England to claim the Throne and his inheritance ... From here [i.e. Haarlem] after the 8th of June in the early morning, this Richard, the White Rose, went – with all his people – to the village and cloister of Egmont. And from there to the island of Texel. But most of his men/ships were passing from the outside along the sea [coast] to Texel and were already there waiting for him and preparing all necessary things they needed for their journey. And on the first day of July with a lucky wind they sailed to Ireland, because he could not or dare not come to England.

The Zeeland chronicler, Jan van Reijgersbergh, also records in his *Dije Cronijcke van Zeelandt* that Richard, 'who was called The White Rose', travelled via Holland to England in the year 1495.[10]

What Preceded Richard's Journey Through Holland?

In mid-January 1495, the Duke of York must have been informed of the apparent treachery of a key supporter and confidant, Sir Robert Clifford.[11] At that time, York was in the Brabant town of Bergen op Zoom (with Duke Albert of Saxony).[12] It seems likely that the first rumours of the betrayal arrived here, since Bergen op Zoom had close trade contacts and rapid communication lines with England. Clifford appeared to have given Henry VII the names of York's supporters among the English nobility. These alarming reports from England must have come as a great shock and provided a considerable setback to the Yorkists' invasion plans.

A second major setback followed about a month later. Henry VII had captured and executed many high-ranking nobles and secret supporters of York, thus depriving Edward IV's son of crucial support and potential help in England prior to his invasion. Among them were Sir Simon Montford, John Radcliffe, Lord Fitzwalter, Henry VII's Steward of his Household and Sir William Stanley, Henry VII's Chamberlain.[13]

If we are to believe the reports of the Milanese ambassadors and envoys in Flanders, made shortly after these dramatic events, it seems that the initial plan to invade England was put on hold and York shifted his focus to Ireland. Their reports show King Maximilian (who was in the Netherlands at the time) had said, 'Duke Richard now wants to go to Ireland, where he has valuable connections ... and where he is recognized as a ruler.'[14]

Other diplomatic correspondence from the Milanese ambassadors dating to the end of February 1495 shows that York – according to King Maximilian – had actually left, probably shortly before or around 1 March 1495.[15]

There may have been several reasons for York's sudden decision to turn to Ireland. One of these is likely to have been to secure the support of the Irish nobility after the disastrous events in England following Clifford's betrayal. However, no convincing evidence has been found to support that York travelled to Ireland in the first weeks of March, or that he had made a serious attempt to do so. By mid-March 1495, Maximilian reported that 'the son of the king of England had built up a strong army to go to England'.[16]

Despite the devastating blow in England, it had apparently been decided to go ahead with the planned invasion. Serious efforts were now made to ready the expedition, raising funds and buying ships, recruiting soldiers and arranging supplies,[17] all of which had been led by experienced military commanders such as Albert of Saxony, Rodrigue de Lalaing and a Spaniard by the name of Quintinck.[18]

The Burgundian chronicler Jean Molinet described these preparations:

Notwithstanding the executions by the king of those who adhered to him [York], ... with the help of his friends he [York] provided the ships, men, provisions and other artifacts. He expected to conquer England because of the great confidence he had in his followers and friends who provided him with help and large grants.[19]

Albert of Saxony, Governor General of the Netherlands, was one of those friends. He was Maximilian's most experienced military commander and strategist in the Low Countries, who had played a key role in organising and financing the expedition.

Initially, York's fleet seems to have assembled in Zeeland, probably with the intention of departing from there to England.[20] However, in the first week of April, a further serious and unexpected problem seems to have prevented the fleet sailing for England. In a reply to Albert of Saxony, written at Worms on 10 April 1495, Maximilian writes, 'We have understood your dear letter and we understand that something has occurred which prevented York's departure.'[21]

That there was indeed an unexpected setback is evident in a letter written by Georg von Ebenstein on 6 April 1495.[22] Here we find Margaret of York at the heart of events. Referring to her as 'the old lady', Ebenstein vividly described her reaction when she heard about the problems besetting her nephew's expedition. He wrote, 'She was sad, and she complained that "Von Jurick" [the Duke of York] as a result was deprived of his kingdom and that he had relied on it.'

What exactly had gone wrong is not made clear. Difficulties raising finance or recruiting sufficient soldiers (who apparently deserted en masse because of payment problems) could have led to the postponement or cancellation of the operation. Yet there may have been a more obvious reason.

On 4 April 1495, the Duke of Saxony was warned about 'the landing of the English in Zeeland'.[23] It seems that Henry VII, through his spy network, had received information about the forthcoming invasion and as a precaution (or a deterrent to intimidate) had despatched English ships.

It is not clear whether the English vessels entered Zeeland waters and engaged the Yorkist fleet. If an action did take place, it was an unforeseen intervention on the part of the English king. Presumably, as a result, Yorkist plans were now altered. This was probably on the advice of Albert of Saxony, with the aim of re-evaluating the local situation and devising an alternative plan in consultation with York.

Following Albert's advice, it was decided to leave Zeeland (on the western coast) and travel by land to the north of Holland. Albert was familiar with this part of the Burgundian Netherlands. He had been based in the Kennemerland region in the north of Holland for an extended period during the Bread and Cheese Revolt of 1492.[24] Remarkably, Albert's active involvement in York's cause seems to have been ignored in existing literature, as well as his personal ties with the young Yorkist claimant.

From York's arrival at Margaret's court in Malines in 1493, the Duke of Saxony and the Duke of York were often in each other's company.[25] Albert seems to have been an important mainstay for Richard. His personal involvement can be seen, for example, in a postscript to the previously mentioned letter from the Burgundian Captain Georg von Ebenstein, 'a servant of York had said that … he [Albert of Saxony] would [much] rather march to England' (instead of Friesland). From this, it can be established that the Duke of Saxony, who had to divide his attention between several wars, had preferred an invasion of England (with York).[26]

The Journey of the White Rose Through Holland in April, May and June 1495

Entries in the 1495 Account Books of the *Grafelijkheidsrekenkamer* of Holland (County Court of Auditors, Dutch National Archive) confirm the narrative set out in the *Divisie Chronicle*, that the 'White Rose' began his journey to the northern part of Holland in mid-April 1495.

The Messenger Expenditure Accounts reveal that around mid-April 1495 various messengers were despatched to several Dutch cities, including Dordrecht, Rotterdam and Leiden. The messengers were carrying letters from the Stadtholder (Steward) of Holland, Jan III of Egmont, in which he requested the cities 'to receive the Duke of York kindly and to show him their friendship, so that when he arrives in his realm, they shall be treated in the same manner'.[27]

At this remove, it is not possible to determine exactly when and from where York left the south of the Netherlands, but he will have departed Zeeland around mid-April.

Haarlem (27 April 1495–8 June 1495)

According to Aurelius, the Duke of York arrived in the city of Haarlem, in the north of Holland, 'in the year 1495, after the octave of Easter' (Monday, 27 April).[28] York had been allowed to lodge in the Commandery of St John in Haarlem for over a month, once again indicating the involvement of Albert of Saxony.

Albert's servant and confidant, Jacob van Barry was the Town Clerk of Haarlem.[29] In this position, Van Barry exercised considerable influence in the City Council. Only with the consent (and at the expense) of the City Council would high-ranking guests have been allowed to stay in the 'Count's Room' at St John's.[30]

Entries in the 1495 Account Book further reveal that York continued to make all necessary preparations in the north of Holland. On 27 May (by order of an official of the heir, Archduke Philip the Handsome), a messenger from the court of Holland was sent from The Hague to Amsterdam to discover whether the ships York had purchased had been delivered to him.[31] A few days later, on 5 June, another messenger was sent to Amsterdam bearing letters from the archduke himself, likely to exert more pressure. The writer also enquired whether the ships that the duke bought had been delivered to him.[32]

At Maximilian's request, Margaret of York had supplied the necessary provisions.[33] These appear in the accounts of Margaret's domain, Voorne. At the beginning of May 1495, Margaret had personally ordered 1,484 tons of beer, brewed and collected in the city of Delft (near The Hague), 'for My Lord, the Duke of York, her nephew'.[34]

Beverwijk (7 June 1495)

On 7 June 1495, York was in Beverwijk.[35] Beverwijk was a small market town about 6 miles north of Haarlem. Since the twelfth century, it had had its own port on the Wijkermeer, with an open connection to the Dutch South Sea (Zuiderzee).[36] Because of a narrow coastal strip, Beverwijk had no open connection with the North Sea. It was therefore protected against any naval attack coming that way. Via the Zuiderzee (past the island of Texel), the North Sea was easily accessible from Beverwijk. Given its strategic proximity to Haarlem, it is probable that the town served as a mustering centre for York's troops, artillery and ships. This assumption is supported by a letter from the Stadtholder and Council of Holland addressed to the Duke of York, 'present there at Beverwijk', with a request to embark and ensure that his servants (men) will not cause any damage to the country.[37]

Egmond Abbey

The following day, York left Haarlem. After visiting the famous Egmond Abbey, the young claimant to the English throne travelled north to the island of Texel.

The Abbey of St Adelbertus in Egmond, founded in the second half of the tenth century, was the oldest abbey in Holland and an important site of pilgrimage.[38] The abbey held the relics of two important Anglo-Saxon saints, St Adelbert and St Jerome of Noordwijk. According to tradition, Adelbert was the son of an English king who renounced his rights and went to Holland as a missionary. The same was true, albeit to a lesser extent, of St Jerome of Noordwijk, who was a son of Anglo-Saxon (Scottish) nobles.[39] Since both saints were of Anglo-Saxon (royal) descent, Prince Richard, Duke of York, would have seen and venerated the holy relics in the abbey and prayed for good fortune.

It is worth mentioning that his father, Edward IV, had venerated the same relics at Egmond Abbey, twenty-five years before, in 1470, when he was on his way south from Texel to Flanders. Shortly before, the exiled monarch had landed, destitute, on the island of Texel following a hasty flight from England. Aurelius, in his *Divisie Chronicle*, noted:

> when the lord of Gruythusen heard this [the arrival on Texel], he ... went to the king [Edward IV] and brought him to Egmont to see the holy relics of Saint Adelbert and others who were born in England.[40]

It turned out that the English king was indeed blessed with good fortune. Five months later, he recovered his crown with a fleet of thirty-six ships amassed in the Burgundian Netherlands.

Texel

Following his visit to the abbey, York travelled to Texel with his supporters.

At the beginning of May, Maximilian had declared publicly that he was 'no longer involved in any way with the ruler of York'.[41] He appears, however, to have had more heart for York's cause than he wished to divulge.

The evidence is contained in a letter written by Maximilian on 17 June 1495 in which he urged his son, the Archduke Philip the Handsome, 'to deliver my lord York 4 pieces of artillery for his intended journey'.[42]

Another entry in the 1495 Account Book of the County Court of Auditors of Holland clearly shows the involvement of King Maximilian shortly before York's departure from Texel. A messenger was sent from The Hague to the island of Texel carrying several 'private' letters from 'der KM' (King Maximilian). The letters, which discussed secret matters, were destined for the Duke of York ('lying on the island of Texel, with the intention of invading England') and were presented by the messenger personally 'into his hands'.[43]

According to Aurelius, most of the ships and men had been waiting for some time at Texel for 'The White Rose' to appear. The invasion fleet must have anchored on the 'Reede van Texel' on the south-east side of the island, where it will have waited for a favourable wind.[44] The choice of Texel as a safe haven seems well considered. Again, the servant of the Saxon duke, Jacob van Barry is present. Van Barry was made Clerk of Texel for life in 1492 as a gift from Albert of Saxony and therefore had significant administrative influence on the island.[45] Furthermore, the 'Reede' was quite isolated from the North Sea and access to the Marsdiep (a waterway between the island of Texel and north of Holland) was very difficult and potentially treacherous for inexperienced captains coming from the west (from the North Sea).

Notes compiled in later years by the English Captain John Aborough, sent by Henry VIII to explore the entrance to the sea channel near Texel, highlights the dangers:

> On the seaward side of this [land] point and the island [Texel] lie the Haaksgronden, which consist of particularly dangerous sandbanks and extend into the sea 6 or 7 miles westwards.[46]

Compared to the open waters of Zeeland, the Duke of York's ships were protected by this natural barrier from hostile English ships.

It is not known how many ships 'The White Rose' gathered at Texel. What is certain is that York, his captains and crews, did not have to wait long for a favourable wind. On 1 July 1495, the sails were set, and one by one the ships sailed into the North Sea, eventually arriving off Deal two days later.

Postscript

The extensive narrative provided by Aurelius in the *Divisie Chronicle* describing the journey of 'The White Rose of York' through Holland proves to be surprisingly accurate. Its detail is corroborated by the contents of various Messenger Expenditure Accounts included in the 1495 Account Book of the County Court of Auditors of Holland.

The route north taken by York and his followers can be reconstructed.[47] Extensive research has been undertaken in the archives of Dutch cities along the route. However, many city archives from 1495 have been lost (sold, or destroyed by fire and acts of war, etc.). Other potentially interesting local sources, including the archives of the Abbey of Egmond, the Commandery of St John in Haarlem and various local chronicles, have also been investigated in the hope to gain further insight into the activities of York and his supporters. Further research is ongoing.[48]

As the safety of a successful crossing from Zeeland could no longer be guaranteed, it can be assumed that on the advice of Albert of Saxony, a more remote and secure place was chosen as the mustering point for the army and fleet for the Yorkist royal heir. That Maximilian entrusted the organisation of the expedition to his most important military commander, Albert of Saxony, demonstrates that he was committed to the invasion plans of 'the young king of England', as he called him, and that he wanted them to succeed.

One might argue that the movement of troops to the north of Holland had a minimal impact on the expedition and the subsequent invasion of England and is therefore of little historical value. While this may be so, the results of this investigation are nevertheless concerned with a larger truth. Until now, the story of Richard, Duke of York, has relied on the interpretation of fragmentary and biased evidence. For the first time in the historiography of this son of York, an extensive and hitherto unnoticed[49] passage in a chronicle has been confirmed by objective primary source research in the Dutch National Archive. Consequently, a reliable reconstruction of the past can now be made.

From this, it may be concluded that the events surrounding the Yorkist invasion of 1495 were not handed down in history as they actually happened. The importance of a continuing search for new and neglected primary source material is thus vindicated as the only means to prevent the acceptance and repetition of non-substantiated narratives.

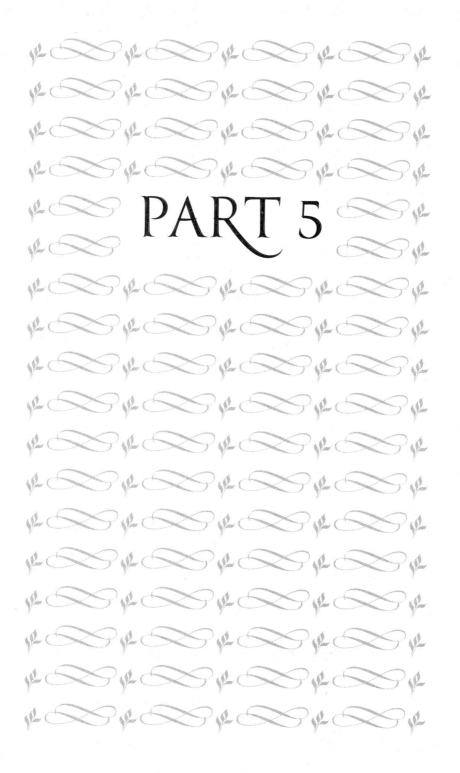

PART 5

16

The Family of Edward V and Richard, Duke of York

As in any police cold-case enquiry, it is important to investigate the actions of those closest to the missing individuals to help shed light on what was going on behind closed doors. The creation of detailed timelines allows us to travel back in time and identify potentially crucial information. Simply put, individual behaviour is the clearest indication of what people believed and (potentially) knew. It is valuable, therefore, to consider the conduct of the immediate family, both as individuals and as a collective family unit.

The Death of Edward IV

There are signs that suggest co-ordinated activity in the weeks immediately preceding and following Edward IV's unexpected death on 3 April 1483, which it had been decided to conceal for nearly a week until Lord Howard arrived in the capital.

King Edward had already handed an inordinate amount of collective power to the queen's Woodville family, whom the contemporary writer Domenico Mancini portrayed as greedy and grasping.[1] Historical biographer Annette Carson records early moves just weeks before the king's death:

While the entire Court and council were caught unawares by Edward's death, this individual had taken all the right steps, at least three weeks before Easter, to ensure his personal position was legally watertight and that machinery was in place for defensive or offensive action if circumstances demanded. This person was the queen's brother Anthony, Earl Rivers.[2]

In February 1483, the king had revised his ordinances for the governance of the Prince of Wales at his base in Ludlow, doubtless framed in conjunction with Rivers. Among new provisions, the queen's younger son, Sir Richard Grey, was added to the personnel who had control of the prince and access to his treasury: in effect, 'nothing was to be done by the prince' without the advice of Rivers, Grey and the prince's tutor, Bishop John Alcock. This afforded a 'virtual monopoly' on the young prince's actions.

It has been argued that Rivers, who had held the leading role of the prince's governor for the past ten years, exploited his authority to obtain (sometimes illegally) extensive powers in Wales and on the English border. He was the foremost nobleman in Wales and the Marches.[3] His nephew, Richard Grey, the prince's half-brother, had already made strides in the same direction: in January, he received the Duchy of Lancaster Lordships of Kidwelly and Iscennen in Wales, doubling his income overnight. Grey was now the 'prince's most active henchman'.[4]

Less than a month before Edward IV's death, on Saturday, 8 March, Rivers wrote to his London agent, Andrew Dymmock, requiring copies of the letters patent that granted him the governorship of the prince, the control of moving him from place to place, and the right to raise troops on his behalf. Yet Rivers had only recently attended Parliament at Westminster and could have requested the desired copies at that time.

In the same letter, Rivers issued a further instruction, handing his authority as Deputy Constable of the Tower of London to his nephew, Thomas, Marquess of Dorset, the Prince of Wales' other half-brother. For a Deputy Constable to reassign his office unilaterally would have been quite irregular,[5] especially since Dorset had wielded nothing approaching such authority in any previous appointment. Possession of the Tower was a vital element if one needed to control the capital and government, being not only London's royal palace but also home to the Treasury, Mint, Armoury and Garrison.

Analysis of Rivers' movements at the time of the king's death strongly suggests he was on his Norfolk estates when he heard the news (see Chapter 3), and that he proceeded to London, where he received the queen's instructions before travelling to Ludlow to inform the young King Edward V of his father's demise.

Meanwhile, the queen and her circle had seized the reins of power by swaying members of the Council in London to act precipitately before the royal dukes (Gloucester and Buckingham) and other senior nobility had time to arrive. Taxes were levied, a hasty coronation arranged for 4 May, and Dorset, as Deputy Constable of the Tower, shared what remained of state funds with his mother's youngest brother, Sir Edward Woodville, to man and equip a sea-going fleet.

Dorset would remain in London, while Woodville, despite orders by the Council to return to port, instead took two vessels (and a vast amount of gold) to the Tudor camp in Brittany. Though he supported Henry Tudor's bid for the crown, their relationship eventually soured, and he did not attend the coronation of his niece, Elizabeth of York.[6]

Referring to decisions taken by the queen's party after Edward IV's death, Mancini writes that Dorset declared, 'We are so important that even without the king's uncle [Gloucester] we can make and enforce these decisions'.[7] As historian Stephen David observes, this bold claim:

> … was not the empty boastfulness it has sometimes been portrayed but a confident assessment based on their experience of ruling Wales and the Marches since 1473 and an assured recognition that in April 1483, they now also controlled the future.[8]

Rivers, using powers to recruit his escort and control his every move, made haste to bring the new king to London in time for the coronation. There followed the events in Northamptonshire (described in Chapter 3), which resulted in various leaders of the king's escort being arrested and imprisoned. The armorial devices on their confiscated weaponry, says Mancini, displayed those of the queen's sons, Dorset and Grey.[9] This again indicates prior preparations, thanks to Dorset making full use of his access to arms and men at the Tower of London.

Frustrated in trying to raise an army at Westminster to seize the king, the remaining Woodville family fled into sanctuary. Their impetuous April coup, followed by flight without any attempt at reconciliation, seems inexplicable unless prompted by their likely concern that King Edward's secret marriage to Lady Eleanor Talbot might be revealed before they had entrenched their position.

Eight weeks later, with the queen's family further implicated in unrest against the government, the writing was on the wall for the imprisoned Rivers and Grey. On Wednesday, 25 June, they were put on trial at Pontefract Castle with Henry Percy, Earl of Northumberland acting as 'their chief judge'.[10] Mancini gives the prevailing view in the capital that their execution was to be effected judicially 'by certain quaestors [prosecutors]'.[11] Sir Richard Ratcliffe, Gloucester's close adherent, had earlier been sent to Pontefract, probably bearing materials relevant to the impending trial.

The New Discoveries

Following the discovery of new evidence supporting the survival of Edward V and Richard of York post-Bosworth, an important new line of enquiry has emerged. We need to examine the actions of the immediate family during the reigns of Richard III and Henry VII in case new insights are revealed concerning the princes' later lives.

Thomas Grey, Marquess of Dorset (1455–1501): Maternal Half-Brother
As the adult half-brother of the princes, Dorset is a significant person of interest. Following Gloucester's seizure of Edward V at Stony Stratford, Dorset took sanctuary at Cheneygates Mansion, in Westminster, with his mother, half-sisters and uncle Lionel. He later absconded, and by 2 February 1485 was in Bruges, Burgundy. Here Dorset sent several messages via the herald, Roger Machado, to the town of Laon in northern France and to his great-uncle, Jacques de Luxembourg, at Porsnay Castle.[12] By Christmas or early 1485, Dorset had received a letter from his mother telling him to return to England and, like her, make his peace with King Richard.[13] At this time, Dorset was in France with the pretender, Henry Tudor. Dorset deserted Tudor but was captured at Compiègne, en route for Flanders.[14]

When Henry Tudor invaded England in early August 1485, he left Dorset in prison in Paris as surety for his loan from the French king. Although not summoned to Henry VII's first Parliament, a petition was raised on Dorset's behalf in its second session (23 January–23 March 1486).[15]

By Whit Sunday, 14 May, Dorset had been allowed to return.[16] He received a commission, several land grants and, in September 1486, attended the christening of Prince Arthur, King Henry's heir.

Later, while rumours circulated of a Yorkist claimant in Ireland, hailed as 'King Edward', Dorset attended Henry's Council at Sheen (around 2 February–3 March 1487).[17] Here, his mother was deprived of her income and possessions.

A few weeks later, in mid-March, King Henry made an urgent journey to the de la Pole and Howard family territories in East Anglia.[18] On his way to join the king, Dorset was arrested in Suffolk, near Bury St Edmunds, and imprisoned in the Tower of London on suspicion of complicity in a new Yorkist plot.[19] It is not known if Dorset helped finance the 1487 invasion.

In early June, King Edward V's invading army marched unopposed past Gleaston Castle, on the north-west coast, which belonged to Dorset's mother-in-law, Katherine Bonville (née Neville, niece of Cecily, Duchess of York).[20] On 16 June, King Edward was defeated and possibly injured or killed. Five months later, on Sunday, 25 November 1487, Dorset's half-sister Elizabeth of York was crowned. Dorset's young son Thomas attended the coronation.[21]

By 21 November 1489, Dorset was released from the Tower.[22] His term of imprisonment spanned one year and four months to (potentially) two years and eight months.[23] By 11 February 1490, Dorset was described as the 'king's councillor'.[24] His incarceration may have affected him, as Vergil describes him as part of Henry's Council with men chosen for their 'prudence, faith and gravity'. He describes Dorset as 'a good and prudent man'.[25] This description is in sharp contrast to Mancini's boastful and arrogant young man of 1483.

Dorset was back in favour but by 22 May 1491, his loyalty to King Henry was again in question. Fifty-five individuals were 'mainprized' (stood surety) for Dorset's loyalty with pledges of very large sums of money. These included John Alcock, Bishop of Ely (£200); John Russell, Bishop of Lincoln (£100); Edward Grey, Viscount Lisle (£1,000); a Doctor Hanswell (£100); Sir Richard Haute (£100); Halneth Mauleverer (£100); and Robert Fabyan, draper (100 marks). These men, all associated with Dorset and Edward IV's sons, comprised merchants, suppliers and a brewer, and possibly even Dorset's own doctor. Moreover, one of those named was the Abbot of Bermondsey, the monastery where Dorset's mother, the former queen, now resided in poverty. The Abbot of Bermondsey was mainprized for £200.[26] By around November 1491, Richard, Duke of York, was welcomed in Ireland as the youngest son of Edward IV.[27]

By June 1492, Dorset, who should have realised he was under surveillance, had managed to displease Henry VII more seriously. To receive a pardon and regain favour, he was placed under an extortionate bond not only for good behaviour but also under compulsion to divulge any treasonous plans that came to his knowledge. In addition to a cash bond of £1,000, he had to yield his son's wardship to the king, find another group of guarantors willing to stand mainprize to the tune of £10,000, and see nearly all his estates forfeited if he reneged.

Having agreed to all this, he received his pardon – but it extended only to the date of his last mainprize, twelve months earlier, and did not extend to Calais, Guînes and Ireland, including Ireland's Treasurer.[28] If Henry wanted to keep Elizabeth Woodville's eldest son in check, he had comprehensively achieved his objective. Dorset was then named as a participant in King Henry's (half-hearted) French expedition of the same year.[29]

But why place Dorset under restraint now? By this time, Thomas Peirse had probably informed Dorset and his mother of Richard of York's survival and arrival in Ireland as the new Yorkist claimant. By 28 February 1493, John Grey, Viscount Lisle, was also bound to Henry VII for £1,000 as surety for Dorset's good behaviour.[30] This strongly suggests that Henry VII intended to deter support for Richard, Duke of York, by threatening suspects and their families with bankruptcy.

Four days after Dorset's restraint, on 8 June, Elizabeth Woodville died in poverty at Bermondsey Abbey.[31] Dorset attended her funeral Mass where he alone offered a piece of gold.[32]

Dorset's actions are the subject of continuing investigations (see Appendix 3). After his mother's death, he adopted the role of a model subject, taking his place on several commissions of the peace. His son, Thomas, was the first to be knighted on All Souls' Day (2 November 1494), when the king's second son, Prince Henry (age 3), was installed as a Knight Companion of the Bath and created Duke of York.[33] Thus, on Edward V's birthday, his brother Richard was stripped of his dukedom and Dorset's son was knighted in celebration.

It was a master class of message and manipulation by the first Tudor monarch. But these actions had little effect on the support being garnered by 'Richard IV' at home and abroad.

By 26 February 1495, Henry VII may have harboured lingering doubts and insecurities concerning Dorset's fealty or may have felt that extra insurance was required. Sir Thomas West, Lord de la Ware (8th Baron Warr, d. 1525), was now entered into a bond of 500 marks for life to ensure Dorset's loyalty.[34] By 26 August 1496, these precautions were augmented with the addition of ten individuals in Devon and Somerset mainprized for further large sums of money in guarantee of Dorset's continued 'allegiance'.[35]

At this time, Richard of England was in Scotland preparing an invasion with the assistance of James IV. Henry's policy towards Dorset seems to have worked. After Richard of England's capture in 1497, Dorset played little part in Henry's administration, receiving on 1 July 1497 tenements and lands in Calais following the death of his uncle, Richard Woodville (see below).[36]

Intriguingly, a few weeks before his death, Dorset had a private dinner with the new Yorkist claimant to the throne, Edmund de la Pole, Duke of Suffolk, just before Suffolk fled to the continent (see de la Pole family further on). Also present was William Courtenay, heir of the Earl of Devon, who showed the new Yorkist heir 'great reverence'.[37] Courtney was the husband of Dorset's half-sister, Katherine of York. Dorset's son was now arrested and imprisoned, first in the Tower and later in Calais.

Dorset died on 30 August 1501. Writs of *diem clausit extremum* were posted for his death on 2 September.[38] He was buried at the collegiate church of St Mary's, Astley, in Warwickshire.[39] His son escaped execution due to King Henry's death.[40] Cecily and Thomas were buried beside him.

Elizabeth Woodville (1437–92): Mother

Elizabeth Woodville, mother of the princes, is a significant person of interest for the enquiry. Her timeline reveals three events which require closer examination.

The first is her decision to take sanctuary at Cheneygates Mansion, Westminster, on 1 May 1483. What led the Queen Mother to take such an unprecedented step during a time of peace? As the young king's mother, Elizabeth could look forward to an honoured place at court and at his coronation together with all his relatives and siblings.

It has been suggested that Elizabeth feared for her life at the hands of Richard of Gloucester. Does this stand up to scrutiny?

The Yorkist kings had no record of executing their women, a practice later pursued under the Tudor dynasty. Elizabeth's flight to sanctuary could elicit sympathy and embarrass her son's government, but the overriding opinion among Londoners, who were aware of the reputation of the queen's relatives, seemed to support Gloucester's new role as Protector and his separation of the young king (at Stony Stratford) from their corrupting influence.

So, did Elizabeth fear some other form of personal attack or punishment? Was she aware of or implicated in plots against Gloucester's life at

Northampton and Stony Stratford? And did she fear the consequences of answering these allegations?

This seems unlikely, because Gloucester was already holding the relevant individuals who were under suspicion. Holding them in prison ought, potentially, to bring the family to its senses – and the negotiating table. Gloucester had taken the precaution of writing to the Council and Mayor of London that all was now well, and this had been generally accepted.

Did Elizabeth fear something else? Mancini offers an account of the death of George, Duke of Clarence in 1478, alleging a deadly feud involving the Woodvilles against Clarence, initiated by his objection to the queen's marriage to King Edward. Mancini tells us that Clarence was 'removed' at the instigation of the queen and that the Duke of Gloucester, 'his feelings moved by anguish for his brother ... was heard to say that one day he would avenge his brother's death. Thereafter he rarely went to court, but remained in his own province.'[41] That Clarence harboured a grudge is undoubtedly true, but we need to examine this accusation closely in relation to Gloucester.

It is important to note that Mancini had no personal experience of England in the 1460s–70s: as we have seen, his account was penned in France on 1 December 1483. The Franco-Italian cleric does not say how these stories of past resentments and overheard threats came to his ears, but he was writing after the October 1483 uprising against King Richard when several rebels fled to the continent.

Michael Hicks, Clarence's modern biographer, makes clear that the evidence of Mancini's text indicates that he knew none of the individuals he described.[42] Moreover, contemporary evidence suggests that Gloucester maintained normal relations with the queen and her Woodville family throughout Edward IV's reign. Furthermore, there is no evidence of tensions between the parties in areas 'where both were important landowners'.[43] To add to this, A.J. Pollard, a specialist in the north of England in the later fifteenth century, produced substantive materials to reveal that Gloucester 'remained *"persona grata"* at court throughout the last five years of his brother's reign, for he lent his name to every royal charter issued between February 1478 and January 1483'.[44]

Mancini (via his informants) goes further with his allegations about Elizabeth Woodville's motives. He tells us that the queen, mindful of accusations that:

> ... according to established custom she was not the legitimate wife of the king, deemed that never would her offspring by the king succeed to the

sovereignty unless the Duke of Clarence were removed; and of this she easily persuaded the king himself.[45]

Considering the events outlined in Chapter 3, which led to Edward V's precipitate coronation on 4 May, it is likely that Elizabeth Woodville (and some of her family) knew about the late king's prior secret marriage to Lady Eleanor Talbot. In this context, the Woodville family's arrangement of a hasty coronation to secure the succession without delay begins to make sense.[46] Once Edward V was crowned, he would have been anointed with the Holy Chrism and God would have entered his body. This religious ceremony was definitive in the eyes of the populace, and even more importantly, it formed a shield around the king and his inner circle. As a fait accompli, it was sufficient to deter any whistle-blower from questioning the king's legitimacy, and from their position of power they could dismiss or take punitive measures against anyone with the temerity to come forward.

The second important incident is Elizabeth's rapprochement with Richard III on 1 March 1484. This directly followed Parliament when the bastardy of Edward IV's children was enacted into law. At this time, King Richard entered into an agreement with Elizabeth in which her daughters were placed in his care (see Appendix 1). By late 1484 to early 1485, Elizabeth had written to Dorset telling him to desert Henry Tudor in France, return to England and make his peace with Richard. Dorset attempted to do so but was apprehended.

Following Richard's death and Henry's marriage to Elizabeth's eldest daughter (Elizabeth of York), Prince Arthur was born on 24 September 1486. Elizabeth Woodville was now grandmother of the future King of England, as well as his godmother.[47] Additionally, her children from her marriage to Edward IV were no longer officially bastards after the 1484 Act of Parliament had been repealed unread in Henry's first Parliament.

Elizabeth Woodville had achieved the highest status and recognition as Queen Elizabeth[48] and received an honoured place at the new Tudor court. Her bloodline on the English throne through Edward IV was secured.

The Rebel Queen

Given such a remarkable transformation in fortune, it is the third significant event in Elizabeth Woodville's timeline which confounds expectations. Around November 1486, rumours of a Yorkist claimant to Henry's throne began to surface: a youth hailed in Ireland as 'King Edward'. There was only one known King Edward (Edward V).

By 2 February 1487, Henry had convened a Council at Sheen Palace at Richmond, London. Here, 'King Edward' was said to be an impostor posing as the young Earl of Warwick – the real Warwick was incarcerated in the Tower of London. If true, this was an easily remedied situation. However, several events indicate otherwise.

First, the actions of Dorset and Lincoln, who were both present at the Council, but more significantly, the measures now decided against Elizabeth Woodville, who was deprived of her possessions and income and relocated to the Abbey of Bermondsey.[49] Vergil remarks that she now led a 'wretched life'.[50]

Elizabeth's jointure and income were awarded to the queen.[51] The reason provided by Henry VII's historian was that King Henry felt aggrieved that Elizabeth had come to terms with Richard III. As many historians have since commented, Henry's sudden remembrance three years after the event stretches credulity. Sir Francis Bacon would later report that she was confined for 'dark and unknown reasons' and that it was dangerous to visit or see her.[52]

Previously, and notably, on 10 July 1486, Elizabeth had taken out a forty-year lease on the Westminster sanctuary at Cheneygates Mansion.[53] She may have enjoyed living there, but the fact that her income was now removed (so she could no longer pay for it and thereby be resident should she require its rights of sanctuary) strongly suggests a retaliatory, or potentially pre-emptive, move on the part of the first Tudor monarch. Henry VII either had information that Elizabeth was using her income to support the king in Ireland, or he suspected the possibility.

Why Elizabeth would support a common 'lad'[54] posing as the son of her former enemy, the Duke of Clarence, thereby acting directly against her own interests and those of her daughter and grandson, was never explained. By contrast, if we consider that the youth in Ireland was indeed her eldest son, Edward V, and Elizabeth knew this, then both her and Henry's actions fall into place. In November 1487, Elizabeth Woodville did not attend her daughter's coronation.[55]

Following the defeat of King Edward and her daughter's subsequent coronation, it seems that Henry VII made some form of rapprochement with Elizabeth, perhaps at his new queen's behest. On 29 December 1487, 'Queen Elizabeth, late wife of Edward IV', was awarded 200 marks by Henry and his government. This was less than a third of that awarded to Elizabeth by King Richard in 1484.[56] It was, however, the same amount awarded to Elizabeth's sister, Katherine Woodville, Duchess of Buckingham, in 1484. At the time of the award, Katherine was the wife of a known traitor who had been executed for treason.

By May the following year, Henry seems to have had second thoughts, awarding Elizabeth 400 marks a year in quarterly instalments.[57] We have no way of knowing, but if Elizabeth was struggling financially (and having to provide for her youngest daughters, the queen's sisters), this increase may also have been at the behest of Henry's queen. Elizabeth Woodville is now described by Henry as 'oure dere moder Quene Elizabeth'. By the end of the year, in peace negotiations with Scotland, Elizabeth was proposed in marriage to James III, and her youngest daughter Katherine of York (aged around 8) was proposed for his son, James. At this remove, it is difficult to assess the seriousness of these negotiations. Elizabeth was 50 and no longer of child-bearing age. King James' death meant that the marriage proposal came to nothing.

Elizabeth Woodville's visits to Henry and Elizabeth's court became less frequent.[58] In 1488 and 1490, Henry awarded Elizabeth some small payments towards her costs and expenses.[59] Elizabeth's final visit was significant. On 31 October 1489, Queen Elizabeth moved into confinement for the birth of her second child. By November, Elizabeth was with her daughter, as was Henry's mother, Margaret Beaufort.

Royal confinement followed fixed procedures and protocol, and was a strictly female-only affair. Yet, while rumours of a second surviving son of Edward IV were surfacing, Elizabeth of York broke all established protocols and allowed her St Pol relative, François of Luxembourg, Viscount Martigues (d.a. 1511), in an embassy from France, to see her.[60] His first cousin, Elizabeth Woodville, was present, as was Margaret Beaufort, Elizabeth's Chamberlain (Thomas Butler, Earl of Ormond) and England's most senior herald, John Writhe, Garter King-at-Arms.

This extraordinary breach of royal protocol may have occurred in order to honour the English queen's visiting relative,[61] but the timing (and Elizabeth Woodville's presence) is highly suggestive of potential royal knowledge concerning the survival of the queen's younger brother, or someone claiming to be him. At this time, Thomas Peirse had long since returned to England. Perhaps her St Pol cousin was putting the queen's mind at rest for the birth by confirming the recent rumours were unfounded?

In November 1491, Richard, Duke of York, arrived in Ireland. We now know that if Thomas Peirse had fulfilled his errand, Elizabeth Woodville knew this to be her youngest son. On 8 June 1492, Elizabeth died at

Bermondsey Abbey, four days after her eldest son, Dorset, had been penalised by the king's bond.[62]

On Sunday, 12 June (Whitsun), Elizabeth was buried with Edward IV at St George's Chapel, Windsor. In her will, she requested no pomp or expense, nor could she pay for it, dying in penury and leaving nothing to her children. Her wishes were followed and only four people attended her burial.[63] Elizabeth of York did not attend her mother's funeral service as she was in confinement at Sheen Palace with her fourth child, whom she named Elizabeth (d. 1495). Elizabeth Woodville did not name Henry VII in her will.

Katherine Woodville, Duchess of Buckingham (1458–97): Maternal Aunt

Katherine was married to Henry Stafford, 2nd Duke of Buckingham. Although Katherine and her children were not involved in Buckingham's attainder after his execution on 2 November 1483, her dower and jointure income were removed. In late October–November 1483, her son was discovered in hiding by Sir James Tyrell and his gentleman servant, Christopher Wellesbourne, and placed in safekeeping.[64]

On 19 December, Katherine was permitted to travel from Wales to London with her children and servants by direct orders of the king.[65] Given the extremity of her descent from high estate, and with her sister now at hand, there is little doubt that Katherine and Elizabeth would have met to comfort each other. There is every likelihood, also, that the widow of the Duke of Buckingham had been aware of his role in arranging for the princes' safety that summer, as evidenced in the Gelderland account (see Chapter 14), long before he was suborned to treason by Bishop Morton.

Faced with a bleak future, Katherine needed support and goodwill, and she had information that could assure her of both while bringing relief to her sister, Elizabeth. With King Richard back in London on 25 November[66] and Elizabeth remaining in sanctuary, it is not known what information may have been imparted to her at this time by the government, and if it was believed. Within weeks of Katherine's arrival, Elizabeth Woodville was engaged in negotiations to leave sanctuary and place herself and her daughters in King Richard's care.

Elizabeth now received a stipend from the king and government, as did Katherine, who was awarded 200 marks annually.[67] Such a relatively small sum suggests that Katherine went to live with family, probably Elizabeth and her young nieces, who were assured of comfortable provision. Her position was not ignored, for she was then awarded a further 50 marks on 24 April 1484.[68]

That her finances did not improve may be supported by William Catesby's will of 25 August 1485. Catesby had been made responsible for the winding up of the duke's estates after his execution, and his will bequeathed to 'my lady of Buckingham' £100 to 'help her children and see my lord's [Buckingham's] debts paid and his will executed'.[69]

After Bosworth, the new king reversed Buckingham's attainder and reinstated Katherine's dower and income. She was married to Henry VII's uncle, Jasper Tudor, newly created Duke of Bedford.[70] It seems there was no love in their relationship: there were no children, and neither remembered the other in their wills.

Katherine and Buckingham had had four children. Their elder son and heir (Edward, 8) was made a Knight of the Bath and placed in the care of Margaret Beaufort, together with his younger brother (Henry, aged about 6).[71] Their two daughters, Elizabeth (7) and Anne (about 3 years old), were allowed to live with her (see Chapter 11). In 1505, Elizabeth married Robert Radcliffe, 10th Baron Fitzwalter, whose father, John (9th Baron), had been executed in 1496 for his support of Richard of England.

In November 1487, Katherine attended the coronation of her niece, Elizabeth of York.[72] By now, those in the know would have been aware of the news, brought secretly to Elizabeth Woodville by Thomas Peirse, that the younger of Edward IV's sons was presently concealed in Portugal. These circumstances are relevant when we consider the subsequent actions of Elizabeth of York as King Henry's queen consort.

Following Jasper Tudor's death in December 1495, Katherine married Sir Richard Wingfield without royal consent.[73] She had no further issue. She died on 18 May 1497[74] and the revenue from her lands was taken into King Henry's hands.[75] Katherine is probably buried at the Wingfield family seat at Letheringham Priory, Suffolk.

Elizabeth of York (1466–1503): Sister

Upon her mother's agreement with Richard III and his government, Elizabeth of York emerged from sanctuary at Cheneygates Mansion, Westminster, on 1 March 1484. A few weeks earlier she had celebrated her eighteenth birthday.

With the pretender Henry Tudor rallying his defeated rebel supporters by vowing to marry Elizabeth, it was an important objective for Richard III's government to find a suitable husband for her (and any of her sisters who might equally serve his purpose). Richard's promise to marry the girls to 'gentlemen born' fulfilled his solemn oath to their mother.

Young Elizabeth seems to have been well treated at Richard's court, and at Christmas 1484 she was honoured at the festivities by being dressed similarly to Queen Anne. There is also some suggestion for Elizabeth of York's acceptance of her illegitimacy and esteem for her uncle, King Richard. In two books signed by Richard as Duke of Gloucester, Elizabeth added her name. On both occasions, she entered 'Elizabeth' without the appellation princess or queen, thus indicating that she wrote during Richard's reign. In one, she signs with a motto 'without changing', in the other with the king's motto, '*loyalte me lye*' (loyalty binds me).[76]

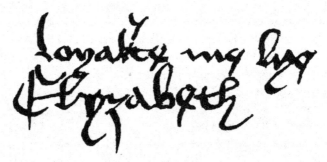

Autograph motto *loyalte me lye* (loyalty binds me) and signature of Elizabeth of York from around 26 June 1483 to 22 August 1485, from French translation of Boethius' *De consolatione Philosophiae*. (British Library MS Royal 20 A xix, f. 195. Redrawn: Philippa Langley)

In 1485, following his queen's death, Richard arranged the betrothal of Elizabeth of York to the Portuguese Duke Manuel of Beja, the cousin of John II of Portugal (with the death of John's heir, Manuel would accede to the Portuguese throne in 1495). We have evidence of Elizabeth's apparent knowledge of the Portuguese marriage in a letter examined by Sir George Buc in his patron's celebrated collection.[77] In her letter, dated late February 1485, an eager Elizabeth apparently requests John Howard, Duke of Norfolk, to mediate with the king in speeding up the matter.

Approaches to Portugal had begun well before Easter (when she may have been moved north), yet malicious rumours were already circulating that Richard planned to marry his niece.[78] This he publicly denied in the 'presence of the mayor and citizens of London' in a 'clear, loud voice'.[79] That these rumours were intended to damage Richard's reputation, and reign, is apparent in the king's vehement denial. To marry his niece, a relative in the first degree, would have been deeply shocking and political suicide. It would also have made a mockery of his election as king: in marrying Elizabeth, Richard would have undermined the grounds upon which he was offered the throne. Furthermore, marrying an English bastard rather than a legitimate foreign princess made no dynastic sense.

Following King Richard's death, the double marriage agreement came to nothing and, on 18 January 1486, Henry VII married Elizabeth of York. On entering England, and with the princes alive, Henry had tried to get out of the marriage, realising the legal predicament it now placed him in.[80] With those who fought for him requiring the marriage and unable to renege on his oath, a short time later the Act of 1484 officially bastardising Edward IV's offspring was repealed.

Elizabeth gave birth to Prince Arthur eight months later. If any at the new Tudor court had looked upon Elizabeth as a useful but ultimately disposable royal consort,[81] the birth of a male heir now cemented her place at the heart of the new regime. The Yorkist uprising on behalf of King Edward in Ireland was beginning around this time, and although her reaction to it is not on record, much has been made of the three-year period between the birth of Arthur and his sister, Margaret, in November 1489.[82] Possibly Elizabeth may have suffered a miscarriage, which wasn't placed on record.

Then came the defeat, injury or possible death of her elder brother in June 1487. Her coronation in the November was marred when several people were killed in a crush, echoing a similar tragedy at Henry's coronation, two years previously, when some of the staging in Westminster Abbey collapsed.[83] In an age of portents and omens, it was an inauspicious sign for the new monarchy. Elizabeth's imprisoned half-brother, Dorset, did not attend the ceremony, nor did her younger sisters (Anne, Katherine and Bridget).

At the emergence of Richard, Duke of York, as the new Yorkist claimant to Henry's throne, Elizabeth had two sons (Arthur and Henry) and a daughter (Margaret). With Richard of England's failed invasion in the autumn of 1496, Elizabeth of York fell ill. She was described as 'a little crazed'.[84]

Richard's invasion in the south-west also failed, and he capitulated to Henry on emergence from sanctuary at Beaulieu Abbey. His wife, Katherine Gordon, was sent to Richmond Palace, assisted by 'guardians' who were 'men of surpassing honesty and goodness'.[85] Katherine was placed in Elizabeth's large household as lady-in-waiting, and one of thirty-two ladies-in-waiting and many other female attendants.[86] Elizabeth was not allowed any contact with Richard. Following his execution, she again fell ill.[87]

In 1501, Elizabeth of York visited the newly extended and remodelled Royal Apartments at the Tower of London. Henry had added 'a bedchamber, a privy closet, and a square new tower – the "King's Tower" – with a private chamber, a library, and large windows over the river'.[88]

On 2 April 1502, Prince Arthur died at Ludlow, leaving his parents grief-stricken. Three months later, on 12 July, Elizabeth planned a residence of her own. She undertook a solo progress, travelling without Henry for the first time in their sixteen-year marriage.[89] Newly pregnant and possibly unwell, Elizabeth journeyed for two and a half months before finally arriving at Raglan Castle in Wales, home of her cousin Elizabeth Herbert, daughter of the late Mary Woodville and the Earl of Huntingdon (after Mary's death, Huntingdon had married Richard III's illegitimate daughter, Katherine Plantagenet). Elizabeth did not visit Ludlow or even Worcester, Arthur's burial place, but travelled to Oxfordshire to Minster Lovell, the former home of Francis, Lord Lovell, and Ewelme, the former great home of her rebel cousins, the de la Pole family, 'now in royal hands'.[90]

These bare outlines of Elizabeth's story reveal little of a life that was at least as traumatic as those of her peers. Her actions in planning a residence separate from her husband also constitute a significant change in behaviour, which is worth investigating.

Going back to her emergence from sanctuary in 1484, Elizabeth was sufficiently mature and politically aware as an 18-year-old to have shared the confidences of her aunt Katherine, Duchess of Buckingham, as to the duke's role in safeguarding her brothers, Edward V and Richard of York. She shared the burden, alongside her mother, of protecting this secret from the king she married and his innumerable agents, who would not have hesitated to eliminate the young men as rivals.

We have noted the gap of three years which separated her first born, Arthur, from her next child, a gap that coincided with the uprising, coronation, invasion and eventual defeat of 'King Edward', followed by Henry VII's scarcely credible story of his capture and employment in his kitchens. At some point in 1487, she would have had news from her mother that young Richard of York was still safe and living in Portugal, so the burdensome secret must still be watched over and protected, year after year.

Another great trauma came with the shock of Richard of York's failed first invasion, when she was so ill as to be described as crazed. The horrors of his eventual execution in 1499, together with her cousin, Edward of Warwick, made her ill again and cannot have failed to scar her psychologically. Perhaps her marriage now meant little more than her devotion to her children, and perhaps the death of Arthur in April 1502 was what broke its last remaining bonds.

In 1502, the year she set up her separate establishment, Elizabeth's records show certain times when she gave funds to the abbess and ladies of the Minories by Aldgate, beside the Tower of London.[91] Analysis of those residing at the Minories reveals a quite extraordinary group of women who collectively knew a great many secrets. They included some who would have known about the princes' clandestine departure in 1483: Anne Montgomery, Sir James Tyrell's aunt; Mary Tyrell, Sir James' sister; and Elizabeth Brackenbury, daughter of Sir Robert Brackenbury, Constable of the Tower at the time.[92]

Others residing there included members of Lady Eleanor Talbot's family, who would have known the truth of Edward IV's pre-contract: Eleanor's sister, Elizabeth Mowbray née Talbot; her sister-in-law, Jane Talbot (married to Humphrey, Eleanor's half-brother); and the Dowager Duchess of Norfolk, who was the most senior member of the Minories ladies.

Elizabeth's gifts of money seem to coincide with her presence at the nearby Tower of London, but there is no record that she ever visited the ladies. If her aim was to show empathy while offering discreet support, it would certainly have been prudent to keep her distance from an establishment that housed so many individuals of long-term interest to the king's agents.

She had only a few remaining months to live. On 2 February 1503, Elizabeth gave birth early, but she and the child, a daughter (Katherine), died. After lying in state for eleven days at the Church of St Peter ad Vincula, she was buried at Westminster Abbey. Overcome with grief, Henry's health never fully recovered. He would also abandon the Tower, 'ensuring its decline as a royal residence'.[93]

Cecily, Duchess of York (1415–95): Paternal Grandmother

Cecily Neville was the tenth child of Ralph Neville, Earl of Westmorland and his second wife, Joan Beaufort.[94] The family home was Raby Castle, near Barnard Castle.

By October 1424, Cecily was betrothed to Richard, Duke of York. She was the mother of two kings of England: Edward IV and Richard III. Both accepted the throne at Baynard's Castle, her London residence. It is not known if Cecily attended Richard's coronation, but their relationship was close, with Richard staying with her for nearly a week at her castle at Berkhamsted on his way to Bosworth.[95]

At Bosworth, Cecily's Neville/Westmorland kinsmen fought for Richard. Following his death, Cecily was careful to avoid Richard's name in more public documents which could be viewed by Henry VII's officials; in contrast to private ones where Richard is described as king and 'worthy king'.[96]

Cecily had eighteen Plantagenet grandchildren. These included King Edward V and Queen Elizabeth of York. Cecily did not attend her granddaughter's coronation but seems to have come to terms with Henry VII and in her will employed flattery to achieve her aim of burial with her husband at Fotheringhay.

With limited surviving materials about Cecily, it is difficult to extrapolate what she may have thought about the two Yorkist claimants to the throne. At her death, she owed £21 to the sanctuary at Colchester where two of her close affinity had taken refuge: John Howard in 1471, during the Readeption (recovery of the throne by Henry VI), and Francis Lovell, following Bosworth.[97] In 1494–95, Cecily's trusted priest and dean of her chapel, Richard Lessy, was released from the Tower of London after being found guilty of misprision of treason for concealing knowledge about Richard of York.[98]

Cecily was buried at Fotheringhay Church beside Richard, Duke of York, and their second son, Edmund, Earl of Rutland. Known for her piety, Cecily was buried wearing an indulgence (a papal remission of punishment for sins).[99]

Lionel Woodville, Bishop of Salisbury (c. 1452/53–84): Maternal Uncle

On 18 April 1483, Lionel Woodville, Bishop of Salisbury, took part in Edward IV's funeral procession.[100] By 9 June, he was in sanctuary at Cheneygates Mansion with his elder sister, Elizabeth.[101]

Lionel seems to have left sanctuary (possibly at around the same time as his nephew, Richard, Duke of York) and come to terms with Richard III's reign. Immediately upon Richard's accession, he was named on a commission for Dorsetshire on 26 June.[102] On 24 July, as Chancellor of Oxford University, Lionel welcomed the king on his royal progress. Over the next two days, the king and court heard disputations on moral philosophy and toured the university.[103]

By 26 August, Lionel was removed from the commission in Oxford, suggesting he was possibly under some suspicion.[104] By 22 September 1483, he was writing letters from Buckingham's manor at Thornbury, Gloucestershire. It is not known if he was there voluntarily or was committed to Buckingham's custody (like Morton).[105]

Lionel involved himself in the October uprising and on 20 October 1483 the university removed him from the chancellorship.[106] He took sanctuary at Beaulieu Abbey.

On 14 February 1484, he was summoned to the king's presence.[107] On 15 March 1484, Thomas Langton was granted Lionel's forfeited temporalities in the Bishopric of Salisbury.[108] In 1484, several plaints for debt were brought against him.[109] Lionel was still alive on 22 July 1484 but had died by 1 December[110] and was buried at Salisbury Cathedral.[111]

Sir Richard Woodville, 3rd Earl Rivers (c. 1446–91): Maternal Uncle

Together with his father and elder brother Anthony, Richard Woodville was pardoned in 1462 by Edward IV for his adherence to the Lancastrian cause.[112] On Anthony's death, Richard became 3rd Earl Rivers. He was the last of his family to hold the title.

In 1465, following Edward IV's marriage to his sister, Richard was made a Knight of the Bath. During the readeption of Henry VI, he was issued a pardon by the Lancastrian government. Richard appeared on several commissions during Edward IV's reign,[113] specifically for Northamptonshire. These were undertaken with the king's brother, Richard of Gloucester.[114]

Although his sister fled to sanctuary following King Edward's death and his younger brother Edward absconded with two ships and some £10,250, Richard is nevertheless listed on a further commission with Gloucester in Northamptonshire on 14 May 1483.[115] It is not known if he served on the commission. Shortly afterwards, he seems to have come under suspicion: five days later, his lands at Wymington in Northamptonshire (now Bedfordshire) were confiscated by Gloucester on the king's behalf.[116]

Richard Woodville seems to have taken part in the October uprising against King Richard and is listed among the rebels at Newbury in Berkshire. In the 1484 Parliament, he is described in the attainder of rebels as 'Richard Widevill late of London Knyght'.[117] It is not known where Richard's London home was located. On 30 March 1485, Richard Woodville was awarded a pardon for life.[118] He did not fight at Bosworth.

Following the accession of Henry VII, Richard's lands at Wymington were restored.[119] He seems to have taken an active role in the early part of King Henry's reign and was present on the king's first progress on 14 March 1486 and at York Minster on St George's Day (23 April 1486), where he is described as Earl Rivers (3rd).[120]

On Sunday, 24 September 1486, at Prince Arthur's christening, 'Richard Wodevile' is listed as an Esquire of the Body.[121] At the coronation of his niece in November 1487, he is again described as Earl Rivers.[122] He did not fight at Stoke Field in June.[123]

Richard Woodville took little part in Henry's later reign and seems to have retired to Northamptonshire.[124] He was not present on the king's second progress in the spring–summer of 1489[125] and died, unmarried, on 6 March 1491, when the earldom became extinct.[126] His lands were bequeathed to his heir and nephew, Dorset. In his will, he sought no prayers for his parents or family members, including his niece, the queen. Richard Woodville is buried at the Abbey of St James in Northampton, 'in a place made ready'.[127]

Sir Edward Woodville (c.1454–88): Maternal Uncle

Sir Edward Woodville was the youngest brother of Elizabeth Woodville. For Edward, see the foregoing and Chapter 3, also Chapter 10 for Henry VII's spy in his household in 1487. For Woodville's non-engagement with Edward V's forces in 1487, see Chapter 19.

On 18 January 1486, Henry VII married Sir Edward Woodville's niece, Elizabeth of York. Shortly afterwards, on 23 January, the 1484 Act of Parliament bastardising Edward IV's children was repealed. Soon after this event, Woodville left for Spain on Crusade to fight against the Moors.

His actions at this time replicated those of his elder brother, Anthony. In 1471, Anthony had travelled to Portugal to fight the Moors, but his request had incurred the slur of cowardice from Edward IV. In 1476, Anthony incurred the same denigration by the Duke of Burgundy when he made his excuses and left prior to the Battle of Morat.[128] Sir Edward's campaigning, coupled with his use of Anthony's title 'Lord Scales' on the continent (see p. 250), suggests he now viewed himself as the head of the family, and might perhaps be interpreted as an attempt to restore the family's name there.

His adoption of this leading role may be further supported by his visit to Portugal on the way back from Spain, when he made a diplomatic intervention with King John II for a new version of a marriage previously agreed with England in 1485. At that time, King Richard III had promised his niece, Elizabeth of York, in marriage to King John's nephew, Duke Manuel de Beja. Sir Edward now proposed marriage to the duke for one of Elizabeth's sisters,[129] though there is no record whether this mission to Portugal had the knowledge or consent of King Henry.

Woodville returned to England in the late summer of 1486 where he attended Prince Arthur's christening at Winchester Cathedral on Sunday, 24 September. With three other lords, he carried the young prince's canopy.[130]

As noted previously, in November 1487, following the Battle of Stoke, Woodville did not attend his niece's coronation. It is not known why. He may have been ill.

On Sunday, 27 April 1488, Woodville was admitted to the Order of the Garter. Within two weeks of this event, he led a force of 800 men across the Channel (from his home on the Isle of Wight) to fight for Brittany against France, causing a diplomatic catastrophe for Henry VII. This is an unusual event which requires further analysis. Why did he risk everything to fight for the Bretons at the apparent height of his success?

It is very possible that he felt a deep sense of loyalty to Brittany after the duchy supported him following his flight from England in May 1483, and this may be the single determining factor. However, as we have seen, Brittany was the ally of Maximilian, who had only recently equipped, at great cost, two fleets to fight on behalf of Woodville's nephew, Edward V, the second fleet being redeployed when France attacked Brittany (see Chapter 13). Woodville also planned a return visit to Portugal, where his other nephew, Richard, Duke of York, resided.

Henry VII had made it clear that to travel to Brittany at this time was forbidden 'on pain of death'.[131] Woodville had, apparently, asked the king on several occasions for permission to travel to the duchy but his requests had been refused. To gather 800 men (including 500 bowmen)[132] takes considerable time so it seems Woodville had already taken steps prior to the Garter ceremony. Significantly, his cousin, the brother of the Earl of Arundel (Woodville's elder sister, Margaret, was married to Arundel) was to follow him.

Henry, however, seized his ships and company and arrested the young knight before he could sail. In his letter to Charles VIII from Windsor on Tuesday, 27 May 1488, an outraged Henry informs us that Woodville's force had been gathered 'secretly and hastily' and that it was formed of 300 men which Woodville 'had drawn from places of sanctuary where they had been for several years on account of their crimes and misdemeanours'.[133] In his apologetic and obsequious letter to the King of France, Henry implies that Woodville's army was full of vagabonds – but his use of the word 'sanctuary' is revealing and strongly suggests many in Woodville's force may have previously opposed Henry and taken sanctuary. King Henry adds, 'all has been done without our knowledge and assent and against our prohibition and interdiction and we are as much displeased as of anything that has ever happened since we have been in this kingdom'.[134]

At Southampton, many men waited to take ship for Woodville. Aboard one, which sailed with 200 men, was 'an ambassador from the King of Scotland who is now in great trouble, together with his son and other Scots Lords'.[135]

Had Sir Edward Woodville survived the Battle of St Aubin du Cormier on 28 July 1488, it seems he may have required refuge for a second time in Brittany. Was Woodville's secondary (and possibly covert) motive to aid Maximilian, and thereby his nephews, Edward V and Richard, Duke of York? Investigations in this regard are ongoing.

Henry VII's letter confirms that Sir Edward had been 'calling himself Lord Scales', a title previously held by Earl Rivers, head of the Woodville family.

John de la Pole, 1st Earl of Lincoln (c. 1460–87): Paternal Cousin

John de la Pole, 1st Earl of Lincoln, was the eldest son of Elizabeth, Duchess of Suffolk (Richard III and Edward IV's elder sister, d. 1503/04), and John, 2nd Duke of Suffolk (d. 1492). In July 1471, Edward IV placed Francis Lovell in the care of the de la Pole family, where it seems he and John (aged about 14 and 11 respectively) formed a lasting friendship.[136]

On 18 April 1475, John (aged about 15) was knighted with Edward V (4) and Richard, Duke of York (2). He also attended the wedding of Anne Mowbray to York in January 1478 and was present at Edward IV's funeral and interment in April 1483. On 6 July, he carried the orb at Richard III's coronation.[137]

Following the death of King Richard's son, Edward of Middleham, Prince of Wales, John was made Lieutenant of Ireland; the office hitherto awarded to the heir-presumptive of the House of York.[138] Based at Sandal Castle in Yorkshire, John was President of the King's Council of the North and in charge of Sandal's Royal Nursery. He was present at the Battle of Bosworth (although incorrectly listed among the dead), but escaped attainder and imprisonment.

On the surface at least, John seems to have come to terms with Henry VII. He was present at York on the king's first progress of May 1486, following the collapse of the uprising led by Lovell and the Stafford brothers.[139] He headed the enquiry into the Staffords' treason and was present at Prince Arthur's christening in September.

It seems, however, that John was acting as a spy at the heart of the Tudor government for his close friend Lovell, raising funds that Christmas which, with others, were sent abroad on 1 January 1487.[140] When the revolt in Ireland on behalf of King Edward became known, John hastened to Flanders to join Lovell at its head. This followed Henry VII's parade of Edward of

Warwick (12) at St Paul's, where John spoke with the boy for some time.[141] By 25 March, Lincoln was sending gold and silver to the north via a servant who was seen at Doncaster.[142]

Given that Warwick was barred by his father's attainder, John (27) was next in line after Edward V and Richard of York. John's presence, together with Francis Lovell, at King Edward V's coronation in Dublin on Sunday, 27 May 1487, shows that he recognised the Dublin King's superior claim to the throne. Two surviving artefacts reveal that, after the death of Edward of Middleham, John had been King Richard's de facto heir. The first is the illuminated de la Pole Pedigree (Genealogical) Roll which records for Richard III 'he justly and lawfully ordained John Earl of Lincoln ... as his lawful heir ... being the next apparent by true succession to the crown of England'.[143] The second is John's seal matrix (see Plate 23). Imprinted in wax, a seal matrix closed (or sealed) a letter or document, giving it legal authority and providing 'visual evidence of status and power'. Dated to 21 August 1484 to 22 August 1485, the seal is larger than any of his de la Pole predecessors' and further records John as 'nephew of Richard III, King of England'. Part of a collection in the British Museum, 'this feature, linking a nephew to the king's person in such a way, is unique in sealing practice'.[144] John died fighting for Edward V at Stoke Field on 16 June 1487. He was buried in one of the unmarked mass graves; a willow stave was said to have been thrust through his heart.[145] It seems his family was not allowed to reclaim the body or were too afraid to ask.

Before 1480, John had married Margaret (d.a. 1524), daughter of Margaret Woodville and Thomas Fitzalan, 10th Earl of Arundel, Lord Maltravers.[146] They had no surviving issue and Margaret never remarried.[147]

The de la Pole Family: Paternal Cousins

Following John, Earl of Lincoln's death and attainder, the family lost their dukedom, which was reduced by Henry VII to an earldom. John's father, Suffolk, was loyal to England's new kings and his mother, Elizabeth, attended her niece Elizabeth of York's coronation. In the years that followed the demise of the two royal 'pretenders', Edward V and Richard of York, Plantagenet de la Pole brothers would each claim the throne of England as rightful heirs and suffer indictment for treason.

Edmund was imprisoned by Henry VII and executed in 1513 by Henry VIII; Richard, also known as 'the White Rose', became an exile and died in battle in France in 1525. Their brother William, although he never claimed the throne, was imprisoned by Henry VII in the Tower of London in 1501 and died there in

1539. Sir George Buc states that their sister, Katherine, Lady Stourton, was also imprisoned at the Tower, where she too may have died by 1513. Glover states that Katherine died in the Tower in 1502, the same year as the capture, trial and execution of Sir James Tyrell.[148] Their sister, Anne de la Pole, was Prioress of Syon [Abbey] where Sir William Stanley's conspiracy on behalf of Richard of York began in 1493 (see Chapter 17). Anne died on 25 April 1501.[149]

Conclusion

The survival of Edward V and Richard, Duke of York, can be supported by the actions of their close family members during the reigns of Richard III and Henry VII.* With the birth of Prince Arthur, the Woodville family returned to favour as the maternal family of England's future monarch, and here they should have stayed. However, what we see is several family members involved in potential activities against King Henry. Significantly, with King Richard III dead, there was no need for any secrecy or fear with regard to the princes' murder (if this was what was believed) and the family could coalesce in vigorous support of the new monarch, in word and deed, as their saviour.

Indeed, this is the traditional view, but as we have seen, it does not stand up to scrutiny. It has been argued that the family's actions were simply real-politik, but this too does not stand up to scrutiny. Any inherent self-interest was for the family members to be Henry's most ardent and loyal supporters.

It has been surmised that Elizabeth Woodville retired to Bermondsey Abbey as she wished to devote herself to a religious life. This suggestion, however, lacks support.[150] Elizabeth's forty-year lease on the sanctuary at Cheneygates Mansion indicates instead that this was her intended long-term residence. Deprivation by a displeased Henry VII seems more likely.

In the next chapter, we will look at the non-family members who were involved in the survival and removal to safety of Edward V and Richard, Duke of York. This will include those involved in their struggle for recognition and their claim for the English throne.

---

* For reasons of space, biographies concerning the least-prominent (and least-documented) family members (sisters Cecily, Anne, Katherine and Bridget of York, and their aunts, Margaret and Mary Woodville) are not included here. For context, Margaret of Burgundy (aunt) is included in Chapter 17.

17

Case Connections

An important component of the investigation is a consideration of what is known about the roll-call of individuals involved, those who were potentially involved and those who were only rumoured to be involved. This may highlight previously unforeseen connections and lead to new lines of enquiry. This is facilitated by means of an extensive person of interest file, allowing individuals to be cross-checked and referenced.

Part of this analysis also includes several individuals who supported both claimants to the throne. This may be important in terms of motive. An example is Sir Richard Harliston (Harleston), Captain-in-Chief of Guernsey and Jersey (and Governor of Jersey) in the Channel Islands.[1]

Harliston was brought up in the household of Richard, Duke of York, (d. 1460) and his support of both claimants[2] has been explained by his apparent loyalty to the House of York. This may be correct and the singular, determining factor. However, we must also consider whether Harliston, a vice admiral, could have been in receipt of intelligence that informed his support. Put simply, was he aware of the princes' removal and survival?

A significant line of the project's investigation focused on the Channel Islands as a potential location for the safekeeping of Edward V.[3] In Jersey, the island's fortress at Mont Orgueil Castle was strengthened by Harliston, and the main entrance tower today bears his name. Orgueil was significant as the coastal stronghold which held out against Henry Tudor's forces after Bosworth; a 'long drawn-out affair' that lasted well into 1486.[4]

Harliston was pardoned on 4 September 1486[5] and Henry VII subsequently rewarded leading Jersey men, with a number placed in Prince Arthur's household. Investigations into Harliston, however, were seriously hampered by the destruction of the Jersey archives in 1502 when the building in which they were housed was engulfed by fire.[6] This took place at the time of Sir James Tyrell's arrest and execution with several significant others. For this reason, Harliston is not included in the following examination.

Thomas More's Narrative and Individuals Named Therein

Thomas More, having heard several versions of the murder of the princes, recounts what he deems the most believable; though, from the sheer number of accomplices named in his story, we might question how many others were named in the versions he rejected. Apparently, More's informants knew the names of some men, like Brackenbury, who had real-life connections with Richard III, so we will do our best to identify any that make historical sense. However, their historical existence should not be taken as confirmation that they did what More's informants said they did.

In brief, his story begins with King Richard's decision to send a message with one John Grene to the Tower of London, with instructions for its Constable, Robert Brackenbury, to despatch the sons of Edward IV. Grene returns with Brackenbury's refusal, which he delivers to Richard III at Warwick.

The king seeks a more willing murderer. A personal attendant recommends James Tyrell, who proceeds to the Tower, where Brackenbury provides access for one night. The princes' sole attendant is named 'Black Will' Slaughter.

Tyrell recruits two men for the job: a knave named John Dighton from his own household, and Miles Forest, one of the princes' guards, a known murderer. With the deed accomplished, Tyrell orders them to bury the bodies deep in the ground at the foot of a staircase and place a great heap of stones on top; this being a night's secret work for two men.

King Richard, however, is dissatisfied and orders the bodies to be moved, for which task Brackenbury appoints a solitary priest whose Herculean labours apparently go unnoticed, and who then dies without revealing their location. To conclude his narrative, More declares that Dighton still lives a free man.

John Grene

Two potential candidates for John Grene were located by Paul Murray Kendall (who dismissed More's story), and two by W.E. Hampton (who felt it would be 'too artless' to disbelieve it).

The first, a Yeoman of Warwickshire, was granted a general pardon on 20 September 1483 for all offences committed before 11 September.[7] He seems to have been the same John Grene who was involved in the provision of fodder for the king's horses, and whose career in this capacity can be traced (under Richard III) from 24 August 1484 to 20 February 1485,[8] and (under Henry VII) from 16 October 1485 to 16 April 1486, from 25 May to 16 November 1487, and 16 November 1487 to 16 May 1488.[9]

A second John Grene was appointed Escheator for the northern counties of Cumberland and Westmorland on 5 November 1482 by Edward IV.[10] On 6 November 1483, Richard III appointed a John Grene Escheator to the counties of Southampton and Wiltshire,[11] probably the same man, who, along with other crown officers, was moved to rebel areas following the October 1483 uprising. Clearly, this Grene was an officer of far higher status than would normally be employed to carry letters to and fro.

On 14 December, he was made Controller of Southampton Port,[12] then in May and December 1484, he was Commissioner of Array for Hampshire and Sheriff of Southampton.[13] On 30 May 1485, he was responsible for the repair of the ship *La Mary*, of Yarmouth.[14]

Grene was a Yeoman of the Chamber to King Richard III and in an undated grant was made Receiver of the Isle of Wight and Portchester Castle and its lordship. The king's grant praises Grene for 'the very trust and confidence that we have in our well-beloved servant'.[15] By 2 December 1485, Henry VII had removed Grene from office.[16]

We also have another John Grene who was resident at Middleham on 10 August 1458.[17] It is impossible to ascertain any relationship with any other John Grene, known or unknown (it was a very common name).

Hampton records a John Grene of Gosfield, Essex, but he was deceased by 30 July and does not fit More's timeframe, which has Grene carrying messages in August.

A final contender for John Grene comes from Cheselerte (Chislehurst), Kent, where he is noted as Sheriff in 1475–76. He died on 16 October 1485 and was related by marriage to Richard's aide, William Catesby, through his uncle, Sir John Catesby. This is another man of senior rank (as Sheriff) and probably of senior age: once again, he was unlikely to be employed as a messenger.

Grene's second wife, Katherine, was the daughter and heiress of John Hynde, the stepson of Ralph Butler, Lord Sudeley, and father-in-law of Lady Eleanor Talbot (née Butler).[18]

Sir Robert Brackenbury (d. 1485)
See Chapter 14 for Brackenbury being named as one of Richard, Duke of York's safe-guarders in the Gelderland manuscript.

Robert Brackenbury of Denton and (later) Selaby, County Durham, entered Richard, Duke of Gloucester's service by about 1477. By 1479, he was Treasurer of the Duke's Household. On 17 July 1483, following Richard's accession, he was made Constable of the Tower of London for life, Master of the Mint and Keeper of the King's Exchange in the Tower.[19]

During the October 1483 uprising, Brackenbury was entrusted with quelling the rebellion in Kent. In March 1484, he was awarded the custody and care of the lions and leopards at the Tower[20] and became an Esquire of the King's Body. Ightham Manor in Kent became his home. At this time, Thomas Bourchier, Archbishop of Canterbury, made Brackenbury his Steward. The archbishop's home was Knole Palace in Kent. Brackenbury and his wife, Agnes, were enrolled within the confraternity of Christ Church, Canterbury.[21]

In April 1484, Brackenbury was a Royal Councillor and appointed vice admiral to Admiral Howard and, as vice admiral, was also one of the department's commissioners.[22] Brackenbury was knighted around Christmas 1484 and made a Knight of the Body.[23]

As we have seen in the city of Canterbury Chamberlain's Accounts for September 1484–85, there is a reference to Brackenbury's return from Calais 'from the Lord Bastard'.[24] In 1484, Pietro Carmeliano dedicated his poem on St Katherine to Brackenbury (St Katherine was the saint of scholars).[25] In the dedication, he describes Brackenbury as the 'wisest of men'.[26]

Brackenbury was killed at Bosworth, fighting in the vanguard with John Howard.[27] His body may have been repatriated to St Mary's Church, Gainford, in County Durham.[28] He was attainted, and his lands were forfeited in the first Parliament of Henry VII. The attainder was reversed in 1489 in favour of his two daughters. His illegitimate son would only inherit if the two daughters died. As a result, Richard III's former Chancellor, Thomas Barowe, left £40 to Brackenbury's son in his will of 1499. At her death, Brackenbury's daughter Elizabeth sold Selaby to pay her debts, including those to the Dowager Duchess of Norfolk, Elizabeth Mowbray (née Talbot), to 'whom I am especially bound'.[29] By this date, Brackenbury's other daughter, Anne, must have been dead as she is not named in the will. Brackenbury's bastard son is also not named.

On his way to Bosworth, Brackenbury was deserted by two retainers from the Tower, who left him in order to fight for Henry Tudor. One of them was Walter Hungerford, an associate of John Norris (see p. 263). Brackenbury's daughter, Elizabeth, was one of the Ladies of the Minories (see Chapter 16).

Henry VII's historian Polydore Vergil attested to Brackenbury's integrity[30] and *The Great Chronicle of London* praised him as a man who acted 'right kindly' and with 'kindness'.[31] By 1540, the Chronicle of Calais described him as 'gentle Brackenbury',[32] an appellation echoed by Shakespeare.

Brackenbury was also connected to William Poche, one of the princes' guards in the Tower (see p. 267). On 14 January 1484, Poche was warranted with Brackenbury and four others to remove the lands and castles of the rebel John Turburvile, of Bradford in Wiltshire, for Turburvile's high treason.[33]

Sir James Tyrell (1456–1502)
See Chapter 8 for a biography, and Chapter 14 for Tyrell named as one of Richard, Duke of York's safeguarders in the Gelderland manuscript.

More's account describes Tyrell as an unknown to the king, who had to be introduced by a page at Warwick in August 1483.[34]

Sir James Tyrell served with Halneth Mauleverer on Commissions of the Peace for Cornwall on 30 December 1483 and 22 November 1484.

Tyrell, Captain of Guînes, was in London on 2 December 1495 to act as a deponent in a legal case brought by Henry VII's leading supporter and victor at Bosworth, John de Vere, 13th Earl of Oxford. Tyrell's deposition failed to support Oxford.[35] It is not known if this event marked Tyrell's card.

On 6 May 1502, Tyrell was executed in London with Sir John Wyndham and an unnamed shipman or sailor.[36] Wyndham was the son-in-law of John Howard, Duke of Norfolk, through his marriage to Howard's eldest daughter, Margaret.[37]

On 9 May, Wyndham's son (thought to be Thomas Wyndham's elder brother) and James Holland, a barber of London, were tried and condemned. At another trial on the same day, Tyrell's eldest son, Thomas; Sir James Tyrell's gentleman servant, Christopher Wellesbourne (see Chapter 8); a Matthew Jonys; and King Henry's Herald Pursuivant Cursum were tried, with Jonys and the herald sent for execution at Guînes. Thomas Tyrell and Wellesbourne remained in prison at the king's grace – Tyrell for two years.[38] It is not known what happened to Wellesbourne. Giles and Christopher Wellesbourne had previously supported the Lovell/Stafford brothers' uprising on behalf of Edward V in 1486.[39]

Investigations into Sir John Wyndham's potential knowledge or involvement in the removal of the sons of Edward IV from the Tower by sea in 1483 are ongoing.

'Black Will' Slaughter

No such person has been discovered, and it seems likely he was an invention for dramatic atmosphere. A William Slatter was found by W.E. Hampton,[40] but he absconded to the continent with Sir Edward Woodville in May 1483.[41] An even less likely candidate is William Slaughter, a canon clerk in Holy Orders and Prebendary of Wedmore in Bishop Stillington's West Country diocese.[42] He died in 1494, when his position was gifted to King Henry's chaplain and doctor of law, Richard Hatton.[43] Since More doesn't name him as a murderer, had 'Black Will' Slaughter existed, he could have laid Henry VII's anxieties about pretenders to rest.

John Dighton

More describes Dighton as Tyrell's horse-keeper, 'a big, broad, square, strong knave', still living, although a candidate for the gallows (yet, surprisingly, More has not divulged this news to the authorities). If we are to believe him, Dighton murdered the princes with an accomplice, Miles Forest.

Two possible historical John Dightons have been found. We can rule out the first, a priest who was awarded the living of Fulbeck in Lincolnshire by Henry VII on 2 May 1487.[44] He seems to have resided in Calais. The second John Dighton was made Bailiff of Ayton in Staffordshire by Richard III on 7 March 1484;[45] he is possibly the same John Dighton named in the will of Sir John Pilkington. Like Dighton, the Pilkington family were loyal supporters of the king who came from Yorkshire.[46] However, was he still alive (and 'in good possibility to be hanged') in 1513–20, and if so, how did More, the Londoner, know this?

Miles Forest (d. 1484)

More's Miles Forest is described as one of the four guards of the princes, a 'fellow fleshed in murder before time', who later 'rotted away piecemeal' at St Martin's in London. None of this is verifiable, but there was a real individual named Miles Forest involved in the safeguarding of the princes whom we met in Chapter 14. Since More's source of information is unknown, we cannot tell whether the blackening of Forest's name, like that of Tyrell, was dreamt up by More or by his source, either of whom might have harboured personal reasons for slandering the Forest family.

A Miles Forest – possibly the real one – can be found based in Yorkshire as Keeper of the Wardrobe at Barnard Castle, a property owned by Richard of Gloucester from 1474. He died in late August–early September 1484, whereupon his wife, Joan, was granted his outstanding salary and, with Edward, Forest's young heir, an annuity of 5 marks.[47] At his death, it seems Joan was pregnant with their second child.

A possible relative, Henry Forest, Yeoman of the Crown, was also in King Richard III's service; his wages were paid by the receiver of Middleham in September 1483.[48] Henry Forest was also Bailiff and Keeper of the Park of Kymberworth, in Yorkshire.[49]

Extensive archival searches have revealed no evidence that Miles Forest was accused of any crime.[50] His wife Joan is said to have resided in Blagraves House, Barnard Castle,[51] which may have been attached to Forest's role as Keeper of the Wardrobe at the castle. (For the tradition of one or more of the princes residing at Barnard Castle, see Chapter 9.)[52]

In December 2020, historian Professor Tim Thornton discovered records indicating that Miles Forest's sons were courtiers at Henry VIII's court, in the service of Cardinal Thomas Wolsey, Lord Chancellor of England, where the family flourished.[53] This, together with a later discovery of a letter potentially connecting one of the Forest sons to Thomas More, was sufficient for Thornton to claim that Miles Forest murdered the princes. He surmised that the Forest sons had revealed their father's crime (regicide) to More at Henry's court. At the time, More was a respected lawyer, Privy Counsellor and man of letters.

On closer examination, however, we must ask whether these much-publicised discoveries really support Professor Thornton's thesis. A recurring problem is the eminence conferred on More by posterity, which leads some historians to suppose his *Richard III* was historical fact. Viewed objectively, this entire proposition rests on the belief that Forest informed his wife that he had killed the princes, and that she then informed their sons. Does it make sense that a murderer and regicide would voluntarily burden his wife with the crime of misprision (the concealed knowledge of treasonous crimes), and that she, in turn, would pass on this dreadful burden to her sons to bear for the remainder of their lives?

Next, we have the assumption that her sons randomly confessed their father's regicide (and their mother's misprision) to Thomas More. Why More? He was not a priest and could not give absolution. And how credible is it that More then decided to commit misprision himself by joining the conspiracy of silence around this astonishing secret? By doing so, he would have opened himself to constant fear of exposure. And for what gain? To help him write a book?

Considering Henry VIII's sensitivity to his royal bloodline and pride in his Yorkist ancestry,[54] the crime of misprision under his despotic regime – especially concealing the murder and regicide of his own uncles – would have been enough to put a much earlier end to Thomas More. Moreover, the legal compulsion to reveal such toxic information exerted an equal obligation on him to advise Chancellor Wolsey that there were such men in his service.

Most baffling of all, since condign punishment would have awaited the Forest family, can we believe they would have chosen to confess their damning knowledge to an ambitious officer of the courts of justice and Privy Counsellor?

Individuals Named in Documentary Evidence (Alphabetical Order)

For reasons of space, the following analysis of individuals involved and highlighted by this work has been edited.

Margaret, Lady Brampton, née Beaumont (Sir Edward Brampton's Wife)

Sir Edward Brampton may have first married Isabel Pecche, a wealthy widow and Midlands landowner (near the Woodville manor of Grafton), but their relationship is unconfirmed.[55] Isabel died in 1480.[56] By 1487, Brampton had married Margaret Beaumont (Beamonde or Boemond),[57] sister of Thomas Beaumont, Archdeacon of Wells Cathedral. By 1507 they had six children: Sir John, Henry, George, Elizabeth, Mary and Jane.[58]

Not much is known about Margaret, but Richard's witness statement and the later Setúbal Testimonies suggest she may have wished to help the young York. A possible connection between Margaret and Francis Lovell through the Beaumont family is currently being investigated. Lovell's grandmother was Katherine Beaumont (née Neville), elder sister of Cecily Neville,

Dowager Duchess of York (see Chapter 16). A 'John Beaumont esquire' (from Cornwall) was also named in Henry VII's attainder of November 1487 (his name coming third after John de la Pole, Earl of Lincoln, and Sir Henry Bodrugan). Beaumont had been present at Edward V's coronation in Dublin and had fought for the young king at Stoke.

At Setúbal in Portugal, on 25 April 1496, Brampton revealed that his wife had met 'Piris' (the Portuguese name attributed to York) at Middelburg where she had fled the plague in Bruges. 'Piris' lived opposite her, working for a craftsman who sold needles and purses. Here, he got to know some of the French boys who worked for her. The youth then went with her on her husband's ship as he wanted to live in their household with their son.

In Portugal, she asked Brampton if he 'wanted him to take him for the household and he answered no, that he had other French boys in service and didn't want any more, but he would place him with a *fidalgo* [nobleman]'. Later, one of Brampton's boys was returning to Flanders and the 'boy' (York) 'wanted to go with him' because Brampton 'did not want to take him in as his son' but 'the ship sailed and he was left behind'.[59]

John Howard, 1st Duke of Norfolk (c. 1425–85)

John Howard was a leading Yorkist noble, soldier, ambassador, shipping magnate and merchant. He died at Bosworth, leading King Richard III's vanguard. He was one of King Richard's closest advisors, described by him on 10 February 1484 as 'oure righte entirely beloved Cousyn'. At this time, Howard had been tasked with bringing John Norris, brother of the rebel Sir William Norris, to the king's presence.[60] Howard was connected to the Norris family through his second marriage in *c.* 1466, as step-father of Sir William Norris (see John Norris on p. 263).

In May and December 1484, Howard and Sir John Everingham were named on Commissions of Array for Norfolk and Suffolk.[61] Howard was also closely connected to Christopher Colyns and King Maximilian.[62] For Howard's connections in France, see Chapter 14.

After Bosworth, Howard's body was repatriated to Thetford Priory, Norfolk, lapped in lead. Following the Dissolution of the Monasteries, it was removed to Framlingham Church, Suffolk, along with his son Thomas.

In 1841, the Howard tombs were opened.[63] The front of what seems to have been John Howard's skull presented a severe wound. The face guard (beaver) of his helmet was reported torn off during combat with the Earl of Oxford, and Howard to have died by a Lancastrian arrow to the face which pierced the brain.[64] He would have died instantly.

For Sir John Wyndam's execution (John Howard's son-in-law) alongside Sir James Tyrell (and including a seaman and barber), see Tyrell, p. 257.

For more on John Howard, see Chapters 3 and 14.

Halneth (Halnath) Mauleverer (d. 1502)

In 1461, Halneth Mauleverer was esquire of the office of the verger who carries the rod before the king at the feast of St George at Windsor Castle. The office was vacated by Halneth and given to William Evington in July 1472.[65]

Halneth, of Allerton Mauleverer, near Knaresborough in Yorkshire, married Jane (sometimes called Joan), a daughter of Thomas Carminewe, and as a result moved south to Ashwater, Devon, in the early 1460s.[66] Halneth was Sheriff of Cornwall in 1470 and of Devon in 1479 and 1483.

He was given the great honour of standing night vigil by Edward IV's coffin as it rested in St George's Chapel on 18 April prior to burial. With Halneth was Christopher Colyns (see p. 278).[67] Halneth was joint Commissioner of Array for Cornwall and Devon in 1484, and an Esquire of the Body to Edward IV and Richard III. He was also an Usher of the Chamber to Edward IV and Master of the Game in the king's parks in Devon.[68]

In November 1483, he sat on a commission 'to arrest and imprison all rebels in the counties of Devon and Cornwall'.[69] In December 1484, Halneth was granted lands in Cornwall by King Richard for his 'good service against the rebels'.[70] In December 1484, he was named on a Commission of Array in Cornwall, and with his brother, Thomas (Sheriff), on a Commission of Array in Devon.[71]

On 17 December 1484, as the king's servant, Halneth was granted the office of Constable of Launceveton (Dunheved) in Cornwall.[72] In 1485, together with his elder brother, Sir Thomas, and his uncle, William (see p. 263), he fought for Richard III at Bosworth. He and William were pardoned by Henry VII on 24 November 1485,[73] and Sir Thomas on 9 November 1485.[74]

On 19 May 1491, Halneth was named with others as being 'mainprized' (stood surety through threat of a large fine) for the loyalty of Thomas, Marquess of Dorset.[75]

Sir Thomas Mauleverer was knighted by Richard of Gloucester in 1480 on the Scottish campaign and made a Knight Banneret during the invasion of 1482.[76] It is probable Thomas' younger brothers, Robert and Halneth, were with him on campaign. Robert (d. 1500) may have also fought for Richard at Bosworth.

In 1486, Sir Thomas was a feed man of the 4th Earl of Northumberland and supported the rebellion of 1487 on behalf of Edward V with Lincoln and Lovell. He was pardoned in 1488.[77] John Pullen/Poleyn (Sir Thomas' brother-in-law, married to his sister, Grace) was also involved in the 1487 rebellion and received a pardon in 1488.[78] Sir Thomas died on or by 4 April 1494.[79] It is not known which Mauleverer sailed with Richard of York's invasion force from Holland and was captured at Deal in Kent in July 1495.

Dame Elizabeth Mauleverer (Thomas' wife) was Lady-in-Attendance on Queen Anne at her coronation.[80] Grace Poleyn was also a gentlewoman of Queen Anne and received livery for Anne's coronation.[81] Her husband, John Poleyn of the Poleyn family of Scotton, near Knaresborough, was Esquire and Sergeant of the Royal Cellar by February 1485.[82] Poleyn (Pullen) was a distant relative of Sir Robert Percy of Scotton.[83] John Vavasour, Gentlemen Usher of Queen Anne's Chamber, was married to Sir Thomas Mauleverer's daughter, Bridget.[84]

Sir William Mauleverer, of Wothersome in Bardsley, West Yorkshire, Commissioner of Array for Kent, was the only son of Robert Mauleverer and uncle of Halneth and Thomas. In August 1484, he was awarded a grant of land in Kent by King Richard III for 'his good service against the rebels',[85] and named in a Commission of Array for the county in December.[86] He died in April 1498. In his will he left a 'little ring' given to him by Richard III to 'Our Lady of Walsingham' (see Chapter 14).

In December 1483 and November 1484, Halneth served with Sir James Tyrell on Commissions of the Peace in Cornwall.[87]

John Norris (Norreys) (d. 10 October 1485?)

Norris (Norreys) of Yatenden, Berkshire,[88] was an Esquire of the Body of Edward IV (with Walter Hungerford).[89] On 11 January 1482, a pardon was issued to Norris and a gentleman of London, John Russe.[90] It is not known if John Russe was any relation to Robert Russe, one of the conspirators in London on 22 July 1483.

At Edward IV's funeral, Norris took part in the short procession from St Stephen's Chapel to Westminster Abbey. By 23 May 1483, he was made Esquire of the Body of Edward V.[91] This appointment was probably made, or at least confirmed, by Richard of Gloucester, as Protector. By 1 August 1483, John and Sir William Norris were named in a commission for Berkshire.[92] In

Leicester, on 23 October, during the autumn uprising, Norris is named with others, including his brother, Sir William, in a proclamation requiring their capture or surrender with pardon.[93]

On 10 February 1484, John Norris was commanded to the king's presence. It seems Norris was quickly apprehended by John Howard, or handed himself in, as he received a general pardon only two days later on 12 February 1484 and escaped attainder.[94] Sir William also received a pardon, but it failed to pass the Great Seal.[95]

A John Norris was dead by 2 July 1491,[96] but he may have been the John Norris who died on 10 October 1485.[97] On 3 July 1495, during Richard of York's invasion at Deal in Kent, a 'John Norrys' was captured and later executed. Described as a Yeoman (gentleman landowner), this may have been Edward IV's Esquire of the Body.[98]

Norris and his family were connected by marriage to John Howard. In January 1467, following the death of his first wife, Howard married Margaret, daughter of Sir John Chedworth. Margaret had previously been married to John Norris senior. John Norris junior seems to have acted as a London agent for Howard in the magnate's shipping business, selling some of Howard's ships and dealing with the sale of freight.[99] It is therefore possible that Howard might have recommended Norris as an attendant and guard of the sons of Edward IV in the Tower. If so, Norris may have known or heard something about the removal of Richard, Duke of York, and his journey abroad.

Norris may have also recounted his knowledge of the elder boy's 'melancholic words' to family members. Did these family members (Sir William and Edward) then interpret the elder boy's distress as something sinister and lend their support to Henry Tudor? Or was the family simply returning to its former Lancastrian allegiance? Sir William Norris had been knighted by Henry VI before the Battle of Northampton and was not one of Richard of Gloucester's 'frendys'.[100] It is also possible that John Norris fought with Howard at Bosworth, thereby the family would ensure that whoever won the day, the family would prosper.

The Norris family was also linked to Francis Lovell by marriage: Lovell's sister, Frideswede, was married to Edward Norris, the son of Norris' elder brother, Sir William.[101] Edward was present for Henry VII at Stoke Field along with his father and was knighted after the battle.[102] It is not known why Frideswede received a grant of 100 marks for life from King Richard III in January 1485, or if she had left Edward Norris by then.[103] If Edward Norris was in the vanguard at Stoke, then he actively fought against his brother-in-law, Francis Lovell.

Sir William Norris is listed among those knighted by Henry VII after Stoke Field. As he was already a knight, this is probably an error for his creation as a Knight Banneret. William was a leader of the Newbury uprising in Berkshire in 1483 in which Richard Woodville was attainted. William fled to the continent and returned with Henry Tudor to fight for him at Bosworth. William was well rewarded by King Henry and was one of the leaders who fought against Richard, Duke of York, in September 1497. William's brother-in-law was John de Vere, 13th Earl of Oxford. William died in 1507.[104]

Henry and Thomas Peirse and the Peirse Family

The Peirse family, of Bedale in North Yorkshire, first come to our attention in a family pedigree of 1634.[105] At this time, Thomas Peirse's great grandson, John Peirse Esq. (d.*c.* 1658), had been appointed a Gentleman Sewer to Charles I.[106] He was in charge of serving dishes at the king's table and sometimes tasting them. A resident of East Greenwich, London (then described as Kent), John Peirse Esq. had also purchased the manor of Bedale in or around 1593. The Manor of East Greenwich had been part of the Manor of Bedale from 1570.[107]

John's father, Henry, had also owned lands in Bedale. He was described in 1621 as a Yeoman, a freeholder of a small, landed estate.[108] John was the first member of the family to hold official office, thereby helping to raise the family's fortunes. His younger brother, Richard (died unmarried), was also Gentleman Sewer to Charles I. In 1637–38, Richard is named as the owner of houses and 170 acres of land in Bedale.[109] By 1654, John's eldest son, John Peirse Esq. of Bedale, is described as an Alderman of London.[110] An address in 1635 is given as St Martin's Parish, near Ludgate.[111] John died unmarried. As a result, the manor of Bedale descended to his great nephew, Henry Peirse Esq. (d. 1759).

The Peirse family pedigree begins with Peter Peirse of Bedale, described as 'Standard Bearer to King Richard the third at Bosworth field where he lost a leg but lived many years after'. Searches for Peter's forebears are ongoing.

Although Peter, as a Christian name, is not recognised in the senior Peirse line, it seems it may have been commonly used within the wider Percy family in northern England. Christopher Hunwick, archivist at Alnwick Castle, brought Picot Percy of Bolton Percy, North Yorkshire, to our attention. Picot seems to have had descendants in the thirteenth and fourteenth centuries called Peter Percy (of Bolton Percy).[112] Other related searches have revealed a fourteenth-century Peter Percy, of Dunsley in North Yorkshire, near Whitby.[113] It is therefore possible that our Peter Peirse may have been a descendant of one of these lines, as a cadet or possibly illegitimate branch. Illegitimacy was very much regarded as a stain on a family at this time and may explain why the Peirse family did not record the antecedents of Peter Peirse. It is notable that the family were happy to record their ancestor's role on behalf of Richard III.

Peter Peirse's son is our Thomas Peirse, with no other siblings recorded. Thomas owned land in Bedale,[114] and it seems likely that he lived to a good age. His son and heir was Marmaduke Peirse of Bedale and Cleveland (d. 1609).[115]

Marmaduke comes to our attention on 27 October 1559 through the grant of a lease on some property in the manor of Bedale by the owner, William Dygby.[116] This was probably a tenement building because on 9 August 1565 the new owners were suing for a year's unpaid rent.[117]

By 1575, 'Marmaduc Pearsey' was serving on the jury for Bedale,[118] and in October 1581, he is named in his brother-in-law's will (Thomas Gaile).[119] The name of Marmaduke's sister is not recorded, nor is there an entry in the Beresford-Peirse family tree. Her daughter is named in Gaile's will as 'Anne' and this may also have been her mother's name.

Thanks to the Beresford-Peirse family (of Bedale), we know that Thomas Peirse had a second son, Christopher Peirse of Burrell. Christopher was buried on 16 August 1597.[120] Nothing else is currently known about Christopher.

It also seems that Thomas had a third son, Richard, which would go on to become a Peirse family Christian name. He was buried in Bedale on 14 April 1573.[121]

In 1511–12, a Thomas Percy was responsible for the keeping of the 5th Earl of Northumberland's house at Wressle Castle and/or Leconfield. He was in charge of all foodstuffs bought for the house in this year and was described as 'Clerk of the Kitchen'.[122] Thomas may have been the son of Peter Percy, a merchant of Scarborough and Hull. Peter had a brother, John Percy, also a merchant in Scarborough.[123] Any connection to the Peirse/Percy family of Bedale currently remains untraced.

Searches to date have uncovered no genealogical record for Thomas' brother, Henry, which suggests he was unmarried and childless when he died in Portugal in 1487. Henry became a popular Peirse family Christian name.

William Puche (Poche) (d.c. March 1484)

On 8 March 1484, William Poche is named as the Keeper of the Little Wardrobe in the Tower of London for life, with two grooms under him.[124] Poche was the 'Keeper of beds and other harness within the Tower'.[125] This may explain later stories of the smothering of the boys between two mattresses. Poche was a Yeoman of the Crown, who lived in the parish of St Mary of Barking in London.[126]

On 14 January 1484, William Poche was warranted with Robert Brackenbury and four others to seize the forfeited lands and castles of the rebel John Turburvile of Bradford in Wiltshire, for Turburvile's high treason.[127] Puche (Poche) is not to be confused with Sir William Pecche (Petch) of Kent (d.c. April 1488).[128]

Henry Stafford, 2nd Duke of Buckingham (1455–83)

Henry Stafford, 2nd Duke of Buckingham, came from a Lancastrian family. In 1460, his grandfather was killed fighting for Henry VI at the Battle of Northampton. In 1466, at the age of 10, he was married to Katherine Woodville (aged about 8), Queen Elizabeth's younger sister. They would have five children (Humphrey died young).

In 1474, as a descendant of Thomas Woodstock, the youngest son of Edward III, Buckingham was awarded Woodstock's royal arms, without quartering[129] and became a Knight of the Garter. However, following his very early return to England from the French invasion of 1475, Buckingham was 'kept conspicuously out of public office'[130] and rarely attended court. He may have entertained pretensions to the throne, hence Edward IV's reluctance to reward him and his fall in favour. It is also not known why Buckingham joined the October 1483 uprising against King Richard (see Chapter 6).

Sir William Tyrwhit (Tyrwyth/Tyrwhite) (c. 1456–1522)

William Tyrwhit seems to have been a trusted servant of the Crown as one of Edward IV's ushers,[131] an Esquire of the Body, and Sheriff of Lincolnshire.[132] Tyrwhit was on a Commission of the Peace for Edward V in Lincolnshire on 14 May 1483.[133]

He was named as King Richard's servant and Esquire of the Body and Steward of the King's Lordship of Caistor in the county of Lincoln on 8 December 1483, with Richard authorising a payment to him (£10) for the offices in October the following year.[134] On 16 November 1483, he was awarded the keeping of Swalefield Park,[135] and in December appointed to commissions in the county of Lincoln to try cases of treason[136] and to a Commission of Array on 1 May 1484.[137]

In March 1485, Tyrwhit was awarded for life the lordship of Seaton, in North Yorkshire, and described as a Squire for the Body.[138] Tyrwhit was granted lands in (rebel) Berkshire by King Richard on 20 February 1485[139] and annuities from the lordship of Freston, Lincolnshire.[140]

Tyrwhit similarly served Henry VII. He was knighted after Stoke Field and described as a 'knyghtes bacheler' at the coronation of Elizabeth of York.[141] During Henry's reign, Tyrwhit was mainly associated with Lindsey in Lincolnshire, where he served on several commissions. On 10 February 1502, he was involved in an action with others against Sir Robert Willoughby of Broke.[142] By 10 March 1505, he was named as Sir William Tyrwhit of Ketelby (Lincolnshire).[143]

Tyrwhit was made Bailiff of Calais in 1491, Knight of the Body (1493), Justice of the Peace (1491–94) and Sheriff of Lincoln in 1494 and 1517. He was also made Knight Banneret at the Battle of Blackheath in 1497. Sir William is buried in Lincoln Cathedral.[144]

Burgundian-Habsburg Nobility

King (Emperor) Maximilian I (1459–1519)

Maximilian was the son of the Emperor of the Holy Roman Empire, Frederick III (1415–93) and his wife, Eleanor of Portugal (1434–67).

After the death of the Burgundian Duke Charles the Bold in 1477, Maximilian married his daughter and heir Mary of Burgundy, through which the Habsburg dynasty rose to prominence in Europe. The young Archduke Maximilian was successful in defending Burgundian unity in a fifteen-year war with France. The birth of his children, Philip (the Handsome) and Margaret (of Austria), secured the Habsburg dynasty in the Netherlands.

In 1482, Mary died in a riding accident. Her death plunged Burgundy into crisis. The nobility and powerful merchant cities in Flanders didn't want to acknowledge Maximilian as their regent, and he was deposed in favour of his son, Philip the Handsome, a minor aged 4. A Regency Council then ruled in Philip's name. The rebellion, however, was put down by Maximilian in 1485.

In 1486, Maximilian was crowned king and elected his father's heir as emperor.

Signature of Maximilian I, 10 March 1497. (Redrawn: Philippa Langley)

In 1487, Maximilian backed Margaret of York in her support of Edward V of England. He and his court provided ships and weapons and a professional army of Zeeland soldiers and German '*landsknechte*'. In that same year, the Burgundian Netherlands were once again in turmoil when France attacked Brittany, Maximilian's ally, requiring the second fleet for Edward V to be diverted.

On 16 December 1490, with the intention of encircling France, Maximilian married 'by proxy' the daughter of his old ally, Anne of Brittany. In 1491, Charles VIII of France, although betrothed to Maximilian's daughter, Margaret of Austria, sent troops to Brittany. Anne surrendered and agreed to marry Charles who annulled his betrothal to Maximilian's daughter.

Maximilian had been embarrassed both as a husband and father. A new war erupted, and Maximilian challenged the King of France to a duel. The Peace of Senlis in 1493 ended the war and Margaret was returned to the Netherlands.

Maximilian fully supported Richard, Duke of York, in his plans to regain the throne of England. From 1493, York received extensive Burgundian recognition and support.

During his regency, Maximilian pursued an ambitious policy of expansion through wars and a clever marriage policy, of which the double marriage between his son, the Archduke Philip, and the Spanish Princess Juana (1496), and his daughter, Margaret, and the Spanish hereditary Prince Juan (1497), is the most famous. Due to a series of unexpected deaths in the Spanish line of succession, the inheritance of the Spanish Empire fell into the hands of the Habsburgs. The Habsburg dynasty became the most powerful in Europe.

Although some aspects of his life, especially his financial mismanagement, were cause for disapproval, he was one of the most popular Roman emperors. Maximilian was buried with honour in the Castle Chapel at Wiener Neustadt in Austria in the Cathedral of St George.

Margaret Plantagenet (of York and England), Duchess of Burgundy (1446–1503)

Margaret was the daughter of Richard, Duke of York, (1411–60) and Cecily Neville (1415–95); sister of Edward IV and Richard III; and the aunt and principal ally and indefatigable supporter of Edward V and Richard, Duke of York.

In 1468, she married the Burgundian duke and lord of the Netherlands, Charles the Bold, and became Duchess of Burgundy. When, in 1470, the Earl of Warwick's restoration of Henry VI forced her brothers Edward and Richard to flee England, she acted as mediator between Duke Charles and King Edward during the latter's exile in the Low Countries. She also regularly represented her husband in difficult negotiations regarding English matters.

In 1477, Duke Charles died at the Battle of Nancy, leaving his country in crisis. A childless Margaret devoted herself to supporting his successors. She also developed an excellent relationship with her stepdaughter, Mary of Burgundy, and played a decisive role as confidante of the young and inexperienced duchess.

Mary of Burgundy expressed appreciation for her stepmother by making a favourable arrangement for Margaret's estate. She wrote:

> Our very dear lady and stepmother ... has always behaved towards our lord father with great prudence, obedience and special friendship, and towards our person and towards our lands and glories with such total and perfect love and benevolence that we will never be able to thank and acknowledge her enough for it.

In the summer of 1480, Margaret returned to England for about three months, staying with King Edward's family at the royal palace of Greenwich and at Coldharbour House, near her mother's home of Baynard's Castle.[145] It was during this visit that she met 7-year-old Richard, Duke of York; a meeting she would later recall in her letter to Queen Isabella of Spain.

After Mary's death in 1482, Margaret took care of her young children, Philip the Handsome and Margaret of Austria. Margaret of York's dowry included Malines (now Mechelen), where she settled and created a court.

As a widow, Margaret could act independently. With the consent and help of Maximilian, she actively supported both Yorkist rebellions. She was determined to install a rightful Yorkist heir on the English throne.

Signature of Margaret of York and Burgundy from 25 August 1493 at Dendermonde. (Bibliothèque Nationale de France. Redrawn: Philippa Langley)

Between 1493 and 1495, the 21-year-old Yorkist claimant, Richard of York, stayed regularly at Margaret's court in Malines with Philip and his younger sister, Margaret. He also stayed at her home at Binche. One of its rooms below the chapel and which led out to the tennis court was renamed 'Richard's room'.[146]

During her life, Margaret showed a strong sense of duty. She was a passionate bibliophile, with a great love of religious (devotional) books and engaged in charitable work.

Olivier de la Marche, poet and chronicler at the Burgundian court, praised 'the daughter of York' as 'that gentle, pleasant woman, beautiful on the outside and inside'.

Later Tudor chroniclers referred to her as the 'diabolicall duches', who was 'lyke a dogge revertnge to her olde vomyte'.[147]

Margaret was buried with great honour in the choir at Mechelen (Malines) Cathedral.

Albert of Saxony (1443–1500)
See also Chapter 15 and Appendix 6.
Albert III, Duke of Saxony was the youngest son of Frederick II, Elector of Saxony[148] and Margaret of Austria, sister of Frederick III, the Holy Roman Emperor.

Little is known about his youth, but he seems to have enjoyed tournaments and other games of knighthood where he showed considerable physical strength and courage from an early age.

On the night of 7–8 July 1455, when the young prince was around 12 years old, he and his 14-year-old brother Ernst were kidnapped. Several knights, who had felt cheated by the boys' father, managed to penetrate the royal residence of the two young princes at Altenburg Castle, in eastern Germany. The princes were captured and taken towards the Bohemian border. However, the kidnapping failed and both boys were freed soon afterwards. This famous event is known in German history as *Der Sächsische Prinzenraub* ('The Saxon Princes Abduction').

In 1464, Albert married Sidonia, daughter of the King of Bohemia. In the same year, after the death of their father, Ernst and Albert ruled Saxony together. In order to receive their lands in fief (feudal service) from the emperor Frederick III, they went to his court. Here Albert stayed for several years, laying the foundation for his life-long loyalty to the Habsburg dynasty.

From 1488 Albert played an important role in the Habsburg Burgundian Netherlands. As a gifted military leader, he was immediately prepared to fight for Maximilian when the latter was imprisoned in Bruges due to the Flemish uprising. After release Maximilian appointed Albert 'General Stadtholder' (the king's deputy), in the Burgundian Netherlands.[149]

In the following years Albert, Duke of Saxony reconquered the counties of Holland, Zeeland, Flanders and the Duchy of Brabant for Maximilian. He also subdued a number of rebellions in the Burgundian Netherlands.

Albert's governorship was regularly extended by Maximilian and in 1491 he was given the great honour of being admitted to the Burgundian Order of the Golden Fleece. In September 1493, he took care of the young prince Richard of York, who had just arrived at Margaret of York's court in Malines.

Albert seems to have been very committed to Richard's cause and supported him financially. In a Charter of 4 October 1493 (see Plates 25 and 26), Richard of York promised to repay Albert for a loan of 30,000 florins (an enormous sum) as soon as he became King of England. The following month, Albert travelled with Prince Richard and his own son Henry to meet King Maximilian, who was in Vienna at the time.

They were often in each other's company and Albert made great efforts to build up Richard's army and fleet, with which 'the new young king', as he was called, would make a first attempt to regain his kingdom in July 1495. Although Albert was also busy with a planned campaign against Friesland, he apparently preferred the mission of the young heir to the English throne. According to a servant of the Duke of York, Albert said 'that he would much rather march into England'.[150]

In 1498, for his dedicated service over many years, Maximilian made Albert governor of Friesland. Two years later, Duke Albert of Saxony, nicknamed 'The Bold', died at the age of 57. He is buried in the Cathedral at Meissen (Saxony).

The Irish Lords

Gerald Fitzgerald, 8th Earl of Kildare (c. 1456–1513)

Gerald Fitzgerald, 8th Earl of Kildare, also known as 'Garret the Great', or 'the Great Earl', supported Edward V, the Yorkist claimant, in 1487. Kildare recruited 4,000 Gaelic *Kerne* (light-armed Irish foot soldiers) for Edward's invasion of England. These were commanded by his brother, Thomas, and would reinforce the 2,000 *Landsknechte* supplied by Margaret of York and Burgundy.[151] The Yorkist army was heavily defeated at Stoke Field, where the Irish suffered heavy casualties including the death of Kildare's brother; Thomas is probably buried in one of its mass graves.

On 23 June 1488, Henry VII sent a commissioner, Sir Richard Edgecombe, to Ireland which had remained loyal to Edward V. On 12 July 1488, Edgecombe held a meeting with Kildare and gave the earl a private verbal message from the English king. Kildare stalled for five days in order to consult with the other members of the Irish Council. The following day, in Christ Church Cathedral, the Bishop of Meath was compelled by Edgecombe to read Pope Innocent VIII's bull against the supporters of King Edward. He also preached a sermon in support of Henry VII's claim to the throne.

On Wednesday, 30 July 1488, Kildare accepted a pardon and recognised Henry VII as King of England.[152] The short reign of Edward V in Ireland was over. Kildare's hesitant dealings with Henry's commissioner, a year after Stoke, may suggest that Edward V survived the battle or, in Ireland at least, was thought to have survived. The content of Henry VII's private verbal message to Kildare is not known.

It is also not known if Kildare was at Greenwich Palace in London in February 1489 when the Irish lords were served by Lambert Simnel but failed to recognise him as the king crowned in Ireland (see Chapter 12).[153] It seems likely that Kildare was not present because in 1490 he evaded a summons to Henry's court 'with the excuse that he could not be spared from the defence of the land'.[154]

By 1491–92, Kildare was implicated in the activities of the second Yorkist claimant, Richard, Duke of York, who was supported in Ireland by Kildare's cousin, the Earl of Desmond. After York left for France, Kildare was dismissed from office as Deputy of Ireland by Henry VII, along with the earl's closest supporters.[155] After refusing to swear an oath of loyalty to the Tudor king in 1493, Kildare was bound by 1,000 marks and summoned again to the English court.

Henry VII now sent a small force to Ireland headed by Sir Edward Poynings. In December 1494, on Henry's orders, Poynings burnt all records in Ireland pertaining to King Edward's coronation and Parliament. In February 1495, after the discovery of his secret communications with the Irish chiefs, Kildare was arrested, attainted by Poynings' Parliament and sent to England, where he was imprisoned in the Tower. Kildare's brother, James, rose in rebellion in Ireland, while his cousin, Desmond, rallied for Richard of York at Munster.[156]

Henry VII's Irish loyalists, the Butlers (Earls of Ormond), helped lift Richard of York's siege of Waterford and thereby broke the resistance. York fled to Scotland. The fight for Ireland had cost Henry VII £23,000.[157]

The English Parliament reversed Kildare's attainder and he married Henry VII's distant cousin, Elizabeth St John. Kildare returned to Ireland as Lord Deputy. Henry VII kept Kildare's son and heir at the English court as surety for the earl's conduct.

In 1504, Kildare returned to England to attend his son's marriage. Father and son returned to Ireland. In 1513, Kildare was shot and wounded on campaign in Ireland. He was buried in his own chapel on the north side of Christ Church Cathedral, Dublin, where twenty-six years earlier he had helped crown King Edward of England. Kildare's chapel and tomb do not survive.

On 13 June 1482, Edward IV described Kildare as 'our dearly beloved cousin Gerald Earl of Kildare, deputy of our beloved and very dear son Richard of Shrewsbury, Duke of York, our lieutenant of our land of Ireland'.[158] Richard III similarly appointed Kildare as deputy to his 'first begotten son' 'Prince Edward' from 19 July 1483, in recognition of Kildare's 'good fame and noble disposition'.[159]

On 21 August 1484, following the death of Richard's son, John de la Pole, Earl of Lincoln and the king's nephew, was made Lieutenant in Ireland, with Kildare confirmed as Lincoln's deputy on 22 September.[160] Following King Richard's death, Kildare was again confirmed as deputy for Jasper Tudor, King Henry's new Lieutenant in Ireland, after first becoming Chief Justice in March 1486.[161]

Kildare's grandson, the 10th Earl, and his four sons by Elizabeth were executed for treason at Tyburn in London by Henry VIII on 3 February 1537.

Maurice Fitzgerald, 9th Earl of Desmond (d. 1520)

For 6-year-old Richard of York's visit to Ireland in December 1479 and probable meeting with Kildare (and Desmond), see Chapters 2 and 14.

Maurice was Kildare's cousin. In December 1487, Maurice's brother, James, 8th Earl (age 28), was murdered.

Maurice Fitzgerald, 9th Earl of Desmond, supported Richard, Duke of York, raising troops on his behalf at Munster in Ireland in 1495. When York's uprising failed, Desmond was taken prisoner but pardoned by Henry VII on 22 August 1497.[162] Thereafter, he was in King Henry's favour.

Desmond was buried at Tralee.

Persons of Interest with Likely Connections

Dr John Alcock, Bishop of Rochester, Worcester and Ely (1430–1500)

Alcock was born at Beverley, North Yorkshire, the son of a Hull merchant. He first came to royal prominence in April 1471 following the Yorkist victory at the Battle of Barnet. It seems likely that Alcock's behaviour during the readeption earned him the favour of Edward IV. It is not known if Alcock joined King Edward and Gloucester in exile.

Alcock was made Keeper of the Rolls of Chancery by Edward IV and was involved in Anglo-Scottish diplomacy. On 8 January 1472, he was made Bishop of Rochester and from 20 September to 18 June 1473 was Keeper of the Great Seal. This was a singular mark of royal favour and trust. The Great Seal (in wax imprint) conferred royal authority. From 10 June to 29 September 1475, during Edward IV's campaign in France, Alcock acted as Chancellor.[163]

From 1473 to 1483, as Bishop of Rochester (1472) and later Worcester (1476), Alcock was tutor to Edward, Prince of Wales (the future Edward V), and President of his Council. In 1481–82, he rebuilt the church of Little Malvern Priory in Worcestershire, installing a stained-glass window of Edward, Prince of Wales.

Following Edward IV's death, Alcock served on the King's Council during Richard III's Protectorate and reign. He is recorded on the progress of 1483 at Magdalen College, Oxford (24–26 July), and seems to have travelled with the king to Worcester, Warwick, York and Grantham (19–20 October).[164] London to Oxford is about 56 miles and approximately two days' travel; it is not known when Alcock left London to join the court, or if he was present when the progress left the capital on 19 July. It is possible that Alcock joined the royal progress at Oxford following the failed abduction attempt at the Tower on 21 July. It is not known if Edward V accompanied him on the journey north to Oxford. In September 1484, Alcock helped negotiate a marriage alliance with Scotland at Nottingham.

Following King Richard's death, Alcock opened Henry VII's first Parliament on 7 November 1485, delivering a sermon as temporary Chancellor. On 6 October 1486, he was promoted to the wealthy see of Ely, when Dr John Morton, Henry VII's closest advisor, became Archbishop of Canterbury. On 6 March 1487, during the Yorkist King Edward's presence in Ireland, Alcock's office of Keeper of the Great Seal was removed from him and awarded to Morton.[165] Following this event, Alcock remained a Royal Councillor but confined his attention to writing, education and building works.

In 1496, Alcock founded Jesus College, Cambridge, having previously founded Hull Grammar School in 1479. He died of the plague at Wisbech Castle in Cambridgeshire and is buried at Ely Cathedral.[166]

Alcock served three kings faithfully. He was later recalled as 'having devoted himself from childhood to learning and piety, made such a proficiency in virtue that no one in England had a greater reputation for sanctity'.[167] At Leicester on 25 August, Alcock was named by William Catesby, prior to his execution, as an executor of his will.[168]

Sir Edward Brampton (c. 1440–1512)[169]

Born Duarte Brandão in Portugal, Sir Edward Brampton converted from Judaism to Christianity with the personal sponsorship of Edward IV as his godfather.[170] In 1484, he was knighted by King Richard as the first man of Jewish origin to receive the honour. Brampton was a soldier, merchant, ship owner and master.

In 1472, Brampton was rewarded with property in London 'for his good service to the king in many battles'. In the following year he was commissioned to raise mariners for service against King Edward's enemies. In 1479, he was a Gentleman Usher of the King's Chamber and by 1481 served under John Howard on the naval expedition against Scotland, commanding a Portuguese carvel. By 1482, he was an Esquire of the King's Body and Captain and Governor of Guernsey in the Channel Islands.

On 11 June 1483, Brampton was shipping goods from London. The ship, the *Salvatour de Porte*, had Portugal listed as its home port. Its captain was Johannis Gomys. As Brampton wasn't the captain on this occasion, it's unclear whether he was on board.[171] As we have seen in Chapter 14, on 25 July as Howard arrived in London (and was appointed admiral), Brampton was awarded, without explanation, £350 (£320,000) from Port subsidies (London, Sandwich and Southampton). On 25 January 1484, he was replaced as Governor of Guernsey by Thomas Rydley (see p. 284).[172]

On 20 August 1484, Brampton was a Knight of the Body and with Christopher Colyns (see p. 278) was awarded an indenture of £100 for twenty years from the Port of London.[173] What these services were for was not specified.

In March and August 1484, he was awarded land in Northamptonshire and London for his 'good service against the rebels'.[174] On 22 March 1485, he was sent to Portugal to negotiate the king's marriage to Joanna, the Holy Princess.[175] Brampton was therefore out of England when King Richard III was killed at Bosworth.[176] He left Portugal and King John on 1 October 1485.[177]

Brampton then settled in Bruges.[178] It is not known if he met Richard, Duke of York, at this time, or if the boy's true identity was revealed to him or his wife (see p. 260). Henry VII's biographer Bernard André, probably repeating gossip and speculation, wrote that 'Peter of Tournai' (aka York) was brought up in England by 'Edward, a former Jew later baptized by King Edward the Fourth' but did not give this Jew a surname or nationality.[179] Brampton returned to Portugal in 1487.

In 1489, Brampton was pardoned by Henry VII, 'provided that the said Edward produce sufficient security in the King's chancery for bearing himself as a faithful liege … towards the king's person and majesty'.[180]

Following the execution in 1495 of Sir William Stanley and several hundred others for their support of Richard of England, on 25 April 1496, at the Setúbal Testimonies in Portugal, which considered the identity of the Yorkist pretender, Brampton revealed his wife's connection to the young man. Regarding the claimant's identity, he said:

… it was the worst evil in the world that he and his brother the Prince of Wales had been killed, and the one they now said [was him] was a youth from a city called Tournai and his father was a boatman who was called Bernal Uberque who lived below the St. Jean Bridge and [the boy] was called Piris.[181]

The Setúbal Testimonies were to be read by Henry VII.[182] Brampton's eldest son, John, was knighted by Henry VII in 1500.[183]

From 1483 to 1484 (exact dates unspecified), a servant called 'Edward' is listed in Brampton's London house. This raises an important question for the project. No surname is given and he is described as 'Portuguese'.[184] Given Brampton's knighthood and considerable rewards by King Richard III at this time, coupled with Edward V's disappearance and what we now know about Richard of York's disguise, with shaven head and poor clothing, does this add up to Brampton having a child in his household that could have been Edward V, hidden in plain sight in the capital for a short period following the July abduction attempt at the Tower? And could André have picked up on some rumour about this and applied it to the wrong boy?

Consequently, Brampton's servant 'Edward' is of interest to the investigation, prior to Edward V being taken to the Channel Islands (Guernsey). (See Thomas Rydley, p.284, and Chapter 18.)

Two further events connected to the Channel Islands, and potentially related to the above, are of interest to the investigation. Before 6 September 1485, less than two weeks after Bosworth, Henry Tudor issued an order to two of his most trusted servants from Jersey (Edmund Weston and Thomas de Saint Martyn) to 'purvey and ordeigne [provide and commission]' at Henry's cost such shipping from the Port of Poole in Dorset as they thought 'suer [dependable] and moost expedient [suitable] for to passe, **in all haste possible**, into oure isle of Garnesey [Guernsey] for suche things as we gave them in charge [emphasis added]'.[185]

On 28 November, Weston and Martyn were rewarded with the joint Governorship of Guernsey for their 'gratuitous [freely given] services rendered at great labour and expense'.[186]

The second event occurred on 6 December 1484 when John Nesfield, King Richard's trusted guardian of Elizabeth Woodville (see Appendix 1), was given a letter of passage by the king to travel to Jersey with two companions. This unusual journey for Elizabeth's guardian was believed to be for 'some important purpose, probably connected with Richard's attempts to win over the Woodvilles at this time'.[187] The 'two persons' accompanying Nesfield are not named.

Christopher Colyns (Colens)
See also Chapter 14.
Christopher Colyns of London was a trusted servant of Edward IV and Richard III and employed by both Yorkist kings on 'business with a

maritime flavour, such as attacking pirates and victualling the king's ships'.[188] A Gentleman Usher to King Edward, on 20 February 1481 Colyns was awarded the commission to collect tax for goods traded through the Port of London by the king (tonnage and poundage).[189]

Colyns was also a friend and business associate of John Howard, who commanded that Colyns be paid £3 from his accounts for an undisclosed reason on 10 April 1482.[190] This may have been related to the voyage of Howard's ship, *The Mary Flour* (Flower) of London. Colyns had received a licence for a cargo of wine from Bordeaux in France and promised Howard a tun of the wine on the ship's return.[191] By 12–13 November 1482, Howard paid a considerable sum (over £18) to Colyns in separate payments over two days for eleven carpets.[192] In December 1482, Colyns received a reward of £20 from King Edward for his diligent service, perhaps as a customer,[193] and in January 1483 he hired and fitted out the carvel *Christopher Lockwood* at Sandwich, crewed by sixty men, to catch pirates who were molesting vessels in the Thames Estuary. Colyns was successful and apprehended John Miles and others of his company: he was paid £3 for his costs and a £97 reward by Richard III in 1484.[194]

At King Edward's death Colyns was honoured as a mourner and on 17 April 1483 took part in the short procession of Edward's coffin from St Stephen's Chapel to Westminster Abbey. In front of the coffin and leading the secular procession was John Howard, carrying King Edward's personal banner of arms. Also in the procession were John Norris and Thomas Tyrell (both referenced in this chapter). Colyns also stood vigil beside the king's coffin as it rested overnight in St George's Chapel. Among those accompanying Colyns at the Night Watch, as the vigil was known, was Halneth Mauleverer.[195]

During King Richard's reign Colyns is described as the king's servant and seems to have been confirmed as a merchant by trade and a draper, but he was more active as a ship's master and outfitter. In early October 1483, Colyns was rewarded by King Richard with a forfeited ship, *Barbara of Fowey*.[196]

Colyns seems to have acted as the king's servant on the seas and was authorised to receive £20 from the Treasurer of Calais 'to content certain soldiers at Guînes'.[197] Colyns was also entrusted with a Privy Seal from the Treasurer and Chamberlains of King Richard's government and the wages of 200 men in his control.[198]

From Easter 1484, he was awarded an annuity of £100 to be paid by the Collector of the Subsidy of the Tonnage and Poundage of the Port of London.[199] Towards the end of 1484, Colyns, by royal command, saw to the wages and supply of 200 men in the king's ship *The Caricon*, and 100 men in *Michael of Queenborough*. The vessels were equipped for a period of six weeks' service from 29 September to 11 November. His costs were substantial at over £194.[200] On an unknown date, Colyns was again rewarded by the king with a further payment from the subsidy of London and paid a much larger sum for 'habilimentes of werre [items of war]'.[201]

By 20 August 1484, Colyns was granted for life the office of Constable of Queenborough Castle in Kent backdated to Midsummer 1483.[202] By 10 April 1485, Colyns' brother, William, was also named as joint Constable of Queenborough Castle.[203]

Colyns was also granted an annuity of £100 for twenty years from Easter 1485 for services to be done by him according to indenture. It was a considerable sum. What these services were was not specified. An identical indenture was granted to Sir Edward Brampton on the same day (20 August 1484).[204] It is probable that Colyns, like Brampton, had significant contacts in France and the Low Countries. Do the simultaneous indentures of Colyns and Brampton indicate a potential involvement in the transport of one or both princes, or at least the use of their ships and captains? Both men were certainly familiar with the ports of London and the continent.

Records of Colyns after Bosworth are scanty. By 21 November 1486, he is described as 'esquire' and 'gentilman' and 'late citizen and draper of London' and granted a pardon by Henry VII, although all his goods were forfeited to the crown.[205] It's possible that Colyns may have left the country post-Bosworth and become a fugitive. It might also be possible that he sailed to Ireland and became part of the Yorkist uprising on behalf of King Edward. The destruction of relevant records means we may never know.

By 1490, Colyn's ship, *Barbara of Fowey* (awarded to him by King Richard), was in the hands of Sir John Treffry, a supporter of King Henry.[206] William, Christopher's brother (also described as 'Draper, London'), is last heard of on 26 June 1488 when he failed to appear to answer a debt.

Christopher Colyns was a ship owner, master, organiser, helper and local agent in the Thames Estuary for both Edward IV and Richard III. He was also (with his brother) far more than a merchant and draper. He was tasked by King Richard to patrol the seas, outfit ships and men for war, ensure payments reached key English fortresses across the Channel in France, control a significant fortress in Kent and command significant numbers of men.

It is also possible that the 'Jane Colyns', the 'servant' and probable nurse of King Richard's son and heir, Edward of Middleham, Prince of Wales, may have been a relative. It is not known what happened to Jane following the king's death at Bosworth.[207]

Thomas Howard, Earl of Surrey, 2nd Duke of Norfolk (1443–1524)
See also Chapter 10.

Following Bosworth, Thomas Howard was the third person to be named in the Act of Attainder at Henry VII's Parliament after King Richard and Howard's father, John, Duke of Norfolk.[208] At his death, Thomas' epitaph recalled that the Lieutenant of the Tower (probably Sir James Radclyf) offered him his freedom in 1487 during the Yorkist uprising in support of King Edward in Ireland.[209] Howard did not take up the offer, probably fearing a trap.

In January 1489, he was released and his (and his father's) attainder was reversed.[210] He was, however, barred from inheriting his lands, other than those in right of his wife. By May, Howard was restored to the earldom of Surrey.[211]

Following the murder of the Earl of Northumberland on 28 April, Howard was sent north to suppress the northern rebels. He became Warden of the East Marches and King Henry's quasi viceroy in the region, residing at Sheriff Hutton Castle.

In 1492, he defeated the northern rebels at Ackworth and gradually recovered his estates. Howard was tasked to array the northern levies against Richard of York's invasion with James IV of Scotland in September 1496, an aborted affair with no clash of arms, owing to York's withdrawal, aggrieved at the Scottish army's treatment of the common people. Howard kept a copy of York's royal proclamation from this time.

By 1501, Howard had returned to court and was made Lord High Treasurer. Despite Howard's zealous show of loyalty to the new regime, the dukedom would not be restored until his victory at Flodden, some twenty-eight years after Bosworth, during the reign of Henry VIII. It seems that Howard's loyalty to the Yorkist kings, and his knowledge of the survival of the sons of Edward IV, remained long in the memory of the new Tudor regime. Following the demise of the Tudor dynasty, Buc noted the bewildered reaction of the Howard family to the stories being told about King Richard.[212]

Francis, Viscount Lovell (c. 1457–92?)
In July 1471, Edward IV placed Francis Lovell in the care of the de la Pole family, where it seems he and their eldest son, John, Earl of Lincoln (aged

about 14 and 11 respectively), formed a lasting friendship.[213] As a child, Lovell was married to Anne Fitzhugh, the northern niece of Richard Neville, Earl of Warwick.

He succeeded to his estates and inheritances at his majority at about 20, becoming Lord of Bedale in Yorkshire, and owner of Minster Lovell, Oxfordshire, among others. By 1480, he was supporting King Edward's campaign against the Scots led by Richard of Gloucester. He was knighted by Gloucester at Berwick in 1481 and likely took part in the 1482 invasion which returned Berwick to England. Following the Scottish invasion, Francis Lovell was made a viscount by Edward IV.

Lovell bore the Third Sword of State at Richard's coronation. He escaped the Battle of Bosworth to take sanctuary at St John's Abbey, Colchester, not far from Sir James Tyrell and the de la Pole homes in Suffolk. Lovell was attainted in Henry VII's first Parliament.

In spring 1486, Lovell led a failed uprising against King Henry in Yorkshire with the apparent aim of kidnapping the new monarch.[214] By April, Edward V was in his care and taken to Ireland. Lovell then travelled to Margaret of Burgundy, where he was soon joined by Lincoln. Here, the two Yorkist lords led the uprising on behalf of Edward V, crowning him in Ireland in May 1487 and attending his Parliament. Lovell escaped the Battle of Stoke with Sir Thomas Broughton and 'many other'[215] and went into hiding.

On 5 May 1488, Broughton is reported to have landed at Ravenglass, on the Cumbrian coast,[216] and by 16 June, soldiers and mariners were 'impressed' to serve on behalf of Henry on *Mare Guldeford* in 'resistance of the king's enemies congregating on the sea'.[217] By 19 June, Lovell fled to Scotland, receiving from James IV a safe conduct along with Broughton, Sir Roger Hartington, Oliver Frank, 'their servants and all others who were of their opinion'. The safe conduct was granted for one year and afterwards at 'the king's pleasure'.[218] By 4 November 1488, James IV issued a further safe passage to 'Richard Harliston, knight, and Richard Ludelay, from Ireland, Englishmen, and 40 persons with them ... at the instance [urgency] of the Lady Margaret, Duchess of Burgundy'. These were rebels who had come from Ireland.[219]

Margaret now sent a herald to Scotland with letters for the Scottish king at 'his command'. The herald arrived on or around 26 November 1488.[220] On 2 February 1490, a herald arrived in Scotland from Ireland on his way to the duchess.[221] Given Lovell's presence in Scotland, together with James IV's communications with Margaret, it seems likely that the Scottish king was aware that the king crowned in Dublin had been Edward V.

According to English records, Lovell was alive, or thought to be alive, from 18 December 1489 to 2 May 1491 when certain properties would have been awarded to him by right of inheritance, had he not been attainted.[222]

On 16 July 1491, a 'simple and pure person' was imprisoned in York for telling 'diverse persons' about the city that he spoke with the 'lord Lovell and Sir Thomas Broghton in Scotland', which he then denied following imprisonment.[223] A letter was sent to Sir Richard Tunstall at Pontefract Castle, one of King Henry's key supporters in the north, to inform him about the event. It is not recorded what happened to the unnamed individual afterwards.

It seems likely that this York account may have been accurate because the first recorded instance of Francis Lovell's apparent death in English records is dated 29 October 1493,[224] but the precise date and location are not known. A commemoration for Lovell formally took place at Magdalen College, Oxford, annually on 17 September, but the significance of this date has, it seems, not been recorded.[225]

However, in the medieval calendar, this is the saint's day for St Lambert, whose name would have resonated in conjunction with Lovell's. Bishop Lambert was murdered at Liège in 709, a victim of political turmoil during the conflict between the Merovingian and Carolingian dynasties, a dispute mainly centred around Tournai and Cambrai. The coincidences of name and place are striking.

In 1534–35, during the reign of Henry VIII, Lovell was said to have 'escaped beyond sea after the battle [Stoke], and to have died abroad'.[226] A full translation reads:

> They say the same Francis was overseas at the time of the attainder [backdated to 20 June 1487], and moreover died after the attainder, but on what day or in what year the said Francis died the appointed judges do not know.[227]

Although no records for Lovell post-1487 have been discovered on the continent or in Ireland, the search for further evidence continues.

On 9 August 1737, a letter from William Cowper, Clerk of Parliament, to the antiquary Francis Peck, concerned the discovery of a man's remains in a large vault or underground room beneath the Lovell family home at Minster Lovell, Oxfordshire. The discovery was made during the construction of a new chimney. The 'entire skeleton of a man, as having been sitting at a table, which was before him, with a book, paper and pen … in another part of the room lay a cap, much mouldered and decayed'.[228] The family judged the remains to be those of Francis, Lord Lovell, but upon what grounds is not recorded.

On 2 March 1486,[229] Minster Lovell had been awarded to Henry VII's uncle, Jasper Tudor, Duke of Bedford (d. 1495), who had been married to the princes' aunt, Katherine Woodville (d. 1497), by Henry VII within a couple of months of Bosworth. Henry VII visited Minster Lovell on 18 January 1494.[230]

Although attainted after Bosworth, Lovell was retrospectively attainted again in October 1495 for his part at Stoke Field in 1487. The reason for this second attainder is unclear and may have provided additional justification for the acquisition and assignment of his property. Lady Lovell, who was alive at the time, was described as 'late wife of the said Francis'.[231] Anne may have died in 1498 but had certainly died by January 1513.[232]

With the emergence of Richard, Duke of York, in 1491, a tradition in Bedale recounts how 'evil' Simon Dygby was given Bedale as an incentive to search the town in order to apprehend and execute Lovell.[233]

Sir Brian Stapleton, of Carleton in Yorkshire, had owned half of the lands at Bedale. Stapleton married Lovell's sister, Joan. Brian and his brother William fought for King Richard at Bosworth. For Lovell's other sister, Frideswede, see John Norris (p. 263).

During Henry VII's reign the official view was that Lovell died at Stoke Field. This was recorded in 1502 by the London merchant Richard Arnold, also by Henry VII's historian Polydore Vergil, and by Edward Hall in his Chronicle of 1548 when Lovell was said to have drowned during his escape from the battle while swimming his horse across the Trent River at Fiskerton.[234]

Thomas Rydley (Ridley)

The Rydley family were based at Ridley Castle at Willimoteswick, in Northumberland by Unthank, the family seat of Sir Nicholas Rydley (also described as Nicholas Rydley Esquire), and nearby Langley Castle, seat of Sir Archibald Rydley.

Nicholas Rydley (d.a. 1491) was Esquire of the Body for King Richard and in 1484–85 was involved in peace negotiations with Scotland. By 1485, he was Constable of Bewcastle. A commissioner and Justice of the Peace, he was granted the office of Bailiff of Tynedale by Henry VII in March 1491. Thomas Rydley's relationship to Sir Nicholas and Sir Archibald is currently unknown, with investigations in this regard ongoing.[235]

On 25 January 1484, Thomas was appointed Captain, Keeper and Governor of the Island of Guernsey by King Richard; the position previously held by Sir Edward Brampton. As Governor, Rydley's residence was the heavily fortified Castle Cornet. Today, the castle is joined to St Peter Port by a Victorian harbour, but at the time of Rydley's governorship, the royal castle, perched high on a rock, was an impregnable island fortress. Surrounded and supplied by the sea, it operated with its own English garrison, language, customs and community.[236]

Castle Cornet is of significant interest to the project as a potential location of Edward V, prior to his removal to Francis Lovell in Yorkshire in April 1486. Sir Archibald (the 'good' Rydley) fought for King Richard at Bosworth.[237] At Easter 1486 (26 March), Edmund Weston became sole Governor of Guernsey for King Henry.[238] It is not known what happened to Thomas, whether he accompanied Edward V to Yorkshire, was present for the king's coronation in Dublin, or joined the rebel force.

Sir William Stanley (c. 1435–95)

The second son of Thomas, 1st Baron Stanley, of Latham in Lancashire, Sir William first came to prominence in his early twenties when he fought for the House of York at the Battle of Blore Heath on 23 September 1459, probably fleeing overseas with the Yorkist leaders. In November, he was attainted a traitor by the Lancastrian Parliament at Coventry. He also fought at Towton.[239]

On Edward IV's accession in March 1461, he became a mainstay of the Yorkist regime, being made Chamberlain of Chester, Constable of Flint Castle and Sheriff of Flintshire for life in May and knighted in July, becoming a Knight of the Body and King's Carver.[240] Sir William was one of the first to declare himself for York in 1471 on Edward's return from exile and was made banneret after the Battle of Tewkesbury. Four years later, he took part in the invasion of France. In February 1483, he was appointed Steward of the Prince of Wales' household at Ludlow, by which time he had gained prominence in North Wales and Cheshire.[241]

In late 1465, Sir William married Joan Lovell (née Beaumont), mother of Francis Lovell (aged about 8). Joan died nine months later, possibly in childbirth with William Jnr.

In 1471, Sir William married another Yorkist heiress, Elizabeth Hopton (d. 1498) and had two daughters, Joan and Catherine.[242] He also had an illegitimate son, Thomas.

Following Edward IV's death, he attended King Richard's coronation[243] and with his elder brother, Thomas, 2nd Baron Stanley, helped suppress the October 1483 uprising. After Buckingham's execution, Sir William succeeded to the duke's former post of Chief Justice of North Wales and by 1484 had acquired Holt Castle.[244]

At the Battle of Bosworth, his intervention on behalf of the pretender Henry Tudor was decisive in securing Henry's crown and, possibly, saving his life. In reward, Henry VII made Sir William his Chamberlain and subsequently (possibly before 27 May 1487, but certainly by 16 November 1489), created him a Knight of the Garter. The stall allocated to him at St George's Chapel was that of Edward IV's youngest son, Richard, Duke of York (see Chapter 9).[245]

Sir William was not present at the Battle of Stoke on 16 June 1487. His elder brother Thomas was also absent (following his usual pattern of behaviour), but this time sent his son, Lord Strange, to fight for Henry VII. Their cousin, Peter Stanley of Hoton, fought for King Edward.[246]

As King Henry watched the ensuing battle from a safe distance, possibly a church tower or windmill at Syerston or Elston, the Stanley rear-guard under Strange failed to engage, despite the vanguard seeming to crumble at one point.[247] Two years later, Sir William raised a large company of men to help King Henry suppress an uprising in Yorkshire, for which he was significantly rewarded. He had, by this time, reputedly become the wealthiest commoner in England.[248]

Sir William's future seemed secure, but in 1495 he was executed for treason. He confessed his guilt (from 14 March 1493)[249] and was found to have sent Sir Robert Clifford to Burgundy three months later to enter the service of the Yorkist claimant (Richard, Duke of York). Clifford had known York as a child and in Burgundy recognised him 'by his face and other lineaments of his body'.[250]

Clifford would send York's supporters to Sir William in England to conspire by 'a certain private sign agreed between them'. Sir William would 'aid and support them with his whole power'. He would 'raise him [York] up to be king of England, and would also depose and destroy the same present lord king [Henry VII]'.[251]

A co-conspirator with Sir William was King Henry's Steward, John Radcliffe, Lord Fitzwalter. Previously, on 14 January 1493, Fitzwalter had agreed to array 500 men on behalf of Edward IV's youngest son and instructed Clifford to urge the young prince in Burgundy to make war on Henry in order to secure the throne.[252]

What brought Sir William to this ignominious end? At Bosworth, he had commanded the Stanley family contingent almost certainly with the knowledge and support of his brother. Thomas, though absent from the battle (see Chapter 10), would become its principal beneficiary, gaining significant rewards, including the earldom of Derby. By contrast, Sir William received no peerage or major landed advancement. Denounced prior to the battle by his nephew, Lord Strange, and proclaimed a traitor by Richard III, Sir William did not join Tudor's ranks, pitching his camp between the two opposing armies,[253] and arriving late to cause Henry 'no small anxiety'.[254] It seems Henry Tudor never fully trusted William Stanley,[255] and may have made him Chamberlain to keep him close.

From 1494, bonds for allegiance were issued against Stanley servants and clients, being evidence of the bondee's support for Sir William's rebellion, with general pardons sought following his arrest.[256]

At Westminster on 6 February 1495, Edward, Duke of Buckingham, handed down the sentence for treason of hanging, drawing and quartering,[257] which was later commuted by Henry. On 16 February at Tower Hill, Sir William was beheaded, bearing himself haughtily, according to observers. Sir William was buried at Syon Abbey, where the rebellion on behalf of Edward IV's youngest son had taken hold.[258] Anne de la Pole (d. 1501) was the prioress at Syon. Having seized all Sir William's lands and goods, King Henry contributed towards the burial.[259]

Following his execution, the Stanley family rallied to write the family history using the ballad tradition and making Sir William at Bosworth into a kingmaker. His granddaughter Joan (Jane), through his son, Sir William Jnr, married a Brereton; in the early sixteenth century, 'The Song of the Lady Bessy' was written by a Brereton.[260] It seemed his surviving line would ensure his name was on the right side of Tudor history.[261]

By contrast, when we dig down, another story reveals itself. With Sir William attainted, his son and heir, Sir William Jnr [262] 'lived out the remainder of his life as a minor country gentleman' and died in relative poverty, three years later, ending the male line of this junior branch. In 1495, Sir William's illegitimate son, Thomas, was placed in captivity for some fifteen years and would not be released until Henry VIII's reign. He then went abroad and joined the last Yorkist claimant, Richard de la Pole.[263] At one time, de la Pole believed him to be a spy.[264]

On 1 June 1487, as King Edward invaded and battle loomed, one of King Henry's courtiers alleged that Sir William had equipped his men in the rebel colours.[265] After Sir William's execution, a gold Yorkist collar of sunbursts and roses was discovered at Holt Castle. This may have been the insignia for his office of Steward to the Prince of Wales (later Edward V).[266]

18

Avenues for Exploration

As the investigation continues, there is also room for reflection and speculation. This may inform new lines of enquiry.

What if that second armada had sailed from Burgundy in support of
King Edward as planned, and executed a pincer move on King Henry's
forces at Stoke?

Henry's reign, and possibly his life, would have ended on 16 June 1487. The
first Tudor monarch would have reigned for 663 days, or 664 if we use Henry's
redating of his reign to 21 August, the day before Bosworth.

However, had events turned against Henry, he may well have escaped. At
Bosworth, Jasper Tudor's absence from the battlefield is believed to indicate
that he was waiting nearby to conduct Henry to safety should the conflict turn
against Henry's general, the Earl of Oxford. Is this what transpired at Stoke?
Was Jasper waiting for Henry in the event of defeat?

The Battle of Stoke has been viewed for centuries with the distortion of
hindsight and through the prism of the later Tudor narrative. A thorough
re-evaluation of this key confrontation and last battle of the Cousins' War is
now required.

Henry VII was not present but watched from a safe distance. It seems he
had learnt his lessons from Bosworth, but also he may not have trusted in
the outcome. Many had deserted Henry's forces prior to the conflict, with
the king himself thought to have fled[1] and only Oxford's vanguard engaged.

The Stanley contingent in the rear-guard and the flank, which included Sir Edward Woodville (probably as commander), took little part, picking off stragglers as the outcome became evident. We are told that the battle was fierce and could have gone either way. Indeed, early reports confirmed victory for the Earl of Lincoln.[2] As at Bosworth, it was Oxford's leadership which secured the day for Henry.

Sir William Stanley, Henry's apparent champion at Bosworth, stayed away. Did he follow his elder brother's example at Bosworth and feign illness, or did he, as he would in 1495, tell Henry that he 'would never take up arms' against Edward IV's son?[3] Did Henry, new and insecure, have little option but to accept Sir William's excuses, thinking it never to be repeated? And is this why Henry's spies watched the younger Stanley for a year or more until his eventual arrest? Henry would never fully trust his erstwhile champion.

Following Oxford's victory at Stoke, over sixty men were knighted, most on the field. Had they all fought in the vanguard? Possibly, but more likely Henry followed his usual pattern of reward and punishment to control England's elite, carefully constructing a potent image of a victorious, rightful king upheld in battle for a second time by verdict of God's judgement.

And what of the men of God? It seems many supported the young claimants to the throne. In 1487, as the newly crowned Edward V made his way through the north-west of England to confront Henry VII, the men of the Church provided succour and rallied to his cause, despite a Papal Bull condemning those who challenged the king's royal title.[4] And in the case of Richard, Duke of York,[5] some ecclesiastics were pardoned or retired, but many were imprisoned; this despite the threat of excommunication obtained by Henry from Pope Sixtus in 1496 should anyone try to wage war against him again. Henry VII had learnt the lessons of both Bosworth and Stoke.

Yorkist servants would rally in significant numbers to support both claimants.[6] Edward IV's master bow-maker, Thomas Mashbrow, stood up for Richard of York. Was he the bowyer who fashioned Howard's gift for the young boy in 1483?[7] And what had driven Elizabeth of York's Yeoman of the Household (Edwards) to join their number?[8]

We come next to the royal houses of Europe. Those who supported Edward V transferred their support to Richard of York. Outwardly, the Spanish monarchs, Ferdinand and Isabella, declared Richard an impostor but their secret communications code for their spies and ambassadors told a different story. Richard's code – DCCCCVII – revealed he was Edward IV's youngest son, Richard, Duke of York.[9] Monarchs would not risk their consecrated legitimacy for an impostor to the royal blood; if they set such an immoral precedent it could then happen to them.

When it came to Richard of York's downfall, Margaret of Burgundy and Maximilian, King of the Romans, later Holy Roman Emperor, would each beg for York's life, humiliating themselves on the world stage before the man on the English throne whom they viewed as a usurper and interloper to the royal dignity. Margaret offered her deepest apology to Henry with a promise of good behaviour and Maximilian his friendship to secure the young prince's life.[10] This included his own letters patent of assurance that York would renounce his claim. To facilitate an agreement in which Henry VII would not put to death his own 'brother in law', the financially pinched monarch offered 10,000 gold florins.[11]

In 1495, Margaret and Maximilian appealed directly to the pope through official legal supplication. The first line of Maximilian's legal address emphatically contradicts Henry's post-Bosworth propaganda and is worth repeating here. It reveals in stark relief events in England following the death of King Richard III at Bosworth:

> Most Holy Father, most Reverend Lord. Whereas of late years, after the invasion and slaughter of Richard King of England, Henry of Richmond occupied that kingdom, and having espoused the daughter of Edward, the late King, brother of said Richard, **causing it to be believed that said Edward had left no male progeny**. [Emphasis added.][12]

With so much on record contradicting the version of history handed down by Henry VII, how has the mythology of the murder of the princes flourished for so long?

Certainly, too many of our historians have failed to question and investigate. To discover the truth, we must set aside conscious bias lest it lead to the dismissal of new material. If the Gelderland document had been investigated when it was first discovered in the early 1950s, our knowledge would have moved on exponentially and it is very likely The Missing Princes Project research initiative would not have been needed.

The loss and destruction of documents in English territories from this period has been a significant factor in hampering our investigations.[13] Henry VII ordered the destruction and burning of every copy of King Richard's title to the throne (and any supporting evidences) on threat of imprisonment. One copy of the King's Title survived, whether through mismanagement or deliberate concealment.[14]

In 1574, during the reign of Henry's granddaughter Elizabeth I, it was reported by John Caius at Cambridge (a founder of Gonville and Caius College) that Henry's historian Polydore Vergil had 'committed to flames as many ancient manuscripts as would have filled a wagon, in order that his faults in his history might not be discovered'. Vergil is similarly reported to have pillaged libraries and sent a shipload of manuscripts to Rome.[15]

In the north of England significant records have been lost. The Patent Roll for the Chancery Records for the Durham County Palatinate (1483–90) for our key period of investigation no longer survive,[16] nor do records from Middleham, Sandal, Sheriff Hutton or Barnard Castle. At Markenfield Hall, near Ripon, home of the Markenfield family with their close connection to the Coldridge investigation, their archive was removed during the Tudor period when the family seat was appropriated (searches for this are ongoing).[17]

In York, its city archives are said to have survived relatively intact because the city fathers refused to select Henry VII's candidate for Recorder. In the spring of 1486, the city chose its own nominee at great risk of incurring the new monarch's displeasure.[18] Yet, as we will see in Chapter 19, following King Henry's visit after the Battle of Stoke, the city's records reveal signs of adjustment and loss. John Rous, the Warwickshire priest, created two handsomely illustrated armorial chronicle rolls during King Richard's lifetime. The roll written in English, with its eulogy of Richard, survives in the British Library. However, the roll written in Latin was edited following the king's death, his image among the group of kings cut out and the text relating his good acts as monarch entirely removed.[19]

In Richard III's book of prayers (his Book of Hours), the rubric to the king's prayer is missing.[20] This is the page which tells you about the prayer and explains what it meant to Richard and why he said it. Following his death at Bosworth, Richard's prayer book was discovered in his tent. Its next owner was Margaret Beaufort, King Henry's mother. It is not known when the rubric was removed.

Unlike other monarchs of the period, King Richard's *Baga de Secretis* (store of secret documents) was found empty. This may have been part of the destruction and burning ordered during Henry's reign, along with the king's will, household records[21] and private correspondence.

One of Henry VII's closest adherents was John Morton. On Henry's victory at Bosworth, Morton's nephew, Robert, was immediately reinstated as Master of the Rolls (records). John Morton was created Archbishop of Canterbury and it is interesting to note that, while all records pertaining to this office exist at Lambeth Palace, those for King Richard's reign are missing.[22]

Records were destroyed and burnt in Ireland on King Henry's orders. In Jersey, the building which held all island records was also burnt to the ground during Henry's reign, at the time of the executions of Sir James Tyrell and significant others – the executions supporting Richard of York's account.

Luckily, whatever form of record management was undertaken by the first Tudor monarch and his circle within the territory he controlled (probably including Calais and Guînes), it did not, apparently, spread to the wider continent – although the loss of certain records in Flanders, such as those for Erasmus and Maximilian previously noted in this work, may be significant. Whether John Morton or his affiliates had access to the repositories in Rome is not known and investigations in this regard are ongoing.

In Ireland, Henry ordered the burning of all records pertaining to King Edward's coronation and Parliament. The destruction took place after a Henrican loyalist, Thomas Butler, was made Keeper of the Rolls of Chancery in Ireland during the King's Pleasure.[23] Butler's specific instructions are not on record.

Together with the destruction of records and control of information, Henry ensured complicity by managing and manipulating points of vulnerability. Hostage-taking was normal practice. York had taken sanctuary at Beaulieu Abbey but with his wife and son (or children) taken by the king, he had no choice but to give himself up.

Henry's skill with extortion is well attested. Bonds and recognizances would be used to great effect to ensure any who fell under suspicion would be controlled, with the threat of crippling fines and bankruptcy extended to friends, family and associates. For a monarch who was paranoid and deeply suspicious, an extensive network of spies further ensured widespread control. At Beaulieu, the heir to England's throne had played one last card. Changing out of the monk's habit he wore as a disguise, Richard, Duke of York, left the abbey sanctuary to meet Henry wearing royal cloth of gold.[24] Previously in 1483, by Act of Parliament, Edward IV had placed into law that cloth of gold could only be worn by the king and queen, the king's mother, his children, and his brother and sisters.[25] The heavy fine for the apparent open violation and disregard of this law is not on record despite Henry's cupidity.

The Question of the Princes' Later Lives

It is possible that Edward V was taken to Suffolk with John Howard on 11 August 1483; or he remained in London in disguise as a servant in Sir Edward Brampton's house;[26] or he was taken north, staying at Francis Lovell's estate at Longdendale in Lancashire and/or taken to Barnard Castle by Sir Robert Brackenbury at some point. It is not known if Edward joined the Royal Nursery at Sandal Castle in Yorkshire for any period of time[27] or resided at nearby Pontefract Castle by early May 1484 and, having reached his majority, visited Calais with Brackenbury later that year.

Was he sent to live in Coldridge in Devon by early March 1485, with John Goddesland, his footman? And did he meet with his mother at Sir James Tyrell's home at Gipping in Suffolk, located a few miles from the port of Ipswich and John Howard's docks. Certainly at some point he was 'expelled from his kingdom' and sent to the Channel Islands.

Researchers constantly come up against references to 'the son of the Duke of Clarence' – the young Earl of Warwick, also named Edward, of course – about whom Henry VII so successfully muddied the waters with his story that this was who the 'feigned boy' of 1487 pretended to be. Was the term 'Clarence's son' used locally to protect Edward's identity and deflect wagging tongues? By late November 1486, gossip in England, perhaps from Henry's spies, already spoke about how 'there will be more speech of' the Earl of Warwick 'after Christmas'.[28]

Certainly, the research of Gordon Smith in 1996 now seems prescient, where he discusses the confession of the priest Richard Simons, named as the *éminence grise* behind the 'Lambert Simnel Affair':

> The changes between Simons's confession in February and Lincoln's Attainder of November 1487 tend to confirm that the character of Lambert Simnel emerged at the end of an *ad hoc* story invented by the English government in response to the events of the 1487 rebellion. Vergil's narrative transposed Lambert back to the start of the conspiracy and to this transposition can be attributed Vergil's mistakes (e.g. Warwick's age ... and the capture of Simons) and the implausibility of the pseudo-Warwick plot ... The conclusion that the king from Dublin was Edward V not only fits the events of the so-called Simnel rebellion of 1487 but also explains the differences in the narratives of Molinet, André and Vergil.[29]

If Edward V was killed in battle at Stoke Field, this was a judicial killing, with his body lying in an unmarked mass grave, most likely beside that of his royal cousin, John de la Pole, Earl of Lincoln. Had willow staves been thrust through his heart as well as Lincoln's? Had he died as an unknown person, without a crown on his helmet to mark him as a target on the field? Had this lesson been learnt from Bosworth? (For future archaeological and DNA investigations of the mass grave at Stoke Field, see Chapter 20.)

Had Lincoln died trying to save the young king's life, or did his sacrifice succeed, and Lincoln's younger brother lead an injured Edward V to safety from the conflict with his face opened by a sword, dagger or halberd strike. Did Edward survive at Coldridge in Devon (see Appendix 3), badly disfigured and unable to communicate but given the identity of John Evans to live his life in peace and obscurity? Was this an agreement made with King Henry on the pleading of Edward's elder sister, the mother of Henry's new young heir? And was it Edward's removal from public and political life that finally allowed his sister to be crowned?

For Richard of York, the story is more grim. Named by Henry VII 'Piers Osbeck' and known to posterity as 'Perkin Warbeck', the lad who was captured and imprisoned was beaten by Henry's men until his face was rendered unrecognisable. Executed in 1499, his lifeless body was cut down, his head struck off and placed on London Bridge for the crows and scavengers. His body is recorded being buried at the nearby Austin Friars,[30] where traitorous nobility were laid to rest. A century later, among the ninety or more markers to all those buried there, the antiquarian John Stow found no indication of Perkin's burial.[31]

In Leicester, upon Richard III's death, Henry VII had failed for ten years to provide a marker for King Richard's grave until Richard of York's emergence presented the political necessity to denote the defeated Yorkist king's resting place after Bosworth. Henry was unlikely to follow the same procedure with the grave of the alleged boatman's son from Tournai. Indeed, would Henry's queen, who probably knew his real identity, allow her brother's grave to be denoted this way in a house of God? Or was York's body removed to the royal vault at Cambuskenneth Abbey near Stirling, as Scottish tradition believes?[32] Was James IV's request granted and the young Yorkist prince buried with quiet dignity and honour in the vault originally intended for the Scottish monarch himself?

Or did King Henry follow the same strategy, deliberate or fortuitous, that had annulled and silenced the elder prince so effectively? Was York beaten so badly to disfigure him permanently so that he too could live out his life as an unknown, unrecognised man? And was he Richard of Eastwell, as some historians have postulated?[33] If so, had this strategy saved his life, as it had his brother's? Was a badly beaten prisoner substituted at Tyburn, a criminal already due to die and sent in York's place, his sentence commuted from disembowelling to hanging? Criminals would have their heads shaved. As we have seen earlier, the man executed on the scaffold at Tyburn on 23 November 1499 did not speak.

And what of Richard's young son with Katherine Gordon? Did he survive to live in obscurity and anonymity? Are the Perkins family of Wales his direct descendants, as claimed?[34] Was this child's life used as leverage to prevent his father, Richard of York, ever revealing his true identity as Edward IV's son?

And finally, is this why Katherine Gordon was never allowed to return to Scotland, for fear of the secrets she might divulge or even mark and honour his grave, and why she went to live in Wales close to the (new) family named Perkins?

The Role of DNA

In 2017, with the help of Dr John Ashdown-Hill, researcher Glen Moran discovered the princes' mitochondrial DNA (mtDNA) sequence.

Moran had discovered an all-female line of descent from Elizabeth Woodville's mother, Jacquetta of Luxembourg, to the acclaimed British opera singer Elizabeth Roberts.[35] Roberts was honoured as the soprano soloist at the Opening Ceremony of the London Olympic Games in 2012, a few short weeks before the lower leg bone of Richard III was uncovered in a council car park in Leicester. Quite uncannily, Roberts bears a remarkable resemblance to her ancestor and namesake, Elizabeth Woodville, the princes' mother.

With the princes' mtDNA and Y chromosome identified (the male Y chromosome through Richard III, their uncle), a simple DNA test of any putative remains will answer this mystery, whether at Coldridge, Eastwell or Cambuskenneth, or if an all-male line of the Perkins family in Wales should come forward. Additionally, if any future development work were to take place in or around the location of the former Austin Friars Church of London, now the Dutch Church, a test could also be carried out on any remains found. Investigations have revealed that an account of exhumation, cremation and reburial of medieval remains (pre-1550) at this site has no apparent evidential basis.[36]

In 1950, following extensive ground-level bomb damage during the Second World War, when the Austin Friars Church was flattened by a parachute bomb, a limited archaeological dig in two locations in the nave removed several post-medieval burials. If this is Richard of York's last resting place, his remains lie undisturbed and may be situated in a location immediately outside the footprint of the current (smaller) modern church.[37] Perhaps future investigations may reveal more.

19

Summary and Conclusion

Summary

This unique enquiry has employed the methodology of a missing person investigation to solve one of the most enduring of historical mysteries: the apparent disappearance of two children in the summer of 1483. The investigation began by examining the time of the disappearance, analysing it moment by moment and using all available contemporary material to place this period under the spotlight. By employing forensic techniques, we went back to their last known location to recreate the past and build an extensive person of interest file of those around them and connected to them. This allowed us to determine who was where, when, with whom, doing what, and with what consequences at the time of the disappearance.

We also analysed exactly what was known about the two missing individuals at the centre of our endeavours to further inform lines of investigation and enquiry. Profiling revealed that both children (male) had large households and were well known. The elder (age 12) was a pre-teen who may not have been as physically robust as his younger sibling. He had an aptitude for poetry and literature and, facially, resembled his father. He seems to have been prone to melancholia which may have related to the onset of puberty and, very likely, the distressing change in his circumstances. Prior to his disappearance, he had been seen by Londoners ceremonially entering the city as the new king and later as he travelled to the Royal Apartments at the Tower Palace. On both occasions he would have been accompanied by leading members of Church, state and commons.

The younger boy (9) presented as a happy and energetic child who was strikingly pretty and considered to be in general good health. He had an aptitude for music, dancing, singing and, it seems, sport, possibly including archery and later tennis. Unlike his elder brother, he lived in the capital. Immediately prior to his disappearance, he was seen by Londoners travelling by barge from Westminster to join his brother at the Tower Palace. The flotilla consisted of at least eight barges and included leading members of Church and state.

Both boys may be described as celebrities and were last seen playing in the gardens of the busy Tower Palace on several occasions. They were blond and seem to have displayed a noticeable degree of charm.

Investigation of the timeline for the disappearance revealed a potential window of two months (18 or 21 July to 20 September), which could be extended to three months (28 October). Intelligence gathering revealed a disparity between local accounts at the time of the disappearance and those from abroad.

Wider analysis revealed that a pretender from France (Henry Tudor) introduced the charge of murder into England immediately prior to the Battle of Bosworth. The accusation of murder then took hold until the demise of the Tudor dynasty, when contemporary documents were investigated and the descendants of several families interviewed. These challenged the Tudor story of murder and presented instead the possibility of survival.

Further forensic analysis of the immediate post-Bosworth period revealed no evidence of murder or witnesses, and a rapid search in the north by Henry Tudor failed to locate the missing individuals, as did his later investigations at the Tower.

Analysis of potential suspects uncovered no obvious motive for murder.

Further investigation uncovered a contemporary blueprint for physical removal of the princes which did not involve or require harm.

As evidence for their survival mounted, the investigation was widened to consider two claimants to the throne. These presented post-Bosworth (in 1486 and 1491 respectively). Both claimants were of the right age and description for the missing individuals. The project then uncovered documented proof of life for both missing individuals: the elder in 1487; his younger sibling in 1493.

Actions Speak Louder than Words

The actions of the princes' mother, Elizabeth Woodville, have never been properly explained. She came to terms with Richard III and his government and advised her eldest son, Dorset, to do the same and thereby desert the pretender Henry Tudor in France. Shortly afterwards, she supported a rebellion against King Henry, ostensibly in the name of a common boy pretending to be the son of the Duke of Clarence, Elizabeth's erstwhile enemy. All this despite her eldest daughter having given birth to a grandson, the heir to the throne of England.

The only explanation for Elizabeth Woodville's actions, and those of Dorset, is the known survival of her sons by Edward IV. Other Woodville family members also acted in ways which contradict the later Tudor narrative. Sir Edward Woodville left England and its new Tudor monarch at what might be viewed as the height of his success. In 1487, he failed to engage with King Edward's rebels and took little or no part in the Battle of Stoke, then was absent from his niece's coronation and finally died in 1488, having taken an armed force overseas to fight for Brittany (Maximilian's ally) – flagrantly disobeying Henry VII's prohibition 'on pain of death'.

Events in York in 1487 have been presented to support the Tudor narrative of an impostor crowned in Dublin who was pretending to be Edward, Earl of Warwick. Much has been made of a document that gave the Dublin King a regnal number of 'VI', which was lodged in the city's archives after the Earl of Northumberland raised a local army to fight for Henry VII against the impostor. Upon forensic investigation, however, the claims made for its authority have been found to be inaccurate.

The document ascribing King Edward the regnal number of 'VI' is a copy and forms part of an introductory description to the originally appended text,[1] with the original text having been lost or destroyed. In extant communications from the Dublin King, he does not assign himself a regnal number; indeed, as king, this followed established procedure.

Those contemporaries reading communiqués would have understood who 'King Edward' was. York had been Ricardian, its city fathers were loyal to King Richard, but their loyalty had transferred to King Henry, who had informed them about the identity of the Dublin King prior to the young king's invasion.

Henry's control of information at this time had been countrywide.[2] Hence, when King Edward asked for help from the city fathers he was refused.

Not all supported the new direction. York recorded many arrests as trouble broke out across the city, with a former mayor murdered.[3]

Significantly, following the withdrawal of Sir Edward Woodville's cavalry from any military engagement with the rebel forces for three days from Doncaster to Sherwood Forest, the city of York declared itself for King Edward.[4] After the Battle of Stoke Henry visited York, issuing a royal proclamation commanding the citizens to keep the peace during his visit.[5] Following his visit, the city wrote its account and lodged the copy of Edward's letter in its records. No mention was made of the city's support for King Edward.[6] It is not known if Henry took King Edward's original letter with him.

Northumberland is another person whose actions were ambiguous. He had raised a northern army and set off to fight for Henry VII, but he returned to York to quell unrest. Two supporters of King Edward shouted the king's name at Bootham Bar, one of the city's gates, and made an assault with a company of horsemen but were quickly put to flight.[7]

Returning with an army of many thousands of men seems a rather heavy-handed response, but perhaps Northumberland suspected the city was under real threat. He waited in York for two days, saw there was no danger – and then took the army north at a time when King Henry was waiting for him in the south. Was the commotion caused by the Scrope Yorkist Lords of Bolton and Upsall at Bootham Bar a feint, intended to force redeployment of the northern levies? Or was it a previously agreed strategy to allow Northumberland to present the appearance of loyalty to the new Tudor monarch without having to fight for him? Northumberland's apparent prescient knowledge concerning the rebels' movements suggests he may have been in contact with them.[8]

We may also reflect on what kind of kings Edward V and Richard IV may have been had their drive for the throne been successful. Their individual characteristics, particularly the love of literature and music, suggests they may have been viewed as Renaissance monarchs, following the example of their father and uncle. Both, it seems, would have also respected and upheld the rule of law.

With the repeal of King Richard's legal title to the throne (Act of Succession) by Henry VII in Parliament on 23 January 1486, Edward V was able to pursue his right to the throne from the first opportune moment. That this was 1486 is evidenced in his only surviving grant in Ireland from August of that year. Here, King Edward clearly states this to be the first year of his reign. Respecting the will of Parliament during that reign would be an important factor for the new king in gaining support, particularly from those in government.

Richard IV's proclamation from Scotland (see Appendix 9) can certainly be viewed as a declaration of his intent as king and here we also see a clear understanding of, and respect for, the rule of law, similarly in obtaining justice. Richard seems to have been a kindly young man, but with perhaps a tendency to naivety as evidenced by his recoil from his invasion of England having witnessed the Scottish army's attack on his people. He was later described as 'intelligent and well spoken'.[9]

On 15 August 1501, twenty months after the execution of Richard, Duke of York, and Edward, Earl of Warwick, members of fifty-one families with lands in Yorkshire worth £40 p.a. or more failed to turn up to be knighted by King Henry. The list was headed by Scrope of Upsall, and included the names of nearly every family of standing in Yorkshire, including Conyers, Fairfax, Franke, Mauleverer, Metcalfe, Neville, Pilkington, Redman, Stapleton and Vavasour.[10]

Conclusion (and Next Steps)

On 2 July 2016, I launched The Missing Princes Project at the Richard III Middleham Festival in the town's collegiate church. I was asked what I hoped to find. I responded that by using the methodology of a missing person investigation and turning over every possible stone, some small pieces of hitherto unknown or disregarded information might come to light and help illuminate the mystery. I was then asked what I would like to find. I replied that I would like to find a witness statement, written by one of the boys and detailing exactly what had happened to them with names and places and verifiable facts. I smiled, and the audience burst into appreciative laughter, clearly hoping for the same seemingly impossible discovery.

Four years later, that would turn out to be exactly what was uncovered by Nathalie Nijman-Bliekendaal in the Gelderland Archive in the Netherlands, and I will never forget sitting at my desk on a bright November afternoon in 2020 reading her email. And yes, I had goosebumps. Six months earlier, on a warm May day, I had experienced the same reaction with an email from Albert Jan de Rooij and his discovery in the archive at Lille in France.

A timeline for the younger missing person, Richard, Duke of York, is now in place. We can track his removal from the Tower of London on or by

11 August 1483, his travels to the island of Texel in 1495, subsequent invasions of England, and his eight-year campaign for the throne.

A timeline for our elder missing person, Edward V, is a significant focus. Current evidence suggests Edward was placed in the Channel Islands on or before late 1485,[11] travelled to Francis Lovell in Yorkshire by April 1486 and was established in Ireland by August of that year. He then seems to have crossed to Burgundy, returning to Ireland with his English and continental forces in May 1487 for coronation, invasion of England and subsequent battle at Stoke Field. As the boys were separated at the Tower on or by mid–late July 1483, Edward's steps from this point to early 1486 are currently unknown (for lines of investigation in this regard, see Chapter 18).

A search for more data concerning Edward V continues in the archives of Burgundy and the Netherlands. What is clear from current evidence was the need for secrecy to maintain the element of surprise for Edward's drive for the throne. Henry VII's spies were everywhere, as evidenced in Sir Edward Woodville's household and the events pertaining to Richard of York's invasion from Burgundy in 1494–95. A mention of George of Clarence's son in Malines by a clerk at Easter 1487 in a financial reckoning, compiled at the end of that year, is currently the only mention of an Edward relating to the family located in the right place and time.

The Lille Receipt of December 1487 supports Edward V's survival at Stoke Field; it recorded no prayers for his soul. Similarly, the action of the Earl of Kildare and the Irish lords six months later, in July 1488, strongly suggests they knew, or believed, King Edward to be alive.

Edward would finally be removed from public and political life on Sunday, 8 May 1491, when his Garter stall at St George's Chapel was reallocated to Arthur, Prince of Wales,[12] who was 4½. We may find that the theory of Edward's post-battle survival could perhaps account for this particular four-year delay.

With the boys separated and Richard, Duke of York's whereabouts and identity kept secret to protect his life following Henry Tudor's victory at Bosworth, was Richard believed to be dead, to have perished in his travels, as his aunt Margaret would later assert to the Spanish monarchs?[13]

If so, all this would be reversed when, following his brother's defeat at Stoke, Thomas Peirse journeyed to bring the news of Richard's whereabouts in Portugal to his mother, Elizabeth Woodville, in the late summer of 1487 – news that soon reached Margaret in Burgundy.[14] But unanswered questions also surround his fate. In prison in 1499, Richard of York was so badly beaten that the Spanish Ambassador believed he would not live long, his face disfigured beyond recognition.[15] The once handsome prince who, like his brother, bore a striking resemblance to their father, Edward IV, would be hanged as a commoner at Tyburn.

If the person hanged at Tyburn was Richard of York, then this too was a judicial killing. He had been tried in the White Hall at Westminster and found guilty of treason. It was never explained how a Tournai boatman's son might be executed for treason against a foreign (English) monarch. The excuse seems to have been that seventeen months earlier, as a servant, he had escaped the royal household.[16] Escape *'from custody'* could be cited under laws of treason, but again, these laws, as devised and accepted in England, applied only to the king's subjects.

And what of the de la Pole family, the princes' royal cousins? Did they decide to speak truth, or hide the princes' new lives in anonymity in order to protect them? And is this why these Plantagenet cousins felt able to launch their own campaigns for the throne?

The de la Pole genealogy roll, incorrectly labelled the 'Lincoln Roll', was created in France sometime after 1492 with additions made after 1513, probably for Richard de la Pole, the last 'White Rose'.[17] Here, Henry VII is placed on an illegitimate line, with his grandfather, Owain Tudor, described as a household servant. The medallion for Edward reveals he died as a youth, without issue and Richard also died without issue.[18] A youth is a young man between the ages of 15 and 24.[19] At Stoke Field, Edward V was 16, in May 1491 he was 20; at Tyburn on 23 November 1499 Richard of York was 26. No further detail is offered.

Phase Two of The Missing Princes Project aims to attempt to answer these questions and, if possible, locate the final resting places of both princes, some clues to which have been discussed in Chapter 18.

The project will continue to commission original research, extend its search of international archives for new and neglected material and continue to request the assistance of families of ancient lineage with private archives.

Our heartfelt thanks go to all those families whose archives have already helped the project. If you have materials relating to our key period of investigation (1483–1509), or which might inform it, please get in touch through the website. Our specialists are waiting for your message. If you are an archivist, researcher or genealogist and have specialist skills in palaeography, Latin or languages (ancient or modern), we are also waiting to hear from you.

At the Middleham Festival in 2016, during the official launch of The Missing Princes Project, I presented an image of the Gordian knot and likened the centuries-old mystery surrounding the Princes in the Tower to the famous challenge faced by Alexander. A second image was that Gordian knot somewhat frayed and opening; a visual representation of my hopes. Never did I dare to believe that, like the Greek legend, we too would expose the two ends of the knot, unravel it and solve the unsolvable mystery. Now the project feels more like a jigsaw puzzle; the major pieces in place, the final ones yet to be found.

As I write these closing words to present The Missing Princes Project's first five-year report, new discoveries continue to come to light. It has been an exciting Phase One of our investigation, Phase Two promises to be equally exciting.

To the dead we owe only the truth.
Voltaire

Philippa Langley MBE

20

Postscript

In the summer of 1987 I was at a conference at Winchester. Going upstairs one afternoon I was suddenly aware of a conversation above me. A well-known historian was shaking with laughter and chortling, 'A book on Lambert Simnel! What next? One on Perkin Warbeck?' Too embarrassed to say anything I turned into the corridor for my room.[1]

Ian Arthurson found the courage to write his book and tell his story. His work did not question the orthodoxy surrounding the identity of the alleged French impostor to the English throne. Whether this helped with his determination to publish is not known by the present writer.

Today, so many of our young historians are not so lucky, or able to be so brave. Those questioning the received wisdom surrounding the reign of Richard III and the two claimants to Henry VII's throne are, at several of our leading seats of learning, patronised, threatened and bullied so they renounce their earlier ideas and conform to the traditional, regurgitated narrative. At one institution, a student was quietly warned that if they questioned anything with regard to the reign of Richard III they would have 'no career at this university'. Another was ridiculed for a paper, rich with research, and informed that their job was not to question but to find new ways of saying the same thing.

Can we imagine, just for a moment, where our scientific discoveries and breakthroughs would be if our students in this particular discipline received the same startling advice?

To all those brave young historians who contact me in despair, please do not give up. You are our next generation and if you can stand firm, change will come and you will make the most remarkable discoveries, as this work has, I hope, attested – all who question do.

A Call to Honour the Fallen

At the Battle of Stoke in June 1487, it is estimated that 5,000 men died fighting for a young King of England and his right to the throne. Their mass graves lay unmarked and unattended. With these unknown warriors may lie the remains of their commanders: John de la Pole, Earl of Lincoln, Martin Zwarte, Thomas Fitzgerald, and possibly Edward V himself.

In 1982, a partial excavation took place for one of these gravepits, located on the 'west side of the Fosse Way (A46) just south of the modern village of Stoke'.[2] I now wish to join historian David Baldwin (d. 2016) in asking for these remains to be re-examined using the most up-to-date techniques and technology so that their stories can now be told; for the remainder of the burial site to be excavated; and for all those uncovered, whether named or unnamed, with their stories told, to receive honourable reburial.

Appendix 1

King Richard's Oath and Promise
Westminster, 1 March 1484 (Modernised)

Memorandum that I Richard by the grace of God King of England and of France and Lord of Ireland in the presence of you my Lords Spiritual & Temporal and you Mayor & Aldermen of my City of London, promise & swear on the King's word & upon these holy Gospels of God by me personally touched that if the daughters of dame Elizabeth Grey late calling herself Queen of England that is to say Elizabeth, Cecily, Anne, Katherine and Bridget will come unto me out of the Sanctuary of Westminster and be guided Ruled & directed by me / then I shall see that they shall be in surety of their lives and also not suffer any manner of hurt by any manner of person or persons to them or any of them in their bodies and persons to be done by way of Ravishment or defouling contrary to their will / nor them or any of them imprison within the Tower of London or other prison / but that I shall put them in honest places of good name & fame / and them honestly & courteously shall see to be well provided for & treated and to have all things required & necessary for their endowment and provision as my kinswomen / And that I shall marry such of them as now being marriageable to gentlemen born / and each of them give in marriage lands & tenements to the yearly value of 200 marks for the term of their lives / and in likewise to the other daughters when they come to lawful Age of marriage if they live / and such gentlemen as shall happen to marry them I shall strictly charge from time to time lovingly to love & treat them as their wives & my kins-women / As they will avoid and eschew my displeasure.

And over this that I shall yearly from henceforth content & pay or cause to be contented & paid for the endowment & provision of the said dame Elizabeth Grey during her natural life at 4 quarters of the year / that is to say at Easter, Midsummer Michaelmas & Christmas to John Nesfield one of the Squires for my Body & for his provision to attend upon her the sum of 700 marks of lawful money of England, by even portions / And moreover I promise to them that if any allegation or evil report be made to me of them or any of them by any person or persons that than I shall not give there unto faith nor credence nor therefore put them to any manner of punishment before that they or any of them so accused may be at their lawful defence and answer.

In witness whereof to this writing of my oath & Promise aforesaid, to your said presences made I have set my sign manual the first day of March the first year of my Reign.

British Library Harleian Manuscript 433, Vol. 3 [f.308b], p. 190: 1 March 1484, Westminster.

Witnesses:

The Three Estates:	Elizabeth Woodville
Lords Spiritual (Bishops)	Elizabeth of York
Lords Temporal (Nobles)	Cecily of York
Mayor of London (Commons)	Anne of York
Aldermen of London (Commons)	Katherine of York
	Bridget of York

Appendix 2

Edward V

Proof of Life, 16 December 1487

I, Jehan de Smet, merchant, maker of wooden objects, living in Malines, declare to have received from Laurens le Mutre, counsellor and receiver of the artillery of the King of the Romans, our Lord, and Lord the Archduke, his son, the amount of 120 *livres*, at the rate of forty groats of the money of Flanders the *livre*, which was owed to me for the quantity of 400 long pikes made of ash, 24 and 23 feet long, clad with good iron in the new fashion/way, finished and sharpened, which the King has had taken away and bought from me in the said place in the month of June, the year one thousand four hundred and eighty-seven and delivered to the Lord of Walhain.

[These pikes were] to be distributed among the German-Swiss pikemen, who were then under the command of my lord Martin de Zwarte, a knight from Germany, to take and lead across the sea, whom Madam the Dowager sent at the time, together with several captains of war from England, to serve her nephew – son of King Edward, late her brother (may God save his soul), [who was] expelled from his dominion – and obstruct the King of the forementioned England in his activities.

These [pikes], at the price of six *sous* of two groats of the said money of Flanders each pike, bought from me by Lienart de La Court, squire, lieutenant of the master of the foresaid artillery, and Andrieu Schaffer, controller of the same, in the presence of the forementioned receiver, amount to the abovesaid sum of 120 *livres*, at the said rate of forty groats the *livre*, with which sum I am satisfied [i.e. which sum I have received].

Witness the signature of Florens Hauweel, secretary of the said Lords, set here at my request, the 16th day of December, in the year one thousand, four hundred and eighty-seven.

Hauweel

We, Lienart de La Court, squire, lieutenant of Lord Jean de Dommarten, knight, counsellor, chamberlain and Master of the Artillery of the King of the Romans, our Lord, and Lord the Archduke, his son, and Andrieu Schaffer, controller of the same, declare to anyone that should know, that Jehan de Smet abovementioned has sold and delivered the pikes clad with iron which, at the order of the King, with our knowledge and consent, have been delivered to the Lord of Walhain, knight, also their [King and Archduke] counsellor and chamberlain, at the price [mentioned/set?] and to be distributed in the manner contained and extensively described in the receipt above, amounting to 120 *livres*, at the rate of forty groats of the money of Flanders the *livre*, which at the above order has been paid by Laurens Le Mutre, also counsellor of the same Lords.

Witness our signatures set here, year and date abovementioned.

De La Court A. Schaffer

A.J. Martin Schwartz Transcriptie, Archives Départementales du Nord, Lille (Departmental Archives of the North, Lille): ADN B 3521/124564.

(Capitals, u and v, and punctuation modernised. With special thanks to Dr Livia Visser-Fuchs.)

Appendix 3

An Ideal Place to Hide a Prince

by John Dike, Lead Researcher,
Coldridge Line of Investigation

Introduction

The Coldridge line of investigation, led by John Dike, in Devon, is important for our ongoing enquiries with significant primary evidence uncovered. Specialist police investigators with many years' experience of cold-case enquiries working within The Missing Princes Project have advised that where coincidences occur, you must also investigate – no ifs, no buts – and here, as you will read below, there are many. In addition, as you will have seen throughout this work, the project cannot afford to ignore any line of enquiry and must turn over every stone we can in search of the truth. We do not have the luxury to make preconceived judgements. As a result, we look forward to John and his team discovering more as their research into this fascinating line of enquiry continues.

Philippa Langley

One can imagine the carnage of Stoke Field, with that gentle English hill littered with the dead and dying, and the cries of injured men and the cawing of feasting crows. And then amid that terrible scene, a young man and a boy are

311

led away, one is wounded and in distress, the other plucked from anonymity and promised food and warmth in the royal kitchens in exchange for silence.

Henry Tudor had won another bloody battle, but his throne was vulnerable. He would need to control public opinion, and that would require devious means. He also had to consider the wishes of his young wife. Strategically, he had already put the brakes on Thomas Grey, Marquess of Dorset, and Elizabeth Woodville, preventing them from assisting the injured young man to take the throne by placing Dorset in the Tower and having Elizabeth constrained at Bermondsey.

Coldridge is a small hilltop village in deepest Devon. It is situated well away from major towns, with Exeter 18 miles distant, Barnstaple 17 miles and Tiverton 16 miles. Medieval access to the village was limited to cart tracks. There was no navigable water nearby. If the imprisoned Dorset wanted somewhere on his own property to secrete his half-brother, he would find no better location.

Although this village is not known for any significant historical events, it has been the source of much interest by historians. Over 100 years ago, the renowned author and church historian Beatrix Cresswell commented on St Matthew's Church:[1]

> Standing on the summit of a steep hill, the church forms one of a line of towers, that, thus situated, are conspicuous landmarks above the surrounding scenery. It is built on a plateau, and around it gather the few cottages, of which the village now consists. In former times it may have been of greater importance. Nothing now remains to explain why this distant, and somewhat dreary spot, should have so fine a church … the portrait of Edward V, is a most unlikely monarch to find in sixteenth century stained glass.

At about the same time Cresswell was writing, Reverend H.J. Hodgson reviewed the church, 'This very interesting building is, for a village church, unusually large … The church seems at one time to be even larger.'

Over the course of many years, the late Professor Chris Brooks and Dr Martin Cherry investigated St Matthews. Their 1992 essay 'The Prince and the Parker' raised several questions:

> Contemporary representations of Edward V in any medium are so rare that the survival of one glass in deepest rural Devon raises intriguing questions as to patronage and purpose … The patron of the chantry remains elusive, being almost wholly absent from the documentary record … Modest as it is

though, this little chantry links Coldridge, far down in the south west, with the turbulent reign of Richard III and the demise of the House of York, and with the dynastic history of the Tudors.[2]

And then in 2007, Peter Bramley responded to the call to Coldridge in his *A Companion and Guide to the Wars of the Roses*:

> Coldridge [awarded four stars by Bramley] may be in the depths of North Devon countryside but, whatever you do, do not miss this one, for this little church contains one of the most fascinating survivals from our story … Why such politically charged stained glass in a tiny Devon church? … So who was John Evans? … Could he have been the real thing?[3]

The reason for this longstanding fascination with Coldridge, as we have seen, centres on the rare Edward V window and its patron, the elusive John Evans. To further this investigation, a team was established in 2018 under the guidance of Philippa Langley and The Missing Princes Project.

The team have taken a narrow, objective focus to look at the origins of the window, the background of John Evans and possible connections with Edward V. The possibility that Edward V had been given the new identity of John Evans, either prior to or after the Battle of Stoke, has been considered and certainly not discounted. Recent evidence has come to light that reinforces this possibility. This submission starts by giving an overview of the evidential base at Coldridge and then discusses this scenario.

Who was John Evans?

John Evans was a man who had been granted a considerable estate – the manor of Coldridge with two farms, Coldridge Barton and Birch, and a sizeable, well-stocked deer park. Brooks and Cherry postulated that he could have been a Yeoman of the Crown and it is true that under Henry VII and Henry VIII there are records of a John Evans (Evan or Jenan) acting at various times as a Yeoman of the Chamber or a Yeoman of the Crown.[4] Henry VIII also had a falconer called John Evans, who was active and had got married around 1530.

Henry VII had formed his Yeomen after Bosworth and they contained many Welshmen, so it is probable that there were a number of Yeomen with variants of the Evans name. However, although many were granted deer parks and estates by the king, there is no record of Coldridge in these.

Evans' predecessor Robert Markenfield is clearly shown as having received the grant of Coldridge estates from Richard III in 1484. If John Evans had been a Royal Yeoman, one would have expected some symbolism of this on his tomb effigy or on other inscriptions in the church. As Brooks and Cherry commented, Evans was elusive and almost wholly absent from the documentary record.

However, we do have information from the Cecily Bonville Estate Records of 1525.[5] This confirms that at that time Evans had estates and the deer park at Coldridge, he had a son, also named John, and another named Humphrey, who in turn had a son, Edmund. There is no factual evidence of where Evans originated from before Coldridge, nor whether he received the grant from Dorset, the owner of the estates prior to his death in 1501, or later, from his widow, Cecily Bonville.

No record has been found of Evans' date of death, but if he was alive in 1525 with grandchildren, then he may have been around 50 to 60 years of age at that time.

The Evans Chantry

By 1511, Evans had constructed a chantry in the church. Chantries were built in the belief that it would hasten one's journey through purgatory and, with

Tomb of John Evans (d. before 1525), Evans Chantry Chapel, St Matthew's Church, Coldridge, Devon. Possible burial location of Edward V. (John Dike)

age expectancy as it was, one would assume that Evans would have completed the building by the age of 40. The chantry contains his tomb monument (see image opposite) with his recumbent effigy carved in Beer stone, looking up at a window containing the Edward V glass and some other stained-glass fragments. He is dressed in armour under a surcoat but there are no indications that he was a knight. The monument is empty of remains.

There is some iconoclasm damage to the figure, with the removal of the hands in prayer and the feet, as well as the head of a cherub. By his left side is a helmet, and to his right a shield with the inscription 'JOHN EVAS'.

Just below the inscription is carefully placed inverted graffiti, which appears to say 'King', and below that are nine inscribed lines. Inverted images, presumably intended to give a hidden comment, are also present in the rood screen, where there are three small, inverted images of a lady with a Tudor headdress. They appear to have long tongues, which could be a reference to the biblical 'sins of the tongue'. These refer to lies, gossip, idle chatter, exaggeration, harsh attacks and uncharitable remarks. As will be seen later, they could be a critical depiction of Margaret Beaufort, mother of Henry VII. Hidden carvings like these are extremely rare and almost unheard of in English churches.

The tomb effigy of John Evans has a pronounced scar across the chin. Closer inspection of this scar reveals the presence of scratch marks outside the line of the scar, indicating that it had been cut with a sharp blade, possibly at a later time than the original sculpture.

Fortunately, there are two pieces of evidence that date the chantry. When it was built Evans equipped this chapel with heavy furniture, and of particular interest are two prayer desks. One was a massive oak structure inscribed, 'Pray for John Evans, Parker of Coldridge, maker of this work in the third year of the reign of King Henry the Eighth'.[6] And on the other desk, 'Pray for the good estate of John Evans, who caused this to be made at his own expense, the second day of August in the year of the Lord 1511'.[7]

By 1930 these desks were in poor condition. The Rural Dean found them jumbled behind the choir stalls and requested that they be sorted out, repaired, renovated and placed in a suitable position, as he considered them very interesting and valuable. A local parishioner undertook this task and decided to combine the remains into just one desk with a facsimile of the first inscription above. As the Evans Chantry is now the vestry, this desk is now in the South Chapel.

It is believed that when Evans referred to 'maker of this work', he was referring to his chantry and probably the rood screen which dates to that period.

Between the Evans Chantry and the chancel is a parclose screen of ornate Breton design. This is a most unusual screen to be found in Devon and is very similar to the parclose screens in the nearby churches of Colebrooke and Brushford. It has been suggested that Evans was the donor of these screens,[8] in which case he must have been involved with Sir John Speke, who, among other estates, held the manors of Wembworthy and Brushford, which bordered Coldridge.

The chantry that Evans constructed has several columns. At the head of these columns is placed the inscription '*Orate pro anima Johes Evans*' – 'Pray for the soul of John Evans'. (Note that Evans is spelt in full, unlike the legend 'Evas' on the tomb.) One column top has the engraving 'IX' next to a crown, possibly referring to the death of Henry VII in 1509 or possibly to the completion date of the stonework.

The Stained Glass

The Coldridge team spent considerable time investigating the origins of the stained glass at St Matthews. As with many churches, all that remained after the iconoclasm of Henry VIII and Edward VI were tiny fragments of the rich window glass that would have adorned the church in 1511 when John Evans built his chantry. It is probable that the Evans family, as wealthy landowners, were able to save images of a mainly secular nature, relating to their family, from hands bent on destruction.

The window in the Evans Chantry has most of the remaining glass. In the bottom left of the window is a fragment of '*Orate pro ...*'. This would indicate that the window still had significance to the Evans family when the fragments of saved glass were placed in it: we may assume that these selected fragments reflected their earnest sentiment to 'Pray for John Evans'.

The window contains two further images. To the left is a full-length portrait of Edward V, and to the right, just the head of another figure that originally would have been of a size, full-length, similar to the Edward V image (see p. 318).

As previous historians have indicated, the presence of a stained-glass portrait of Edward V in a small and remote Devon village raises many questions. There are only two other glass portraits of Edward that date from that time; one is in the Royal Window, Canterbury Cathedral, *c.* 1482 (now a later copy, post-1660s); the other is in the East Window, Little Malvern Priory Church, *c.* 1482. And there are two paintings, one in the Oliver King Chantry, St George's Chapel, Windsor, *c.* 1493; and one in miniature, of Lord Rivers presenting his book to Edward IV and family (*The Dictes and Sayings of the Philosophers*, later printed by Caxton, 1477).

The Authenticity of the Edward V Portrait

There have been suggestions that the Edward V portrait was really depicting Edward VI, but that was discounted many years ago, first by Reverend Sabine Baring-Gould (1834–1924), an author of over 1,200 publications and composer of 'Onward Christian Soldiers', then Beatrix Cresswell,[9] and more recently, Brooks and Cherry.[10]

The glass has been dated to the late fifteenth or early sixteenth century and shares design features with the glass at the Church of St Michael, Doddiscombsleigh, Devon, which was believed to have been created by ateliers in the Exeter glass workshops prior to 1500. If Evans completed his chantry in 1511 then this date is assumed as likely for the Edward V glass.

Above the crowned figure of Edward is a floating larger crown containing an ermine lining. Most unusually, the ermine is not spotted with the usual heraldic depictions of stoats' tails, but the spots are shown as deer, possibly a hidden message linking the Coldridge Deer Parker with royalty. The deer spots total forty-one which, if subtracted from 1511, would give a figure of 1470, the year that Prince Edward was born. The ermine cloak on the main figure has the traditional stoats' tails markings.

The church records refer to an early letter from the Keeper of Ceramics at the Victoria & Albert Museum, 'I should hesitate to suggest whether parts of it are restored (the large crown must, however, have been separate from the figure) ... The inscription seems to read 'Prenys Eduard the feyte, which must surely read fifth ...' (Prince Edward the fifth).

The Large 'Floating' Crown

The concept of the floating crown above a monarch who was apparently never actually crowned is repeated in the painted image at St George's Chapel , but in that painting there is only one crown present. It is believed that the floating crown at Coldridge was one of the post-Reformation remnants that were rescued and replaced in appropriate positions when the windows were repaired during the reign of Mary I. As there were few remnants of stained glass left, it is easy to see why the floating crown would have been positioned above the Edward V image, and confirms that whoever did it was in no doubt that the image actually depicted Edward, but the fact that he was already wearing a crown suggests that this was not its original position.

A comparison of the dimensions of the floating crown with the central bay of the larger chancel window shows that this could have been its original location. It is more likely that the floating crown was originally above a coat of arms or a royal badge; it would be too large to be over another image similar to the Edward V portrait in the Evans Chantry.

The Coldridge estates were passed from the Bonvilles to the Greys. Their coats of arms included a coronet, not a crown carrying the royal insignia depicted on the Coldridge crown. If this was part of a royal coat of arms, it would be most unusual in a small, remote village. One might assume that such a motif would indicate the presence in the area of a person of royal stature and that the rare deer spots in the ermine may provide a link to the Coldridge Deer Parker.

This crown also contains the Yorkist emblem of a falcon in a fetterlock, which was probably a badge of Edward V.[11] This would indicate the presence in the church of at least two images dedicated to the prince, which is highly significant. The Falcon and Fetterlock was also the badge of Edward V's grandfather, Richard, Duke of York (d. 1460), and was used by Edward IV.

The Small Portrait
Of great interest is the fragment of glass in the Evans chapel that portrays just the head and shoulders of a man. This person bears a resemblance to the carved image of John Evans on the tomb. This depiction is most unusual in

Surviving fragment of stained-glass window, Evans Chapel. Portrays head and shoulders of a man with injury to his mouth and chin. Bears resemblance to the carved image of John Evans on tomb. (John Dike)

that it appears to be drawn from life, 'warts and all'. In particular, the mouth appears to lack lips, exposing the teeth, and there is a line across the chin that could depict a scar similar to the one on the tomb effigy.

Brooks and Cherry considered that this image either depicted John Evans, or it could be a very rare image of Richard III.[12] Their publication suggested that an image of Richard III would be an example of Tudor propaganda by local factions objecting to him taking the throne, with the image made more grotesque by removing a lip and twisting the countenance in the interests of deformity.

This fragment of the portrait appears to show a crown, similar to the floating crown in the Edward V portrait, being carried in front of the chest. Brooks and Cherry were assisted by David Evans, who reproduced the crown as it might have been. They considered the idea that this was an image of a royal person, in their opinion Richard III stealing the crown of England, but propaganda of this type would have little effect in such an isolated location, so it is more likely to be a person subject to more local sentiments.

A study of a facially injured Edward V is thought to be a more likely candidate, but this would obviously raise the very intriguing question of the real identity of John Evans, as his tomb effigy has a similar injury. The facial injury raises important questions. A deep cut in this area of the chin would render the mentalis muscle useless. This muscle is located at the tip of the jaw:

> The mentalis muscle supports the lower lip and chin pad. Its damage results in chin and lower lip ptosis with resultant excessive lower tooth show.'[13]

This injury would have exposed the teeth (as seen in the second portrait), making it difficult to articulate, and would have been facially disfiguring.

John Evans, the Deer Parker

We know from the inscriptions on the old benches that John Evans had been granted the position of the Coldridge Deer Parker. Contemporary records show that the deer park, located at the rear of the church, was held by John Evans in 1525.[14] 'The said park contains in circumference 3,000 paces, and by view of the officers there are now 140 beasts of the chase vis bucks and does … and good wood.'

Tristram Risdon wrote, in 1632, 'In this parish was not long since a park, garnished with goodly woods and timber; now so wasted, that in future time the place may better brook his name for want thereof.'[15] However, it may have been in better condition when '*Parcus de Colrudge*' was granted to James Bassett by Mary I in 1557 after she executed the previous owner, Henry Grey, 1st Duke of Suffolk.

The award of the deer park to Evans was a prestigious appointment and gave him the ability to enjoy the benefits of timber and venison in return for the administration of the park. He would also be instructed to give venison to persons selected by Dorset or Cecily Bonville as gifts or in return for favours. Evans was also granted the flour mill, Parker's Mill, adjacent to the park, which was powered by a leat from the River Taw and provided flour to the village.

Medieval Symbolism in the Church

There are many items in the church that could be considered representational of the House of York. There are several floor tiles that were produced at the Barnstaple tileries early in the sixteenth century and have been credited with showing that these tileries were in production much earlier than was at first thought. The swan motif is fairly common in West Country churches, but the Rose of York and the Sun in Splendour seen at Coldridge show a strong link to the House of York. In addition to the tiles, there are many carved oak roof bosses probably depicting the Yorkist Rose, and one that shows the Sun in Splendour. There would appear to be a deliberate attempt here to make a Yorkist statement, because in the window adjacent to this boss there is a salvaged fragment of a similar badge in stained glass.

Robert Markenfield: A Strange Assignment

On 1 March 1484, Elizabeth Woodville, no longer queen and now referred to as Dame Elizabeth Grey, left sanctuary at Westminster Abbey with her daughters after Richard III publicly swore an oath guaranteeing their safety and good marriages for her daughters. Thomas Grey, Marquess of Dorset, Elizabeth's eldest son by her first marriage, had previously fled the same sanctuary. On 3 March 1484, Robert Markenfield, an associate and servant of the king, from Ripon in Yorkshire, was granted the Coldridge estates and sent there:

> Grant, during pleasure, to the King's servant Robert Markynfeld of the office of keeper of the park of Colrigge, Co. Devon, in the King's hands by the forfeiture of Thomas, late Marquis of Dorset, receiving the accustomed fees from the issues of the Manor of Colrigge with all other profits.[16]

1. Earliest known (copy) portrait of Richard III (1452–85), *c.* 1510. Society of Antiquities, London. Panel portrait. See Plate 10. (Bridgeman Images)

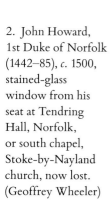

2. John Howard, 1st Duke of Norfolk (1442–85), *c.* 1500, stained-glass window from his seat at Tendring Hall, Norfolk, or south chapel, Stoke-by-Nayland church, now lost. (Geoffrey Wheeler)

3. Six-year-old Edward (V), Prince of Wales (1470 to after 1487), c. 1477, with his mother, Queen Elizabeth Woodville, and father, Edward IV. Anthony Woodville, Earl Rivers (kneeling), second from left. Figure (standing) in blue believed to be Richard, Duke of Gloucester. Lambeth Palace, London. (© Lambeth Palace Library / Bridgeman Images)

4. Eleven-year-old Edward (V), Prince of Wales, c. 1482, stained-glass window, Little Malvern Priory, Worcester. Wearing circlet crown of a prince. The priory was rebuilt at this time by John Alcock, Bishop of Worcester, tutor to Edward and President of his household. (Steve Carse for The Missing Princes Project, 5 April 2022)

5. Edward V age 16 from coronation (Sunday, 27 May 1487), *c*. 1500, stained-glass window, Coldridge Church, Devon. Wearing crown of a king and holding the royal sceptre. Coldridge was owned by Edward V's half-brother, Thomas Grey, 1st Marquess of Dorset (d. 1501), and his wife, Cecily Bonville (d. 1529). (John Dike)

6. & 7. Edward (V), Prince of Wales (right) and Richard, Duke of York (left), after 1660s, Royal Window, Canterbury Cathedral. Following restoration, Edward and Richard are shown in closed crowns of a king. Original window, *c*. 1482, children of Edward IV depicted in circlet crowns. (Geoffrey Wheeler)

8. Twenty-year-old Richard, Duke of York (1473–99?), *c.* 1494, Tournament Tapestry, Musée des beaux-arts de Valenciennes, France. York (centre, facing) depicted at royal tournament with Burgundian royal family, with his aunt Margaret of York and Burgundy on his left. Margaret holds a gilly flower at York's heart. The gilly flower (carnation) was the emblem of York's mother, Elizabeth Woodville (d. 1492). Mark visible at Richard's right eye. (RMN-Grand Palais / René-Gabriel Ojeda / RMN-GP / Dist. Photo SCALA, Florence)

9. Pencil sketch (*c.* 1560) of 20-year-old Richard of York, *c.* 1494, from painting (uncredited). Searches are ongoing for the painting. Reveals mark by right eye and hair detailed as 'blon' (blond). Sketch probably by herald Jacques le Boucq. Arras, France. (Bridgeman Images)

10. One of the earliest known (copy) portraits of Edward IV (1442–83), *c.* 1510, Society of Antiquaries, London. Panel portrait. Note resemblance to Richard, Duke of York (youngest son), see Plate 9. (Bridgeman Images)

11. Elizabeth Woodville (1437–92), mother of Edward V and Richard, Duke of York. Earliest known (copy) portrait, *c*. 1513–30, Royal Collection. (Royal Collection Trust)

12. Margaret of York and Burgundy (1446–1503), *c*. 1468, Louvre Museum, Paris. Sister of Edward IV and Richard III, and aunt of Edward V and Richard, Duke of York. Leading supporter of both Yorkist claimants to the English Crown. (Musée du Louvre)

13. Maximilian I (1459–1519), 1519, by Albrecht Dürer, Kunsthistorisches Museum, Vienna, Austria. Leading supporter of Edward V and Richard, Duke of York. Holy Roman Emperor (1508–19). (Kunsthistorisches Museum)

14. Tower of London, 1480s. Contemporary image from manuscript of poems by Charles, Duke of Orléans (1394–1465). Many of the poems were written while the duke was imprisoned at the Tower (1415–40). Image shows a number of scenes, including the duke writing poetry in the White Tower and gazing out of a window. Reveals White Tower apartments. Artistic style suggests illustrator was Dutch. From manuscript, Bruges. (The Picture Art Collection / Alamy Stock Photo)

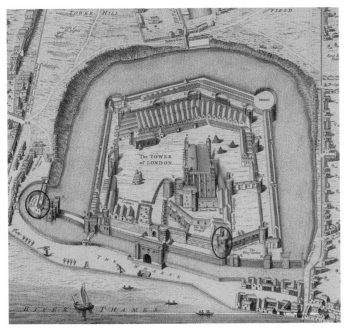

15. Tower of London, Survey 1597; image, 1742. Royal Apartments, Lanthorne Tower, circled in blue (note 'Privy Garden' where princes were probably seen shooting arrows). Lions Tower, circled in green, where Richard of York was housed nearby in July 1483. St Katherine's is located to the east. Buildings were added to southern aspect of the central White Tower, demolished in the 1670s. (© British Library Board. All Rights Reserved / Bridgeman Images)

16. Tower of London entrance, moat and drawbridge. Lions Tower: semi-circular area by moat. Artist's reconstruction by Ivan Lapper. (Historic Royal Palaces)

17. Medieval carvel-built ship, similar to vessel which transported 9-year-old Richard, Duke of York, to France from the Tower of London in mid-July to early August 1483. Travel was organised by John Howard, Duke of Norfolk, Earl Marshal and Lord High Admiral of England. York was cared for by Peirse brothers Henry and Thomas. Manuscript image (sixteenth century) of Edward (IV) landing in Calais in exile in 1459.

Carvel-built: relatively small, fast sailing into the wind with two to three masts. Due to the bottom of the ship protruding below the surface of the water by only a small distance, it is extremely manoeuvrable. Crew size: seven up to fifteen, including passengers. Bears 120 tons of cargo and could be armed with a weapon. Being small with a shallow keel enables it to sail upriver and close to shore. Average length: 23–25m (75–81ft). Image possibly carvel or carrack (broader and less manoeuvrable). Carracks may have been used for Edward V's invasion fleet of 1487. (Musée Thomas Dobrée-Musée Archéologique, Nantes, France / Bridgeman Art Library (Ms. 18 f. 109v.); description of carvel-built ship, thanks to Jean Clare-Tighe)

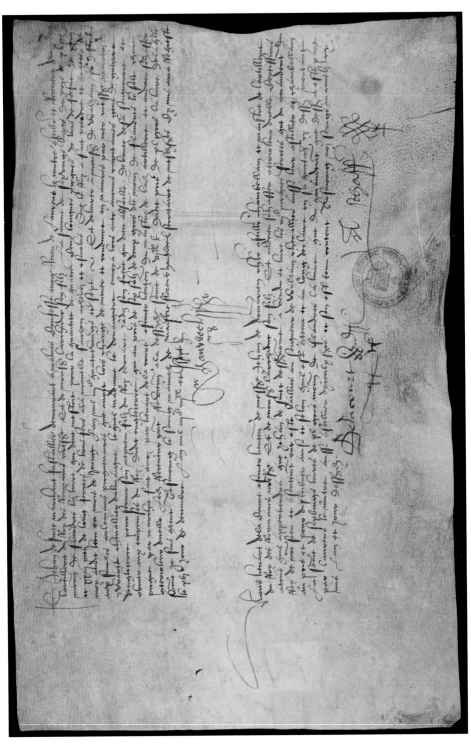

18. Edward V, Proof of Life, 16 December 1497: 'to serve her nephew – son of King Edward, late her brother (may God save his soul), [who was] expelled from his dominion.' (Archives Départementales du Nord, Lille, France, ADN B 3521/124564)

19. Sunday, 27 May 1487, 16-year-old Edward V is carried in triumph at his coronation in Christ Church Cathedral, Dublin. Edward is carried as a young man by the giant William D'Arcy of Platten (Great Darcy). Edward was likely of a slim (gracile) build, similar to Richard III (his uncle). From James Ward mural, 1913, Dublin City Hall. (Courtesy of Dublin City Library & Archive)

20. Christ Church Cathedral, Dublin, site of Edward V's coronation. Edward was crowned on the same (holy) day as the coronation of his mother, Elizabeth Woodville, at Westminster Abbey, twenty-two years earlier (the Sunday after Ascension). All records pertaining to Edward V's coronation and Parliament were destroyed on the orders of Henry VII. (Philippa Langley)

21. (left) Obverse, Great Seal of Edward V, 13 August 1486. Seal affixed to grant patent to Peter Butler, Sheriff of Kilkenny. Witnessed by Edward's 'very dear cousin', Gerald, Earl of Kildare, Governor of Ireland. It remains one of the few surviving artefacts from Edward V's reign. Edward V's image can be seen on the front, crowned and seated on a throne. (National Library of Ireland, Dublin: MS UR 016658, Ref. D 1855)

22. (right) Reverse, Great Seal of Edward V. It shows the royal arms of leopards and lilies quartered, covered with an arched (closed) crown of a king. (National Library of Ireland, Dublin)

23. Matrix seal of John de la Pole, Earl of Lincoln, dating from 21 August 1484 to 22 August 1485. Circular 3 0/9in. Lincoln was Richard III's heir following the death of Edward of Middleham, Prince of Wales. After Parliament repealed *Titulus Regius* on 23 January 1486, Edward V superseded his claim. Leading supporter of Edward V. (British Museum, No. 1838,1232.16)

24. Matrix seal of John de Vere, 13th Earl of Oxford (1442–1513), following restoration in 1485. Circular 2 5/8in. Victor of the battles of Bosworth (1485) and Stoke (1487). (© The Society of Antiquaries of London)

25. Charter and letter patent of Richard of England, Duke of York, with royal seal, 4 October 1493. Acknowledgement of a loan from Albert of Saxony of 30,000 florins and signed 'Richard of England', with royal monogram. Includes seals (and signatures) of York's supporters, Sir Robert Clifford and William Barley, Esquire (Clifford's father-in-law). (Sächsisches Staatsarchiv, Hauptstaatsarchiv Dresden, 10001 Ältere Urkunden, Nr. 9005 [Saxon State Archives, Main State Archive, Dresden, Germany] (SHA))

26. Royal signet seal of Richard of England depicting the shield of royal arms of leopards and lilies quartered and covered with the arched (closed) crown (cross at top) of a king. Arms are encircled by Yorkist roses and suns (in splendour), with the letter 'R' at the base, placed between a rose and sun. The seal survives intact. (SHA, Nr. 9005)

27. Richard, Duke of York, Proof of Life, *c.* 1493. Witness statement, page 1: 'They swore by honour and oath to Duke Howard, as mentioned before, to hide me secretly until certain years were past.' It is one of four pages (including cover page). (Gelders Archief, Arnhem, Netherlands, 0510, Nr. 1549 Diverse charters/diverse aanwinsten)

28. Margaret of York and Burgundy's Palace at Binche (Belgium). 'Richard's room', at the arch in the centre of image, was located beneath the chapel and led out onto a tennis court. (Philippa Langley)

29. Cloth of gold sample (15 x 17cm), Italian, late fifteenth century. Richard, Duke of York, left sanctuary at Beaulieu Abbey to meet Henry VII wearing cloth of gold, which was permitted only to royalty in the late fifteenth century. Gold (or sometimes silver) threads were woven into a precious fabric, usually silk, creating a stiff and heavy (and very expensive) material. (Victoria and Albert Museum, London, Acc. No. 1062–1900)

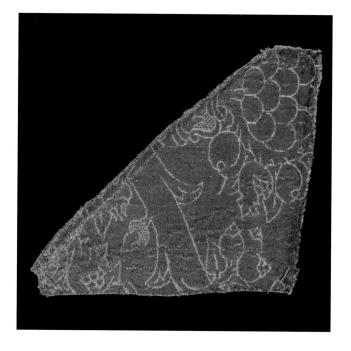

30. Tyburn, London, an ancient place of execution and probable execution site of Richard, Duke of York, on 23 November 1499 (aged 26). 'Tyburn Tree' was the colloquial name for the famous Tyburn gallows. This stone marker is located in the pavement at the top of Edgware Road. (Philippa Langley)

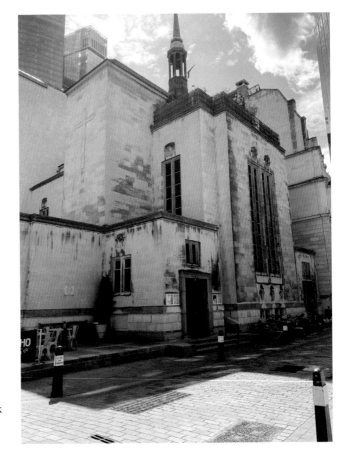

31. The site of Austin Friars church, now the Dutch Church, London. The original medieval friary church was rebuilt following a fire in 1862, but was then flattened by a parachute bomb during the Blitz in the Second World War. It was rebuilt (with a slightly smaller area) in 1950–54. It is the probable burial location of Richard, Duke of York (in exterior passageway). (Philippa Langley)

32. Coat of arms,
Francis, Viscount Lovell KG
(c. 1457–?92).

33. Coat of arms,
John de la Pole, Earl of Lincoln KG
(c. 1460–87).

34. Coat of arms,
Sir William Stanley KG
(c. 1435–95).

35. Coat of arms,
Sir Edward Woodville KG
(1454/8–88).

(All coat of arms images: Thanks to College of Arms, London (assistant to York Herald) for verification of arms depicted.)

36. Dutch Research Group with Philippa Langley at Cramond, Edinburgh (9 September 2017). Langley's Looking For Richard Project began at Cramond in February 2009. L–R: William (Wim) Wiss, Albert Jan de Rooij, Nathalie Nijman-Bliekendaal, Philippa Langley, Jean Roefstra. (Photo Jean Roefstra)

37. Philippa Langley and Rob Rinder filming *The Lost Princes* (working title) documentary at Binche, Belgium. L–R: Andrea Bertelli (Drone Operator), Antoine Paichard (Camera Assistant), Emmanuel Clermont (Runner/Driver), Florrie Reeves (Assistant Producer), Dr Emilia Chodorowska (Producer), Janice Sutherland (Director), Matt Kennedy (Director of Photography), Jean Roefstra (Dutch Research Group), Joël Flescher (Sound Recordist), Nathalie Nijman-Bliekendaal and Zoë Maula (both Dutch Research Group), Philippa Langley and Rob Rinder. Luca Biagiotti (not in shot) (Drone Operator). (Photo Luca Biagiotti)

Robert Markenfield was a brother of Sir Thomas Markenfield of Markenfield Hall, Yorkshire. Our knowledge of Robert is very limited. In 1468 a priest at Ripon Cathedral, Thomas Hawk, left Robert his jerkin and helmet, battleaxe and sword.[17] The same priest, who had been disgraced for adultery and possibly helped by the Markenfield family, also left many of his household items to Sir Thomas and his mother, Margaret.

Sir Thomas was a loyal retainer to Richard III and fought at Bosworth. As Professor A.J. Pollard states:

> Sir Thomas Markenfield, who was born around 1447 and died in 1497, is celebrated for his attachment to Richard III ... he was rewarded with a grant of confiscated estates in Somerset to the value of £100 p.a ... and was made Sheriff of Yorkshire.[18]

It has been reported that both Thomas and Robert were favoured by the king, but it is very strange that Robert was only granted this small manor and deer park in deepest Devon. Was there a special assignment given to him by the king that was associated with the deal struck with Elizabeth Woodville? Did Robert Markenfield follow the wishes of the mother of the two princes and take Edward V to Coldridge to be known as John Evans?

To add to this intrigue, we will see that Robert Markenfield will become involved with another local landowner and associate of John Evans, Sir John Speke, who in 1497 will receive a heavy fine for assisting Richard of England, the brother of Edward V.

Sir John Speke and Richard of England

Sir John Speke (1442–1518) held lands in Somerset and Devon; in particular, the manors of Heywood, at Wembworthy, and Brushford, which adjoin the manor of Coldridge. His son, John (1468–1524), who succeeded him, was on the same side as Robert Markenfield in 1495 in a land dispute at Wembworthy.[19]

In the 1516 will of Sir John there are mentions of bequests of money and a horse to a Peter Markenfield, who may have been a son of Robert and obviously in good standing with the Spekes. Without doubt, Evans and the Spekes would have been associates and there is no evidence to show that they were not friends.

The tomb of Sir John Speke in the Speke Chantry at Exeter Cathedral bears a striking similarity to the Evans tomb, although it is much more ornate.

As previously mentioned, Evans and Speke would have collaborated on the installation of the parclose screens at Coldridge and Brushford.

The involvement of Sir John Speke with Richard of England is of particular interest: for assisting him in 1497, Speke received the very heavy fine of £200 from Henry VII. The rebellion on behalf of Richard of England involved a Cornish uprising attacking the city of Exeter, initially by trying to enter the north gate. The fifteenth-century route to the north gate would have taken Richard from Okehampton to Crediton via Down St Mary and Copplestone, passing very close to Coldridge and Wembworthy. Speke may have offered Richard rest and refreshment on his estates prior to the final 20-mile march to Exeter and the involvement of John Evans may have been very possible.

The presence of two images of the Sun in Splendour – of a similar design to those in the livery of Edward IV – in the stained glass at Speke's church at Wembworthy, further suggests an affinity between Speke and the House of York. It should be noted that Sir John Speke had married Alice, one of the daughters of Sir Thomas Arundell. Arundell was a relative through marriage to Sir James Tyrell.

Sir Henry Bodrugan, Coldridge and Edward V

It is significant that Bodrugan, one of the most controversial characters that ever came out of Cornwall, had links to Coldridge and was a supporter of Richard III and the House of York. Robert Markenfield was granted the manor and deer park of Coldridge on 3 March 1484. A month later, on 8 April 1484, a Sir Henry Bodrugan (also known as Trenowith) was given Coldridge as well as other estates in Devon.[20]

In the uprising of October 1483, Sir Richard Edgecombe of Cornwall had joined the Duke of Buckingham in his revolt against King Richard. Sir Henry Bodrugan, acting for the king, had besieged him at Cotehele. Vastly outnumbered, the desperate Edgecombe managed to break through the cordon and escape to France, where he joined Henry Tudor. It is unclear what role Markenfield played from that point in Coldridge, but possibly he was working for Bodrugan, as he was still in the area in 1495.

This was not the first time that the Bodrugans had an involvement in Coldridge. In 1331, Joan Bodrugan married Henry Champernon, who held Coldridge among his estates.

Henry Bodrugan was a colourful character whose actions appeared to jump between a kind benefactor and responsible Cornish ruler and that of a pirate and robber. Contemporary records show that in February 1486 he was in the favour of Henry VII and put to chasing down Cornish pirates.[21] But in February 1487, a warrant was issued for his arrest for sedition and in May 1487 Bodrugan attended the Dublin coronation of King Edward.

In November 1487 he was attainted, and his land then passed to Sir Thomas Lovell (no relation to Francis) in April 1488. Presumably Dorset's land, including Coldridge, went to Lovell before it went back to Dorset. Lovell was Chancellor of the Exchequer, fought against the Yorkist forces at Stoke and was noted for extortion under Henry VII.

Could Sir Henry Bodrugan have been the man who managed the transportation of the young Edward V from Devon to the Dublin coronation, or more likely, some of his supporters? Three facts may support this: Bodrugan attended the coronation; he owned the Coldridge estates at that time; and he also owned two suitable ships moored in Devon or Cornwall, the *Mary Bodrugan* and the *Barberye*, both ideal for sailing up the coast to Ireland.

William Darcy, Robert Markenfield and the Coldridge Connection

During the Dublin coronation on 27 May 1487, Edward V was carried on the shoulders of 'Great Darcy of Platten'. William Darcy, a leading Anglo-Irish statesman, was from a family that originated in England. Of the family remaining in England, Philip, 6th Lord Darcy, had a daughter Margery, who married Sir John Conyers.

Conyers had been a loyal retainer to Richard of Gloucester, later Richard III. In 1438, Sir John and Margery had a daughter, Eleanor, who would marry Sir Thomas Markenfield and thus be sister-in-law to Robert Markenfield of Coldridge.

John Goddesland

'We have strong presumptive evidence that Prince Edward certainly was alive in March 1485, which is up to a year and a half after the period when More and others say that he and his brother were put to death,' said John Bayley in 1830.[22] His comment is based on the following record. On Wednesday, 9 March 1485 the King's Signet Office records, 'A warrant to Henry Davy to deliver to John Goddeslande fotemane [footman] unto the lord Bastard two dublettes of silk oon jaket of silk oone gowne of gloth two shirtes and two bonetes [hats]'.[23]

As we have seen, some have attributed this grant of clothing to King Richard's bastard son, John of Gloucester. However, John (unlike Edward V) was not a lord (see Chapter 5, note 39). 'Lord Bastard' would have also been a courtesy title for Edward V as the former king and Prince of Wales.

Recent research has revealed that the surname Goddesland is unusual. It originated within 15 miles of Coldridge and was, until only recently, 'restricted to North Devon'.[24] There was a John Goddesland recorded at Burrington, 8 miles from Coldridge in 1524[25] and a John Goddesland recorded as resident in Coldridge in 1569.[26] As this was a rare and localised name at that time it is possible that the Burrington Goddesland was the same person mentioned in the Signet Office record.

The Royal Connection

The evidence presented above shows a viable link between Coldridge, John Evans and the House of York and Edward V. In particular, the presence of two royal images is significant. The Edward V portrait in the Evans Chantry, and what was probably a royal coat of arms carrying the Yorkist Falcon and Fetterlock badge of Edward V in the chancel, sends a strong message.

It is true that in a major church or cathedral, where the footfall would justify these representations, one might expect to see the images or messages that exist at Coldridge, but not in a tiny village in Devon that was difficult to access in the early sixteenth century. In fact, images this strong representing Edward V do not exist anywhere other than Coldridge. One can only assume that the reasons for this imagery were very local. There is also the pattern of historical events that add depth to a royal connection.

Who was Responsible for all the Yorkist Imagery in the Church?

John Evans carried out extensive works in the church at Coldridge, as well as the funding of the parclose screens at nearby Brushford and Colebrooke. It is also thought that he was responsible for the magnificent early sixteenth-century rood screen at Coldridge, regarded by many as the finest in Devon.

His personal chantry required major construction work involving the insertion of new pillars and a realignment of the roof. This work must have been very expensive, and Evans would have needed significant funds to achieve it. The Barnstaple floor tiles and the stained-glass images date from the early part of the sixteenth century. The desk inscriptions confirm that Evans completed 'this work' by 1511 and the first pillar of his chantry, when viewed from the chancel, has the engraving 'IX' followed by a crown symbol, which could indicate that the major stonework was in place by 1509, the year Henry VII died.

Some have suggested that Dorset was responsible for all the Yorkist imagery at Coldridge, but as he died as early as 1501, this would not be possible, and we must conclude that Evans was the major player in this.

Was John Evans Really Edward V? The Facts that Support the Theory

The absence of any early records for Evans, a person who must have had sufficient standing to warrant the level of grants he received, suggests secrecy. The Coldridge estates were owned by Dorset, maternal brother of Edward V and Richard, Duke of York. Coldridge would have been ideal as a remote and inaccessible place in which to locate Edward if by arrangement with Richard III or Henry VII.

Richard III sent his associate, Robert Markenfield, to Coldridge two days after his reconciliation with Elizabeth Woodville. The presence of royal imagery depicting Edward V, and numerous Yorkist badges and motifs, in this remote church in a tiny village is unique. The tomb exhibits the message 'EV(AS)', with the inverted inscription 'KING' below it. If 'AS' was a truncated 'ASA', it would spell 'in sanctuary' in Latin. Even 'EVAS' reversed has significance as the word SAVE (*saven, c.* 1200), with the meaning to protect or rescue from harm.

There are three unique inverted portraits of a Tudor lady hidden in the rood screen, which could be a caricature of Margaret Beaufort, the mother of Henry Tudor. On the Evans tomb, the face resembles the small portrait in the window, and both exhibit facial damage, possibly a battle wound. The small portrait carries a royal crown and wears an ermine collar. The floating crown is thought to have been originally placed above a royal badge or coat of arms in the chancel. This royal crown has the Falcon and Fetterlock badge of Edward V (and his grandfather and father). The ermine spots are shown, uniquely, as deer, linking them to the deer parker. The forty-one deer could suggest, if subtracted from the 1511 date of the chantry, the birth of Edward V in 1470. Bearing in mind prevailing life expectancy, the age of 41 would have been an appropriate age for Evans to finish his chantry.

A Possible Scenario

The premise of The Missing Princes Project is to examine evidence afresh and objectively on a cold-case basis. The investigation at Coldridge has hopefully been presented in that way. However, it is important to consider what the evidence might mean and to examine viable scenarios that would fit the facts presented. This is one such scenario; there may well be others.

In an agreement between Richard III and Elizabeth Woodville in March 1484, she and her daughters leave sanctuary. As part of this agreement, and on the understanding that his very life depends upon it, her elder son is to be placed in a secure location and given a new name.

Robert Markenfield is tasked with taking Edward to Coldridge, where he is given the name John Evans. After Henry VII's repeal of Edward's illegitimacy, Markenfield and Evans hide for a short time at Markenfield Hall in Yorkshire, meeting with Francis Lovell. The landowner, Sir Henry Bodrugan, then supports Evans (Edward V) and his coronation in Ireland when, in 1487, Elizabeth Woodville and Dorset conspire with others, including John, Earl of Lincoln, to retake the throne. Henry VII becomes aware of this and puts Dorset in the Tower and constrains Elizabeth at Bermondsey Abbey.

Edward V is crowned as King Edward in Dublin. At the Battle of Stoke he is led from the field with a facial injury, possibly caused by a blow from a sword across the chin. The injury may have been inflicted deliberately after the battle to limit the potential for Edward to ever challenge the throne again. He gives the name 'John' on the battlefield as there is an agreement that he should revert to the role of John Evans of Coldridge.

In 1497, Richard of York appears. During the advance on Exeter, Richard camps at Wembworthy, on the land and with the support of Sir John Speke, and meets his brother Edward V at Coldridge. Dorset and Robert Markenfield may have been involved.

As Edward is badly disfigured and has difficulty speaking, it has long been agreed that Richard becomes the new heir and makes his bid for the throne. To achieve this, Richard needs to take the walled city of Exeter and make this a base in which he can build local support. The attack fails and Edward, who is in grave danger, settles in Coldridge as John Evans and distances himself from the political arena for good.

Appendix 4

The Dendermonde Letters, 25 August 1493

Margaret of Burgundy to Queen Isabella of Spain

From the dowager duchess of Burgundy to the Queen

Most serene and most excellent Princess and honourable cousin, I entirely commend me to Your Majesty.

Last year, the illustrious Earls of Desmond and Kildare, chief Lords of Ireland, and other lords of the island at the same time, wrote to me that the second son of Edward, formerly king of England, my most beloved brother, by name Richard Plantagenet Duke of York, whom everyone thought was dead, was still alive and was with those Earls in Ireland safe and held in great honour. They affirmed this with letters corroborated by their seals and with a sacred oath. They prayed that I might be willing by the right of affinity and blood, to offer aid and resources to the same Duke of York and promised they would also help him. This was for me a sort of dream and ravings.

However, after this Duke of York was recently invited to France by the King of France, as the son of King Edward and as his cousin, I sent certain men who would recognise him as easily as his mother or his nurse, since from their first youth they had been in service and intimate familiarity with King Edward and his children. These men too with a most sacred oath affirmed that this man was the second son of King Edward, and they cursed themselves with great oaths, if it should turn out otherwise, and were ready to endure every torment and great physical pains of every kind.

At last the Duke of York himself came to me out of France, seeking help and assistance. I recognised him as easily as if I had last seen him yesterday or the day before, the reason being that I had seen him long ago in England, and that was not by one or two general signs, but by so many visible and specific signs that hardly one person in ten hundred thousand [a million] might be found who would have marks of the same kind. Then I recognised him by the private conversations and acts which had taken place between him and me, which undoubtedly no other person would have been able to guess at. Lastly I knew him by the questions and conversations of others, to all of which he responded so aptly and skilfully that it was obvious and easy to see that this was he whom they thought had died long ago.

I indeed for my part, when I gazed on this male Remnant of our family – who had come through so many perils and misfortunes – was deeply moved, and out of this natural affection into which both relationship and the rights of blood were drawing me, I embraced him as my only nephew and my only son. And I decided either to aid him in his right as far as my resources allowed, or at least maintain and take care of him. But what can I do a woman and a widow, bereft of father and so many mighty brothers? For after all the disasters in our most unfortunate family, after the fall of our House from the summit of Royalty, what aid, what help still lies in me? Can I do other than implore the faith, justice, kindness and mercy of most powerful princes who are closely related to me?

So most excellent princess, Lady and cousin, since Your Majesty has surpassed the queens of all the ages in greatness of soul, in justice, in prosperity, in achievements, and we indeed are connected by relationship and blood affinity, I pray and implore Your Majesty to show compassion for our calamities and our losses and not allow the throne of England to be tyrannously usurped by that wicked invader, in which he actually does wrong to your family as much as ours.

Be so kind as to make our case to the Most Serene King, Your Highness's consort, so that, together with Your Excellency, he will show favour, where he can, to this man, bound to him by blood and affinity, and continuously support him with good will and aid. For if, by divine assistance, he should recover his inheritance (which with the help of the nobles of England, we hope may happen) he guarantees and promises that he shall be bound by even greater closeness, alliance, allegiance and friendship to Your Majesties and Your Kingdoms than in the past was his father King Edward, and that I assure. And that I too will most readily offer allegiance to both Your Majesties, whom may the Loving God preserve according to your prayers.

Written from my town of Dendermonde, the 8th before the calends of September [25th August], 1493.

To the Most Excellent Majesty
Cousin Margaret of England Duchess of Burgundy, Brabant etc.
Count of Flanders, Artois, Burgundy [Franche Comté], Hainaut, Holland, Zealand, Namacia [?]
[signature] Margaret

Bibliothèque Nationale de France (BNF), *Fonds Espagnol 318, F. 83 ligne 69.* Translation from Latin on behalf of The Missing Princes Project by Maria G.L. Leotta. Examined by Dr Betty Knott, 6 February 2021.

Richard Plantagenet to Queen Isabella of Spain

Most Serene and Excellent Princess, My Lady and Cousin, worthy of all honour, I commend myself most earnestly to Your Majesty.

When the first-born son of the former King [of England] of blessed memory, my lord and beloved parent, the Prince of Wales that is, had been killed in a pitiable death, and I too, being about nine years of age had been handed over to a certain lord to be killed, it pleased the Divine Mercy that that lord, taking pity on my innocence, preserved me alive and unharmed, though he first bound me by an oath taken upon the Sacred Body of Our lord, that I would not for a certain number of years reveal to anyone my name, lineage and family.

So he sent me abroad with two men who were to have the direction and custody of me. Thereafter, an orphan bereft of father and brother, kings both of them, an exile from kingdom and country, despoiled of my inheritance and all my fortune, a fugitive amidst great dangers, I lived a miserable life in fear and grief and sorrow, and for nearly eight years lurked in hiding places throughout various countries. At last one of those men who had care of me died, the other was sent back to his country and never seen again.

And so, still hardly more than a boy, alone and destitute, I stayed for time in the kingdom of Portugal. After that, I sailed to Ireland, where I was acknowledged by the illustrious lords, the Earls of Desmond and Kildare, my blood-relations. Also I was accepted with joy and honour by other chief men of the island. After that, when the King of France enticed me with many ships and provisions, promising resources and support against Henry of Richmond, the wicked usurper of the Kingdom of England, I came to the aforesaid King of France, who received me with due honour as kinsman and well-wisher. When he did not produce the promised aid, I took myself to the illustrious princess, my Lady the Duchess of Burgundy, sister of my father, and my beloved aunt.

She in accord with her courteous and virtuous nature embraced me with all kindness and honour, and at the same time for her sake the Most Serene King of the Romans and his son the Archduke of Austria, and the Duke of Saxony, all my dear blood-relations, together with the kings of Denmark and Scotland, who sent ambassadors to me offering friendship and alliance. Leading men of the Kingdom of England who abominate the arrogant and wicked tyranny of this Henry of Richmond did the same in secret.

Truly, Most Serene Princess, my Lady and my blood-kin, in accord with the claims of our kinship and of your own renowned excellence, seeing that this surpasses the other princes of the world in justice, achievement and prosperity, it is only right and proper, no less than other princes, to grieve at our situation and support us with true affection.

And so I beg and beseech Your Majesty to use your influence with your Most Serene Spouse, to the end that he, together with Your Clemency, may pity the great calamities that have befallen our family, and with influence, resources and aid support me and mine in my right, which is yours also.

For I promise that, if the Divine Grace restores me to my hereditary kingdom, I shall be more closely associated in friendship with both Your Majesties than King Edward was, also that I and my kingdom shall be ever ready to do your pleasure.

Fare well, Noble Majesties.
From the town of Dendermonde, Aug. 25, 1493
[Signed] Richard

Egerton_ms_616_f003r. Translation from Latin on behalf of The Missing Princes Project: Dr Betty Knott, 3 January 2019.

Appendix 5

Richard, Duke of York: Proof of Life, *c.* 1493

[Page 1]

Here we follow the Duke of York, son, and heir to king Edward the fourth, Richard, his son, delivered from the Tower of London where he has been for a while.

First of all, I remember that my dearest lady and mother, queen Elizabeth, delivered me from sanctuary of Westminster into the hands of the Archbishop of Canterbury, and other men, also from the states of the country, under commitment of certain promises made by him under oath to bring me back to the same sanctuary.

Which Archbishop brought me to my uncle of Gloucester. And so I was brought to my brother who was already there, in the Tower of London.

Item [... several knights?] and squires were waiting for us there, of whom I think I remember that John Norris was one, and William Tyrwyth another. Item on the first night, shortly after these guards were relieved, they took leave of us with great melancholy and sadness. To these guards my brother often said melancholic words. Among other things he said and prayed my uncle of Gloucester to have mercy on him, for he was just an innocent person.

And then we were delivered to Brackenbury, and then to sir James Tyrrell, and then to the Duke of Buckingham, by whose orders we were separated.

And so they ordered my lord Foriest, Hamelett Maleven and Wylliam Puche by whom I was secretly taken into a room in a place where the lions are kept. There I was for such a long time, that Lord Howard, later made Duke of Norfolk, came to me and encouraged me. [At last?], he ordered the guards – described above – to leave and then brought two other men to me. They were called, they said so themselves: Henry Parcij and Thomas Parcij. They swore by honour and oath to Duke Howard, as mentioned before, to hide me secretly until certain years were past …

[Page 2]

… and that I would be placed under supervision by them for certain years. Then they shaved my hair and put a poor and drab skirt on me. And shortly after that they left the Tower with me and went to Saint Katherine's. There they took a boat and rowed aboard a small and narrow ship already waiting there.

And sailed to the sea and came ashore in the dunes of Boulogne-sur-Mer.

And from there we went to Paris. We stayed there for a long time. Till the moment I was noticed by English folks there. And so we travelled from there to a city called Chartres and from there to Rouen, to Dieppe and various other cities and places in France. And finally, we got to Hainaut.

From there in Brabant […?] Malines, Antwerp, Bergen for a period of certain years. And from there I went to Zeeland […?] Middelburg until Edward Brampton's wife was ready to sail us to Portugal.

[I sailed together with the prescribed Parcij's in a ship of their own.. ?]. To be able to tell [later?] [that they were on the same ship [with me], they knew a distinguishing feature of me, namely that I played the clavichord.]

And then we arrived in Lisbon. From there I sent the aforementioned Thomas Parcij to England, to my lady my mother with certain distinguishing features and also with certain messages. Shortly afterwards

[Page 3]

Henry Parcij became ill with the plague. During his illness, he told me that when he died, I would have to travel to Ireland to the lords of Kyldare and Desmond and also told me how I should rule the country. Then he died, may God save his soul.

Shortly afterwards I found a ship from Brittany that wanted to sail to Ireland. The master of the ship sailed me to Ireland as he himself has testified and will testify more fully – at all times – when questioned.

There I found several of my acquaintances, among them the lord of Kyldare, Garret the Great and many others. There I was recognized for who I was and treated as such.

And there I stayed for a while until my cousin the King of France contacted me and made a firm promise to assist and help me to claim my rights. However, when I arrived in France, I found the opposite. So I left, and went to my dearest aunt, the duchess of Burgundy. She recognized my rights and honesty. And by the grace of God, I received help, honour and comfort from my dear friends and servants that in a short time I will obtain my right to which I was born.

[Cover (page 4)]

A [record?] and so forth (etc) how the Duke of York, son, and heir of King Edward the fourth, was delivered from the Tower of London and where he has been since then.

Modern English translation of the transcribed text of the Gelders manuscript by Nathalie Nijman-Bliekendaal, Research Report 21 November 2020: Gelders Archief, 0510 'Diverse Charters en Aanwinsten [Various Charters & Acquisitions]', nr 1549: *Verhandelingen over de lotgevallen van Richard van York, ca 1500* [Treatises on the fates of Richard of York c. 1500], four written pages in total. With copy from the sixteenth century.

Appendix 6

Richard of England: Dresden MS, Signature and Royal Seal, 4 October 1493

Pledge of Payment to Duke Albert of Saxony

Chapter 14, p. 196, note 30, and Plates 25 and 26

Richard, by the grace of God, Duke of York, son and heir of our most revered lord and father, Edward IV, late King of England and France and Lord of Ireland, to each and everyone who shall see or hear this present writing, greetings.

Know that we, considering intimately the friendly and gratuitous benevolence shown and to be shown in the future many times as well to us as to other friends and those loyal to us, by the very powerful Prince Albrecht, Duke of Saxony, and lieutenant of the most excellent princes, Maximilian, King of the Romans, and his son, Philip, Archduke of Burgundy, our dearest kinsmen, as well as the supervisor and governor of all the dominions, lands, and tenements of the said Philip in these parts, are bound and by those present firmly obliged to the same Duke of Saxony to pay, or cause to be paid, the sum of thirty thousand florins, each florin being valued at twenty patards, within three months after the acquisition of our Kingdom of England.

For the said payment, we bind strictly and faithfully ourselves, our heirs, and executors, and all our goods by those present. And for greater security of the said payment, our kinsman, Lord Robert Clifford, knight, as well as William Barley, Esquire, our servant, are also obliged by their good will on our behalf in this writing.

In witness of which matter, both we, the aforementioned Duke of York, and the aforesaid Lord Robert and William, have affixed our seals, signed with our own hands, on the fourth day of October, in the year of our Lord one thousand four hundred ninety-three (4 Oct 1493).

Nathalie Nijman-Bliekendaal, Research Report, 18 February 2019.
English translation (updated): Professor Henrike Lähnemann, 18 August 2023.
Sächsisches Hauptstaatsarchiv (Saxon State Archive) (SHA), Dresden, 10001, Altere Urkunden, Nr_09005.

Duke Albert of Saxony (1443–1500), deputy to King Maximilian. Known as 'The Bold'. Leading supporter of Richard, Duke of York. Possible father figure.

Analysis: Prof. Henrike Lähnemann, 18 August 2023

The parchment with the seals is kept doubly wrapped: outside a modern archival blue cardboard folder (21st cent.), inside a blue paper wrapper with the call number 9005 which is probably from the time when the Staatsarchiv was established, i.e. 1834; glued to the front is a brown (rag) paper label which looks older – probably from the time of the 1702 established 'Königlich geheimes Archiv'; this has a summary of the content of the charter and retains the spelling of the names: 'Literae Ricardi, Dei Gratia Ducis Eboraci filii, et Regis Angliae hæredis, quibus profitetur, et firmiter se, suosque hæredes obligat, Albright, Duci Saxoniae, assignatisve suis, triginta millia florenorum solvere. Dat: 4 die Octobris 1493. in membrana tribus silligis appensis. Letters of Richard, by the Grace of God Duke of York, son and heir of the King of England, in which he professes and firmly binds himself and his heirs to pay thirty thousand florins to Albrecht, Duke of Saxony, or those he assigns. Given on the 4th day of October 1493, on parchment with three seals attached.'

This summary was included as the basis for the edition by Friedrich Langenn in his history of Duke Albert of Saxony (1838), p. 554. The original punctuation has been reintroduced and two transcription mistakes corrected: ‚vel' replaced by ‚seu'; ‚florena' instead of ‚florenus'.

www.digitale-sammlungen.de/de/view/bsb10020114?page=566&q=clifford.

Appendix 7

Trois Enseignes Naturelz,
27 November–12 December 1493

by Zoë Maula, Dutch Research Group

In gaining the support of Yorkists and royalty alike, Richard, Duke of York, was aided by the existence of three distinguishing physical features. Maximilian I appears to have been convinced by these '*trois enseignes naturelz*'. This becomes clear from a document uncovered in the *Österreichische Staatsarchiv* (Austria State Archive) and dated between 27 November to 12 December 1493.[1] This reads (in extract):

> ... for the king has found through truthful enquiries, made in several family trees, that my lord the duke of York, who is with him at the moment, is the true legitimate son and heir of the said late King Edward. And my lord the Duke of York offers to present himself in England before King Henry and all the princes and subjects of the realm and show several signs by which those who knew him in his youth would recognize him, and **especially three natural marks which he has on his body and which cannot be counterfeited, that is: his mouth, one of his eyes and a mark he has on his thigh.** And if it is found that he is not at all [what he says he is] he is content that justice be done on him as it should be done in such a case, by way of hostages who will be held hostage on his behalf. If it happens that he is found [to be] son and heir as he claims, he will be received as king, or at least no harm will be done to him. In that case he will no doubt be able to return to where he came from or [go] wherever it pleases him. [Emphasis added.][2]

The document appears to be a first draft for an instruction[3] to unnamed Burgundian envoys going to Henry VII to mediate between Henry and the Duke of York. However, as an actual letter or record of these envoys being received by King Henry is yet to be found, it is not known whether such an embassy took place.

More significantly, this document presents the earliest documentary evidence of Richard of York's three physical marks. Until now, English sources often vaguely refer to them as 'natural marks' by citing Heinrich Ulmann's book *Kaiser Maximilian I*,[4] or more explicitly, as 'mark under his eye', 'slightly raised or prominent upper lip' and 'a mark on his breast', as stated in the later Setúbal Testimonies.[5]

According to historian Ann Wroe, Maximilian's letter, which Ulmann cites, might have said more if it had not been lost. It is highly certain that this document is Maximilian's letter, which Ulmann discovered, making this the first record of Richard, Duke of York's claim to the English throne through his three physical marks. Namely, his mouth, one of his eyes and a mark on his thigh.

For Margaret of York's verification of her nephew's physical marks (signs) and her own recognition of them from his childhood, see Margaret's letter to Queen Isabella of Spain of August 1493, Appendix 4: The Dendermonde Letters. Also, Chapter 14, note 84 and Chapter 17, note 250.

Zoë Maula, TMPP Research Report, 14.12.2020: Österreichische Staatarchiv – AT-OeStA/HHStA RK Maximiliana 41-3-2. Translation thanks to Dr Livia Visser-Fuchs.

Appendix 8

Maximilian I

Legal Supplication to Pope Alexander VI on Behalf of Richard, Duke of York, 22 September 1495 (Modernised)

Most Holy Father, most Reverend Lord

Whereas of late years, after the invasion and slaughter of Richard King of England, Henry of Richmond occupied that kingdom, and having espoused the daughter of Edward, the late King, brother of said Richard, causing it to be believed that said Edward had left no male progeny, obtained from your Holiness's predecessor, Innocent VIII., of pious memory, letters confirming him in the possession of his kingdom, and purposing that all persons disputing the said Henry's right to his kingdom, or waging war on him, were to be excommunicated; therefore the most illustrious Lady Margaret, sister of the aforesaid Edward and Richard, and wife of the late most illustrious Charles Duke of Burgundy, our father-in-law (perceiving that she as well as Richard, her brother Edward's son, – who, lest he should be put to death by the occupiers of the kingdom, has hitherto often hidden himself, wandering over the world as an unknown exile, – were without cause violently injured and aggrieved, being excluded from their right), our very dear mother-in-law did appeal forthwith against those confirmatory letters, in the name of herself and of her nephew, the aforesaid Richard Duke of York, and of all others whom it might concern.

Similar confirmatory letters denouncing excommunication having been lately obtained from your Holiness, in the same manner – the truth

339

being suppressed – the said most illustrious Margaret and her nephew appealed, and committed the prosecution of the appeal to our ambassador, Philiberto Naturelli, requesting our recommendation and assistance with your Holiness,

We, perceiving the aforesaid confirmations and excommunications to be surreptitious and frivolous, as they could not exclude others from their right without hearing them; and as the said Richard Duke of York is the born son of Edward, the legitimate and true deceased King, and it is evident he has excellent right [*optimum jus*] to that kingdom; which things had they been known both to the pious memory of Innocent VIII., as also to your Holiness, similar letters would doubtless not have been conceded; we have thought fit to write to your Holiness, that this said matter, which is of such great moment, may be more carefully examined, and that what was ill conceded be revoked, or that you will clemently hear such other things as our said ambassador, Philibert, will more fully declare by word of mouth, providing and administering justice, so that said most illustrious Lady Margaret, and others whom it concerns, may, both from sense of justice and through our recommendation, obtain from your Holiness their right, and that for conscience sake [*ex serupulo conscientiæ*] we may see them freed from both sentences of excommunication. And your Holiness, whom may God preserve, will perform an act just and holy, and most agreeable to us.

From our city of Worms, 22nd September 1405 [*sic* 1495]. Maximilian, by divine clemency, King of the Romans, ever august King of Hungary, Dalmatia, Croatia, etc., Archduke of Austria, etc.

[On the external corner] Letter of Maximilian, presented by his ambassador, Philibert, the 18th of October 1405 [*sic* 1495]

Original from 'Appendix: Miscellaneous 1495', in *Calendar of State Papers Relating to English Affairs in the Archives of Venice, Volume 4, 1527–33*, edited by Rawdon Brown (London, 1871), pp. 482–83. British History Online, www.british-history.ac.uk/cal-state-papers/venice/vol4/pp.482-483

Appendix 9

Richard IV's Proclamation, September 1496

(Modernised)

In the autumn of 2020, The Missing Princes Project began an investigation into a quite remarkable document – Richard of England's proclamation from Scotland in September 1496. Here, he introduced himself as the youngest son of Edward IV and rightful King of England, King Richard IV. Project member Dr Judith Ford agreed to investigate this important contemporary source.

Judith's investigation now reveals several new discoveries – in the document's provenance and connection to the Howard family, but also in Richard of England's message within the proclamation that may relate to Richard III, and which Sir Francis Bacon would later recognise as such. The proclamation champions the good rule of the old Yorkist order, which King Richard (IV) now intended to restore for the benefit and welfare of his people. In doing so, he would remove Henry VII, his 'extreme mortal enemy', who had 'by subtle false means' obtained the crown. Richard adds that 'as soon as he [Henry] had knowledge of our being alive, imagined, compassed and wrought all the subtle ways and means he could devise to our final destruction'.

Judith has uncovered the most contemporaneous copy, which is held in the National Library of Wales. Richard of England would be denounced by the Tudor government as a boatman's son from Tournai in France and given the names 'Perkin Warbeck', 'Piers Osbeck', 'Pierce Osbeck', 'Petyr Osbek', 'Piris (Pedro) Osbeque', 'Piris Uberque', 'Styenbek' and 'Pierrechon de Werbecque'.

The Proclamation

Richard by the grace of God King of England & of France, Lord of Ireland, Prince of Wales, to all those who see, hear or read this proclamation we send greetings. In our tender age we escaped, with God's help, from the Tower of London, and were secretly taken overseas (to various countries), where we remained for a number of years. Then Henry, son of Edmund Tudor, created Earl of Richmond, son of Owen Tudor, who was born in Wales in lowly circumstances, came to our realm of England, and by dishonest means obtained the Crown that was rightfully ours.

Henry Tudor is our mortal enemy. As soon as he found out that we were alive, he tried various means to bring about our destruction. Not only has he tried to trick you by declaring that we are an imposter, and giving us false names, he has also tried to prevent us from reaching this realm. He has offered large sums of money to the rulers of several countries to apprehend us, and has tried to persuade some of our personal servants to murder us, and to persuade others, such as Sir Robert Clifford, to leave our service and our cause. In order to fund these malicious intentions he has exacted money from the people of this realm to their great detriment and impoverishment. Yet, by God's grace, we have safely crossed land and sea and are now with the high and mighty prince, our dearest cousin the King of Scots, who, without any inducement, has kindly and lovingly supported us and has crossed into England with us. We shall openly show ourselves to you and expose Henry Tudor's lies. Everyone of reason and discretion will understand that Tudor would not have gone to the aforesaid expense and trouble if he really believed that we are an imposter. Regarding yourselves, it is the intention of our dearest cousin [the King of Scots], that if he sees our subjects and vassals giving us sufficient allegiance and support to defeat our enemies, he is determined to return quietly with his forces to Scotland without inflicting any suffering on the inhabitants of England.

In order to bolster his false position Henry Tudor has caused to be murdered many nobles of our realm, whom he feared, and whose loyalty he doubted. These include Lord Fitzwalter, Sir William Stanley, Sir Robert Chamberlain, Sir Simon Mountford, Sir Robert Ratcliffe, William Daubeney, Humphrey Stafford and many others who have paid dearly with their lives. Some nobles are now in the Sanctuary and Henry Tudor has long kept in prison our right entirely beloved cousin Edward, son and heir to our uncle the Duke of Clarence, as well as other nobles, withholding from them their rightful inheritance in order to stop them giving us their rightful support. He has also forced certain of our sisters, and the sister of the Earl of Warwick, as well as other ladies of royal blood, to marry his own kindred and supporters of low estate, thus undermining the established nobles who were most likely to support us. The only people he trusts and favours are wretches of low birth such as Bishop Foxe, Smyth, Bray, Lovell, Oliver King, Sir Charles Somerset, David Owen, Rysley, Sir John Turberville, Tyler, Robert Lytton, Guilford, Cheyne, Emson, James Hobert, John Cutt, Garth, Hanson, Wyatt and other such wretches and villains, who by clever means and by robbing the people, have been the principal agents of the misrule that now pertains in England.

We have also been reliably informed that Tudor, with complete disregard for the wealth and prosperity of this realm and with regard only for his own safety and well-being, has sent his adherents out of this country with the nation's treasure, so that he can take personal possession of it, if he is forced to flee. This will bring peril and insecurity to the whole population. In order to protect yourselves and the well-being of this land it is necessary for you to use every means and effort to prevent Henry Tudor escaping. Whoever apprehends him will be rewarded according to their estate and degree, so that the most lowly will be given a thousand pounds in money, as well as property with the yearly value of 400 marks in perpetuity.

We are also aware of the great offences daily committed by Henry Tudor and his adherents in destroying the liberties and authority of our holy mother church to the great displeasure of almighty God, besides committing manifold treasons, abominable murders, manslaughters, robberies, extortions, the daily robbing of the people by the imposition of tithes, taxes, feudal levies, benevolences, and other unlawful exactions to the great detriment of this realm. We will make it our personal responsibility to protect you and redress the damage done to you by Tudor's administration. We will act, not as a stepmother but as a true mother who sees their child languishing or in peril, and we will put an end to misrule, and punish those responsible. We will also by God's grace and the help and assistance of the great lords of royal blood, and with the counsel of otherwise people of approved policy, prudence and experience, ensure the proper administration of justice based on the good laws and customs that were established by our noble predecessors the Kings of England, according to their original purpose and meaning. Those who have been wrongly disinherited will find justice, and all other wrongs and injuries, both spiritual and temporal, inflicted on the subjects of our realm will be redressed.

Trade with other countries will be conducted in a manner that will benefit the whole realm and all the aforementioned levies and unlawful impositions and exactions will be exposed and abolished except in those circumstances that have been established by custom and use.

We desire that all those who have actively or covertly acted against us since the reign of Henry Tudor (excepting those who have plotted to kill us), will receive a full pardon and have their rightful lands and goods restored to them if they henceforth support us with their bodies and their goods. Be assured that those who continue to stand with our enemies and act against us will be treated as traitors and rebels and punished accordingly. Those subjects who aid and support us to the best of their ability, or provide food for our forces (for which they will be paid) we will treat lovingly and justly, provided that upon hearing our proclamation, they will, according to their duty and honour, equip themselves for battle and join us wherever we shall happen to be. In so doing, they shall find us to be their right, especial and singular good lord and their services will be rewarded as they deserve.

R

National Library of Wales: BL, Harley MS 283, ff.123v–124v. Transcription on behalf of The Missing Princes Project by Dr Judith Ford, 14 June 2021. Copy dated 1616.

For Judith Ford's transcription and article on the proclamation, see 'The King's Speech' at: www.revealingrichardiii.com/two-pretenders. html#kings-speech

Appendix 10

Maat, and Black & Hackman Reports

'Bones in the Urn', 14 June 2018, 11 November 2021

The Maat Report (2018)

Background

In August 2017, leading Dutch bioanthropologist Professor George Maat agreed to undertake an analysis of images and skiagrams (X-ray images) taken of bones discovered in London in the mid-seventeenth century. Maat was approached to do the analysis by Dutch archaeologist Jean Roefstra. Although the analysis was done blind in order to eliminate any potential prejudice, the analysis was on behalf of Philippa Langley's The Missing Princes Project. The bones in question had been exhumed and investigated in the early twentieth century when fifteen black and white photographs and five skiagrams were taken and a report written by an osteologist and dental expert.

For the present analysis, Maat was given copies of the original photographs and skiagrams, and the original twentieth-century report. The report was redacted to include factual information only, in order to eliminate any historical references and bias from the early twentieth-century analysis.

Summary of Findings

Analysis of the photographs of the remains concluded the Minimum Number of Individuals (MNI) present as being two.

However, the 'Bones of Which Exact Identification is Uncertain' section from the twentieth-century report contains some ambiguous information. This comes from the following line of the original report: 'the lines of union of the three primary parts of the vertebrae still apparent'. Probably, the reporters mean the fusion line between both halves of the arch and the fusion lines of both neuro-central junctions (overall age interval 3–24 years). But if the reporters mean the fusion lines between the vertebral body with arch and the two circular epiphyses (fusing 18–24 years of age), then there is a third, much older, individual in the assemblage. But no other bones typical for such a maturation phase were seen or reported.

The age range of the set of remains called 'PS1' is recorded as being from 9.5–12.5 years, with the second set, 'PS2', being from 7–11 years. It is likely that PS1 is the more mature and therefore has a more advanced calendar age, but this is not certain from this analysis. The age range in terms of calendar age deviation per maturity/development phase may vary between the two sets of remains within a 3–4-years-wide range age gap.

The photographs do not show any anatomical structure giving a clue on the sex development of the contributors to this assemblage of remains. The photographs depict individuals who are both developmentally too immature to show distinct sex features. However, the development of the older set of remains (PS1) suggests it is more likely this person is female, since the assessed age at death concords better with the supposed fusion time of the distal epiphysis of metatarsal I (also marked PS1). In terms of the younger set of remains (PS2), nothing can be seen in the X-ray images with regard to the lower canine tooth (unerupted) in the lower jaw as being an indicator of sex as it is too small/slender.[1]

The assessed age at death of the detected individuals that contributed to the assemblage does not exclude consanguinity. Only DNA analysis may produce a calculated conclusion on this issue.

No indications were found on the cause of death, and no date (period) for the age of the remains. The presence of large Wormian bones does not indicate any particular date (period) for the remains.

Conclusion

Minimum Number of Individuals present is two (with a possibility of three, as above), with one set of remains (PS1) more likely to be female than male. Consanguinity between the two main sets of remains is possible via the age range. No cause of death indicators were present, and no date (period) age for any of the remains was identifiable.

'Analysis of Bones Discovered in London in the Mid-C17th and Exhumed in the Early C20th for Investigation – Summary of a Modern Analysis' by Professor George Maat (14 June 2018)

The Black & Hackman Report (2021)

Papers presented for comment by Philippa Langley:

1. Tanner, L.E., and Wright, W.W., 'Recent Investigations Regarding the Fate of the Princes in the Tower', *Archaeologia*, 84: 1–26 (1934).
2. Hammond, P.W, and Whyte, W.J., 'The Sons of Edward IV: A Re-examination of the Evidence on their Deaths and on the Bones in Westminster Abbey', in P. Hammond (ed.), *Richard III: Loyalty, Lordship and Law* (London: Richard III and Yorkist History Trust) pp. 121–70 (1986).
3. Molleson, T., 'Anne Mowbray and the Princes in the Tower: A Study in Identity', *The London Archaeologist*, 5: 258–262 (1987).
4. Ashdown-Hill, J., 'Hypodontia?' in *The Mythology of the 'Princes in the Tower'*, Chapter 28, pp. 187–93 (2018).
5. Moran, G., 'The Search for the MtDNA of the Princes', *Bulletin*, December 2018, pp. 41–44.

Statement

We provide this report based only on the papers above and do so in the light of forensic standards.

The Tanner and Wright paper raises some interesting questions.

1. Within the paper, the bones have been 'assumed' to be of the Princes but there is no evidential proof to support.
2. The questions asked in this paper exhibit confirmation bias, i.e., 'If the bones are human are they of two boys of an age with the Princes?' More appropriate questions would be: Are the remains human? How long have the individuals been deceased? Are the remains intact? How many

individuals are represented? Are the remains male or female? What is the age at death for the remains? What are the predicted heights of the individuals? Is there evidence of pathology or trauma? Is there evidence of a cause of death? Can DNA be extracted?

3. Additional questions might include: Does history tell of other children who died in the Tower? Have the bones been dated? Surely all that can be inferred is that they died before 1674 which assumes that the bones found in the box in 1674 are the ones interred in the urn? What were the dimensions of the box in which the bones were found? Was it big enough just for bones or was it large enough to take the bodily remains of the individuals? Were there any indications on the inside of the box that might have been left by the decomposition of soft tissue? Was the box retained?

4. Tanner and Wright's examination of the contents of the urn reported that two individuals were represented and that they were of two children some 2–3 years apart in age.

5. It is unfortunate that the photographic and radiographic images are incomplete.

6. The age of the older child was predicated on the maturation of the axis (C2) and the first sacral vertebra (S1). C2 was 'without the apical part of the odontoid process'. This does not mean that the ossiculum terminale had not formed, only that it had not yet fused as the apex may simply not have been recovered. A bifid odontoid process is present in most individuals younger than 12 years of age (although it can be older) – in agreement with Tanner and Wright. However, an ossiculum terminale persistens Bergmen can occur where fusion does not take place. A separate bone can also arise as a result of trauma. The rationale for why the C2 could have originated from the older child has some validity, but it should be borne in mind that match fitting a C1 to a C2 is not necessarily reliable given the incongruity of the joint surfaces.

Age was also assigned based on the maturation of the first sacral vertebra. The laminae of the vertebra were 'still half an inch apart' which the authors take as corroboration of an age less than 13 years. If the laminae are to fuse, then they will do so variably between the ages of 7 and 15 years. However, these laminae may not fuse and remain patent throughout life, as described by Molleson (1987). This is referred to as spina bifida occulta. It should be noted that all aspects of age estimation in juvenile are sex dependent with the females reaching a comparable stage of maturation to males, around 2 years earlier.

Therefore, determining the sex of the remains is paramount to establishing a confident estimation of age at death.

7. Much was made of age determination from the teeth and evidence from the alveolar bone. Only the right half of the mandible was available for the younger child and both maxillae and mandible were present for the older child although all teeth were missing. In the younger child, the maturation of the incisors was determined from the alveolar sockets. The canine was unerupted with the root described as half formed. The first premolar was unerupted (as seen from radiograph) and the root half formed. The second premolar was unerupted with the crown only formed and this is confirmed from the radiograph. The crypt for the first molar is present, but the tooth is not. The second molar was found loose in the urn, was represented by the crown only with no sign of root formation. Fig 4 in their report shows the second molar in position, presumably after a retro fit. The suggestion was that age at death was between 9 and 11 years, which is not unreasonable, but we would widen the range to between 8–12 which is more in keeping with Molleson's suggestion. There were no teeth available for the older child and age was undertaken by analysis of alveolar morphology alone – this is not something that would be advocated in a forensic investigation. The crown of an alleged third molar was found separate in the urn. It was identified as being from the left side and about 'one third formed'. On the basis of the alveolar status and an alleged third molar, the individual was aged to between 12 and 13 years. Whilst we do not disagree that this is a possibility, we would by necessity, given the nature of the material, widen the age range from between 12–15 years, again largely in keeping with the views of Molleson.

8. In relation to age estimation, the figures of the ribs, clavicles and scapulae appear to confirm the juvenile nature of the remains but it is unfortunate that there are no descriptions of the glenoid surfaces of the scapulae as they may have assisted in age estimation.

9. The presence of Wormian bones were offered as evidence on consanguinity as was the presence of hypodontia (absence of tooth formation). Whilst it is accepted that both features have a genetic predisposition, it is a large leap to accept their presence/absence as evidence to support consanguinity.

10. Mention was made of a stain on the facial skeleton of the younger individual. Whether it is a blood stain would require laboratory analysis and

we would not comment on whether such staining could be evidence of suffocation using a pillow.

11. Height was calculated at 4ft 10ins and 4ft 6.5ins using tables available at the time. It was suggested from the bones that they were 'of slender form' but this is not something that would be suggested in a forensic context as it is unreliable to predict body mass from bone alone.

12. The suggestions as to the position of the bodies within the box are supposition.

13. Page 22 states that the lines of union of the three primary parts of the vertebrae were still visible and attributed this to the older of the two individuals – we believe that could be the case for either individual. Within the section on the skull, we do not recognise the description surrounding the fusion pattern associated with the jugum sphenoidale and the pre-sphenoid.

14. Page 23 – measurements. A clavicle of 113mm is consistent with a child of around 12–14 years and one of 96mm is consistent with a child of around 8–10 years. A humeral length of 242mm is consistent with a child of around 9–11 years and one of 222mm is consistent with a child of around 8–10 years. An ulnar length of 195mm is consistent with a child of around 9–10 years and one of 182mm is consistent with a child of between 8–9 years of age. A femoral length of 383mm is consistent with a child of around 12 years (lengths thereafter include epiphyses) and a length of 345mm is consistent with a child of between 9 and 11 years. A tibial length of 306mm is consistent with a child of around 11–12 years and a length of 274mm is consistent with a child of around 9–10 years of age.

15. In relation to the summary on page 24:
    1. No comment.
    2. There was nothing presented that 'confirms' identity as set against modern forensic standards.
    3. Consanguinity is possible but not certain.
    4. We would question the stain being blood.
    5. The older child was aged at between 12–13 years. We would widen this range to 9–15 years based on the evidence available.
    6. The age of the younger child was given as between 9–11 years. We would widen this range to 8–12 based on the evidence available.
    7. An additional point is that there is no evidence to support the suggestion that both sets of remains are male.

In forensic terms we would agree that the remains in the photographs and radiographs are human. We would agree that they are not complete, some elements are missing and some are fragmented. We would agree that at least two individuals are represented. We would agree that both are juvenile with one being aged between around 9–15 years and the other most likely being somewhat younger, between around 8–12 years. There is no evidence to support sex of either of the sets of remains. There is no scientific evidence to support a date of death. There is no strong evidence to support consanguinity.

Hammond and Whyte (1986):

1. Hammond and Whyte introduce a question as to whether the remains found in 1674 are the same as the remains interred in 1678. In forensic terms, a chain of custody would have been set up to ensure that such doubt could not be introduced.

2. There is a reasonable argument that neither Tanner nor Wright were working 'blind' as both were aware that they could be looking at the bones of the Princes and were therefore subject to the possibility of both conscious and unconscious bias.

3. The authors are correct to debate the value of using modern day standards to age archaeological material. Individuals developed under different nutritional, environmental and pathogen burdens and so are not directly comparable. For this reason we have extended the possible age ranges and cannot be prescriptive.

4. Sex estimation from the juvenile pelvis is not considered viable in forensic investigations.

Molleson (1987):

1. Molleson addresses the issue of the sex of the skeletal remains and confirms that estimation of this in juvenile individuals is 'notoriously unreliable'. She considered sexual dimorphism in the dentition which exists prior to pubertal change and so is influenced less dramatically than skeletal elements. She also considered 'relative' differences in development both dentally and skeletally. Neither approach would be acceptable for forensic identification and the only approach we would take for sex determination from juvenile remains is through DNA analysis.

2. Evidence of consanguinity. As with Tanner and Wright, she considered Wormian bones and hypodontia. Neither approach would be

acceptable as a forensic standard for establishing consanguinity which would require DNA analysis.

3. Both Warwick (Roger) in his paper on Anne Mowbray, and Molleson mentioned 'a rare anomaly' of an alleged distal epiphysis which was partly fused to the shaft of each of the first metacarpals. These have since been shown to be a normal process of maturation where there is no separate epiphysis.

4. Molleson considered the dentition and the alveolar evidence as well as bone maturation and bone lengths. It is interesting that the author does not attempt to give a final age range and only states that 'the skeletons are those of juveniles'.

5. The report states that 'the odontoid process of the axis or second cervical vertebra is not ossified'. This is misleading as the odontoid process is clearly ossified and I suspect that Molleson means the ossic-ulum terminale. We cannot say whether the ossiculum was ossified, all we can say was that it had most likely not yet fused and perhaps had understandably not been recovered with the remains.

6. We are unclear how Molleson reached the conclusion that '... and one wishes to propose that they died or were killed at the same time, the most likely period that is compatible with the dental and skele-tal age for both skeletons would be some time in the year 1484'. An estimation of the date of death for forensic purposes would require laboratory testing.

Ashdown-Hill (2018):

1. The paper summarises that via hypodontia it cannot be proved that Anne Mowbray was related to either of the Tower skeletons.

Moran (2018):

1. The premise of this paper is that mtDNA testing is required to answer some of the unresolved questions and we would agree with this.

Recommendations for further tests should a re-examination be granted. These should be as non-invasive as possible but it is important to state that most are destructive in nature:

1. Full photographic and radiographic catalogue be taken. 3d scans of the bones would also make the material available for study without recourse to further disturbance of the remains.
2. mtDNA analysis be undertaken for the sake of genealogical relationship matching.
3. Nuclear DNA analysis to be attempted to determine sex of the remains.
4. Dating methodologies be employed.
5. Isotope analysis be employed that could assist with dietary and geographical origins.

Views on previous publications relating to the 'Princes in the Tower', prepared by Professors Sue Black and Lucina Hackman, 11 November 2021.

Timelines

Please note: All timelines follow the modern calendar year of 1 January–31 December, not the medieval calendar of 25–24 March.

1483: Protectorate

March 1483	London: Thomas, Marquess of Dorset, secures Tower and armoury.
Friday, 28 March–Sunday, 30 March 1483	Westminster, London: Edward IV falls ill.
Wednesday, 2 April 1483	Westminster: Edward IV sends letter to John, Lord Howard at Stoke-by-Nayland, Suffolk.
Thursday, 3 April 1483	Westminster: death of Edward IV.
Friday, 4 April 1483	Howard receives Edward IV's letter.
Sunday, 6 April 1483	City of York receives news of Edward IV's death.
Monday, 7 April 1483	York Minster: dirge sung for Edward IV.
	Howard leaves Stoke-by-Nayland with fifty-plus men.
Wednesday, 9 April 1483	Howard arrives at Westminster.
	Death of Edward IV announced.

Monday, 14 April 1483	Ludlow: Edward V informed of king's death.
	North: Gloucester probably informed of king's death.
Wednesday, 16 April 1483	Edward V's letter: no mention of Edward IV's will or Gloucester's Protectorate.
Thursday, 17 April 1483	Two-week anniversary of Edward IV's death: king's funeral begins.
	York Minster: Requiem Mass for Edward IV. Gloucester leads north in allegiance to Edward V.
Friday, 18 April 1483	St George's Chapel, Windsor: burial of Edward IV.
Before Sunday, 20 April 1483	London: meetings of Woodvilles and Councillors; Gloucester's Protectorate set aside.
	Sir Edward Woodville awarded control of English fleet; Dorset empowered to raise forces.
c. *Tuesday, 22 April 1483*	York: Gloucester and 200–300 northern retinue in mourning leave for rendezvous with Edward V at Northampton.
Thursday, 24 April 1483	Ludlow: Edward V leaves with Rivers and escort of 2,000 for rendezvous with Gloucester at Northampton.

Tuesday, 29 April 1483	Northampton: Gloucester arrives, joined by Rivers and companions.
	Buckingham and escort arrive later.
	Edward V's party overnights at Grafton Woodville, escort billeted at Stony Stratford.
	Richard Grey and company arrive at Grafton.
Wednesday, 30 April 1483	Rivers, Grey and others arrested.
	Edward V returns with Gloucester to Northampton.
Thursday, 1 May 1483	Northampton: Edward V received by dignitaries.
	Rivers and Grey taken north.
	London: after failing to raise an armed force, Elizabeth Woodville takes sanctuary at Westminster.
	Southampton: Edward Woodville impounds £10,250 in gold from a ship.
Saturday, 3 May 1483	First month-mind of Edward IV's death; Howard arranges two masses.
	Edward V at St Albans with Gloucester and Buckingham.
Sunday, 4 May 1483	London: Edward V enters capital with Gloucester and Buckingham.
	Edward V resides at Bishop's Palace.

Monday, 5 May–Saturday, 10 May 1483	King's Council: Gloucester appointed Protector of Realm.
	Edward Woodville ordered to return with fleet.
	Howard sends thirty-eight men home.
Monday, 19 May 1483	Edward V moves to Tower of London for coronation on Sunday, 22 June.
Friday, 23 May 1483	King's Council: leading members deliver draft oath for Elizabeth Woodville's safety if she agrees to leave sanctuary.
Tuesday, 3 June 1483	Second month-mind of Edward IV's death; Lady Howard gives offerings.
Monday, 9 June 1483	King's Council: decision to recommend Parliament to continue Protectorate after coronation.
	Edward Woodville absconds.
Tuesday, 10 June–Wednesday, 11 June 1483	Protector appeals for help from north against Woodville plots.
Friday, 13 June 1483	Weapons in King's Council; plot against Protector uncovered.
	Hastings executed; Morton and Rotherham arrested.
Monday, 16 June 1483	Tower: Richard of York joins Edward V in Royal Apartments.

1483: Constitutional Crisis

Tuesday, 17 June 1483	King's Council: Edward V's coronation postponed to 9 November 1483.
Wednesday, 18 June 1483	Last signed warrant by Edward V.
Friday, 20 June 1483	Last (London) documents naming Edward V as king.
	Edward Grey, Viscount Lisle, joins Gloucester.
Sunday, 22 June 1483	London: sermons preached proclaiming illegitimacy of Edward IV's children and naming Gloucester rightful heir to the throne.
Wednesday, 25 June 1483	Gloucester petitioned to become king by Three Estates of Parliament.
	Pontefract: trial and execution of Rivers and Grey by Northumberland.
Thursday, 26 June 1483	Gloucester accepts election and assumes throne as King Richard III.
Saturday, 28 June 1483	Letter sent to Calais verifying King Richard's election by Three Estates.
	Richard III signs first grant at Cittie of London.
	Howard created Duke of Norfolk and Earl Marshal of England.
	Coronation: clothing prepared for 'Lord Edward, son of King Edward'.
Friday, 4 July 1483	Gloucester and Anne Neville move to Tower prior to coronation.

Sunday, 6 July 1483	Westminster Abbey: joint coronation of Richard III and Queen Anne.
Monday, 7 July – Saturday, 12 July	Greenwich Palace: coronation jousts and celebrations.
Tuesday, 15 July 1483	Buckingham created Lord High Constable of England.
Thursday, 17 July 1483	Robert Brackenbury appointed Constable of Tower of London.
Saturday, 19 July 1483	Royal progress leaves London for Windsor.

The Survival of Edward V

(From 6 July, Coronation of Richard III)

Saturday, 28 June– Thursday 3 July 1483	Richard III coronation; clothing made for (and delivered to) 'Lord Edward, son of late king Edward the fourth' (and his henchmen).
Friday, 18 July 1483	Seventeen men paid for their service to Edward IV and 'Edward Bastard late called king Edward Vth' (no prayers offered for Edward V).
Monday, 21 July 1483	Abduction attempt at Tower.
	Probable date that Buckingham orders brothers separated.
	York resides in or near Lions Tower; Edward's whereabouts unknown.
Thursday, 24 July 1483	Howard arrives in London to carry out king's orders.

Friday 25 July 1483	Howard appointed Admiral of England.
	Sir Edward Brampton granted £350 from Ports.
c. Saturday, 2 August 1483	York's departure arranged by Howard; Edward's whereabouts remain secret.
Thursday, 7 August 1483	Howard writes to his son, Thomas, with King Richard at Warwick.
	Princes in safekeeping.
Monday, 11 August 1483	Howard leaves London for Suffolk and progress to Walsingham.
c. Monday, 15 September 1483	York: Langton letter.
	Princes alive.
Friday, 19 December 1483	King Richard: Katherine Woodville, Duchess of Buckingham, to travel to London.
Tuesday, 23 January–Friday, 20 February 1484	Parliament: *Titulus Regius* (Act of Succession) Richard III.
Monday, 1 March 1484	Elizabeth Woodville reconciles with King Richard, places daughters in his care.
Wednesday, 10 March 1484	King Richard (via Langton) writes to Pope Innocent VIII concerning 'secrets of my heart'.
Thursday, 11 March 1484	King Richard (via Langton) writes to Charles VIII of France to explain 'certain matters concerning us'.

Saturday, 1 May 1484	York: Popplau delivers letter to King Richard from Margaret of Burgundy.
	Popplau reports 'sons of princes' kept at Pontefract Castle 'just as close as if in captivity', believes Edward IV's sons kept in secret place.
Saturday, 24 July 1484	Sandal Castle, Royal Nursery: 'children together at breakfast'.
Tuesday, 2 November 1484	Edward V's majority (fourteenth birthday).
November 1484	'Lord Bastard riding to Calais.'
	Brackenbury returned 'from the Lord Bastard'.
Wednesday, 1 December 1484	'Edward bastard late called King of England the fifth' (no prayers for Edward V offered in government records).
Monday, 6 December 1484	John Nesfield travels to Jersey in Channel Islands with two unnamed persons by letter of passage from King Richard.
Wednesday, 9 March 1485	Signet Office: order to deliver clothing to 'John Goddeslande fotemane [footman] unto the lord Bastard'.
Monday, 22 August 1485	Bosworth: death of Richard III, Howard and Brackenbury.
Tuesday 23 August–Sunday 28 August 1485	Henry Tudor searches north.

Saturday, 3 September 1485	London: Henry Tudor proclamation, 'If there were a claimant to the crown by descent from King Edward. He was to show himself; and he [Henry] would help him to get crowned'.
Sunday, 30 October 1485	Westminster Abbey: Henry Tudor crowned Henry VII.
Monday, 23 January 1486	Henry VII Parliament: repeals official bastardy of Edward IV's children.
	Edward V (15) now able to claim inheritance/throne.
Tuesday, 27 February 1486	Langton in Malines, Burgundy.
Thursday, 20 April 1486	Yorkshire: Francis Lovell rebellion.
Tuesday, 25 April 1486	Midlands: Lovell rebellion on behalf of King Edward.
Saturday, 29 April/Sunday, 1 May 1486	Guernsey: King Edward set free, travels to Yorkshire, placed in safe-keeping of Lovell.
Monday, 10 July 1486	London, Westminster: Elizabeth Woodville takes out forty-year lease on Cheneygates Mansion.
Sunday, 13 August 1486	Edward V issues grant of office in Ireland.
	Dates reign from summer 1486 in Ireland.
After Friday, 29 September 1486	Henry VII sends Herald to Ireland on 'his secret business'; Edward V interviewed by Herald.
	Lovell and Edward V cross to Burgundy.

Wednesday, 29 November 1486	Henry VII receives word of Yorkist uprising with many enemies on the sea and ships taken; arrests made in Henry's household.
Wednesday, 27 December–Monday, 1 January 1487	Burgundy: King Maximilian obtains war chest.
	Money provided to rebels abroad by Lincoln, Abbot of Abingdon and others.
c. *Friday, 2 February–Saturday, 3 March 1487*	News of King Edward in Ireland reaches England.
	Elizabeth Woodville deprived of possessions and income, sent to Bermondsey Abbey.
Sunday, 18 February–Monday, 19 February 1487	London: Edward, Earl of Warwick, (11) taken out of Tower and exhibited.
Friday, 9 March 1487	Lincoln flees the 'kynges grace' and joins Lovell.
Mid-March 1487	East Anglia: Henry VII makes urgent journey to de la Pole and Howard family heartlands; Dorset arrested nearby, imprisoned in Tower.
Sunday, 25 March 1487	Lincoln sending gold and silver north.
Wednesday, 18 April 1487	Clerk entry for 'son of Clarence' (meaning Edward V) in Malines, Burgundy.
End of April 1487	Burgundy: Preparations for Edward V's invasion of England under way with Margaret and Maximilian.

Saturday, 5 May 1487	Rebels from England arrive in Ireland.
Tuesday, 15 May 1487	Middelburg, Holland: First Burgundian-Habsburg fleet on behalf of Edward V sails to Ireland.
Friday, 25 May 1487	Ireland: Burgundian-Habsburg fleet arrives.
Sunday, 27 May 1487	Christ Church Cathedral, Dublin: Coronation of Edward V (aged 16).
	Burgundy: second Burgundian-Habsburg fleet prepared for Edward V.
c. Tuesday, 29 May 1487	Dublin: Edward V's Parliament.
	Waterford: coins for King Edward minted.
Monday, 4 June 1487	Piel Island, north-west England: Edward V's armada invades England.
Early June 1487	Burgundy: second fleet for Edward V diverted to Brittany by Maximilian.
Friday, 8 June 1487	Masham, North Yorkshire: King Edward writes to city of York.
	City denies King Edward access.
Tuesday, 12 June 1487	York: Northumberland's army leaves city, heads south to Henry VII.
	Yorkists attack city gates and cry 'King Edward'.
	Northumberland returns army to York.
Thursday, 14 June 1487	York: Northumberland's army departs, heading north.

Saturday, 16 June 1487	Battle of Stoke.
	Edward V's death/injury/escape?
	Death of Lincoln.
	Lovell 'put to flight' with 'many other'.
	Northumberland and Stanley brothers not present.
	Lincoln's sister, Katherine de la Pole, imprisoned in Tower of London.
c. *Friday, 9 November 1487*	London: boy captured at Stoke Field named as 'Lambert Simnel'.
	Date of King Edward's coronation (Sunday 27th) recorded as Thursday (24th).
	Household plot against Henry VII foiled, four of king's servants hanged at Tower Hill.
Sunday, 25 November 1487	Coronation of Elizabeth of York; Elizabeth Woodville, Sir Edward Woodville and Dorset not present.
Sunday, 16 December 1487	*Proof of life, Edward V.*
	Burgundy: receipt from Maximilian's court for delivery and payment of pikes for the army that Margaret of York 'sent at the time (across the sea) *to serve her nephew, son of King Edward*, late her brother' (no prayers offered for Edward V).
Thursday, 19 June 1488	Scotland: James IV issues safe conduct to Lovell and English rebels.

Monday, 23 June 1488	Henry VII sends Sir Richard Edgecombe on urgent mission to Ireland to issue pardons, guarantee loyalties and recognition of Henry as king.
Saturday, 12 July 1488	Dublin, Ireland: Edgecombe gives Kildare secret verbal message from Henry VII.
	Kildare stalls for time; privately consults with Irish Council.
Wednesday, 30 July 1488	Kildare recognises Henry VII as king; other Irish lords follow.
	Reign of King Edward in Ireland comes to an end.
January 1489	Thomas Howard released from Tower under oath of allegiance.
February 1489	London: Irish lords visiting Henry VII do not recognise 'Lambert Simnel' as Dublin King.
On or before Saturday, 21 November 1489	Dorset released from Tower.
Sunday, 8 May 1491	St George's Chapel, Windsor: Edward V's Garter stall allocated to Prince Arthur (aged 4½).
	Political death of Edward V.

The Survival of Richard, Duke of York

Monday, 16 June 1483	Tower: Richard of York joins Edward V in royal apartments.
Monday, 21 July 1483	Tower: abduction attempt.
	Princes taken into care of Brackenbury, Tyrell involved.
	Probable date Buckingham orders boys separated.
	York moves into accommodation in or near the Lions Tower.
Thursday, 24 July 1483	Howard arrives in London to carry out king's orders; visits York at Tower.
Friday 25 July 1483	Howard appointed Admiral of England.
	Sir Edward Brampton granted £350 from Ports.
c. *Saturday, 2 August 1483*	York sails to France with Henry and Thomas Peirse.
c. *Wednesday, 6 August 1483*	York arrives in Paris.
Thursday, 11 March 1484	King Richard (via Langton) writes to Charles VIII of France to explain 'certain matters concerning us'.
c. *September 1484*	Henry Tudor and followers arrive in Paris.
	York (aged 11) moves south and then to northern France.

c. *End of* 1484	York arrives in (Burgundian) Hainault; resides in nearby French city of Tournai.
	Tournai: York said to receive education at Cathedral Choir school.
c. *Christmas 1484–early 1485*	France: Dorset with Henry Tudor.
	London: Elizabeth Woodville writes to Dorset to make peace with King Richard.
	Dorset deserts Tudor, is captured at Compiègne, en route for Flanders.
Monday, 22 August 1485	Bosworth: death of Richard III, Howard and Brackenbury.
Saturday, 3 September 1485	London: Tudor proclamation 'claimant to the crown by descent from King Edward to show himself; and he [Henry] would help him get crowned'.
Sunday, 30 October 1485	Westminster Abbey: Henry Tudor crowned Henry VII.
Monday, 23 January 1486	Henry VII Parliament: repeals official bastardy of Edward IV's children.
	Edward V and Richard of York able to claim inheritance/throne.
End of April 1487	Burgundy: York and Peirses sail to Portugal with Sir Edward Brampton's wife.
Saturday, 16 June 1487	Battle of Stoke.
	Edward V's death/injury/escape?

Late summer 1487	Portugal: news reaches York of defeat of Edward V.
	York (aged 14) sends Thomas Peirse to Elizabeth Woodville.
	Thomas Peirse remains in England.
Early 1488	Henry VII sends spies to Portugal.
Wednesday, 30 July 1488	Reign of King Edward in Ireland comes to an end.
Tuesday, 4 November 1488	Scotland: James IV issues safe passage to English rebels from Ireland at 'urging of Margaret of Burgundy'.
August 1489	Henry VII sends Richmond Herald to Portugal.
Monday, 17 August 1489	York reaches majority (sixteenth birthday).
November 1489	London: last recorded appearance of Elizabeth Woodville at court; unprecedented meeting during Elizabeth of York's confinement.
Monday, 16 November 1489	Windsor, Black Book: by this date York's Garter stall allocated to William Stanley.
	Political death of York as duke and heir to throne.
On or before Saturday, 21 November 1489	Dorset released from Tower.
c. 1489–90	Portugal: Henry Peirse advises York to travel to Ireland to Lords Kildare and Desmond (who helped his brother).
	Peirse dies of plague.

Tuesday, 2 February 1490	Scottish Treasurer's Office: records item to 'the herald that come from Ireland and past [proceeded] to the Duchess of Burgundy'.
Thursday, 19 May–Sunday, 22 May 1491	London: Halneth Mauleverer and others stand surety for Dorset's loyalty.
c. November 1491	York (18) sails to Ireland.
Monday, 4 June 1492	Dorset receives pardon, required to give wide-ranging guarantees of loyalty to King Henry and report any treasons and conspiracies in writing.
	Dorset's heir (Thomas, 14) made King Henry's ward.
Friday, 8 June 1492	Bermondsey Abbey: death of Elizabeth Woodville.
After Tuesday, 10 July 1492	Henry VII loyalist, Thomas Butler, made Keeper of the Chancery Records in Ireland.
Summer 1492	York to France at French King Charles VIII's invitation/offer of support.
October 1492	Paris: 100 English supporters join York.
Saturday, 3 November 1492	Peace treaty of Étaples prevents support by Charles VIII.
	York leaves France.
Late 1492	York with Margaret of Burgundy.

Monday, 14 January–Thursday, 14 March 1493	London: Lord Fitzwalter to array 500 men on behalf of York as king.
	Sir Gilbert Debenham and Sir Humphrey Savage join rebellion for York.
	Sir William Stanley joins rebellion for York as titular head.
Sunday, 25 August 1493	Dendermonde, Burgundy: York and Margaret write to Queen Isabella of Spain to confirm his identity and request support.
Late summer–early autumn 1493	*Proof of life, Richard, Duke of York.*
	Burgundy: York gives full account of his story, beginning at the Tower.
	Nobles and many others in England flock to him, including Elizabeth of York's Yeoman.
7 December 1493	Vienna: York attends funeral of Frederick III, Holy Roman Emperor; first official public appearance; Maximilian recognises York as King Edward's heir.
Summer 1494	York rises against King Henry.
Monday, 1 December 1494	Ireland: all records of Edward V's coronation and Parliament destroyed on Henry VII's orders.
Mid-January–February 1495	London: English nobles arrested and executed, including William Stanley and Sir Simon Montford.
Saturday, 4 April 1495	Zeeland: English ships threaten York's invasion fleet.

Friday, 8 May 1495	York fleet moved to Texel, northern Holland.
	Burgundy: Margaret's supplication to Pope Alexander VI on behalf of her nephew, York.
Wednesday, 1 July 1495	Texel: York's invasion fleet sails to England.
Friday, 3 July 1495	Lands at Deal, Kent.
	100-plus of York's men killed or captured.
	Approximately 400 executions follow.
c. *Tuesday, 7 July 1495*	York's fleet arrives in Ireland.
Saturday, 12 September 1495	London: four Dutchmen supporting York hanged in river at St Katherine's.
Mid-September 1495	Henry VII undertakes inquisition against all Irish in England, specifically London.
	All Irish nationals, including women and children, to be accounted for.
Tuesday, 22 September 1495	Burgundy: Maximilian's supplication to Pope Alexander VI on York's behalf.
Late November 1495	Scotland: York at court of James IV.
Mid-January 1496	Scotland: York marries James IV's kinswoman, Katherine Gordon.

September 1496	York issues proclamation as King Richard IV.
	Invades northern England with James IV.
	Invasion fails.
	Elizabeth of York unwell.
c. *Monday, 3 July 1497*	Ayr: York leaves Scotland with three ships; James IV to attack Henry VII's forces from north, York from south-west.
	Henry VII spends over £60,000 on defending England from York.
c. *25 July 1497*	York in Ireland.
Thursday, 7 September 1497	York invades England at Cornwall, marches to Devon.
	Invasion fails.
	Takes sanctuary at Beaulieu Abbey.
Thursday, 5 October 1497	York leaves sanctuary wearing royal cloth of gold.
	Meets Henry VII in Taunton, Devon, and is captured.
Wednesday, 8 November 1497	Metz: Maximilian begs Henry for York's life, offers 10,000 florins to help save him.
After 18 November 1497	York guarded at Sheen and Westminster Palace.
	Forbidden to meet Elizabeth of York or have conjugal relations with wife.
Wednesday, 22 November 1497	London: York paraded as French impostor.

Saturday, 9 June–Wednesday, 13 June 1498	York escapes. York is captured and imprisoned in the Tower. York is placed in shackles and beaten, his face broken.
August/September 1499	Burgundy: Margaret writes apology to Henry VII to save York's life.
	Maximilian offers Henry his friendship to save York's life.
Tuesday, 12 November 1499	Plot discovered to free York and Warwick from Tower.
	Warwick to make York king.
Saturday, 16 November 1499	London, White Hall, Westminster: York tried for treason.
Thursday, 21 November 1499	London, Great Hall, Westminster: Warwick tried for treason.
Saturday, 23 November 1499	York (26) hanged at Tyburn as French impostor 'Perkyn Osbeck'.
Thursday, 28 November 1499	Warwick (24) beheaded at Tower.
	John of Gloucester (approx. 30) secretly killed in Tower.
December 1499–January 1500	Elizabeth of York (33) unwell.

Abbreviations

The place of publication is London unless otherwise stated.

ADN	Archives Départementales du Nord, Lille, France.
André	Bernard André, *The Life of Henry VII*, Daniel Hobbins (ed.) (2011).
Beloved Cousyn	*Richard III's 'Beloved Cousyn': John Howard and the House of York*, John Ashdown-Hill (Stroud, 2009).
Bennett	*Lambert Simnel and the Battle of Stoke*, Michael Bennett (Gloucester, 1987).
BHO	British History Online.
BIHR	*Bulletin of the Institute of Historical Research.*
BNF	Bibliothèque Nationale de France.
Buc	*The History of King Richard the Third* by Sir George Buc, Master of the Revels (1619), Arthur Kincaid (ed.) (2023).
Bulletin	*Ricardian Bulletin*, magazine of the Richard III Society.
Campbell	*Materials for a History of the Reign of Henry VII*, Reverend William Campbell (ed.) (1873).
CCR	Calendar of the Close Rolls.
CFR	Calendar of the Fine Rolls.
CPR	Calendar of the Patent Rolls.
Coronation	*The Coronation of Richard III: The Extant Documents*, Anne F. Sutton & P.W. Hammond (eds) (Gloucester, New York, 1983).
Crowland	*The Crowland Continuations 1459–86*, Nicholas Pronay & John Cox (eds) (1986).
Crown & People	*Richard III: Crown and People*, J. Petre (ed.), Richard III Society (Gloucester, 1985).

De But   'Chronique d'Adrien De But' ('Chronicon ab anno 1465 usque ad 1487') in *Chroniques relatives à l'histoire de la Belgique sous la domination des ducs de Bourgogne*, I, pp. 581–310, J. Kervyn de Lettenhove (Brussels, 1870).

DI   *Dickon Independent*, magazine of the Gloucester Branch, Richard III Society.

Divisie Chronicle   *Die cronycke van Hollandt, Zeelandt ende Vrieslant*, Cornelius Aurelius (Jan Seversz, 1517), The Hague, Royal Library, KW 1084 A6.

DNB   *Dictionary of National Biography, 1885–1900*, en.wikisource.org/wiki/ Dictionary_of_National_Biography_1885–1900.

Early Historians   *Richard III and His Early Historians 1483–1485*, Alison Hanham (Oxford, 1975).

EHR   *English Historical Review*.

GC   *The Great Chronicle of London*, A.H. Thomas & I.D. Thornley (eds), (1938, reprint 1983).

Harley 433   *British Library Harleian MS 433*, R.E. Horrox & P.W. Hammond (eds) (Gloucester, 1979–1983).

Heralds' Memoir   *The Heralds' Memoir 1486–1490: Court Ceremony, Royal Progress and Rebellion*, Emma Cavell (ed.), (Donington, 2009).

HHSA   Haus-, Hof- und Staatsarchiv, Wien, Austria.

Hicks   *Edward V: The Prince in the Tower*, Michael Hicks (Gloucester, 2003).

Historical Notes   'Historical Notes of a London Citizen, 1483–1488' by Richard Firth Green, *EHR* (July 1981), Vol. 96, No. 380.

Howard Books   *The Household Books of John Howard, Duke of Norfolk, 1462–1471, 1481–1483*, Anne Crawford (ed.) (Stroud, 1992).

Itinerary   *The Itinerary of King Richard III 1483–1485*, Rhoda Edwards (1983).

JHA   *Journal of the Historical Association*.

LMA Common Council 9   London Metropolitan Archives, City of London, COL/CC/01/01/009: Court of Common

	Council, City of London Corporation, Journal 9.
Maligned King	*Richard III: The Maligned King*, Annette Carson (Stroud, 2008, 2013).
Mancini	*Domenico Mancini: de occupatione regni Anglie*, Annette Carson (trans./ed.) (Horstead, 2021).
Memorials	*Memorials of the Wars of the Roses: A Biographical Guide*, W.E Hampton (Gloucester, 1979).
Molinet	*Chroniques de Jean Molinet 1474–1504*, five volumes, J.A. Buchon (Paris, 1827–28).
More	*St Thomas More: The History of King Richard III and Selections from the English and Latin Poems*, Richard S. Sylvester (ed.) (New Haven, 1976).
Mythology	*Mythology of the Princes in the Tower*, John Ashdown-Hill (Stroud, 2018).
NAH	National Archives, The Hague, Netherlands.
NYCRO	North Yorkshire County Record Office (Northallerton).
ODNB	*Oxford Dictionary of National Biography* (Oxford, 2004).
Orme	'The Education of Edward V' by Nicholas Orme, *BIHR*, November 1984, Vol. LVII, No. 136, pp. 119–30.
PROME	*Parliament Rolls of Medieval England* (Woodbridge, 2005); British History Online: www.british-history.ac.uk/no-series/parliament-rolls-medieval
Protector & Constable	*Richard, Duke of Gloucester as Lord Protector and High Constable of England*, Annette Carson (Horstead, 2015).
RI XIV	*Regesta Imperii XIV Maximilian I (1486/1493–1519)*.
Ricardian	*The Ricardian*, academic journal of the Richard III Society.
Road to Bosworth	*Richard III: The Road to Bosworth Field*, P.W. Hammond & Anne F. Sutton (1985).
Rot. Parl.	*Rotuli Parliamentorum, ut et petitiones et placita in Parliamento* (Rolls of Parliament).

Royal Funerals	*The Royal Funerals of the House of York*, Anne F. Sutton and Livia Visser-Fuchs with R.A. Griffiths (2005).
Secret Queen	*Eleanor, The Secret Queen: The Woman Who Put Richard III on the Throne*, John Ashdown-Hill (Stroud, 2009, 2016).
SHA	Sächsisches Hauptstaatsarchiv, Dresden, Germany.
TMPP	The Missing Princes Project.
TNA: PRO	The National Archives: Public Record Office.
Vergil-1	*Polydore Vergil's Life of Richard III: An Edition of the Original Manuscript*, Stephen O'Connor (ed.) (Westoning, 2021).
Vergil-2	*The Anglica Historia of Polydore Vergil 1485–1537*, Denys Hay (ed.) (1950).
Weightman	*Margaret of York, the Diabolical Duchess: the Woman Who Tried to Overthrow the Tudors*, Christine Weightman (Oxfordshire, 2012).
Wroe	*Perkin: A Story of Deception*, Ann Wroe (2003, 2004).
York Books	*The York House Books 1461–1490*, Lorraine C. Attreed (ed.) (Stroud, 1991).

Notes

Front Matter

1   Philip Lindsay, *King Richard III: A Chronicle* (1933), frontispiece.

Introduction

1   Leicester University, 27 April 2015, *Annual Review 2014–2015*, p. 9.

2   Annette Carson (ed.), *Finding Richard III: The Official Account of Research by the Retrieval and Reburial Project* (2014), pp. 20–21.

3   *Ibid.*, pp. 25–7; Langley & Jones, *The Lost King: The Search for Richard III* (2022, first published as *The King's Grave*, 2013), pp. 247–48. From David Baldwin, 'King Richard's Grave in Leicester', *Transactions of Leicestershire Archaeological and Historical Society* (1986), 60, pp. 21–24; *Leicester Mercury*, 8 October 2002, p. 10. Plaque erected by the Richard III Society.

4   No unevenness is apparent in the drawings from life by John Rous, nor in diary of Niclas von Popplau, who met Richard in 1484. Philippa Langley & Doris Schneider-Coutandin, 'Niclas von Popplau: Lost in Translation?' Part Two, *Bulletin*, March 2021, pp. 39–47 (p. 43).

5   'Bones in Urn "not related to Richard III"', *The Times*, 27 June 2016; Ashdown-Hill, *Eleanor* (2016), pp. 249–52.

6   Theya Molleson, 'Anne Mowbray and the Princes in the Tower', *London Archaeologist*, 1987, Vol. 5 (10), pp. 259–60 (A.H. Brook, 'A unifying aetiological explanation for anomalies of human tooth number and size', *Archvs Oral Biol.*, 29, 1984, pp. 373–78).

7   Michael Hicks & Martin Biddle, 'Was the Skeleton in the Leicester Car Park Really Richard III?', *BBC HistoryExtra*, 6 May 2014.

8   'King Richard III: DNA and Genealogical Study Confirms Identity of Remains …', Leicester University, 2 December 2014.

9   Ashdown-Hill, *The Mythology of Richard III* (2015), pp. 171–76.

10 Executive Producers, Nick Kent, Sue Jones.

11 Oxford Film & TV website, 2015.

12 Anna Leszkiewicz, 'Richard III: the Princes in the Tower' (Channel 4, March 2015) review, *Daily Telegraph*.

13 Michael Jones, *The Black Prince* (2017), pp. 367, 371–73, Appendix, 'Black Propaganda and the Sack of Limoges', pp. 405–08 (Pépin's discovery, p. 408).

1. The Missing Princes Project: A Cold-Case Investigation

1 Rachael Stark, 'A Song of Ice and Fire: the Retold Story of King Richard III', *Court Journal*, Vol. 22, Autumn 2017, pp. 37–39.

2. The Missing Princes: Edward V and Richard, Duke of York

1 TNA C 66/530. See also H.M. Carey, *Courting Disaster: Astrology at the English Court and University in the Later Middle Ages* (1992), Appendix III, p. 257. Gloucester Cathedral, MS 21, f.9v, 'Edward V Astrological Chart' shows he was born on 2 November 1470 at 4.06 p.m. For Dr John Argentine, see Rhodes, *Argentine: Provost of Kings*, 1967, p. 12), thanks to Marie Barnfield. Also, Rosemary Horrox, *ODNB*; Hicks, pp. 54, 177. *Crowland*, p. 123 records the incorrect date.

2 TNA E 404/71/6; Horrox, *ODNB*.

3 A.J. Hibbard, *An Account of Richard (Plantagenet), Third Duke of Gloucester and Third King of England, of that Name & The Most Noble Order of the Garter* (2016), p. 16.

4 James Gairdner, *DNB*.

5 CPR 1467–77, p. 283; Gairdner, *DNB*; Horrox, *ODNB*; Josephine Wilkinson, *The Princes in the Tower* (2013), p. 13; Hicks, p. 83.

6 Hicks, pp. 61–63.

7 Charles Ross, *Edward IV* (1974, 1997), p. 197.

8 Hicks, p. 75.

9 Stephen David, 'Ludlow and the Woodvilles and What Richard of Gloucester Had to Fear', *DI*, No. 120, July 2021, pp. 6–10 (p. 7); *Mythology*, pp. 29–33.

10 David, *op. cit.*, p. 8.

11 *Protector and Constable*, Appendix IX, p. 95.

12 David, *op. cit.*, p. 7.

13 Orme, p. 129.

14 Hicks, pp. 65–66.

15 Horrox, *ODNB*.

16 Hicks, pp. 68–69.

17 Horrox, *ODNB*; Scofield, *Edward the Fourth* (2016 reprint), Vol. 2, p. 125, n. 1. His knighting on 7 May is unverified. Hicks, p. 64, n. 12, gives 18 April. See notes 19, 42, 49.

18 See *Mythology*, pp. 23–24 for Edward being sickly/doubts over the succession (see Chapter 7).

19 BL, Add MS 6113 f. 74v; poss. later copy of lost contemporary heraldic account is found in Collection Wriothesley, son of John Writhe Garter, KoA 1477. Thanks to Marie Barnfield.

20 Hicks, p. 59. Other nobles also paid homage. Charles Ross, *Richard III* (1988), p. 35, cites the occasion incorrectly.

21 Hicks, p. 57.

22 Horrox, *ODNB*; Howard Books, Vol. 2, pp. 3–12.

23 Hicks, p. 67.

24 *Mancini*, pp. 54–55.

25 *Molinet*, Vol. 1, Chapter 100, p. 402. Trans. thanks to Isabelle Lloyd (5.9.2019).

26 *Mancini*, pp. 41–43, alleges Edward IV's melancholia. See also *Crowland*, pp. 149–51.

27 Orme, pp. 124–25. See *Protector & Constable*, pp. 95–100 for full 1483 ordinances; also Wilkinson, *The Princes in the Tower*, pp. 18–19.

28 Orme, p. 124.

29 *Protector & Constable*, p. 97.

30 Orme, pp. 127–29.

31 Orme, p. 123.

32 *Mancini*, p. 65.

33 *Crowland*, p. 149.

34 Lambeth Palace Library, MS 265 f.vir. DNA research indicates the eye colour of Richard III was probably blue as per SAL portrait. Elizabeth of York's eyes were brown as per Royal Collection, RCIN 403447.

35 For a closer view, see The Missing Princes Project: www.revealingrichardiii.com/johnson.html

36 John Ashdown-Hill discusses Canterbury glass at www.johnashdownhill.com/johns-blog/2017/11/6/does-the-royal-window-at-canterbury-cathedral-show-us-what-edward-ivs-two-sons-really-looked-like

37 *Mancini*, p. 49.

38 *Mancini*, p. 65.

39 D.R. Carlson, *English Humanist Books* (1993), p. 41.

40 For Richard's birth, see Scofield, Vol. 2, p. 60 n. 4. See also Gairdner, *DNB*, Vol. 48; *Gentleman's Magazine*, Vol. 101, Part 1, Jan. 1831, p. 25.

41 Wroe, pp. 58, 61.

42 Horrox, *ODNB*; W.A. Shaw, *Knights of England: A Complete Record*, 1906, Vol. 1, p. 136. See also note 17.

43 Hibbard, *An Account of Richard (Plantagenet), Third Duke of Gloucester and Third King of England, of that Name & The Most Noble Order of the Garter*, pp. 17–18.

44 *Mythology*, p. 26; *Excerpta Historica*, pp. 366–79.

45 *Excerpta Historica*, p. 371; Wroe, pp. 65–66.

46 Scofield, Vol. 2, p. 205 n. 1.

47 Scofield, Vol. 2, pp. 204–06.

48 *Mythology*, p. 37. Papal dispensation for consanguinity was made to Pope Sixtus IV.

49 BL, Add MS 6113 f.74v. See notes 20 and 21.

50 Wroe, p. 59, he is also described as Banneret/Knight of the Body to the King. Of numerous Thomas Greys, one attended Richard III's coronation (*Coronation*, pp. 350–51); A. Compton Reeves, 'The Foppish Eleven of 1483', *Medieval Prosopography*, Aut. 1995, Vol. 16, No. 2, pp. 111–34 (pp. 127, 134); *Memorials*, pp. 185–86, p. 203 offers other candidates.

51 Wroe, p. 58.

52 *Mythology*, pp. 116, 280 n. 1 (Howard Books, Vol. 2, p. 348). Poynes' identity is unclear. For Sir Robert Poyntz of Gloucester, see *Memorials*, p. 64; *Royal Funerals*, pp. 26, 38.

53 Gairdner, *DNB*.

54 See Chapter 14, note 96, for Richard of York in Ireland in December 1479.

55 Wendy Moorhen, 'Anne Mowbray: In Life and Death', *Bulletin*, Spring 2005, pp. 24–26.

56 Ross, *Richard III*, p. 36 n. 51.

57 See Chapter 3, note 17, for Edward IV's date of death.

58 *Crowland*, p. 159.

59 *Mythology*, p. 115; Kingsford, *Stonor Letters and Papers*, Vol. 2, p. 161.

60 Hicks, p. 129.

61 Barrie Williams, 'Rui de Sousa's Embassy and the Fate of Richard, Duke of York', *Ricardian*, June 1981, pp. 341–45. Also, TMPP Research Report: 'The Movements of Rui de Sousa', Rosemary Swabey, 12.7.2019.

62 Wroe, pp. 59, 60, 525.

63 *Molinet*, Vol. 1, Chapter 100, p. 402.

64 *Mythology*, pp. 116, 280 n. 11 (Howard Books, Vol. 2, p. 348).

65 Wroe, pp. 40, 525.

66 BNF, *Fonds Espagnol* 318, f.83, line 69. Margaret of Burgundy's letter to Queen Isabella of Spain, Dendermonde, 25 August 1493 (trans. Maria Leotta, 11.3.2020). Text ed./trans. by Dr Betty Knott, Snr Hon. Research Fellow in Classics, Glasgow University (6.2.2021). See Appendix 4.

3. 1483: Two Weeks, One Summer

1 That Elizabeth Woodville would have resided in the dining hall at College Hall (Abbot's Court complex) is highly unlikely, whereas she had taken sanctuary in Cheneygates Mansion within the complex in 1470 where she gave birth. In 1486, she returned to Cheneygates with a forty-year lease. Thanks to Eileen Bates (2.12.2021).

2 *Crowland*, p. 159. For Howard, see *Vergil-1*, p. 6. For payments for river boats travelling the Thames, see Howard Books, Vol. 2, p. 402.

3 A contemporary witness describes the young prince as 'merry', see Chapter 2.

4 *Protector & Constable*, p. 57 n. 182 (LMA Common Council 9, 17 June 1483).

5 *Mancini*, pp. 67, 110 nn. 151, 152.

6 *Mancini*, pp. 69, 113–14 nn. 165 & 166. *Crowland*, p. 159, has Richard claiming the throne by pretext. For his election as king, see Chapter 7.

7 *Mancini*, p. 69, 116 nn. 179 & 180.

8 *Protector & Constable*, Appendix III, p. 85.

9 This period spanned brief interruptions in 1470–71 of about eleven months.

10 Annette Carson, The Mysterious Affair at Stony Stratford (11 June 2021), pp. 1–25 (p. 2), tinyurl.com/27k4vm86

11 *Protector & Constable*, p. 7.

12 *Ibid.*, p. 24.

13 *Ibid.*, p. 25.

14 Ian Mortimer, 'Richard II and the Succession', *JHA*, Vol. 91 (303), July 2006, pp. 320–36.

15 Mortimer, p. 332.

16 Mortimer, p. 333.

17 Howard Books, Vol. 2, pp. 389, 398: the date of death is supported by the Howard family's observances of King Edward's first month's mind (3 May, payment for two Masses) and second month's mind (2 June, payment for Lady Howard's offerings at St Antholin Church, London, for three days, 2–4 June). For payments for offerings on his first Sunday in London following the king's death, see *ibid.*, p. 384. His death is also recorded as 3 April by Jean Molinet, *Mythology*, pp. 41–44, 217, 272 n. 5.

18 Howard Books, Vol. 2, p. 378; *Beloved Cousyn*, pp. 82, 164. Given the distance to Suffolk, Edward would have written the letter two days earlier.

19 On 9–10 May, Howard sent thirty-eight men home to Suffolk and Essex: Howard Books, Vol.2, pp. 390–91; *Beloved Cousyn*, p. 88. He also sent his servant, Browning, home on 15 May: Howard Books, Vol. 2, p. 392.

20 Howard Books, Vol.2, p. 383.

21 *Mancini*, pp. 43, 82 n. 8; *Crowland*, p. 151.

22 *Crowland*, p. 153.

23 *York Books*, Vol. 1, pp. 281–82.

24 See *Mancini*, pp. 51, 91 n. 61 for questions surrounding this being Hastings.

25 Howard Books, Vol. 2, p. 384; *Beloved Cousyn*, p. 83.

26 *Crowland*, p. 151.

27 Anne Crawford, *Yorkist Lord: John Howard, Duke of Norfolk* (2010), p. 98; Linda Clark, *ODNB*: born *c.* 1411, aged about 72. Already, in 1469, he is described as an old man who might be 'happy to dye' any moment (N. Davis, *Paston Letters and Papers of the Fifteenth Century* (2004), I, 337).

28 *Royal Funerals*, pp. 14–17, 22, 31.

29 Hammond & Sutton, *Richard III: The Road to Bosworth Field*, pp. 89–91; *Rot. Parl.*, vi, pp. 204–06. For Richard's successful 1482 Scottish campaign and retrieval of Berwick, Edward IV in Parliament 1483 awarded him an unprecedented palatinate that included Westmorland, Cumberland and parts of Scotland.

30 NYCRO, ZBA 17/1/1 f.3, Bedale, North Yorkshire: Court of Francis Lovell, 15 April 1483, dated first year of the king's reign (a scribal error names King Edward IV, which cannot be reconciled with Lovell's age). Bedale, which Lovell only inherited in 1474, was the adjacent manor and lordship to Middleham, Richard's apparent main residence and family home. Gloucester's letter took some days to be received/discussed in London by the King's Council on or around 20 April. See note 53.

31 *Mancini*, p. 51.

32 *Mancini*, p. 53, who asserts that Henry Stafford, Duke of Buckingham, also wrote suggesting he join the king travelling to London, incorrectly assuming Buckingham and Gloucester travelled eastward together, p. 94 n. 76.

33 *Crowland*, p. 155, reported that in York, Gloucester held a funeral ceremony and swore all the nobility of those parts in fealty to the king's son: 'he himself swore first of all'.

34 *York Books*, Vol. 1, p. 282. On 24 April, the York Council proposed sending a man to London to attend upon Gloucester and request the king to pardon their annual toll fee.

35 *Mancini*, p. 97.
36 *Mancini*, p. 95 n. 81; Carson, The Mysterious Affair at Stony Stratford, p. 12.
37 Carson, The Mysterious Affair at Stony Stratford, pp. 13, 15.
38 *Itinerary*, p. 1.
39 Hicks, pp. 65, 75. Rivers was appointed by ordinances of 1473, 1483. The prince resided at Ludlow from 1473, aged about 3; his signet warrants are normally dated there from 1474.
40 To be arbitrated by Gloucester's 'Council Learned'. C.E. Moreton, 'A Local Dispute and the Politics of 1483', *Ricardian*, Vol. 8, No. 107, December 1989, p. 1 (thanks to Marie Barnfield).
41 *Maligned King*, p. 16. *Crowland*, p. 151, records King Edward fell ill at 'about Easter-time'. Easter Sunday was 30 March.
42 Hall Book 2, NRO KL/C 7/4, see notes 46, 49; *Coronation*, p. 14.
43 *Crowland*, p. 155.
44 *Crowland*, pp. 153–55.
45 *Crowland*, p. 155, describes them as 'horse' and a 'force'. *Mancini* pp. 53, 95 n. 80 describes them as 'companions', whereas Gloucester's smaller escort is 'a large force of soldiers'. Carson notes these distorted descriptions both here and in Vergil, *Maligned King*, p. 53 n. 6.
46 The haste of the coronation is recorded by *Crowland*, p. 153, *Mancini*, p. 53 and Edward V himself, see notes 42 and 49.
47 *Mancini*, p. 53.
48 *Protector & Constable*, pp. 1, 2.
49 Hall Book 2, NRO KL/C 7/4: a copy of a letter in the King's Lynn Archives (transcription Marie Barnfield) indicates Edward knew of his father's death by 14 April. The letter was apparently received a week later and read to the Council on 24 April.
50 Carson, The Mysterious Affair at Stony Stratford, p. 8.
51 Ibid.
52 (Quote) *Coronation*, p. 15; *Mancini*, p. 51.
53 *Protector & Constable*, p. 52.
54 *Mancini*, pp. 55, 96. *Crowland*, p. 157.
55 *Crowland*, p. 155, writes that Rivers was to submit everything to Gloucester's judgement. Carson argues this is inconsistent with decisions in London, *Maligned King*, p. 52. For Rivers' companions, see *Mancini*, p. 53.
56 *Mancini*, p. 53.
57 *Crowland*, pp. 154–55; *Mancini*, p. 53, 95 n. 81; *Beloved Cousyn*, pp. 86–87.
58 GC, p. 230.
59 *Mancini*, pp. 55, 59.
60 *Crowland*, p. 157.
61 *Harley 433*, Vol. 2, p. 25.
62 Thanks to Christopher Tinmouth (31.12.2019). *Crowland*, pp. 157, 161; Rous' translation, *Early Historians*, p. 118.
63 *Ibid.*, p. 119; Rous, *Historia* (*c.* 1490). Northumberland acted as 'their chief judge'. *Mancini*, p. 65, gives the prevailing view in the capital that their execution was to be effected judicially 'by certain quaestors' (prosecutors). Also see Chapter 16, note 11.

64 *Memorials*, pp. 117–18, thanks to Dr Judith Ford. See Langley, 'Part 4. The Fate of the Sons of King Edward IV: The Aftermath of Bosworth 22 August to 3 September 1485', *Bulletin*, September 2020, p. 44 and n. 47. Also, *GC*, p. 230, records 'Sir' Richard Haute (with Vaughan and Grey) taken into 'safe keeping' at this time; however, plain 'Richard Haute' entered into a bond with William Catesby on 17 June, probably for good behaviour; *Coronation*, p. 23. No record of his incarceration exists, so if he was taken, he was later released. For Haute as Controller of the prince's Ludlow household and disambiguation, see *Maligned King*, p. 52.

65 Those who 'abetted' Edward's 'lustfulness' are named as Sir Richard Grey, Thomas Grey, Marquess of Dorset, and Sir Edward Woodville, in *Mancini* pp. 47–49. Also named is Lord Hastings, at mortal enmity with Dorset and vying for each other's mistresses.

66 *Mancini*, p. 57.

67 *Mancini*, p. 59.

68 *Mancini*, p. 55; Carson, The Mysterious Affair at Stony Stratford, p. 23.

69 *Itinerary*, p. 2.

70 *Itinerary*, p. 2; Carson, The Mysterious Affair at Stony Stratford, p. 24.

71 *Road to Bosworth*, p. 103 (for the Stallworth letter, see note 86). Neither Mancini nor Crowland mentions Lionel Woodville.

72 *Mancini*, p. 57.

73 *Mancini*, pp. 57, 99 nn. 101 & 102.

74 C.P. Wilkins, *ODNB*. Figures for Scottish invasion force can be found in Edward Hall's *Chronicle* (1809), p. 331 (thanks to Dr Sandra Pendlington).

75 *Mancini*, p. 57.

76 *Mancini*, pp. 59, 100 n. 109.

77 *Mancini*, pp. 59, 100 n. 111.

78 *GC*, p. 230.

79 *Crowland*, p. 157.

80 *Mancini*, pp. 59, 101–02 n. 116.

81 *Coronation*, p. 17.

82 Howard Books, Vol. 2, pp. 390–91; *Beloved Cousyn*, p. 88. Howard sent his servant Browning home on 15 May, Howard Books, Vol. 2, p. 392.

83 Edward V signed '2 grants this day, in the Cittie of London and Tower of London', indicating his move to the Tower: *Grants of King Edward the Fifth*, Camden Society Old Series (1968), pp. 16–17; *Harley 433*, Vol. 3, pp. 3, 4, 6.

84 Grants, p. 17; *Beloved Cousyn*, p. 91.

85 *Protector & Constable*, p. 67; *Coronation*, p. 19.

86 *Road to Bosworth*, p. 102. Canon Simon Stallworth, letter of 9 June 1483: 'The Quene kepys stylle [still] Westminstre'.

87 *Ibid.*, p. 102, Stallworth letter.

88 *Ibid.*, p. 103.

89 *Ibid.*, p. 102, Stallworth letter.

90 *York Books*, Vol. 1, p. 284. The muster was planned for Wednesday, 18 June.

91 *Protector & Constable*, p. 102.

92   *Coronation*, p. 18 suggests it was formulated between 13 May and 5–10
      June; transcribed in *Protector & Constable*, Appendix X, pp. 101–06. For the
      protectorate to last until the king comes of age, see p. 106.

93   Historical Notes, p. 588; *Mancini*, pp. 74–76, 106 n. 132.

94   *Mancini*, p. 63.

95   *Vergil-1*, pp. 7–10, has the knights in the 'next chamber'.

96   *Coronation*, pp. 21–22. For dating the Cely note to March 1483, see *Mythology*,
      Chapter 13, pp. 75–78.

97   Historical Notes, p. 588.

98   *Protector & Constable*, pp. 71–73; *Mancini*, p. 106 n. 132.

99   Sir Henry Ellis, *Three Books of Polydore Vergil's English History*, 1534 (1844),
      pp. 180–81; *Early Historians*, p. 167.

100   'Ballad of Bosworth Fielde', line 236.

101   Matthew Lewis, *Richard III: Loyalty Binds Me* (2018), pp. 273–74.

102   *Mancini*, pp. 36–37.

103   *Mancini*, p. 159.

104   *Crowland*, p. 159.

105   *Mythology*, p. 115; Kingsford (ed.), *Stonor Letters and Papers*, Vol. 2, p. 161.

106   *Mancini*, p. 99 n. 100, for Gloucester's respect of sanctuary, October 1483,
      when rebels claimed sanctuary at Beaulieu. On the abbey's sanctuary rights
      being ascertained, 'the fugitives remained there unmolested'. Sanctuaries under
      Henry VII and VIII first became sealed prisons then lost all rights.

107   Hicks, p. 151: interestingly, the grant was countersigned.

108   *Mythology*, pp. 220, 292–93 nn. 50 & 60, Appendix 1, 'Edward V Timeline';
      CCR 1476–85, pp. 304, 306.

109   *Coronation*, p. 25.

110   Judith Ford, 'A Vale of Mysrye: The Will of Dr Ralph Shaa',
      Bulletin, September 2021, pp. 52–55.

111   *Coronation*, p. 26.

4. The Disappearance: A Timeline

1   *Coronation*, p. 46.

2   *Itinerary*, p. 4.

3   CPR 1476–85, p. 364; Horrox, *ODNB*. Brackenbury was simultaneously
     appointed Master & Worker of the King's Moneys and Keeper of the Exchange
     in the Tower.

4   *Beloved Cousyn*, pp. 96, 166.

5   *Harley 433*, Vol. 2, p. 2. Paid out of the Honour of Tutbury, named as: Edward
     John, John Melyonek, Sir Olyvere Underwode, Maister Robert Cam, Maister
     Smythe, Sir William Sulby, Sir Richard Prestone, Sir William Luce, Richard
     Holme, John Martyn, Edward Wakefield, Henry Muschamp, John Londone,
     John Buntynge, Thomas Blaydesmith, Robert Ham and Thomas Coke.

6   J.A.F. Thomson, 'The Death of Edward V: Dr Richmond's Dating
     Reconsidered', *Northern History*, 26:1 (1990), pp. 207–11 (p. 210), cites the same

description of 'Edward Bastard', etc. in a payment of 15 July 1483 to Dr John Gunthorpe, Keeper of the Privy Seal.

7   Orme, p. 123.

8   Various records list Dr John Alcock, former tutor and President of Edward V's Council, as present with the king on progress from at least 24–26 July at Oxford, see Chapter 17.

9   Giles may have been paid off in November 1483 (see note 30): N. Orme, *English Schools in the Middle Ages* (1973), p. 27 (thanks to Dr David Johnson). See *ibid.*, n. 1 for A.B. Emden, *Biographical Register of the University of Oxford to A.D.1500* (1958), Vol. 2, p. 842, likely identification as 'Jo. Giles granted an annuity of £20 for his good service in instructing the king's sons, Edward, prince of Wales and Richard, duke of York, in grammar, 1 May 1476' (CPR 1467–77, p. 592). See *Harley 433*, Vol. 3, p. 194 for John Giles as a royal tutor (may be dated 1 March 1485 if folios are chronological) – an extensive list of fees and wages granted out of the crown and underwritten by Edward IV names Master John Gilys (Giles) 'enformer of the kinges children', so he may have been royal tutor in the north at this time. Others listed with him continued their roles during Richard's reign. See *Harley 433*, Vol. 2, p. 26, for Giles as 'Archediacone of Londone and Collector of the pope', with a payment undated but placed among materials for Sept–Oct 1483. Ordinances for the children at Sandal Castle are recorded on 24 July 1484 (*Harley 433*, Vol. 3, pp. 114–16) and mention no tutor, but the absence of a tutor would have been highly unusual. Perhaps significantly, only six days later, Master Giles received an annual payment of £20 for life (CPR 1476–85, p. 481), which was originally granted by Edward IV. For heightened security at the Sandal Royal Nursery, see Philippa Langley and Doris Schneider-Coutandin, 'Niclas von Popplau: Lost in Translation? (Part One)', *Bulletin*, December 2020, p. 5, nn. 27, 30–33.

10   *Itinerary*, p. 5.

11   The Feast Day of St Anne, see *Beloved Cousyn*, p. 98.

12   *Itinerary*, p. 5; Howard Books, Vol.2, p. 412. Travel by night is indicated by a payment for the 'burnynge of a torche'.

13   Howard Books, Vol. 2, p. 416.

14   CPR 1476–85, p. 363.

15   Howard Books, Vol. 2, p. 415. Howard's payment to the 'master of the barge' indicates part of his return to London was by river.

16   Howard Books, Vol. 2, p. 416; SAL MS 77, f.73, 75. At the feast day of St Anne, Howard's steward paid for an item at Crosby's Place where activities were in progress under Howard's supervision (25 July).

17   TNA, C81/1392 No.1; NPG Exhibition Catalogue 1973, p. 98; *Road to Bosworth*, p. 125.

18   Vernon Harcourt, '*The Baga de Secretis*', *EHR* (1908), Vol. 23, No. 91, pp. 508–29. The first reference to the *Baga de Secretis* occurs in the Controlment Rolls of King's Bench, Edward III, c. 1345. They were canvas bags containing legal documents pertaining to 'criminal proceedings at the suit of the crown'. The first extant *Baga* date from Edward IV in a treason trial against Burdett and Stacey, 1477. At this point, there is a 'division of these records into privy bags'. The records of Edward of Warwick's treason trial in 1499 were placed in Henry VII's *Baga* and locked in a special closet

with three keys: for the Lord Chief Justice, Attorney General and Master of the Crown Office. Indictments of Warwick, plus the trial of rebels supporting Richard of England in 1499 were later discovered in a box containing indictments from the reign of Henry V.

19 There may have been a deliberate campaign under Henry VII to destroy records that were potentially embarrassing to his regime and supporters: A.J. Hibbard, 'The Missing Evidence', *The Court Journal*, Vol. 26, Autumn 2019, p. 27. King Richard's *Baga de Secretis* may have been lost or destroyed by Robert Morton, Master of the Rolls, nephew of Henry VII's close advisor, John Morton.

20 Carson, in *Maligned King*, pp. 153–55, proposes this 'enterprise' was the plot reported by Stow in *Annales of England* (1631), pp. 459–60. See also Charles Samaran (ed./trans.), *Thomas Basin: History of Louis XI* (1963–1972), Vol. 3, Chapter 2, pp. 229–39 (p. 235), trans. thanks to Jonathan Mackman. Basin's account, written in Breda or Utrecht in January 1484: 'Around fifty men from London had conspired for their [princes'] release, truly believing that, with them beginning the business, the whole city would rise up with them to accomplish it, but when they had no support their effort ceased and came to nothing, and four of them were captured and beheaded.' Carson suggests Crosby's Place was prepared for an ad hoc treason trial under the jurisdiction of the Constable's Court. For the presiding officer being Earl Marshal John Howard, see *Protector & Constable*, pp. 23–25, 71 n. 244. This may be supported by the purchase of two brigantines (armoured jackets) by Howard's retainer William Schell on 29 July: see Howard Books, Vol. 2, p. 418.

21 Howard Books, Vol. 2, pp. 420, 423. On 6 August, after such a trial, Howard paid for 26 tonnes of 'fermyng' (hay/straw), a very large amount that may be indicative of the industrious activities over the past few days at Crosby's Place. Stow has the trial taking place at Westminster, with heads displayed on London Bridge, but no such contemporary record exists (Constable's Court records are very scarce). Whatever the conspiracy discovered or foiled, it must have been carefully kept from public knowledge: a wise precaution to maintain calm during the king's absence.

22 Robert Ruff (Russe), Sergeant of the Mace, London, who 'has suffered for treason' and 'who was put to death for treason': TNA, C 1/64/124 (1483–85), '*Lucasse vs The Mayor of London*. The mayor and sheriffs of London for a Bond to John Mathewe and William White, sheriffs, as surety for Robert Ruff [Russe], their sergeant of the mace, who has suffered for treason' (research by Hilary Jones, Richard III Forum, 2016: thanks to Dr A.J. Hibbard). See also TNA, C 1/64/35 (1483–85): 'Action brought by John Mathew, mercer, and William White, draper, late sheriffs of London, on a bond of complainants as surety for Robert Ruffe, sergeant to the said late sheriffs, who was put to death for treason.' The documented (but undated) Lucasse case mentioning Ruff/Russe is important since it confirms his existence and office, also that he was accused of treason at the relevant time (thanks to Terri-Kate Lee, 25.5.2022).

23 *Early Historians*, p. 122. John Rous, Warwickshire priest and Neville family retainer, writes of Richard's royal progress: 'And then he went to Worcester and finally Warwick where the Queen joined him from Windsor.' Her departure from London is calculated using general travel times for a 76-mile

journey from Windsor to Warwick. Richard was in Warwick from around 8–14 August (*Itinerary*, pp. 5–6).

24 *Beloved Cousyn*, pp. 105–06.

25 *Harley 433*, Vol. 3, p. 24. Sasiola joined the royal party on 8 August at Warwick. For the knightings, see *Harley 433*, Vol. 1, p. 2; *Early Historians*, p. 122; For Edward of Middleham, see Hammond, *The Children of Richard III* (2018), *op. cit.*, p. 33, also *The Rous Roll* (1980), p. 60.

26 Hammond, *op. cit.*, pp. 32–34, 81–82.

27 BRO, Ref. No.CC/2/2, 'The Maire of Bristowe I's Kalendar', ff.129r, 129v, 130r (f.129v), appreciation to Bristol Archives, 7.8.2018; Lucy Toulmin Smith, *The Maire of Bristowe I's Kalendar by Robert Ricart Town Clerk of Bristol 18 Edward IV* (1872), p. 46. For the mayoral year, see Evan Jones, *The Smugglers City* (Bristol University, 2004) www.bristol.ac.uk/Depts/History/Maritime/ Sources/1480ricart.htm

28 *Crowland*, p. 163: 'people round about the city of London and in Kent, Essex, Sussex, Hampshire, Dorset, Devon, Somerset, Wiltshire and Berkshire.'

29 *Itinerary*, p. 10.

30 CPR 1476–85, p. 378; for whether to pay Giles off or for tutelage to continue in the north at Royal Nurseries (Sandal/Sheriff Hutton), see note 9 and Langley & Schneider-Coutandin, *op. cit.*

31 *GC*, p. 234. Mayor Edmund Shaa left office on 28 October 1483.

32 Some seventeen years later, around 1500, Burgundian chronicler Jean Molinet, Ch. 100, p. 402, wrote: 'Pierre' and 'George' (meaning Edward and Richard) '… were prisoners for about five weeks; and through the Captain of the Tower, the Duke Richard had them secretly killed and made to disappear' (trans. thanks to Isabelle Lloyd, 5.9.2019). Five weeks from 16 June is 21 July. See Chapter 5.

33 The suggested timeline for disappearance excludes a full analysis of Ricart's Kalendar (see Chapter 5).

5. The Sources: Missing, Murdered, Maintained

1 For the Cely note as a rumour in March 1483, see *Mythology*, Chapter 13, pp. 75–78. The 'Lord Prince' ('troubled') was previously identified as Richard, Duke of York (Hanham, *Cely Letters 1472–1488* (1975), p. 286). Ashdown-Hill clarifies that this title is reserved for the Prince of Wales, while York is referred to as duke, see for example *GC*, p. 231; note 89; Historical Notes, p. 588; note 94. (*Mancini*, p. 107 n. 135, agrees with Hanham, pointing out the note was far from being a carefully considered document.)

2 Philippa Langley, 'The Accession of Richard III (Part One)', *Bulletin*, March 2019, pp. 39–43 (p. 40).

3 The letter is undated but the contents suggest it was written around mid-September: J.B. Sheppard (ed.), 'Christ Church Letters' (1877), *Camden Society*, p. 100. For a date after 12 September, see A.F. Sutton and L. Visser-Fuchs, 'Thomas Langton's Letter to William Selling, 15 September 1483', *Ricardian*, Vol. 31 (2021), pp. 46–72 (p. 58).

4   D.P. Wright, *ODNB*.

5   Matthew Lewis, *Richard III: Loyalty Binds Me* (2018), pp. 311–12, 435.

6   Sutton & Visser-Fuchs, *op. cit.*, p. 50.

7   *Mancini*, p. 14.

8   *Mancini*, p. 15.

9   Household Ordinances: Edward V had a physician and surgeon at all times, see Orme, pp. 123, 129.

10   Bertram Fields, *Royal Blood* (1998), pp. 10, 130; Matthew Lewis, *The Survival of the Princes in the Tower* (2017), pp. 41–42. *Mancini*, p. 95, describes Argentine as *medicus*. A.B. Emden, *A Biographical Register of the University of Cambridge to 1500* (1963), pp. 15–16, suggests his M.D. was received at Padua, Italy by 1485. Like Mancini, Argentine spoke Italian as well as Latin. Unrecorded in England under Richard III, Emden, p. 16 has him in Henrician England on 6 October 1485. Thanks to Marie Barnfield for the Argentine Papers (Dennis E. Rhodes, 1967) and Francisca Icaza for the Emden copy, Damian Riehal Leader (1988, 1994) and Rhodes, *Provost Argentine of King's and his Books* (1956). Loss/destruction of the records has negated searches for alumni of possible universities including Padua. Fifteenth-century scientific tracts belonging to Argentine are currently at Gloucester Cathedral (including Johann Mueller, *Calendarium. Venice: Erhardus Ratdolt, 9 August 1482*) and were printed near Padua 1482–85. This may suggest Argentine was at Padua (school of medicine) during that time (see Emden). Argentine searches, with thanks to Francisca Icaza.

11   *Mancini*, pp. 17, 41. Mancini warns, 'You should not expect from me the names of individuals and places, nor that this account is complete in all particulars.'

12   *Mancini*, p. 65. Contrary to the inaccuracy in Armstrong's translation, Mancini did not write that Richard 'destroyed Edward's children and then claimed for himself the throne', which contradicts Mancini's inability to ascertain their fate.

13   Former Spanish Ambassador Diego de Valera reports to Ferdinand and Isabella on 1 January 1486, 'three thousand Englishmen' fled to France following the October 1483 uprising. Figures may be somewhat exaggerated, but his account confirms that English rebels were in France at that time: Elizabeth Nokes and Geoffrey Wheeler, 'A Spanish Account of the Battle of Bosworth', *Ricardian*, No. 36, March 1972, pp. 1–5 (p. 2).

14   *Mythology*, p. 24.

15   J. Masselin (ed.), *Journal des Etats-généraux de France tenus à Tours en 1484* (Paris, 1835); Alan Harding, *Medieval Law and the Foundations of the State* (OUP, 2002), p. 284. Rochefort's speech was 'Reported in great detail by Jean Masselin, a deputy from the bailliage of Rouen who played a leading part in the proceedings'.

16   Harding, *Medieval Law*, p. 284, translates *faventibus* as 'by approval'.

17   The exclamation mark has been removed as it was not present in Masselin's original account (Masselin, *Etats-généraux*, p. 38).

18   Samaran (ed./trans.), *Basin: History of Louis XI* (1963), Vol. 3, p. 234.

19   Livia Visser-Fuchs, 'English Events in Caspar Weinreich's Danzig Chronicle, 1461–1495', *Ricardian*, Vol. 7, No. 95, December 1986, pp. 310–20 (p. 316).

20   *Harley 433*, Vol. 3, p. 190.

21 Langley and Schneider-Coutandin, 'Niclas von Popplau: Lost in Translation? (Part Two)', *Bulletin*, March 2021, pp. 39–47 (pp. 39, 46) www.revealing-richardiii.com/niclas-von-popplau.html

22 *Crowland*, p. 171.

23 *Itinerary*, pp. 15–16.

24 Hammond, *The Children of Richard III*, p. 82, translates this as 'servants'. Cooper had mistranslated it as 'minstrels' (see note 25).

25 C.H. Cooper, *Annals of Cambridge, Volume 1* (1842), p. 230.

26 The York/Warwick age difference was a relatively small eighteen months. For this source in relation to Niclas von Popplau, see Philippa Langley and Doris Schneider-Coutandin, 'Niclas von Popplau: Lost in Translation? (Part One)', *Bulletin*, December 2020, pp. 46–53, www.revealingrichardiii.com/niclas-von-popplau.html

27 *Mythology*, pp. 102–03. Ashdown-Hill interprets Latin *nuper*, as regards Edward the 'bastard', as meaning 'late' rather than 'former/recently', and presents this source as confirming the death of Edward V. The word 'bastard' was later scratched out.

28 CPR, p. 375.

29 *Harley 433*, Vol. 2, p. 70.

30 Sean Cunningham, *Richard III: A Royal Enigma* (2003), pp. 50–51, for tax collection for Trinity Term, first year of Richard III (his regnal years began on 26 June). Since Trinity Term ran from early June to the end of July, this gives the document's end date as 25 June 1484.

31 CCR, p. 396 (thanks to Ian Rogers, 30.6.2018).

32 Gordon McKelvie, 'The Bastardy of Edward V in 1484: New Evidence of its Reception in the Inquisitions Post Mortem of William, Lord Hastings', *Royal Studies Journal*, 3, No. 1, 2016, pp. 71–79 (p. 74).

33 McKelvie, 'The Bastardy of Edward V', pp. 71, 72, 74.

34 Peter Hammond and Anne F. Sutton, 'Research Notes and Queries', *Ricardian*, Vol. 5, No. 72, March 1981, p. 319: Chamberlains Accounts, City of Canterbury, Michaelmas 1484–Michaelmas 1485, f.26.

35 *Harley 433*, Vol. 2, p. 211; John Bayley, *The History and Antiquities of the Tower of London* (1830), p. 343.

36 Sir Clements Markham, *Richard III: His Life and Character* (1906, repr. 1968), p. 237; Rymer's *Foedera*, XII, p. 265, 'Pro filio bastardo regis' … Dilecti Filii nostril Bastardi, Johannis de Gloucestria (thanks to John Dike, Coldridge Research Group).

37 As a bastard, John could inherit nothing, i.e., it would only have been by his father's creation that he might have held any title, which had not (yet) been done. Members of the nobility were sometimes referred to as 'lord' or 'prince' as a courtesy title, but not in official crown documents.

38 For Henry Davy as Richard III's tailor, see *Coronation*, p. 333.

39 *Ibid.*; *Archaeologia*, 1, p. 367. Also, *Coronation*, pp. 171–72: 'To Lorde Edward, son of late Kyng Edward the Fourthe, for his apparaill and array' and 'To the henxemen [henchmen] of the said Lord Edward for theire apparaill and array'. It is possible that Edward V attended the coronation of his uncle, or certainly it

was planned for (Lewis, *The Survival of the Prices in the Tower*, p. 54). For delivery of clothing and dating, note 125.

40 Dr A.J. Hibbard, TMPP Research Report, 22.11.2020. Also, John Dike, 'Coldridge': one-name.org/name_profile/godsland.

41 Horrox, 'Henry Tudor's Letters to England During Richard III's Reign', *Ricardian*, Vol. 6, No. 80, March 1983, pp. 155–58 (p. 155); Caroline Halsted, *Richard III* (1844, reprint 1980), Vol. 2, pp. 424, 566, Appendix NN; BL, Harleian MS 787, f.2. The letter is undated but has been attributed to around November 1484–Spring 1485.

42 Nokes and Wheeler, 'A Spanish Account', p. 2.

43 Langley and Schneider-Coutandin, 'Lost in Translation? (Part Two)', pp. 39–40.

44 The highlighted text reads in German: 'Darauf der König seinen Schatz und alle grosse Herren, als des Königes Kinder und der Fürsten Söhne verwahrt werden, welche den Gefangenen gleich gehallten werden.' Taken from a 1712 copy of Popplau's manuscript (Piotr Radzikowski [ed.], Reisebeschreibung Niclas Von Popplau, Ritters, bürtig von Breslau, Trans-Krak [1998], p. 53). Adapted from translations for TMPP by Doris Schneider-Coutandin; Annette Carson; Dr Eleoma Bodammer, Senior Lecturer in eighteenth- and nineteenth-century German literature, Edinburgh University; Professor Henrike Lähnemann, Chair of Medieval German Literature & Linguistics, St Edmund Hall, Oxford University. For full discussion, see Langley and Schneider-Coutandin, 'Lost in Translation? Part One'.

45 Hammond, *The Children of Richard III*, p. 50; Langley and Schneider-Coutandin, *ibid.*, n. 18.

46 Radzikowski, *op. cit.*, p. 53 n. 155: 'Pontefract Castle was the prison and place of execution of many representatives of great dynasties.' (Trans. thanks to Bodammer and Lähnemann.)

47 Reputedly a favourite residence of Henry Bolingbroke (before he usurped the throne), but his children were born elsewhere.

48 Langley and Schneider-Coutandin, 'Niclas von Popplau: Timeline', p. 2: www. revealingrichardiii.com/niclas-von-popplau.html

49 Langley and Schneider-Coutandin, 'Popplau: Timeline', p. 6.

50 Langley and Schneider-Coutandin, 'Lost in Translation? (Part One)', p. 6.

51 Langley and Schneider-Coutandin, 'Lost in Translation? (Part Two)', pp. 39, 40, 42.

52 *Mythology*, pp. 109–11, records a Papal Requiem Mass for King Edward at the Sistine Chapel on 23 September 1483. Ashdown-Hill suggests this may have been for Edward V, but corroboration has not been found. Such a significant public Requiem would have been remarked in England and on the continent. It seems likely the Papacy was observing the twenty-four weeks' mind of Edward IV's death, which some accounts record as 8 April (e.g., Bristol and Colchester, *Mythology*, p. 42; BRO, Ref. No. CC/2/2, 'The Maire of Bristowe I's Kalendar', f.129r). Bristol as a port is significant. For the London account, see Historical Notes, p. 588; *Early Historians*, p. 108; Lyell (ed.), *Acts of Court*, p. 146.

53 In the north, Popplau visited only Doncaster and York, see Langley and Schneider-Coutandin, 'Popplau: Timeline'. For the possible detour to view

Pontefract Castle on the way to York, see Langley and Schneider-Coutandin, 'Lost in Translation? (Part One)', p. 50.

54 For locations with traditions concerning the princes, see Chapter 9.

55 Andrew Breeze, 'A Welsh Poem of 1485 on Richard III', *Ricardian*, Vol. 18, 2008, pp. 46–53 (p. 52).

56 Horrox, 'Henry Tudor's Letters', p. 157.

57 Breeze, 'Welsh Poem', p. 47.

58 *Maligned King*, pp. 318–19: 'unnaturall, mischievous and grete Perjuries, Treasons, Homicides and Murdres, in shedding of Infants blood, with manie other Wronges, odious Offences and abominacions ayenst God and Man and in espall oure said Soveraigne Lord'; *Rolls of Parliament*, vi, pp. 275–78.

59 Michael Hicks, 'The Second Anonymous Continuation of the Crowland Abbey Chronicle 1459–86 Revisited', *EHR*, Vol. 122, No. 496, April 2007, pp. 349–70.

60 *Crowland*, p. 163.

61 Langport further reflected the words of Henry's Parliament but used them regarding Rivers, Grey and Vaughan, who he incorrectly asserted were 'beheaded without any form of trial', the 'second shedding of innocent blood' (after Hastings) (*Crowland*, p. 161).

62 Some writers have assigned this note to either 1483 or 1484 but this is inaccurate. The earliest date for this to be recorded as the marginal note would be upon completion of the following mayoral year of September 1484–September 1485, so the earliest it could have been written was September 1485, following Bosworth. Ricart's employment as Clerk of Bristol before 1489 means it could have been added anytime up to this point or when Ricart's handwriting apparently ends in 1506 (see note 86 for 1502–03). Later dating is supported by Ricart's entry for 1484 recording Buckingham's execution (2 November 1483), which was within the new mayoral year so is recorded correctly. The place to have noted the rumour of the princes' death in 1483 within the main text was before, or directly after, Buckingham's execution. For the marginal note added after Richard's death, see Peter Fleming, 'The Maire of Bristowe I's Kalendar', *Bristol Record Society*, Vol. 67, 2015, pp. 1–74 (p. 25). Fleming believes the main Kalendar entry for King Richard was also written after his death but information in the main text does not suggest this. For Ricart's handwriting, see Evan Jones, *The Smugglers City* (University of Bristol, 2004) www.bristol.ac.uk/Depts/History/Maritime/Sources/1480ricart.htm

63 BRO, Ref. No. CC/2/2 'Kalendar', ff.129r, 129v, 130r (f.129v), thanks to Bristol Archives, 7.8.2018. See also Toulmin Smith, *The Maire of Bristowe I's Kalendar by Robert Ricart*, p. 46.

64 D. Mario Penna, *Biblioteca de Autores Españoles*, Vol. 1, '*Prosistas Castellaños del XV siglo*' (Madrid, 1959). Trans. thanks to Marie Barnfield (23.7.2018). See also Nokes & Wheeler, 'A Spanish Account', p. 2.

65 David Johnson, 'Ardent Suitor or Reluctant Groom? Henry VII and Elizabeth of York. Part Two: Reluctant Groom', *Bulletin*, March 2020, pp. 37–41 (pp. 37, 39). The second session of Henry's Parliament sat on 23 January 1486: www.revealingrichardiii.com/the-pre-contract.html

66 Carlson, *English Humanist Books*, p. 58. Carmeliano presented his new work
    (*Suasoria Laeticiae*) to Henry VII on or shortly after the birth of Prince Arthur,
    Henry's heir (b. 19 September 1486) and received Henry's first pension on
    27 September (Henry married Elizabeth of York on 18 January).
67 J.B Trapp, *ODNB*.
68 *Mancini*, p. 22; Carlson, *op. cit.*, pp. 45, 58, is incorrect that Carmeliano
    received no patronage from King Richard. Carmeliano's praise of Richard
    prefaces work on St Katherine dedicated to him, with copy gifted to
    Brackenbury which survives (Carlson, pp. 38, 42–45).
69 Carlson, pp. 37, 58, 195, 203.
70 Carlson, pp. 48–49, 52. Carmeliano (speaking as the spirit of Henry VI)
    rhetorically accuses Richard of putting the princes 'to the sword' himself, and
    with that act, piercing Henry's wailing ghost equally (lines 91–92), trans. thanks
    to Annette Carson; see p. 49 for Carlson's erroneous assertion that Carmeliano
    meant (literally) that Richard deployed the sword 'with his own hand'. For
    Carmeliano's connection to John Morton and the Morton family, see Anne F.
    Sutton and Livia Visser-Fuchs, 'Richard III's Books XIV: Pietro Carmeliano's
    Early Publications', *Ricardian*, Vol. 10, No.132, March 1996, pp. 346–86
    (pp. 347, 350, 360, 369–72).
71 António S. Marques, 'A Little Known Portuguese Source for the Murder of the
    Princes', *Bulletin*, Spring 2007, pp. 31–32 (p. 32). Although this source is placed
    in 1488, it is not known when the notes were written, likely for a memoir. Notes
    exist today as sixteenth and seventeenth-century copies. Álvaro Lopes de Chaves
    died after 1 January 1490. Thanks to António Marques.
72 Visser-Fuchs, 'English Events in Caspar Weinreich's Danzig Chronicle,
    1461–1495', p. 320 n. 28.
73 Annette Carson (in personal correspondence) challenges the date of 1486
    that is generally assumed for Rous' *Historia Regum Angliae*, preferring around
    1490. Internal evidence indicates that when writing the date of Bosworth
    he left the last digit blank – '148★' – returning later to insert '5'. It seems
    inconceivable that within months he could have forgotten the year of Henry's
    accession. Further, it is unlikely he could have completed this major chronicle
    immediately on the heels of his two Rous Rolls (see note 74).
74 *Early Historians*, pp. 120, 123 (trans. Rous' *Historia*). In earlier works – two
    Rous Rolls, written in English and Latin during Richard's reign – he had
    lauded King Richard as a legitimate and benevolent king, but when Henry
    ascended the throne, Rous (who held the Latin version) acted quickly to
    edit it and denigrate Richard. His *Historia*, later still, was considerably more
    venomous. For the English and Latin versions of the Roll see *Maligned King*,
    pp. 332–33, 335. Also, Chapter 18.
75 *Early Historians*, p. 120.
76 Wroe, pp. 402, 525.
77 *Molinet*, Chapter 100, pp. 402–03. Trans. thanks to Isabelle Lloyd (5.9.2019).
78 *Molinet*, Chapter 100, p. 404.
79 Thanks to Isabelle Lloyd, TMPP (20.9.2019), who writes, '*Suppediter*' is an
    old French [*ancienne langue française*] verb meaning '*vaincre*' or '*fouler aux pieds*'.
    '*Suppedité*' translates into English as either 'vanquished' or 'trampled underfoot'.

Molinet might have intended either. Given the descriptive accounts of Richard's demise, 'trampled on' has been preferred.

80 *Molinet*, Chapter 101, p. 409.

81 See Chapter 4. Five weeks from when Richard of York left sanctuary on 16 June was 21 July 1483.

82 Describing the Battle of Bosworth, Molinet names the Captain of the Tower as 'Lord of Bracqueben' (Brackenbury): Chapter 101, pp. 407–08.

83 Medieval St Paul's was destroyed in the Great Fire of London, 1666.

84 Prince Arthur was invested Prince of Wales on 29 November 1489, aged 3.

85 André, p. 20.

86 *Early Historians*, p. 109. Ricart's marginal note 'put to silence' in his Kalendar, 1502–03, may have derived from this published work. See note 62.

87 S.J. Gunn, 'Early Tudor Dates for the Death of Edward V', *Northern History* (1992), p. 214. Further editions of Pynson were printed in 1514, 1519 and 1527; the same information is recorded by Robert Redman's edition of 1525.

88 M.T.W. Payne, 'Robert Fabyan's Civic Identity', *The Yorkist Age*, Harlaxton Medieval Studies XXIII (Donington, 2013), pp. 275–86; *GC*, pp. 236–37; London Metropolitan Archives MS.

89 *GC*, p. 231.

90 *GC*, p. 232.

91 *GC*, p. 234. Fabyan misreports the rumoured death of Queen Anne 'by poisoning' at Easter 1484 (her death *recte* 1485).

92 *GC*, pp. 236–37.

93 For dating of the copy, see Historical Notes, p. 587.

94 Historical Notes, p. 588.

95 Henry Ellis (ed.), *The New Chronicles of England and France by Robert Fabyan* (repr. from Pynson's 1516 edition, 1811), pp. 668–69. Thanks to Marie Barnfield. For the *New Chronicles* making use of French source, see Robert Gauguin's *Compendium* (Paris, 1497); C.S.L Davies, 'Information, disinformation and political knowledge under Henry VII and early Henry VIII', *Historical Research*, Vol. 85, No. 228, 2012, pp. 228–53 (p. 238).

96 Hammond, 'Research Notes and Queries', *Ricardian*, Vol. 3, No. 46, September 1474, pp. 12–13 (p. 13).

97 *Maligned King*, pp. 336–37. Also published in 1548 and used by Edward Hall in compiling his *Union of the Two Noble Families* (1548, 1550).

98 Michael Jones (ed.), *Philippe de Commynes Memoirs, 1461–1483* (1972), pp. 354–55.

99 *Ibid.*, pp. 396–97.

100 Thomas Frognall Dibdin (ed.), *The Pastime of People, Or, The Chronicles of Divers Realms, and Most Especially of the Realm of England* (1529) by John Rastell (d. 1536), (1811), pp. 293–94, 297, www.revealingrichardiii.com/tyrells-confession.html

101 Philip Morgan, 'The Death of Edward V and the Rebellion of 1483', *Historical Research*, Vol. 68, No. 166, 1995, pp. 229–32 (p. 229). Trans. thanks to Annette Carson.

102 J.A.F. Thomson, 'Death of Edward V', *Northern History* (1990), p. 207. By this calculation, Edward IV died on 14 April, but the cartulary records it as

9 April 1484 (C.F. Richmond, 'Death of Edward V', *Northern History* (1989), p. 278).

103 This may have been copied from Wynkyn de Wordes *Chronicle of Kings* (1530) as it includes the same information (Gunn, *Early Tudor Dates*, pp. 213–14).

104 Richmond, *op. cit.*, p. 278.

105 Richmond, *op. cit.*, see p. 278 for Latin text.

106 Hammond, 'Research Notes and Queries', *Ricardian*, No. 43, Dec. 1973, pp. 15–16. From Armourers and Braziers Company, Court Book 1 (p. 10 modern transcript), largely written by William Gonn in 1532, probably from old records: source Claude Blair, V&A Museum. Thanks to Dr Tobias Capwell (24.2.2019).

107 W.J. Connell, *ODNB*.

108 *Vergil-1*, p. 18.

109 *More*, pp. lxxxv–vi. For More's account as a dramatic narrative, see 'Sir Thomas More's Satirical Drama', *Early Historians*, pp. 152–90. See also Josephine Wilkinson, *The Princes in the Tower* (2013), pp. 122–28. More's friend Erasmus noted that as a young man More would write plays and act in them, pp. 121–22 n. 35 (Erasmus, *Opus Epistolarum*, 4.16). As a dramatic account and literary work, see C.S.L. Davies, *op. cit.* pp. 241–42; W.H. Sewell, 'Memoirs of Sir James Tyrell', *Proceedings of the Suffolk Natural History and Archaeological Society*, Vol. 5, Part Two, 1878, pp. 157–59. See also S.B. House, *ODNB*, p. 2 for More as a young actor; p. 5 for irony in *Richard III*; p. 7 for satire in *Utopia*; p. 12 for More's writing of worldly events compared to a stage play; and p. 24 for 'theatrical metaphors' in his *Richard III*.

110 For John Morton, see Chapters 8, 17 and 18.

111 From 1472–73 Tyrell was a Councillor for Richard, Duke of Gloucester (Horrox, *ODNB*). In 1479, he became the duke's Chamberlain (memorandum/letters patent, 28 April, TNA, SP 46/139 f.167).

112 *Recte* knighted 1471 by Edward IV after the Battle of Tewkesbury; in 1482, he was made Knight Banneret during the Scottish campaign by Richard, Duke of Gloucester (*ODNB*).

113 *More*, pp. 84, 88–89.

114 Translation Halsted, *op. cit.*, Vol. II, pp. 180–81, n. 3, which notes Francis Bacon recorded the same reports. Thanks to Annette Carson for sources.

115 Jan Reygersbergh's 'Dye Cronijck van Zeelandt', 1551 (*The Chronicle of Zeeland*), p. 121r: objects.library.uu.nl/reader/index.php?obj=1874-214708&lan=e n&lan=en#page//91/43/30/9143305280806983450175476565627324050519.jpg/ mode/1up.

116 Raphael Holinshed, *The Chronicles of England, Scotland and Ireland* (1577), Vol. 2, p. 1405 (thanks to Michael Alan Marshall for source, 6.7.2015). Following Holinshed's death in 1580, an extended edition of his *Chronicles* was published 1587, augmented to before 1586 (ed. Ellis, 1808), Vol. 3, p. 422. See also Philippa Langley, 'The Fate of the Sons of King Edward IV: Robert Willoughby's Urgent Mission, Part One', *Bulletin*, March 2020, p. 45.

117 In 1623, Shakespeare's First Folio moved the play from tragedies to histories, with the title changed to *The Life and Death of Richard III*. Shakespeare's *Richard III* is still known as a history. Similarly, *King Lear* underwent a change

– from history to tragedy. Shakespeare in 1608 called it '*The True Chronicle History*', clearly as part of its draw for his audience (King Lear, of course, did not exist). Lear, having a character arc, does not conform to a tragedy.

118 Bertram Fields, *Royal Blood*, p. 20; Speed, *Historie of Great Britaine* (1611, 1623, 1632), p. 731.

119 Fields, *op. cit.*, p. 20.

120 *Maligned King*, p. 346.

121 A.N. Kincaid, Sir William Cornwallis the Younger, The Encomium of Richard III (1977).

122 See Buc, pp. 120–22, for Morton as 'the chief instigator and prime submover of all these treasonous detractions and the ringleader of these detractors and vitilitigators of King Richard'; pp. cxxii–iii, cxli–ii for the known existence among antiquarians of Morton's Latin pamphlet (Sir Edward Hoby said Sir William Roper had the original) and their belief that More took his account from it. The Ropers were heirs of both Morton and More. See S.B. House, *ODNB*, p. 2, for More being educated in Morton's household, which he entered in *c.* 1489, aged 11. Markham, *op. cit.*, pp. 169–71, records that Sir John Harington, poet, in his *Metamorphosis of Ajax* (1596), had heard that More's work was written by Morton. Markham believed More's English version was 'dictated or inspired by' Morton, citing that the author speaks of the deathbed of Edward IV as an eyewitness (when More was aged 5). Markham adds that More's account ends abruptly at the exact point when Morton left England.

123 Buc, pp. 138–39.

124 Francis Bacon, *The History of the Reign of Henry the Seventh*, Roger Lockyer (ed.) (1971), p. 40. Elizabeth of York was crowned on 25 November 1487, over two years after Henry.

125 'To Lord Edward, son of late King Edward the Fourth, for his apparel and array, that is to say ...' (long list of clothing follows). Page title: 'The delivery of diverse stuff delivered for the use of Lord Edward and of his henchmen.': *Coronation*, p. 171 (for dates Friday 27 June–Thursday 3 July: pp. 25–6). Also see: *Mythology*, pp. 86–9.

126 Horace Walpole, *Historic Doubts on the Life and Reign of Richard The Third* (1768, repr. 1974), pp. 70–71. In 1793, following the barbarity of the French Revolution, Walpole added a postscript concerning the atrocities of the Terror. Fields, *op. cit.*, p. 21: 'He made it clear, however, that while I *can* believe ... [that Richard might now have behaved so abominably] ... I do not say I do.' Walpole's postscript has since been subverted by some writers as meaning he did change his view.

127 Walpole, *Historic Doubts*, p. 71.

128 For more on early Tudor accounts see C.S.L. Davies, *op. cit.*

129 Buc, pp. 140, 142. Buc thought Edward V was sickly and died young and could find no mention of him in Flanders (unlike his brother, York).

130 For the importance/implication of French support for Henry Tudor, see Mike Ingram, *Richard III and the Battle of Bosworth* (2019).

6. The Suspects: Means, Motive, Opportunity, Proclivity to Kill

1 P.M. Jones, *ODNB*. This may be supported by his disappearance from academic life at this time, and survival of his astrological charts for Edward IV and Edward V; Carey, *Courting Disaster*, pp. 256–57; Gloucester Cathedral, MS 21, f.9v. Only an approved person would be allowed to compile such charts. Thanks to Marie Barnfield for source (11.2.2022).

2 For Argentine as Edward V's physician, see Rhodes, *John Argentine Provost of King's*, Appendix A, p. 25; MS Rawlinson B.274, Bodleian Library, Oxford (seventeenth century).

3 M.J. Trow, *The Killer of the Princes in the Tower: A New Suspect Revealed* (2021). For the accusation of poisoning of Isabel, Duchess of Clarence, see Scofield, *Edward the Fourth*, Vol. 2, p. 187. For the suspected poisoning of Edward IV, see R.E. Collins, 'The Death of Edward IV', in J. Dening, *Secret History* (1996), pp. 138–92.

4 S.J. Gunn, *ODNB*, 'Henry VII'; Michael K. Jones and Malcolm G. Underwood, *The King's Mother: Lady Margaret Beaufort, Countess of Richmond and Derby* (1992, 1995), pp. 23–26, from 7 Henry IV cap. 2; *Stat. Realm*, ii, 151; Mortimer Levine, *Tudor Dynastic Problems 1460–1571* (1973), p. 126.

5 In 1483, Henry Tudor stood about thirtieth in the succession, akin today to Arthur Chatto (who descends from a legitimate line). For the French proclamation of Tudor (incorrectly) as the son of Henry VI, see note 41.

6 Her husband, Thomas, Lord Stanley (d. 1504), accompanied King Richard on progress (his son, Lord Strange, is named at York). See note 24.

7 In 1483, John de la Pole was 23, Edward 18, Edmund 12, Humphrey 9, William (and Geoffrey?) 5 and Richard 3 (estimated ages).

8 *Harley 433*, Vol. 2, p. 7.

9 Jones & Underwood, *The King's Mother*.

10 Wroe, pp. 79–80, writes that Warwick is 'naive, querulous and childlike' from reported conversations in 1499. Wroe, p. 542, cites *Vergil-2*, p. 115n: 'And Earl Edward, who had been imprisoned since childhood, so far removed from the sight of man and beast that he could not easily tell a chicken from a goose, although he had deserved no punishment by his own wrongdoing and had been brought to this by another man's fault', www.philological.bham.ac.uk/polverg/. This may offer a (literal) meaning that Warwick was merely unaware which types of poultry arrived on his plate during his long confinement. It might also have been useful to question his mental faculties should he recognise the pretender as his cousin of York. For apparent lucid conversations, see Wroe, pp. 473–74, 477–78. *Vergil-2*, p. 19, when exhibited in 1487 at St Paul's, he spoke to 'many important people'; p. 117 for Warwick involved in Tower plot 'quite innocently'; see *Vergil-2*, p. 119 for his description as a 'worthy youth'.

11 Jones & Underwood, *The King's Mother*, pp. 86–88. With thanks to Mike Jones.

12 Buc, pp. 163, 322.

13 For the murder of Edmund, Earl of Rutland (brother of Edward IV and Richard III), following his capture after the Battle of Wakefield in 1460, see Matthew Lewis, *Richard, Duke of York* (2016), p. 308. Their father, Richard,

Duke of York, fell at the battle (p. 307). At the Battle of Tewkesbury, Edward
of Lancaster was killed in the field or rout (Lewis, *Loyalty Binds Me*, p. 139).

14 Anne Crawford, 'John Howard, Duke of Norfolk: A Possible Murderer of
the Princes?', *Ricardian*, Vol. 5, No. 70, Sept 1980, pp. 230–34; *Yorkist Lord*,
pp. 111–14; Howard Books, Vol. 2, p. 394.

15 For Henry's character, interrogation of prisoners and torture during his reign,
see Thomas Penn, *Winter King: The Dawn of Tudor England* (2011), pp. 78,
82–83.

16 GC, p. 250. In London, in October 1494, Henry VII pardoned several
convicted rioters.

17 Philippa Langley and Michael Jones, *The Lost King: The Search for Richard III*
(2013), pp. 195, 202–03. For Henry not being present at Stoke Field, see
Bennett, p. 98.

18 Those known to be executed were John Bracher and his son (after the battle);
John Buck at Leicester on 24 August; William Catesby and 'a few others' at
Leicester on 25 August. For Leicester, see *Vergil-1*, p. 56.

19 John Throsby, *The History and Antiquities of the Ancient Town of Leicester* (1792),
p. 63.

20 Wroe, pp. 488–91; Markham, p. 275. For the trap at the Tower, see Wroe,
pp. 473–86. The pretender 'Perkin Warbeck' was executed for treason. As a
supposed French citizen of Tournai, treason directly against the English Crown
was not legally feasible, which explains the engineered treasonable offence
of attempted escape. For Warbeck under the obedience of the Archduke of
Austria and Burgundy, see Wroe, p. 189.

21 For the apparent disappearance of the children of Richard of England (Perkin
Warbeck) and Lady Katherine Gordon, see Wroe, pp. 298, 327, 374, 422, 453,
482, 506; and for their possible survival in Wales, see p. 506.

22 Imprisonment, especially without charge, was rare in the fifteenth century.
Henry VIII incarcerated Henry Pole, the 14-year-old Plantagenet heir, and,
withdrawn into the recesses of the Tower with his tutor and servants removed,
he was never seen again. It was rumoured he starved to death in 1542 (as an
adult): see Langley and Jones, *The Lost King*, pp. 230–31.

23 Buc, pp. 170, 323. For John Gloucestre, merchant in Calais in 1505, and others
of that name, see Hammond, *The Children of Richard III*, p. 47.

24 Prior to leaving London on royal progress on 19 July, Earl Marshal John
Howard visited Buckingham's London home on three to six occasions (Howard
Books, Vol. 2, p. 410). In light of the Gelderland document (see Chapter
14), which speaks of Buckingham and Howard acting in concert to secure
the safety of the princes while the king was on progress, these meetings may
suggest discussions between the two dukes to agree a *modus operandi* if action
became necessary. Buckingham would need to be consulted in advance because
his immediate commission from Richard was to oversee the incarceration
of Bishop Morton at Brecon Castle. For Buckingham not being at Oxford
(24–26 July), see W.D. Macray, *A Register of the Members of St. Mary Magdalen
College, Oxford*, New Series, Vol. 1 ('Fellows to the Year 1520') (1894),
pp. 11–12. See also Robert C. Hairsine, 'Oxford University and the Life and
Legend of Richard III', *Crown and People*, pp. 307–32, (p. 309).

25 *More*, p. 92. More says King Richard aimed to murder Buckingham at Gloucester. For reports of an argument, see p. 90.

26 For reasons of space, we are addressing motives attributed to Buckingham by Tudor accounts. Other motives that were attributed later include: (a) to rid Richard of the threat they posed; (b) doing so to disguise his real motive of revenge on Edward IV, his Woodville queen and their line (for Buckingham's anti-Woodville hostility, see *Mancini*, p. 53, p. 94 n. 75); (c) fear of reprisals if Tudor overthrew Richard, instilled by Bishop Morton who was in his custody (Ross, *Richard III*, p. 115).

27 For Buckingham's proclamation at the time of the October uprising, see *Crowland*, p. 163. Searches for its existence are ongoing.

28 *Road to Bosworth*, p. 145 for King Richard's handwritten postscript naming Buckingham 'the most untrue creature living'.

29 Ross, *Edward IV*, p. 166.

30 W.J. White, 'The Death and Burial of Henry VI: A Review of the Facts and Theories, Part I', *Ricardian*, Vol. 6, No. 78, Sept 1982, pp. 70–80 (p. 71).

31 *Ibid.*, p. 71.

32 For this work no longer being considered a chronicle or by John Warkworth (*c.* 1425–1500), see Wikipedia.

33 White, 'Death and Burial of Henry VI, Part II', *Ricardian*, December 1982, p. 117.

34 White, 'Death and Burial of Henry VI, Part I', pp. 70–71; for John Rous on 23 May, see p. 73.

35 *Ibid.*, p. 74.

36 *Ibid.*, p. 75.

37 *Ibid.*, p. 71.

38 Ross, *Edward IV*, p. 166.

39 Hanham found that if Henry VI was murdered as per Crowland, the culprit was thought to be alive at time of writing [*recte* November 1485 since the redating of the second continuation], because the chronicler prayed for the murderer to be granted time to repent. Hanham, pp. 95–96, mentioned Radclyf as a possible murderer.

40 Andrew Breeze, 'Welsh Poem', *Ricardian*, 2008, pp. 46–53 (pp. 47, 49).

41 Michael Jones, *Bosworth 1485*, pp. 123–25, letter from Charles VIII to the town of Toulon, where Tudor is described as '*fils du feu roi Henry d'Angleterre* [spelling modernised]'; Alfred Spont, '*La marine française sous le règne de Charles VIII*', *Revue des Questions Historiques*, new series, 11, 1894, p. 393. See also *PROME*, 'Henry VII: November 1485, Presentation of the Speaker [3]': 'Afterwards, the same lord king [Henry VII], addressing the aforesaid commons in person and demonstrating that his coming to the right and crown of England was as much by lawful inheritance as by the true judgement of God in giving him victory over his enemy in battle'. Thanks to David Johnson. For Henry VI described as Henry VII's 'uncle', see CFR 1485–1509, p. 28, 11 December 1485.

42 David Johnson, 'Coercion or Compliance: Richard, Duke of Gloucester and Elizabeth, Countess of Oxford', *Ricardian* (2024, forthcoming), with thanks to Dr Johnson for early sight of this paper.

43 Christine Carpenter, *ODNB*.

44 *Mancini*, p. 63. Mancini locates this as being in mid-June, around the time Richard of York joined his brother at the Tower. Anne Neville arrived in London on 5 June 1483 (*Coronation*, p. 19). Warwick's whereabouts 1481–83 are unknown, and nothing is known about his elder sister Margaret's (1473–1541) early life. She is not recorded at the coronation on 6 July.

45 See Chapter 5. For 9–11 March 1484 in Cambridge, see C.H. Cooper, *Annals of Cambridge, Volume 1* (1842), p. 230; *Itinerary*, pp. 15–16.

46 David Buss, *The Murderer Next Door: Why the Mind is Designed to Kill* (2005). Professor of Psychology at Texas University (Austin), Buss surveyed 5,000 people and found that 91 per cent of men and 84 per cent of women had thoughts of killing someone, often hypothesising very specific victims and methods. In collaboration with a leading forensic psychiatrist, Buss cites numerous examples from an FBI file of more than 400,000 murders, with a highly detailed analysis of 400.

7. Richard III: King by Right – The Evidence

1 For consideration as figureheads for insurgency, see Chapter 11.

2 *Coronation*, p. 25.

3 *Maligned King*, pp. 112–13. Until Dorset absconded, he had Warwick's wardship and marriage. Warwick then brought to the household of Richard's wife, Warwick's aunt Anne Neville. Though the putative threat from Warwick was scarcely less than from the princes, he was well treated throughout Richard's reign. For Warwick knighted in York on 8 September 1483, see Chapter 4. For his presence with Richard and Anne in Cambridge in March 1484, see Chapter 9.

4 Cases were not infrequent due to the informality of most marriages. Settlement was subject to civil law for circumstantial evidence and canon law, which governed the sacrament of matrimony. In canon law, a sin could be compounded by later sin. For a full examination, see R.H. Helmholz, 'The Sons of Edward IV: A Canonical Assessment of the Claim that they were Illegitimate' in P.W. Hammond (ed.), *Richard III: Loyalty Lordship and Law* (1986), pp. 106–20.

5 Edward IV put himself beyond reach of expiation by both his marriages being secret. Not only was secrecy illicit under Church law, but the knowingly deceitful secrecy of the second marriage compounded his sins. He died without regularising the situation, leaving a disastrous outcome for his heirs.

6 *Secret Queen*, p. 129.

7 Dr David Johnson, Philippa Langley, Dr Sandra Pendlington, 'More than just a canard: the evidence for the precontract', *Bulletin*, September 2018, pp. 51–52.

8 *Rot. Parl.*, Vol. 6, p. 241. The Text of *Titulus Regius* can be found at www.revealingrichardiii.com/the-pre-contract.html#titulus-regius

9 *Harley 433*, Vol. 3, p. 29. For the discovery of the Parliamentary Act of Succession (1484), see Chapter 18, note 14.

10 The Chronicle as far as Bosworth was completed in November 1485. See Michael Hicks, 'The Second Anonymous Continuation of the Crowland

Abbey Chronicle 1459–86 Revisited', *EHR*, Vol. 122, No. 496, April 2007, pp. 353–54.

11 *Crowland*, p. 161.

12 Michael Hicks, *ODNB*. For Stillington's family tree, see W.E. Hampton, *Crown & People*, p. 170.

13 Michael Jones (ed.), *Philippe de Commynes, Memoirs of the Reign of Louis XI*, pp. 353–54, 397.

14 *Secret Queen*, Appendix 1, p. 209.

15 Year Book 1, Henry VII, Hilary Term, plea 1. Year Books recorded legal reports. Only the bishopric of Bath and Wells could be meant by 'Bishop of B', see listing in J.T. Rosenthal, 'The Training of an Elite Group: English Bishops in the Fifteenth Century', *Transactions of the American Philosophical Society*, Vol. 60, No. 5, 1970, p. 50.

16 *Rot. Parl.*, Vol. 6, p. 292.

17 Year Book, *ibid.*, plea 1.

18 *Rot. Parl*, Vol. 6, p. 288.

19 Gairdner, *Richard III*, p. 92.

20 *Secret Queen*, p. 213.

21 *Coronation*, p. 23.

22 *Secret Queen*, pp. 81, 213, 325 n. 32.

23 Philippa Langley, 'The Accession of Richard III: Two Sources Supporting the *Titulus Regius* and Pre-contract Crisis of June 1483. Part One: The English Source', *Bulletin*, March 2019, pp. 39–43: www.revealingrichardiii.com/the-pre-contract.html

24 Walter Ullmann (ed.), *Liber Regie Capelle* (Henry Bradshaw Soc.,1961), Vol. XCII, pp. 40–41. See pp. 24–38 for Recognition in coronation ceremonies in England and France. French kings removed Recognition from coronations, 'certainly from the ordo of Rheims (*c.* 1270) onwards', see p. 34.

25 *Coronation*, pp. 204 n. 19; BL, Add MS. 18669. For dating, see *Coronation* pp. 204, 212, etc.

26 *Coronation*, p. 204. The Acclamation comes at the end of the Recognition when the people (congregation) signify their loud and enthusiastic approval for the coronation.

27 *Coronation*, pp. 212, 224 n. 120.

28 *Coronation*, pp. 204 n. 19, 212; BL, Add MS. 18669.

29 *Coronation*, pp. 4, 204, 207.

30 *Coronation* – deletions/marginal notes in the manuscript indicate adjustments, including the substitution of the Bishops of Exeter and Ely for key roles that were traditionally performed by the Bishops of Bath and Wells and Durham as supporters, see p. 219 n. 72.

31 *Coronation*, p. 218. Asaph may have been chosen for the Acclamation. Also note 56.

32 *Coronation*, pp. 218–19. Text modernised: for original, see note 23.

33 *Coronation*, pp. 20–21 n. 68. Three bishops were absent – Lionel Woodville, Bishop of Salisbury, John Morton, Bishop of Ely, and Thomas Rotherham, Archbishop of York. Salisbury was in sanctuary following the failed Woodville

coup; Ely and York were imprisoned in Wales as accomplices in the Hastings plot (*Crowland*, p. 159).

34 *Coronation*, p. 214 n. 11, e.g., the Mayor of London, Sir Edmund Shaa.

35 *Coronation*, p. 285.

36 *Coronation*, p. 280 n. 130. Grafton's list concludes, 'And at the other bords sat dyvers noble and worshipfull personages.'

37 www.telegraph.co.uk/news/uknews/royal-wedding/8154425/Westminster-Abbey-a-royal-wedding-venue-steeped-in-history.html (accessed 3 January 2019).

38 *Harley 433*, Vol. 3, pp. 25–28, 35–38, 47–51 for early communications in 1483. For letters to Ireland concerning Richard's son as Lieutenant of Ireland (19 July) conveyed by William Lacy, see pp. 36–38; to Philip, Duke of Burgundy (30 July), see pp. 26–28. See the response from James III of Scotland (9 September) on pp. 47–48. See also pp. 52–53 for safe conducts for eleven of King James' ambassadors with sixty others.

39 C.A.J. Armstrong, *Usurpation* (1969), p. 134 n. 112: the celebration in Bruges was impossible on 6 July as Philip the Fair was paying a state visit.

40 *Harley 433*, Vol. 3, p. 26. King Louis says, 'Dear Cousin, I have seen the letters that your White Boar messenger had for me and I thank you for the news that you gave me and if I can be of any service to you I would do it with very good heart because I very much want to have your friendship. And I commend you to God (farewell), my Cousin, written at Montilz Les Tours the 21st day of July.' Trans. thanks to Clive Atkinson.

41 Louis had sent his letter via Buckingham Herald, as Richard's earlier reply to Louis of 18 August indicated, 'My Lord Cousin, I have seen the letters that you sent me by Buckingham Herald'. Richard's letter to Louis on 20 August showed that Blanc Sanglier was still at Louis' court. For both letters, see *Harley 433*, Vol. 3, p. 28, trans. thanks to Marie Barnfield.

42 *Harley 433*, Vol. 3, pp. 23–26.

43 *Harley 433*, Vol. 3, p. 24. Sasiola communicated Queen Isabella's antipathy to Edward IV for 'his refusing of here [*sic*]', 'and taking to his wiff a wedowe of England'. Sasiola seemingly had no issue speaking ill of Edward IV's marriage, even within the general dictates of diplomatic language. Elizabeth Woodville is not referred to as his queen.

44 *Harley 433*, Vol. 3, p. 24. Sasiola had joined the royal party on 8 August at Warwick. Richard knighted him on 8 September in York (*Harley 433*, Vol. 1, p. 2.), when he invested his son Prince of Wales.

45 *Mancini*, p. 67.

46 *Mancini*, p. 69.

47 *Mancini*, p. 67.

48 Philippa Langley, 'The Accession of Richard III: Two Sources ... Part Two: The French Source', *Bulletin*, June 2019, pp. 34–36: www.revealingrichardiii.com/the-pre-contract.html

49 Masselin (ed.), Journal des Etats-généraux de France 1484; Harding, Medieval Law, p. 284.

50 en.wikipedia.org/wiki/Mad_War (accessed 2 January 2019).

51 *Ibid.* The revolt or 'Mad War/Silly War' was also known as the 'War of the Public Weal'. It encompassed 1483–88, beginning with Charles VIII's reign when Louis d'Orléans (Louis XII) tried to seize the regency.

52 Harding, *Medieval Law*, p. 284, translates this as 'approval'.

53 Masselin, pp. 37, 39. Trans. Albert Jan de Rooij (December 2017).

54 *Coronation*, p. 204.

55 *Coronation*, p. 204 n. 23. For the removal from publication of the king's recognition speech, see L.G. Wickham Legg, *English Coronation Records* (Westminster 1901), Chapter 18, p. 196 (also 'Little Device', Chapter 20, p. 219, for mention of King Richard's Recognition speech when describing Henry VII's coronation). Legg refers only to its opening and closing lines: 'Sirs, here present is Richard, rightful and undoubted inheritor to the crown' and 'Yea, yea, yea, so be it; King Richard, King Richard, King Richard.'

56 *Coronation*, p. 218 n. 67. In a marginal note is written 'Assop' for the Bishop of St Asaph (Richard Redman). For which coronation, it is unclear, though a later Henry VII insertion suggests Asaph may have been considered to carry the patten (as he had done for Richard), but his name was deleted, see p. 219 n. 74, p. 217 n. 45. A key supporter of Richard, it is unlikely he participated in Henry VII's coronation. He was not summoned to Parliament in November 1485 but received a pardon on 22 February 1486 (R.K. Rose, *ODNB*).

57 *Coronation*, pp. 257 n. 24, 266–67. See also Grafton, *Hardyng's Chronicle* (1543, ed. Ellis 1812).

58 In his *Chronicle at Large* (1569, ed. Ellis 1809), Vol. 2, p. 113, Richard Grafton referred to Richard's accession as a 'mockish election', so possibly he decided against publishing the Recognition.

59 This also included the Heralds' largesse. *Hardyng's Chronicle*: '... the kynges champion, making a proclamacion, that whosoeuer woulde saye that kyng Richarde was not lawfullye kyng, he woulde fighte with hym ... and threwe downe his gauntlet ... After that the herauldes cryed a largesse thryse in the halle.'

60 *Hardyng's Chronicle*, ed. Ellis, pp. 517–18; Grafton, *Chronicle at Large*, Vol. 2, pp. 115–16; *Hall's Chronicle* (1548, ed. Ellis 1809), pp. 375–76; *Holinshed's Chronicles of England, Scotland and Ireland* (1577, augmented to 1586, ed. Ellis 1808), Vol. 3, pp. 399–400. Neither *GC*, p. 233, nor Fabyan, *New Chronicles of England and France In Two Parts* (1516, ed. Ellis 1811), p. 670, mentions the coronation or the Challenge in Westminster Hall and Heralds' largesse. See above and *Coronation*, pp. 260, 277.

61 Ullmann, *Liber Regie Capelle*, pp. 80–81. Trans. thanks to Dr Betty Knott (6.1.2019): '... the king meantime standing in his place and turning to the four sides of the said dais while the priest addresses the people, and when they according to custom give their consent and cry out with one voice "So be it, so be it" and "Long live the king", gladly proclaiming the name of the said king, then the choir shall sing ... etc.' See also Legg et al., *English Coronation Records*, p. 85; *Coronation*, p. 202; Daron Burrows, 'The Anglo-Norman Coronation Order of Edward II' in *Medium Ævum*, Vol. LXXXV, No. 2, 2016, pp. 278–313 (p. 289, lines 25–40), trans. thanks to Clive Atkinson.

62 D. Johnson, 'The King's Royal Title: A Tale of Two Parliaments', *The Court Journal*, Richard III Society, Scottish Branch, Vol. 29, Autumn 2022, pp. 11–16.

63 *PROME*, 'Henry VII: November 1485, Part 1': '... be it ordained ... by authority of this present parliament, that the inheritance of the crowns of the realms of England and of France, with all the pre-eminence and royal dignity pertaining to them, and all other lordships belonging to the king [etc.] ... abide in the most royal person of our present sovereign lord King Henry VII, and in the lawfully begotten heirs of his body, and in no-one else, thus to endure forever'.

64 S.B. Chrimes, *Henry VII* (1972), p. 62. Henry's acclaimed biographer describes it as 'a masterpiece of terse assertion which, as a statement of the fait accompli, could scarcely have been bettered.'

65 E.F. Twinning, *The English Coronation Ceremony* (1937), pp. 90–91. For the double coronation of George VI and Queen Elizabeth: 'the king is presented to the east and is said Garter Principal King at Arms in a loud voice: "Sirs, I here present unto you King ____, the undoubted King of this Realm: Wherefore all you are come to this day to do your homage and service, are you willing to do the same?" The people signify their willingness and joy by loud and repeated acclamations of "God save King ____!" The Archbishop of Canterbury and Herald then proceed to do the same on each side.' See also, *The Coronation of Her Majesty Queen Elizabeth II* (King George's Jubilee Trust, 1953), p. 31.

66 Norman Davis, *The Paston Letters and Papers of the Fifteenth Century*, Part II (2004); Christine Carpenter, *Kingsford's Stonor Letters and Papers 1290–1483* (1996). Note also Thomas Langton, Bishop of St David's famous letter (September 1483) to William Selling, Prior of Christ Church, Canterbury. Sir William Stonor was present at the coronation (*Coronation*, p. 272). It is probable that Thomas Langton was also present (see p. 46), believed to have processed carrying the eagle ampulla at the pre-coronation vigil. If Sir George Browne's cryptic/undated letter to John Paston III was written during Richard's reign, it probably refers to their secret support of the October rebellion. Paston's actions tend to suggest Lancastrian/Oxford sympathies and/or attachments. For Browne's letter, see Carpenter, p. 443: 'Loyalty Always. By your honourable G. Browne, Knight. It shall never come out for [from?] me.' Transcription thanks to Wendy Johnson (6.01.2019).

67 See 'Introduction' for the massacre at Limoges; Jones, *The Black Prince* (2017), pp. 367, 371–73, Appendix, pp. 405–08. For Pépin's discovery (2014), see p. 408.

68 A.M. & A.J. Salgado (eds), *Alvaro Lopes de Chaves, Livro de Apontamentos (1438–1489), Codice 443 da Colecção Pombalina da BNL* (Lisbon, 1983), pp. 254–56. Thanks to Annette Carson. See also Barrie Williams, 'The Portuguese Connection and the Significance of "the Holy Princess"', *Ricardian*, Vol. 6, No. 80, March 1983, pp. 138–45.

8. Sir James Tyrell's Confession: Fact or Fiction?

1 On 2 December 1495, Tyrell's age is confirmed as 40. See M.A. Hicks, 'The Last Days of Elizabeth Countess of Oxford', *EHR* (January 1988), Vol. 103, No. 406, p. 89. From a statement in a court case where Tyrell offered evidence, a calculation of Tyrell's age on 6 May 1502 when executed makes him 46. Consequently, his birth year is here amended to 1456 (for *c.* 1455 see Horrox, *ODNB*). Some writers have suggested a slightly earlier date of *c.* 1450, perhaps due to Tyrell's age at the Battle of Tewkesbury, see note 6.

2 *Maligned King*, p. 190 n. 24, from *Harley 433*, Vol. 2, p. 187.

3 *Ibid.*, p. 190 n. 25. Carson aptly calls this vast sum a 'king's ransom'. From *Harley 433*, Vol. 2, p. 191.

4 *More*, pp. 88–89.

5 Joanna Laynesmith, *Cecily Duchess of York* (2017), p. 96. William Tyrell (James' father) had been Richard, Duke of York's Receiver General.

6 If Tyrell's age was recorded correctly in December 1495 (see note 1), he was aged about 16 when he fought at Tewkesbury. This could be suggestive of his calibre and ability, the 'greatness, reputation and personal bravery' described by his biographer, Reverend W.H. Sewell (see above and notes 11 and 71).

7 TNA, SP 46/139/fo167, Letters Patent of Richard, Duke of Gloucester, 28 April. On 10 February 1480, Thomas Salle was appointed as Tyrell's deputy. For Robert Brackenbury (d. 1485) as Duke Richard's Treasurer at this time, see Horrox, *ODNB*. Richard knighted Brackenbury around Christmas 1484.

8 W.E. Hampton, 'Sir James Tyrell', *Crown & People*, p. 214; CPR 1476–85, p. 241: 'Grant for life to Elizabeth Darcy, lady mistress of the king's nursery. For her good service to the king and his consort the queen and his son the prince, of a tun of wine yearly in the port of London.' Elizabeth Tyrell, wife to Sir Robert Darcy, was daughter of Sir Thomas Tyrell (*c.* 1411–76) and Anne Marney. Widowed in 1469, Elizabeth married Richard Haute of Kent (*c.* 1470), son of William Haute and his second wife, Joan Woodville, who was Elizabeth Woodville's aunt. Elizabeth Darcy would become mistress of Prince Henry's Nursery (1491) – the future Henry VIII (Alison Weir, *Elizabeth of York* (2013), pp. 299, 533 n. 44) – from Exchequer Records E404.

9 Hampton, *ibid.*, p. 205; CPR 1476–85, p. 317. Tyrell shared the office of Vice Constable with Sir William Parr and Sir James Harrington (CPR 1476–85, p. 317).

10 For Tyrell's children, see Hampton, *ibid.*, pp. 212–13, family tree. They are named as Sir Thomas Tyrell, James, William and Anne. Only William seems not to have married. For Margery Tyrell, who married Richard Garneys, see www.geni.com/people/Anne-Tyrrell/6000000008064424506. *ODNB* records only Tyrell's son Thomas, who was arrested with his father in 1502. For the pre-nuptial agreement of 1469 at Lanhern for Tyrell to marry Ann, daughter of Sir John Arundel, see TNA, AR/1/835.

11 Reverend W.H. Sewell, 'Memoirs of Sir James Tyrell', *Proceedings of the Suffolk Natural History and Archaeological Society*, Vol. 5, Part Two, 1878, pp. 125–80 (see pp. 133–34). During the search for his rebel father, 5-year-old Edward Stafford had his head shaved and was dressed as a girl to avoid capture. See also

Hampton, *op. cit.*, p. 205. Following Richard's death, Edward and his younger brother Henry were placed in the household of Margaret Beaufort. For Edward Stafford and Tyrell's trial, see note 18.

12 Horrox, *ODNB*.

13 *Ibid.*, Tyrell was in dispute with his brother-in-law, Arundel, over his wife's right to these lands. In 1469, he had married Anne, daughter and heir of John Arundel of Lanherne, Cornwall, by his first wife Elizabeth, daughter of Thomas, Lord Morley. Tyrell had been made Knight of the Shire in 1478. For children, see note 10.

14 In 1488, Tyrell's office of Sheriff of Glamorgan was returned.

15 Thanks to Marie Barnfield (Walsh), Richard III Discussion Archive (2007), for this possibility: www.richardiii.org.uk/topic/9114/Tyrell%27s+two+Pardons. For Giles and Christopher Wellesbourne, see W.E. Hampton, 'Opposition to Henry Tudor after Bosworth', *Crown & People*, p. 174.

16 Campbell, Vol. 1, pp. 460, 503. Tyrell's first pardon is sandwiched between John Smyth and William Welles of Warwick, both indicted for involvement in the Stafford brothers' uprising in the West Country and Worcester as Lovell headed to Yorkshire (TNA, KB9/127 m.9, KB 9/138 m.4, KB 9/127 m.9, KB9/127 m.10). Thanks to Marie Barnfield for sources (see note 15). Following Bosworth, Lovell and the Staffords had taken sanctuary in St John's Abbey, Colchester, not far from Tyrell's home at Gipping, Suffolk. The second pardon, end-dated 12 July, names Tyrell first in a long list of those from Guînes Castle and garrison, including John Bonyngton, William Bondeman, William Rose, John Lichfield, John Thirlewal the elder (of York), fourteen yeomen and eight soldiers (Campbell, pp. 503–05). As Tyrell remained in post, his pardons may have been to assure the new king of his loyalty.

17 *Rot. Parl.*, Vol. 6 (1472–1504), p. 545 – he was attainted during Henry VII's Parliament of late 1503 to 1 April 1504. Edmund de la Pole, Earl of Suffolk, is named first in the attainder, with William Courtney (d. 1511), heir of the Earl of Devon, and William Pole and Richard Pole of Wingfield, Suffolk. James Tyrell is named fourth in a list including eleven further names, and reads, 'with diverse other evil disposed persons, falsely and traitorously imagining and conspiring the death and destruction of the King our Sovereign Lord, and the subversion of this his Realm, and for which false and traitorous purpose, divers of them were and be before divers of the King's Commissioners of Oyer determiner in several Shires within this Realm, severally convicted and attainted of high Treason'. A second list of those attainted for high treason includes the late Lord Audley and Edward, Earl of Warwick, with Sir James and a further thirty-seven names.

18 CPR 1494–1509, pp. 506–07. Tyrell's reversal reads, 'the said James having been convicted in Guildhall London ... of diverse offences committed 1 July 14 Henry VII [1499], and at other times, and afterwards beheaded'. For Tyrell's son, Thomas (1475–1551), 'the said Thomas having been convicted in the white hall within the king's palace at Westminster ... of treason committed in December, January, February and March, 17 Henry VII [1502]'. There is no doubt that Sir James' trial had been a show trial. He was arraigned before every leading member of Henry VII's court and its nobility, including the Mayor of

London, John Shaa. Of interest to the project is that they were led by Edward Stafford, Duke of Buckingham, Thomas, Marquess of Dorset, Henry, Earl of Northumberland, and Thomas Howard, Earl of Surrey, among others.

19 See Arthur Kincaid's seminal paper setting out the proto-drama concept, 'The Dramatic Structure of Sir Thomas More's *History of King Richard III*', *Studies in English Literature 1500–1900: Elizabethan and Jacobean Drama* (Rice University, Houston, Texas) Vol. 12, No. 2, Spring 1972, pp. 223–42. Thanks to Annette Carson.

20 Sewell, pp. 146–47, for Grafton's imprisonment in 1537 for the notoriety of his work. Sewell notes remarks by Henry Ellis (editor of Vergil and several sixteenth-century 'chronicles') about Grafton's two different editions of *Hardyng's Chronicle*, both printed in January 1453 and 'differing in almost every page'. Rastell, in the preface to the 1557 edition of *More*: 'Which worke hath bene before this time printed … very much corrupte in many places' (*Early Historians*, p. 198).

21 *Early Historians*, Appendix, pp. 198–219, for Hanham's detailed account of the many versions of More's *Richard III*. See also Kendall, p. 421, and C.S.L. Davies, p. 243 for publication in 1557.

22 *Ibid.* Also, for example, Wilkinson, pp. 113–28, and *More*, pp. xv–xvi.

23 Sewell, pp. 156–59. Also for example, *Early Historians*, p. 201, and Wilkinson, pp. 116–21.

24 For example, Jürgen Meyer, 'An Unthinkable History of King Richard III: Thomas More's Fragment and his Answer to Lucian's Tyrannicide', *The Modern Language Review*, Vol. 109, 2014, pp. 629–39.

25 *More*, p. 85.

26 *More*, p. 88.

27 *More*, p. 89.

28 *More*, p. 84.

29 Hampton, *Crown & People*, Appendix I, p. 209 n. 39, from Sewell, pp. 172–76.

30 Hampton, p. 209 n. 40, from James Gairdner (ed.), *Memorials of Henry VII* (1858), p. xxxvi.

31 *GC*, p. 237.

32 Extracts from Volume 2 of Vergil's original manuscript have been printed in two separate publications: folios 214v–235 in *Vergil-1*; and subsequent folios in *Vergil-2*, pp. 2–146.

33 *Vergil-1*, p. 18.

34 *Vergil-2*, p. 13.

35 *Vergil-2*, p. 15 for 'restore'; Latin *restituendo*, p. 14.

36 *Vergil-2*, p. 67.

37 *Vergil-2*, pp. 69–71.

38 *Vergil-2*, p. 87 'restored'; Latin *restitueretur*, p. 86.

39 *Vergil-2*, p. 127.

40 Translation by Caroline Halsted, *Richard III* (1844), Vol. 2, pp. 180–81 n. 3. Halsted notes that Sir Francis Bacon recorded the same reports (see note 46). Thanks to Annette Carson.

41 Buc, pp. 120–22 for Morton as 'the chief instigator and prime submover of all these treasonous detractions and the ringleader of these detractors and

vitilitigators of King Richard'. See Chapter 5, note 111, for Morton as More's source.

42 Following Henry VII's accession, John Morton was made Lord Chancellor in March 1486. On 6 October 1486, he was made Archbishop of Canterbury. In 1493, following Henry's innumerable appeals to Rome, Morton was made Cardinal by Pope Innocent VIII. He died of the plague at Knole House, Kent, on 15 September 1500. He was buried at Canterbury Cathedral, although his grave is believed to be empty. Stoneyhurst College in Lancashire holds a skull said to be Morton's (Isolde Martyn, 'How Posterity Beheaded Morton: The Case of the Missing Head', *Ricardian*, Vol. 9, No. 118, September 1992, pp. 311–14). For a recent examination of the skull, see Martyn, 'Cardinal Morton's Skull', *Bulletin*, December 2015, pp. 59–62.

43 Buc, p. 165.

44 For several individuals called John Green, see Hampton, 'Sir James Tyrell', *Crown & People*, pp. 210–11.

45 Buc, p. 167.

46 Bacon, *Henry the Seventh*, (Lockyer, ed.) p. 40. When discussing the first days of Henry VII's reign and his claim to the throne by conquest, rather than descent of blood or Act of Parliament, Bacon records, 'at that time secret rumours and whisperings – which afterwards gathered strength and turned to great troubles – that the two young sons of King Edward the Fourth, or one of them, which were said to be destroyed in the Tower, were not indeed murdered but conveyed secretly away, and were yet living'.

47 For the possibility that Thomas More may have encountered the sons of Miles Forest in the course of royal business, see Tim Thornton, 'More on a Murder: The Deaths of the "Princes in the Tower", and Historiographical Implications for the Regimes of Henry VII and Henry VIII', *JHA*, 28 December 2020, pp. 1–22. For an analysis of whether this had implications for More's assertion that Richard III murdered the sons of Edward IV, see Matthew Lewis, 'The More I Read' in 'Matt's History Blog': mattlewisauthor.wordpress. com/2021/02/07/the-more-i-read/ (accessed 7.2.2021). See also Joanna Laynesmith, 'Miles Forest and the Princes in the Tower', *Bulletin*, June 2021, pp. 22–23; *Bulletin*, September 2021, pp. 29–30 (Thornton), and p. 3 (Philippa Langley).

48 For searches for the remains of the boys at the Tower of London, see Buc, p. 139: 'there was much and diligent search made for their bodies at the Tower. And all these places were opened and digged where it was said or supposed their bodies were laid. But they could never be found by any search.' John Rastell also recorded searches, see *The Pastime of People, Or, The Chronicles of Divers Realms, and Most Especially of the Realm of England 1529* (ed. Dibdin, 1811), p. 293: 'because the bones of the said children could never be found buried, neither in the Tower nor in no other place'.

49 Bacon, pp. 138–39. See p. 211 for nobles arrested with Tyrell on suspicion of treasonous association with pretender Edmund de la Pole; see also *Vergil-2*, p. 125.

50 *Coronation*, p. 176.

51 *Coronation*, p. 178.

52 *Coronation*, p. 82.

53 Buc, pp. xxxix, liv–lv. For the letter from Elizabeth of York to John Howard,
    1st Duke of Norfolk, see pp. c–civ, 191, 333–34. For the old manuscript
    book, see p. 163: 'For I have read in an old manuscript book it was held for
    certain that Dr Morton and a certain countess, conspiring the deaths of the
    sons of King Edward and some other, resolved that these treacheries should
    be executed by poison and by sorcery.' Following the execution of John
    Buck [sic] after the Battle of Bosworth, the Buck family was taken into the
    care and protection of the Howard family (p. xvii). Thomas Howard, Earl of
    Arundel and Surrey (later 5th Duke of Norfolk) was Sir George Buc's patron
    to whom Buc's *History* was dedicated (p. 3). Buc requested his protection so
    that none might take offence at his *History* (p. 4). For sources including the
    Earl of Oxford, John, Baron Lumley, and Baron Darcy, etc., see pp. cxliv–v.
    For Henry Howard (in 1583) expressing the Howard family's 'strong sympathy
    and sense of gratitude, baffled by what had been written about Richard III
    by the "authorities"', see p. cxxvii. For Buc's use of the Crowland Chronicle
    manuscript, Tower Records, College of Arms, Parliament Rolls and memorials,
    etc., see p. cxl. For all Buc's sources, see pp. cxx–cxliv.

54 *Op. cit.*, p. 139. For a commentary on Bacon's supposed royal source, see Susan
    Leas, 'As the King Gave Out', *Ricardian*, Vol. 4, 1977, pp. 2–4. For a John
    Dighton, priest, see Chapter 17.

55 For how the TV documentary came about, see Philippa Langley, 'The Tyrell
    Confession', *Bulletin*, June 2021, p. 49, www.revealingrichardiii.com/tyrells-
    confession.html

56 CPR 1494–1509, pp. 506–07, for Tyrell's trial. Also see notes 17 and 18.

57 For more, see Annette Carson, 'After 500 years of controversy we may finally
    have solved the mystery of the Princes in the Tower!', tinyurl.com/47pxaf3f

58 For Tyrell's commissions for Edward IV, see CPR 1467–77, pp. 492, 606.

59 Halsted, Vol. 2, p. 187 n. 3., from P. Vergilii, *Anglicæ Historiæ libri XXVI* (1534),
    p. 569. Thanks to Marie Barnfield.

60 Among differing translations, the Halsted rendering is preferable for the more
    accurate translation of *migrasse* as 'migrated' in the active voice, rather than
    'had been conveyed', which assumes agency by some unnamed person. Thanks
    to Annette Carson for clarifying variations in Vergil's editions and thanks to
    Christopher Tinmouth for transcriptions/research.

61 James Gairdner, *Letters and Papers Illustrative of the Reigns of Richard III and Henry
    VII* (1863), Vol. II, pp. 335–36, 'XVII: Fines Levied on Warbeck's Adherents'.

62 Hampton, *Crown & People*, pp. 204–05. Thanks to John Dike of Coldridge
    Research Group and for copy of Speke's will. Also see p. 214 for James
    Haute's support of Richard III. Haute was a former Esquire of the Body
    to Edward IV and a close relation of the Woodvilles and several rebels in
    the October 1483 uprising.

63 Wroe, p. 177.

64 Sir Frederick Madden, *Documents Relating to Perkin Warbeck, with Remarks on his
    History* (1837), p. 25. See also *Archaeologia*, Vol. 27, 1838, p. 178. Taken from a
    detailed written report to Henry VII from Frenchman Bernard de Vignolles,
    dated Rouen, 14 March 1495 (New Style 1496): 'the said Prior of St John has
    been two or three times, once a twelve-month, to the house of Sir Thomas

Tirel … and among other things the Prior began to speak how King Edward had formerly been in the said house, to which the said Sir Thomas replied, that it was true, and that the King had formerly made good cheer there, and that he hoped, by God's will, that the son of the said Edward should make the like cheer there … and during the above discourse the said Bernard and Sir John Thonge [Thweng?] were present.'

65 Horrox, *ODNB*, Tyrell family.
66 Wroe, pp. 177–78, 185, 228.
67 *ODNB*, ibid.
68 Audrey Williamson, *The Mystery of the Princes* (1978), p. 91: 'that the princes and their mother Elizabeth Woodville lived in the hall by permission of the uncle', a tradition going back 'well before the eighteenth century and was handed down from generation to generation' – revealed to Williamson in 1973 by a relative of the Tyrells, Kathleen Margaret Drewe.
69 *Maligned King*, p. 183.
70 *Harley 433*, Vol. 2, p. 187. See note 2.
71 Sewell, p. 179.
72 For Tyrell's children, see note 10.
73 Davies, p. 242; Matthew Lewis, *The Survival of the Princes in the Tower* (2017), pp. 29–31 (and see pp. 29–30 for transcript of Rastell), revealingrichardiii.com/tyrells-confession.html
74 Sewell, p. 152; Rastell, *Pastime*, pp. 293–94, 297: 'Immediately after his coronation, the grudge, as well of the lords as of the commons, greatly increased against him [King Richard], because the common fame went that he had secretly murdered the two sons of his brother, King Edward IV in the Tower of London.' Tyrell is not mentioned in Rastell's account of any reign, including Richard III's (pp. 297–99), although he erroneously gives the name 'Sir Thomas Tyrell' (p. 274) to Sir Thomas Kyriell, who was famously executed after 2nd St Albans (1461).

9. Windsor Coffins and a Westminster Urn

1 Henry Emlyn, St George's Chapel E.16/9, SAL (1790); *Royal Funerals* (burial of George) pp. 47–57, Mary, pp. 58–65.
2 Without title 'Duke of Bedford', see *Royal Funerals*, p. 48.
3 Edward Legge, Dean of Windsor (1805–16), 'Arrangements for installation of Prince of Wales' (SGC X.23). Timeline: Kate McQuillian, Archivist & Chapter Librarian, St George's Chapel (18.10.2021).
4 Art Ramirez, TMPP Research Report, 24.2.16.
5 Eileen Bates: sparkypus.com/2020/08/03/those-mysterious-childrens-coffins-in-edward-ivs-vault/.
6 1790 report: 'This vault escaped the examination of the paviours.' Thanks to Kate McQuillian, St George's Chapel, as above.
7 A.J. Hibbard, An Account of Richard … & Order of the Garter.
8 Hibbard, *ibid.*, p. 21. Edward V's stall was reassigned to Henry's heir, Prince Arthur. Richard, Duke of York's was reassigned to Sir William Stanley.

9 *Maligned King*, pp. 208–11. See also Lawrence E. Tanner & William Wright, 'Recent Investigations regarding the Fate of the Princes in the Tower', *Archaeologia*, 1935, Vol. 84, pp. 1–26, (pp. 10–11). For the new open area, see note 26.

10 As propaganda to shore up Charles II's reign when he was labelled a tyrant for the revenge killings of his father's executioners, or as potential hoax, see Richard Unwin, *Westminster Bones: The Real Mystery of the Princes in the Tower* (2015).

11 Given by Tanner & Wright, p. 12, as the time needed to make the urn, but four years is an inordinate time, particularly for royal architect Sir Christopher Wren.

12 'Analysis of Bones Discovered in London in the Mid-C17th and Exhumed in the Early C20th for Investigation – Summary of a Modern Analysis' by George Maat (14 June 2018).

13 Theya Molleson, 'Anne Mowbray and the Princes in the Tower: A Study in Identity', *London Archaeologist*, Vol. 5, No. 10, 1987, pp. 258–62, suggests (pp. 259–60) a dental link between the elder skull in the urn (which she assumed belonged to Edward V) and Lady Anne Mowbray (wife of the younger prince, related to them in the third and fourth degrees) through hypodontia – congenitally missing teeth. Suggested by Tanner & Wright, hypodontia had already been discounted in 1965 by leading orthodontist Martin Rushton. See 'The Teeth of Anne Mowbray', *British Dental Journal*, Vol. 119, 1965, p. 35 (and note 14). Following the discovery of Richard III, this dental connection was also disproved by Ashdown-Hill (see note 15).

14 P.W. Hammond and W.J. White, 'The Sons of Edward IV: A Re-Examination of the Evidence on Their Deaths and on The Bones in Westminster Abbey', *Richard III: Loyalty, Lordship and Law* (1986), pp. 121–70 (see note 18), quoted orthodontist Martin Rushton in ruling out significant hypodontia (p. 125); he also commented on the size of the crown on the lower permanent canine of the younger skull (p. 122), and the development of the elder remains, offering the possibility, in both cases, of them being female.

15 *Mythology*, 'Hypodontia?', pp. 187–93, 289 n. 4.

16 Glen Moran, 'The Search for the MtDNA of the Princes', *Bulletin*, December 2018, pp. 41–44.

17 Sue Black and Lucina Hackman, 'Views on previous publications relating to the 'Princes in the Tower', The Missing Princes Project (11.11.2021).

18 Wright, despite claiming it was a blood stain, conceded an inability to prove it was even human blood (*op. cit.*, p. 18 n. 2). Hammond & White, 'Sons of Edward IV', p. 128: 'Here, with the cause of death ... Wright far exceeded the bounds of what was permissible.' Bill White (d. 2010) was a leading osteologist and founder member of the British Association of Biological Anthropology and Osteoarchaeology.

19 Geoffrey Parnell, 'The Roman and Medieval Defences and Later Development of the Inmost Ward, Tower of London: Excavations 1955–77', *Transactions of the London & Middlesex Archaeological Society*, Vol. 36, 1985, pp. 1–80.

20 For example, W.J. White, 'Research Notes and Queries', 'The Examination of Skeletal Remains: Henry VI and the 'Princes', *Ricardian*, Vol. 6 , No. 80, March 1983, pp. 159–61.

21 Tanner & Wright, pp. 9–10.

22 Richard Davey, *The Tower of London* (1910, 1914, 1919), p. 36. Thanks to Francisca Icaza.

23 'Velvet-weaving techniques were developed between the 12th and 13th century and there is a consensus among the scholars that it occurred almost simultaneously in Persia, China and in Europe.' Thanks to Silvija Banić, V&A Museum, Textiles Curatorial Team (16.5.2022); Dr Mariam Rosser-Owen, Curator Middle East, Asian Department; and Katie Dungate, Administrator, Collections Care and Access. For velvet church vestments in 1250, see Herbert Norris, *Church Vestments: Their Origin and Development* (1949), p. 80.

24 Seán Ó Súilleabháin, 'Foundation Sacrifices', *Journal of the Royal Society of Antiquaries of Ireland*, Vol. 75, No. 1, March 1945, pp. 45–52; www.oxfordreference.com/view/10.1093/oi/authority.20110803095830880.

25 Geoffrey Parnell, *The Tower of London* (1993), p. 22. By 1171–72, the King's Apartments were repaired by Henry II.

26 *Ibid.*, pp. 65–68. Charles II's demolition of the medieval Royal Apartments began on 3 April 1668 and was completed in the 1670s. Buildings including the Jewel House were removed to form a clear and open corridor around the White Tower to safeguard its ordnance and powder magazine.

27 *Maligned King*, p. 208. Tanner & Wright, p. 8 n. 2, from a note signed by Knight, dated 1674 and written into a copy of Yorke's *The Union of Honour*; repeated in print by Francis Sandford, *Genealogical History of the Kings of England* (1677), p. 402.

28 Parnell, *Tower of London*, pp. 13–15, 67–68. Demolition began at the south-west corner on 10 March 1674, with the remains of children discovered on 17 July.

29 Parnell, pp. 13, 17. For Colchester Castle, see p. 19.

30 Parnell, p. 16.

31 *Maligned King*, pp. 211–13, Figures 15–18, detail p. 204.

32 *Maligned King*, pp. 200–203. Also 'Notes on Opening the Urn': tinyurl.com/ye5sytzr. For the fate of the young Henry Pole at the Tower (holds the same mtDNA as the princes), see Philippa Langley and Michael Jones, *The Lost King*, p. 231 and John Ashdown-Hill, *The Private life of Edward IV* (2017), p. 238.

33 *Coronation*, p. 369. Believed to be around 16 years old.

34 Ordinances for the Royal Household in the North: *Harley 433*, Vol. 3, p. 114; Hammond, *The Children of Richard III*, p. 33. At Edward of Middleham's investiture on 8 September 1483 in York, Edward, Earl of Warwick and John of Gloucester (Richard's nephew and bastard son respectively) were knighted with him. This confirms these three were either domiciled in the north or travelled north at the time of the royal progress. Edward of Middleham was not present at Richard III's coronation on 6 July, which is confirmed by the Middleham accounts (Hammond, p. 22). Henry Lovell, Lord Morley (b.*c.* 1466) would die at the Battle of Dixmunde on 13 June 1489, supporting Brittany against France.

35 *Harley 433*, Vol. 2, p. 2.

36 *Itinerary*, p. 4.

37 At Oxford: *Itinerary*, p. 5; Robert C. Hairsine, 'Oxford University and the Life and Legend of Richard III', *Crown & People*, pp. 307–32 (p. 309). At

Worcester and Warwick (5–14 August): *Early Historians*, p. 122. At York (29 August–20 September): Hammond, *The Children of Richard III*, pp. 29, 65–66, Appendix III; Bedern College Statute Book (late fifteenth century), York Minster Library, p. 48. At Grantham (19–20 October): *Itinerary*, p. 9, CCR, No.117, from CCR 1476–85, pp. 346–47, Kent Archives (thanks to Jean Clare-Tighe). Also *Foedera XII*, p. 203.

38 Williamson, *op. cit.*, p. 91, see note 36.

39 Richard III made Tyrell Steward of Llandovery Castle following Buckingham's execution and gave the town a Royal Charter in 1485 (*Harley 433*, Vol. 1, pp. 160, 256). See also, 'Presentation of Freedom of the Borough of Llandovery to HRH the Prince of Wales' (June 1985), Barton Library downloads, topographical. Thanks to Christine Forbes (21.7.2017).

40 A.J. Pollard, *North-Eastern England During the Wars of the Roses* (1990), p. 357.

41 Thanks to local residents, Elizabeth Watson and Kim Harding.

42 Richard's remarkable Charter to Scarborough in spring 1485 made it into a 'shire incorporate'. See Ross, *Richard III*, p. 58, 'a dignity only previously enjoyed by such major towns as London, Bristol and Norwich'. Original vellum is held in Scarborough Collections. Also, for Scarborough under Richard III, see *Harley 433*, Vol. 1, p. 249. Scarborough Castle, on the coast, was heavily fortified and its Constable was William Tunstall, see Pollard, *op. cit.*, p. 387. Under Henry VII Scarborough lost its county status.

43 en.wikipedia.org/wiki/Francis_Lovell_1st_Viscount_Lovell (accessed 9.2.2020). In 1474, Lovell inherited a large estate, including Bedale, a possession of the Stapleton family, adjacent to Middleham – this might be the source for the tradition. Thanks to Dr A.J. Hibbard. The Stapleton family arms appear on Lovell's Garter stall plate in St George's Chapel.

44 Thanks to Sharon Lock, also Garry Smith, Curator (Collections), Tameside Metropolitan Borough for Portland Basin Museum, Ashton-under-Lyne (13.4.2016).

45 Campbell, Vol. 1, p. 322, grant made on 25 February 1486. A significant question is whether Sir William Stanley discovered information regarding the fate of one or more of the sons of Edward IV during his tenure as Lord of Longdendale, following Lovell's lordship.

46 Michael J. Bennett, *ODNB*. At his trial, Sir William Stanley confessed to treason. See also T.B. Howell, *Complete Collection of State Trials for High Treason and Other Crimes etc.* (1816), Vol. 1 (1163–1600), 'The Trial of Sir William Stanley, Knight, for High Treason: 10 Hen. VII. AD 1494–5 [Hall and Lord Bacon]', pp. 277–84.

47 *Vergil-2*, pp. 73–77.

48 *Ibid.*, pp. 73, 79. Also Buc, p. 161.

10. To Kill a King: The Aftermath of Bosworth

1 Men from the battle reached London (around 100 miles) within two days on the 24th (see note 3). The three-day journey is calculated on factors including Henry's journey from Leicester–Coventry on 24 August, approx. 24 miles

in a day. See notes 22 and 25 for revictualling his forces. A mounted force could travel 40 miles a day, as evidenced by Richard Ratcliffe's journey from London–York on 10 June 1483, a distance of approx. 195 miles in four to five days (*York Books*, Vol. 2, *loc. cit.*, pp. 713–14). The force despatched from Leicester on 23 August (Cotton; Windsor Herald) covered about 100 miles to the outskirts of York in time to meet the city fathers on 24 August. If Henry took heavy ordnance to London, it may have taken about four or five days, covering up to 20 miles a day (during the Napoleonic Wars an army with ordnance could march up to 30 miles a day). John Sponer covered Bosworth to York in a day, which was 108 miles (*York Books*, Vol. 1, pp. 368–69). For information on gaited (ambling) horses travelling up to 20mph, see en.wikipedia.org/wiki/Horses_in_the_Middle_Ages and petticoatsandpistols.com/tag/how-far-a-horse-can-travel-in-a-day

2 *Vergil-2*, pp. 3–5: '… was greeted with the greatest joy by all. Far and wide the people hastened to assemble by the roadside, saluting him as king and filling the length of his journey with laden tables and overflowing goblets.'

3 Mike Ingram, *Richard III and the Battle of Bosworth*, p. 51; LMA Common Council 9, f. 81d, 82r. Though an organised fighting force, some doubt the London men were sent, but their presence fighting for Richard is indicated by London's description of Henry as 'rebell', the martial law immediately imposed, the speed of the men returning to confirm the king's death and the enormous sums paid to Henry by the city on his arrival and coronation. Thanks to the late Mike Ingram.

4 Ingram, *Richard III and the Battle of Bosworth*, p. 207; LMA Common Council 9. See also Ralph A. Griffiths and James Sherborne, *Kings and Nobles in the Later Middle Ages* (1986), pp. 193–94.

5 Margaret M. Condon, 'More than the Sum of Its Parts. The London Customs Accounts 1400–1510, a major new resource', *Ricardian*, Vol. 29, 2019, p. 109. On 28 August 1485, the Common Council of London sent delegates to meet with the new king. The previous day, Henry had granted himself London's customs and subsidies.

6 Ingram, *op. cit.*, p. 207. Also, *Vergil-2*, p. 5: 'as he [Henry] entered the city: trumpeters went in front with the spoils of the enemy, thundering forth martial sounds'.

7 For immediate post-Bosworth events in York and a copy of Henry's proclamation, see *York Books*, Vol. 2, *loc. cit.*, pp. 734–39.

8 Bob Pritchard, *The Battle of Bosworth: Nobles and Knights Profiles* (2018), p. 54. At Bosworth with King Richard, the herald was believed to be Richard Slack (d. 1502): *York Books*, Vol. 2, *loc. cit.*, p. 736, the city fathers' reward to Windsor Herald for his 'comfortable words'. Slack was made Keeper of Claverdon Park, Warwickshire.

9 Pritchard, p. 38. Sir Roger Cotton (Cotam) is believed to have fought for King Richard and been knighted by him (when Duke of Gloucester) for the Scottish campaign of 1482. See W.C. Metcalfe, *A Book of Knights Banneret, knights of the Bath and knights bachelor made between the fourth year of King Henry IV and King Charles II* (London, 1885), p. 7, archive.org/details/bookofknightsban00metcuoft/page/n10 (thanks to Dr Sandra Pendlington). By

21 September 1485, Cotton was Sheriff of the counties of Glamorgan and Morgannock; by 17 December, Master of the Horse to 'the queen' (Elizabeth of York); by June 1486, he was awarded the Constableship, Stewardship and Honour of the Lordship and Castle of Clare, a significant Yorkist property in ownership of Cecily, Duchess of York (Campbell, Vol. 1, pp. 36, 220, 479).

10   This would seem to be King Richard's boar device/possible battle standards retrieved from Bosworth by Windsor Herald, perhaps a direct reference to Vergil's 'spoils of the enemy' (see note 6).

11   *York Books*, Vol. 2. *loc. cit.*, p. 738.

12   Philippa Langley, 'Robert Willoughby: A Short Biography', *Bulletin* (March 2020), pp. 48–51. Available at: www.revealingrichardiii.com/case-study.html.

13   *Vergil-2*, p. 3. For 10-year-old Warwick incorrectly described as 15 (the age of Edward V), see Philippa Langley, 'The Fate of the Sons of King Edward IV: Robert Willoughby's Urgent Mission, Part One', *Bulletin*, March 2020, pp. 42–47 (p. 42) www.revealingrichardiii.com/case-study.html, from Gordon Smith, 'Lambert Simnel and the King From Dublin', *Ricardian*, Vol. 10, No. 135, Dec. 1996, pp. 498–536 (p. 502 n. 10). The age discrepancy was first raised by Barrie Williams, 'Lambert Simnel's rebellion: how reliable is Polydore Vergil?', *Ricardian*, Vol. 6, No. 79, December 1982, pp. 118–23 (p. 120). Vergil also incorrectly describes Warwick as 'sole survivor' of George of Clarence – his sister, Margaret, was 12 at the time. Married in November 1487 (aged 14) to King Henry's cousin, Sir Richard Pole, by 1505 (now widowed), she was out of favour and living at Syon Abbey, Isleworth by London.

14   Sandal Castle is about 82 miles from Leicester Castle; Sheriff Hutton is 113 miles. Though unaccountably unrecorded, Henry would have been negligent not to send to the Sandal Nursery. For its importance, see Philippa Langley, 'Niclas von Popplau: Lost in Translation? Part One', *Bulletin*, December 2020, pp. 48–49, www.revealingrichardiii.com/niclas-von-popplau. html. For other daughters of King Edward, see note 21.

15   For Willoughby's post-Bosworth mission to Sheriff Hutton, see Langley, 'Fate of Sons, Part One'. Described as Henry VII's 'first act' (James Gairdner, *Henry The Seventh* (1889), p. 31).

16   *York Books*, Vol. 2, *loc. cit.*, p. 735. For Northumberland's post-Bosworth imprisonment and oath to Henry for release on 6 December 1485, see Campbell, Vol. 1, pp. 198–99. For his heir taken into Henry's custody, see Pollard, *North-Eastern England*, p. 362, but the source remains untraced – Pollard may have confused Northumberland with the Earl of Westmorland and his heir, who were taken into custody on 5 December 1485 (Campbell, Vol. 1, pp. 196, 311; CCR 1485–1500, p. 22). For Northumberland being released by 18 December, see *York Books*, Vol. 1, p. 391.

17   *York Books*, Vol. 2, p. 735.

18   *York Books*, Vol. 1, pp. 373, 392, for 14 October 1485 and the Council's openly recorded description of Richard as 'King', the 'moost famous prince of blissed memory'; also, their refusal on 18 December to elect King Henry's chosen candidate as Recorder of York. Consequently, York's City Archives survived relatively intact.

19 Willoughby's urgent mission may be explained by Northumberland's control of the Eastern Marches; his chief seat was Leconfield, about 34 miles from Sheriff Hutton, so he would have been aware of any children domiciled there. Moreover, if the account of Diego de Valera, from 1 March 1486 (within six months of Bosworth) is to be believed, the 'Lord of Tamorlant' (Northumberland) aimed to marry his daughter to Warwick may be borne out by Northumberland's delay in reaching the Battle of Stoke to support Henry. Anthony Goodman and Angus Mackay identify Northumberland as 'Tamorlant' in 'A Castilian Report on English Affairs, 1486', *EHR*, Vol. 88, No. 346, January 1973, pp. 95–96. Valera's letter is translated by Nokes & Wheeler in 'A Spanish Account'. Valera was a Spanish nobleman and servant of Ferdinand and Isabella. Thanks to Marie Barnfield (23.7.2018). Northumberland's will, dated 27 July 1485, seems to indicate the intention to participate in the Battle of Bosworth, See 'A Selection Of Wills From The Registry At York', Vol. III, *The Surtees Society*, 1865, pp. 304–10 (with thanks to Dr Heather Falvey). Of the seventeen knights named therein, ten are known to have fought for King Richard and seven seem not to have participated or are untraced. For Henry VII's personal interrogation of prisoners, see Penn, *Winter King*, p. 82.

20 The key northern stronghold of Pontefract Castle is about 83 miles from Leicester Castle. Sandal Castle is about 8–9 miles from Pontefract Castle. See notes 13 and 14.

21 Campbell, Vol. 1, p. 311. The children were placed in the care of Henry's mother, Margaret Beaufort, to whom he granted £200 on 24 February 1486 for her late 'keeping and guiding' of the daughters of Edward IV and the young Duke of Buckingham and Earls of Warwick and Westmorland (see note 16). Beaufort kept them a few months from September to December/January. For her custody of Buckingham's sons (3 August 1486), see Campbell, p. 532. Henry VII's delayed arrival in London has been attributed to the Sweating Sickness (Hairsine, 'Oxford University'). However, this sickness reached Oxford only at the end of August/early September, then took hold in London during September (Historical Notes, p. 589; thanks to Dr Judith Ford). Henry, in London by 3 September, would scarcely have entered had the sickness been there.

22 *Crowland*, p. 161.

23 Coventry Leet Book/Mayor's Register, p. 531, 'payment to divers persons for stuff sent to the field of King Richard': archive.org/details/coventryleetboo00unkngoog/page/n554

24 Anne F. Sutton, '*Camera principis*: Good Government, Industry and Ceremony in Richard III's Coventry', *Ricardian*, Vol. 29, 2019, pp. 66, 78, 83. Leading citizens Robert Coleman and Thomas Maideford fought for Richard. Thomas was injured and may have captained the Coventry contingent (p. 83).

25 Griffiths & Sherborne, *Kings and Nobles*, p. 194.

26 Coventry Leet Book, pp. 194–95. Henry received a gold cup and £100 from the city, plus payments for bread, wine and ale. See also *The Lost King*, p. 217: 110 gallons of wine to please Henry's large contingent of French mercenaries (cf. 4.5 gallons of ale).

27　Henry's army carried three banners to London: St George, the Welsh Dragon and the Dun Cow. The latter was the banner for Coventry and Warwickshire. See Griffiths & Sherborne, *Kings and Nobles*, p. 197 (it also had a very slight association with Henry's maternal Beaufort family). Coventry being the nearest city to the battle in Warwickshire, and having supported Richard, Henry's imagery told a clear story of victory. The acquisition of the Dun Cow banner, whether from the battlefield or while securing Coventry's submission, seems to explain the detour, ensuring the message of capitulation was evident as Henry's forces passed by.

28　Sutton, *op. cit.*, pp. 63, 67.

29　*Ibid.*, pp. 50, 69–70 (also for the young Edward V, as Prince of Wales, asserting himself as a warrior in 1481).

30　The distances from Leicester and Coventry to London (Shoreditch) were similar (98 and 93 miles).

31　Gairdner, *op. cit.*, pp. 32–33; André, p. 31. André correctly records the date as a Saturday (this is confirmed as Saturday in other reports). Henry waited until 6 September for his first grant to be presented (Campbell, p. 6).

32　*Vergil-2*, p. 3.

33　See note 1 for journey time to York (195 miles) at 40 miles a day.

34　Langley, 'Robert Willoughby's Urgent Mission, Part One', p. 42.

35　C.P. Wilkins, *ODNB*. Edward Woodville was (probably) the youngest child of Richard Woodville, Earl Rivers.

36　He was made Knight-Banneret by his commander, Richard, Duke of Gloucester.

37　*ODNB:* in May 1483, Woodville had taken two royal ships with 200–300 soldiers/archers, plus £10,250 in gold appropriated from a vessel lying at harbour (Horrox, *Financial Memoranda*, p. 211). This figure amounted to 15 per cent of royal revenues, a similar figure having financed the 1482 invasion of Scotland.

38　*ODNB*, also *Crowland*, p. 181. Woodville is described as 'a most valiant knight', one of the 'chief men' of Henry's army and listed before Willoughby.

39　In September 1485, he awarded Woodville the captaincy of the Isle of Wight and restored his command of Portchester Castle.

40　Bennett, pp. 95, 98–99, 131; *Heralds' Memoir*, pp. 30, 112. Molinet, who says Woodville supported Henry VII, reports him on the right wing with cavalry, which seems only to have picked off stragglers from the main battle engaged by the Earl of Oxford. For information regarding only the vanguard being engaged, see Bennett, p. 99. Molinet also reports Woodville's contingent fleeing the Yorkist forces (for reasons unknown), a few days prior to the battle (Bennett, pp. 81, 82, 130).

41　27 April 1488.

42　*ODNB*. All were killed except one boy: the disaster brought about the end of independent Brittany. Ironically, Woodville's death in a cavalry charge would mirror that of King Richard.

43　*Vergil-1*, p. 36. In autumn 1484, Henry escaped Brittany (to France) with only his most trusted followers. Woodville was left behind.

44 For the spy, see Wroe, p. 44, from PRO, E 404/80 (numbered 467). Henry's spy was 'a Scot with a beard'. (For the transcription, thanks to Marie Barnfield.) For Woodville's plans to travel to Portugal, see the updated translation by António S. Marques of his article 'Álvaro Lopes de Chaves: A Portuguese Source', *Bulletin*, Autumn 2008, p. 27, from MS 1163/Codex 443 *da Colecção Pombalina da Biblioteca Nacional de Lisboa*: '… and while [we were] waiting for the coming of this Count Scales who had written to the king [John II] that he should bring this marriage and other matters to conclusion, he [Woodville alias Scales] went to Brittany'.

45 TNA, PRO E 154/2/4, 10 December 1484, for list of Catesby's armour and weaponry.

46 Daniel Williams, 'The Hastily Drawn-up Will of William Catesby, Esquire, 25 August 1485', *Transactions of the Leicestershire Archaeological & Historical Society*, Vol. 51, 1975–76, pp. 43–51.

47 *Ibid.*, p. 49. 'My lordis Stanley Strange and all that blod help and pray for my soule for ye haue not for my body as I trusted in you.'

48 Penn, *op. cit.*, pp. 82–83.

49 *Maligned King*, pp. 307–08; *Calendar* of Papal Registers Relating To Great Britain and Ireland: Vol. 14, 1484–1492, ed. J.A. Twemlow (London, 1960), British History Online; Richard Mackinder, *Bosworth: The Archaeology of the Battlefield* (2021), pp. 49–50; Glenn Foard and Anne Curry, *Bosworth 1485: A Battlefield Rediscovered* (2013), pp. 50, 56.

50 Ellis, *Three Books of Vergil*, pp. 224–25. John Stow, *The Annals of England* (1592), p. 783 follows Vergil: Catesby executed with 'diverse others'.

51 John Throsby, *The History and Antiquities of the Ancient Town of Leicester* (1792), p. 63.

52 *Crowland*, p. 183; *Vergil-1*, p. 58; Ellis, *op. cit.*, p. 225.

53 Howard had fought at Barnet in 1471, was wounded and unable to fight at Tewkesbury. In 1482, he took part in the invasion of Scotland, then helped quell the October 1483 uprising against King Richard. In 1513, he would command the English army at Flodden.

54 Buc, p. xvii. John Buck (*sic*) (Sir George's great-grandfather) may have been a retainer of Thomas Howard's wife, Elizabeth Tilney, given his family's earlier Tilney connections. His children were taken into Howard's protection after Bosworth and brought up at his manor in Suffolk. Robert Buck (*sic*), Sir George's grandfather, knew Howard well and fought for him at Flodden; see also Buc, p. 116. John Buck is listed among those attainted for high treason in Henry VII's first Parliament (*PROME*, 'Henry VII: November 1485, Part 1').

55 Buc, p. xvii.

56 Buc, pp. 107–08. Thomas Howard was attainted for high treason at Henry VII's first Parliament, losing his title and lands. All who fought against Henry could be indicted for treason following Henry's back-dating of his reign to the day before Bosworth. Thomas was third to be named in the Act of Attainder (after Richard III and John Howard) – *Rot. Parl.*, vi, pp. 257–58 (n. xxix).

57 Buc, pp. xvii–xix (also notes 54 and 55).

58 *Vergil-2*, pp. 5, 7.

59 Buc, p. 108.

60   Campbell, Vol. 1, pp. 208, 392. Payment for Howard, as Earl of Surrey, for his imprisonment in the Tower, dated 9 December 1485, and 8 March 1486 for special pardon permitting detention in any prison at the Crown's pleasure.

61   *York Books*, Vol. 2, *loc. cit.*, pp. 735–36. Henry Tudor's proclamation after the battle (read in York on 25 August) was a particularly clever ruse in immediately presenting the Yorkist cause as hopeless, flushing out Howard. A dead man could not protect family and affinity, nor hope to retain lands and titles. Viscount Lovell and the Earl of Lincoln also appeared among the dead, whereas both clearly survived.

62   Buc, p. 108. Interestingly, Buc makes it clear that according to his grandfather, Robert Buck (*sic*, a friend of Howard's), many Yorkists were executed in Leicester and, had Howard been captured, he would have suffered similarly. This seems to accord with Throsby and suggests more executions at Leicester than were supposed. For more on the hanging of the Bracher father and son after the battle, see *Crowland*, p. 183.

63   *Mancini*, p. 63: 'she surrendered the boy, trusting in the word of the cardinal of Canterbury, that the boy should be restored after the coronation: indeed the cardinal, suspecting no treachery, had so persuaded the queen'.

64   Linda Clark, *ODNB*. Bourchier appointed as his steward the king's close associate Robert Brackenbury (Constable of the Tower of London) in March 1484. Brackenbury and his wife Agnes were also enrolled in the confraternity of Christ Church, Canterbury, a great honour (Horrox, *ODNB*). From F.R.H Du Boulay (ed.), *Registrum Thomas Bourgchier ... 1454–1486*, CYS, 54 (1957).

65   Horace Walpole, *Historic Doubts on the Life and Reign of King Richard the Third* (1768, repr. 1974), pp. 59–61.

66   Sutton & Visser-Fuchs, 'Thomas Langton's Letter to William Selling', p. 61 n. 51.

67   All Hallows, Bread Street, and All Hallows, Gracechurch (Lombard Street): D.P. Wright, *ODNB*.

68   D.P. Wright (ed.), 'The Register of Thomas Langton, Bishop of Salisbury 1485–1493', *Canterbury and York Society*, 1985, p. xii.

69   Sutton & Visser-Fuchs, 'Thomas Langton's Letter', p. 64.

70   D.P. Wright, *ODNB*.

71   Susan Troxall, 'Thomas Langton, Richard III's Bishop', Part Two, *Bulletin*, March 2018, pp. 33–39 (p. 37 n. 32). From R. Percival Brown, 'Thomas Langton and his Tradition of Learning', *Transactions of the Cumberland & Westmorland Antiquarian & Archaeological Society*, New Series, Vol. 26, 1926, pp. 15–246, for full Latin transcription of Langton's will.

72   David Johnson, 'Reluctant Groom', *Bulletin*, March 2020, pp. 37–41; P.D. Clarke, 'English Royal Marriages and the Papal Penitentiary in the Fifteenth Century', *EHR*, Vol. 120, No. 488, September 2005, p. 1025.

73   Buc, p. 139. Rastell (1529) also seems to indicate a search, see Chapter 5; also Chapter 8, n. 48.

74   CPR 1485–94, pp. 12, 126. Lynom was appointed Receiver at Middleham on 29 July 1486 (thanks to Ian Rogers).

11 In Living Memory: The Mortimer Heirs – A Blueprint

1   Grant of 19 February 1401: 330 marks for Edmund and Roger from the lordship of Clare, Suffolk: J.L. Kirby (ed.), *Calendar Signet Letters, Henry IV and Henry V (1399–1422)* (HMSO, 1978), pp. 25–26 (C81/1356, No. 8); CPR 1399–1401, p. 380. First noted 20 Sept 1400 – Sara Kondol-Hanna, TMPP Research Report, 'Mortimer Chronology: Original Sources' (2.11.2019), p. 7.

2   Chris Given-Wilson, *Henry IV* (2016), p. 264.

3   Under the care of Sir John Pelham (d. 1429), CPR 1405–08, p. 276; CPR 1408–13, pp. 149, 202: Kondol-Hanna, *op. cit.*, pp. 22–23, 28, 30.

4   Horrox, *ODNB* – York returning to favour by October 1405 and in favour on 8 December when his land was restored; James Tait, *DNB*, Vol. 45 – on 7 October, Henry IV ordered York brought to him after apparent rumours of his death.

5   R.A. Griffiths, *ODNB* (2008).

6   In 1402, with the king's children, John (13) and Philippa (8), Edmund was 11 and Roger 10 (CPR 1401–05, p. 108; Kondol-Hanna, *op. cit.*, p. 12).

7   CFR 1399–1405, p. 61; CFR 1405–13, pp. 230, 241; CPR 1399–1401, p. 380; CPR 1401–05, pp. 108, 406; CPR 1405–08, p. 408; CPR 1408–13, pp. 149, 202, 350; CPR 1413–16, p. 45; Kondol-Hanna, pp. 6, 9–10, 12, 25, 28, 30–34.

8   CPR 1401–05, p. 30; CCR 1399–1402, pp. 527–28; CPR 1399–1401, pp. 546–47; Kondol-Hanna, pp. 8–9, 11.

9   Margaret Pollard was nursemaid to both boys. She and her husband were former servants of their father, Roger Mortimer, 4th Earl of March (d. 1398) (CPR 1399–1401, p. 475; Kondol-Hanna, pp. 7, 11).

10   CPR 1405–08, p. 173 (13 May 1406); Kondol-Hanna, p. 22. The girls' mother Eleanor, Countess of March, died in October 1405.

11   www.wikitree.com/wiki/Mortimer-257 Douglas Richardson. From various sources, including Harpenden's tomb monument, Westminster Abbey.

12. Edward V: Proof of Life

1   For a list of all those attainted at Henry VII's Parliament of 1487 and pardoned, see David Baldwin, *Stoke Field: The Last Battle of the Wars of the Roses* (2006), Appendix 1, pp. 123–25. As key supporters of the house of York, the Irish lords and Earls of Kildare and Desmond might be added to this list.

2   Jan Reygersbergh, *Dye Cronijck van* Zeelandt [*The Chronicle of Zeeland*] (1551), (digital) p. 123: 'In the same year [1487] in the month of May, the fifteenth day, captain Merten de Swarte [Martin Zwarte] went from Aremuyen [Arnemuiden] with many men of war to England, where he was defeated a short while later', objects.library.uu.nl/reader/index.php?obj=1874-214708&lan= en#page//25/73 /41/25734125922173294290517646744035980316.jpg/mode/1up

3   The date of the crowning of King Edward is on Sunday, 27 May 1487, and not Thursday, 24 May (as recorded by Henry VII's Parliament). This is derived from a number of sources, including the Red Book of Ireland; Randolph Jones in *Bulletin*, June 2009, pp. 42–44 and *Bulletin*, September 2014, pp. 43–45. See

also *Academia* (2015), pp. 185–209, esp. Appendix 1: 'The Revised Coronation Date of Lambert Simnel', pp. 207–09. In the fifteenth and sixteenth centuries, a Sunday was the appropriate day for a coronation. If Reygersbergh is correct about the date of departure of the Yorkist fleet from Middelburg (Arnemuiden) on 15 May 1487, then this supports the supposition that the coronation took place on 27 May, rather than 24 May. In the Middle Ages, a ship could sail by sea at an average speed of 2 knots, measured over day and night. This rule is also used about the fleet of Henry V by Ian Friel in *Henry V's Navy: The Sea-Road to Agincourt and Conquest 1413–1422* (2015). In twenty-four hours, a ship could sail approx. 50 nautical miles or 90km. However, this was seldom the case because medieval ships could not sail close to the wind as do modern yachts. They also suffered from leeway, i.e., displacement as a result of the set and drift of currents, but it does provide some tools to determine travel time. The distance from Middelburg (Arnemuiden) to Ireland (Wexford, in the south) around the point of Cornwall is more than 621 nautical miles (1,150 km), so it could be done in ten days if everything went well. The final leg from Land's End to Dublin could have gone fast with a good wind. Knowing this, it is highly unlikely the Yorkist fleet arrived before the (widely accepted) coronation date of 24 May, for which the sailing route would need to have been completed in less than nine days; this is highly unlikely given the above explanation. Special thanks to Dutch historian Ad van der Zee for sharing his expertise on 'Maritime Heritage in the Late Middle Ages' with the Dutch Research Group.

4   Bennett, pp. 89–103.

5   '[King Richmond] marched against him, with a large army and won the battle and killed the boy who would be king' – Livia Visser-Fuchs, 'Caspar Weinreich's Danzig Chronicle 1461–1495', *Ricardian*, December 1986, pp. 310–20 (p. 317). Weinreich was a seagoing merchant during the years of Yorkist rule, who made contemporary notes – though neither official nor especially reliable – recording news and rumours of the day. In his two entries for 1487, Weinreich identifies this 'boy who would be king' as the son of the Duke of Clarence (as he is often described in European records), but nowhere does Weinreich suggest that the pretender was an impostor. Of interest is his offering two strangely incorrect versions of a name attached to the pretender ('Jores' and 'Jorgen'), not encountered as his Christian name in any other report of his identity. However, the chronicle survives only in a copy made, and in places 'improved', by a sixteenth-century transcriber, who may have had difficulty making out the writing in Weinreich's manuscript. It is possible that in the original, the author wrote the Dutch word for 'York': not a name the transcriber would automatically have expected, which may explain why he made two different attempts at transcribing it. Weinreich could have rendered the name 'York' in Middle Low German (the language of the Hanseatic League) in a bewildering variety of medieval spellings, all beginning with the letter 'J' (e.g., 'Jorick', 'Jor(c)k' or 'Jorgk'). Understandably, English translations have followed the transcriber's logic in assuming it was a Christian name and have rendered it 'George'. This is unlikely to have been Weinreich's intention, as elsewhere when he means 'George', he actually writes 'Georg(e)'.

See State Archives of Gdańsk, copy of the notes of sea captain Caspar Weinreich (by Stenzel Bornbach): APG 300, R/LI,q 32, pp. 57–76 (1486/1487), 135–46 (1494/1495). The identification of this word as 'York' is supported by Weinreich's consistent references to Henry VII, not by his regnal name but by his title 'Richmond'. Thus, his likely intention was to identify the dynastic challenger to 'King Ritzmundt', in the name of the previously ruling house of York.

6 However, Adrien De But (see note 12) says the 'Dublin King' was led away to safety from the battlefield by his cousin, Edmund de la Pole, Duke of Suffolk (1471–1513) and taken to Guînes – 'The Young Duke of Clarence was also captured, but the Duke of Suffolk, who liberated him by stealth, took him overseas and took refuge in Guînes' (pp. 674–75, trans. from Latin by Dr. Betty Knott for TMPP). Edmund de la Pole succeeded to the ducal title in 1492, being the younger brother of John, Earl of Lincoln, who died at Stoke. For potential battlefield injury (facial), see Appendix 3, The Coldridge Investigation.

7 For the early contradictory accounts from Henry VII's government regarding the identity of the pretender in Ireland, see Gordon Smith, 'Lambert Simnel and the King from Dublin', *Ricardian*, Vol. 10, No. 135, December 1996, pp. 499, 514, 520; three accounts for the identity, p. 518.

8 The Register of the Archbishop of Canterbury contains a record of this imposture of Warwick, being the confession of a priest (William Simonds) before the convocation of Canterbury on 17 February 1487 in (medieval) St Paul's Cathedral, London: '… he [Simonds] himself abducted and carried across to places in Ireland the son of a certain organ-maker of the university of Oxford; and this boy was there reputed to be the earl of Warwick'. See Bennett, p. 9, Appendix (a). Henry VII's subsequent decision to publicly show the real Warwick immediately afterwards, also at St Paul's (described in *Vergil-2*, pp. 18–19), seems to confirm his underlying propaganda motives.

9 The earliest surviving source that gives 'Lambert Simnel' as the name of the Dublin King is the Act of Attainder against John de la Pole, Earl of Lincoln, in November 1487 (after the Battle of Stoke). See John Ashdown-Hill, *The Dublin King* (2015), Chapter 5: 'Lambert Simnel', p. 77. An extract of this attainder (from *Rot. Parl.*, vi, pp. 397–98) is added as Appendix (f) in Bennett, pp. 124–26.

10 The son of a 'joiner' appears in the Act of Attainder 1487 (Bennett, p. 125; Ashdown Hill, *Dublin King*, p. 77; Lewis, *The Survival of the Princes in the Tower*, p. 109). The 'Son of a baker or tailor' is from Bernard André (in *Dublin King*, p. 22). For 'son of either a baker or a shoemaker', see Bennett, Appendix (j), p. 132.

11 Hitherto attributed to 1486, the date is now amended to 1487: Nathalie Nijman-Bliekendaal and Koen Vermeulen, TMPP Research Report, 7.8.2020, from *City Account Mechelen (Malines) 1486–1487* (from f.153r), 'Gifts with the procession of Saint Rumbold and of the Holy Sacraments'. The relevant entry says, 'Also 8 stopen of whine presented to the son of Clarentie (Clarence) from England …' (information from Koen Vermeulen, archivist, Malines City Archive). The City Account runs from 1 November 1486 (All Saints Day) to

1 November 1487. The two processions of Saint Rumbold each year normally took place on the Wednesday after Easter and on or around 1 July. Though undated in the City Accounts for 1486–87, the missing dates can be narrowed down to 18 April 1487 (the Wednesday after Easter) and 1 July 1487. As preparations for the Yorkist invasion took place in spring 1487, prior to Stoke Field in June 1487, if we assume 'the son of Clarence' to have been its leader, this points to the gift of wine being presented to him during the Easter-tide procession of April 1487. However, the identity of 'the son of Clarence', as understood in the Low Countries, remains somewhat unclear when we consider that the Yorkist rebellion in 1487 was in favour of Edward V, not a real or counterfeit Edward of Warwick. It may simply have been a misnomer that took hold in common parlance.

12 De But (b. 1437), pp. 674–76, 678. The chronicle is his original work, continued until his death on 24 June 1488. It describes events he witnessed or learnt from reliable sources. When he wrote, he was living in Ter Duinen Abbey, Koksijde, on the Flemish west coast, near Calais and Guînes, which were both under English Tudor rule at the time. It seems likely he received his 'first-hand' information from the English who were present there. See also Véronique Lambert, *Chronicles of Flanders 1200–1500*, 'Chronicles written independently from "Flandria Generosa"', pp. 128–30, published in *Verhandelingen der Maatschappij voor Geschiedenis en Oudheidkunde te Gent XIX* (1993).

13 NAH, The Hague, County Accounts of Holland (*Grafelijkheidsrekenkamer*), Margaret of York's Domain Account Voorne, Account of Jan Michielszoon, 5 January 1487–5 January 1488, register number access: 3.01.27.02, inv. nr 3337, f.105r. This describes all the income and expenses of Margaret's Dutch domain, Voorne. The specific entry describes heavy costs for a large group of men to help '*De Hertoghe van Clarens* [The Duke of Clarence], who was of their noble blood and her brother's son and by right succession and honour entitled to the crown of England'. (NB: In comparison with the Lille document, it is unsigned, undated and written by a clerk.)

14 See note 8.

15 John de la Pole, Earl of Lincoln, was also in London at the time and saw the young Earl of Warwick on this occasion (Bennett, p. 51), 'which himself [Lincoln] knew and daily spoke with him at Sheen before his [Lincoln's] departing [from England]' (*Heralds' Memoir*, p. 109). In his September 1496 proclamation from Scotland, Richard of England (Edward V's brother) confirms that his 'Right entirely wellbeloved' cousin, Edward (Earl of Warwick) has long been held a prisoner by Henry VII and 'yet keepeth' there. See Appendix 9. Transcription by Judith Ford available at www.revealing-richardiii.com/two-pretenders.html

16 For in-depth analysis of the contemporary materials for the Dublin King and his identification as Edward V, see Gordon Smith, pp. 498–536, and Matthew Lewis, *Lambert Simnel and Edward V* (July 2018), pp. 1–10 at www.revealingrichardiii.com/two-pretenders.html and at mattlewisauthor.wordpress.com/2018/07/24/lambert-simnel-and-edward-v

17 It seems there was a campaign deliberately undertaken during the reign of Henry VII to destroy any records that might have proved embarrassing to the

new regime and its supporters: A.J. Hibbard, 'The Missing Evidence', *Court Journal*, Vol. 26, Autumn 2019, p. 27 at www.revealingrichardiii.com/archival-destruction.html

18 Albert Jan de Rooij, TMPP Research Report, 5.5.2020, from ADN, B 3521, nr 124564. Thanks to Dr Livia Visser-Fuchs for the original French transcription (16.7.2020). See the image of the receipt at Plate 18.

19 During the reign of King Maximilian, the Artillery Department was divided, and a separate Treasurer for War appointed. This Treasurer was permanently responsible for all military expenses. However, the responsibility for all artillery expenditure, such as ammunition, weapons and transport, remained with the '*Recette de l'Artillerie*'. From the end of the fifteenth century, these accounts and the accompanying accounting documents form a separate collection, kept in the archives in Lille.

20 John Glymes of Bergen, Lord of Walhain (1452–1532), was the second son of Jan II of Glymes, Lord of Bergen op Zoom (1417–94). Various members of the Glymes family, among them Henry of Glymes, Bishop of Cambrai, fulfilled key positions at the Burgundian-Habsburg courts under Maximilian I, his son, Philip the Handsome, and Charles V. In 1487, Walhain was a member of the Financial Council of King Maximilian. After his father's death in 1494, he became Lord of Bergen op Zoom (John III). He maintained close links with the English envoys and kings (just like his father, John II) as the prosperity of Bergen op Zoom was heavily dependent on trade with England. See Carl H.L.I. Cools, '*Mannen met Macht, Edellieden en de Moderne Staat in de Bourgondisch-Habsburgse landen, c. 1475–c. 1530*' (2000), p. 310 at pure.uva.nl/ws/files/3087234/11364_Thesis.pdf

21 In the continental accounts/records, Margaret of York (1446–1503) is often referred to as '*Madame la Douagiere* [Madam Dowager]'. For more on Margaret of York, see Chapter 17.

22 For the complete French transcription of the Lille Receipt and translation into modern English, see Appendix 2.

23 'And there was taken the lad that his rebels called king Edward' (*Heralds' Memoir*, p. 117), see also Bennett, p. 129, where the Heralds' report dated 1488–90 (BL Cotton MS, Julius B.XII, f.27d-29d, amending John Leland, *Collectanea*, Vol. V, ed. Hearne [Oxford 1774], pp. 212–15) is added as appendix (h). For the boy from Stoke Field being called 'John', see *Heralds' Memoir*, p. 117, and Lewis, p. 1. It is quite possible that the 'John' who was captured after the battle refers to King Richard's base-born son, John of Gloucester, see also Chapter 6 for John's incarceration in the Tower of London and probable death there in 1499.

24 'And anon after his departure the Lord Scropes of Bolton and Upsall, constrained as it was said by their folks, came on horseback to Bootham Bar, and there cried "King Edward".' See appendix (c) in Bennett, p. 123; June/July 1487, York House Books 6, f.98–99d; A. Raine (ed.), *York Civic Records*, Vol. 2, Yorkshire Archaeological Society, Record Series 103 (1941), pp. 22–24; *York Books*, Vol. 2, p. 572. Entries date the city's report of the rebellion to 8–17 June 1487.

25 Patent Roll 2, Henry VII [*sic*], nr 7 (National Library of Ireland, MS UR
    016658, Ref: D 1855) chancery.tcd.ie/document/patent/2-Henry-VII/7.
    Written in Latin and issued and sealed in the name of 'King Edward' (see
    Plates 21 and 22). In this letter patent, Peter Butler is granted by 'Edward,
    by the grace of God, King of England, France and Ireland ... the office of
    sheriff of our County of Kilkenny...' It was witnessed 'by our very dear
    cousin, Gerald, Earl of Kildare ... at Dublin, on the 13th day of August in the
    first year of our reign'. The document has been noticed by several historians,
    their views differing as to whether the year of its issuance was 1486 or 1487.
    The grant itself offers no clue, but those who attribute it to 1487 tend to be
    those who subscribe to the centuries-old orthodoxy that 'King Edward' was
    not Edward V. Thus, it is usually relegated to a curiosity emanating from a
    period of turmoil and shifting loyalties. More recently, John Ashdown-Hill
    (*The Dublin King*) and Randolph Jones (see below) have argued that 'King
    Edward' was Edward, Earl of Warwick – an identification that fails in the
    face of the Maximilian I receipt. Gordon Smith (*op. cit.*, pp. 516, 533 n. 124)
    concludes that issuing patents in the name of the rebels' king in 1487 *after* the
    Battle of Stoke was unlikely, with the most unforced interpretation being
    that the patent of 13 August was issued under King Edward V in 1486. In
    any case, if still at liberty in August 1487, he would have had more pressing
    concerns than appointing an Irish Sheriff under the royal seal. Historians have
    also comfortably ruled out the writ belonging to April–June 1483 or to the
    reign of the Tudor Edward VI. Whichever way Edward V may have chosen to
    begin his regnal year (and there are several possibilities), August 1486 accords
    naturally with most variations. Another argument of Ashdown-Hill and
    Jones that requires discussion is that 'King Edward' was known as Edward VI.
    Ashdown-Hill's argument relies on an entry in the York city records which,
    upon forensic investigation, is unreliable. The entry giving King Edward the
    regnal number 'VI' does indeed exist, but is a copy of a *scribal introduction*, in
    other words, a description of a text (a letter from King Edward) originally
    appended, which has been lost or destroyed (see Chapter 19); therefore we are
    left with the numeral 'VI' occurring only in the scribe's words without any
    means of checking their accuracy: *York Books* Vol. 2, p. 570 (York Archives:
    Y/COU/1/1/4 f.97 r). In extant communications from the Dublin King,
    he never assigned himself a regnal number; indeed, as king, this followed
    established procedure. Jones also claims the regnal number 'VI' was recorded
    in another document no longer extant, i.e., a membrane in the now-destroyed
    fifteenth-century Irish Exchequer Memoranda Roll. There are three modern
    notes of it (made in the 1820s, 1855 and 1912–15), of which the most reliable
    is the repertory by Rolls Office Clerk William Lynch in the 1820s, where
    his notes contain a reference to a regnal year '/1 Ed 6/' ('New Evidence for
    'Edward VI's' Reign in Ireland?', *Bulletin*, Sept 2014, pp. 43–45). The later
    two, less-satisfactory notations may well have copied this first one since it
    provided a ready-made translation of the Latin original. (N.B. On the grounds
    that two sources giving the same information are better than one, Jones argues
    that because the membrane is recorded with differing reference numbers
    in the modern notes, there must have been two identical membranes in the

original Roll, both containing exactly the same information about exactly the same writ. Two identical membranes are far less likely than a case of modern confusion over numbering of the single original, considering the way medieval manuscripts have a history of being routinely assigned different (or erroneous) reference numbers, depending on their binding and filing over the years by collectors, clerks and catalogue-makers.) As to the reference '/1 Ed 6/', the two forward slashes surrounding the regnal year (which don't occur around other regnal years on the same page) are important: they are probably Lynch's system of carets indicating an interpolation or interlineation that he observed had been added *after* the entry was first engrossed in 1487–88. As such, the words could have been added at any time between the fifteenth and nineteenth centuries.

26 David Johnson, 'Reluctant Groom', *Bulletin*, March 2020, pp. 37–41, reveals how Henry VII did not legitimise Elizabeth of York until the second session of Parliament on 23 January 1486, after their marriage on the 18th. Also available at: www.revealingrichardiii.com/the-pre-contract.html

27 Annals of Ulster, author unknown, U1485.22, celt.ucc.ie/published/T100001C. html. It is noteworthy that the word 'expelled' is used in the Lille Receipt. Clearly, 'the son of King Edward' had been expelled from his dominion, his exile being further recorded in the Annals of Ulster for the year 1487, which mention his probable crossing to Ireland: 'A great fleet of Saxons came to Ireland this year to meet the son of the Duke of York, who was exiled at this time with the Earl of Kildare' (*op. cit.*, U1487.12). It is unclear who is meant by 'the son of the Duke of York', as after Bosworth no sons of the late Duke of York (1411–60, former Lieutenant of Ireland) remained alive, but the Irish records cited in this chapter fit his grandson, Edward V.

28 Smith, pp. 517–19; Lewis, p. 9.

29 Smith, pp. 503, 516: '… would best fit Edward V, since he is described as a young man and in exile'. Also: Jan Reygersbergh's 'Dye Cronijck van Zeelandt', 1551 (*Chronicle of Zeeland*), p. 121r: objects. library.uu.nl/reader/index.php?obj=1874-214708&lan=en&lan= en#page//91/43/30/914330528080698345017547656273240505919.jpg/ mode/1up.

30 Lewis, p. 2.

31 For a full analysis of contemporary sources, see Chapter 5.

32 Lewis, p. 6. From André, p. 45.

33 Randolph Jones, 'The Extraordinary Reign of "Edward VI" in Ireland, 1487–8', *Bulletin*, September 2021, pp. 48–56 (p. 49, n. 22). Following his journey to Ireland, Yonge was made Somerset Herald for life (CPR 1485–1494, p. 460).

34 Matthew Lewis, TMPP Research Report, 22.8.2018. From J.S. Brewer (ed.), 'Henry VIII: August 1526, 11–20; 2405. Ireland', in *Letters and Papers, Foreign and Domestic, Henry VIII*, Vol. 4, 1524–1530 (1875), pp. 1066–81 (p. 1075), 17–18 August 1526.

35 Lewis, from Bernard André, pp. 5–6; for Henry VIII briefing note and Pope Innocent VIII, p. 4.

36 Philippa Langley, TMPP Research Report, 27.5.2022. Ascension is the fortieth day after Easter Sunday when Jesus ascended into heaven. Latin terms used for

the Christian feast (*ascensio* and *acensa*) signify that Christ was raised up by his own powers.

37 Sir John Thomas Gilbert, *History of the Viceroys of Ireland: With Notices of the Castle of Dublin and Its Chief Occupants in Former Times* (1865), p. 606 n. 3: 'All records, processes, stiles, pardons, liveries, acts, and ordinances of Council, and all other acts done in the "Laddes" name annulled, and persons keeping, concealing, or receiving them after proclamation deemed traitors attainted.' Henry VII's deputy in Ireland, Sir Edward Poynings, ordered the destruction on Henry's behalf in the Parliament of 1494. Thanks to Randolph Jones for transcription and identifying BL, Add. MS 4801 (8.9.2021). See also Smith, p. 515.

38 This logical consequence is supported by the recently rediscovered (contemporary) manuscript in the Gelderland Archive in the Netherlands concerning the fate of the younger son of Edward IV, Richard, Duke of York: Nathalie Nijman-Bliekendaal, TMPP Research Report, 21.11.2020. See also Chapter 14.

39 In a private paper of instruction at Sheen, 10 August 1494, given by Henry VII to 'Richmond, otherwise Clarenceux King of Arms' (Roger Machado, his confidential envoy to France), Henry writes, 'And it is notorious that the said garçon is of no consanguinity or kin to the late king Edward, but is a native of the town of Tournay, and son of a boatman, who is named Werbec': Frederic Madden, 'Documents Relating to Perkin Warbeck, With Remarks on his History', *Archaeologia*, Vol. 27 (1837), pp. 12 n.y. 13. It is interesting to note that in his 'official confession' a few years later, Perkin confesses that he is 'the son of a controller' named 'Osbeck' – an echo of the job-switching applied to 'Lambert Simnel' who, according to Henry VII, started his career as 'the son of an organ maker' and very soon afterwards (John de la Pole, Act of Attainder, November 1487) is described as 'the son of a joiner'. See also notes 10 and 23.

13. The Yorkist Invasion of 1487: Edward V and the Second Fleet

1 This chapter is the result of original research in the Low Countries by the Dutch Research Group of Philippa Langley's The Missing Princes Project. Thanks are due to everyone of the Dutch Research Group for their support and valuable insights, and to Philippa Langley for assistance with queries, drafts and editing. Thanks also to Nathalie Nijman-Bliekendaal, particularly regarding Margaret's Domain Accounts.

2 Zoë Maula, 'The Glymes and the Yorkist Invasion of 1487' (research paper: 19.6.2021), *Bulletin* (forthcoming).

3 Ibid.

4 Zoë Maula, 'John II of Glymes, Lord of Bergen op Zoom (1417–94) at the Court of Richard III in May 1484: A Puzzle Solved', *Bulletin*, December 2020, pp. 54–58; Zöe Maula, 'Richard's Dutch Visitor Revealed', *Bulletin*, June 2022, pp. 32–33.

5   Anne F. Sutton, *The Mercery of London: Trade, Goods and People, 1130–1578* (2019), p. 319.

6   Nathen Amin, *Henry VII and the Tudor Pretenders* (2021), p. 97.

7   NAH GRR (*Grafelijkheidsrekenkamer* [Chamber of County Accounts] of Holland), Register number access: 3.01.27.02, inv. nr 3337, domain account '*Grafelijk Huis*', 'Margaret of York', Voorne, f.101r, Accounts of Jan Michielszoon, 5 January 1487–5 January 1488. This describes all income and expenses of Margaret's Dutch domain, Voorne (hereafter, NAH GRR 3337).

8   NAH GRR 3337, f.101r.

9   Christine Weightman, *Margaret of York: The Diabolical Duchess* (2009) p. 50.

10 Amin (2021), p. 97.

11 ADN, Serie B 3523, nr 124846. Letter dated 10 April 1486 (1487, New Style), from Margaret of York to the artillery collector directly, requesting 60 pavois. Maximilian added at the bottom of the letter, with his hand, 'action without excuse'.

12 West-Brabants Archief, Archief Schepenbank, *Register van rentebrieven en recognitiën 1487*, 12 April, Inv. Nr. 302, f.126.

13 www.bankofengland.co.uk/monetary-policy/inflation/inflation-calculator. Calculation based on livres Parisis (= English pound). If paid in livres Tournois, the value in English pounds would be 1.25 times the amount (3,125 English pounds = £2.7 million): thanks to Wim Wiss.

14 West-Brabants Archief, City Accounts Bergen op Zoom 1487, p. 72 (RH page): westbrabantsarchief.nl/collectie/archieven/scans/NL-BozWBA-boz%20-%20 0005/2.6.2.1.1.14/start/50/limit/50/highlight/22. 'In April of these accounts, the city council meets on the request and desires of my lord of Bergen and his son lord of Walhain, to sell 9,315 Brabantse gulden with a rent tariff of 16 penningen, which are guaranteed by the same lords and city, and of which the sold 1,500 Livres were received and handed over to our lady dowager.'

15 West-Brabants Archief, City Accounts, *ibid.*, p. 34 (LH page): westbrabantsarchief.nl/collectie/archieven/scans/NL-BozWBA-boz%20-%20 0005/2.6.2.1.1.14/start/0/limit/50/highlight/34

16 Albert Jan de Rooij, TMPP Research Report, 5.5.2020.

17 ADN, B 3521, f.124.564. For analysis, see Chapter 12.

18 Jan Reyghersberg, *Dye Cronijck van Zeelandt* [*The Chronicle of Zeeland*] (1551) (digital) p. 123: 'In the same year (1487) in the month of May, the fifteenth day, captain Merten de Swarte (Martin Zwarte) went from Aremuyen (Arnemuiden) with many men of war to England, where he was defeated a short while later.' objects.library.uu.nl/reader/index.php?obj=1874-214708&lan=en#page//15/76/04/1576046872594871071192833030090422682459.jpg/mode/1up.

19 West-Brabants Archief, City Accounts, *ibid.*, p. 73 (RH page): westbrabantsarchief.nl/collectie/archieven/scans/NL-BozWBA-boz%20-%20 0005/2.6.2.1.1.14/start/0/limit/50/highlight/34

20 Regarding the pikemen from the Lille Receipt sailing to England as intended, research continues – Maula, 'The Glymes and the Yorkist Invasion of 1487'; see notes 2 and 3.

21 NAH GRR 3337, Chapter 'Other expenses of pensions of the servants from my gracious lady …' f.112r.

14. Richard, Duke of York: Proof of Life

1 Gelders Archief, 0510, '*Diverse Charters en Aanwinsten*', nr 1549: *Verhandelingen over de lotgevallen van Richard van York, ca 1500* [Treatises on the fates of Richard of York *c.* 1500]. Four written pages, with a copy from the sixteenth century. Includes photocopied correspondence between P.J. Mey and Professor D. Th. Enklaar. Nathalie Nijman-Bliekendaal, TMPP Research Report, 21.11.2020.

2 In 1951, Dr P.J. Mey was 'Master of the Charters' at the State Archives, Gelderland.

3 For this correspondence, see note 1.

4 Tim Thornton, 'More on a Murder: The Deaths of the "Princes in the Tower", and Historiographical Implications for the Regimes of Henry VII and Henry VIII', *JHA*, 28 December 2021, pp. 1–22. This made headlines in several newspapers, reporting sensationally that this proved Richard III was behind the murder of the princes. For a response, see Joanna Laynesmith, 'Miles Forest and the Princes in the Tower', Research news and notes, *Bulletin*, March 2021, pp. 22–23. See note 46.

5 The only known account is a copy of the official confession of Perkin Warbeck, stating that from his arrival in the town of Cork in Ireland he was called 'Duke of York' by some English and Irish noblemen, who persuaded him against his will to adopt the persona of the second son of Edward IV, see note 7.

6 One of Henry's first claims that he was the 'son of a boatman' is in a private paper of instruction (Sheen, 10 August 1494) to 'Richmond, otherwise Clarenceux King of Arms' (Roger Machado, his confidential envoy to France): 'And it is notorious that the said garçon is of no consanguinity or kin to the late king Edward, but is a native of the town of Tournay, and son of a boatman, who is named Werbec': Frederic Madden, 'Documents Relating to Perkin Warbeck, With Remarks on his History', *Archaeologia*, Vol. 27, 1837, pp. 12 n.y. and 13.

7 The full text of the confession can be found in *GC*, p. xvii. Also, f.18v-19r (f.264v-265r), pp. 284–86; C.L. Kingsford, *Chronicles of London* (1905), pp. 219–22/BL, Cotton Vitellius MS. A XVI f.169r-170v. The original confession has not survived.

8 Diana M. Kleyn, *Richard of England* (2013), p. 2.

9 Translation from Caroline Halsted, *Richard III* (1844), Vol. 2, pp. 180–81 n. 3, where Halsted also notes that Sir Francis Bacon recorded the same reports. Thanks to Annette Carson.

10 Buc, p. 142, also p. 138: 'but some others … say that these young princes were embarked [in] a ship at Tower Wharf, and that they were conveyed from hence into the seas and … were safe on shore beyond the seas'.

11 Reygersbergh, *Dye Cronijck van Zeelandt* [*The Chronicle of Zeeland*] (1551) p. 121r: 'In the same year King Edward the fourth, with this name king of England died. And he left two sons and one daughter behind. And these rightful heirs

were expelled from England': objects.library.uu.nl/reader/index.php?obj=1874-214708&lan=en#page//91/43/30/91433052808069834501754765627324050519.jpg/mode/1up.

12 From a close contemporary copy of the proclamation, Griffith Collection, National Library of Wales, Carreglwyd Estate Archive, Series 1/695 (1496). Located/transcribed for TMPP by Dr Judith Ford (5.6.2021), who notes that many of his papers came 'into [Griffith's] hands during his residence in the Earl of Northampton's household [and] remained in [them] after [the earl's] death': Historical Manuscripts Commission, 5th Report, 1876, p. 406. Henry Howard, Earl of Northampton (d. 1614), was the great-grandson of Thomas Howard, 2nd Duke of Norfolk (d. 1524); the family possibly obtained copies of the proclamation through Thomas Howard's tenure in the north for Henry VII at the time (Judith Ford, 'Richard of England's Proclamation', *Bulletin*, March 2022, pp. 46–51). See Appendix 9.

13 For example, Buc, Kleyn (as above), Horace Walpole, Sir Clements Markham, Bertram Fields, Matthew Lewis, et al.

14 Trans. Nathalie Nijman-Bliekendaal, November 2020.

15 K.J.W. Peeneman, Rijksarchief in Gelderland (Gelderland Archive), 0510, various charters, various acquisitions: www.archieven.nl/nl/zoeken?mivast=0&mizig=210&miadt=37&micode=0510&milang=nl&miview=inv2#inv3t1. The Gelderland manuscript was added to the collection 'Various Acquisitions' of the former State Archive, Gelderland, which comprises acquisitions outside existing categories that are not substantial enough to be archived individually.

16 BL, Egerton MS. 616, f.003r. Trans. Dr Betty Knott (6.1.2019), see Appendix 4.

17 At first glance, the language of the narrative resembles Middle Low German, the written language of the Hanseatic merchants (1300–1500) then spoken in northern Germany and eastern Netherlands. Interestingly, the Gelderland manuscript is kept in Arnhem, one of the twenty-two Dutch Hanseatic cities in the eastern Netherlands area.

18 See Howard Books, Vol. 2, p. 426 for retrospective payments on 11 August detailing four outfits for humble children of the stables: 'The Stabill: Item to Rychard Thaylor for makyng of iiij chylder of the stabylles gownes, ij.s.' See note 59.

19 'Boene' is the northern French coastal town Boulogne-sur-Mer. The old (middle) Dutch name was Bonen/Beunen, derived from Latin *Bononia*.

20 'Bergen' is Bergen op Zoom, a small Dutch city near Antwerp, which belonged to the Duchy of Brabant during the Burgundian and Habsburg-Netherlands period. From the mid-fourteenth century it held two annual fairs where English cloth and wool were traded.

21 Horrox, *ODNB*. For Brampton being awarded £350 by King Richard on 25 July 1483, see *Beloved Cousyn*, pp. 98, 167 n. 83; CPR 1476–85, p. 366 (granted from customs and subsidies of the Port of London, Sandwich and Southampton). This vast sum was awarded to Brampton on the same day that Howard was made Admiral of England with 'certain specified powers', see note 56. See Howard Books, Vol. 2, p. 246 for Edward Brampton being indented with Howard on 26 February 1481 to the king's service (Scottish campaign)

by sea with the English fleet into Scotland. £350 = £320,000 today: www. nationalarchives.gov.uk/currency-converter/#currency-result

22 See note 24.

23 Maurice Fitzgerald, 9th Earl of Desmond (d. 1520) supported Perkin Warbeck/ Richard, Duke of York. He was imprisoned afterwards but pardoned by Henry VII on 22 August 1497. See 'The Earls of Desmond (continued)', *Kerry Archaeological Magazine*, Vol. 4, No. 17, Oct. 1916, p. 56; also Wikipedia.

24 Gerald Fitzgerald, 8th Earl of Kildare (*c.* 1456–1513), S.G. Ellis, *ODNB*. Aka 'Garret the Great' or 'the Great Earl', he openly supported the Yorkist claimant in 1487, and was later suspected of supporting Richard, Duke of York, as heir to the English throne. He was arrested and imprisoned in the Tower in November 1494, and returned to Ireland as Lord Deputy upon being freed in 1496.

25 Charles VIII (1470–98) was King of France from 1483 (age 13).

26 BNF, *Fonds Espagnol* 318, f.83, line 69. TMPP translation by Maria Leotta and Dr Betty Knott, 11.3.2020 and 10.2.2021: gallica.bnf.fr/ark:/12148/ btv1b52503046g/f326.item. The letter from Margaret of England, Duchess of Burgundy, etc., to the Queen of Spain, written in Dendermonde on 25 August 1493, in which she describes why she is convinced of the true identity of her royal nephew, Richard. See Appendix 4.

27 From mid-1493, Maximilian I, King of the Romans, took care of Richard, Duke of York, 'whom he firmly believed to be the son of King Edward IV of England'. Venice, 1496: *Calendar of State Papers Relating To English Affairs in the Archives of Venice, Vol. 1, 1202–1509*, ed. Rawdon Brown (1864), nr 665. Letter of the Venetian Ambassador Zacharia Contarini, written at the court of Maximilian, Nordlingen, Germany, on 6 January 1496. His conviction is evident in that 'Richard of England' was the only person allowed to escort Maximilian during his festive ride to church upon the blessing of his marriage on 16 March 1494 (Wroe, p. 152); *Regesta Imperii* online, *RI XIV*, 1, nr 478. Richard, Duke of York, also frequently stayed at the court of Margaret of York in Malines, 1493–94, spending a great deal of time with Maximilian's son and heir, Philip the Handsome.

28 For Albert, Duke of Saxony, see Chapters 15 and 17.

29 Engelbert II of Nassau (1451–1504), Count of Nassau and Vianden, Lord of Breda, Chamberlain to Maximilian and (later) his son, Philip the Handsome. A leading military leader, Engelbert was made President of the Grand Council (1494) and Stadtholder General (1496, 1501–03).

30 Two highly respected noblemen at the courts of Maximilian and Philip lent enormous sums to Richard of England: (1) Albert of Saxony, Charter '*Dat 4 die Octobris 1493*', signed by 'Richard of England' and bearing his royal seal and monogram, also signed by 'Rb Clyfford' and 'Wyllelm Barley', with their respective seals (SHA (Dresden), 10001, Altere Urkunden, Nr 9005, see: Appendix 6, images 13a, 13b); (2) Engelbert II of Nassau: Charter dated 9 March 1494 (1495, New Style), signed by 'Richard d'Engleterre, Duc de York' (HHSA, 3036, *Koninklijk Huis Archief* [Royal House Archive], Inv. A2, Nr. 468). Note that Engelbert's loan has previously been attributed incorrectly as a payment to Richard III instead of 'Richard of England', Duke of York. Special

thanks to Zoë Maula. See also Steven Thiry, 'Counterfeited Jewels Make the True Mistruste', *De constructie van een "vorstelijk imago"*: *Perkin Warbeck in de Nederlanden en het Heilige Roomse Rijk'*, *Tijdschrift voor Geschiedenis*, 124e jaargang, 2011, p. 165 n. 47.

31 *Divisie Chronicle*, f.416r. On 'The White Rose' traversing Holland, April–May–June 1495, see Chapter 15; also *Mythology*, pp. 133–34.

32 *Divisie Chronicle*, f.427r: *'daer hi int openbaer gerecht wert mitten swaerde* [where he was publicly justiced with the sword]'. In England, this term could mean 'killed deliberately'.

33 *Royal Funerals*, pp. 16, 35; also *Harley 433*, Vol. 1, pp. xxiii n. 99, xliv (for Edward IV); *Harley 433*, Vol. 3, p. 9 (for Edward V).

34 CPR 1476–85, pp. 159, 342. Also p. 540 for Tyrwhite as Esquire of the Body to Richard III; *Heralds' Memoir*, p. 120, for Tyrwhite being knighted on 16 June 1487 after Stoke Field.

35 André, in Gairdner (ed.), *Memorials of King Henry the Seventh* (1858, repr. 1966), pp. 65, 66. For the cited text (trans. from Latin), see Ian Arthurson, *The Perkin Warbeck Conspiracy, 1491–1499* (1994), p. 59.

36 *Mancini*, pp. 65, 108 n. 144.

37 *GC*, p. 234.

38 *Beloved Cousyn*, pp. 98 and 167 n. 88. From TNA, C81/1392 No.1: Catalogue for the NPG Exhibition 1973, p. 98. Also see *Road to Bosworth*, p. 125 n. 99 and *Maligned King*, pp. 153–55.

39 CPR 1476–85, p. 122; *Coronation*, p. 371. For Halneth Mauleverer (Malyverer) as Esquire of the Body to Richard III, see CPR 1476–85, pp. 502, 503.

40 Kingsford/Vitellius A XVI, 1495, p. 206; also *GC*, p. 259. For the Mauleverer family, see Chapter 17.

41 André, p. 62. Also see note 138.

42 *GC*, p. 260.

43 TNA, PRO B 11 11 381, transcription thanks to Heather Falvey, *Surtees Society*, Vol. 53, p. 182; Robert Waters, *Genealogical Memoirs of the Extinct Family of Chester of Chicheley their Ancestors and Descendants* (1878), Vol. 1, p. 205. For William as uncle to Halneth and Thomas, see 'Visitations of the North *c.* 1480–1500', *Surtees Society*, III, 1930, pp. 71–72, Ashmole 831, f.39r, v. For William Mauleverer and Richard III, see Keith Dockray, 'Richard III and the Yorkshire Gentry', *Richard III: Loyalty, Lordship and Law* (1986), pp. 46–68 (p. 61).

44 *Harley 433*, Vol. 1, p. 153; also, CPR 1476–85, p. 386. For Poche as 'Yoman … of the parish of St. Mary, Berking (Barking), London', see CFR 1471–85, p. 310. William Poche of Barking, London, is not to be confused with Sir William Pecche of Kent (d. 1488): CFR 1485–1509, p. 310.

45 Poche being 'keeper of the beds and other harness within the Tower of London' may explain the princes allegedly 'smothered between two feather beds': T.F. Dibdin (ed.), *The Pastime of People, Or, The Chronicles of Divers Realms, and Most Especially of the Realm of England (1529) by John Rastell (d. 1536)* (1811), p. 292, revealingrichardiii.com/tyrells-confession.html. Also see *More*, p. 88, and Buc, p. 138. For the earliest account of the smothering between two quilts/beds, see *Molinet*, Vol. 2, pp. 402, 403.

46 Thornton, 'More on a Murder', see note 4. The findings were used to accuse Forest as undoubted murderer (owing to presence of Forest's two sons at Henry VIII's court under Wolsey), but actually indicate the exact opposite, with key investigative enquiry questions unaddressed: see Chapter 17.

47 Johan Huizinga, *Erasmus*, 12th edn (2017), pp. 35, 36.

48 Henry of Glymes (1449–1502) was son of John II of Glymes (1417–94), Lord of Bergen op Zoom and older brother of John III of Glymes. Henry was Bishop of Cambrai 1480–1502. In 1479, Margaret of York appointed him Court Chaplain. See Cools, *Mannen met Macht*, *op. cit.*, p. 308, and this book, Chapters 12 and 13.

49 Desiderius Erasmus, *The Correspondence of Erasmus, Letters 1–141*, Vol. 1, Letters 33, 37, 39, 41, 42.

50 Huizinga, pp. 47–56. Erasmus' first stay in England was early summer 1499 to early January 1500. On 23 November 1499, Perkin Warbeck was executed at Tyburn, London. At his execution, 'Warbeck's' former written confession was '*shewid*' (shown) to the crowd: *GC*, p. 291. It is usually asserted that he 'spoke' his confession, so there is an important distinction to be made here: Middle English '*schewin*' is 'to look, look at, exhibit, display'. '*Shew*' was still in use in the early twentieth century.

51 CPR 1461–67, p. 47, and CPR 1476–85, pp. 365, 460. Keeper of the Lions and Leopards at the Tower was Sir Ralph Hastings, which was granted under Edward IV and confirmed by Richard III on 10 August 1483. For his general pardon on 18 August 1483, see CPR 1476–85, p. 365. A similar role, 'Keeper of the Lions, Lionesses and Leopards', was granted for life to Robert Brackenbury on 10 March 1484. See CPR 1476–85, p. 405 (likely due to Ralph being located at Guînes Castle, Calais). For Hastings' connection to support for Richard of England, see Wroe, pp. 189, 252.

52 *Beloved Cousyn*, pp. 100 and 168 n. 99. Were the four men deliberately executed on 5 August at Tower Hill (rather than Tyburn) as a clear warning to those working within the Tower against further plots? And does the place of execution also imply both boys had now left the Tower? In the Gelderland Manuscript, Richard, Duke of York, mentions no executions.

53 See H.M Office of Works, Tower of London Plan: (2747), 105NN/14 I (*c.* 1937–38), thanks to Matt Oliver. At this time, Howard's London home was located in Stepney, at the riverside hamlet of Ratcliffe, now Limehouse. See Howard Books, p. xxii (thanks to Jean Clare-Tigue). For Howard and a house called La Toure (the Tower) in London, see Anne Crawford, *Yorkist Lord* (2010), pp. 111–12, also Chapter 6. Howard may also have had access to the previous (Mowbray) Duke of Norfolk's home on the Thames at Broken Wharf, though Crawford states that Howard did not change his London address when he became a peer (p. xxii).

54 Anne Crawford, *The Career of John Howard, Duke of Norfolk 1420–1485*: core. ac.uk/download/pdf/78865333.pdf. Also, Howard Books, pp. xxvi–xxix.

55 See note 38.

56 CPR 1476–85, p. 363. See note 21.

57 Howard Books, Vol. 2, p. 423.

58 For Howard's letter to his son Thomas, Earl of Surrey, on 7 August: Howard Books, Vol. 2, p. 420. See note 107.

59 'Outfits for humble children', see Howard Books and note 18.

60 Searches for Henry and Thomas Percy have yielded no results in the archives of Alnwick Castle or Petworth House and the Leconfield Estate, also Arundel Castle and Castle Howard: thanks to Ralph Percy, Duke of Northumberland, Christopher Hunwick, Max Percy, Lord Egremont, and Alison McCann, who also assisted with searches for Peter Percy (see note 69). Thanks also to Diana Percy, Craig Irving, John Martin Robinson, Christopher Ridgway; and to Gabriel Damaszk for the search of the Raby Castle archives.

61 Howard Books, Vol. 2, p. 471. For more on the brothers see Howard Books, pp. xv, xvii, xxi, xxiv and xl.

62 W.E. Hampton, 'Sir Robert Percy and Joyce his wife', *Crown and People*, pp. 184–94 (family tree on pp. 190–91).

63 For example, Anne Percy (Fitzallen) was companion for ten years to Katherine Gordon, Richard of York's wife. See Wendy E.A. Moorhen, 'Four Weddings and a Conspiracy: The Life and Times and Loves of Lady Katherine Gordon, Part 2', *Ricardian*, Vol. 12, No. 157, June 2002, p. 459.

64 Thanks to Marie Barnfield for the Percy of Scotton pedigree: 'Visitations of the North' *c.* 1485, p. 68; MS Ashmole 831, f.38r; MS Dodsworth 81, p. 159. Sir Robert Percy may have had uncles named Richard and Thomas (Thomas is described as a 'Presbiter', priest); or perhaps they were Robert's younger brothers. No one in his family named Henry can be located for this period. See also note 60. Thanks to genealogist Carol Ann Kerry-Green for searches of Northallerton, Leeds, Beverley and Hull archives, also Nick Dexter at Kew.

65 Francis Lovell became Lord of Bedale, North Yorkshire, in 1474, upon the death of his paternal grandmother, Alice Lovell (Deincourt): Ross, *Richard III*, p. 49. For the Barony of Bedale, see IPM of Alice Lovell (Deincourt) in John Caley (ed.), *Calendarium Inquisitionum Post Mortem Sive Escaetarum* (1828), Vol. IV, p. 365 (thanks to Marie Barnfield). Also: archive.org/details/dli. granth.74587/page/374/mode/2up

66 Philippa Langley, TMPP Research Report, 7.7.2021. The pedigree of the Peirse family of Bedale (Bedall) is from *The Visitation of London* (1634), p. 149: freepages.rootsweb.com/~enzedders/history/peirselondon.jpg. Thomas' father is recorded as 'Peter Peirse Standart Bearer to King Richard the third at Bosworth field where he lost a legge but liued many yeres after'. Beneath this is Peter's son, 'Thomas Peirse of Bedall', and beneath this is Thomas' son, 'Marmaduke Peirse of Bedall in Com. York and of Clineland [Cleveland]'. It seems that by the mid-eighteenth century the name was pronounced 'Pierce', see Durham County Record Office, Ref. D/X 487/1/165 (1759), records transferred from Darlington Library (part 3).

67 NYCRO, ZBA 17/1/1 f.3, Bedale, Court of Francis Lovell, 15 April 1483: '*Eidem arabiliem eadem iii acram? // Thome/Henricus Peirs ibidem// Reddendo pro acram 30s 4d // sua soluit pro Martinmas* [The same arable land of three acres of the aforesaid Thomas/Henry Peirs. Rent for the acres at 30s 4d he pays for Martinmas].' N.B. f.3r also mentions '*Pactus inter Pearsy et R(ichar)di // Qui Ed(wardi?)*' – an agreement between a 'Pearsy' (Percy) and 'Richard', 'who

Edward(?) … [MS damaged] … 16d' [the '16d' reference appears immediately
above the name 'Pearsy']; seems to form the first part of Folio 3.' Thanks to
Dr Christopher Tinmouth for translation and transcription, TMPP Research
Report, 20.12.2021.

68 For the ducal coronet in the Peirse family pedigree, see *Visitation of London*,
p. 149; John William Clay, *Dugdale's Visitation of Yorkshire, with Additions* (1666)
(1899), Vol. 3, p. 35. For Marmaduke's eldest son, see Peirse family pedigree
for Hutton Bonville Parish, Allertonshire, North Yorkshire in *Topographer
and Genealogist* (1846), Vol. 1, pp. 509–11 (p. 510): Foundation for Medieval
Genealogy (FMG), Ref. No.: S-1618.

69 For Peter Percy: acknowledgements as note 60; also, thanks to Christopher
Hunwick for raising Picot Percy of Bolton Percy, North Yorkshire. Picot seems
to have had descendants in the thirteenth and fourteenth centuries named
Peter Percy (of Bolton Percy): Charles Travis Clay (ed.), *Early Yorkshire Charters*
(1963), Vol. 11, 'The Percy Fee', pp. 7–8, 104–18. Related searches have revealed
a fourteenth-century Peter Percy of Dunsley, North Yorkshire. Thanks to
NYCRO for the genealogical archive papers of the Beresford-Peirse family of
Bedale, including ZBA 5, 17, 20.

70 The name Marmaduke, particularly common in Yorkshire in the Middle
Ages, means 'servant/devotee' of Madoc. It may refer to the Irish St Madoc,
or alternatively, the legendary Welsh (bastard) Prince Madoc. The earliest
textual reference to his legend attributes the discovery of America to Madoc
in 1170 and stems from late-fifteenth-century England in a poem written
by Meredudd Ap Rhys (*c.* 1420–*c.* 1485), a well-known poet in his lifetime:
biography.wales/article/s-MERE-APR-1450. There seems to be evidence
that the discovery of America (by Welshmen) must have come in the year
1477, during the reign of Edward IV, fifteen years before Columbus: Arthur
Davies, 'Prince Madoc and the Discovery of America in 1477', *The Geographical
Journal*, Vol. 150, No. 3, November 1984, pp. 363–72. Presumably, 'the
legend of Madoc' gained popularity owing to onset of the era of great
overseas voyages and discoveries, quite probably the (Welsh) Tudors used the
Madoc story as propaganda, challenging Spanish/Portuguese claims to the
New World. Revival of the name Marmaduke may have resulted. See www.
bangor.ac.uk/oceansciences/about/facilities/madog/prince_madog.php.en. For
the story of Madoc, see en.m.wikipedia.org/wiki/Madoc. For the name
Marmaduke associated with Madoc from Saint Máedóc, see en.wikipedia.org/
wiki/M%C3%A1ed%C3%B3c_of_Ferns.

71 Family Search website: www.familysearch.org/search/record/results?q.
anyDate.from=1471&q.anyPlace=Lazenby&q.surname=Peirse

72 Sir Walter Besant, *Medieval London* (1906), Chapter 20, 'St Katherine's By The
Tower', pp. 334–41; thanks to Jean Clare-Tighe.

73 For Howard's career at sea/ships/shipping interests, see Howard Books,
pp. xxii–xxv, xxvi. The description of the vessel as a 'small and narrow
ship' could indicate one that is carvel-built. By the mid-fifteenth century,
shipwrights had moved to carvel-built vessels, but some may still have been
built clinker style according to local tradition. Carvel-built should not be
confused with the caravel, a small, highly manoeuvrable sailing ship developed

in the fifteenth century by the Portuguese. Coastal ships such as a balinger and barge were seagoing vessels. A dogger was a smaller, two-masted vessel and a crayer was usually a medium-to-large, single-masted vessel; both were used for fishing and trading. The foregoing may eliminate other vessel types from investigation and potentially indicate ownership. Thanks for the advice on medieval vessels to Dr Craig Lambert, Research Fellow at Southampton University Marine Institute and Assoc. Professor in Maritime History, and his medieval shipping database with information on shipping routes from England to the continent and information on English ports including the Port of London. Source: Jean Clare-Tighe, TMPP lead researcher on shipping.

74 Crawford, pp. 180, 181.

75 Maxime F. de Montrond, Notre-Dame de Boulogne-sur-Mer, son pèlerinages et ses fêtes (1887).

76 C.S.L. Davies, 'Richard III, la Bretagne et Henry Tudor (1483–1485)', *Annales de Bretagne et des pays de l'Ouest*, Vol. 102, No. 4, 1995, p. 34.

77 In the fifteenth century, Tournai had a thriving cloth trade and was a major supplier of tapestries. It was a so-called 'free city', surrounded by the powerful Burgundian counties Hainault and Flanders, but under the jurisdiction of the French kings.

78 *Rot. Parl.*, vi, p. 276; CPR 1485–94, pp. 133–34.

79 Campbell, Vol. 1, pp. 208, 392. The payment for Howard (as Earl of Surrey) for his imprisonment in the Tower is dated 9 December 1485, and 8 March 1486 for a special pardon enabling his detention in any prison at the Crown's pleasure. Sir Robert Percy of Scotton died with King Richard at Bosworth (*Memorials*, 'Sir Robert Percy', pp. 185, 193 n. 16). His son (also Robert) fought for King Edward at the Battle of Stoke (Bennett, p. 125).

80 David Johnson, 'Reluctant Groom', *Bulletin*, March 2020, pp. 37–41, reveals Henry VII did not legitimise Elizabeth of York until the second session of Parliament on 23 January 1486, after their marriage on the 18th: www.reveal-ingrichardiii.com/the-pre-contract.html

81 The text in the 'official' confession (note 7) reads: 'And after this the said Berlo set me w a merchaunt in Middelburgh to service w whom I dwelled from Christmas unto Easter; and than I went into Portyngale in the company of Sir Edward Bramptons wif in a ship which was called the Quenes ship.'

82 Wroe (p. 19) indicates date of the journey to Portugal seems to be sometime after Easter 1487.

83 According to Zeeland chronicler, Reygersbergh, the Yorkist fleet left for Ireland from Arnemuiden on 15 May 1487. See Chapter 12 and note 2. In the fifteenth and sixteenth centuries, Arnemuiden was a small but important harbour city and outer port of Middelburg. Near the same time and place, 'Richard, Duke of York' left for Portugal (see note 82). For the involvement of the city and lords of Bergen op Zoom in the first Yorkist invasion, see Chapter 13.

84 Zoë Maula, TMPP Research Report, 14.12.2020. See Appendix 7: Maximilian's letter of late 1493, regarding 'three natural marks which he [York] has on his body, and which cannot be counterfeited', i.e., 'his mouth, one of his eyes and a mark he has on his thigh'. Also, Appendix 4: Margaret's letter to

Isabella of Spain regarding York's marks (August 1493). Several other sources also mention the striking body features of Richard of York, among others, the Setúbal Testimonies of 25 April 1496 (Wroe, Appendix, p. 525). Another contemporary source mentions a deviant (left) eye. In a letter to the Duke of Milan on 21 October 1497, the Milanese Ambassador reports, 'his left eye rather lacks lustre' (Milan, 1497, no. 548 in Allen B. Hinds (ed.), *Calendar of State Papers & Manuscripts in Archives & Collections of Milan 1385–1618* (1912), pp. 310–14, www.british-history-ac.uk/cal-statepapers/milan/1385-1618

85 See Chapter 2.

86 State Archives Courtrai: 'Collection Jacques Goethals-Vercruysse', Manuscripts, inv. 111, f.188v-189r.

87 Wroe, pp. 394–97.

88 Wroe, p. 24, pp. 525–58, Appendix (see note 84).

89 Wroe, p. 47: '... *Vimos alcar Branca Rosa, por Rey muytos dos Ingleses* ... [We saw the White Rose, acclaimed as King by many of the English, and it was a wonderful thing that in days, not in months, he gathered people of the highest birth to him. He called himself their natural King, and gave the King battle on the field, but he was defeated and sentenced to hanging, because they thought he was not such a man].' Poem from Resende, *Miscêlanea.*

90 Wroe, p. 44 (her p. 43 timeline for Edward Woodville's visit to Portugal should read 1486–87).

91 *Journals of Roger Machado, Embassy to Spain and Portugal, AD 1488* in Gairdner, *Memorials Henry VII, op. cit.* Wroe (p. 44) discovered that Machado, a Portuguese, was sent to Portugal 'for certain causes', apparently alone, in August 1489, before joining the official delegation that left England in December 1489, seemingly to spy. Gemma L. Watson, who did extensive research on Machado, regards him as an elusive and largely unexplored character in English history, best known as Henry VII's Richmond King of Arms. She writes that because of his past, heralds and scholars have generally assumed he came to England with Tudor in 1485, but closer inspection of English sources reveals that from 1471–83 Machado was living in England and serving as Leicester Herald for Edward IV, Edward V and Richard III ('Roger Machado, Perkin Warbeck and Heraldic Espionage', *The Coat of Arms*, 3rd Series, 10, 2014, pp. 51–68).

92 *Universidada de Lisboa, Chronology Calamities – PWR Portugal, 1488/1489:* Outbreak of plague in Lisbon, 1491: Plague throughout Portugal: pwr-portugal.ics.ul.pt/wp-content/uploads/Chronology_of_Calamaties.pdf

93 The 'official' confession (note 7) reads: 'And than I put my silf in service w.a. Breton called Pregent Meno, the which brought me w hym into Ireland.'

94 For identity: Richard of England's Proclamation of September 1496 – see Appendix 9 and note 102.

95 Wroe, pp. 228, 229.

96 Ferns Diocesan Archive, Wexfordiana, Volume 7: 'Extracts from Calendar of Memoranda Rolls of the Exchequer', digital page 22 of 493. Specific entry records: – 20 Edward IV – 'Sir Jac. Kettyng, prior of the Hospital of St John of Jerusalem in Ireland appointed to be head constable of Dublin castle. Witnes Ric Salop [Shrewsbury] Duke of York at Dublin 22 Dec 19 year'. Prior

James Keating (d.a. 1495) supported both Yorkist invasions (1487 and 1495). He was a close supporter of Richard, Duke of York, from the very start of the conspiracy and firmly committed to the Yorkist cause. See Wroe, pp. 185, 231.

97   See notes 26 and 84. Also Appendices 4 and 7.

98   R.C.H. Lesaffer, 'The three peace treaties of 1492–1493', in H. Duchhardt & M. Peters (eds), *Kalkül-Transfer-Symbol: Europäische Friedensverträge der Vormoderne, Institut für Europäische Geschichte Mainz* (2006), p. 51.

99   See letter from Margaret of England to Queen Isabella of Spain, written in Dendermonde, 25 August 1493, note 26. See also Appendix 4.

100 Regarding the mention of the killing of the 'Prince of Wales' (Edward IV's elder son) in the Dendermonde letter, Matthew Lewis argues that if Richard, Duke of York, were to launch his assault on the throne as Edward IV's younger son, he would have to explain why it was not his elder brother making the bid. Lewis asserts that Margaret's pressing concern was to present Richard as the legitimate heir of the house of York, hence the senior heir must be represented as already dead. He offers the possibility that neither boy was murdered, but they were separated to ensure their safety and minimise their potential to be figureheads for rebellion until Richard III's reign was secure, with each boy maybe given the story that the other was killed but that he was spared in order to frighten him into obeying the requirement of silence. Lewis derives another interpretation from the Dendermonde letter that possibly Edward V died or was captured at Stoke Field in 1487, but Margaret and Richard, Duke of York, wanted to divert attention from the failed first Yorkist revolt: Lewis, *The Survival of the Princes in the Tower, Murder, Mystery and Myth* (2017), pp. 125–27. See also *Maligned King* (2008), Chapter 9, esp. pp. 172–75.

101 Weightman, pp. 151–53.

102 Judith Ford, 'The King's Speech: Richard of England's Proclamation', *Bulletin*, March 2022, pp. 48–53: www.revealingrichardiii.com/two-pretenders.html#kings-speech Appendix 9.

103 Gairdner, *Memorials Henry VII, op. cit.*, Appendix A, pp. 393–99: Lambeth Palace Library CM VI/31. Trans. for TMPP, thanks to Dr Shelagh Sneddon, 1.11.22. For Richard III's proclamation of 1485, see *Road to Bosworth*, pp. 208–10. For the 1484 proclamation, which included Dorset's name, see *Maligned King*, pp. 284, 286.

104 Wroe, p. 208. Maximilian described these as 'surreptitious and frivolous'. See Appendix 8.

105 Wroe, p. 208, Appendix: 'Miscellaneous 1495', *Calendar of State Papers Relating To English Affairs in the Archives of Venice, Volume 4, 1527–1533*, ed. Rawdon Brown (1871), pp. 482–83: www.british-history.ac.uk/cal-state-papers/venice/vol4/pp482-483. See Appendix 8.

106 Howard Books, Vol. 2, p. 417. Accounts dated this day (22 July) record payment for a gift of venison from Sir John Everingham to Howard, the only time Everingham is mentioned in the Howard Books.

107 For Howard's letter to his son, Thomas, Earl of Surrey, on 7 August, see Howard Books, Vol. 2, p. 420. The words 'A leter' are written in Howard's own hand, which could indicate its importance. Thomas was with King Richard at Warwick on the royal progress.

108 Howard Books, Vol. 2, p. 421.

109 CPR 1476–85, p. 363. Howard was made Admiral of England, Ireland and Aquitaine with 'certain specified powers and the accustomed fees'. This seems to confirm a plan to get the boys out by ship. Thanks to David Johnson for his analysis of the wording of the grant of High Admiral of England from 1461–85, including that of Richard, Earl of Warwick, on 2 January 1471: CPR 1467–77, p. 233 (23.6.21).

110 'Quellen Und Darstellungen Zur Hansischen Geschichte', Hanseatic History Association, founded in 1871, Vol. 74, Part III, Number 6, pp. i, viii–xi, 64. Also Stuart Jenks, The London Customs Accounts (2016), Part III, 'York 1461–85', pp. vii–140. Thanks to Jean Clare-Tighe.

111 CFR 1471–85, p. 264. This may have been a joint appointment with Robert Fitzherbert (23 July 1483). Thanks to Jean Clare-Tighe.

112 Harley 433, Vol. 3, p. 59. See note 124. Thanks to Sharon Lock (5.1.2018).

113 Howard Books, Vol. 1, p. 368; Vol. 2, pp. 384, 396, 401, 419. For Edward Neville, see Vol. 1, pp. xv, 218. Transcription of George Neville, Lord Abergavenney's will by Dr Judith Ford, 5.8.2021, who notes: Neville asks Archbishop Morton to be the supervisor of the document. Will most notable for conveying Neville's status as a member of the old nobility; he asks, for example, that his will be fulfilled for the sake of his soul and for 'the honor of [his] blood'. Neville had six surviving sons and died c. July 1492.

114 Howard Books, Vol. 1, pp. 184, 245, 471, 472; Vol. 2, p. 283. Jean Clare-Tighe, TMPP Research Report, 9.1.2022.

115 Beloved Cousyn, pp. 98, 167 n. 83: CPR 1476–85, p. 366, see note 21. On this day, a 'Thomas Brampton' is appointed to the Port of Lenne: CPR 1476–85, p. 403. Also, a Robert Mannyng is appointed by the king to provide workmen for the Palace of Westminster and Tower of London: Beloved Cousyn, pp. 98, 167 n. 82: CPR 1476–85, pp. 365. Had both royal palaces received damage during the abduction attempt? The Treasury was already so depleted by recent Woodville activities that Gloucester was providing subsidy from his own revenues.

116 Howard Books, Vol. 2, p. 246, item for 26 February 1481 reads: 'The xxth yere of the king (Ed. The iiijth) – Edward Brampton indented with Lord Howard to do the king servisse on the see with xl. men wel harnessed for xvj wekes.'

117 CPR 1476–85, p. 481.

118 Roth, 'Perkin Warbeck', p. 155.

119 In 'The list and index of Warrants for Issues 1399–1485' from TNA, PRO (1964), Christopher Colyns and John Howard are mentioned jointly in connection with operations against piracy (p. 364). Separate specific reference to Colyns in 'naval operations against rebels and pirates in 1483' (p. 360) may well refer to orders by the Protectorate Council (conducted by Brampton, 14 May 1483) to recall the English fleet taken to sea by Sir Edward Woodville: Harley 433, Vol. 3, p. 2: 'xiiii Maij, Item a lettre to Edward Brampton, John Wellis, and Thomas Grey, to go to the see with shippes to take Ser Edward Wodevile'.

120 Buc, p. cxxvii.

121 Buc also records what may have been another long imprisonment – that of Katherine de la Pole, sister of John, Earl of Lincoln: pp. 212, 345; see also Chapter 16.

122 Raphael Holinshed, *The Chronicles of England, Scotland and Ireland* (1577), Vol. 2, p. 1405. Thanks to Michael Alan Marshall for the original source (6.7.15).

123 *Harley 433*, Vol. 3, p. 59. Thanks to Sharon Lock (5.1.2018).

124 *Ibid.*, p. 62, 11 March 1484. Thanks to Sharon Lock (5.1.2018).

125 An entry in the Malines City Archives shows Thomas Langton, Bishop of Salisbury ('*bisschop van Salebry*') was in Malines in 1486 receiving '4 stopen whine' given at the Saint Rombout and/or Holy Sacraments Procession: City Account Mechelen (Malines), 1 November 1485–1 November 1486. This concerns the so-called 'doubles' (contemporary copies of the Malines City Account) kept in the Royal Archives Belgium, Brussels – online: inv.nr V132, 41271, f.154v. On the same folio, Margaret of York is also mentioned as recipient of a gift of wine. Nathalie Nijman-Bliekendaal, TMPP Research Report, 15.12.2020.

126 In 1494, Thomas Langton, Bishop of Winchester, was part of a cell centered on John Kendal, Prior of the Order of the Knights of St John of Jerusalem in England, who secretly supported the claims of Richard, Duke of York: Wroe, p. 185; see also D.P. Wright (ed.), 'The Register of Thomas Langton, Bishop of Salisbury 1485–1493', *Canterbury and York Society* (1985), p. xiii.

127 *Molinet*, Chapter 101, p. 409. Significantly, no pro-Tudor history records these early post-Bosworth proclamations: Vergil, Hall, Holinshed, Grafton, More, et al. Also, see Langley, 'Part 1. Fate of the Sons of King Edward IV', *Bulletin* (March 2020), p. 45.

128 CPR 1485–94, p. 127, 16 August 1486.

129 Wroe, pp. 139, 549; TNA: PRO E405/79, mem. iv; Peter Camilletti: TMPP Research Report, 16.6.2017, p. 3. Thomas Lyneham, Richard III's former lawyer, undertook the investigation.

130 *Rot. Parl.*, vi, p. 492.

131 For Simon Digby as Lieutenant of the Tower, see Birmingham Library Archives, MS 3888/A647, 23 December 1496, from letters patent granting Digby the manor of Coleshill in Warwickshire. See also Wroe, pp. 220, 466 (incorrectly called Constable of the Tower: Constable at this time [1485–1513] was John de Vere, Earl of Oxford). See Wroe, p. 559: TNA:PRO KB/9/78, litigation of 22 August 1493–21 August 1495 and Thomas Bagnall statement with 'Master Digby being present'. Kingsford, *op. cit.*, pp. 204, 227 for 'M. Dygby', meaning 'Master' Digby (p. 331 for Hall's description of Sir John Digby in this role, which seems mistaken, as Sir John would not be 'Master' but 'Sir' or 'knight'). Kingsford, p. 227 for M. Dygby also described as 'Marshall of the Tour', perhaps where the confusion with Constable arose. Simon Digby's responsibility was day-to-day activity in the Tower, or possibly both Digby brothers (Simon and John) had roles at the Tower.

132 Wroe, pp. 466, 469, 478, 480, 488 (sources, pp. 584–85).

133 CPR 1494–1509, p. 131. Sir John Digby (d. 1533) was knighted 16 June 1487 by Henry VII after Stoke Field: *Heralds' Memoir*, p. 119; Bennett, p. 129.

134 Birmingham Library Archives, MS 3888/A 757, 27 October 1542, 'Covenant between Reynolde [Reginald] Dygby of Coleshill co. Warwick, esq, [Simon Digby's son and heir] and John Dygby of Kettleby co. Leics, esq, [Reginald's son and heir] re payment of annual rent of 20 marks from issues of Manor of Bedale, co. York'. Thanks to Bill Hare of Bedale for the source. The Digby family genealogy/pedigree can be found in John Burke, *A Genealogical and Heraldic History of Commoners of Great Britain and Ireland* (1838), Vol. 4, pp. 461–62.

135 For the death of Everard Digby (1410–61) of Tilton and Drystoke (Stoke Dry), Leicestershire, and three of his (Tilton) brothers at Towton, see John Wilkes, *Encyclopaedia Londinensis* (1811), Vol. 9, p. 535. For the death of 'Everard Dykby late of Stokedry in the shire of Rutland Squire' at Towton, see *Rot. Parl.*, v, pp. 476–78. For the death of Rowland Digby at the Battle of Sandal (1460), see Alex Leadman, *Battles Fought in Yorkshire* (1891), p. 88. With thanks to Louise Whittaker of the Battlefields Trust.

136 In all awards, Simon Digby is described as 'esquire' or 'squire', see note 131, also CPR 1476–85, p. 125; *Harley 433*, Vol. 3, p. 196; *Rot. Parl.*, vi, p. 361; CPR 1494–1509, p. 44.

137 'A History of the County of York North Riding' (1914), Vol. 1, 'Bedale Parish', pp. 291–301: www.british-history.ac.uk/vch/yorks/north/vol1/pp291-301. For the Digby family pedigree, see John Nichols, *The History and Antiquities of the County of Leicester*, Vol. II.i, (1795) p. 261. The uprising aimed to place the Catholic monarch, Mary, Queen of Scots, on the English throne.

138 *Vergil-2*, pp. 73, 77, 83, 109, 117–19; Buc, pp. 161–62. Buc was in no doubt that Perkin Warbeck was the younger son of King Edward IV. For Richard Grafton's confirmation of the pretender as the younger son of King Edward, see p. 162. Buc records: 'Richard Grafton affirmeth this. In Flanders, saith he and most of all, here in England, it was received for an undoubted truth, not only of the people but also of the nobles, that Perkin was the son of King Edward IV. And they all swore and affirmed this to be true.' For Vergil's statement about nobles 'believing Peter to be Edward's son Richard', see *Vergil-2*, p. 67. Among the nobles arrested at Henry's court were Sir William Stanley★, John Radcliffe, Lord Fitzwalter★, Sir Simon Mountford★, Sir Thomas Thwaites, William Daubeney★, Robert Ratcliffe★, Richard Lacy, Sir George Neville, Sir John Taylor, Sir Thomas Challoner, Thomas Bagnol, Henry VII's Sergeant Ferior★ and Elizabeth of York's Yeoman, Edwards★, Corbet★, Sir Quentin Betts★ and Gage★, plus 200 more. Those marked with asterisks were executed along with 200–300 others: Kingsford, *op. cit.*, pp. 203–07, 227–28, plus several Dutchmen, pp. 206–07. Those arrested were condemned for treason, although priests, priors, provincials and deans of the Church escaped execution as men of the cloth. For the execution of Henry's Serjeant Ferior and Elizabeth of York's Yeoman (Edwards), see *GC*, pp. 283–84. For Edward IV's bow-maker, Thomas Mashborwth (Mashbourth/Marsburgh), who was executed a few days before Richard of England, see *GC*, p. 291; *Chronicles of London*, p. 227; Wroe, p. 177.

139 Chapter 12.

15. The Journey of the White Rose to the Island of Texel, April–July 1495

1 Analysis of new archival sources discovered in the Low Countries by the Dutch Research Group in 2017.

2 For the will signed in Malines, 24 January 1495, see HHSA AUR 1495 I 24. He styles himself 'We, Richard, by the grace of God, King of England and France'. Full text in D.M. Kleyn, *Richard of England*, Appendix III, p. 236. A royal seal was originally attached, which is now lost. It is described in *Codex Diplomaticus*, Vol. IV (Frankfurt & Leipzig 1758), p. 505: *inscriptio: SECRETVM SIGILLVM RICARDI QVARTI* [Richard IV] *REGIS ANGLIE et Francie et Domini Hibernie ...*

3 Among others: Kingsford, *Chronicles of London*/Vitellius, pp. 205–07; *Vergil-2*, pp. 81–83; *Molinet*, Vol. 5, pp. 50–52; Bacon, *Henry the Seventh* (Lockyer, ed.), pp. 152–53; Gairdner, *Richard III*, pp. 359, 360.

4 Three modern authors who undertook detailed/extensive research into Richard/Perkin mention Vlissingen or Zeeland as the fleet's port of departure: Arthurson, *The Perkin Warbeck Conspiracy*, p. 110; Nathen Amin, *Henry VII and the Tudor Pretenders* (2020), p. 204; Ann Wroe, p. 236.

5 *Regesta* (RI OPAC), 1 April 1495, *RI XIV*, 1, nr 1482. Correspondence between Maximilian and Albert of Saxony shows the latter in Zeeland around 26 March 1495 (*phintztag nach dem Sonntag 'Oculi'*), probably overseeing the fleet's imminent departure: SHA, 10024 *Geheimer Rat* (Geheimes Archiv) Loc. 08497/02, *König Maximilians I schreiben an Herzog Albrecht zu Sachsen, kaiserlichen Majestät statthalter (in den Niederlanden)*, letter nr 73. Two other contemporary sources show York's servants and soldiers present in Zeeland, April/May 1495: *Bronnen voor de geschiedenis der dagvaarten van de Staten van Zeeland 1318–1572*, nr 1287b: resources.huygens.knaw.nl/retroboeken/dagvaarten_zeeland/#page= 210&accessor=toc&accessor_href=http%3A%2F%2Fresources.huygens.knaw. nl%2Fretroboeken%2Fdagvaarten_zeeland%2Ftoc%2Findex_html%3Fpage %3D0%26source%3D1%26id%3Dtoc&source=2. See also J.H. de Stopelaar, *Inventaris van het Oud Archief der stad Middelburg 1217–1581*, (1883), p. 185, nr 697: letter of 25 May 1495 from Philip the Handsome to Mayor/Aldermen of Middelburg (Zeeland) requesting 'no excise duty be levied on beer consumed by the Duke of York's servants, and that they should be treated as if they were his own servants': books.google.nl/books/about/Inventaris_van_het_Oud_ Archief_der_Stad.html?id=PvmlzzGaTh8C&redir_esc=y

6 Edward IV departed from Vlissingen to recapture England from Henry VI (1471), and a fleet in favour of 'King Edward' departed from Middelburg (Arnemuiden) to challenge Henry VII (1487). See Chapter 12.

7 Except for Flemish historian Steven Thiry, whose article mentions this specific passage from Aurelius: 'Counterfeited Jewels Make the True Mistrusted'.

8 Aka 'Cornelis Geritsz of Gouda', Aurelius was born in Gouda around 1460, and died in August 1531. He studied at the universities of Cologne, Leuven and Paris, returned to Holland and became an Augustinian canon. As a friar, he stayed in various monasteries. In 1495 he was prior of the monastery of St Martin on the Donk, near Schoonhoven. He was also a humanist scholar,

and friend of Erasmus from 1489: K. Tilmans, *De Divisiekroniek van 1517, Bourgondische-Habsburgse deel (div. 29–32)*, (2003) pp. 10, 11: karintilmans.nl/pdf/dk29-32.pdf.

9   *Divisie Chronicle*, div. 32, f.316r: resources.huygens.knaw.nl/retroboeken/divisie kroniek/#page=0&accessor=thumbnails&view=homePane Div. 29–32 – this is a contemporaneous Holland part of the chronicle, largely an original account of events, apparently without referring to any previous writings. Descriptions in div. 32 encompass the White Rose's journey through Holland, and must reflect Aurelius' own experiences from observation, from witnesses and/or from hearsay.

10   *Chronicle of Zeeland* (trans.): 'In the year MCCCC XCV [1495] in July Richard who was called the white Rose/king Edwards son of England crossed Holland and went to England to receive his father's inheritance': objects.library.uu.nl/reader/index.php?obj= 1874-214708&lan=en#page//72/28/77/72287723489789 7383298709333694636913619.jpg/mode/1up, p. 130 (RH page).

11   Sir Robert Clifford (1448–1508), a Yorkshire knight, staunch Yorkist under Richard III and leading supporter of the Duke of York from early 1493. In late 1494, he betrayed all the names of his co-conspirators to Henry VII, receiving a pardon and considerable reward. He served Henry VII from 1495 as Master of the King's Ordnance: Wroe, pp. 181–82, 184, 222–23, 369 and Chapter 17.

12   On 12 January 1495, 'the Duke of York' and 'the Duke of Saxony' received a gift from the City Council of Bergen op Zoom: West-Brabants Archief, City Accounts Bergen op Zoom 1495: westbrabantsarchief.nl/collectie/archieven/scans/NL-BozWBA-boz%20-%200005/2.6.2.1.1.20/start/0/limit/50/highlight/44, p. 44 (LH page).

13   For nobles who supported York in 1495 and were subsequently arrested/executed, see Chapter 14, note 138.

14   *Regesta*, 11 February 1495, *RI XIV*, 1, nr 1329.

15   *Regesta*, 24 February 1495, *RI XIV*, 1, nr 1346; 28 February 1495, *RI XIV*, 1, nr 1360; 1 March 1495, *RI XIV*, 1, nr 1362.

16   *Regesta*, 18 March 1495, *RI XIV*, 1, nr 3311.

17   *Regesta*, 1 April 1495, *RI XIV*, 1, nr 1482.

18   For Albert of Saxony (1443–1500), see Chapter 17, pp. 271–73. Rodrigue de Lalaing was the bastard son of Antoine de Lalaing (d. 8.1.1470), a descendant of the Hainaut noble family De Lalaing. Antoine was the younger brother of the famous Burgundian knight, Jacques de Lalaing, *le bon chevalier* (1420–53). Rodrigue was an experienced military commander under Maximilian I and later Archduke Philip the Handsome (Philip legitimated him 1505). For army captain Quitinck, see *Kroniek van Holland* (anonymous), *Dit is die historie van Hollant (1477–1534)*, written around 1540, Royal Library, The Hague: 76 H 42, p. 119 – 'and among the other captains was also Quitinck, who had served this country for a long time'. In Kingsford, p. 207, Quitinck is 'a Spaniard called Quyntyne', one of York's captains arrested at Deal, Kent. He was beheaded at Tower Hill on 7 September 1495.

19   *Molinet*, Vol. 5, p. 50.

20   See note 5.

21   HSA, 10024, *Geheime Rat, loc. Cit.*, letter nr 71.

22 *Ibid.*, letter nr 67.

23 Arthurson, *op. cit.*, p. 110.

24 In 1491, peasants in the north of Holland revolted against Jan III of Egmond, Stadtholder of Holland, rejecting tax increases put in place regardless of pre-existing food shortages and economic malaise in Kennemerland and West-Friesland. Protests received support from cities in other regions: Haarlem, Beverwijk and Alkmaar, they were known as the 'Cheese and Bread People'. Habsburg-leaning Jan III requested Maximilian to send an army to the north of Holland under the command of Duke Albert of Saxony, who finally defeated the rebels on 15 May 1492.

25 Albert, Duke of Saxony, currently Stadtholder General of the Habsburg-Netherlands, was a loyal companion of Richard, Duke of York, and regularly seen in his company. E.g. *Regesta, RI XIV*, 1, nrs 185, 478, 485, 1482, 2761, 2820; City Accounts of Bergen op Zoom 1494–95, boz-0005, inv nr 765, p. 44 (LH page); also Chapter 14, notes 30 and 31.

26 See note 22. Thanks to Paul Baks, whose works include '*Saksische heerschappij in Friesland, 1498–1515, dynastieke doelstellingen en politieke realiteit*' (1999). Baks kindly explained some of the Ebenstein letter: Ebenstein, one of Maximilian's military commanders with his own army of mercenaries, was apparently told by one of York's servants that the mercenaries were saying Albert preferred to march against England. Ebenstein, fearing for a campaign planned against Friesland, alerted Duke Albert. However, on 15 June 1495, Maximilian ordered Ebenstein and his mercenaries to Italy to support the Duke of Milan (ruling out engagement in an invasion of Friesland or England). The Duke of York left for England from Texel on 1 July 1495, possibly with a smaller army than expected.

27 NAH, *Grafelijkheidsrekenkamer*, Reg. nr: 3.01.27.02, inv. nr 191, 'Accounts of the Steward General of Holland, Thomas Beukelaar, 1 January 1495–31 December 1495' (hereafter NAH GRR), f.102r, translations:
(1) 'The aforementioned Joris rynouts son who on Easter eve ~~18 April anno XCV~~ travelled from The Hague to the city of Leiden with certain private letters from the Stadtholder General of Holland, containing the request to receive the Duke of York kindly and to show him their friendship, which he will repay, when he has arrived in his realm.'
(2) 'The aforementioned Jan Pieters son, who on 21st day of April anno XCV travelled with similar private letters to the cities of Rotterdam, Delft and Dordrecht containing and telling similar recommendations as stated above.'

28 See note 27. The welcoming of the Duke of York in Dordrecht, Rotterdam, Delft and Leiden around mid-April indicates he was proceeding to the city of Haarlem and, according to Aurelius, arrived after the octave of Easter (27 April).

29 Jacob van Barry (d. 31.1.1500) was an official at the Court of Holland, a servant and representative of the Duke of Saxony in Holland from 1486 to at least 1499. In 1493, on the duke's intercession, he received the Clerkship of Haarlem as well as Texel for life: S. ter Braake. *Met recht en rekenschap: de ambtenaren bij het Hof van Holland en de Haagse Rekenkamer in de Habsburgse Tijd (1483–1558)*, (2007): hdl.handle.net/1887/12449, p. 365.

30 W. Cerutti, Van Commanderij van Sint-Jan tot Noord-Hollands Archief, Geschiedenis van het klooster en de kerk van de Ridderlijke Orde van het Hospitaal van Sint-Jan van Jeruzalem in Haarlem (2007), p. 156.

31 NAH GRR, 191, f.104v: Trans.: 'The aforementioned Willem Wouters son, who on the 28th day in May anno XCV, travelled from The Hague with certain private letters from the Stadtholder General and council of Holland to the city of Amsterdam, containing and telling how the official from Brussels had come, in the name of my gracious lord, to the aforementioned lords to ensure that the ships which the Duke of York had purchased and lying before the aforementioned city [Amsterdam] would be delivered to him.'

32 NAH GRR, 191, f.105r: Trans.: 'The aforementioned Willem Jans son, who on the 5th of June in the above-mentioned year, travelled to the city of Amsterdam with certain private letters from my gracious lord, containing that they should deliver the ships which the aforementioned duke had bought.'

33 *Regesta*, 1 April 1495, *RI XIV*, 1482: 'KM [King Maximilian] hopes that the old woman of Burgundy [Margaret of York] will provide the provisions and everything else, as promised.'

34 NAH GRR, 3346, Domain Account *Grafelijk Huis* Margaret of York, Voorne, f.44v, Accounts of Boudijn Willemszoon, 1 January 1495–31 December 1495: '… *uut laste en bevele van mijner gnadige vrouwe* [Margaret of York] *aldair hadde doen brouwen voor mijne her den hertoge van Yorck hare Neve ende ome t selve bier te doen scepenen*'. Thanks to Zoë Maula for the source.

35 NAH GRR, 191, f.105r: Trans.: 'The aforementioned Hemrick Faes, who on the 7th of June in the aforementioned year, travelled from the Hague to the town of Beverwijk and to the Duke of York – who was there – with certain private letters from the Stadtholder and the council of Holland, requesting that he should embark his men and order them not to harm these lands.'

36 In 1276, the Count of Holland, Floris V (1254–96) had granted Beverwijk market rights. Thereafter, its port was mainly used for the export of local products. Ships were moored directly alongside the '*Platinckdijck*' (dike) or on wooden jetties. Significant losses of archives make the reliable reconstruction of the town's local history challenging. Thanks to Alfred Schweitzer, a local historical expert of the region of Kennemerland in North Holland (including Haarlem and Beverwijk), for generously providing information about Beverwijk in the (late) Middle Ages.

37 See note 35.

38 E.H.P. Cordfunke, E. Den Hartog, G.J.R. Maat & J. Roefstra, *De Abdij van Egmond, Archeologie en duizend jaar geschiedeni* (Zutphen, 2010), pp. 11, 12, 63.

39 G.N.M. Vis, Marco Mostert & Peter Jan Margry, Heiligenlevens, Annalen en Kronieken: geschiedschrijving in middeleeuws Egmond (Hilversum, 1990), p. 48.

40 *Divisie Chronicle*, div. 30, f.328r. For Edward IV's journey from Texel through Holland to Flanders in 1470, see J. Huizinga, '*Koning Edward IV van Engeland in Ballingschap*', *Verzamelde Werken. Deel 4. Cultuurgeschiedenis II* (1949), www.dbnl. org/tekst/huiz003verz05_01/huiz003verz05_01_0026.php. Also, Antoon P.R. Obermann & H. Schoorl, '*Koning Edward IV van Engeland op Texel*', *Regionaal-historisch tijdschrift 'Holland', 13e jaargang*, No. 1, February 1981.

41 *Regesta*, 5 May 1495, *RI XIV*, 1, nr 3406.

42 HHSA, AT-Oesta/HHstA RK Maximiliana 4-3-20: Maximilian's letter of instruction to Jacques of Gondebault for his son, Archduke Philip, 17 June 1495: 'to deliver my lord York 4 pieces of artillery for his intended journey'. Thanks to Zoë Maula for the source.

43 NAH GRR, 191, f.94v. Trans.: 'The aforementioned Walraven Potter, who travelled from The Hague to the island of Texel with certain private letters from KM [King Maximilian] to the person of the Duke of York lying there in order to travel to England, has presented the aforementioned letters concerning certain secret matters, of which there is no need to make any further mention here, in his [York's] hands and then waited for his answers.' This is the last entry for December 1495 but unfortunately does not indicate the date the bailiff was sent to Texel. It is impossible for York to be on Texel in December 1495 as his presence in Scotland on 20 November 1495 seems confirmed: Thomas Dickson et al. (eds), 'Accounts of the Lord High Treasurer of Scotland', *Scottish Records Series, 1877* (Edinburgh, 1877–1978), Vol. 1, 1473–98. E.g. see p. 256 of f.71a–79a: 'Expens made apone the Kingis Persoun sen the last compt in Striueling, guhilk wes the xviij day of Nouember, in the jere of God j""iiijlxxxxv jeria'; also p. 263, f.82 a.b.: 'Expens maid apone Prince Richard of England and his seruitos, fra his cumin in Scotland, quhilk wes the xxviij day of Nouember, in the jere of God j""iiijlxxxxv jeris; apud Striueling'. This may possibly be a clerical mistake, i.e., a 'forgotten' entry, for which there was no place on the proper page (the 2nd half of June 1495), which the clerk added afterwards to a page that had enough blank space (thus ensuring his account book could be closed correctly).

44 See part of map of Texel made by Jan Scorel in 1551, giving a unique general view of the site shortly before 1500. On the left side above can be seen the exact sheltered place where York's fleet was waiting.

45 For Jacob van Barry, see note 29.

46 Obermann & Schoorl, 'Edward IV op Texel', pp. 11 and 12. In September 1539, King Henry VIII sent two shipmasters, Richard Couche and John Aborough, to explore the route via Marsdiep, along Texel to Zuiderzee, for the conveyance of his bride-to-be, Anna van Cleef (Cleves) from Harderwijk. The notes and chart made are preserved, see Alwyn Ruddock, *The Earliest Original English Seaman's Rutter and Pilot's Chart* (Cambridge University Press, 2010), online at The Journal of Navigation: www.cambridge.org/core/journals/journal-of-navigation/article/abs/earliest-original-english-seamans-rutter-and-pilots-chart/0222E55BDE7070B2DD9ABF39D48E9AFA

47 See the map on p. 14 for map of Holland.

48 Thanks to Alfred Schweitzer (note 36) and Jean Roefstra, historical archaeologist at *Stichting Historische Archeologie*, for help in finding information about York's stay in Haarlem and Beverwijk, May–June 1495.

49 Aside from Thiry, see note 7.

16. The Family of Edward V and Richard, Duke of York

1   *Mancini*, pp. 49, 51, 55.

2   *Maligned King*, pp. 40–41.

3   David, 'Ludlow and the Woodvilles', *op. cit*, pp. 6–10.

4   David, *op. cit.*, p. 9; Orme, p. 124. For the Prince of Wales' Household Ordinances, revised in 1483, see *Protector & Constable*, pp. 95–100.

5   *Protector & Constable*, pp. 48–49.

6   *Heralds' Memoir*, pp. 120–21.

7   *Mancini*, p. 53.

8   David, *op. cit.*, p. 10.

9   See *Mancini*, p. 55, for Grey 'come out to the king from the city'; p. 59 for 'wagons loaded with arms bearing the devices of the queen's brothers and sons'.

10 *Early Historians*, p. 119: Rous, *Historia* (*c.* 1490).

11 *Mancini*, p. 65. The Crowland author (p. 161), who is resolutely anti-northern, remarks 'without any form of trial'. Surprisingly for an English chronicler (perhaps typically for his prejudices), he fails to mention Gloucester's judicial powers as Constable of England or his right to deputise Northumberland.

12 *The Memorandum Book of Roger Machado* (College of Arms, MS Arundel 51, f.19–28), compiled 1484, 1485. Trans.: 'Memorandum that I left the city of Bruges to go to My Lord Jacques de Luxembourg and My Lady of Mans in the service of my aforementioned Lord, My Lord the Marquis the second day of February 1484 [1485 New Style].' Also: 'Item, My Lord the Marquis instructed me to travel for x [10] days on horseback with his messages from the city of Bruges to the city of Lan in Lanoy and to the castle of Porsnay *-j lb. xiij s iiij d.*' Jacques de Luxembourg, Lord of Richebourg, Viscount of Lannoy (1426–87) was great-uncle of the princes and uncle to Elizabeth Woodville (her mother's brother). She was seemingly on good terms with him; he had led an embassy from the Burgundian Netherlands to England in 1465 for her coronation. Nathalie Nijman-Bliekendaal, TMPP Research Report, 6.12.20. See note 58.

13 C.L. Kingsford, *DNB*.

14 *DNB*: Dorset was apprehended for Tudor by Humphrey Cheney.

15 *PROME*, Rosemary Horrox (item 44 [49]). Dorset, though not summoned to the Parliament, had his attainder reversed, with the petition probably in the second session, 23 January–March 1486: *Rot. Parl.*, vi, pp. 315–16. However, a punitive proviso denied exemption from the Act of Resumption and he was restored only to lands acquired through inheritance or marriage.

16 *Heralds' Memoir*, pp. 88–89.

17 *Ibid.*, p. 108; Bennett, p. 50.

18 *Heralds' Memoir*, p. 109.

19 *Vergil-2*, p. 21. Bacon, *Henry the Seventh* (Lockyer, ed.) p. 64.

20 Neil Whalley, TMPP Research Report from: CPR 1461–67, p. 118 (1462); *Rot. Parl.*, VI, pp. 107–08 (1474); W. Farrer & J. Brownbill (eds), *Victoria History of the County of Lancaster* (1914), Vol. VIII , p. 302, n. 100 (1498). Thanks also: Isobel Sneesby. Following Lord Bonville's death at the Battle of Wakefield

(1460), Katherine married William, Lord Hastings (1462). Katherine died on 12 February 1504 when Gleaston and Aldingham passed to Cecily Bonville.

21 *Heralds' Memoir*, p. 146. Dorset's name was omitted from the list of nobles present; see p. 148 for the presence of his son, Sir Thomas Grey.

22 CCR 1485–1500, p. 122. Dorset was granted the office of Steward of Claveryng, Essex.

23 CCR 1485–1500, p. 67. On 19 July 1488, Dorset was awarded several grants which may indicate his release at this time. *Heralds' Memoir* (before Easter 1490) does not record Dorset's release.

24 CCR 1485–1500, p. 122.

25 Vergil, 1555, Book XXVI; see *Vergil-2*, p. 6n. Dorset's (apparent) improved behaviour may suggest the need to keep his head down.

26 CCR 1485–1500, pp. 180–81.

27 GC, p. 285.

28 CPR 1485–94, p. 388; CCR 1485–1500, pp. 177–78.

29 *Vergil-2*, p. 52.

30 CPR 1485–94, p. 425. Lisle's mother Joan Grey also received a pardon.

31 John Nichols, *A Collection of all the Wills, now known to be extant, of the Kings and Queens of England (1780)*, pp. 350–51; TNA, PRO B 11/9/207, 10 April 1492. Thanks to Dr Heather Falvey.

32 David MacGibbon, *Elizabeth Woodville: A Life* (1938, 2014), p. 163. Elizabeth's daughter, Anne of York, offered the Mass penny.

33 CCR 1485–1500, p. 237.

34 CCR 1485–1500, p. 246. In 1494, Baron West's heir, Thomas, had married Elizabeth Bonville, daughter and co-heiress of John Bonville, Esquire of Shute, Devon.

35 CCR 1485–1500, p. 289. This includes the Earl of Devon (£1,000) and Sir John Arundell (his son-in-law, 500 marks).

36 CPR 1494–1509, p. 110.

37 W.E. Hampton, 'The Ladies of the Minories', *Crown & People*, pp. 195–202 (pp. 199, 202 n. 17).

38 CFR 1485–1509, p. 316.

39 *Memorials*, pp. 189–92. This is the tomb monument of Sir Edward Grey, Lord Ferrers of Groby (d. 1457). Thanks to Dr Tobias Capwell.

40 Wroe, p. 504.

41 *Mancini*, p. 45.

42 *Maligned King*, p. 26.

43 *Mancini*, p. 86 n. 33; J.L. Laynesmith, *Cecily, Duchess of York* (2017), p. 153.

44 *Mancini*, pp. 86–87. Only later did Richard, as king, perhaps from newly accessed evidence, intimate in correspondence that the Woodvilles had acted unlawfully to bring about certain executions: J. Ashdown-Hill and A.J. Carson, 'The Execution of the Earl of Desmond', *Ricardian*, 2005, pp. 70–93.

45 *Mancini*, p. 45.

46 *Maligned King*, pp. 65–66.

47 *Heralds' Memoir*, pp. 104–05.

48 *Heralds' Memoir*, p. 104.

49 *Vergil-2*, pp. 17–19; *Bacon, Henry the Seventh*, pp. 58–59. The Council at Sheen took place around 2 February–3 March 1487; *Heralds' Memoir*, p. 108.
50 *Vergil-2*, p. 6.
51 Campbell, Vol. 2, pp. 148–49.
52 Bacon, pp. 59–60.
53 J. Armitage Robinson, *The Abbot's House at Westminster* (1911), p. 22. Thanks to Eileen Bates for source, 12.11.2021.
54 *Heralds' Memoir*, p. 117.
55 *Ibid.*, p. 147. For Henry's attendance at Elizabeth of York's coronation, see p. 140. A stage was erected near the high altar where Henry (and his mother) watched behind latticework.
56 Campbell, Vol. 2, p. 225.
57 *Ibid.*, pp. 319–20.
58 Weir, *Elizabeth of York*, p. 292.
59 Campbell, Vol. 2, pp. 322, 555.
60 James Gairdner, *DNB*: Leland, *Collectanea*, Vol. 4, pp. 239, 249. See note 12.
61 fr.wikipedia.org/wiki/Fran%C3%A7ois_de_Luxembourg_(p%C3%A8re)
62 Nichols, *Collection of Wills*, pp. 350–51 (see note 31).
63 Prior of Sheen Charterhouse (John Ingleby); (Dr Thomas) Brent, Elizabeth's chaplain; Edmund (Edward) Haute, her executor/cousin; Grace, bastard daughter of Edward IV, and 'an other gentilewoman': MacGibbon, *op. cit.*, p. 162. Richard Woodville died the previous year: *Royal Funerals*, p. 68.
64 See Chapter 8.
65 *Harley 433*, Vol. 2, p. 63.
66 *Itinerary*, p. 10.
67 *Harley 433*, Vol. 1, p. 213.
68 *Harley 433*, Vol. 2. p. 130.
69 Williams, 'Will of William Catesby', p. 49 nn. 82–83.
70 *Rot. Parl.*, vi, p. 284.
71 Campbell, Vol. 1, p. 311; C.S.L Davies, *ODNB*.
72 *Heralds' Memoir*, pp. 134, 141, 147.
73 *ODNB*.
74 Ibid.
75 E101/414/16 f.82r (Revenues of Lands),1497. Thanks to Lynda Pidgeon.
76 Visser-Fuchs, 'Where did Elizabeth of York find Consolation?', *Ricardian*, Vol. 9, 1993, pp. 469–71: BL, Harleian MS y 49; BL, MS Royal 20 A xix f.195.
77 For Elizabeth of York's letter relating to Portuguese marriage, see Buc, pp. 330–31.
78 For Richard's denial of the rumour of an intended marriage, see David Johnson, 'The Remarkable Rise of Sir Richard Ratcliffe', *Court Journal*, Autumn 2021, pp. 14–16 (p. 16); *Road to Bosworth*, p. 199 n. 167; L. Lyall & F. Watney (eds), *The Acts of Court of the Mercers' Company 1453–1527* (Cambridge, 1936), pp. 173–74.
79 *Crowland*, p. 177.
80 David Johnson, 'Ardent Suitor or Reluctant Groom? Henry VII and Elizabeth of York. Part Two: Reluctant groom', *Bulletin*, March 2020, pp. 37–41: www.revealingrichardiii.com/the-pre-contract.html.

81 Lynda Pidgeon, *Brought Up of Nought: A History of the Woodville Family* (2019), pp. 226, 311. The Papal Bull Henry obtained from Pope Innocent VIII 'appears to have given him a "let out" clause, with or without children by Elizabeth'.

82 For Henry and Elizabeth's children, see Weir, *op. cit.*, pp. 348–49.

83 *Heralds' Memoir*, p. 136.

84 Weir, *op. cit.*, p. 329: Henry VII Privy Purse.

85 André, p. 69.

86 Weir, pp. 278–80; Calendar State Papers, Spain, and Privy Purse Expenses; Appendix II, pp. 471–76.

87 Weir, p. 358; *Calendar State Papers*, Spain.

88 Weir, pp. 422–23. In 1506, Henry added the gallery recorded as 'the Queen's Gallery' (see 1597 plan), p. 546 n. 59.

89 Weir, p. 409.

90 For Elizabeth's progress, see Weir, *op. cit.*, pp. 409–15.

91 Nicholas Harris Nicolas, *Privy Purse Expenses of Elizabeth of York: Wardrobe Accounts of Edward the Fourth* (1830, 1972 facs. edn), p. 8. Elizabeth's Accounts record sums given to the abbess, her ageing servant and three nuns at the Minories on 1 May 1502 when Elizabeth was at the Tower Palace. See note 87 for Elizabeth's further sums to the same (7 November 1502, when again at the Tower).

92 Hampton, 'Ladies of the Minories', *Crown & People*, pp. 197–99.

93 Weir, pp. 426, 440.

94 Christopher Harper-Bill, *ODNB*.

95 Langley and Jones, *The Lost King* (2022, 2013), p. 165; Jones, *Bosworth 1485: Psychology of a Battle* (2002), pp. 82, 105, 109. For Richard's only surviving letter to his mother on 3 June 1484, following death of his son, see *Road to Bosworth*, pp. 193–94; *Harley 433*, Vol. 1, p. 3.

96 *Lost King*, pp. x–xi, 280; Joanna Laynesmith, 'Remembering Richard', *Bulletin*, June 2016, pp. 27–28; also 'In the Service of Cecily, Duchess of York', *Bulletin*, September 2017, pp. 54–56.

97 Laynesmith, *Cecily*, p. 165.

98 *Ibid.*, p. 169.

99 *Ibid.*, p. 179. While visiting Fotheringhay, Elizabeth I became aware of the decay to Cecily's and Richard's monuments. In 1573, their coffins were exhumed and reburied with new monuments, observable today.

100 *Royal Funerals*, pp. 17, 36.

101 *Coronation*, p. 20.

102 J.A.F. Thomson, 'Bishop Lionel Woodville and Richard III', *Historical Research*, Vol. 59, Issue 139, May 1986, pp. 130–35 (p. 132); CPR 1476–85, p. 559.

103 Robert C. Hairsine, 'Oxford University and the Life and Legend of Richard III', *Crown and People*, p. 309.

104 Thomson, *op. cit.*, p. 132; CPR 1476–85, p. 569.

105 J.A.F. Thomson, *ODNB*.

106 Thomson, 'Lionel Woodville', p. 134; *Epistolae Academicae Oxon*, ii, pp. 489–90.

107 *Harley 433*, Vol. 2, p. 92.

108 CPR 1476–85, p. 387; *Rot. Parl.*, vi, p. 250.

109 Ian Rogers, www.girders.net; source AALT (CP40no888).

110 *Harley 433*, Vol. 2, p. 177.

111 *Memorials*, p. 203.

112 Scofield, *Edward the Fourth*, Vol. 1, p. 178 n. 1. Thanks to David Santiuste.

113 For commissions in 1480 (Bedford Castle, Bedfordshire, Oxford) and February 1483 (Berkshire), see CPR 1476–85, pp. 212, 553–54, 569.

114 CPR 1476–85, p. 567.

115 Ibid.

116 *Harley 433*, Vol. 3, p. 216.

117 *Rot. Parl.*, vi, p. 246.

118 *Harley 433*, Vol. 1, p. 266; CPR 1476–85, p. 532.

119 *Rot. Parl.*, vi, pp. 273–74

120 *Heralds' Memoir*, pp. 71, 81; also *Rot. Parl.*, vi, p. 273 (Henry VII, 1st Parliament).

121 *Heralds' Memoir*, p. 102.

122 Ibid., p. 146.

123 Ibid., pp. 111–20.

124 CPR 1485–94, pp. 494–95 for Commissions of the Peace in Northamptonshire before 27 November 1490.

125 *Heralds' Memoir*, pp. 166–71. Richard Woodville was last listed on a Commission of the Peace for Northamptonshire on 27 November 1490: CPR 1485–94, p. 495.

126 IPM, Henry VII, Vol. 1, No. 681. Thanks to Peter Hammond for source.

127 N.H. Nicholas, *Testamenta Vetusta* (1826), Vol. 2, p. 403. Thanks to Dr Heather Falvey. Richard Woodville's will was written on 20 February 1490 (1491 New Style) and proved on 23 March 1492 (poss. error for 1491). See also Carol Dougherty and Peter Charnley, 'The Magic of Medieval Wills, including Richard Woodville', *Bulletin*, March 2021, pp. 60–64 (pp. 62–63); also, Reverend R.M. Serjeantson and W.R.D. Adkins (eds), *Victoria History of the County of Northampton* (1906), Vol. 2, p. 128.

128 Portugal: James Gairdner, *The Paston Letters* (1986), Vol. 1, p. 263. For Morat, see Scofield, Vol. 2, p. 165.

129 Elaine Sanceau, *The Perfect Prince: A Biography of the King Dom João II* (1959), pp. 296, 297.

130 *Heralds' Memoir*, p. 103.

131 Louis de la Trémoille, *Correspondance de Charles VIII et de Ses Conseillers Avec Louis II de la Trémoille Pendant la Guerre de Bretagne (1488)* (Paris, 1878) pp. 238–39. Letter from Henry VII to Charles VIII of France, Windsor, 27 May 1488: gallica.bnf.fr/ark:/12148/bpt6k5600572n.texteImage (trans. thanks to Annette Carson).

132 A stone monument in Brittany records who fought in the battle that ended its independence: Christopher Wilkins, *The Last Knight Errant: Edward Woodville and the Age of Chivalry* (2010), pp. 164 n. 34, 216.

133 Trémoille, *Correspondance de Charles VIII*, p. 238, 'hors des franchises' means 'out of sanctuary'. Trans. thanks to Dr Michael K. Jones.

134 Trémoille, p. 239.

135 Wilkins, *The Last Knight Errant*, p. 153. See Gairdner, *Paston Letters*, Vol. 6, pp. 111–12, William Paston's letter of 13 May 1488.

136 CPR 1469–77, pp. 261, 312.

137 Rosemary Horrox, *ODNB*.

138 CPR 1476–85, p. 477. The de la Pole Roll (inaccurately called the 'Lincoln Roll') is a family genealogy from 1496 held at Rylands Library, Manchester University. The Roll, though confusing the information around the appointment, reveals that the family viewed it as creating John heir presumptive. Dating and name correction thanks to Alice Johnson, TMPP Research Report, 19.5.2022. For the original dating to 1484, see Philip Morgan, '"Those Were The Days": A Yorkist Pedigree Roll', in Sharon Michalove & A. Compton Reeves (eds), *Estrangement, Enterprise and Education in Fifteenth Century England* (1998), pp. 107–16 (p. 116).

139 Rosemary Horrox, *ODNB*.

140 Bennett, pp. 51, 146 n. 25. Money for Edward V, to aid Lincoln, was sent abroad (via a John Mayne) by John Sant, Abbot of Abingdon, Oxfordshire (19 miles from Lovell's home at Minster Lovell). On 30 March 1487, a report in York had Lincoln wishing to join the rebels when he was last in the city in April 1486 (with Henry VII): *York Books*, Vol. 2, p. 542.

141 *Vergil-2*, p. 19. See also: Wendy E.A. Moorhen, 'The Career of John de la Pole, Earl of Lincoln', *Ricardian*, Vol. 13, 2003, pp. 341–58 (p. 356). Lincoln 'daily spoke with him' (Warwick) at Sheen (from Morton's Register). See also *Heralds' Memoir*, p. 109.

142 *York Books*, Vol. 2, pp. 541–42.

143 The Roll incorrectly records this being an announcement at King Richard's Parliament in 1484. Richard's Parliament took place in the medieval year of 1483, prior to his son's death (in 1484). Trans. thanks to Marie Barnfield, 22 October 2021. For the de la Pole Pedigree Roll: Ryland's Library: Latin MS 113. Also see Chapter 19.

144 Dickon Whitewood, 'The Seal Matrix of John de la Pole, Earl of Lincoln', *Bulletin*, June 2016, pp. 54–56. BM No. 1838, 1232.16. Whitewood is Project Assistant for the British Museum Seals Project.

145 Bennett, p. 101.

146 Maltravers fought for Richard III at Bosworth. He was made godparent to Prince Arthur in November 1486. He failed to participate at Stoke Field, but was Chief Butler at Elizabeth of York's coronation in November 1487 (as he had been at Elizabeth Woodville's, Henry VII's and very probably Richard III's, see *Coronation*, p. 44). *Heralds' Memoir*, pp. 104, (119–20), 136, 147.

147 Horrox, *ODNB*.

148 Buc, pp. 212, 345.

149 The Martyrology of Syon Abbey, BL, Add. MS 22285, f.36r; for Anne's burial at Syon, see f.191r. Thanks to Francisca Icaza.

150 John Ashdown-Hill, *Elizabeth Widville, Lady Grey: Edward IV's Chief Mistress and the 'Pink Queen'* (2019), pp. 182–86.

17. Case Connections

1   E.L. O'Brien, *ODNB*; C.S.L. Davies, 'Richard III, Henry VII and the Island of Jersey', *Ricardian*, Vol. 9, No. 119, December 1992, pp. 334–42 (p. 335).

2   *ODNB.* Harliston took part in both invasions: Edward V's in 1487, and Richard of York's in 1495 (Davies 'Jersey', p. 336). He died in *c.* 1497, probably in Malines. Margaret of Burgundy paid for his burial with full honours (Bronwyn Matthews, *Les Chroniques de Jersey* (2017), p. 55; *Cæsarea: The Island of Jersey* (1840), p. 20).

3   C.H. Williams, 'The Rebellion of Humphrey Stafford in 1486', *EHR*, Vol. 43, No. 170, 1928, pp. 181–89 (p. 183 n. 5). Contemporary reports from 1 May 1486 stated the claimant to the throne ('Edward, Earl of Warwick') had been 'delivered to the foresaid Francis [Lovell] by David Philip and Matthew Baker from the isle of Guernsey and so continually conducted from county to county into the foresaid county of York … and that Humphrey Stafford would go with all haste and ride with a great multitude of people to the said Francis, to maintain, comfort and abet, and also support, the foresaid Francis and all others aiding the foresaid Francis in order to destroy the person of the Lord King [Henry VII]' (King's Bench, KB 9/138 m.12; thanks to Marie Barnfield). For the trial of the rebels on Wednesday, 17 May 1486 (the Wednesday after Whitsun), see KB 9/127, m.7; also *Coram Rege Roll*, Mich. 4 Hen.VII, rex, rot.3: aalt.law.uh.edu/AALT2/H7/KB27no909/aKB27no909fronts/IMG_0248.htm

4   Davies, 'Jersey', p. 337.

5   *ODNB*; *Materials*, Vol. 2, p. 30; CPR 1485–94, p. 141.

6   Marguerite Syvret and Joan Stevens, *Balleine's History of Jersey* (Revised and Enlarged) (1950), p. 67. Jersey investigation thanks to Valérie Noël, Lord Coutanche Library, Société Jersiaise; Susan Freebrey and Linda Romeril, *Archive dé Jèrri*, and Charlie Malet de Carteret, St Ouen's Manor. Guernsey investigation thanks to Nathan Coyde, Archives Manager, States of Guernsey. See also Wroe, pp. 91, 136–37, 177, 239.

7   CPR 1476–85, p. 464; *Harley 433*, Vol. 1, p. 89.

8   CPR 1476–85, p. 513.

9   CPR 1485–94, pp. 25, 151, 174.

10   CFR 1471–85, pp. 246, 268.

11   CFR 1471–85, p. 277; CPR 1476–85, pp. 403, 523.

12   CPR 1476–85, p. 403.

13   W.E. Hampton, 'Sir James Tyrell', *Crown & People*, p. 210. For Tyrell as Sheriff of Southampton (8 December 1484), see CPR 1476–85, p. 491.

14   CPR 1476–85, p. 544.

15   *Harley 433*, Vol. 2, p. 33.

16   CFR 1485–1509, p. 15.

17   CCR 1454–61, pp. 337–38. Thanks to Marie Barnfield, 1.7.22.

18   Hampton, *op. cit.*, p. 211.

19   CPR 1476–85, p. 364.

20   Ibid., p. 405.

21   Rosemary Horrox, *ODNB*; Du Boulay, *Registrum Bourgchier*, p. 54.

22   CPR 1476–85, pp. 891–92
23   Horrox, *ODNB.*
24   Peter Hammond and Anne F. Sutton, 'Research Notes and Queries', *Ricardian*, Vol. 5, No. 72, March 1981, p. 319; Chamberlains Accounts, City of Canterbury, Michaelmas 1484–Michaelmas 1485, f.26.
25   Anne F. Sutton & Livia Visser-Fuchs, *Richard III's Books* (1997), p. 64. Carmeliano's 'Life of St Katherine' was dedicated to Richard III, Robert Brackenbury and John Russell, Bishop of Lincoln and Chancellor of England. For Brackenbury's dedication, see pp. 69–71.
26   Carlson, *English Humanist Books*, p. 44.
27   J.G. Nichols (ed.), *The Chronicle of Calais in the Reigns of Henry VII and Henry VII to the Year 1540* (Camden Society 35, 1846), p. 1; *Molinet*, I, pp. 434–36.
28   *Memorials*, p. 51, from Brackenbury's bastard son Robert's will: my 'bodie to be buried within the parish churche of Gainforthe besides my father'.
29   Horrox, *ODNB*; TNA, PRO PROB 11/14, f.1630. Elizabeth's will does not mention her sister, Anne.
30   *Vergil-1*, p. 18.
31   *GC*, pp. 237–38.
32   Nichols, *loc. cit.*
33   *Harley 433*, Vol. 2, p. 212.
34   *More*, p. 86.
35   For Tyrell's deposition, see Hicks, 'Elizabeth, Countess of Oxford', p. 310. Further details of Tyrell's involvement can be found in Dr David Johnson, *Ricardian*, 2024 (forthcoming), with appreciation for advance sight.
36   Reverend W.H. Sewell, 'Memoirs of Sir James Tyrell', pp. 125–80 (p. 176).
37   W.E. Hampton, 'Sir Robert Percy and his Wife', *Crown & People*, p. 187.
38   Sewell, *op. cit.*, pp. 176–77; *GC*, p. 319.
39   Moorhen, 'John de la Pole', p. 354.
40   CPR 1485–94, p. 78.
41   *Harley 433*, Vol. 1, p. 48.
42   Hampton, *op. cit.*, p. 214.
43   CPR 1494–1509, p. 13.
44   CPR 1485–94, p. 173.
45   CPR 1476–85, p. 436.
46   Hampton, p. 210.
47   *Harley 433*, Vol. 2, p. 160; Vol. 1, p. 216.
48   *Harley 433*, Vol. 2, p. 25.
49   CPR 1476–85, p. 512; *Harley 433*, Vol. 1, p. 191.
50   Thanks to Margaret Watson, TMPP Research Report, 16.5.2018, pp. 1–24 (p. 16).
51   *Ibid.*, pp. 2, 9–10. A former owner of the property, Victor Walton, asserted he held an ancient document transferring possession of Blagraves and High Shipley (Barnard Castle) to Forest from King Richard. It is unclear whether this was as king or duke, or whether this began the tradition in the town. It was owned by Walton prior to the Second World War: North Yorkshire and Cleveland Vernacular Buildings Study Group, *Report No. 948* (1983), p. 1. Thanks to archivist David Cook, 21.6.22.

52 Thanks also to Daniel Blagg, great-great-great-grandson of Joseph Blanchett Brackenbury (b. 1788). Family tradition recalls: 'the princes were not murdered by Richard III. Sir Robert had secreted them to "his other castle in the north of England" before the Battle of Bosworth. They were there when the battle took place and were then sent on for their safety to other secret places. If anyone killed them, it was Henry Tudor.' Daniel adds, 'Some years ago I spotted a short article in an American newspaper that stated that researchers in the Yorkshire archives had found documents from a castle there governed by Sir Robert Brackenbury, where suddenly in 1485 the expenses skyrocketed for unusual items like "fine cloth for clothing for their highnesses the princes", and better food, etc.' Investigations into this continue, including at Barnard Castle (Brackenbury Tower).

53 Tim Thornton, 'More on a Murder', *JHA*, 2020. For the response, see Chapter 8, Note 47.

54 Davies, 'Information, disinformation ... etc.' pp. 228–53. For Henry VIII's pride in his Yorkist ancestry, see p. 250.

55 Horrox, *ODNB* (Sir Edward Brampton).

56 Barrie Williams, 'Sir Edward Brampton: The Portuguese Years', *Ricardian*, Vol. 6, No. 84, March 1984, pp. 294–98 (p. 295). For the Isabel Pecche relationship, see Horrox, *ODNB*.

57 Margaret has been referred to as Catherine de Bahamonde (Roth, 'Sir Edward Brampton', *Transactions Jewish Historical Society of England*, 1945–51, Vol. 16). However, a history of the Carmelite Order in Portugal, written in the 1580s, notes that Sir Edward and his wife, Margarita Beamonda, endowed the Order's Chapel of St Sebastian. Such great donors would scarcely have been incorrectly recorded: Barrie Williams, 'Research Notes and Queries', *Bulletin*, March 1986, pp. 226–29 (p. 228). Thanks to Marie Barnfield.

58 F.W. Weaver, *Somerset Medieval Wills* (1901), p. 112 – Thomas Beaumont (Beamonde) will, d. 1507.

59 Wroe, pp. 526–27.

60 *Harley 433*, Vol. 2, p. 91.

61 CPR 1476–85, pp. 490, 897.

62 Howard Books, Vol. 2, p. 312: '... my Lord ... payed to Curteys for havenge owt the gret seale for my Lord to Flaundres, for the mater of the Dewke of Astryche [Duke of Austria]' (12 November 1482).

63 John Ashdown-Hill, 'The Opening of the Tombs of the Dukes of Richmond and Norfolk, Framlingham, April 1841: the Account of Revd J.W. Darby', *Ricardian*, Vol. 18, pp. 100–07 (p. 103).

64 For the report of Howard's death by arrow to the brain, see *Bosworth Field: A Poem* by Sir John Beaumont, (*c.* 1582–April 1627) of Grace Dieu, Leicestershire, published posthumously by his son in 1629: Nichols, *History and Antiquities of the County of Leicester*, Vol. IV.ii, 'The Hundred of Sparkenhoe' (1811), pp. 559–63 (p. 561). See also, William Hutton, *The Battle of Bosworth Field* (1788), pp. 101–02. Thanks to Ken Hillier for the sources. See also *Yorkist Lord*, p. 133. A stained-glass window that was once in Tendring Hall, Howard's main residence (Suffolk), indicates he had fair hair.

65 CPR 1461–67, pp. 25, 269.

66 Horrox, *Richard III: A Study of Service*, p. 200.
67 *Royal Funerals*, pp. 16, 26, 35, 39. In the night vigil with Halneth and Colyns was also Sir William Parker, standard bearer for Richard III at Bosworth.
68 CPR 1476–85, p. 122, 29 August 1478.
69 *Ibid.*, p. 371.
70 *Ibid.*, p. 502.
71 *Ibid.*, p. 490.
72 *Ibid.*, p. 503.
73 CPR 1485–94, p. 39.
74 Ibid.
75 CCR 1485–1500, p. 181.
76 Metcalfe, *Book of knights … etc.* Thanks to Dr Sandra Pendlington. Also: W.E. Hampton, 'Opposition to Henry Tudor after Bosworth', *Crown & People*, p. 174.
77 *Coronation*, p. 371; CPR 1485–94, p. 225.
78 Thomas Stapleton (ed.), Plumpton Correspondence: A Series of Letters, Chiefly Domestick, written in the reigns of Edward IV, Richard III, Henry VII and Henry VIII (1839), p. 55.
79 CFR 1485–1509, p. 198. Thanks to Heather Falvey.
80 *Coronation*, pp. 371, 168, 170.
81 *Coronation*, pp. 386, 168.
82 Stapleton, *op. cit.*, pp. 45, 46. Also *Harley 433*, Vol. 1, p. 260 and Vol. 2, p. 224; *Coronation*, p. 386.
83 *Coronation*, p. 386.
84 *Coronation*, p. 408. For the best pedigree see J. Foster (ed.), *Visitations of Yorks 1584–5* (1875), p. 345.
85 CPR 1476–85, p. 515.
86 *Ibid.*, p. 490.
87 *Ibid.*, p. 556.
88 *Ibid.*, p. 458.
89 Horrox, *Richard III: A Study of Service*, p. 105.
90 CPR 1476–85, pp. 247–48.
91 *Harley 433*, Vol. 3, pp. 8–9; Hungerford, Vol. 1, p. 48.
92 CPR 1476–85, p. 395.
93 *Ibid.*, p. 371.
94 *Ibid.*, p. 458.
95 Horrox, *op. cit.*, p. 221 n. 141.
96 CPR 1485–94, p. 345.
97 Maskelyne and H.C. Maxwell Lyte, 'IPM Henry VII, Entries 101–150', *Calendar of Inquisitions Post Mortem: Series 2*, Vol. 1, Henry VII (London, 1898), pp. 41–60: www.british-history.ac.uk/inquis-post-mortem/series2-vol1/pp41-60. Thanks to Heather Falvey. Also TNA C/142/1/110 and C/142/1/132.
98 Arthurson, *The Perkin Warbeck Conspiracy*, Appendix B, p. 221. For yeoman as gentlemen in royal service, see Horrox, *Richard III: A Study of Service*, pp. 240–41 – with thanks to Annette Carson.
99 Crawford, *Yorkist Lord*, pp. 47, 168. See Howard Books for more on the Norris family's long connection with John Howard.

100 Kenneth Hillier, 'William Norris', *Crown & People*, pp. 128–33 (pp. 129, 130).
101 Horrox, *Study of Service*, p. 221, fn. 141.
102 Bennett, p. 129.
103 CPR 1476–85, p. 508.
104 Hillier, *Crown & People*, p. 132.
105 *The Visitation of London* (1634), title page and p. 149 for Peirse family pedigree.
106 *Visitation of London*; also *Dugdale's Visitation of Yorkshire*, Vol. 3, pp. 35–36. Although there is no reason to doubt the grant of the Sewer office (it would have been corroborated for *Visitations* of 1634 and 1666), there is no record of a John or Richard Peirse holding this office. A 'J. Peirce' is listed as Groom of the Great Chamber in Ordinary Without Fee, 9 November 1668. These grooms served as court messengers, numbered between 10–14, with a salary of £40: courtofficers.ctsdh.luc.edu/CHAMBER2.list.pdf (p. 44).
107 NYCRO, ZBA 5/1/13.
108 Francis W. Steer (ed.), 'The Common Paper: Subscription to the Oath, 1613–28' in *Scriveners' Company Commons Paper 1357–1628 With A Continuation To 1678* (1968), pp. 54–62, www.british-history.ac.uk/london-record-soc/vol4/pp54-62; also p. 211. John Peirse is described as 'son of Henry Peirse of Bedale, co.Yorks, yeoman'. Thanks to Marie Barnfield for distinguishing yeoman (land)/Yeoman (militia).
109 NYCRO, ZBA 5/1/61.
110 Carol Kerry-Green, CKG Genealogy, TMPP Research Report, 5.8.2021, p. 4; lease of lands in Bedale to the Stapleton family, 2 December 1654, see U DDCA/15/3, Hull History Centre.
111 NYCRO, ZBA 5/5/1–2.
112 Charles Travis Clay (ed.), *Early Yorkshire Charters* (1963), Vol. XI, 'The Percy Fee', pp. 104–18.
113 *Ibid.*, pp, 7–8 n. 13; *Whitby Cartulary*, ii, pp. 384–85 (No. 438).
114 Carol Kerry-Green, TMPP Research Report, 29.7.21; Survey of the Manor of Bedale, 1618: U DDCA2/57/1, Hull History Centre.
115 Hardy Bertram McCall, *The Early History of Bedale in the North Riding of Yorkshire* (1907), p. 68. Marmaduke died on 6 March 1609, see NYCRO, ZBA 20/1.
116 NYCRO, ZBA 5/1/9.
117 NYCRO, ZBA 5/1/12.
118 NYCRO, ZBA 17/1. Thanks to Carol Kerry-Green, 10.11.21.
119 Marmaduke received 40s, his son Henry 40s, also George and Anne Peerse 'my sister's children 40s each', Christopher Peers 20s, his children 40s among them: Hardy Bertram McCall, *The Early History of Bedale in the North Riding of Yorkshire* (1907), p. 68. Thanks to Carol Kerry-Green for the Peirse/Percy timeline: TMPP Research Report, 29.7.2022.
120 Thanks to Lady Jadranka Beresford-Peirse for the Peirse family tree, 25.9.2021.
121 For Richard Peirse (Pearse), d. 1573, see Family Search website: www.familysearch.org/search/record/results?q.anyDate.from=1471&q.anyPlace=Lazenby&q.surname=Peirse
122 For the Council at Wressil, see 'The 5th Earl of Northumberland's Household Book', Monday, 30 September 1512. This Household Account began in 1512,

so possibly Thomas was already employed earlier. Thanks to Christopher Hunwick, Archivist at Alnwick Castle, 2.3.2021. See also Thomas Percy, 'Regulations & Establishments of the household of Henry Algernon Percy, 5th Earl of his castle Wresil & Leconfield' (1827), pp. 1–2 (Carol Kerry-Green, Peirse/Percy timeline: TMPP Research Report, 29.7.2022.)

123 *Surtees Society*, Vol. 53, pp. 183–85. The Scarborough Peter Percy's sons are Peter, Thomas and William, his wife is Allison. Peter's brother, John Percy, is a merchant of Scarborough. His son is Robert, daughters Margaret and Elizabeth, and wife Elin. Robert's children are Gregory, Peter, Margaret, Elyn and Kateryn.

124 *Harley 433*, Vol. 1, p. 153.

125 CPR 1471–85, p. 386. Poche was granted the position for life on 8 March 1484 at Westminster.

126 CFR 1471–85, p. 310. William Poche was described as Yeoman of the parish of St Mary of Barking in a mainprise grant, 18 February 1485.

127 *Harley 433*, Vol. 2, p. 212.

128 CFR 1485–1509, p. 71. The date of death for Sir William Pecche of Kent is recorded as 14 April 1488.

129 C.S.L. Davies, *ODNB*; Rodney Dennys, *Heraldry and the Heralds* (1982). Thanks to David Santiuste.

130 Davies, *ODNB*.

131 CPR 1476–85, p. 159. Tyrwhite, as the 'king's servant', received a grant from Edward IV on 24 July 1479.

132 CPR 1476–85, p. 342. Tyrwhite received a pardon from Edward IV on 27 February 1483 for all offences committed by him.

133 CPR 1476–85, p. 565.

134 *Ibid.*, p. 540. *Harley 433*, Vol. 2, p. 167.

135 *Harley 433*, Vol. 2, p. 35.

136 CPR 1476–85, p. 393.

137 Ibid., p. 398.

138 *Harley 433*, Vol. 2, pp. 210, 211.

139 CPR 1476–85, p. 512.

140 *Harley 433*, Vol. 1, p. 112.

141 *Heralds' Memoir*, pp. 120, 148.

142 CPR 1500–1509, Vol. 2, p. 64.

143 *Ibid.*, p. 174.

144 *Memorials*, p. 109.

145 Weightman, pp. 134–35.

146 Wroe, pp. 301, 518.

147 Weightman, p. 153.

148 An Elector was one of the highest-ranking princes of the Holy Roman Empire who was solely entitled to elect the Roman-German king (until 1806). In the original form there were seven electors, three of them spiritual (archbishops of Mainz, Trier and Cologne) and four secular (Bohemia, Palatine, Saxony and Brandenburg). www.historisches-lexikon-bayerns.de/Lexikon/EN:Electors. For Albert: Dr P.C. Molhuysen and Prof. Dr P.J. Blok, 'Albrecht van Saksen', *Nieuw Nederlandsch Biografisch Woordenboek* (1911), Deel 1.

149 The General Stadtholder was a deputy of the absent sovereign in a certain area of his realm. This official's powers were not limited to military matters but also extended to administration and justice. The Stadtholder oversaw the troops and was responsible for recruitment and armament. He also carried out diplomatic missions. From 1452 onward the word 'General' was added to the title of Stadtholder. See: A. van Cruyningen, *Stadtholders in de Nederlanden van Holland tot Vlaanderen (1448–1879)*, p. 12.

150 See Chapter 15.

151 Steven G. Ellis, *ODNB*.

152 Randolph Jones, 'The Extraordinary Reign of "Edward VI" in Ireland, 1487–8', *Bulletin*, March 2021, pp. 48–56 (pp. 53–54).

153 Ashdown-Hill, *Dublin King*, p. 155; *The Book of Howth* (1871), p. 189. For 1489 as the date of the meeting at Greenwich, *Dublin King*, pp. 155–56. For 1494 as the date of the meeting, see Randolph Jones, 'Henry VII, the lords of Ireland and the two pretenders', *Bulletin*, September 2022, pp. 72–76 (p. 75).

154 Ellis, *ODNB*.

155 Ibid.

156 Ibid.

157 Ibid.

158 *Statute Rolls, Edward IV* (22), pp. 897–901. Thanks to Randolph Jones.

159 *Harley 433*, Vol. 3, p. 36.

160 CPR 1476–85, p. 477; *Harley 433*, Vol. 3, pp. 111–12.

161 CPR 1485–94, p. 84. Kildare was Deputy by 25 September 1486. Circle, 'A Calendar of Irish Chancery Letters *c.* 1244–1509', Trinity College, NAI MS 2011 1 196: chancery.tcd.ie/roll/2-Henry-VII/patent.

162 'The Earls of Desmond (contd)', *Kerry Archaeological Magazine*, Vol. 4, No. 17, October 1916, p. 56.

163 R.J. Schoeck, *ODNB*.

164 For Oxford, see *Itinerary*, p. 5; Hairsine, 'Oxford and Richard III', *Crown and People*, pp. 307–32 (p. 309). For Worcester and Warwick (5–14 August), see *Early Historians*, p. 122. For York (29 August–20 September), see Hammond, *The Children of Richard III*, pp. 29, 65–66; Appendix III, 'Bedern College Statute Book', p. 48. For Grantham (19–20 October), see *Itinerary*, p. 9; CCR No.1171 (membrane 13d); CCR 1476–85, pp. 346–47; also *Foedera* XII, p. 203. CCR source thanks to Jean Clare-Tighe.

165 Schoeck, *ODNB*.

166 *Memorials*, p. 26.

167 Schoeck, *ODNB*.

168 D. Williams, 'Will of William Catesby', p. 49.

169 For Brampton's death in 1512 (not 1508), see B. Williams, 'Sir Edward Brampton', *Ricardian*, March 1984, p. 297; *Grande Enciclopédia Portuguesa e Brasileira*. Brampton may have died in England.

170 J.L. Bolton (ed.), *The Alien Communities of London in the Fifteenth Century: The Subsidy Rolls of 1440 and 1483–4* (1998), p. 74; CPR 1485–94, p. 274.

171 Stuart Jenks (ed.), *Quellen und Darstellungen Zur Hansischen Geschichte*, Hanseatic History Association, Part III, No. 6, 2016, p. 57; *Neue Folge*, Vol. 74, Part III,

No. 6; www.hansischergeschichtsverein.de. Thanks to Jean Clare-Tighe (24.8.2021).

172 CPR 1476–85, p. 413.

173 *Ibid.*, p. 481.

174 *Ibid.*, pp. 416, 479.

175 B. Williams, 'Portuguese Connection', p. 141.

176 Rosemary Horrox, *ODNB*.

177 B. Williams, 'Sir Edward Brampton', *Ricardian*, p. 296.

178 Wroe, p. 22.

179 André, p. 60; Bolton, *Alien Communities: Subsidy Rolls 1483–4*, pp. 73–74. No French servant is recorded in Brampton's household.

180 Wroe, p. 197.

181 Wroe, p. 526. For questions regarding the Setúbal Testimonies, see p. 41.

182 Wroe, p. 20.

183 Horrox, *ODNB*; Weaver, *Somerset Medieval Wills*, p. 112. The 'John and Thomas Brampton' who supported Richard of England had no connection to Sir Edward and Lady Margaret Brampton (Wroe, p. 178).

184 *Alien Communities*, p. 74. Brampton's London house was in Broad Street Ward. See also 'England's Immigrants 1330–1550', TNA, E 179/242/25 [1407]. Backdated to 25 June 1483.

185 Davies, 'Jersey', pp. 336 n. 18, 341, from Campbell, *Materials*, I, p. 316.

186 *Ibid.*, from *Materials*, I, p. 186. Also: CPR 1485–94, p. 46.

187 *Ibid.*, pp. 335 n. 10, 340.

188 Horrox, *Study of Service*, p. 8.

189 CFR 1471–85, p. 199.

190 Howard Books, Vol. 2, p. 38.

191 *Ibid.*, p. 41.

192 *Ibid.*, p. 312.

193 Colin Richmond, 'Royal Administration and the Keeping of the Seas, 1422–1485' (Thesis, University of Oxford, 1963), p. 522. Thanks to Jean Clare-Tighe. See also note 194.

194 Richmond, Thesis, Chapter 5 ('The Pattern of Naval Activity') p. 96.

195 *Royal Funerals*, pp. 16, 26, 35, 39.

196 *Harley 433*, Vol. 1, p. 256.

197 *Ibid.*, p. 258.

198 *Ibid.*, p. 275.

199 *Ibid.*, p. 212.

200 Richmond, p. 522 n. 5; PRO E404/78/3/49.

201 *Harley 433*, Vol. 1, p. 180.

202 CPR 1476–85, p. 481.

203 *Harley 433*, Vol. 2, p. 213.

204 CPR 1476–85, p. 461.

205 CPR 1485–94, p. 142.

206 Freepages.rootsweb.com/~treevecwll/family/msrfowey1700.htm; *Rot. Parl.*, vi, pp. 246–47 for Treffry attainted by Richard III; for the attainder reversed by Henry VII, see p. 273.

207 *Harley 433*, Vol. 2, p. 25 ('Cs [100 shillings] to Jane Colyns for hire hole yere wages ending at Michelmess' from Middleham Accounts, 25 Sept. 1483) and Vol. 1, p. 224 (annuity 'ten markes for terme of her lyf of the Revenues of Wakefield'), possibly dated *c.* October 1484, therefore the annuity is likely granted following the death of Edward of Middleham. For Jane Colyns as the prince's possible nurse, for wages paid and offerings while with him at nearby religious houses (Coverham, Jervaux, Fountains Abbey, etc.), see Hammond, *Children of Richard III*, pp. 20, 23–24.

208 *Rot. Parl.*, vi, p. 276.

209 Howard's epitaph at www.luminarium.org/encyclopedia/thomashow-ardepitaph.gif. For the Tower, see Campbell, Vol. 1, p. 207, and Howard's costs there, p. 208.

210 *Rot. Parl.*, vi, p. 410.

211 CPR 1485–94, p. 285.

212 Buc, p. cxxvii.

213 CPR 1469–77, pp. 261, 312.

214 *Crowland*, p. 197. At York, Henry was 'nearly trapped by the cunning of the enemy'.

215 *York Books*, Vol. 2, p. 573 (17 June 1487), Lovell 'discomfetid and fled'; *Heralds' Memoir*, p. 118, Lovell 'put to flight'.

216 *York Books*, Vol. 2, p. 460.

217 Gairdner, *Letters &Papers Henry VII*, Vol. 2, p. 370.

218 Sheilah O'Connor, 'Francis Lovel and the Rebels of Furness Fells', *Ricardian*, Vol. 7, No. 96, March 1987, pp. 366–70 (p. 368 n. 23); J.B. Paul (ed.), *Register of the Great Seal of Scotland* (1882), Vol. 1424–1490, p. 370, item 1738: NAS02024 C2-12-00004.

219 Thanks to Marie Barnfield and Sharon Lock; Paul, *Register of the Great Seal of Scotland*, Vol. 1424–1490, p. 381, item 1796; O'Connor, in 'Francis Lovel and the Rebels of Furness Fells', records this inadvertently as December (p. 368 n. 26).

220 Thomas Dickson (ed.), *Scotland, Chronicle and Memorials: Account of the Lord High Treasurer* (1877), Vol. 1, 1473–1498, p. 99. Thanks to Marie Barnfield and Sharon Lock.

221 Dickson, *op. cit.*, p. 130. Thanks to Marie Barnfield and Sharon Lock.

222 CPR 1485–94, pp. 304, [298], 305, 307, 351.

223 O'Connor, *op. cit.*, pp. 368–69 n. 27; Angelo Raine (ed.), *York Civic Records* (1941), Vol. 2, *Yorkshire Archaeological Society Records Series*, Vol. 103, p. 75.

224 O'Connor, *op. cit.*, p. 369 n. 29; IPM Henry VII (1898), Vol. 1, p. 345, No. 803. Henry VII 8 (1493). From inquiry into the holdings of a John Samuell, which O'Connor records as 1492.

225 Thanks to Sharon Lock, investigations with Magdalen College (4.7.18).

226 *Notes and Queries* (1878), 5th Series, Vol. 10, pp. 28–29, Gairdner entry citing IPM Henry VIII 26, No. 110, Francis Lovell.

227 David Baldwin, 'What Happened to Lord Lovel?', *Ricardian*, Vol. 7, No. 89, June 1985, pp. 56–65 (p. 58 n. 15), *Notes and Queries* (1878), n. 226.

228 For the skeleton at Minster Lovell, see Baldwin, 'What Happened?', pp. 60–44.

229 CPR 1485–94, p. 64.

230 Henry visited Minster Lovell from Woodstock, see D.A. Luckett, 'The Thames Valley Conspiracies against Henry VII', *Historical Research*, Vol. 68, p. 171, citing E101/413/13 or BL, Add. MS 7099 f.14. Thanks to Marie Barnfield and Sharon Lock. Jasper Tudor was likely then in residence.

231 O'Connor, *op. cit.*, pp. 366–70 (p. 369 n. 29); *Rot. Parl.*, vi, p. 503.

232 historytheinterestingbits.com/2019/11/16/ guest-post-anne-fitzhugh-lovell-by-michele-schindler/

233 Thanks to Bill Hare, Bedale, June 2021: Hare, 'Bedale and the Wars of the Roses: Viscount Francis Lord Lovell, Lord of Bedale, Last Stand', p. 19.

234 Baldwin, *op. cit.*, p. 57; *Vergil-2*, p. 25.

235 TMPP Genealogical Report, thanks to Kate Smith.

236 Gregory Stevens Cox, *Guernsey's Medieval Castles* (2012), pp. 8–10, 13, 18, 21–22.

237 *Ballad of Bosworth Fielde*, line 260. Also Hutton, *Battle of Bosworth Field* (1788, 1999), p. 127. Nicholas Ridley may have also fought at the battle.

238 CPR 1485–94, p. 144. Easter 1486: Thomas de Saint Martyn was appointed Gentleman Usher of King Henry's Chamber with an annuity of £12. See also note 185.

239 Michael K. Jones, 'Sir William Stanley of Holt: Politics and Family Allegiance in the Late Fifteenth Century', *Welsh Historical Review* (1988), pp. 1–22. For the Battle of Hexham 1464, see James Tait, *DNB*.

240 *Coronation*, p. 399

241 Jones, 'Stanley', pp. 5–6.

242 Jean M. Gidman, 'The wives and children of Sir William Stanley of Holt', *Ricardian*, Vol. 9, No. 116, March 1992, pp. 206–10 (family tree on p. 207). N.B. The Leycester line is in error; Tait, *DNB*. See also Jones, 'Stanley', p. 20.

243 *Coronation*, pp. 271, 399.

244 M. J. Bennett, *ODNB*.

245 A.J. Hibbard, *An Account of Richard … & Order of the Garter*, pp. 21, 38. Richard, Duke of York, received his Garter stall in 1475 (at 1 year and 8 months old) (p. 18). Edward V's Garter stall was not filled until Sunday, 8 May 1491, when it was allocated to Prince Arthur (at 4 years, 7½ months old), even though stalls had become vacant earlier. Edward had received his stall in 1471, aged about 6 months (p. 16). George Frederick Beltz, *Memorials of the Order of the Garter* (1841), p. clxvii (No. 233: Henry VII), assigns Sir William to the order before 27 May 1487. No reason is given for this end-date, other than assumption that Richard, Duke of York, was killed in 1483.

246 Baldwin, *Stoke Field*, Appendix I: 'The Rebels of 1487', pp. 123–25.

247 Bennett, pp. 98–99.

248 Bennett, *ODNB*.

249 Bennett, *ODNB*; T.B. Howell, *Complete Collection of State Trials for High Treason and Other Crimes etc.* (1816), Vol. 1 (1163–1600), 'The Trial of Sir William Stanley, knight, for High Treason: 10 Hen. VII. AD 1494–5 [Hall and Lord Bacon]', pp. 277–84; *Vergil-2*, p. 75. For date, see W.A.J. Archbold, 'Sir William Stanley and Perkin Warbeck', *EHR* (1899), Vol. 14, pp. 529–34 (p. 530). Latin trans. thanks to Dr Shelagh Sneddon (2.12.22).

250 Wroe, p. 137.

251 Archbold, *op. cit.*, pp. 530–31 (trans. Sneddon).

252 Wroe, p. 181.

253 Tait, *DNB*.

254 *Vergil-1*, p. 54.

255 Tait, *DNB*.

256 TNA, C/54/376/001–2 (translation thanks to Dr Shelagh Sneddon). Also T. Thornton, *Cheshire and the Tudor State 1480–1560* (2000), p. 177. The Bonds and Recognizances research for TMPP and Sir William's 'rebellion' from CPR 1494–1509, p. 16 (17 March 1495), with thanks to Dr Judith Ford.

257 As Constable, Thomas Stanley would have presided over treason trials but is not named (at Westminster). Buckingham is named, with Dorset next and others: Archbold, *op. cit.*, pp. 530–31. For Thomas Stanley presiding over the treason trial on 20 February (at Westminster) for Sir Humphrey Savage and others, see Archbold, p. 532.

258 Wroe, p. 181, at Syon House.

259 Jones, 'Stanley', p. 21 n. 91. Also, Tait, *DNB*.

260 Jones, 'Stanley', p. 20 nn. 86, 88.

261 *Vergil-2*, p. 75, for later mitigation of the narrative surrounding Sir William's treason.

262 It is unknown whether William Jnr was by Sir William's first or second wife: Gidman, *op. cit.*; 'Research Notes and Queries', Vol. 10, No. 124, pp. 21–22. Sir William Jnr married Joan Massey of Tatton, see note 242, family tree. Also see Tait, *DNB*.

263 Jones, 'Stanley', pp. 20–21 nn. 88, 93.

264 Jan Mulrenan, 'Thomas Stanley, a bastard's tale', *Bulletin* (December 2018), p. 50 n. 17, from British History Online: J.S. Brewer, *Letters and Papers Henry VIII* (1864), Vol. 2, pp. 1156–1172.

265 Michael J. Bennett, 'Henry VII and the Northern Rising of 1489', *EHR*, Vol. CV, No. 414, January 1990, pp. 34–59 (p. 44 n. 3.); C.G. Bayne & W.H. Dunham (eds), *Select Cases in Council of Henry VII* (1958, Seldon Society), pp. 85–87; this search thanks to Francisca Icaza.

266 Jones, 'Stanley', p. 18 n. 74; TNA, E 154/2/5.

18. Avenues for Exploration

1 *Heralds' Memoir*, p. 116. For Henry fleeing the conflict, see Bennett, p. 82.

2 Bennett, pp. 122, 131, letter of Henry VII to Pope Innocent VIII, 5 July 1487; *Molinet* (1490).

3 *Vergil-2*, p. 75, reported response in 1495: 'if he [Sir William] were sure that the man was Edward's son he would never take up arms against him'.

4 Bennett, p. 72.

5 Wroe, p. 179; Arthurson, *The Perkin Warbeck Conspiracy*, pp. 85, 221; Kingsford, *Chronicles of London*, p. 203; André, p. 64.

6 Baldwin, Stoke Field, Appendix 1, 'Rebels of 1487', pp. 123–25; Athurson, pp. 204–05; Wroe, pp. 176–81.

7   Aka Mashborough/Marsburgh. *GC*, pp. 219, 446; *Mythology*, pp. 116 n. 11, 280; Howard Books, Vol. 2, p. 348. Marsburgh was the keeper, maker and provider of the king's bows in the Tower, Calais, Ireland and elsewhere: CPR 1467–77, p. 420, thanks to Ian Rogers; Athurson, p. 209. He seems to have served in the same role under Richard III.

8   *GC*, pp. 284 and 291.

9   Matthew Lewis, *The Survival of the Princes in the Tower*, p. 207.

10 Wroe, pp. 468, 471–72.

11 Wroe, pp. 431–32.

12 Rawdon Brown, *Calendar Relating to English Affairs/Venice, Vol. 4, 1527–1533*: 'Appendix: Miscellaneous 1495', pp. 482–83 (British History Online). See Appendix 8.

13 For list, see A.J. Hibbard, 'The Missing Evidence', *Court Journal*, Vol. 26, Autumn 2019, p. 27, www.revealingrichardiii.com/archival-destruction.html

14 The *Titulus Regius* first came to light as an abstract made by William Camden and published in his *Britannia* edition of 1607. Camden's published abstract consisted of notes taken from an earlier abstract of the Act of Succession, which is extant in BL, MS Add. 33216, ff.370–72, of which the author is unknown but may have been William Bowyer, Keeper of the Records in the Tower of London in the 1560s (David Weil Baker, 'Jacobean Historiography and the Election of Richard III', *Huntington Library Quarterly*, Vol. 70, No. 3, September 2007, pp. 311–42 [pp. 313, 321 n. 50]). The Act was first published in full by John Speed, *The Historie of Great Britaine*, 1611: see Buc, pp. xlviii, xlix.

15 Jeremy Potter, *Good King Richard?* (1983), p. 101. Thanks to Lesley Lambert.

16 A.J. Pollard, *Richard III and the Princes in the Tower* (1991), p. 233.

17 Thanks to Janet Senior, researcher and archivist at Markenfield Hall, 1.9.2022. In 1601, seventy-nine boxes, a coffer and two bags of archive material were removed from Markenfield Hall by the last Tudor monarch.

18 *York Books*, Vol. 2, pp. 475–76, 478–79.

19 Anne F. Sutton & Livia Visser-Fuchs, *Richard III's Books* (1997), p. 146 n. 51.

20 Eaedem, *The Hours of Richard III* (1990), pp. 68–70.

21 Horrox, *Richard III: A Study of Service*, p. 145.

22 Dr Sandra Pendlington and Patricia Payne, 'Research: Cardinal Archbishop Thomas Bourchier', *Court Journal*, Vol. 19, Spring 2016, pp. 22–29 (p. 29). Records missing: 1482–86. The Bourchier Register is still available, as are some of the Knole House records.

23 CPR 1485–95, p. 386.

24 Wroe, pp. 359, 573. 'Milan: 1497', in *Calendar of State Papers and Manuscripts in the Archives and Collections of Milan 1385–1618*, ed. Allen B Hinds (London, 1912), pp. 310–341. BHO: www.british-history.ac.uk/cal-state-papers/milan/1385-1618/pp310-341 [accessed 30 January 2021].

25 *Rot. Parl.*, vi, p. 220. Fine imposed for violation of cloth of gold (Sumptuary) law was £20. For the eleven named courtiers close to Edward IV exempt from the law and with royal authority to wear cloth of gold, p. 122. Also: A Compton Reeves, 'The Foppish Eleven of 1483', *Medieval Prosopography*, Autumn 1995, Vol. 16, No. 2, pp. 111–34.

26 See Chapter 17: Sir Edward Brampton; Howard Books, Vol. 2, p. 426. Retrospective payments were made on 11 August 1483 for four outfits for humble children of the stables. See Chapter 14.

27 Langley and Schneider Coutandin, 'Lost in Translation?' (Part One), p. 49; *Ibid.* for Sandal Castle Nursery as a highly controlled and secure location.

28 Stapleton, *Plumpton Correspondence*, p. 54: 29 November 1486.

29 Smith, 'Lambert Simnel and the King from Dublin', p. 520; thanks to Eileen Bates.

30 *GC*, p. 291.

31 Wroe, p. 499.

32 Wroe, p. 511.

33 Baldwin, *The Lost Prince: The Survival of Richard of York* (2007). For Jack Leslau's theory of the survival of both princes, see Lewis, *The Survival of the Princes in the Tower*, pp. 210–33. Ongoing investigations thanks to TMPP members, Carl Holdcroft and James Leslau.

34 Wroe, p. 506.

35 Glen Moran, 'The Search for the mtDNA of the "Princes"', *Bulletin*, December 2018, pp. 41–44; *Mythology*, pp. 204–07, Appendix 4b, pp. 264–66.

36 Wendy Corbett Kelley, TMPP Research Report, 11.5.2017.

37 *Ibid.* An outdoor passageway may mark the original location of the south aisle ('West Winge') of the fourteenth-century Austin Friars church where York is believed to be buried.

19. Summary and Conclusion

1 *York Books*, Vol. 2, p. 570. This is the only surviving contemporary document that ascribes to him the regnal number 'VI', see Chapter 12, n. 25.

2 Bennett, p. 70.

3 *York Books*, Vol. 2, pp. 574–82.

4 Bennett, p. 81. See note 6.

5 *York Books*, Vol. 2, pp. 586–87.

6 Bennett, p. 148 n. 29.

7 *York Books*, Vol. 2, p. 572.

8 Bennett, p. 78.

9 'Milan: 1497', in *Calendar of State Papers and Manuscripts in the Archives and Collections of Milan 1385–1618*, ed. Allen B Hinds (London, 1912), pp. 310–41. BHO: www.british-history.ac.uk/cal-state-papers/milan/1385-1618/pp310-341 [accessed 30 January 2021].

10 BL Add MS 24513, f. 148-1: source and transcription thanks to Marie Barnfield. NB: Metcalfe may be 'Metham'. Also: Mason Metcalfe, 'The Metcalfes of Nappa Hall: Inside the House of Metcalfe', *Bulletin*, September 2022, pp. 48–54 (p. 54) 109 families should read 51. From: Walter C. and Gilbert Metcalfe, *Records of the Family of Metcalfe, formerly of Nappa in Wensleydale* (1891), pp. 36–37; *Collectanea Hunteriana*, 'Abstract of Record in the Queen's Remembrances' Office', Richard III, Henry VII, Additional MS 24618, Vol. 6, fo. 148.

11 C.H. Williams, 'The Rebellion of Humphrey Stafford in 1486', *EHR*, Vol. 43, No. 170, 1928, pp. 181–89 (p. 183 n. 5). The Yorkist pretender is recorded as

coming from the island of Guernsey. The Governorship of Guernsey included Alderney, Sark, Herm and Jethou: CPR 1476–85, pp. 818 (1482), 413 (1484). Searches continue.

12 A.J. Hibbard, *An Account of Richard ... & Order of the Garter*, p. 16. Edward, Prince of Wales, received his Garter stall on 23 April 1471, aged nearly 6 months.

13 See Appendix 4.

14 Wroe, p. 91.

15 Wroe, p. 469.

16 Stapleton, *Plumpton Correspondence*, pp. 141–42, note a. The trial was before Sir John Sely, Knight Marshal, and Sir John Turbervile, Marshal of the Marshalsea (the Palace Court for household servants).

17 Alice Johnson, TMPP Research Report, 'The "Lincoln" Roll: Does it truly fit the criteria of a piece of propaganda?', 19.5.2022. Forthcoming publication in *Bulletin*.

18 Iiif.biblissima.fr/collections/manifest/197399e5ad696aa5d11ac5e0ef6b821fd ddab14e (trans. thanks to Marie Barnfield). There is no medallion for Edward of Warwick.

19 Middle English: the part of life following childhood.

20. Postscript

1 Arthurson, *The Perkin Warbeck Conspiracy 1491–1499*, p. vii.

2 David Baldwin, *Stoke Field*, Appendix IV, pp. 133–34.

Appendix 3 An Ideal Place to Hide a Prince

1 Handwritten notes on Coldridge Church are in Crediton Library (*c.* 1910). As a local historian, Cresswell published three books on antiquities and churches in Exeter and Devon from 1908–10.

2 Chris Brooks and Martin Cherry, 'The Prince and the Parker', *The Journal of Stained Glass*, Vol. 26 (1992, rev. 2003), p. 17. Lecturers at Exeter University investigated the connection between Edward V and Coldridge.

3 Peter Bramley, *A Companion Guide to the Wars of the Roses* (2011), p. 107, focuses on associated physical remains.

4 Brooks and Cherry, 'The Prince and the Parker', p. 20.

5 1525 survey of lands (rental) of Cecily Bonville, Marchioness of Dorset (d. 1529): Somerset Heritage Centre, T\PH\st/1525. This contains an early record of the land and manor leased by John Evans at Coldridge.

6 E. Ashworth, *Notes on Some North Devon Churches*, Vol. 5, Part 1 and Part 7 (1887). Ashworth was a leading English artist/architect from Devon who built, restored and visited many churches and left a large archive.

7 Ibid.

8   Donald P. White, *Elaboration: Artisans and Ideas in the Devon Parish* (2010),
    p. 168. 'Some elite benefactors who engaged in dispersed benefaction appear
    to have employed the same principal artisans for each of their initiatives. This
    strategy further blurred the differences in design from parish to parish and
    object to object. It is possible that the Coldridge parclose screen standing next
    to the 1538 [?1511] box pews and obviously constructed by the same group of
    Anglo-French carvers was also initiated by John Evans.'

9   See note 1.

10 Brooks and Cherry, 'The Prince and the Parker'.

11 With thanks to York Herald, College of Arms. Also: John Burke, Bernard
    Burke, *A General Armory of England, Scotland, and Ireland* (1842).

12 Brooks and Cherry, p. 11.

13 Michael J. Yaremchuk, MD, 'Commentary on: Chin Ups and Downs:
    Avoiding Bad Results in Chin Reoperation', *Aesthetic Surgery Journal*
    (1 March 2017), Vol. 37, Issue 3, pp. 264–65, doi.org/10.1093/asj/sjw266.

14 Somerset Heritage Centre, T\PH\st/1525.

15 Tristram Risdon, *The Chorographical Description, or, Survey of the County of
    Devon, with the City and County of Exeter*, p. 370. Circulated in manuscript form
    for almost eighty years before it was published in 1632. The source of the
    description of the deer park is unknown.

16 CPR 1476–85, 3 March 1484, p. 879. N.B. The term 'King's Servant' would
    apply to senior members of his household.

17 Lawrence C. Duggan, *Arms Bearing and the Clergy in History and Canon Law of
    Western Christianity* (2013), p. 198, highlights the military role of clergy and
    parishioners: e.g. Coldridge Church maintained armour and weapons.

18 Pollard, *Sir Thomas Markenfield and Richard III* (2018), pp. 1, 10, 11, posits the
    development of a personal bond with Richard of Gloucester when Thomas
    entered his service, which may have extended to Robert Markenfield.

19 'Court of Common Pleas', Henry VII, CP40 No 931 (1495), image 142. An
    Edmund Gyll took out a plea at Wembworthy for trespass against John Speke
    Jnr, Robert Markenfield, yeoman, and three farm workers.

20 *Harley 433*, Vol. 2, pp. 124–25: 'Sir Henry Bodrugan … shall enter and take
    possession of the manors, towns and lordships before specified [including
    Coldridge]'.

21 CPR 1485–94, p. 105. Bodrugan was commissioned with others on
    26 February 1486 to arrest John Gaye and William Bruer for pirating two ships
    of a foreign but friendly country, Almayn (Cornish for Germany).

22 John Bayley, *The History and Antiquities of the Tower of London* (1830), p. 343,
    already the raised queries that one of the princes still lived.

23 *Harley 433*, Vol. 2, p. 211. Davy was the king's tailor.

24 Dr A.J. Hibbard, TMPP Research Report, 22.11.2020. Peter Armstrong
    (one-name.org/name_profile/godsland/): 'The Godsland surname is thought to
    be locative and comes from an area in the parish of Cruwys Morchard, Devon
    known as Gogland. C. Spiegelhalter in *A Dictionary of Devon Surnames* quotes
    this origin for the name and cites Wm. de Goggalond, 1329.'

25 T.L. Stoate (ed.), *Devon Lay Subsidy Rolls 1524–1527* (1979), p. 123. At
    Burrington, a John Goddyslond had the designation 'W1', a category that

included servants and workers on deer parks. Dorset (and subsequently Cecily Bonville) had land and tenants here.

26 T.L. Stoate and A.J. Howard (eds), *The Devon Muster Roll for 1569* (1977), p. 109. This listed all those able to fight on a commission of array. John Goddesland, possibly son of the John Goddesland of interest, is listed as bellman or billman.

Appendix 7 Trois Enseignes Naturelz, 27 November–12 December 1493

1 Zoë Maula, TMPP Research Report, 14.12.2020. Trans. thanks to Dr Livia Visser-Fuchs.

2 *RI XIV*, 1, n. 136: *Regesta*, www.regesta-imperii.de/id/1493-11-27_1_0_14_1_0_136_136; and *RI XIV*, 1, n. 176: *Regesta*, www.regesta-imperii.de/id/1493-12-12_2_0_14_1_0_176_176. Nicolo di Cesare, the Milanese envoy, reports from Vienna on on 12 December 1493 that Maximilian has tried mediation between Henry VII and the Duke of York, but the English King remains distrustful. This document must therefore have been written between 27 November, when the Duke of York came to Maximilian's court requesting aid, and its despatch on or after 12 December 1493. Appreciation to Dr Manfred Hollegger, Deputy Project Manager of the *Regesta Imperii XIV*, for sources and kind insights.

3 Using characters typical of a French or Burgundian writer, the letter was probably written at the Burgundian court or by one of Maximilian's 'French' clerks: most likely, Antoine Waudripont, who is often revealed as author of Maximilian's letters in the *Regesta*. Appreciation again to Dr. Manfred Hollegger.

4 Wroe, p. 132.

5 *Ibid.*, p. 133.

Appendix 10 Maat, and Black & Hackman Reports: 'Bones in the Urn', 14 June 2018, 11 November 2021

1 See 'The Sons of Edward IV: A Re-Examination of the Evidence on their Deaths and on the Bones in Westminster Abbey' by P.W. Hammond and W.J. White, in *Richard III: Loyalty, Lordship and Law* (Yorkist History Trust, 1986, 2000), p. 152.

Bibliography

Arthurson, Ian, *The Perkin Warbeck Conspiracy 1491–1499* (Sutton Publishing, 1994, 1997).

Ashdown-Hill, John, *Richard III's 'Beloved Cousyn': John Howard and the House of York* (The History Press, 2009).

Ashdown-Hill, John, *Eleanor: The Secret Queen: The Woman Who Put Richard III on the Throne* (The History Press, 2009, 2016).

Ashdown-Hill, John, *The Dublin King* (The History Press, 2015).

Ashdown-Hill, John, *The Mythology of the Princes in the Tower* (Amberley, 2018).

Ashdown-Hill, John, *Elizabeth Widville, Lady Grey: Edward IV's Chief Mistress and the 'Pink Queen'* (Pen and Sword History, 2019).

Attreed, Lorraine C., *York House Books 1461–1490* (Alan Sutton for Richard III and Yorkist History Trust, 1991).

Bacon, Francis, *The History of the Reign of Henry the Seventh*, edited by Roger Lockyer (Folio Society, 1971).

Baldwin, David, *Stoke Field: The Last Battle of the Wars of the Roses* (Pen & Sword, 2006).

Baldwin, David, *The Lost Prince: The Survival of Richard of York* (The History Press, 2007).

Bayley, John, *The History and Antiquities of the Tower of London: With Memoirs of Royal and Distinguished Persons, Deduced from Records, State-Papers, and Manuscripts, and from Other Original and Authentic Sources* (Jennings & Chaplin, 1830).

Bennett, Michael, *Lambert Simnel and the Battle of Stoke* (Alan Sutton, 1987).

Bolton, J.L., (ed.), *The Alien Communities of London in the Fifteenth Century: The Subsidy Rolls of 1440 and 1483–4* (Richard III & Yorkist History Trust with Paul Watkins, 1998).

Buchon, Jean Alexandre C., *Chroniques de Jean Molinet 1474–1504*, five volumes (Paris, 1827–28).

Burke, John, *A Genealogical and Heraldic History of Commoners of Great Britain and Ireland* (1838).

Campbell, William (ed.), *Materials for a History of the Reign of Henry VII* (Longman, 1873).

Carlson, David R., *English Humanist Books: Writers and Patrons, Manuscript and Print 1475–1525* (University of Toronto Press, 1993).

Carpenter, Christine, *Kingsford's Stonor Letters and Papers 1290–1483* (Cambridge University Press, 1996).

Carson, Annette, *Richard III: The Maligned King* (The History Press, 2008, 2013).

Carson, Annette (ed.), *Finding Richard III: The Official Account of Research by the Retrieval & Reburial Project* (Imprimis Imprimatur, 2014).

Carson, Annette, *Richard, Duke of Gloucester as Lord Protector and High Constable of England* (Imprimis Imprimatur, April 2015).

Carson, Annette, *Domenico Mancini: de occupatione regni Anglie* (Imprimis Imprimatur, 2021).

Cavell, Emma (ed.), *The Heralds' Memoir 1486–1490: Court Ceremony, Royal Progress and Rebellion* (Richard III and Yorkist History Trust with Shaun Tyas, 2009).

Chastelain, Jean-Didier, *L'Imposture de Perkin Warbeck* (Office de Publicité, 1952).

Chrimes, S.B., *Henry VII* (Yale University Press, 1999).

Clay, Charles Travis (ed.), *Early Yorkshire Charters* (Yorkshire Archaeological Society, 1963).

Cooper, Charles Henry, *Annals of Cambridge, Volume 1* (Cambridge University Press, 1842).

Crawford, Anne (ed.), *The Household Books of John Howard, Duke of Norfolk, 1462–1471, 1481–1483* (Alan Sutton for Richard III and Yorkist History Trust, 1992).

Crawford, Anne, *Yorkist Lord: John Howard, Duke of Norfolk c. 1425–1485* (Continuum, 2010).

Cunningham, Sean, *Richard III: A Royal Enigma* (TNA, Richmond Surrey, 2003).

Davis, Norman, *The Paston Letters and Papers of the Fifteenth Century, Part II* (Oxford University Press, 2004).

Edwards, Rhoda, *The Itinerary of King Richard III 1483–1485* (Alan Sutton Publishing for the Richard III Society, 1983).

Ellis, Henry (ed.), *Three Books of Polydore Vergil's English History Comprising the Reigns of Henry VI, Edward IV and Richard III* (Camden Society, London, 1844).

Fabyan, Robert, *The New Chronicles of England and France in Two Parts* (Pynson's edition, 1516; ed. Henry Ellis, London, 1811).

Fields, Bertram, *Royal Blood: King Richard III and the Mystery of the Princes* (ReganBooks, 1998; Sutton Publishing, 2000).

Foard, Glenn, and Curry, Anne, *Bosworth 1485: A Battlefield Rediscovered* (Oxbow, 2013).

Gairdner, James (ed.), *Memorials of Henry VII* (1858).

Gairdner, James, *Letters and Papers Illustrative of the Reigns of Richard III and Henry VII*, Vols I and II (Longmans, 1861 & 1863).

Gairdner, James, *The History of the Life and Reign of Richard the Third to which is Added the Story of Perkin Warbeck from Original Documents* (Longmans, 1878).

Gairdner, James, *Henry the Seventh* (MacMillan & Co., 1889).

Gairdner, James (ed.), *The Paston Letters* (1904; Gloucester: reprint Alan Sutton Publishing, 1986).

Gilbert, John Thomas, *History of the Viceroys of Ireland* (Dublin: James Duffy, 1865).

Grafton, Richard, *The Chronicle of John Hardyng ... Together with the Continuation by Richard Grafton* (1543; ed. Henry Ellis, London, 1812).

Grafton, Richard, *Grafton's Chronicle at Large* (1558; London: ed. Henry Ellis, 1809).

Griffiths, Ralph A., and Sherborne, James, *Kings and Nobles in the Later Middle Ages* (St Martin's Press, 1986).

Hall, Edward, *The Union of the Two Noble Houses of Lancaster and York* (1548; London: ed. Henry Ellis, 1809).

Halsted, Caroline, *Richard III as Duke of Gloucester and King of England*, Vols I and II (1844; Alan Sutton, 1980).

Hammond, P.W. (ed.), *Richard III: Loyalty, Lordship and Law* (Richard III and Yorkist History Trust, 2000).

Hammond, P.W., and Sutton, Anne F., *Richard III: The Road to Bosworth Field* (Constable London, 1985).

Hammond, Peter, *The Children of Richard III* (Fonthill, 2018).

Hampton, W.E., *Memorials of the Wars of the Roses: A Biographical Guide* (Alan Sutton Publishing for the Richard III Society, 1979).

Hanham, Alison, *Richard III and His Early Historians 1483–1485* (Clarendon Press, 1975).

Hanham, Alison (ed.), *The Cely Letters 1472–1488* (Oxford University Press, 1975).

Hay, Denys, *The Anglica Historia of Polydore Vergil 1485–1537* (Royal Historical Society, 1950).

Hibbard, A.J., *Richard (Plantagenet) Third Duke of Gloucester and Third King of England, of that Name, & the Most Noble Order of the Garter* (2016).

Hicks, Michael, *Edward V: The Prince in the Tower* (Tempus Publishing, 2003).

Hobbins, Daniel (ed.), *Bernard André: The Life of Henry VII* (1500; Italica Press, 2011).

Holinshed, Raphael, *The Chronicles of England, Scotland and Ireland* (1577; extended edition 1587; ed. Henry Ellis, 1807–08).

Horrox, Rosemary, *Richard III: A Study of Service* (Cambridge University Press, 1989).

Horrox, Rosemary, and Hammond, P.W. (eds), *British Library Harleian MS 433, Vols 1–4* (Richard III Society, 1979–83).

Ingram, Mike, *Richard III and the Battle of Bosworth* (Helion and Company, 2019).

Jones, Michael (ed.), *Philippe de Commynes Memoirs, 1461–1483* (Penguin, 1972).

Jones, Michael K., *Bosworth 1485: The Psychology of a Battle* (Tempus Publishing, 2002).

Kendall, Paul Murray, *Richard III* (1955; reprint Sphere Books, 1972).

Kincaid, Arthur (ed.), *The Encomium of Richard III by Sir William Cornwallis the Younger* (1616; Turner & Devereux, 1977).

Kincaid, Arthur (ed.), *The History of King Richard the Third* (1619) by Sir George Buc, Master of the Revels (Society of Antiquaries, Richard III Society, 2023).

Kleineke, Hannes, and Hovland, Stephanie R., *The Estate and Household Accounts of William Worsely, Dean of St Paul's Cathedral 1479–1497* (Richard III and Yorkist History Trust with Shaun Tyas, 2004).

Kleineke, Hannes, and Steer, Christian (eds), 'The Yorkist Age: Proceedings of the 2011 Harlaxton Symposium', *Harlaxton Medieval Studies*, Vol. XXIII (Shaun Tyas and Richard III and Yorkist History Trust, 2013).

Kleyn, D.M., *Richard of England* (Jacobyte Books, 2001, reprint 2013).

Lamb, V.B., *The Betrayal of Richard III* (The History Press, 2015).

Langley, Philippa, and Jones, Michael, *The Lost King: The Search for Richard III* (first published as *The King's Grave*) (John Murray, 2013, 2022).

Lewis, Matthew, *Richard, Duke of York: King By Right* (Amberley, 2016).

Lewis, Matthew, *The Survival of the Princes in the Tower* (The History Press, 2017).

Lewis, Matthew, *Richard III: Loyalty Binds Me* (Amberley, 2018).

Lindsay, Philip, *King Richard III: A Chronicle* (Ivor Nicholson & Watson, 1933).

Mackinder, Richard, *Bosworth: The Archaeology of the Battlefield* (Pen & Sword, 2021).

Markham, Sir Clements R., *Richard III: His Life and Character* (Smith Elder & Co., 1906; reprint Redwood Press, 1968).

Matthews, Bronwyn, *Les Chroniques de Jersey* (Société Jersiaise, 2017).

McCall, H.B., *The Early History of Bedale in the North Riding of Yorkshire* (Elliot Stock, 1907).

Nicolas, Nicholas Harris, *Privy Purse Expenses of Elizabeth of York: Wardrobe Accounts of Edward the Fourth* (William Pickering, 1830; Frederick Muller, 1972).

Nicols, John Gough, *Grants of King Edward the Fifth* (Camden Society, AMS Press, 1968).

O'Connor, Stephen, *Polydore Vergil's Life of Richard III: An Edition of the Original Manuscript* (1513; Richard III Society, 2021).

Page, William (ed.), *A History of the County of York, North Riding* (Victoria County History, London, 1914).

Parnell, Geoffrey, *The Tower of London* (English Heritage, B.T. Batsford, 1993).

Parnell, Geoffrey, *The Tower of London: Past & Present* (The History Press, 1998, revised edition 2009).

Penn, Thomas, *Winter King: The Dawn of Tudor England* (Penguin, 2011).

Percy, Ralph, Duke of Northumberland, *Lions of the North: The Percys of Alnwick Castle: A Thousand Years of History* (Scala Arts & Heritage Publishers, 2019).

Petre, J. (ed.), *Richard III: Crown & People* (Richard III Society, Gloucester, 1985).

Pollard, A.J., *North-Eastern England During the Wars of the Roses: Lay Society, War, and Politics 1450–1500* (Clarendon Press, 1990).

Pollard, A.J., *Richard III and the Princes in the Tower* (Alan Sutton Publishing, 1991).

Pritchard, Bob, *Battle of Bosworth: Nobles and Knights' Profiles* (Instaprint Rugeley, 2018).

Pronay, Nicholas, and Cox, John (eds), *The Crowland Chronicle Continuations 1459–1486* (Richard III and Yorkist History Trust, 1986).

Rastell, John, *The Pastime of People or the Chronicles of Divers Realms; and Most Especially of the Realm of England* (1529; ed. Thomas Frognall Dibdin, 1811).

Ross, Charles, *Richard III* (Methuen, 1981, 1988).

Rous, John, *The Rous Roll* (William Pickering, 1859; Alan Sutton Publishing, 1980).

Sanceau, Elaine, *The Perfect Prince: A Biography of the King Dom João II* (Barcelos, 1959).

Santiuste, David, *Edward IV and the Wars of the Roses* (Pen & Sword, 2010).

Schofield, John, *Medieval London Houses* (Yale University Press, 1995, 2003).

Scofield, Cora L., *The Life and Reign of Edward the Fourth: King of England and France and Lord of Ireland*, Vol. 2 (Fonthill Media, 2016 reprint).

Speed, John, *History of Great Britain* (London, 1611).

Stapleton, Thomas (ed.), *Plumpton Correspondence: A Series of Letters, Chiefly Domestick, Written in the Reigns of Edward IV, Richard III, Henry VII and Henry VIII* (Camden Society, 1839).

Stevens Cox, Gregory, *Guernsey's Medieval Castles* (Toucan Press, 2012).

Stow, John, *Annales or a General Chronicle of England* (1592, 1631).

Sutton, Anne F., and Hammond, P.W. (eds), *The Coronation of Richard III: The Extant Documents* (Alan Sutton Publishing, 1983).

Sutton, Anne F., and Visser-Fuchs, Livia, *The Hours of Richard III* (Sutton Publishing, 1990, 1996).

Sutton, Anne F., and Visser-Fuchs, Livia, *Richard III's Books* (Sutton Publishing, 1997).

Sutton, Anne F., and Visser-Fuchs, Livia, with Griffiths, R.A., *The Royal Funerals of the House of York at Windsor* (Richard III Society, 2005).

Sylvester, Richard S. (ed.), *St Thomas More: The History of King Richard III and Selections from the English and Latin Poems* (Yale University Press, 1976).

Syvret, Marguerite, and Stevens, Joan, *Balleine's History of Jersey* (Société Jersiaise; Phillimore, 2011).

Thomas, A.H., and Thornley, I.D. (eds), *The Great Chronicle of London* (George W. Jones, London, 1938; Alan Sutton Publishing, 1983).

Throsby, John, *The History and Antiquities of the Ancient Town of Leicester* (1792).

Toulmin Smith, Lucy (ed.), *The Maire of Bristowe I's Kalendar by Robert Ricart Town Clerk of Bristol 18 Edward IV* (Camden Society, 1872).

Trémoille, Louis de la, *Correspondance de Charles VIII et de Ses Conseillers Avec Louis II de la Trémoille Pendant la Guerre de Bretagne* (1488) (Paris: 1878).

Tucker, Melvin J., *The Life of Thomas Howard, Earl of Surrey and Second Duke of Norfolk 1443–1524* (Mouton & Co., 1964).

Walpole, Horace, *Historic Doubts on the Life and Reign of King Richard the Third* (1768, reprint 1974).

Weightman, Christine, *Margaret of York: The Diabolical Duchess* (Amberley, 2009).

Weir, Alison, *Elizabeth of York: A Tudor Queen and her World* (Ballantine Books, 2013).

Wilkins, Christopher, *The Last Knight Errant: Edward Woodville and the Age of Chivalry* (I.B. Tauris & Co., 2010).

Wilkinson, Josephine, *Richard: The Young King to Be* (Amberley, 2008, 2009).

Wilkinson, Josephine, *The Princes in the Tower* (Amberley, 2013).

Williamson, Audrey, *The Mystery of the Princes* (Amberley, 1978, 2010).

Wroe, Ann, *Perkin: A Story of Deception* (Vintage, 2004).

Contributors

Nathalie Nijman-Bliekendaal (Joined Project: 7 July 2016)

Nathalie Nijman-Bliekendaal, a Dutch national, graduated from the University of Leiden in 1993, where she studied (criminal) law. She started her career at the Court of Appeal in the Hague and after four years provided legal support to victims of crime, first at the Criminal Injuries Compensation Authority and later at Victim Support Netherlands. After having worked successfully in this field for many years, in 2016 she left to follow her heart and real passion – European medieval history – eventually becoming the Lead Researcher of The Missing Princes Project Dutch Research Group. Nathalie's current research is focusing on the genealogy of the 'Van Weerbeke/De Werbeque' family from Oudenaarde and Tournai (and their apparent linkages with the cities of Bruges and Gent (Flanders)), and finding new source material in Portugal related to the Duke of York's Portuguese years.

Jean Roefstra (Joined Project: 30 November 2016)

Jean Roefstra, a Dutch national, studied archaeology and castle science at Utrecht University (privatissimum classes Prof. Dr. J.G.N. Renaud). Jean regularly collaborates with forensic anthropologists and taught at the Criminal

Investigation Department (police) about archaeological clues in the excavation and identification of human skeletal remains. He worked for thirty-five years as a historical archaeologist at the National Service for Archaeological Soil Research in North Holland. He is Chairman of the Historical Archaeology Foundation (SHA). From 2006, he worked on the excavations at Egmond Abbey. He also participated in the re-excavation, dating and identification of the Counts of Holland and their families with Professors George Maat and Erik Cordfunke. Since 2000 he's worked as Deputy Archaeological Deposit Holder for the Province of North Holland. Jean has published extensively.

John Dike (Joined Project: 8 January 2018)

John Dike is a professional electrical engineer, now retired from the electricity supply industry, who is passionate about history. He regularly presents several talks on various historical subjects and has written books relating to local history. His *Bristol Blitz Diary* (1982) was recommended reading by the Imperial War Museum as a source of information on urban warfare. He adopts an analytical style to historical research in an attempt to acquire a truth that is not always present in the written narrative. It was while writing about Coldridge in Devon that he came across the significant evidence of a possible connection between the village and Edward V and joined Philippa Langley's The Missing Princes Project. John is Lead Researcher of the project's Coldridge Research Group with fourteen members.

Zoë Maula (Joined Project: 17 July 2019)

Zoë Maula is a Dutch national and graduate from Leiden University with a bachelor and master's degree in Japan studies with a specialisation in Japanese pre-modern history. Whilst Zoë's specialisation might differ from the focus of The Missing Princes Project, British history of the fifteenth and sixteenth century has always fascinated her and ignited her interest due to its parallels with the Warring States Period (1477–1568) of Japanese history. Zoë's current research focus is the Van Glymes family and the secret ciphers of the Holy Roman Emperor Maximilian I and the Spanish monarchs, Isabella and Ferdinand.

Acknowledgements

Over the past thirty years I have been researching the life and times of Richard III. This book is the result of two journeys: the first an investigation of all known source materials, the second, the search for new and neglected material in archives around the world. Such an ambitious search required an army and it is this army to whom our most grateful thanks are extended. In particular to the Dutch Research Group led by Nathalie Nijman-Bliekendaal with members Zoë Maula, Albert Jan de Rooij, Jean Roefstra and William Wiss. Their commitment and dedication has been unwavering. Our thanks go in particular to Nathalie and Albert, their extraordinary discoveries changing what we know. Nathalie would also like to thank: *Drs* Paul Baks, Leanne Erras, MA, Marjolein Jacobs-Driessen, MA, Dr Fred van Kan, Zoë Maula, MA, Jean Roefstra, *Mr* Albert Jan de Rooij, Irene Rooker, MA, *Drs* Alfred Schweitzer, Koen Vermeulen, MA, *Drs* William Wiss and *Drs* Ad van der Zee (Dutch academic titles in italics).

The Missing Princes Project in America was launched by its lead, Sally Keil, in November 2018. The goal was to scour libraries, institutions and archives in the US and Canada for primary source documents dated between 1483 and 1509. More than twenty-three people participated. With thanks to its top researchers: Maureen Chelak, Evelyn Fair, Jim Minor, Amy Odenbaugh, Jean Pivetz, Suzanne Sage, Julie Stafford, Denise Testa, and Tish Wolter. The 'stars' of the project were Linda McLatchie who searched fifty-two libraries,

Sally Keil who went through 101 and Bobbie Franks who delved into the archives of 146 institutions. Recently concluded, The Missing Princes Project in America represents a remarkable research achievement.

With special appreciation to the Coldridge Research Group in Devon led by John Dike and its team of eleven dedicated researchers: Jessica Bailey, Rosalind Bailey, Eileen Bates, Diane Bosley, Ian Churchward, Donna Egan, Lyn Green, Helen Ingram, Terri-Kate Lee, Julie Stafford and Beth Williams.

Grateful thanks are extended to the Somerset Branch Research Group in Wells led by Kieran Molloy and its dedicated researchers, including Louisa Purcell, Christine Simpson, Helena Smith, Keith Stenner, Rosemary Swabey, Cathy Symons and the late Hugh Warren.

Special thanks are also extended to the ancient families and their archivists who have generously aided our researches: Lady Jadranka Beresford-Peirse, Julie Biddlecombe-Brown, Daniel Blagg, David Brackenbury, Lord Gerald and Lady Emma Fitzalan-Howard, Christopher Hunwick, Craig Irving, Isabel Keating, Charlie Malet de Carteret, Seigneur of St Ouen, Jersey, Alison McCann, Ali McGrain, Alan McKerchar, Diana Percy, Max Percy, Lord Egremont, Ralph Percy, 12th Duke of Northumberland, Malcolm and Sue Rayfield, Christopher Ridgeway, John Martin Robinson, Lady Hetti Ronaldshay, David, Lord Willoughby de Broke and Ruth Wrigley.

The debt owed to the more than 300 members of the project is legion, too numerous to mention here, but they all have my deepest gratitude. Many of their names are recorded in this work. Particular gratitude to: Naomi Asukai, Marie Barnfield, Tracy Branagan, Sharon Camilletti, Annette Carson, Abigail Cherry, Jean Clare-Tighe, Suzanne Court-Oak, Michele Cross, Annette Davies, Iain Farrell, Dr Judith Ford, Amanda Geary, Gwendolen Godfrey, Nicola Heathcote, Mark Hicks, Francesca Icaza, Alice Johnson, Randolph Jones, Wendy Corbet Kelley, Lesley Lambert, Joanne Larner, Maria Grazia Leotta, Isabelle Lloyd, Sharon Lock, Satu Mannonen, Dan Moorhouse, Marion Moulton, Matt Oliver, Dr Alan Pendlington, Dr Sandra Pendlington, Art Ramirez, Lucy Roberts, Ian Rogers, Matthew Rolfe, Michele Schindler, Sandra Secchie, Kate M. Smith, Carol Southworth, Elena Taborri, Kirsteen Thomson, Dr Christopher Tinmouth, Lindsay Trenholme, Elizabeth Watson and Neil Whalley.

I am incredibly grateful to all the specialists who gave their time and expertise: Clive Atkinson, Silvija Banić, Dame Professor Sue Black (Baroness Black), Dr Eleoma Bodammer, Dr Tobias Capwell, Dr Heather Falvey, Peter Field, Professor Lucina Hackman, Peter and Carolyn Hammond, Dr A.J. Hibbard,

Ken Hillier, the late Mike Ingram, Dr David Johnson, Wendy Johnson, Carol Ann Kerry-Green, the late Dr Arthur Noel Kincaid, Dr Betty Knott, Sara Kondol-Hanna, Professor Henrike Lähnemann, Dr Greg Lambert, Dr Joanna Laynesmith, Matthew Lewis, Professor George Maat, Richard Mackinder, António Marques, Isolde Martyn, Wendy Moorhen, Toni Mount, Peter O'Donoghue (York Herald), Dr Lynda Pidgeon, Professor Compton A. Reeve, Dr Mariam Rosser-Owen, David Santiuste, John Saunders, Doris Schneider-Coutandin, Léonie Seliger, Dominic Sewell, Gordon Smith, Dr Shelagh Sneddon, Isobel Sneesby, Susan Troxell, Maureen Tyrell, Christopher Vane (Chester Herald), Dr Livia Visser-Fuchs, Louise Whittaker and Diana Withee.

With gratitude to all the archivists, librarians, museum curators and employees, custodians of ancient properties and local historians and researchers whose names are too many to list here but with thanks in particular to: Jennifer Allison, Clare Brown, Nathan Coyde, the late Ian Curteis, Gabriel Damaszk, Laurence Delsaut, Katie Dungate, Susan Freebrey, Bill Hare, James Harte, Alicia Hendrick, Cindy Hopkins, Joanne Iddison, Dr Bob Irving, Camille Koutoulakis, Louise Christine Larson, Dr Eckhart Leisering, Kate McQuillian, Graham Mitchell, Valérie Noël, Kris Palmer, Tom Richardson, Clare Rider, Rosanne Rietveld, Linda Romeril, Jan and Mike Saunders, Elizabeth Scudder, Janet Senior, Garry Smith, Kimberley Starkie, Nora Thornton, Marine Vasseur, Emily Ward, Anne Warsönke, Dickon Whitewood, Professor Peter Wiegand and Marc Yates.

My thanks also to all the project members from the police and judiciary for their continuing advice and analysis: Jayne Adams, Peter Camilletti, Gary Edginton (USA), Jeff Goodwin, Carl Holdcroft and Graham Roberts. Those working in our intelligence services and Ministry of Defence whose names cannot be recorded here for security purposes, you know who you are.

I would also like to thank my literary agent Charlie Viney and all those at The History Press who believed in this book: Claire Hopkins (commissioning editor), Cynthia Hamilton (head of PR and marketing), Chrissy McMorris (editorial manager), and my independent publicist Angela Martin. With thanks also to Georgia Holmes (senior acquisitions editor) at W.F. Howes for commissioning the audiobook and Alistair George (audiobook producer) in my home town of Edinburgh for making it happen.

Finally, my heartfelt thanks go to the three people who helped make this book possible: Dr David Johnson for kindly reading the early draft of each chapter and for his helpful suggestions, comments and additions. Likewise to Annette Carson who checked (and edited) the extensive endnotes so critical to this work and identified and aided a number of clarifications within the text. And to Director Janice Sutherland who gave me the belief and impetus to place my journey on screen. Thank you.

For the onscreen story: with especial thanks to those who gave their time and elucidation: Nathen Amin, Dr Tracy Borman, Mallaurie Dandois (archivist), Professor Henrike Lähnemann, Matthew Lewis, Dr Elizabeth Norton, Dr Janina Ramirez, Irene Rooker, MA, (archivist) and Dr Ann Wroe, and with especial gratitude to Emily Shields, Commissioning Editor at Channel 4, Malcolm Brinkworth (executive producer and chief executive officer, Brinkworth Productions), Xander Brinkworth (executive producer), Dr Emilia Chodorowska (producer), Florrie Reeves (assistant producer), Matt Kennedy (director of photography), Janice Sutherland (director), and the inimitable Rob Rinder who I now have the honour to call friend. Thank you for sharing my journey.

This book is dedicated to all those who seek truth, and to the memory of Richard Plantagenet (1452–85) whose good name is now returned to him.

Requiesce in pace.

Index